W9-AFL-565

Plant Morphogenesis

McGRAW-HILL PUBLICATIONS IN
THE BOTANICAL SCIENCES

Edmund W. Sinnott, *Consulting Editor*

There are also the related series of McGraw-Hill Publications in the Zoological Sciences, of which E. J. Boell is Consulting Editor, and in the Agricultural Sciences, of which R. A. Brink is Consulting Editor.

PLANT MORPHOGENESIS

Edmund W. Sinnott

STERLING PROFESSOR OF BOTANY, EMERITUS
YALE UNIVERSITY

McGRAW-HILL BOOK COMPANY, INC.

New York   Toronto   London

1960

PLANT MORPHOGENESIS

II
57585

To the Memory of

HERMANN VÖCHTING

PIONEER IN PLANT MORPHOGENESIS

Preface

The present volume is an outcome of the author's concern with the problems of plant morphogenesis for over 40 years. During that time he has followed the literature in this field with some care and has seen the subject grow from a relatively minor aspect of botanical science to a much wider recognition as one of the central concerns of biology. New techniques and fields of work have developed in it over the years, and its contacts with other sciences have grown much closer. Few discussions of the subject as a whole have appeared, however, and no extensive synthesis of its content has been made. The book that follows is an attempt to do this and to organize the field of plant morphogenesis so that it can be studied and taught as an integrated discipline.

This is no simple task, and botanists will doubtless disagree as to how it should be accomplished. The method adopted here is first to discuss plant growth, emphasizing descriptive and experimental work on cells and meristems. This is followed by a survey of the various categories of morphogenetic phenomena—correlation, polarity, differentiation, and the rest—mobilizing under each the major facts that are known about it and the work of the chief contributors to the field. This portion is largely descriptive and serves to pose problems for consideration. It is followed by a third section that discusses the major factors operative in the control of plant development and is primarily concerned with physiological and genetic questions. It touches these broad subjects, however, only so far as they are concerned with morphogenetic problems and then only in a brief and rather summary fashion. Too frequent repetition of material in the three sections is avoided by numerous cross references.

Throughout the book no attempt is made to go at all completely into most of the topics. From the vast literature on subjects of concern to plant morphogenesis, however, a considerable bibliography has been compiled by means of which the reader is introduced to the more important publications where detailed information may be found. In this bibliography many important earlier papers of general and historical interest have been cited, but emphasis has been placed on relatively recent ones. Where available, review papers have been cited. There is some unavoidable repetition of material but this has been reduced by frequent use of cross references. The book is designed primarily for reference, though by means of such a presentation more teachers may be encouraged to offer courses in this field.

To many individuals the author is indebted for good counsel and assistance in many ways. His thanks are due especially to his former colleague Dr. Robert Bloch, who for some years collaborated with him in the present project. Professor Ralph H. Wetmore has read a portion of the manuscript and made valuable suggestions, as has the author's colleague Prof. Arthur W. Galston for the chapter on Growth Substances. Various problems have been discussed with many others, and to all these the author is grateful. For the positions taken on particular issues and the opinions expressed, however, he assumes full responsibility, as he does for any errors of fact, attribution, or citation which may appear and which are hard to eliminate completely from a book of this sort.

For several years Mrs. Charlotte Reeder has assisted in compiling information, in abstracting papers, and, through her genius for orderliness, in keeping the project from bogging down under the sheer weight of its material. To her the author is greatly indebted. Other assistants have been associated with the work from time to time, and their help is here thankfully acknowledged.

For financial assistance, and especially for grants from the Eugene Higgins Trust, the author wishes to express his gratitude to Yale University and its Provost, Edgar S. Furniss.

The illustrations have been taken from the work of many individuals. In every case the source from which they come has been acknowledged in the caption, but the author here offers his further thanks for the privilege of using them. For specific figures he is indebted to the editors of *Endeavour,* the authorities of the Boyce Thompson Institute for Plant Research, the Department of Plant Pathology of the University of Wisconsin, Triarch Botanical Products, the W. Atlee Burpee Company, Dr. G. R. Zundel, and Rutherford Platt.

This book has been a long time in the making. It proved to be such a time-consuming task that the author was not able to bring it to completion until his retirement from academic duties a few years ago. He hopes that this long period of ripening may have improved its quality and increased its value to those who use it.

Edmund W. Sinnott

Contents

ix

CHAPTER 1

Introduction

A study of the form and structure of living things has a perennial interest, not only for biologists but for everyone. It appeals to the aesthetic in us. Philosophers have been concerned with it since the time of Plato, who distinguished between matter and form and believed that spirit was inherent in the latter. Most naturalists owe their first interest in animals and plants to the almost infinite variety of forms which these display and which make possible their identification. Although morphology (Goethe's term), the science that deals with form, has lost the commanding position it once held, following the advent of physiology and the disciplines that connect biology with the physical sciences, it still remains the foundation for any thorough knowledge of living things. We must all be morphologists before we can be biologists of any other sort.

In a famous sentence Charles Darwin paid tribute to morphology by calling it the very soul of natural history. How curious it is, he remarked, that the hand of a man and of a mole, the leg of a horse, the paddle of a porpoise, and the wing of a bat, despite the great difference in their functions, should all be formed on the same basic pattern. Specific bodily forms and structures had long been used to distinguish the major groups of plants and animals and were also the basis of that "idealistic" morphology which so intrigued Goethe and the biologists of his day. Darwin, however, saw in the science of comparative morphology something far more significant—a strong support for the doctrine of evolution, for only by assuming a common ancestry for each of the groups that show a common pattern of bodily form could these similarities be explained. Form was widely acknowledged as the most distinctive character on which the phylogenetic relationships of organisms could be based and a truly natural system of classification constructed.

The study of organic form, however, poses a problem deeper still, and one concerned with the very character of life itself. From the facts of embryology it is evident that in the development of an individual there occurs as regular a progression of changes in form as has taken place in evolution. Indeed, the theory of recapitulation called attention to some

1

interesting parallels between the two. In a study of form in organic development the biologist has the great advantage of dealing with a process that is going on under his eyes and is thus susceptible to experimental attack. An organism is not static but displays a continually unfolding series of changes during its life. It has been well described as a "slice of space-time." As knowledge about organic development increased, biologists came to realize that development is not only an orderly unfolding but that in this process all parts of the growing individual are closely correlated with the rest so that an organized and integrated system, the *organism,* is produced. Differences in rate of growth and in character of the structures developed are evident, but these various changes do not occur independently. They keep in step with one another. When form changes, it does so in a regular and predictable fashion. Still more significant, the experimental embryologist is able to show not only that these relationships are to be seen in normal development but that they persistently tend to be restored if development is disturbed. An organism is an essentially fluid system through which matter is continually moving but which nevertheless maintains a constant form much as does a candle flame or a waterfall.

In the various physiological activities of the living organism there is evident the same coordination so manifest in bodily development. What occurs in an individual is not simply a series of unrelated metabolic processes, but these are tied together in such a precise fashion that the life of the organism is maintained in a steady state. Just as the normal progress of development tends to be restored if it is disturbed, so the normal state of physiological organization tends to be maintained at a constant level. This regulatory process of *homeostasis* is recognized as one of the major facts of physiology.

Organic form is thus the visible expression of an inner relatedness characteristic of life at every level. This can be most simply designated as *biological organization* and is the most important problem that confronts students of the life sciences. Form may be thought of not only as the soul of natural history in the sense that it provides a measure of evolutionary relationship but as the soul of all biology, since it provides the most obvious and easily accessible manifestation of the basic characteristic of life.

Biological organization is to be seen most distinctly in bodily development. It is obvious that, to produce an individual with a specific form and structure, growth must be more rapid in some directions than in others and must form tissues and organs of different character in different places. Embryology has shown how precisely the activities in one part of the developing individual are related to those in every other part. Few happenings in nature are as fascinating to watch as the unfolding and growth of a leaf or a flower from a tiny primordium, especially when this is speeded up to our eyes by time-lapse photography. Every step is co-ordinated with all the others as though a craftsman were molding it according to a plan. Within the whole, the cells and other subordinate parts do not develop independently but all are knit together into an organized system.

How all this is accomplished and a specifically formed organism produced is not yet understood, although specific parts of the process are now well known. Most metabolic activities are yielding to biochemical analysis; students of gene action find that specific substances are produced by specific genes, and the nucleic acids, with their remarkable properties, are recognized as being at the very foundation of life itself. How all the various metabolic and developmental activities are related in such an orderly fashion, however, and proceed without interference or confusion so that, step by step, an organism is produced poses a problem of a very different kind. Relations, not chemical changes, are the facts to be explained. The problem must be approached experimentally but one should recognize that this may require the development of techniques and ideas not yet explored.

The biological science concerned with this dynamic and causal aspect of organic form is evidently different from either morphology, physiology, or embryology, though partaking of all three. It deserves a name of its own. The Germans usually call it *Entwicklungsmechanik,* a name proposed by Wilhelm Roux. This great zoologist is looked upon as the father of the science of zoological morphogenesis. He founded the *Archiv für Entwicklungsmechanik der Organismen,* a journal which now occupies 16 feet of library shelf and contains a vast amount of material, chiefly on the animal side. Elsewhere this science has often been termed experimental morphology or experimental embryology. British biologists sometimes refer to it as causal morphology. In recent years it has generally been given a more appropriate name than any of these—*morphogenesis.* The derivation of this word is obvious—the origin of form. Who first used it is not certainly known but Ernst Haeckel employed the cognate form morphogeny (*Morphogenie*) in 1859. Some have employed this term in a strictly descriptive sense, essentially as synonymous with developmental morphology. More commonly and properly, however, it includes, in addition to a discussion of purely descriptive facts as to the origin of form, a study of the results of experimentally controlled development and an analysis of the effects of the various factors, external and internal, that determine how the development of form proceeds. In other words, it attempts to get at the underlying formativeness in the development of organisms and especially to reach an understanding of the basic fact of which form is the most obvious manifestation—biological organization

itself. It is in these senses that the term morphogenesis will be used in
the present volume.

Each of the major biological subsciences is intimately related to the
others. One cannot study genetics apart from physiology, for example,
or physiology from morphology, or taxonomy and evolution from all
these. It may well be maintained, however, that morphogenesis, since it is
concerned with the most distinctive aspect of life—organization—is the
crossroads where all the highways of biological exploration tend to converge. Its subject matter deals with some of the most elusive and intract-
able phenomena in science, but it is here that the greatest discoveries of
the future are likely to be made. These will be significant not only
for biological problems but for many others that man faces. Even
philosophy, long concerned with problems of form, is still gaining
from this source fresh insights into its chief task, an understanding of
life.

More study has been given to morphogenetic problems with animals
than with plants. A great advantage of animal material is that in many
groups the egg is discharged into water and the embryo develops there,
at least through its earlier stages, and is thus easily accessible for observation and experiment. Among higher plants, on the contrary, all the early
development of the embryo takes place within the ovule, surrounded by
many layers of tissue and relatively inaccessible. The result has been that,
save for rather special material like the egg of *Fucus* which can be
treated much like that of an animal, very little morphogenetic work has
been done on plant embryos. Modern techniques, however, by which
it is possible to grow the embryos of some higher plants to maturity in
culture, are making the science of experimental plant embryology a more
fruitful one.

Workers with plants have a number of advantages, however. In plants,
permanently embryonic regions, the meristems, are available for study.
At the tip of shoot and root and in the cambial layers these are indeterminate and produce new plant structures almost indefinitely. Such
meristems are usually numerous or extensive on the same plant so that
ample material for the study of development, identical in genetic constitution, is available. Growth and differentiation in the development of
a plant are thus continuing processes and not limited to a single and
often brief life cycle.

Organs such as leaves, flowers, and fruits, which are determinate in
growth, pass through a cycle closely comparable to that of individual
animals, and morphogenetic problems can also often profitably be studied
in them. The fact that they are usually produced in abundance on a
single plant is a further advantage, for here the investigator need not be
concerned about genetic diversity in his material but can study strictly

comparable organic forms under a wide range of environmental conditions.

Another important difference between botanical and zoological material is concerned with the behavior of individual cells during development. In animal embryos many cells are relatively free to move about so that certain morphogenetic changes are due to movements of cells or cell groups rather than to differences in relative growth. In plants above the simplest types, on the contrary, cells are almost always attached firmly to their neighbors so that morphogenetic movements have no part in development. Changes of form are the result of differences in the location or orientation of cell divisions or in the size or the shape to which the individual cells grow. This makes the study of morphogenetic problems somewhat simpler in plants because development leaves a record of its course in the structure of the growing system itself.

Most plant cells have rather firm walls as compared with animal cells, and the structures that they produce are therefore not as soft and plastic as in many animals. A plant part tends to hold its form rather well and can thus be measured more easily and accurately. Its anatomical structure is also less fluid. Certain organs, such as woody stems and hard-shelled fruits, retain their form when dead and dry and can then be kept for study without the necessity for special preservative treatment.

Plant material is generally more tractable than that of animals, is easily grown, and lends itself readily to experiment. Because of their stationary habit, plants are more susceptible to changes in environmental influences, notably water and light, than are animals, and the morphogenetic effects of such factors may be studied more easily in them.

The organization of a plant, too, is much looser than that of most animals. The individual organism is less sharply marked and specific, and its powers of regeneration are far greater. Its structural plan is simpler, for the stationary habit of most plants renders unnecessary several organ systems found in animals, notably a digestive tract, excretory organs, musculature, and a nervous system. Morphogenetic problems can therefore be studied in plants uncomplicated by the physiological complexities inseparable from animal life. The absence of a nervous system, which has such an important role in animal development, is of particular advantage, for developmental processes in plants are under the control of relatively unspecialized protoplasm, and they may thus be studied most directly and at their simplest level. There is no reason to believe that the fundamental phenomena of the development of form are not as manifest in these relatively simple systems as in the more complex ones of animals.

What is now called morphogenesis came first into prominence in the late decades of the nineteenth century after the early enthusiasm over the idea of evolution had given place to a more sober realization that it did not provide a solution for all the problems about living things. The list of men working primarily with animal material includes some of the most brilliant names in the science of zoology. In plant morphogenesis, most of those who made important early contributions were chiefly engaged in other fields, especially morphology, physiology, and pathology. Here are remembered the classical studies of Hanstein on meristems and their derivatives, of Winkler on chimeras, of Haberlandt on plant hormones, of Küster on abnormal growth, of Klebs on the effects of the environment, of Goebel on the general area to which he gave the name of organography, and many others.

It is to Herman Vöchting, however, long Professor of Botany at the University of Bonn, that botanists owe the first thoughtful discussion of such problems as polarity, differentiation, and regeneration. His "Organbildung im Pflanzenreich," published in 1878, is a classic and may be said to have founded a new field of botanical investigation. It deserves to be read by all students of development even today. About the turn of the century the zoologist Hans Driesch stated his often-quoted aphorism, "The fate of a cell is a function of its position," which in a few words sums up a central fact of biological organization. What few botanists know is that Vöchting, in a book written 20 years earlier, said the same thing in almost the same words.[1] Other botanists also made important contributions here. Much of the work of men such as van Tieghem, Jost, Sachs, Pfeffer, Schwendener, and Strasburger was on problems that we should now call morphogenetic.

Most studies in plant morphogenesis have been made with vascular plants—pteridophytes, gymnosperms, and angiosperms. It should be remembered, however, that many of these problems can be approached more directly through work on the lower ones. Polarity, for example, is manifest in its simplest form in some of the filamentous algae. The very beginnings of differentiation are to be seen in the lower thallophytes. Almost every cell in some of the bryophytes may easily be induced to regenerate. The problem of the development of form is nowhere posed more directly than in the formation of the remarkable fruiting bodies of some of the myxomycetes and of the higher fungi. These more primitive plants are proving to be ideal material for the study of many problems in physiology and genetics, and although they have been rather neglected in morphogenesis, they offer abundant opportunities for fruitful work in this field.

The science of plant morphogenesis has never received a comprehen-

---

[1] Die jeweilig zu verrichtende Function einer Zelle wird in erster Linie durch den morphologischen Ort bestimmt, den sie an der Lebenseinheit einnimmt. *Organbildung im Pflanzenreich*, 1878, p. 241.)

sive formulation. To bring together in a single volume a discussion of the various phenomena that distinguish it and of the factors that have been found to affect the development of plants, together with a bibliography of some of the most important publications dealing with the subject, should help to give it recognition as a distinctive botanical discipline. To attempt this is the purpose of the present volume.

Morphogenesis is such an immense subject, however, covering most of the territory of biology, that to organize its facts and its problems in a logical and reasonably compact fashion is a matter of much difficulty. The method used here is to divide the subject into three parts. First is presented a brief discussion of plant growth as a necessary introduction to morphogenesis proper, placing particular emphasis on its cellular basis and on the activities of the meristems. The remaining subject matter is then divided into two sections: first, the various phenomena of plant morphogenesis and the more important studies that have been made on them and, second, a brief account of the morphogenetic factors that have been found to affect the development and form of plants. In the first there are chapters on Correlation, Polarity, Symmetry, Differentiation, Regeneration, Tissue Mixtures, and Abnormal Growth. In the second are discussed the effects of light, water, temperature, and other physical factors; inorganic and organic substances (especially growth substances); and finally the various genetic factors. There is a concluding chapter on the problem of Biological Organization.

At the end of the book is a selected list of references to some of the more important books and papers on the subject. This obviously must be far from complete since the literature is enormous and scattered through most of the fields of botany. An attempt has been made to include, both in text and references, some of the important early work, not alone for its intrinsic but also its historical value. In the more rapidly advancing fields, where many of the results from older studies have now been superseded, only a relatively few of the earlier papers are mentioned, and there is considerable representation of recent work. Aside from bringing the subject up to date, these later papers through their bibliographies will give the student a means of entry into the literature of a given field. Opportunities for further research, particularly in areas now less popular than in the past, are so numerous that the author has felt justified in calling attention to some of them from time to time.

The problem of deciding which pieces of work to include in a discussion of this sort and which to omit has been very difficult. Among those mentioned there are doubtless some that will be regarded by many readers as relatively unimportant. The omission of others will be criticized. It is hoped, however, that the papers chosen will provide a fair picture of accomplishment in plant morphogenesis. A considerable number of review papers are cited which help summarize results in particular fields. No one person, and certainly not the present writer, is competent to give a thoroughly informed and authoritative judgment on the relative worth of the wide variety of investigations here discussed. It is hoped, however, that one service of the book will be to introduce its readers to the subjects of these studies even though in some cases a piece of work can be given little more than mention.

Since there is no sharp line between morphogenesis and its neighboring fields of morphology, physiology, genetics, and the chemical and physical sciences, much of the advance in it will doubtless be made, as in the past, by men whose chief concern is with one of these other disciplines; but as morphogenesis becomes better organized and as more opportunities for training and research in it are offered by our colleges and universities, there will be more students whose primary interests are directed to it. More than other biological sciences, perhaps, morphogenesis will need to maintain close contact with a wide variety of other fields, for few can hope to be competent in its entire area. To develop this comprehensive subject fruitfully will require the active cooperation of many sciences, and by this means the morphogenetic point of view can thus help to integrate all of biology.

PART ONE

Growth

CHAPTER 2

Growth in General

The process of organic *development,* in which are posed the chief problems for the science of morphogenesis, occurs in the great majority of
cases as an accompaniment of the process of growth. The association between these two activities is not an invariable one, for there are a few
organisms in which growth is completed before development and differentiation are finished, but far more commonly the form and structure
of a living thing change while it grows. Knowledge about growth is
therefore necessary for an understanding of development, and any discussion of morphogenetic problems in plants should be preceded by a
discussion of plant growth in general. This is the purpose of the first
few chapters of the present volume.

Definition of Growth. The term "growth" has been variously defined
by biologists. For some (Hammett, 1936)[1] it includes not only increase
but also the accompanying phenomena of progressive differentiation.
Most regard this definition as too inclusive and would limit it in one respect or another. Since much of the increase in volume is brought about
merely by gain in amount of water, increase in dry weight might seem to
be the best measure of growth, but sprouting seeds kept in the dark will
"grow" into large, etiolated seedlings through intake of water though
their dry weight actually decreases. In one sense these sprouts have
grown, but in another they have not. The fundamental fact in all growth,
of course, is the self-multiplication of living material, a process of much
biological significance. For this reason, growth might best be defined
as increase in amount of protoplasm. Even if we could agree, however,
as to what constitutes protoplasm (whether vacuoles, for example, are
parts of it), it would be impossible, as a practical matter, to measure
this. Furthermore, in every organism, and particularly in every plant,
there is much material (such as cell walls and starch grains) which is an
integral part of the organism but which presumably is not living, and it
seems illogical not to regard increase in such material as part of growth.

[1] For bibliographic information concerning books and papers referred to in the text,
see Bibliography, pp. 461 ff.

11

In most multicellular organisms growth is accomplished chiefly by cell multiplication, and to some observers this process seems to be an essential part of growth. In the cleavage of many animal eggs and in similar processes in plants, however, there is a great increase in cell number but none in the actual material which constitutes the "growing" structure, and whether such cellular increase should be regarded as growth is a question. In the case of the female gametophyte in the megaspore of *Selaginella,* and especially of the young embryo which develops there, growth of an organized structure by cell multiplication certainly occurs, but at the expense of material stored in the spore. Where an entire mass is cut up into cells, as in the development of a male gametophyte in a microspore, one may doubt as to whether this should be called growth at all. What definition of growth one adopts depends on the particular problem with which he is concerned.

For the study of morphogenesis, the most important aspect of growth is the *permanent increase in volume* of an organ or organism, regardless of how it is accomplished, and this is the sense in which the term will here be used. The ultimate problem—the self-multiplication of living material—is one primarily for the student of physiology and reproduction, but it is the gross and geometrical result of such growth with which morphogenesis is chiefly concerned.

Growth in Plants. In most plants, the process of growth is different in one important respect from that in animals. The typical mature plant cell is surrounded by a relatively stout cellulose wall which under ordinary conditions prevents any further cell division or growth save in exceptional circumstances. The cells are rather firmly cemented together and thus unable to move about or migrate. Plant tissues are therefore incapable of growth and renewal except through the activity of thin-walled, relatively undifferentiated embryonic regions, or *meristems,* where occur the divisions that produce new cells and the changes by which these attain their final size. These meristems are rather sharply localized. In plant axes where growth is continuous and often indeterminate, growth in length is controlled chiefly by the activity of meristems at the tip of each root or stem. The older portion of the axis, having once attained maturity, does not make further growth in length. A tree increases in height only at the tips of its twigs and not elsewhere. In the stems of some monocotyledons, however, growth of the stem in length may continue for a time by the activity of *intercalary* meristematic regions at the base of each internode. Perennially growing roots and stems increase in thickness through the activity of a lateral meristem, or *cambium,* situated between xylem and phloem, by which the growth of both these tissues is accomplished. There are other sharply localized meristematic regions, such as the phellogen, or cork cambium.

In organs which (unlike the axes) have a limited or determinate growth, such as leaves, flowers, or fruits, the meristems are usually not localized but are *diffuse*, so that the whole organ, or most of it, is growing throughout and not at any particular point. Such structures have a growth cycle of their own, much as does an animal body, and when they reach maturity all their tissues stop growing and there is no embryonic region set apart by which further growth may be accomplished.

Graphical and Mathematical Analysis of Growth. One of the most obvious facts which a study of growth reveals is that it does not proceed at a constant rate. Many factors influence this rate, but under normal and favorable conditions a growing organ or organism undergoes a characteristic course of increase, first growing slowly, then with increasing speed, and finally slowing down again until growth stops entirely.

It is possible to picture this graphically in various ways. In Table 2-1 are presented the data for the increase in diameter of a gourd fruit from its early state as a small ovary primordium until maturity. If these diameters are plotted as ordinates against time in days, the growth curve shown in Fig. 2-1 results. This is an S-shaped, or *sigmoid*, curve and is typical of most growing organisms, both plant and animal, though it is subject to much variation. It presents the changing *size* of the growing organ throughout its course but does not give a very clear picture of the changing amounts of daily growth. If daily increments are plotted in the same way against time, the curve in Fig. 2-2 results. These increments are small at first, then progressively larger, and then smaller again.

Such graphical representations of growth have long interested biologists and mathematicians, who have endeavored to analyze them in mathematical terms and thus obtain clues as to the character of the growth process itself. In many cases such analyses have proved helpful in providing a simple statement of the course of growth, but there are so many variables involved in growing organisms that one can hardly expect to express their increase completely in an equation.

Table 2-1. Growth of a Gourd Fruit from a Small Primordium to Maturity

Date	Diameter, mm.	Date	Diameter, mm.
July 30	2.4	Aug. 9	30.0
" 31	3.1	" 10	35.2
Aug. 1	3.9	" 11	40.0
" 2	5.1	" 12	43.8
" 3	6.5	" 13	46.0
" 4	8.4	" 14	47.0
" 5	11.0	" 15	47.5
" 6	14.0	" 16	47.9
" 7	18.0	" 17	48.0
" 8	23.5	" 18	48.0

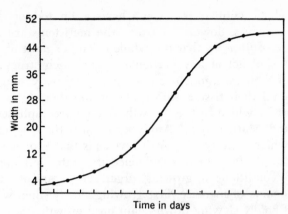

F₁ɢ. 2-1. Sigmoid growth curve. Fruit diameters in Table 2-1 plotted against time in days.

The first period of growth, in the most typical instances, shows the regular acceleration of a mass increasing, so to speak, at compound interest, the growth during any period being a constant proportion or percentage of the amount already present, and the "interest" being compounded continuously. In Table 2-1 it will be observed that for the first 10 days the increase in diameter each day is an approximately constant proportion of the diameter of the day before, though the daily incre-

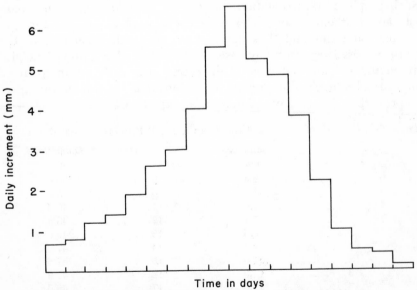

F₁ɢ. 2-2. Graph of daily increments in fruit diameter, from Table 2-1.

ments themselves continually increase. The equation for "compound-interest" growth is the familiar one

$$P_1 = P_0 e^{rt}$$

where P_1 is the size at any time t; P_0 the size at the beginning of growth; e the base of the natural logarithms, 2.18; and r the rate of growth (interest or exponential rate). This can be expressed, by using common logarithms, as

$$\log P_1 = \log P_0 + \log e\ (rt)$$

To find r for the first 10 days in Table 2-1, we substitute in this equation as follows:

$$1.4771 = 0.3802 + 0.4343 \times 10r$$

$$r = \frac{1.4771 - 0.3802}{10 \times 0.4343} = 0.25$$

This is the rate of diameter increase per day at which, continuously compounded, this fruit is growing, expressed as a per cent of its previous growth. If the logarithms of the successive size of gourd fruits in Table 2-1 are plotted against time (or the data plotted on semilogarithmic paper) the graph in Fig. 2-3 results. Here the growth for the first 10 days is seen

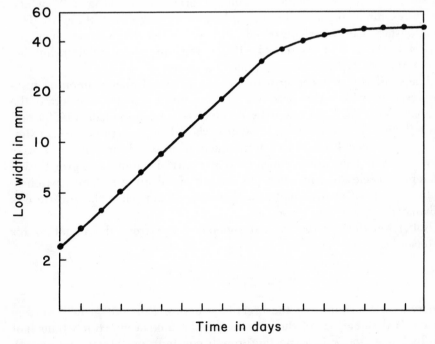

Fig. 2-3. Curve of the logarithm of fruit diameter in Table 2-1 plotted against time in days.

to fall along an essentially straight line, showing that the fruit was growing at a constant exponential rate. The slope of the line is a measure of this rate.

The resemblance between such organic growth and compound-interest increase has long been noted, but it was particularly emphasized by V. H. Blackman (1919). He proposed the term *efficiency index* for the "interest rate" in such growth. That living things in the early stages of their development should grow in this way is not surprising, for if embryonic material is self-multiplicative, the increase per unit of time should be proportional to the growing mass.

To explain the rest of the growth curve is more difficult. Evidently growth cannot proceed in any organism at a continually accelerating rate, if for no other reason than that building material would soon be used up. The gradual slowing down and final cessation of growth are far too regular a process, however, to be due to mere exhaustion of materials. A plant or animal provided with a superabundance of nutrients will rarely exceed the size characteristic for its species. Each organ or body has a specific growth cycle through which it passes, and the second part of this cycle, in which growth is falling off in rate, is much like the first part in reverse, so that the entire growth curve thus tends to be symmetrical. In such a case the periodic increments form a curve (Fig. 2-2) which much resembles the so-called *normal* curve, or curve of probability. This relationship has been observed and discussed by various workers, especially Pearl and his school (1915), but any causal relationship between the two types of curves is not easy to see.

The similarity between growth and the chemical phenomenon of autocatalysis, in which the products of a catalytic process accelerate the process itself, has been noted by many observers. Robertson (1923) and his followers have attempted to analyze the whole growth curve as a simple (monomolecular) autocatalytic reaction by which an enzyme breaks down a mass of substrate. During the first part of the process, growth will therefore accelerate, but when the amount of substrate becomes seriously reduced, rate of growth will also be reduced, and when the substrate is exhausted, growth will cease.

Robertson derives the typical sigmoid curve from the equation for autocatalysis:

$$\log \frac{x}{A - x} = k(t - t_1)$$

where x is the volume of the organic structure (amount grown) at any time t; A the final size of the structure; t_1 the time at which it attains half its final size; and k is a specific growth constant, or exponential growth rate.

The essential feature of this growth equation is that the rate of growth is determined by the amount of growth which is yet to occur. This implies that the final size is established at the start of growth, either by the amount of available building material or in some other way. If only one "master reaction" were concerned, the course of growth might well follow Robertson's equation, but there are evidently many substances involved and many processes going on simultaneously which probably make the growth process too complex to be analyzed by any one reaction.

Growth curves for certain organs and organisms fit Robertson's equation fairly well (Reed, 1927). For others the fit is not so close. In a structure which in its growth fits the equation perfectly, the rate of exponential

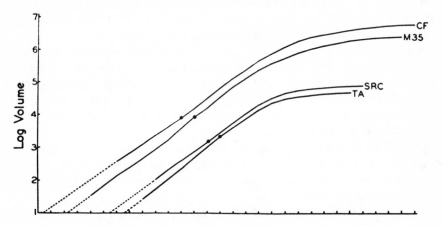

FIG. 2-4. Growth of large and of small fruits in *Cucurbita*. Log of fruit volume plotted against time in days. Early growth in all races is at a constant rate (straight line) the slope of which here is the same in large and small races. Solid circle, time of flowering. (*From Sinnott.*)

growth will constantly decrease (since it is proportional to the amount yet to grow, which is decreasing) so that the curve of the logarithm of size against time will be convex from the beginning. When the rate is relatively low the difference between this and the straight line of constant exponential growth at first is not great, since the absolute amount of growth in these early time intervals is slight. In many growth curves, such as those of fruits of various races of cucurbits presented by Sinnott (1945*b*), the early growth is at a constant exponential rate and shows no indications of convexity of line (Fig. 2-4). Furthermore, large and small fruits which are here compared grow at essentially the same rates but for very different durations. Under these conditions, Robertson's formula would require that the length of time between half size and maturity should be the same for all races, but actually in the small-fruited races this period is much less than in the large-fruited ones.

The mathematical analysis of growth involves many complexities and has been developed in much greater detail than is possible in the present brief discussion. For a fuller treatment of this subject the reader is referred to the work of Pearl (1939), D'Arcy Thompson (1942), Erickson (1956), and others.

It is evident that no single mathematical statement will express all types of growth nor perhaps any of them with complete exactness. Growth is a very complex process involving many variables, and it is not to be expected that it can be compressed into a single equation. Even if it could be, this would not tell us a great deal for, as D'Arcy Thompson well says, a formula "which gives a mere coincidence of numbers may be of little use or none, unless it go some way to depict and explain the *modus operandi* of growth." That growth under some conditions proceeds as at compound interest and at others like an autocatalytic process is of some importance in providing a clue to the mechanism of growth, but so far mathematical analysis has added comparatively little to our understanding of the fundamental character of growth itself. For this we must look to a more concrete study of the growth process in terms of genetics, biochemistry, and physiology.

Variation in Growth. Many structures do not show the simple sigmoid growth discussed in the preceding section. Just as the smooth course of growth in mammals is interrupted by birth and by puberty, it is modified in various ways in plants. In fruits of peach and cherry, for example, Tukey and Young (1939) and others have shown that after these structures are partly grown there is then for some time no increase in volume. This is the period in which the endocarp, or "stone," is being formed. Later the fruit begins to enlarge again, so that a curve like that in Fig. 2-5 results. Duncan and Curtis (1942) have shown a somewhat similar growth curve in the fruit of certain orchids where one epoch of growth is associated with meiosis and a later one with seed maturity. In vegetative structures, aside from annual periods, there are also sometimes discontinuous cycles, as in the pear shoots studied by Reed (1927), where there may be three such in one season. The dandelion scape shows a somewhat similar growth pattern (Chao, 1947). It is rapid during flower development, much slower after the flower opens, and then accelerates greatly as the fruit becomes mature.

Borriss (1934a) reports that etiolated stipes of *Coprinus* show a marked periodicity of growth with maxima 3.5 to 4.5 hours apart. This and similar cases may be manifestations of endogenous rhythms such as have frequently been reported in other processes (p. 322).

In many plants, particularly herbaceous ones, growth is not evenly distributed throughout the length of the stem. Thus in tobacco (Wolf, 1947) and in maize (Heimsch and Stafford, 1952) the internodes are progressively longer from the base to about half way up the axis and then are progressively shorter to the apex. The distribution of growth in a developing leaf blade also shows local differences (Avery, 1935). Many alterations in form arise from local changes in growth.

Determinate and Indeterminate Growth. In most animals, growth is part of a definite life cycle and produces a determinate structure. In many plants, on the other hand, the growth of the body is essentially indetermi-

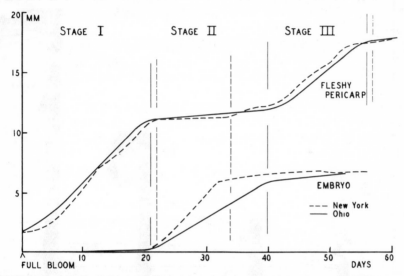

FIG. 2-5. Intermittent curves of growth of a cherry fruit from flowering to maturity. (*From L. D. Tukey.*)

nate and, within certain limits, may go on indefinitely through the activity of terminal and lateral meristems. Even such theoretically unlimited growth (such as that of a tree in height or a vine in length), however, usually reaches a limit and in its growth follows a curve which is S-shaped. In some plants, such as the sunflower and most grasses, height is not indeterminate but is limited by a terminal inflorescence, and stem growth in such cases is typically sigmoid. Lateral organs, such as leaves and fruits, which do not grow by localized meristems have still more definite growth cycles and are quite comparable to single animal individuals and show similar growth curves. Examples of these are fruits (Fig. 2-1), leaves (Wolf, 1947), and ovules and embryos (Rietsma et al.,

1955). Plants provide examples of all types of growth from that in loosely organized, essentially indeterminate structures to highly organized and sharply determinate ones and therefore are particularly good material for a study of the mechanism by which growth, presumably free and continuous in primitive organisms, becomes controlled and molded into a definite cycle or pattern. Such cyclical, controlled growth is one manifestation of the general phenomenon of biological organization.

Growth and Size. The size that an organism attains is often an important factor in determining the character of its development, and size is intimately related to growth. Differences in ultimate size may be due

Fɪɢ. 2-6. Diagram of growth of stipe and pileus of the common mushroom, *Agaricus campestris*. Homologous points are connected by lines. Growth is most active in the region intermediate between base and apex. (*From Bonner, Kane, and Levey.*)

to differences in rate or in duration of growth or in both of these. Little is known in plants as to the relation between growth and size. The increased size of heterozygous corn plants is apparently associated with a higher growth rate (Whaley, 1950), and this may be true rather generally for size difference in indeterminate structures. In determinate ones such as the fruit, however, rate may not be important. The great size differences between small-fruited and large-fruited cucurbits of the same species studied by Sinnott (1945*b*) are due in almost every case to differences in *duration* of growth, for growth rate is essentially the same in all of them (Fig. 2-4). This difference in duration applies to all recognizable parts of the growth cycle—from primordium to flowering, from flowering to the end of exponential growth, and from this point to growth cessation.

Growth in plants has usually been studied in the higher forms because of their generally larger size and the greater ease with which observations can be made upon them. Some lower plants, however, offer good opportunities for growth studies. Borriss (1934*a*) found that growth is not evenly distributed in the sporophore stalk of *Coprinus* but is progressively more rapid toward the apex. This has been confirmed by Bonner, Kane, and Levey (1956; Fig. 2-6), who find that, after the early stage, growth is accomplished chiefly by elongation of the cells of the hyphae. By dusting the tips of young sporangiophores of *Phycomyces* with starch grains and recording changes photographically, Castle (1958) has analyzed the distribution of growth here, both as to longitudinal and circumferential increase. The ratio between these two components is not constant but changes with location on the sporangiophore.

Brown, Reith, and Robinson (1952) examined the mechanism of growth in plant cells, both in intact organs and by culture of isolated fragments. Lindegren and Haddad (1954) found that in yeast cells growth rate is constant and that it begins and ends abruptly, thus differing from growth in most higher organisms.

Physiology of Growth. The essential fact in growth is the increase in amount of the various components of the organism. This results from the self-multiplication of its essential portions, the genes and their basic constituents, the nucleic acids. Everywhere syntheses are involved. This general field is closer to physiology than to morphogenesis. Also essentially physiological are problems concerning the rate and duration of growth. These traits may be affected by many factors, some in the genetic constitution of the plant and others coming from its environment, such as temperature, light, water, and chemical substances of many kinds. To consider these aspects of growth would require much space and is outside the purpose of the present volume. The physiology of plant growth has been frequently discussed, as by Thimann (1954).

It is not growth itself that is of morphogenetic importance but its relative distribution, for this is what determines form. Richards and Kavanagh (1945*a*) call attention to the fact that a study of growth by geometrical changes alone, as is commonly done, does not tell the whole story. Density (mass per unit volume) and volume may be increasing at different rates in different regions. The forces of stretching and compression that result may affect the distribution of growth. Under the discussion of various factors in the latter part of this book, growth and its control will from time to time be mentioned, but as part of a larger problem. This problem is the development of a specifically formed and organized plant body. One of the leading students of morphogenesis has recently expressed this well:

I think, after we have surveyed the facts, that the whole subject of growth will seem bigger than the chemistry of synthesis, and that it will be more likely that this latter will seem a small (although important) part of a larger scheme in which growth is used here and there, sometimes encouraged, sometimes discouraged, and in such a way that a consistent, whole, individual organism is created in an orderly and masterful fashion. (J. T. Bonner, 1952*a*, p. 61.)

CHAPTER 3

The Cellular Basis of Growth

One of the great biological generalizations of the nineteenth century is the cell theory, commonly attributed to the botanist Schleiden and the zoologist Schwann and formally stated in 1839. This was a recognition of the fact that all organisms are composed of living units, the cells. The theory provided a common foundation for a study not only of structure but of growth (cell multiplication) and development (cell differentiation). It has served as a unifying concept for all biology, somewhat comparable to the atomic theory in the physical sciences.

The implications of the cell theory for morphogenesis are important. In the minds of those who promulgated it, it meant that the cell is the true biological individual and that an organism is the result of the activities of its constituent cells. That the cell is thus the primary agent of organization is the opinion of some biologists today. In such a view the organism is looked on as a sort of cellular state, built by the cooperative efforts of its citizens among whom, as in a human society, there is a high degree of division of labor. In support of this idea are cited cases such as that of certain of the slime molds, where some thousands of individual cells (myxamoebae), entirely independent in the early stages of the life cycle, become aggregated into a cellular mass and then by their mutual interactions build up a fruiting body of a specific size and form (p. 223).

Other biologists, however, believe that the true individual is the *organism*, essentially a mass of protoplasm divided into cellular units. Such division has the advantage that it makes possible the differentiation of parts and the segregation of various physiological activities within particular cells. The organism may thus be said to make the cells rather than the cells to make the organism. In this conception the multicellular plant body is to be thought of as having arisen not through the aggregation of individual cells, originally separate, but by cellular multiplication.

That this *organismal theory* gives a better picture of the growth and activities of plants and animals is suggested by the high degree of coordination and self-regulation that exists in a living thing. The production of individuals essentially alike by a variety of developmental routes in regeneration is difficult to explain as a result of the interaction of essentially independent units. The cellular society, if it is one, must have a strong central government which regulates the activities of its individual members. A certain amount of self-differentiation undoubtedly exists, in which a given organ or structure, once its development has begun, proceeds more or less independently of the rest, but the parts are usually interdependent. The problem of organization, the central one for biology, can be attacked more hopefully by a study of organized systems as wholes than simply of the units of which these are composed.

There are obviously considerable differences in the degree and level of organization. In plants with indeterminate growth, especially in some of the lower groups, the "individual" is little more than a colony of cellular individuals, which are so nearly independent that if isolated they will produce new plants directly. Among higher forms it is much more closely organized. Even here one can hardly tell, in types such as strawberries and many grasses, for example, which spread by stolons or rootstocks, how much should be regarded as a single individual. In many cases, however, growth is determinate, the number of parts is relatively constant, and the individual is a distinct and specific thing. In no plants does it reach the high level of organization that most animals display.

In support of the concept that the organism is the developmental unit, one may point to the many cases in plants where, as in the alga *Caulerpa,* a very considerable degree of differentiation occurs into "roots," "stems," and "leaves" but where there are no cellular boundaries at all. The whole plant is a coenocyte, a simple mass of cytoplasm in which great numbers of free nuclei are embedded or move about. In other algae where the general character of the plant body seems to be similar to this, some species have uninucleate cells, others multinucleate ones, and others are entirely coenocytic, with no cell walls save where reproductive organs are formed. In most of the true molds, or *Phycomycetes,* the hyphae are multinucleate and not divided into cells, and this is true of certain of the higher fungi also. In some other algae and fungi the partitions across the filaments are incomplete and have a central perforation through which cytoplasm can flow, so that there is no true cellular structure. In the developing endosperm of the higher plants there is usually at first a large number of free nuclei in a mass of cytoplasm, but these gradually become separated from each other by the growth of walls.

The difference between these two views of the relation between the cell and the organism is of much importance for morphogenetic theory. The individual cells are certainly significant, particularly in physiology, and their presence makes possible much useful analysis of developmental processes, but just how a group of cells develops into an *organism* still remains the central problem.

CELL DIVISION

Growth of plants and animals, in the last analysis, is an increase in amount of living stuff in them, but this growth is almost always accompanied by an increase in the number of their cells. This takes place by the process of cell division, which thus assumes much significance for problems of growth and differentiation. The precise method by which new cells are formed was not understood for some time after the cell theory was established. In the seventies of the last century a number of botanists and zoologists, Strasburger prominent among them, made clear the mechanism of mitosis and the leading part played by the nucleus in cell division.

Division does not take place in all parts of the plant individual. In higher forms it is limited chiefly to apical and lateral meristems and to

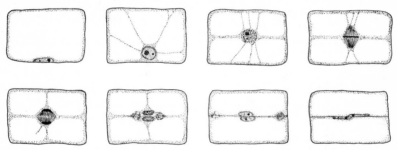

FIG. 3-1. Division of a vacuolate cell showing the development of the phragmosome, which precedes the cell plate. (*From Sinnott and Bloch.*)

the growing regions of determinate organs, though there may be cell division under certain conditions in other parts of the plant.

Division is usually studied in small-celled meristematic regions where the cells are not vacuolate or have only small vacuoles. In many cases, however, particularly in the rib meristems of root and shoot and below wounds, cells that are relatively large and in which a vacuole occupies the bulk of the cell may continue to divide. In such cases the nucleus moves from near the wall to a position in the center of the cell, where it is held by strands of cytoplasm. Here it undergoes mitosis. The position where the cell plate, and later the cell wall, will form is usually indicated early by a plate of cytoplasmic strands, the *phragmosome*, which extends across the cell and in which the nucleus is embedded (Sinnott and Bloch, 1941; Figs. 3-1, 3-2). The cell plate itself is laid down later by the *phragmoplast*, a group of fibers which are a continuation of the fiber system between the nuclei at telophase. This spreads across the cell, following the course of the phragmosome where the latter is present. In side view, as in the dividing cambium cells figured by Bailey (1920*a*), the phragmoplast appears in section as two spindles at the edge of the developing cell plate. In face view it looks like a cytoplasmic "halo." The phragmosome and the phragmoplast, and the function of each in cell division, have sometimes been confused. The difference is made clear by Esau (1953*b*, her Fig. 3-10). In some dividing vacuolate cells, such as those of the cambium, the phragmosome is either absent or has not been observed.

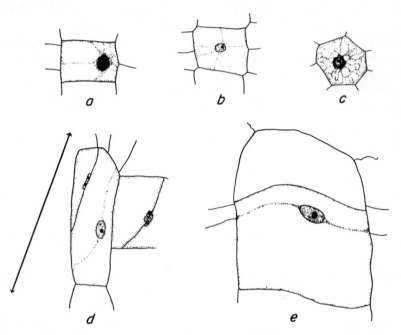

Fig. 3-2. Phragmosomes in various cells, *a–c*, normal tissue; *c*, in face view showing anastomosing strands; *d, e*, mature cells near wound face beginning to divide. (*From Sinnott and Bloch.*)

The significance of the cytoplasm in cell division has been emphasized by Mühldorf (1951). The general problems of cell division in plants are treated at length in Tischler's monumental book (1951).

The factors that determine whether a cell will divide or not are various and have been much discussed. The size of the cell itself is evidently one of these factors. In actively meristematic regions, the dividing cells are usually of about the same size. This means that each daughter cell, after division, enlarges until it reaches the size at which its mother cell divided, and then itself divides. After division ceases, the cells usually expand considerably.

Size in dividing cells is by no means always constant, however. Wagner

(1937), studying the distribution of mitoses in root tips, found that these occurred not only in the small cells at the apex but in the progressively larger ones back from this until division ceased. Incidentally, he reported that in many cases dividing cells are not evenly distributed through the meristematic region but tend to occur in several waves, moving backward from the tip (Fig. 3-3).

In developing cucurbit ovaries during the period of cell division there is a progressive increase in the size of the dividing cells in each region (epidermis to placental region), and this increase is greater in successive tissues from the epidermis inward (Sinnott, 1939; Fig. 3-4). The daughter cells from a division must therefore increase to a size somewhat greater than that at which their mother cell divided before they themselves divide again. The largest cells to divide were many times the volume of the smallest ones.

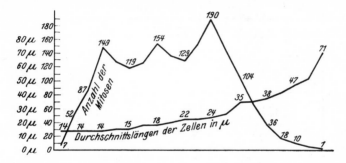

Fig. 3-3. Changes in cell length in microns (lower line) and frequency of mitoses (upper line) at successive distances from the root tip (at left) in periblem of onion root. (*From Wagner.*)

Another factor in division, emphasized especially by zoologists, is the ratio of nucleus to cytoplasm (the *nucleoplasmic* ratio). R. Hertwig (1908) believed that, as a cell grows, the cytoplasm increases faster than the nucleus so that a tension is set up which is finally relieved by the division of the cell. This restores the equilibrium of nucleus and cytoplasm, since presumably the size of the nucleus is at once restored. Popoff (1908) was able to remove some of the cytoplasm from certain cells by micropipette and found that these divided more slowly than their untreated sister cells, as one would expect on Hertwig's theory. There is little evidence from meristematic plant cells that a changing nucleoplasmic ratio is significant in cell division, though perhaps it may be. In larger and vacuolate plant cells it is difficult to measure the cytoplasm since it is distributed in a thin layer lining the wall. The *cytonuclear* ratio (volume of cell to volume of nucleus), however, can be determined. In vacuolate cells of progressively larger size the volume of the nucleus tends to keep pace with the *surface* of the cell and thus perhaps with the volume of the cytoplasm if the thickness of the cytoplasmic layer is constant (Trombetta, 1939; Fig. 3-5). This suggests a relationship which in earlier stages may have a bearing on cell division.

An important element in growth and development is the rate at which cell division takes place. This is essentially a physiological problem and

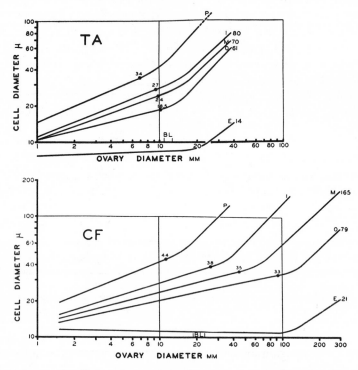

Fig. 3-4. Relation of cell diameter to fruit diameter in *Cucurbita pepo*. TA, small-fruited race. CF, large pumpkin. In early development, cell size increases less rapidly than fruit size, showing that division is occurring. Later growth is by cell enlargement. Solid circles, cell diameter (in microns) at last division. Final cell diameter at end of each line. Lowest curve, epidermis; next higher, outer wall; next, middle wall; next, inner wall; uppermost, placental region. (*From Sinnott.*)

involves various internal and external factors, some of which will later be discussed. There are certain techniques by which it can be measured, however, which are of importance for the student of morphogenesis.

Root tips are especially favorable material for this. Brumfield (1942) recorded the rate of division in the apical meristems of small roots by photographing the surface cells at measured intervals of time, and this has since been done by others (p. 78). A method for measuring rate of increase in cell number by macerating the root meristem and counting the

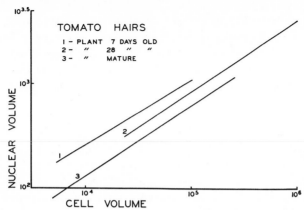

Fig. 3-5. Logarithmic graph of relation of nuclear volume to cell volume in cells of stem hairs of tomato. Nucleus increases about two-thirds as fast as cell. (*From Trombetta.*)

numbers of cells at intervals has been developed by Brown and his students (p. 41). Erickson (1956) has analyzed mathematically the rate of division in certain root tips.

In growing gourd fruits Sinnott (1942) determined cell number by dividing tissue volume by cell volume and found that increase in cell number takes place at approximately the same rate in epidermis, outer wall, inner wall, and placental region, regardless of the marked differences in cell size in the four. Cell division in the epidermis takes place at the rate necessary to maintain a constant cell size, and this tissue may thus serve in a sense as a pacemaker for division in the whole ovary primordium. Jahn (1941) has made a detailed study of the localization and degree of cell division and cell expansion in the epidermis of growing internodes of *Vicia faba*.

CELL SIZE

The size of plant cells is obviously an important element in growth, differentiation, and other morphogenetic problems. Cells are relatively small objects, presumably because the ratio of surface to volume, and thus the ease of exchange of material between a cell and its environment, is inversely proportional to its size. Cells with high metabolic rates tend to be very small, and large cells are relatively inactive. Rapidly dividing cells, for example, are much smaller than those of storage parenchyma. There is a wide range in cell size among various tissues of a plant. In meristematic regions they are often as small as 1,000 cu. microns or less but in pulp of watermelon may be almost a million times this volume. Strasburger (1893) believed that the nucleus has a certain "working sphere" and that this limits the size to which a particular cell will grow.

Studies of comparative cell size have often been made but chiefly on mature cells. This problem, however, is one that must be attacked developmentally. Two processes are involved in it: the rate and amount of growth or increase in size in a given region and the rate and duration of cell division there. Cell size is the result of the relationship between these. The faster the cells divide, in proportion to the total amount of growth, the smaller will they be, and vice versa.

At the end of a cell division each daughter cell is about half the volume of its mother cell. At this time it begins to enlarge, and if it is in a meristematic region it will soon divide again. Where division rate is relatively rapid, the cells may divide before they have time to enlarge to the size of their mother cells, and cell volume decreases, as in some early embryos. Sometimes the new cells do not expand at all and a process of cleavage takes place, much as in the first stages of many animal embryos, where the egg is cut up into a mass of smaller and smaller cells. In plants such cleavage may be seen in endosperm formation; in the development of the female gametophyte within a megaspore; in the renewal of meristematic activity in large, mature cells during regeneration; and elsewhere. Where cell enlargement is relatively rapid, the cells will become larger than their mother cells before they divide again and cell size in the meristematic region will increase. Thus in growing gourd ovaries, where the tissues are still meristematic and the cells all start from a very small size, they gradually enlarge, though not as fast as the ovary itself. In most roots, dividing cells increase in size with increasing distance from the root tip.

In their detailed analysis of the growth of the oat coleoptile, Avery and Burkholder (1936) found that in the outer epidermis cell division ceased after the organ was first initiated, so that during all later growth cells here elongated greatly, sometimes becoming 150 times as long as at the beginning. The inner tissues, however, grew in part by cell multiplication until the coleoptile was 10 to 20 mm. long. There were progressively fewer divisions from the subepidermis inward. Thus at maturity the longest cells were in the outer epidermis, the shortest in the layer next below it, and the cells then increased in length toward the inner layers (Fig. 3-6).

In some meristems, especially the vascular cambium, the size of dividing initials may undergo permanent increase. Sanio (1873) and others since his time have found that xylem cells in trees have different lengths at different distances from the center of the trunk or from the ground and that these differences are mainly established in the fusiform initials in the cambium from which the mature cells develop.

Most increase in cell size, however, comes after the final division. In plants, as contrasted with animals, this increase may be very great. Usually it is related to the absorption of water and increase in size of the vacuole. Differences among tissues in mature cell size are very considerable and are one of the most important aspects of differentiation. In tissues where division persists relatively late there is little time for cell expansion before maturity is reached, and the cells remain small, as is often the case in the epidermis. Where division ceases early, as in storage parenchyma, the cells grow to a much greater size. In many axial structures there is a gradient from without inward, the cells becoming progressively larger toward the center either because of more rapid increase or earlier cessation of divi-

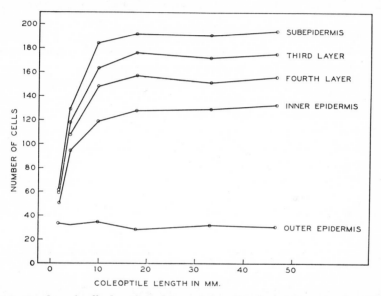

Fig. 3-6. Number of cells, lengthwise, in various cell layers of the oat coleoptile at six stages in its growth. There is evidently no division in the outer epidermis after the coleoptile begins its development, and division ceases early in the other layers, though there are differences among them in the frequency of division. (*From Avery and Burkholder.*)

sion. This is not always the case, for the epidermis may have larger cells than the other tissues, as Avery and Burkholder found in the *Avena* coleoptile.

There is a question as to just where in the cycle of cell division growth actually occurs. Abele (1936) distinguishes between *Teilungswachstum*, growth during division itself, and *Streckungswachstum*, growth after division has ceased. There is certainly a considerable visible increase in size during prophase but not much more until telophase. Of course the duration of these phases must be taken into account. It is probable that non-aqueous material increases at a constant rate throughout growth. Sinnott (1945a) found that in gourds there was no change in rate of growth of the ovary, as measured by gain in dry weight, at the time when cell division ceased and cell expansion began (Fig. 3-7).

Cell Size and Organ Size. There are several important implications of the problem of cell size for morphogenesis. One is that of the relation between the size of an organ or body and the size of the cells that compose it. Is a body large because its cells are large or because they are more numerous? This problem was discussed by Gregor Kraus in 1869 in connection with his work on structural changes during etiolation, but Sachs (1893) and his student Amelung (1893) seem to have been the first to attack it directly. Sachs called attention to the fact that the size of a cell

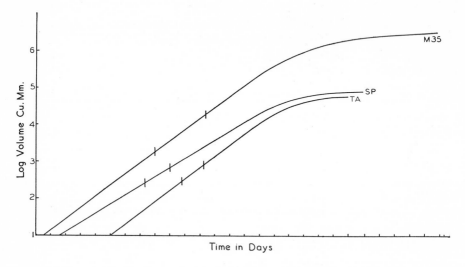

Fig. 3-7. Relation of cell division and cell enlargement to growth. Logarithm of ovary volume plotted against time for three races of *Cucurbita* differing in fruit size. The period between the vertical bars is that during which cell division ceases. To the left of it, growth is by cell division; to the right, by cell enlargement. Despite this change, the rate of growth at this period remains constant. (*From Sinnott.*)

must be closely related to its physiological activity and that cells of a particular tissue should thus be expected to be of about the same size. If this is so, size in a plant would be related to the number rather than the size of its cells. His measurements supported this conclusion. Amelung made a much larger series of measurements and found the same general result, although he observed a good many cases where cell sizes differed considerably between comparable plants or tissues.

The problem is not quite as simple, however, as these early workers thought. It is true that most of the size differences between plants, especially those in the indeterminate axial structures, result from differences in cell number. In determinate organs, on the other hand, notably in bulky structures such as tubers and fruits, the greater size is due to an increase in both the number and the size of their cells. Lehmann (1926) found a positive correlation between the size of a potato tuber and that of its cells. Since the increase in cell size was by no means proportional to that in tuber size, it was evident that large tubers have more as well as larger cells. The same relations are found in tomatoes (Houghtaling, 1935). A more detailed study of this problem, in large-fruited and small-fruited races of gourds, was made by Sinnott (1939; Fig. 3-4). Here cell size increases in the young ovary but much less rapidly than organ size, showing that cell division is taking place. During this period there is more increase in cell size in the larger races. The size at which the cells divide steadily increases. At about the time of flowering, however, division in most of the young fruit ceases, first in the central region and then progressively outward, so that nearly all later fruit growth is by cell expansion. In large-fruited races the period of cell division and that of cell expansion are both longer than in small-fruited ones, so that the greater size of the former is due to both more and larger cells. This general developmental pattern was found by Riley and Morrow (1942) in *Iris* ovaries and fruits, by W. H. Smith (1950) in apple fruits, by Ashby and Wangermann in leaves (p. 210), and by others. In avocado fruits, however, cell division in the fruit wall continues to some extent until maturity (Schroeder, 1953*b*). In general, larger fruit size results from an extension, so to speak, of all parts of the developmental history.

In several genera Ullrich (1953) studied the relation between epidermal cell size and leaf size in the series of successive leaves up the stem. He found that the size of the cells decreases steadily whereas that of the leaves increases for several nodes and then decreases. Thus there is no close relationship, at least in this tissue, between cell size and organ size. Under unfavorable conditions, however, both tend to decrease together. A somewhat similar variation in the correlation between cell and organ size has been reported in wheat (Nilson, Johnson, and Gardner, 1957).

It is noteworthy that tissues differ considerably in the relation of the size of their cells to that of the organ of which they are a part. This relation is usually closest in storage parenchyma and least in the epidermis. In general, as Sachs pointed out, cells that are physiologically important, like most of those in the leaf blade, are relatively constant in size and show little relation to the size of the organ. In mosses, unlike higher plants, cell size and leaf size are usually rather closely proportional to each other, cell number being much more constant.

Size relationships sometimes extend below the level of the cell. The ratio of cell size to nuclear size has already been mentioned here. Both Budde (1923) and Schratz (1927) found a rather close correlation between the total surface area of the plastids and the volume of the cell.

Möbius (1920), however, observed no relation, in 215 species, between chloroplast size and that of cells or organs. Irmak (1956) confirmed this.

There are other complications in the problem of cell size, some of which are of morphogenetic significance. One involves the dwarfing of plant structures. This has been discussed in a number of early papers, among others by Gauchery (1899), Sierp (1913), Oehm (1924), Sinoto (1925), and Abbe (1936). It is generally agreed that where dwarfing is the result of unfavorable environmental conditions cell size is reduced, though not equally in all structures. A scanty water supply chiefly affects the second phase of cell enlargement in which considerable quantities of water normally are absorbed. The problem is complicated by the fact that dwarfing is often the result of genetic as well as environmental influences.

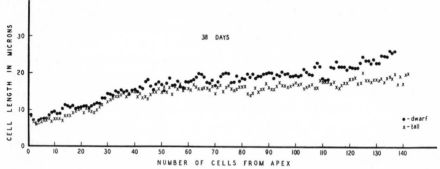

Fig. 3-8. Relation of cell size to plant height. Length of successive cells along the terminal meristematic region of a dwarf race (above) and a tall one (below) of tomato. Cells of the dwarf are somewhat longer because they attain maturity, and thus stop dividing, at an earlier stage. The tall plants have many more cells. (*From Bindloss.*)

Genetic Factors. The relation of genetic factors to cell and body size is complex and will be discussed more fully in a later chapter (Chap. 19). Genetic analyses of size differences in plants have been made repeatedly but the histological effects of gene and chromosome differences are widely various. Most genetically large plants are so because of more rather than larger cells. Thus in the tall races of *Lycopersicon* and *Zinnia* studied by Bindloss (1942) there are many more cells, lengthwise, than in dwarf races, though the cells are somewhat shorter (Fig. 3-8). In other cases, however, cell size is involved. Thus the difference between large-leaved sugar beets and small-leaved vegetable beets is due chiefly to the greater cell size of the former. What is inherited here is evidently the amount of postmitotic expansion, for the meristem cells are the same size in both. Von Maltzahn (1957) found that the difference in size of vegetative structures between large and small races of *Cucurbita* was related to both cell size and cell number.

Some "giant" races, however, owe their large size to larger cells. The first instance of this was reported by Keeble (1912) in a mutant of *Primula sinensis*. Tischler (1918) found a similar case in the reed *Phragmites communis*, and here large cell size was accompanied by larger than normal chromosome size, a fact reported by others (Schwanitz and Pirson, 1955). Much more commonly, giant forms with large cells result from polyploidy (p. 436). The first case of this to be observed was *Oenothera gigas* of de Vries, which was found to be a tetraploid. Many similar examples are now known. Tetraploids are not always giant in character, however, and many polyploid series in nature show no difference in body size or cell size. Sinnott and Franklin (1943) found that in young tetraploid gourd fruits the *gigas* condition, both as to ovary and cells, is present until after flowering but that later growth is reduced so that at maturity there are no great size differences between diploid and tetraploid (p. 439). A diploid giant moss race reported by von Wettstein (p. 437) returned to normal size of cell and organ after a few years of vegetative propagation.

The increased cell size due to polyploidy is not uniform but is considerably greater in some tissues than in others. In the diploid moss races produced by von Wettstein (1924) the ratio of size increase from the $1n$ to the $2n$ was found to be characteristic for each race (p. 437). In general, the increase of organ size due to polyploidy is not as great as the increase in cell size, since cell number tends to be somewhat reduced.

Increased cell size may also result from increased number or bulk of chromosomes (p. 445), quite apart from polyploidy (Navashin, 1931; Lorbeer, 1930), and from extra or accessory chromosomes (Randolph, 1941; Müntzing and Akdik, 1948). Particular chromosomes, when present in trisomics, have different effects on cell size (and on other characters), presumably because of the specific genes which they contain (p. 447). Geitler (1940) observed that chromosome volume was correlated with nuclear volume and that in some tissues the chromosomes were more than four times as large as in others. In species of four genera, Mrs. Sax (1938) found that cell size was correlated with the chromosome number of the species but that in three others there was no such correlation. Somatic polyploidy or polysomaty (p. 441) is a factor of importance both for cell size and for differentiation.

Cell size has been found to be inherited in a number of lower plants, as in yeast (Townsend and Lindegren, 1954).

Heterosis is usually not related to an increase in cell size (Kostoff and Arutiunova, 1936).

Cell Size and Position. Many workers have found a great variation in size among comparable cells in the same plant. Often this is not random but follows a certain pattern. The problem has been studied most intensively in the size (chiefly length) of cells in the xylem of woody plants.

Sanio (1872, 1873), working with pine, was the first to attack this problem intensively. He came to several general conclusions, the more important of which are the following:

1. Tracheids increase in length from the center of the trunk or branch toward the outside through a number of annual rings but finally reach a constant size.

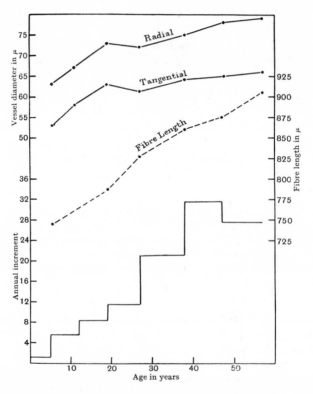

FIG. 3-9. Relation of vessel diameter and fiber length to annual increment and age in trunk of *Acer pseudoplatanus*. (*From Desch.*)

2. This final tracheid size increases from the base of the trunk upward to a maximum at a specific height and then decreases somewhat.

3. The final size of tracheids in a branch is less than in the trunk but depends to some extent on the position of the branch.

Sanio's "laws" have been confirmed by most workers since his time (Kribs, 1928, and others). Bailey and Shepard (1915), however, found that, although the length of tracheids increases from the pith outward in a number of conifers, it does not reach a constant size but fluctuates rather widely, falling and rising in cycles, perhaps climatic ones. Laing (1948), Bissett, Dadswell, and Wardrop (1951), and Bannan (1954) report that tracheid length tends to be less where the growth of the tree in diameter is rapid, presumably because of the more frequent pseudotransverse divisions of the cambial initials. Tracheid length is largely determined by length of the cambial initials (Bailey, 1920*b*).

Dicotyledonous woods follow the same general pattern as conifers but the situation is more complex because of the greater variety of cell types (Desch, 1932; Fig. 3-9; Kaeiser and Stewart, 1955). Fibers may increase considerably in length over their cambial initials (Chattaway, 1936) but vessel segments do not (Chalk and Chattaway, 1935). In storied woods neither fibers nor parenchyma cells show any tendency to increase in length from the pith outward (Chalk, Marstrand, and Walsh, 1955). In all growth rings of pine, Echols (1955) finds a close correlation between the fibrillar angle in the cell wall and tracheid length. The subject of fiber length in woody plants has been reviewed by Spurr and Hyvärinen (1954*b*).

EXPERIMENTAL STUDIES

The division and enlargement of cells are essentially problems in the physiology of growth, a subject too extensive to discuss here in any detail. Much experimental work has been done, however, on certain aspects of cell growth which are of particular morphogenetic interest and which it will be profitable to review briefly.

The role of growth substances (Chap. 18) is particularly important. Auxin was first recognized because of its stimulation of cell enlargement, and in many cases it also affects cell division. Other substances are effective here. Jablonski and Skoog (1954) observed that the cells of tobacco pith tissue in culture did not divide even under optimum amounts of auxin unless extracts from vascular tissue, coconut milk, or certain other things were added. This suggested that a substance specific for cell division but different from auxin was here operative, and such substances, the kinins, are now recognized. Gibberellin especially influences cell size. Wound hormones induce division in many mature cells. The presence of vitamin C seems to be related to cell expansion (Reid, 1941). Lutman (1934) assembled a mass of data on the effects of various inorganic substances on cell size. The stimulating and inhibiting influences of these various chemical factors are key problems in the physiology of development.

Metabolic factors are also important. Oxygen consumption is related to cell division (Beatty, 1946). Interesting observations here have been reported by Transeau (1916) for the seasonal distribution of various species of *Spirogyra*. These differ markedly in the size of their cells, those of the largest being about 150 times the volume of the smallest. The small-celled forms are the first to appear in the spring, when temperatures are low, and the larger-celled ones come on progressively as the season grows warmer. This presumably is because of the higher metabolic rate of the smaller cells which results from their greater ratio of surface to volume.

Progressive physiological changes (p. 210) seem also to be involved. In successively higher leaves on the stem of *Ipomoea*, Ashby and Wangermann (1950; Fig. 3-10) found that the cells became smaller and suggest

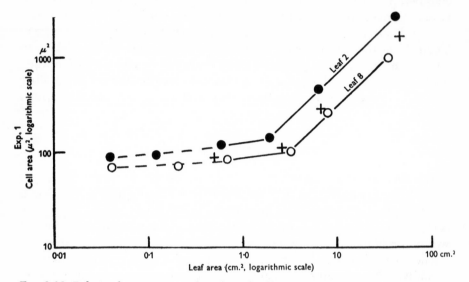

FIG. 3-10. Relation between area of epidermal cells and of leaf lamina in developing leaves of *Ipomoea caerulea,* plotted logarithmically. Solid circles, second leaves; crosses, fifth leaves; empty circles, eighth leaves. Early growth is chiefly by cell division, since cell size increases little. Later growth is by cell enlargement since cells and lamina grow at the same rate. Compare with Fig. 3-4. Cell size becomes smaller in successive leaves. (*From Ashby and Wangermann.*)

that this is symptomatic of a process of aging in the apical meristem. This problem of possible senescence in plants has other implications for cell size. Benedict (1915) presented evidence that in a number of vegetatively propagated plants, notably *Vitis*, cell size tends progressively to decrease with the age of the clone, a fact interpreted by him as the result of senescence. He believed that the "running out" of certain varieties was due to this cause, but it has now been shown that in many cases such a change is due to virus infection. Benedict's results have had some confirmation, notably by Tellefsen (1922) and Bergamaschi (1926) in studies of cuttings from trees of different ages. Ensign (1921), however, found no correlation between age of plant and vein-islet area (and thus cell size).

Even growth habit may involve differences in cell size, for H. B. Smith (1927) reports that annual sweet clover has considerably larger cells than does the biennial race.

Correlation (p. 95), a sufficiently vague term to describe certain phenomena about which we understand little, also affects cell size. In various growth compensations, removal of an organ results in greater growth of another one and often in larger cells there. In "topped" tobacco plants (where the terminal flower cluster has been removed) Avery (1934) found that the leaves on the upper third of the stalk grew larger and that much of this extra growth was due to increase in cell size (Fig. 3-11). Lindemuth (1904) removed and rooted mature begonia leaves and ob-

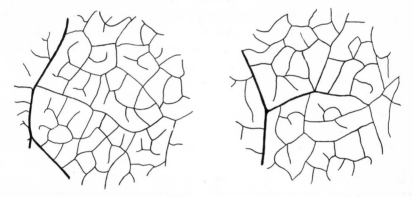

Fig. 3-11. Effect of topping a tobacco plant. Portion of the vein network in the twentieth leaf from the tip. At left, untopped; at right, topped. The leaves from topped plants are larger and have more space between the veins because of increased cell size. (*From Avery.*)

served that they then increased considerably in size, chiefly because of cell enlargement. While they were attached to the plant this presumably was prevented by "correlative inhibition." Similar results have been reported by others. In linden leaves, however, which had been induced to grow much larger than their normal size by the removal of other leaves, Ewart (1906) found the increase to be due chiefly to a larger number of cells.

Factors within the cell itself are doubtless related to the onset of its division. Cytoplasmic viscosity generally rises in prophase, falls in metaphase, and rises again in telophase. Molè-Bajer (1953) has explored the effect of artificially increased viscosity of cytoplasm in slowing down the rate of mitotic division. Gustafsson (1939) found that the difference between meiotic and mitotic division was related to the degree of hydration of the nucleus. The effect of dehydration in checking mitosis has also been reported by Molè-Bajer (1951).

Osmotic concentration of the cell sap was observed by Becker (1931) to be inversely proportional to cell size and to number of chromosome sets in polyploid moss protonemata.

Various external factors are important both for the division and the enlargement of cells. Light frequently tends to check division, and ultraviolet radiation may inhibit it. The hypothetical mitogenetic rays of Gurwitsch (1926) and his school were thought to stimulate mitosis. The effect of light on cell size has been emphasized by Straub (1948). Most of the elongation of etiolated plants (p. 309) is due to increase in cell length. Giese (1947) has reviewed 300 papers dealing with the effects of various kinds of radiation on the induction of nuclear division.

Temperature, so important in many protoplasmic processes, has an effect on mitosis. P. C. Bailey (1954) has shown that in *Trillium* the maximum rate of cell division takes place at considerably lower temperatures than does the maximum rate of increase in root length. Burström (1956) reports that under higher temperatures the final cell length in roots is less because of the shorter period of cell elongation.

Wagner (1936) found evidence that gravity influences mitosis. In root tips placed horizontally he observed that after about an hour there was a marked increase of mitoses on the upper side, so that the very tip of the root bent down. After 4 hours mitoses were equally distributed, and after 10 to 12 hours they were more abundant on the lower side and the tip straightened out again. These changes were quite independent of the geotropic bending due to auxin and cell expansion, which was evident much farther back from the tip. When plants were grown on a clinostat, Brain (1939) observed in lupine seedlings that cells of the cortex, endodermis, and pith in the hypocotyl were larger than those of upright plants but that in the radicle they were smaller.

In some cases pressure stimulates division, as can be seen in the cortical tissues through which a lateral root pushes its way (Tschermak-Woess and Doležal, 1953).

Water is of marked influence in determining cell size. The amount of it available often determines how much a cell can expand (Thimann, 1951). Zalenski and others (p. 325) have observed that at successively higher levels on a plant the cells of the leaves are smaller, presumably because of their inability to become fully turgid while they were expanding. Water may have other effects. Funke (1937–1939) found that if some water plants are put into deep water their petioles elongate rapidly by cell expansion, sometimes lengthening tenfold in 2 days.

The role of the wall in cell growth has been much discussed. Does the wall merely stretch under the pressure of an expanding vacuole or does it grow independently of this? Burström (1957 and earlier papers) presents evidence that cell elongation is not primarily a matter of water uptake but is due to growth of the cell wall. He believes that this occurs in two steps, the first a plastic stretching of the wall and the second the production and deposition of new wall material. Auxin promotes the first but probably inhibits the second. Others believe that auxin, known to stimulate cell enlargement, directly increases the plasticity of the wall and thus its extensibility (Heyn, 1940). This view has found recent support (p. 412).

It obviously is necessary to know just how the wall grows and particularly whether this is by apposition of new material on its inner face or by intussusception throughout. Green (1958), using techniques for measuring radioactivity, treated elongating *Nitella* cells with tritium (H_3) and found by test that the inner part of the wall became radioactive. The outer portion, which was not, grew thinner as the cell lengthened, thus suggesting that new cell wall material was being laid down only on the inside and not throughout.

Rate of wall thickening sometimes has a direct effect on plant size. Thus in a dwarf mutant of *Aquilegia* (Anderson and Abbe, 1933) this trait was found to be due to the precocious thickening of its cell walls (p. 426).

The important problem of the relation of deoxyribonucleic acid to cell division has often been investigated. Grundmann and Marquardt (1953) determined the content of DNA in successive phases in the mitotic cycle of the nuclei of periblem cells of the root tip of *Vicia*. This increases steadily throughout the interphase. It is reduced at telophase since it is roughly proportional to nuclear volume.

Brown and his students have used various modern techniques for a study of the problems of the multiplication and growth of cells. Brown and Rickless (1949), for example, cut off *Cucurbita* root tips of equal length (1.6 mm.) and grew them in culture for 3 days, taking samples every 12 hours. These tips were macerated, and in a haemacytometer the total number of cells and the number of nonvacuolate cells were counted. From these counts, together with a measurement of the length of each root examined, it was possible to determine the rate of cell division and the index of extension (ratio of root length to number of vacuolate cells). This method is subject to a number of errors, particularly from the assumption that only the nonvacuolate cells were dividing. However, it gave consistent results, and these were in general agreement with the more laborious method of measuring cell size and volume from microtome sections. The authors found that there was no division in the absence of sugar in the culture medium and that the rate of division increased with the addition of sugar and inorganic salts and even more with the addition of yeast extract. At 15°C the rate of division was higher than at 5 or

25°. The greatest increase in cell size was with sugar and mineral salts. Yeast extract tended to decrease extension.

Brown and Wightman (1952) grew root tips of pea 3.0, 6.0, and 10.0 mm. long in sterile culture and found that the peak rate of division occurs later and that its peak value is greater the shorter the initial tip. They conclude that cell division in the meristem depends partly on synthesis of metabolites there and partly on a supply of metabolites from more mature regions of the root.

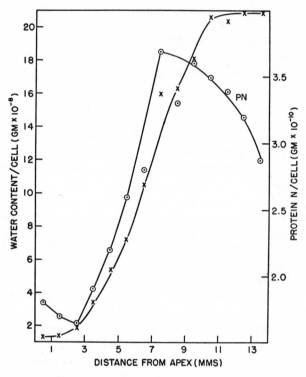

Fig. 3-12. Changes in protein (circles) and water content (crosses) of bean-root cells at increasing distances from the root apex. (*From Brown and Robinson.*)

A basic problem in this field is that of protein synthesis. Brown and Broadbent (1950) sliced a series of root tips into segments 0.2 to 0.8 mm. thick and in each successive section determined the number of cells, the protein content, the dry weight, and the amount of respiration. During development from the meristematic to the fully extended state the average cell volume increased thirtyfold and there was an increase in protein content and in respiration (Fig. 3-12).

Genetic factors are concerned in cell activities in many ways. Beadle (1931), for example, found a gene for supernumerary divisions in maize;

Moewus (1951), one for cell division in *Protosiphon* which is linked to sex manifestation; and Nickerson and Chung (1954), one in yeast that seems to block the sulphydryl mechanism of division. Dörries-Rüger (1929) grew protonemata from the spores of plants produced by various combinations of genome and plasmon in mosses, among races developed in Wettstein's laboratory. She cut off and cultured the tip cells of these protonemata and recorded marked differences in the rate of cell division in the filaments growing from them, thus comparing the effects of different genotypes under the same environment.

PLANE OF CELL DIVISION

Cell size and cell number are important elements in growth and differentiation, but the problem of form is primarily dependent not on these factors but on the relative *directions* in which growth occurs. These, in turn, are closely related to the planes of cell division in the developing tissues. Whatever determines the position of the new cell wall between two daughter cells will determine the direction in which these cells expand, since this direction will normally be at right angles to the new wall. At the time of cell division, therefore, the direction of growth in this particular region of the meristem is determined. If plant cells could change their relative positions, as is possible in many animal tissues, the deciding factor in the direction of growth would often be cell movement rather than plane of cell division.

The position of the cell plate at telophase, and thus of the new cell wall, follows the position which the equatorial plate of chromosomes finally assumes at metaphase. The mitotic figure may roll around somewhat before it settles down to a permanent position, but there must be something that determines that position. This raises the question as to whether the plane of division is controlled by whatever decides the final orientation of the mitotic figure or whether this, in turn, is itself determined by other factors. That the latter may be the case is suggested by the way in which vacuolate cells divide. In such cells a series of cytoplasmic strands forms a loose diaphragm, the phragmosome, across the cell, and in the middle of this the nucleus is supported. In tissues where the plane of division can be predicted, observation shows that the position of this diaphragm is the one which the future cell wall will occupy. The diaphragm is laid down considerably before the nucleus enters metaphase, and the metaphase plate of chromosomes may not at first lie parallel to the diaphragm, though it finally does. This seems to indicate that the plane of division is determined early and for the cell as a whole rather than by factors acting on the mitotic figure alone. There is also evidence that the mother cell, before division, begins to elongate at right angles to the direction in which it will divide. All this raises the fundamental question as to whether morphogenetic factors operate directly on each dividing cell or whether relative directions of growth, and thus form, are determined by factors affecting the entire growing organ, the whole mass of living stuff, and that the degree and manner in which this is cut up into cells are a secondary result. This is simply another aspect of the main problem raised by the cell theory.

Factors Determining the Plane of Cell Division. Many suggestions have been made as to the factors that determine the position of a new cell wall. Years ago Hofmeister (1863) stated the general rule which bears his name, that growth precedes division and that the new wall is at right angles to the long axis of the mother cell. There are many cases, especially in parenchymatous tissue, where this rule holds, but frequent exceptions to it occur in which the new wall is *parallel* to the long axis. An extreme example of this is the longitudinal division of very long cambial initials. Sachs (1878) noted that in most dividing cells the new wall meets the old one at an angle of 90°, even though this requires that the new wall be curved, and proposed this as a rule for cell division.

About a decade later a number of biologists were impressed by the close resemblance between many cell configurations and masses of soap bubbles. The behavior of molecules in liquids and the principle of surface tension were then being worked out by physicists. One of the implications of surface tension is that, because of molecular forces acting at their surfaces, liquids tend to pull themselves into forms with the smallest possible surface area. This is why drops of liquid, for example, or soap bubbles are spherical. The principle of least surfaces was applied to liquid film systems by the physicist Plateau (1873), who showed that in a mass of bubbles the partition walls in every case arrange themselves so that they have the least possible area. He also observed that where walls intersect there are only three at a given point and that the angles between them tend to be 120°, the point at which surface forces are in equilibrium.

The biologists Berthold (1886) and Errera (1888) applied this principle to young cell walls, assuming that these walls in the beginning are essentially weightless liquid films. The rather striking resemblance often observed between a mass of cells and a mass of bubbles on this assumption is easy to understand. Some interesting implications of the principle of least surfaces for the problem of cell division have been developed by D'Arcy Thompson (1942).

Only a few examples need be cited here. If, in a cubical box, the sides of which are liquid films, a film partition extends across the middle, the partition will be flat. If it is gradually moved toward one of the sides so that the two "cells" become more and more unequal in size, it will suddenly shift to a position across a corner of the box and, as seen in section,

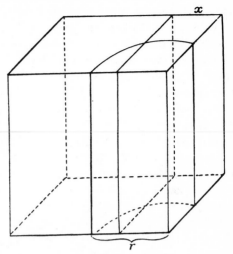

Fig. 3-13. Hypothetical cube of film with a film partition moving from left to right across it. When a position is reached 31.8 per cent of the distance from the right-hand side, this partition slips into the corner and becomes curved, as shown. (*From D'Arcy Thompson.*)

will now be curved instead of straight as it was before (Fig. 3-13). The point where this shift occurs is the point where the wall, now (in section) a quarter of the circumference of a circle, has the same length that the flat partition wall had, for the wall will have the least possible area that will enclose the volume of the smaller "cell," the latter now being part of a cylinder. If this smaller cell is then made still smaller, the wall that separates it from the larger one will continue to be curved and to be less than any other wall area that could bound the volume of the smaller cell.

Just where the point of shift from flat wall to curved will occur can be calculated by determining the point at which (before the shift) the length of a curved wall (a quarter of the circumference of a circle) across the corner will be the same as that of the flat partition wall. Both will enclose the same area. If it is assumed that each side of the cube, and thus the length of the flat partition, equals 1, then

$$\frac{2\pi r}{4} = 1 \qquad 2\pi r = 4 \qquad \text{and} \qquad r = \frac{4}{2\pi} = 0.637$$

The area of a quarter circle with this radius is $\pi(0.637)^2/4 = 0.318$. This also is the area of the smaller rectangular cell just before the shift. Thus the distance from the partition wall to the side wall, when it shifts from straight to curved, is 0.318 of the diameter of the cube. Experiments with films essentially confirm this theoretical expectation. In cases of unequal division of actual cells, such as the formation of companion cells in sieve tubes, the new cell is usually cut out of a corner of the old one, as this theory of least surfaces requires.

Many dividing cells in plants and animals are spherical, and here the application of the liquid film theory is particularly interesting. In the division of an egg into two equal cells, for example, the position of the wall between the two daughter cells, if they behave like soap bubbles, can be determined. This new wall should form an angle of 120° with the tangent to the circumference of each daughter cell at the point where these meet the partition wall, since this is the position where the surface forces will be in equilibrium and where the film system thus is stable. It is obvious geometrically that this wall is in such a position that the distance between the centers of the two new cells is equal to their radii (Fig. 3-14). When a single spherical cell, such as an egg or an algal cell, divides thus equally, the position of the two daughter cells relative to each other is approximately what this theory demands.

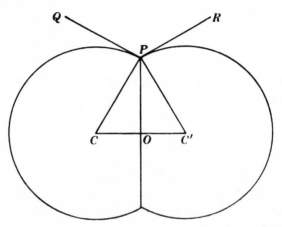

Fig. 3-14. Stable partition and walls of minimum surface assumed by two equal bubbles which are in contact. Angles *OPQ* and *OPR* are 120°. The distance between the centers equals the radii. (*From D'Arcy Thompson.*)

Where such a divided bubble divides again but now by a partition at right angles to the plane of the first one, these two walls usually do not meet at an angle of 90° but there is a readjustment in the film system so that they meet at 120°, the stable position. Arrangements like that of Fig. 3-15*d* may thus result, which resembles a group of actual cells. Anyone familiar with cellular structure and who draws a bit of it comes almost instinctively to make the cell walls intersect at angles of about 120°, much as they would if they were liquid films.

Where a spherical bubble is divided unequally, the curvature of the partition wall can be calculated. Since the pressure is inversely proportional to the radius of curvature, a small bubble pulls itself together, so to speak, more strongly than a larger one. Thus $P = 1/R$, where P is the pressure and R the radius. The pressure that determines the radius of the partition wall between unequal bubbles is thus the difference between the pressure of the smaller bubble and that of the larger one. If R equals the radius of the partition wall, r' that of the smaller bubble, and r that of the larger one, then $1/R = 1/r' - 1/r$, or $R = rr'/(r - r')$. In other words, the radius of the partition wall is the product of the two bubble radii divided by their difference. If two bubbles have radii of 3 and 5, for example, that of the partition wall will be 7.5. In spherical cells of unequal size which are dividing, the new wall does tend to have this theoretical radius.

Where the dividing cell has a relatively firm wall, however, as in microspores within which a small prothallial cell is cut off, the situation is different, since only the new dividing wall now acts as a liquid film. It will be curved and will occupy a position such that it intersects the old wall at the stable position of 90°. If the linear distance between the two

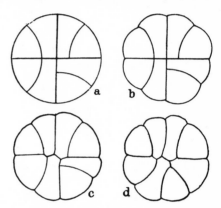

Fig. 3-15. Plate of eight cells (or bubbles) assuming a position of equilibrium where cell surfaces are of minimum area. (*From D'Arcy Thompson.*)

points of intersection (as seen in section) and the radius of the large cell are known, the radius of curvature of the new wall can readily be calculated.

There are other cases of division walls, notably in "rib" meristems where the cells are in parallel rows and growth is strongly polar, which may also be interpreted on the liquid-film theory even though the resemblance to a bubble system is much less close. In such rows of cells it can be observed that the new cross walls, even in the phragmosome stage, always tend to avoid a position that would put them opposite a cross wall in an adjacent row (Fig. 3-16) and would thus bring four walls together, unstably, at a point. The walls are always "staggered," like bricks in a wall. This often prevents a new wall taking its natural position, which would divide the cell into two equal parts. The angles between the walls are larger than 90° but do not reach the theoretical 120°. It may be that surface forces are operative in pulling the new wall away from the intersection point with an old one and thus tending to form an angle of 120°, even though the longitudinal walls, which are relatively firm, remain essentially straight and the theoretical angle cannot be attained.

The theory that the position and curvature of dividing cells are what they would be if the walls were liquid films lends itself to some interesting geometrical analyses, for which the reader is referred to Thompson's book. Giesenhagen's work (1905, 1909) also has a discussion of the theory and its applications. Various experiments with actual liquid films have been reported by van Iterson and Meeuse (1942), and Matzke (1946) has discussed the role of surface forces in determining cell shape. There is no doubt that the configurations of the cells in an actively growing mass often do resemble a system of bubbles, for there are usually no more than three walls intersecting at a point and the angles between them tend to approximate 120°. The young walls are at least semiliquid, so that

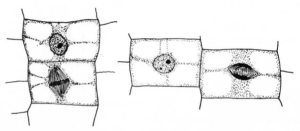

Fig. 3-16. Walls in dividing cells (as shown by position of phragmosome) tend to avoid continuity with adjacent partition walls. (*From Sinnott and Bloch.*)

surface forces are doubtless operative to some extent in determining their position. In any morphogenetic analysis the least-surface theory therefore must certainly be taken into account. It greatly oversimplifies the problem, however, and fails to explain some facts with which the student of plant development is confronted. Among the chief objections to it are the following:

1. The theory in its simplest form is applicable only to weightless liquid films, and young cell walls obviously are not such, though they may approach this condition. To account for their position the theory would require correction.

2. Many division walls are formed in positions different from those which the theory demands. Often the new walls are parallel to the longer axis of the cell instead of at right angles to it. The most extreme case of this occurs in dividing fusiform initials at the cambium which are 50 times or more as long as wide but which nevertheless divide lengthwise.

3. The early wall formed by the cell plate, and certainly the phragmosome which precedes it in vacuolate cells, are not at first continuous films and would thus not follow the law of least surfaces.

4. In many cases, as often in the unequal division that cuts off a stomatal mother cell, the new wall is at first straight instead of curved and becomes curved only later, as the turgor of the cell increases.

5. Frequently, as in growing cork layers, the new division wall is laid down exactly opposite a partition wall in an adjacent cell so that four walls do come together at a point (p. 195). This also happens in tissue which is to form aerenchyma and in which the cells are in regular rows with cross walls opposite. Here, however, at the point where the four walls meet, a small air space (which later may enlarge) is commonly formed by the pulling apart of the walls so that the wall angles do tend to reach the theoretical 120°.

6. In a system of film bubbles increasing in number by the formation of new walls, the equilibrium least-surface configuration is reached by a shifting of the wall positions within the film system. This involves some gliding or sliding of the bubbles in relation to each other. Such a change could happen in animal tissues where the cells are free to move about, at least to some degree, but would be impossible in most plant tissues, where they are cemented to one another.

For these reasons it is clear that the theory of surface forces alone is by no means sufficient to explain all the facts as to the position of new cell walls and the planes of cell division. Other physical factors are doubtless involved in determining these events. Among them pressure is important. Kny (1902) found that pressure applied to a dividing cell forced the mitotic figure into a position in which its long axis was oriented at right angles to the direction of the pressure, and the new wall consequently was parallel to this direction. This fact, incidentally, makes an important contribution to our knowledge of the character of the cytoplasm, at least at this time in the history of the cell. If the cytoplasm were essentially fluid, pressure from without should not change the orientation of structures in it but would do so if the cytoplasm had a structural framework. Other evidence for the conclusion that walls are formed parallel to pressure on the cell can be found in the cortex of the young stems of many woody plants. Here the cells tend to be elongated tangentially, presumably because of the pressure exerted by the expansion of the vascular cylinder below through cambial activity. If these cells divide again, radial walls, parallel to the direction of cambium pressure, are often to be seen. As Kny points out, however, in cambial cells, which are presumably under radial pressure, division is chiefly periclinal (at right angles to the pressure) instead of anticlinal. This he attributes to "inner factors." In the case of radial divisions in the phellogen, Bouygues (1930) concludes that pressure is not a factor.

The plane of division is evidently related to the polarity of the cell and is further discussed under this topic (p. 131). It has been studied particularly in the egg of *Fucus*. Here centrifugal force, light, electricity, and gradients in concentration of various substances have been found to affect this plane.

In certain colonial blue-green algae and flagellates, in pollen mother cells, and in some other cases where division in all the cells is simultaneous and in the same plane, the planes of each successive division tend

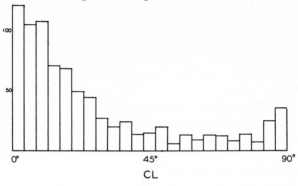

CL

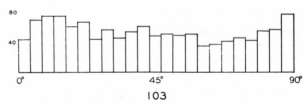

103

Fɪɢ. 3-17. Distribution of angles between mitotic spindles and longitudinal axis of the ovary in an elongate type of cucurbit fruit (above) and an isodiametric one (below). There is evidently a higher proportion of divisions nearly at right angles to the axis (spindles with low angles) in the former. In the latter, divisions are approximately equal at all angles. (*From Sinnott.*)

to be at right angles to each other so that a regular pattern of cells in twos, fours, eights, sixteens, and so on, all in one plane, is produced. Between divisions the cells tend to grow but not enough to make them isodiametric, so that the next division is at right angles to the longer axis of the cell, as it would be in a least-surface configuration (Geitler, 1951). Division in three planes sometimes occurs, producing cubical colonies.

In many instances there is no obvious explanation for the particular plane in which a cell divides, and we are forced to attribute this to genetic factors. Steward (1958) finds that in cells freely suspended in culture the planes of division are highly irregular and unpredictable, since such cells are not subject to the organizing restraints that are operative in the normal plant body.

The forms of most plant structures are presumably related to the planes in which their constituent cells divide. In a few cases this relationship has been demonstrated. Thus in ovary primordia of elongate gourds such as *Trichosanthes* and the "club" variety of *Lagenaria*, Sinnott (1944) measured in the growing ovary the angles between the mitotic spindles and the longitudinal axis of the primordium and found that there were many

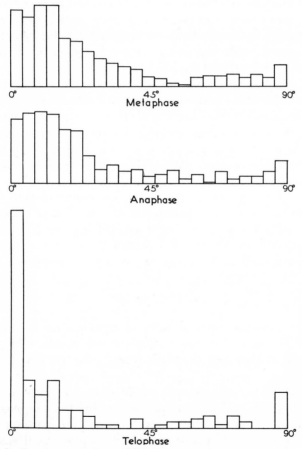

Fig. 3-18. Angles between mitotic spindle and ovary axis in metaphases, anaphases, and telophases in *Trichosanthes*, the snake gourd, where the great preponderance of divisions are transverse and thus predictable as to orientation. The mitotic figure evidently becomes more stabilized in direction as mitosis proceeds. (*From Sinnott.*)

more of them parallel to the primordium axis, in the direction of growth in length, than at right angles to it, in the direction of growth in width. In isodiametric ovaries, however, spindle angles were almost equally distributed between 0 and 90° to the axis (Fig. 3-17).

The question arises as to just what determines the plane of cell division in cases like this. It cannot be simply the orientation of the mitotic spindle, for this can be shown to change during mitosis. Thus in the fruit of *Trichosanthes*, which is very long and narrow, practically all the divisions are transverse to the long axis and their orientation can thus be predicted. The spindles in metaphase, however, are by no means all parallel to the axis but vary considerably. In anaphase the variation is much less, and in telophase the cell plates are almost all transverse (Fig. 3-18). Evidently the spindle rolls about somewhat during mitosis (as it has been seen to do in living material of other forms) but finally settles into position. What this position will be seems to be determined by the cytoplasmic body since, in vacuolate cells, the phragmosome is formed at prophase in the position of the final cell wall (p. 25).

Something certainly controls not only the plane of cell division but the distribution of divisions and the amount and character of cell expansion. Whatever this may prove to be, it is concerned with the origin of organic form. If one looks at a section through a young and growing plant structure, such as an ovary primordium, he sees a mass of cells of various shapes and dividing in many planes. Here chaos seems to reign. When he observes how such a structure develops, however, and finds that it is growing in a very precise fashion, each dimension in step with all the others, he comes to realize that this is not the seat of chaos but of an organizing control so orderly that a specific organic form is produced. This realization is one of the most revealing experiences a biologist can have and poses for him the major problem that his science has to face.

CELL SHAPE

One of the simplest manifestations of organic form is in the shape of individual cells. This obviously involves plane of cell division, cell size, polarity, microstructure of the wall, genetic constitution, and other factors.

Since the cell, at least at first, is a fluid system, its natural shape, other things being equal, is that of a sphere, for this has the least surface in proportion to its volume. Most cells, however, are parts of tissues and thus are closely packed against neighboring cells on all sides. This results in a modification of the basic spherical shape to that of a polyhedron with flattened sides, each representing a plane of contact with an adjacent cell. How many faces should such a cell have, and what sorts of polygons should these faces be? At first it was believed that cells were 12-sided figures, since when spheres are stacked together like cannon balls, each touches 12 others. Lord Kelvin (1887, 1894), approaching the problem mathematically, showed that when space is divided into similar units, each with a minimum area of partition and with stable angles, each unit will be a 14-faced figure or a tetrakaidecahedron and that eight of its faces will be hexagons and six will be squares. This, he thought, was what the shape of a cell in pith or similar tissues theoretically should be. F. T. Lewis (1923 and others) found that the average number of faces in such cells was, indeed, close to 14 but that only very rarely did a cell with this number of faces show eight hexagons and six squares.

This problem has been studied with particular care by Matzke and his students and reported in a series of papers. The results have been briefly reviewed by Matzke (1950), who cites the more important papers from his laboratory. The general conclusion is that parenchyma cells do tend to have 14 sides but that "ideal" ones, conforming to Lord Kelvin's rule, occur very infrequently. Matzke points out that many factors other than mathematically ideal space-filling are involved in determining cell shape, among them pressure, surface forces, differences in cell size, direction of cell division, unequal growth, and genetic constitution. The problem is being attacked developmentally by an analysis of cell shapes at the meristem (Matzke and Duffy, 1956). In dividing cells, the number of faces here rises to about 17 and in daughter cells drops at first to between 12 and 13. The total cell population has an average number of about 14 faces.

In more specialized tissues there is a wide variety of cell shapes. Palisade cells are elongated at right angles to the leaf surface. Most cells of the vascular and conducting tissues are elongated parallel to the axis. Hairs and glandular cells have many forms. Some cells expand equally on all sides. Others, like root hairs, grow only at one point. Still others, such as the more fantastic sclereids, have many growing regions (Foster, 1955, and others). Galston, Baker, and King (1953) found that benzimidazole promotes the transverse as opposed to the longitudinal extension of cortex cells in the pea epicotyl. Doubtless the polarity, or polarities, of the cell and the plasticity, elasticity, and microstructure of its walls are involved in shape differences.

Tenopyr (1918) found that in leaves of different shapes the shapes and sizes of cells were constant. Rüdiger (1952), however, observed that in tetraploid plants the subepidermal cells of leaves, hypocotyls, and other organs were not only absolutely but relatively wider than in diploids, a fact which he relates to the greater relative width found in most tetraploid organs as compared with diploid ones.

Even in microorganisms where the cells are free from contact with others, they often display shapes by no means spherical. Many unicellular green algae and the simpler fungi are examples of this. Von Hofsten and von Hofsten (1958) have explored the effect of various factors on cell shape and thus on vegetative characters in the ascomycete *Ophiostoma*. In the development of cell shape genetic factors are doubtless important, and these appear to control cytoplasmic patterns, wall differences, and other factors. Cell shape is one aspect of the more general problem of differentiation.

Much of morphogenetic significance can be learned from a study of individual cells. A knowledge of their relations to each other, and particularly of the way in which they form cell aggregates, is still more important. This involves the general problem of meristematic activity, the subject of the next chapter.

CHAPTER 4

Meristems

In many of the morphogenetic problems which they present, plants and animals are very similar. The fundamental physiological differences that distinguish these two groups of living things, however, produce a number of developmental differences between them. Among these, that in method of growth is conspicuous. Because of their ability to synthesize food from inorganic substances, plants have developed, in all forms but the smallest and simplest, a body which is nonmotile and anchored to the soil or other substratum. This doubtless resulted, during the course of evolution, from the fact that motility in a plant is not necessary for obtaining food, as it is in animals.

The motility of animals requires that their skeletons be jointed and the rest of their bodies relatively soft and plastic. Plants, however, gain the necessary rigidity not by a specially differentiated skeleton but by a thickening of the walls of most of the cells. This is especially conspicuous in the fibrovascular system of higher plants but it occurs in other tissues. The plant cell wall, because cellulose is characteristically deposited in it, is a much firmer structure than the rather tenuous membrane which surrounds typical animal cells. As a result, plant tissues themselves are also firmer, save in exceptional cases such as certain short-lived floral parts. As a consequence of this distinctive character, most plant cells, as soon as their final size is reached, become locked up, so to speak, in a firm box of cellulose. Such a cell ordinarily does not divide further, or if it does its daughter cells cannot expand, so that mature plant tissue usually grows no more. In almost every part of the soft-celled animal body, on the contrary, growth occurs not only during development but in the restoration and repair of tissues throughout the life of the individual. It should be remembered, however, that under certain conditions a plant cell or a group of cells may become embryonic again and begin to divide (p. 232), setting up a new growing region. There is no doubt that most cells—perhaps all—are potentially able to do this. What prevents it is not simply mechanical confinement by the wall but so-called correlative factors that limit each cell to the development appropriate for its particular place in the organism.

If a plant is to grow, this must be accomplished by allowing some of its cells to escape the general fate and remain capable of division, progressively forming new tissues but preserving a remnant that persists in a perpetually embryonic condition. The plant body grows in size by the activity of such localized growing points or regions, the *meristems,* which are centers of cell division and cell expansion.

The axis of the plant grows in length by a meristem at the apex of stem and root, and in width by a sheath of lateral meristem, or cambium. Determinate organs such as leaves, however, rarely have sharply localized meristems but enlarge throughout much of their extent, as an animal body does, until growth ceases. Meristems are obviously of much interest to the student of plant morphogenesis. They provide, in a sense, a continuous embryology for the plant and offer an important point of attack on the problems of plant development.

APICAL MERISTEMS

In the simplest plants, the lower algae and fungi, growth is hardly localized at all. Cells capable of division are either present throughout the plant body or in considerable portions of it, and nothing which might be called a meristem is to be found. In *Spirogyra,* for example, growth in length of the filament is produced by cell division almost anywhere in it. In such a membranous type as *Ulva,* growth results from divisions at right angles to the surface throughout most of its area. In coenocytic forms, the whole thallus enlarges, and growth is not related to cell division at all.

In some of the simpler filamentous brown algae, however, growth in length is limited to the tip of the filament, which is occupied by a single large cell. This divides transversely, and a series of daughter cells is thus produced from its basal face. They and their daughter cells divide a few more times, but division finally ceases. The only permanently embryonic cell is the apical one, which thus dominates the development of the plant body. Branches originate by the lengthwise division of this apical cell (Fig. 4-1).

In types like *Fucus,* with larger and more complex plant bodies, growth still originates by the activity of an apical cell, which occupies the base of a terminal notch in the thallus. This cell cuts off daughter cells from its two lateral faces. From these and their descendants are formed the various tissues of the thallus. A fern prothallium grows in much the same way, developing under the control of the meristematic region in the notch. This control may be relaxed, however, and almost any cell in the structure may begin to divide. Many prothallia never form the typical heart-shaped structure.

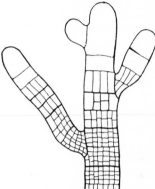

FIG. 4-1. Terminal portion of the alga *Sphacelaria,* showing how thallus is produced by activity of the apical cell and its descendants and how a branch originates. (*From Haberlandt.*)

Throughout the bryophytes, the ferns, the horsetails, and many of the lycopods, growth of the plant body is governed by the activity of apical cells, one at the apex of the shoot and the other at the apex of the root. These cells are usually pyramidal with the base of the pyramid outward, and division takes place parallel to the three inner sides of the pyramid. Most growth of tissues results from the later division of these daughter cells and their descendants, but growth seems to be initiated and dominated by the apical cell (Figs. 4-2, 4-3). It is not clear, however, just what the function of the apical cell is. Wetmore (communication to the author) states that he has very rarely seen an apical cell dividing and he suggests that these cells may function as do the groups of large cells just below the apex of root and shoot in angiosperms, which are thought to be centers of metabolic activity. Most of the actual cell division in the meristems of these lower vascular plants takes place in the cells just be-

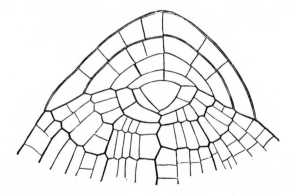

FIG. 4-2. Longitudinal section through apex of a fern root, showing origin of tissues from the apical cell. (*From Sachs.*)

side or below the apical cell. In ferns, lycopods, and horsetails this considerable body of embryonic cells at the apex of the axis somewhat resembles the terminal meristems of higher plants.

Among bryophytes, the origin and arrangement of the leaves and the structure of the various tissues can usually be traced back to precise divisions of the apical cell and its daughter cells so that there is a very definite pattern of cell lineage in the plant body. This is especially diagrammatic in such a form as *Sphagnum,* where the two markedly different types of cells in the leaves can be seen to originate in differential cell divisions. Such a precise cell lineage is less conspicuous in higher

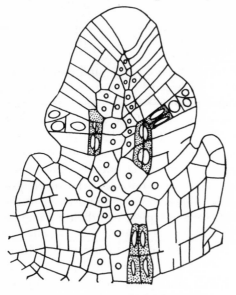

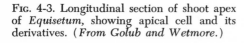

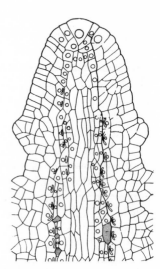

Fig. 4-3. Longitudinal section of shoot apex of *Equisetum,* showing apical cell and its derivatives. (*From Golub and Wetmore.*)

Fig. 4-4. *Selaginella wildenovii.* Median longitudinal section of young shoot, showing apical cell and its derivatives. (*From Barclay.*)

forms but often can still be traced even there. In one species of *Selaginella* (Barclay, 1931), for example, the derivation of the epidermis, cortex, pericycle, endodermis, and vascular cylinder can be traced back to direct descendants of the apical cell (Fig. 4-4).

Although the distribution of the leaves and the general organization of the shoot are determined in many of the lower forms by the activity of the apical cell and the arrangement of its derivatives, Golub and Wetmore (1948) found that in *Equisetum* there is no relation between the cellular pattern of the apex and that of the mature axis derived from it.

In a few of the lower vascular plants, notably *Lycopodium,* no single apical cell can be distinguished, and the same is true of most gymnosperms and angiosperms. Instead, the meristem at the tip of both root and shoot consists of a considerable group of embryonic cells. Many of these divide actively during the growth of the plant, and they produce all the tissues of the axis (save those formed by later cambial growth) as well as the leaves and branches.

Much attention has been paid in recent years to the structure, organization, and activity of apical meristems, particularly in the ferns and seed plants. These regions of persistent embryonic character have often been compared to animal embryos. Botanists have tried to find a correspondence between their structure and that of the parts that grow from them so that the developing plant might be analyzed in terms of embryonic regions, as zoologists have been able to do by using the germ layers established in the animal embryo. A wide variety of plant meristems have been studied and compared, but differentiation into layers as precise in their fate as ectoderm, mesoderm, and entoderm seems rarely to occur. Some botanists, however, do regard meristematic layers as true germ layers (Satina, Blakeslee, and Avery, 1940).

Although these apical meristems do not provide a precise classification of plant tissues, much information of importance for morphogenesis may be derived from them. Observation of the way in which meristems have produced the various tissues and organs of plants has been of service in the solution of problems in growth, differentiation, and phyllotaxy. Plant meristems offer the great advantage that a single plant may produce many of these embryonic regions, which are thus genetically identical. Though small, meristems are open to direct experimental investigation, and this has already provided results of much morphogenetic significance.

The apical meristems of shoot and root, though alike in many respects, show certain characteristic differences, and further consideration of their structure and activity will be more profitable if each is considered by itself.

THE SHOOT APEX

The length of the growing region in the shoot is considerably greater than in the root and may often extend over a region of several centimeters. Cell division persists longer in some tissues than in others and usually stops first in the pith. No very sharp line is to be found between the developing region and the mature portion behind it. The strictly meristematic zone, however, where cell division chiefly occurs, is usually limited to a few millimeters or less, and most growth of the stem in length results from cell elongation back of this.

The tip of the meristem in seed plants is usually a rounded, dome-shaped mass of cells around the base of which the leaf primordia appear in succession (Fig. 4-5). Some earlier investigators reported the presence of apical cells here but later work did not confirm this. Newman (1956), however, finds dividing cells in the very center of the apical dome in *Tropaeolum* and *Coleus* and believes that they are to be regarded as true apical cells. A similar situation has been reported in certain roots.

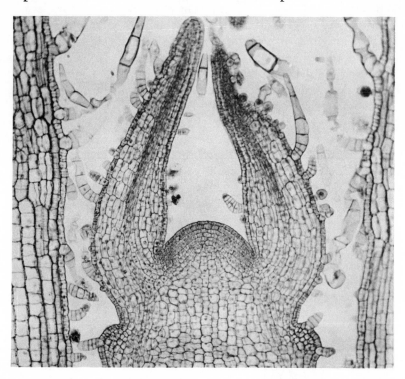

Fig. 4-5. Longitudinal section through shoot apex of *Coleus,* showing meristem, leaf primordia, and two bud meristems. (*Courtesy Triarch Botanical Products.*)

Much attention has been paid to the structure of the dome itself. Hanstein (1868) was the first to give careful study to the shoot meristem. He noted the presence in it of well-marked layers of cells and distinguished three regions, or *histogens,* each of which, he believed, gave rise to a particular tissue or tissues of the stem. The outermost, or *dermatogen,* is a single layer and produces the epidermis. Under this, several layers thick, is the *periblem,* giving rise to the cortex. The innermost core, or *plerome,* without well-marked layers, forms the vascular cylinder and pith (Fig. 4-6).

This hypothesis would have important implications for morphogenesis

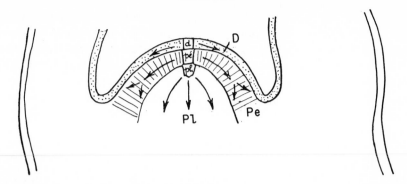

Fig. 4-6. Diagram of shoot apex according to Hanstein's interpretation. D, dermatogen; Pe, periblem; Pl, plerome. (*After Buvat.*)

if it could be supported. There is now much evidence, however, that no constant relation exists, valid for all plants, between these "histogens" and the structures formed by them. Some of this evidence comes from direct observation, as in Schoute's (1902) studies on the origin of the vascular cylinder. Some is derived from the structure of periclinal chimeras (p. 268) in which the layer or layers derived from one graft component can be distinguished by the size of their cells from those coming from the other, a distinction that persists in the mature structures and is a

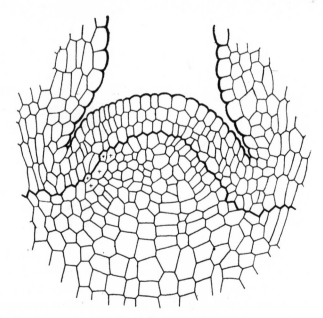

Fig. 4-7. *Vinca minor.* Longitudinal section through shoot apex, showing three-layered tunica and unlayered corpus beneath it. (*From Schmidt.*)

useful means of determining their particular meristematic origin. Evidence from these sources shows that a particular tissue may come from one meristematic layer in one plant and from another in another plant.

Hanstein's histogen theory has largely been superseded by another, first proposed by Schmidt (1924; Fig. 4-7). This recognizes an outer zone of layered cells, usually from one to four cells thick, the *tunica,* covering a core of unlayered cells, the *corpus.* The tunica-corpus theory does not maintain that either of these regions produces specific organs or tissues but describes the common type of organization of the shoot apex (see Reeve, 1948).

The significance of layering in the meristem has often been overemphasized. Whether or not a layer is formed depends on the plane of division of the meristematic cells. When the apical initials always divide

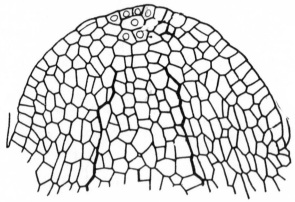

Fig. 4-8. Longitudinal section of shoot apex of *Torreya californica,* showing almost complete absence of layering. (*From Johnson.*)

anticlinally they obviously will produce a layer, and its growth will be entirely growth in surface. Where divisions occur in other planes or irregularly, layers are not produced. Specific factors such as mechanical pressure (p. 49) which influence plane of division may thus determine the presence and number of layers. If the central region of the meristem is growing faster than the surface, the latter will be subjected to pressure, its cells will tend to divide parallel to the direction of that pressure, and a layer will be formed. Perhaps this is the only real significance of the layered structure. It is noteworthy that the shoot meristems of many gymnosperms (Korody, 1938, and others; Fig. 4-8) show little or no layering but that they produce structures in a perfectly normal fashion. Layering as such, in the sense of marking out particular regions of the meristem that are significant morphogenetically, seems to be of much less importance than many workers have regarded it.

Fɪɢ. 4-9. At left, shoot apex of *Abies pectinata,* semidiagrammatic. At right, diagram of confocal parabolas as postulated by Sachs from such an apex as that of *Abies.* (*From Sachs.*)

Even though layering may not be of primary significance, the general pattern formed by the planes of cell division in the meristem is of interest. Reinke (1880) and Sachs (1878) many years ago called attention to the fact that the divisions approximately at right angles to the surface of the meristem and axis and those parallel to it tend, if extended, to form two sets of essentially parabolic curves with a common focus just below the apex of the meristem (Fig. 4-9). This somewhat diagrammatic interpretation of the situation has largely been neglected by recent writers. Such a pattern can be found both in shoots and roots, however, though it is often inconspicuous in small meristems. Foster (1943) called attention to the observations of these early workers in his study of the broad apices of certain cycads; and Schüepp, both in his volume on meristems (1926) and in a later paper (1952), has emphasized it. The pattern made by these two series of curves is modified as they

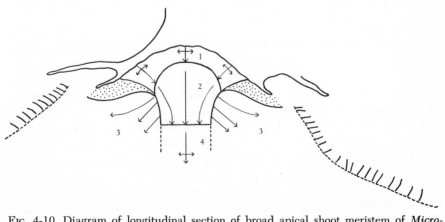

Fɪɢ. 4-10. Diagram of longitudinal section of broad apical shoot meristem of *Microcycas.* 1, initiation zone; 2, central mother-cell zone; 3, peripheral zone; 4, zone of rib meristem. Arrows represent lines of convergence of cells. (*From Foster.*)

suffer displacement, transversely and longitudinally, if growth is more rapid in some regions and directions than in others. In such broad apices as those of *Microcycas*, the normal pattern has been greatly modified and the tip flares out in a fan-like fashion (Fig. 4-10). What these facts mean morphogenetically we do not know, but they show that the growing apex has a pattern of organization which develops in a precise fashion.

The shoot meristem is by no means homogeneous or structureless in other particulars. In recent years many students have come to recognize a rather uniform series of *zones* within it, distinguished not primarily by layers or planes of cell division but by differences in the character of their cells. A general survey of zonation in vascular plants has been made by Popham (1951), who, from his own work and a long series of published descriptions of meristems, has grouped them into seven classes.

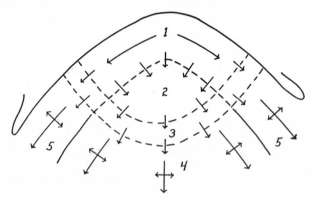

Fig. 4-11. Diagram of zonation in the shoot apex of *Chrysanthemum morifolium*. 1, mantle layer; 2, central mother-cell zone; 3, zone of cambium-like cells; 4, rib meristem; 5, peripheral zone. (*From Popham and Chan.*)

In the vascular cryptogams there are one or more apical cells or a surface meristem, with tissues below sometimes differentiating into a central and a peripheral meristem. Among seed plants, four or five zones can be seen (Fig. 4-11). These are a surface zone, or mantle, including two to several cell layers and corresponding roughly to the tunica; a zone of subapical mother cells, irregular in shape, often rather highly vacuolate and dividing less rapidly than the surrounding ones; a central zone giving rise to the rib meristem and pith; and a peripheral zone just outside this, producing cortex and procambial tissue. In some plants, just below the mother-cell zone there is a somewhat cup-shaped arc of cells stretching across the axis, the cambium-like zone. Popham and Chan (1950) and Popham (1958) have described a typical case of this last type. The particular functions of these zones are not well understood but they doubtless differ physiologically. The subapical mother-cell zone is perhaps comparable to a somewhat similar region in the root (p. 78) where the rate of protein synthesis is lower than in surrounding cells.

An attempt to follow cellular changes at the surface of living shoot apices has been made by Newman (1956), using *Tropaeolum* and *Coleus*. By an ingenious technique he was able to follow and draw, for as long as 9 days, the divisions of individual surface cells. At the very tip of the meristem he observed that divisions were frequent and believes that in this region there is a small group of cells that may be regarded as apical cells. His results fail to confirm those of Lance (1952), who reported that divisions were infrequent at the very apex, as Plantefol's theory (p. 156) assumes.

There is a considerable literature dealing with the structure of the shoot meristem in particular plants and under different conditions. Much of this has morphogenetic interest. Cutter (1955), for example, finds that the organization of shoot apices in eight saprophytic and parasitic species of angiosperms is essentially like that in plants with normal nutrition. Boke in a series of papers (1955 and earlier) described the stem apices and shoot histogenesis in a series of xerophytes, especially Cactaceae. Stant (1954) compared the shape of the shoot meristem in five species of monocotyledons and found a relationship between this character and the growth habit of the plant. In general, where the meristem is long and narrow, as in *Elodea*, the plant has well-developed internodes. Where it is relatively short and wide, as in *Narcissus*, the stem is much reduced and the internodes very short. The size of the apical dome is essentially the same in cucurbits with large fruits as in those with small fruits, and differences in organ size do not appear until a short distance below the tip of the meristem (von Maltzahn, 1957). The difference between the single-gene maize mutant "corn grass" and normal corn arises in the meristem, the mutant having a relatively larger meristem and a more rapid production of leaf primordia (Whaley and Leech, 1950). Rouffa and Gunckel (1951) examined 54 species of Rosaceae but found no significant relation between the number of tunica layers and the taxonomic position of the plant. The development of the shoot meristem from its early appearance in the embryo has been studied by various workers (Reeve, 1948; Spurr, 1949; and others).

The implications of results from the study of the shoot apex for morphological problems, especially the nature of the leaf, have been considered by various observers. Philipson (1949) believes that the evidence from this source supports the idea that the leaf is an enation and not a consolidated branch system.

Leaf primordia are formed in regular sequence below the dome of the shoot apex, and it is here that many of the structural characters of the plant seem to be determined. The period between the initiation of two primordia (or two pairs, if the leaves are opposite) is termed a *plastochron* (Askenasy, 1880; Schmidt, 1924). These periodic changes in the meristem can be seen best in opposite-leaved forms. As the two primordia begin to appear, the apical dome between them becomes relatively flat. When they have developed further but before another pair appears, the dome bulges upward again and reaches its maximal surface area. In the lower vascular plants the primordium arises from one or more of the surface cells of the meristem but in the higher ones it develops as a swelling on the side of the apex at the base of the dome, generally as the result of periclinal divisions in one or more layers below the surface one. The term *plastochron index,* for the interval between corresponding stages of successive leaves, has been proposed (Erickson and Michelini,

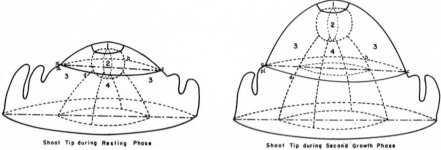

Shoot Tip during Resting Phase   Shoot Tip during Second Growth Phase

FIG. 4-12. Diagram of shoot tip of *Abies concolor.* At left, during resting phase. At right, during second growth phase. That portion of the shoot apex above plane *abcd,* which marks the level of the youngest leaf primordium, has a very different zonal topography in the two stages. 1, zone of apical initials; 2, mother-cell zone; 3, peripheral zone; 4, zone of central tissue. (*From Parke.*)

1957) as a better measure of the stage of development of a growing shoot than is its chronological age. In many plants the shape and structure of the meristem change somewhat with the season (Parke, 1959; Fig. 4-12).

The phyllotaxy of a shoot is determined by the arrangement of the leaf primordia around the axis. This phyllotactic pattern has been studied developmentally in the meristem, both through observation and experiment, by a number of workers (Chap. 7). The regularity and precision with which the leaf primordia arise at the shoot apex are evidence that this region has a high degree of organization.

Branches are formed from meristems arising in the axils of the leaf primordia. They are at first much smaller than the main apical meristem but do not differ essentially from it. Whether the potentially meristematic tissue here will grow into buds and whether these buds will produce branches are dependent in most cases on the stimulatory or inhibitory influence of auxin or other growth substances (p. 386). The development of axillary buds has been discussed by Sharman (1945) and by Garrison (1955), who finds that they originate from a region of residual meristem. After the organization of an apical meristem in the bud, the procambial strands develop acropetally into the leaf primordia, as does the phloem. Xylem forms at several loci and develops in both acropetal and basipetal directions (p. 204).

When the shoot is producing leaves, the meristematic dome is relatively low and rounded but when flower buds begin to be formed it becomes steeper and more elongate. Flowers arise as modified branches, and the floral parts develop from a series of primordia (Fig. 4-13). In the forma-

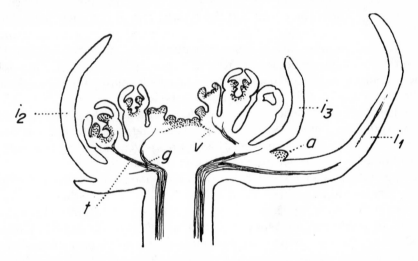

Fig. 4-13. Longitudinal section through young inflorescence, showing stages in development of floral primordia. *i*, bract; *t*, trace to primordium; *v*, procambial strand. Most active meristematic areas are stippled. (*From Philipson.*)

tion of more complex inflorescences, however, the meristem changes markedly. Since growth in length usually ceases at this time, what is formed is essentially a determinate structure rather than an indeterminate one like that of the vegetative shoot. What its character will be is decided by the size and number of the flowers and the character of the inflorescence. Various factors, notably the carbohydrate-nitrogen ratio and the photoperiod, determine whether the meristem forms vegetative or reproductive structures (p. 184). For accounts of the development of the reproductive apex, see papers by Grégoire (1938), Philipson (1948), Gifford and Wetmore (1957), and others.

The shoot meristem is not constant in size but changes during development. In the young embryo it is very small, and it enlarges as the plant grows. At the onset of reproductive maturity or at the end of the life cycle it often becomes reduced again in size. In maize, a plant essentially determinate in its growth, Abbe and his colleagues (1951a, 1951b, 1954) have studied the size of the apical shoot meristem (above the first leaf primordia) and the size and number of its cells as these change with time. In plastochrons 7 to 14 (the seedling stage until just before flowering) the apex increases by a constant amount in each plastochron but the duration of the plastochron decreases exponentially, from a length of 4.7 days to one of 0.5 day. Cell size is essentially constant throughout, so that all growth is by cell multiplication. The growth rate per plastochron accelerates exponentially. In the five or six plastochrons during early embryogeny, on the contrary, the duration of successive plastochrons *increases* and the growth rate of the apex decreases.

Sunderland and Brown (1956) have determined the cell number and average cell volume in the meristematic dome and the first seven primordia and internodes, back from the apex, in the shoot of *Lupinus*. The primordia increase exponentially in successive plastochrons but there is little increase in cell volume in the internodes.

Cell shape in the shoot apex of *Anacharis* (*Elodea*) has been studied by Matzke and Duffy (1955) with particular reference to the number of faces. These range from 9 to 21 and are in general agreement with the shape of cells in other undifferentiated tissues.

For a statement of conditions in the apical meristem of the shoot in ferns the reader is referred to Wardlaw (1945). This author has also published an extensive series of papers on experimental and analytical studies of pteridophytes, many of which are cited in his books (1952a, 1952b) and in later papers by himself and his colleagues. The shoot meristems of gymnosperms are described by Camefort (1956) and Johnson (1951). General accounts of this region in the angiosperms, with reviews of the literature, have been written by Foster (1939, 1949), Sifton (1944), Philipson (1949, 1954), Popham (1951), Buvat (1952), and Gifford (1954).

The ontogeny of a typical shoot apex (*Xanthium*) has been described in detail by Millington and Fisk (1956).

EXPERIMENTAL STUDIES ON THE SHOOT APEX

Early work on the shoot apex was primarily descriptive, and much of this still continues. It has been concerned with apical cells, planes of division, cell lineages, layering, zonation, and the relations of the meristem to differentiation and organ formation. This work has been of great value morphogenetically for it has provided a fund of information as to the structure and developmental activity of this determinative region of the plant, but it has yielded little knowledge of the meristem as a living and functioning center of morphogenetic activity.

In recent years, however, an increasing number of workers have used experimental methods to attack the problems of the meristem with techniques like those which have proved so fruitful in the experimental embryology of animals (Wetmore and Wardlaw, 1951). This part of the plant is a perpetually embryonic region and thus offers many advantages for work of this sort. Most shoot meristems are minute, however, and so enfolded by protective structures that experimental work upon them has had to await the development of specialized techniques. Means for direct operative attack on the meristem have now been developed and have begun to yield valuable results. In this work the Snows, Wardlaw, Ball, Wetmore, and their colleagues have been particularly active. The methods of tissue culture have recently added a wealth of information. Biochemical analysis by means of experiments with growth substances, chromatographic techniques, and other methods is yielding further knowledge of meristem physiology. This experimental work has powerfully supplemented earlier descriptive studies.

Direct operations on the meristem involve procedures of much delicacy and are performed under a lens by tiny scalpels. Pilkington (1929) seems to have been the first to do such work. She split the meristem of *Lupinus* down the middle and found that each half regenerated a normal meristem so that the original axis was now divided into two branches. Ball (1948), also using *Lupinus,* divided the meristem into four parts longitudinally and each of the four, by regenerative development, was able to produce a normal shoot. Later (1952*a*) he went still further and split the meristem into six strips. Each of these, unless it was below a minimum size, regenerated a new meristem and shoot, though leaf formation was somewhat delayed and vascular tissue was poorly differentiated until leaves had developed.

A major problem here is to find to what extent the meristematic tip is autonomous and thus independent from the tissues below it in development. In a fern, *Dryopteris,* Wardlaw (1947 and other papers) isolated the apical meristem from the adjacent leaf primordia by four longitudinal incisions (Fig. 4-14). It was thus continuous with the rest of the plant only by the parenchyma of the pith below it, all the vascular tissue having been severed. Despite this isolation, the meristem continued to grow and to produce leaf primordia and leaves. Whatever material entered it came through undifferentiated parenchyma. Provascular tissue was developed below the tip but this did not make connection with the vascular bundles in the stem below.

Ball (1948) did much the same thing in *Lupinus,* isolating the central axis of the meristem by four deep incisions. In this axis, however (unlike all cases studied in the ferns), vascular bundles were regenerated in the former pith tissue and became connected basipetally with the vascular system of the axis below. A normal shoot was thus restored. Similar results were obtained by Wardlaw (1950) with *Primula*. Furthermore, Ball (1946) succeeded in growing complete plants from isolated apices in sterile culture, and this has now been done repeatedly in other cases, both with ferns and seed plants (see Wetmore, 1954).

As a result of such experiments it is now generally agreed that the shoot apex is totipotent and independent of the rest of the plant. This is hardly surprising since many—perhaps all—cells are totipotent under favorable conditions. The subjacent tissue must have some influence on the apex, however, since from below there come into it not only water

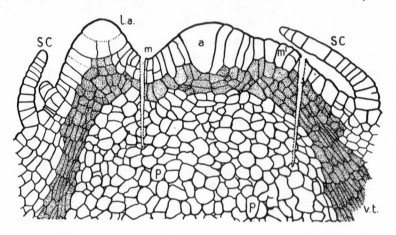

FIG. 4-14. Longitudinal median section through the stem apex of *Dryopteris*, showing how the region around the apical cell (a) has been isolated by deep cuts extending through the vascular tissue (v.t.). (*From Wardlaw.*)

and nutrient materials but specific substances of morphogenetic importance. The induction of flower buds at the meristem, for example, results from a hormone brought thither from the leaves. There evidently must be a reciprocal relation between the shoot meristem and the axis below it for both are parts of the same integrated organic system.

The shoot apex has a morphogenetic role which goes beyond regeneration, however, for it exerts a strong influence on the differentiation of tissues and organs in the region adjacent to it. By a long series of experiments reported in many papers (see Wardlaw, 1952a, 1952b, and Cutter, 1958) Wardlaw and his colleagues have made important contributions to a knowledge of this differentiation. Much of the work was done on the apical meristems of ferns. In *Dryopteris*, Wardlaw (1949b) determined the region where the next leaf primordium would arise (through its place in the phyllotactic series) and then isolated it from the apical cell by a deep tangential cut. Under these conditions a *bud* rather than a leaf primordium developed. Evidently some influence coming from the apex determines whether a new lateral outgrowth will form the dorsiventral primordium of a leaf or the radially symmetrical, potentially indeterminate one of a bud, a discovery of much importance not only morphogenetically but morphologically. Cutter (1956) has found that the three youngest primordia respond in the same way but that older ones do not. These same young primordial areas (in *Osmunda*) if excised and grown in culture will form buds and finally mature plants, whereas the older areas, if cultured, will grow into typical leaves (Steeves and Sussex, 1957). There is evidently a point before which the lateral structure has the potentiality to form either a bud or a leaf, but after a certain early stage has been reached its fate is determined.

Wardlaw has extended these studies further (1956*a, b*). When incisions between apex and primordium were so shallow that the prevascular strands were not cut, a leaf primordium still developed, suggesting that this incipient vascular tissue is a pathway for morphogenetic stimuli. When deep cuts were made on the radial and *abaxial* sides of a primordium site, thus without isolating it from the apex, a leaf grew from it, but this usually showed abnormally rapid growth.

In flowering plants results like these were not obtained, for isolated primordia do not develop into buds but into dorsiventral leaves or radially symmetrical leaf-like structures (Sussex, 1955). However, Cutter (1958) found that in *Nymphaea* and *Nuphar* (favorable material because of their large meristems), although tangential cuts separating a primordium from the apex did not change it to a bud, buds under these conditions were formed more often and very close to the primordium. The critical time for the determination of the fate of a primordium thus seems to be earlier in flowering plants than in ferns.

The problem of phyllotaxy is closely related to conditions at the meristem, for the arrangement of the leaves is presumably determined by the distribution of their primordia. This subject will be discussed more fully in the chapter on Symmetry, but it should be mentioned here that the experimental work of the Snows and of Wardlaw on the factors that determine where a given primordium shall arise has yielded much information. It is evident that the apex has an important influence on the differentiation of primordia, but whether the exact determination of the position of these structures results from chemical, mechanical, or geometrical factors is still not clear. Experimental manipulation of the meristem is a hopeful way of approaching this problem directly.

The differentiation of vascular tissue seems to depend on a stimulus, probably a growth substance, passing basipetally from the apex. The influence of buds on the production of vascular tissue below them is well known. When growth of an adventitious bud is induced in the epidermis, for example, a vascular strand usually differentiates in the parenchymatous tissue below it which establishes connection with the vascular tissue of the leaf or stem (p. 245). More direct experimental evidence on this problem is available from other sources. When Camus (1944, 1949) grafted a bud of endive into root callus in culture, provascular strands were formed below it. Camus attributes this to the effect of auxin (and possibly other substances) produced by the bud. Wetmore and Sorokin (1955) and Wetmore (1956) have shown much the same effects from lilac buds grafted into lilac callus in culture. Here the amount of provascular tissue induced in the callus below was much increased if auxin was also added.

Wardlaw (1952c) has called attention to the important effects on stelar structure which are related to the strength of the meristematic stimulus in the development of vascular structures. When leaf primordia in ferns are removed, gaps in the vascular ring below are much reduced. In this way it was possible to transform the axis of the normally dictyostelic *Dryopteris* into a solenostelic form with a continuous ring. By further reducing the size of the meristem through isolating it on a small piece of tissue, even a protostelic condition was produced. The basis for such important morphological differences thus seems to be in the degree of development of the meristem.

In recent years the physiology of these tiny shoot apices has also begun to be investigated. Growth substances are evidently synthesized there, but just what these are and how they act are still not known. Ball (1944) found that when auxin in paste was applied to the meristem apex of *Tropaeolum* no changes were produced in it, presumably because of the large amount of native auxin present; but below the tip hypertrophied tissues, multiple leaves, and abnormal development of vascular tissue appeared. The role of growth substances at the meristem involves many important problems in plant physiology and morphogenesis (Chap. 18).

By use of the techniques of paper chromatography, information is being gained as to the biochemistry and particularly the nitrogenous components of apical meristems. Some of the pioneer work here is described by Steward and others (1954, 1955) and by Wetmore (1954). The meristematic region is well supplied with free amino acids. The basic ones, arginine and lysine, are more abundant in the tip of the meristem than in tissues farther back, in the primordia, leaves, and stem. A substantial beginning has been made toward a knowledge of the distribution of these substances and similar ones, as well as of DNA and various enzymes, throughout the meristematic region and at different stages in its development. Something is thus being learned about the chemical as well as the histological organization of the shoot apex.

The techniques of tissue culture have also proved to be very useful for a knowledge of meristem physiology. It has been found (Wetmore, 1954), for example, that the shoot apex of vascular cryptogams, when cultured with only inorganic substances and sucrose, will produce entire plants but that they will grow better if supplied with auxin and some nitrogen source other than nitrates. Angiosperm apices (*Syringa*), however, will not grow in this simple medium, but if coconut milk and casein hydrolysate are added, the tips root, and growth is much better. When in the culture medium the same amino acids and amides are provided, and in the same proportions, as are found in meristem tissue, growth is still very slow and far from normal. Evidently something more is necessary.

Wetmore's demonstration (1954) that when apices of sporeling ferns are cultured with successively higher concentrations of sucrose the leaves that they produce correspond to those formed in progressive stages of normal ontogeny (p. 222) shows the important morphogenetic and morphological implications of nutritional factors.

The rates of metabolic processes in the shoot apex have also been investigated. Ball and Boell (1944), using the Cartesian-diver technique by which it is possible to measure the rate of respiration in tiny bits of living tissue, compared this rate in the apical dome of cells, the region just below this where the first primordia are appearing, and a third region below this (Fig. 4-15). In *Lupinus*, respiration was most active at the tip and progressively less so below. In *Tropaeolum*, however, there was *less* respiration in the extreme tip than in the region below it. The occurrence of a descending metabolic gradient in the plant apex thus seems not to be universal.

These various experimental studies on the shoot meristem have directed attention even more strongly to this embryonic region. Many believe that it is of primary importance for development and that in it the major problems of morphogenesis, at least as far as the shoot system of vascular plants is concerned, come sharply to focus. This conclusion is supported by the facts that the apex is autonomous, a small portion of the tip of it being able to produce an entire plant; and that if it is removed, the development of the tissues below it finally stops. It is recognized, however, that certain structures, such as leaf primordia beyond a certain stage, are partially removed from its control since they will develop independently in culture and are thus self-differentiating.

Ball has compared the shoot apex to an organizer such as has been postulated in animal embryology. Such, in a sense, it is, but the comparison is not very exact since the organizer is a part of the embryo which controls the development of the rest, wheeras the shoot apex

corresponds to the whole embryo itself and thus to the organism in miniature. Recent work shows more and more clearly that the apex is an
organized system (Wardlaw, 1953*b*, 1957*a*) with a structure that is not
only histologically but biochemically integrated. Before this structure
can control development it must *itself* develop. Growth *of* the meristem

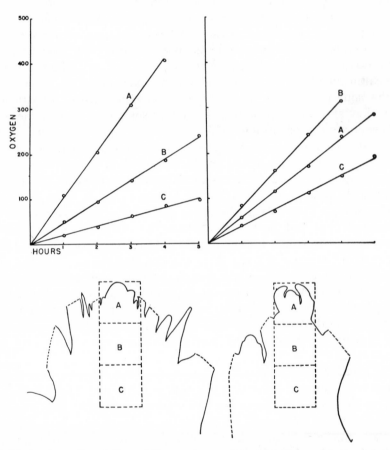

Fig. 4-15. *Lupinus albus,* left, and *Tropaeolum majus,* right. Below, location of A, B,
and C pieces in the two shoot apices. Above, oxygen consumption of these three
pieces in milliliters of O_2, at successive hours in the apparatus. In *Lupinus* there is a
gradient from A to C but in *Tropaeolum* the oxygen consumption is greater in B than
in A. (*From Ball and Boell.*)

precedes that *from* the meristem. The initiation of a meristem may take
place in various ways—from the tip of a young embryo, from adventitious
buds by regeneration, or from groups of cells or even single cells—but in
every case from simple and undifferentiated tissue.

A study of the origin of meristematic centers within masses of tissue in culture promises to be enlightening. Here Steward and his collaborators (1958) have done some significant work. They were able to grow in culture dissociated phloem cells from the root of carrot. Some of these produced multicellular masses. When a mass reached a certain size there formed in it a sheath of cambium-like cells enclosing a nest of lignified elements such as often is found in tissue cultures. In this spherical nodule there developed a root meristem and then a shoot initial opposite it. Thus an embryo-like structure was formed which was able to grow into an entire normal carrot plant. Steward emphasizes the fact that the change from random cell multiplication to organized development and the formation of meristems comes only after the group of inner cells has become enclosed by a wall of outer ones which cuts it off from direct access to the coconut-milk medium outside and subjects these inner cells to physical and presumably physiological restraints. Before this happens they multiply irregularly and form simply an unorganized callus-like mass. Such studies open up an important line of attack on the problem of the origin of organized meristems. It will not be possible to understand the role of meristems in development until we learn through experiments like these how such an organized apical system comes into being.

THE ROOT APEX

The apical meristem of the root differs in several respects from that of the shoot. It is relatively short, the elongating region of the root rarely exceeding a millimeter in length. No lateral organs have their origin at the apex, and thus there are no rhythmic changes here as in the shoot. The lateral roots arise farther back, in the pericycle, and push out through the cortex. The apical meristem produces not only the structures of the root itself but, from its outer surface, the root cap, or calyptra. Root meristems received much attention in the early work of Eriksson (1878), Flahault (1878), Holle (1876), Janczewski (1874), and van Tieghem and Douliot (1888).

In those lower vascular plants where shoot growth is centered in an apical cell, the root grows in the same way (Fig. 4-2). In the higher plants, however, although there is a meristem which is in many respects like that of the shoot, there is less uniformity in its organization. In most roots there are seen well-marked layers and to these some workers have applied Hanstein's terminology. The direct origin of particular tissues from particular layers is not uniform, and the same objections to regarding the layers as histogenetic ones may be made as for the shoot. The presence of the root cap prevents smooth and continuous layering over the root apex, and this is probably the reason why periclinal chimeras are not found in roots.

In many forms growth seems to be centered in a small group of cells. Brumfield (1943) produced specific chromosomal changes in root-tip cells of *Crepis* and *Vicia* by X radiation which could be recognized in the descendants of these cells farther back along the root. They were found to form wedge-shaped sectors of the entire root, including parts of the root cap, epidermis, cortex, and vascular cylinder (p. 268). Such a sector usually occupied about a third of the area of the root cross section, and Brumfield concluded that there were about three cells at the tip from

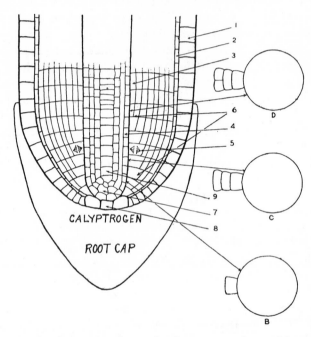

FIG. 4-16. Longitudinal diagram of root development as observed by Williams. The tissues all arise from a small group of cells at the very tip. 1, epidermis; 2, hypodermis; 3, endodermis; 4, pericycle; 5, mitotic figure; 6, young cortical cells; 7, stelar initials; 8, dermatogen; 9, metaxylem initial. B, C, D, transverse diagrams showing origin of cortical cells from a single cell of the endodermis. (*From B. C. Williams.*)

which all the tissues of the root were derived, though these cells could not be recognized in sections of the root apex. Von Guttenberg (1947) later presented evidence from a considerable variety of dicotyledonous plants that there is a *single* apical cell that gives rise to the whole root and which thus is comparable to the apical cell of lower vascular plants, but this has received little confirmation.

Popham (1955*a*) found in *Pisum sativum* a transverse row of meristematic initials across the root apex that gives rise to all the tissues of the root and the cap, and Clowes (1954) observed a somewhat similar condition in *Zea*. Both these workers believe that Brumfield's results can better be explained on the assumption of such a small meristematic center than of a group of apical cells, thus far unobserved. Clowes (1950) found meristematic layers in the root tip of *Fagus* that seemed discrete enough to be called histogens.

Williams (1947) observed in many roots of vascular plants a rather simple pattern of development. The epidermis, hypodermis, and endo-dermis could all be traced back to a small group of cells at the very tip of the plerome. The endodermal row, coming from this, gives rise by re-

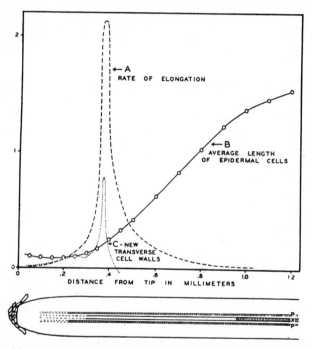

FIG. 4-17. *Phleum* root tip. Graph showing rate of root elongation (A), average length of epidermal cells (B), and new transverse cell walls (C), at various distances from the root tip. (*From Goodwin and Stepka.*)

peated tangential divisions to the cortex. This accounts for the fact that the cortex, particularly in its inner layers, is often made up of radial rows of cells (Fig. 4-16). A second small group of cells, just *below* the plerome tip, produces all the stelar tissues. The progress of cell division, par-ticularly in the surface layer and the cortex, was followed by Wagner (1937) by means of tracing cell groups, or "complexes," each of which had descended from a single meristematic cell. Sinnott and Bloch (1939) studied cell division in living root tips of small-seeded grasses by camera-lucida drawings. Brumfield (1942) continued this work by the use of photography, and the situation was analyzed more fully by Goodwin and Stepka (1945; Fig. 4-17) and Goodwin and Avers (1956). Erickson and Goddard (1951) used still more refined photographic methods. The location and rate of cell division in the root offer problems of considerable complexity.

There are a number of developmental patterns in the root apices of seed plants. They have been classified into various "types" by Janczewski (1874), Kroll (1912), and Schüepp (1926). These are well described in Esau (1953*b*, p. 116). In the structure of the root apex there is obviously less uniformity than in that of the shoot.

The development of the apical meristems in both root and shoot from their first appearance in the early embryo has been studied by a number of workers. A typical example is described in *Pseudotsuga* by G. S. Allen (1947).

Root tips, with the regions just behind them, were among the first materials to be used for plant-tissue culture (p. 296) and much has been learned through this technique as to the physiology of the root. In many plants, for example, the root cannot synthesize thiamin but depends for this vitamin on a supply produced in the shoot.

Mention has already been made (p. 41) of the work on the physiology of the root meristem by Brown and his colleagues, who determined the changes that take place in the activity of the apical cells in various regions, particularly as to growth rate, respiration rate, and protein synthesis. In a general discussion of this work, Brown, Reith, and Robinson (1952) show that there is a considerable difference in the composition of the proteins at different distances from the apex. Jensen (1955) has also made a biochemical analysis of the cells near the root tip in *Vicia faba*.

Clowes (1956, 1958) discovered between the active meristematic region and the root cap a cup-shaped group of cells, the *quiescent center* (Fig 4-18), which from their appearance divide rarely. He reports that these cells synthesize DNA more slowly than do the surrounding ones. They presumably have some specific metabolic function. Jensen and Kavaljian (1958) have made a census of cell divisions in the root tip of *Allium cepa*. They found a definite apical initial region where there are few divisions and agree with Clowes that these have a low DNA content. Cell division is slower to start in the axial than in the peripheral region of the tip. They report a very definite daily periodicity in division, with a maximum about noon.

The growth-substance relations of growing roots have received much attention (p. 391). Auxin and various synthetic substances stimulate the initiation of root primordia but usually check the later growth of the root. Auxin tends to be basipetal in its flow, a fact that helps to account

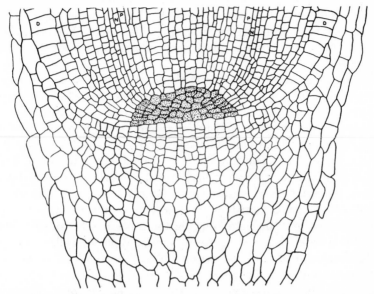

F<small>IG</small>. 4-18. Median section of root tip of *Zea,* showing the quiescent center (stippled). Its cells are physiologically different from the surrounding ones and seem rarely to divide or grow. (*From Clowes.*)

for the normal preponderance of roots at the base of the plant axis. A high carbon-nitrogen ratio (p. 366) also favors root growth. Torrey (1950) presents evidence that a growth substance, not auxin, is produced in the root and moves toward the apex, stimulating the formation of lateral roots.

Intercalary Meristems. Growth of an axis in length may sometimes take place at other points than its tip, by the activity of an *intercalary* meristem. Thus in many monocotyledons cell division persists in the base of an internode when it has ceased elsewhere, and the stem elongates all along its course, somewhat like an extending telescope (Prat, 1935). The gynophore of the peanut, which carries the young fruit down and into the ground, grows in a somewhat similar way, as has been described by Jacobs (1947). Such material is excellent for a study of the relations of cell division and cell elongation to growth.

LATERAL MERISTEMS

The Vascular Cambium. Apical meristems govern growth in length and produce those tissues commonly called *primary.* Their cells tend to be arranged in longitudinal rows, each row being the descendants of a single meristematic cell. In woody plants, the root and stem axes continue to grow not only in length but in diameter. This is accomplished chiefly by the activity of another meristem, quite different in character, the vascular cambium. The tissues that such meristems produce are termed *secondary*.

The vascular cambium is a sheath of embryonic cells extending from the beginning of secondary growth in the shoot tip to a corresponding position in the root. It arises between the xylem and the phloem of the primary vascular bundles and forms xylem on its inner face and phloem on its outer one. Each cambium cell produces a radial row of daughter cells on either side. The tissues thus formed can usually be recognized by this cell pattern, though it may sometimes be altered by the marked increase in diameter of certain cells, notably the vessels and sieve tubes.

Cells of the apical meristem are relatively uniform, varied though their products may be. Cambium cells, on the other hand, from the beginning are differentiated into two quite dissimilar types of cells, corresponding to the longitudinal and transverse cellular systems in vascular tissue. Those cambium cells that produce tracheids, fibers, sieve cells, and other elements of the longitudinal system are termed *fusiform initials* and are usually much elongated in the dimension parallel to the axis. The *ray initials* are much smaller and essentially isodiametric and produce the rays in wood and phloem.

The fusiform initials, especially those destined to form tracheids and fibers, may be from 50 to 100 times as long as wide. Often they do not differ greatly in length from the mature cells that they produce, though in some cases the fibers of the summer wood may become much longer than their initials (Bosshatd, 1951). Most of the divisions of these initials must be longitudinal and tangential since only in this way can additions be made to the width of the axis. The division of such an elongate cell violates Hofmeister's law. It is a remarkable process and was first clearly described by I. W. Bailey (1920*a* and *b*; Fig. 4-19). The nucleus, usually in the center of the cell, divides mitotically. Between the two daughter nuclei the cell plate is then laid down by the *phragmoplast,* an extension of the system of fibers at telophase. This appears in longitudinal section as two sets of fibers (sometimes called *kinoplasmosomes*) connected by the cell plate, one moving upward and one downward until the basis of the new division wall has been completed. An account of division in cambial cells was also given by Kleinmann (1923) in a paper written during the war and without a knowledge of Bailey's work.

Since the circumference of the axis continually increases, it is necessary, if the cambium cells are not to enlarge in tangential diameter, that they increase in number by occasional radial divisions. In storied cambia, where the initials are in tiers, this is done by radial divisions much like the tangential ones. More commonly, however, the initial cell divides by an obliquely radial (*pseudotransverse*) wall, and the daughter cells move past one another until the two initials reach normal length and lie side by side tangentially. The number of such divisions is usually more than enough to make the number of initials conform to the enlarging circumference of the cambium (Bannan, 1953). In many cases the daughter cells fail to maintain themselves, and the rows of cells coming from them are pinched out and gradually disappear (Bannan and Bayly, 1956). This process is so regulated, however, that the normal tangential diameter of the mature cells is essentially maintained. The length of the vascular elements originating from the cambium is also regulated to an approximately constant size.

FIG. 4-19. Early stages in the division of a cambial cell, near the middle of a long initial. The nucleus has divided, and the cell plate is being formed by the fibers of the kinoplasmosome (*k*). (*From I. W. Bailey.*)

The change in relative position of these enlarging cambial daughter cells involves a problem in cellular readjustments that is of importance morphogenetically. In 1886 Krabbe published a monograph on what he termed "sliding growth," presenting evidence that during the differentiation of tissues there was a good deal of change in intercellular position brought about by the slipping or gliding of one cell past another. This is common in animal embryology, where cells are more plastic and often migrate for some distance, and is responsible for many of the changes that take place in the development of these organisms. Its occurrence in plants might therefore be expected and was generally accepted as true for some time. Krabbe was supported in his position by some other botanists, notably Neeff (1914) and Grossenbacher (1914).

Priestley (1930) criticized Krabbe's conclusion and believed that all intercellular changes were brought about by what he termed "sym-

plastic" growth, a rather vague concept that there is a readjustment
of all the cell walls operating in one "common framework" and with
no slipping between adjacent ones. Sinnott and Bloch (1939, 1941) studied
living and growing tissues of young roots where the gliding of one
cell past another would be recognized, if it occurred, by alterations in
relative wall positions and found no evidence for it. They suggested

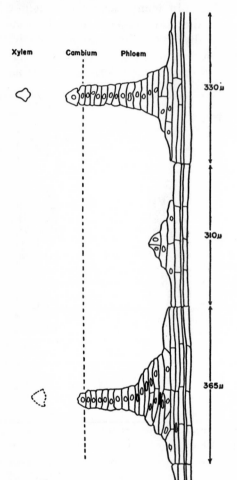

Fig. 4-20. Origin of ray initials in gymnosperms. Radial sections from *Thuja*,
showing progressive subdivisions of fusiform initials and the consequent origin
of several ray initials. (*From Bannan.*)

that changes in intercellular relationships come about by *intrusive* growth
limited to a particular region (such as the tips of cambial cells), so
that the cell may grow in between its neighbors without requiring that
it slide past them. Bannan and Whalley (1950) have shown how this
is accomplished in elongating fusiform initials. Schoch-Bodner and Huber
(1951) present evidence that the phloem fibers of flax, which become very

long, grow not only by cell stretching as the internode elongates but also by localized growth at both tips, as a result of which the fibers push in between adjacent ones. In the readjustments thus made necessary it is essential that where pits are present the pit fields in adjacent cells develop opposite each other, since there must be a corresponding opening in each wall. This evidently takes place after the relative position of the walls has become fixed. The problem of "sliding growth" has been discussed at length by Meeuse (1942).

The increasing circumference of the axis also requires that the number of rays be continually increased if the proportion between rays and verti-

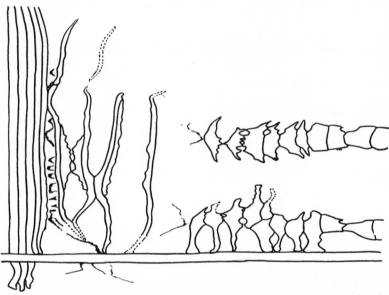

FIG. 4-21. Radial section of wood of *Chamaecyparis,* showing transitional cell types associated with the origin of a ray from a fusiform cell. (*From Bannan.*)

cal elements is to be maintained. The origin of new rays has been described for gymnosperms by Bannan (1934 and Figs. 4-20 and 4-21) and by Barghoorn (1940*a* and Fig. 4-22) and for certain angiosperms by Barghoorn (1940*b* and Fig. 4-23). A new ray arises from a short cell cut out of the radial face of a fusiform initial, the nucleus first migrating to the particular place where the new daughter cell is to be produced. The height of the ray is then increased by transverse divisions of this cell and its products, and its width by radial divisions. High rays may break up into shorter ones. The rays as seen in tangential section maintain an almost constant distance from one another. How this is accomplished is described by Bannan (1951).

The cambial region is obviously a much more active and plastic one than early workers regarded it. New initials are being produced and others are disappearing. Rays are being formed, fusing and dividing. Changes and rearrangements are continually taking place among the initials. The two sides of the cambium are forming quite different types of cells, and further differentiation within the xylem and the phloem is beginning. All these changes, however, are so well coordinated and regulated that a specific pattern of structure, constant enough for taxonomic purposes, is produced and maintained. There are few places in the plant where histological differentiation can be so well studied as in the products of the vascular cambium.

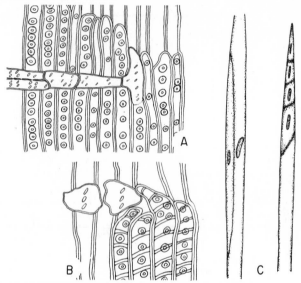

Fig. 4-22. Radial sections of wood of *Ginkgo* (A) and *Amentotaxus* (B and C), showing relation of young ray to ends of wood cells. (*From Barghoorn.*)

The cambium proper consists of a single row of cells, though on the xylem side there are usually several rows of mother cells, developed from it, which by their division produce the xylem. Relative activity in xylem and phloem production differs considerably in different forms. In *Thuja*, Bannan (1955) found that phloem began to develop later than xylem but then continued at a steady rate. In larch, however, Knudson (1913) had reported that phloem development preceded that of xylem, though the most rapid growth of each took place at the same time. In *Acer*, Cockerham (1930) and Elliott (1935) observed that the first cambial divisions formed the spring type of sieve tubes. This was followed by xylem growth, during which no new phloem was formed. As xylem production ceased, a second phase of phloem development occurred in which the

smaller summer sieve tubes were formed. The various steps in the development of xylem from cambium to heartwood, with particular reference to
changes in the cell wall, have been described by Bailey (1952). Ladefoged (1952) has published a detailed study of cambial activity and wood
formation in six conifers and 13 hardwoods in Denmark, based on observations from March to November.

The character of cambial products, particularly on the xylem side, as
to the number and size of the cells and the thickness of their walls, is
influenced by various factors though the precise effect of these has had

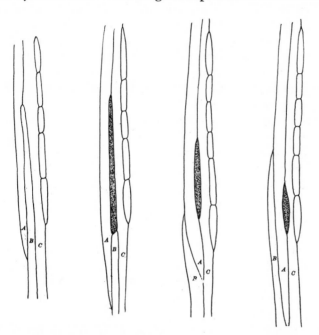

Fɪɢ. 4-23. Origin of ray initial in an angiosperm. Serial tangential sections of wood of
Trochodendron, showing origin of ray initial (stippled) from the end of a fusiform
initial. (*From Barghoorn.*)

little experimental study. In temperate climates, during the cold weather
of much of the year cambial activity ceases. The contrast between the last
formed wood of one season and the first of the next makes it possible to
identify boundaries of the annual rings formed in each season. These are
absent in regions where growth is continuous. The relations between
climatic factors, particularly annual rainfall, and the width of these rings
has been studied (Glock, 1955, and others). Lines of denser wood within
an annual ring may be related to rainfall differences in a single season
(Dobbs, 1953). Injuries from frost, fire, and insect attack can also be
recognized by their effects on the growth ring. These changes in the

products of the cambium, through the permanent record they leave in the tree, are of importance in the study of past climatic changes and in the dating of ancient timbers, and have been actively studied especially by Schulman (1956) and others in the Laboratory of Tree Ring Research.

The course of cambial activity differs among various plants. In herbaceous ones it is associated with vegetative growth and generally ceases at flowering (Wilton and Roberts, 1936). In most woody plants, growth of the new shoots in length is complete or nearly so before there is much cambial activity. The age of the tree may make a difference in woody plants, for Messeri (1948) observed that in old trees cambial divisions began a month earlier in the twigs than in the main stem whereas in young ones they started simultaneously throughout. In most conifers and in ring-porous angiosperms, cambial growth begins at about the same time throughout the stem (Wareing, 1951). In diffuse-porous angiosperms, however, division starts just below the buds at about the time they open and proceeds downward into the branches and then the trunk (Cockerham, 1930; Priestley, Scott, and Malins, 1933). This is apparently related to the production of auxin in the buds, for there is a close relation between the appearance of auxin there and the onset of cambial activity (Avery and others, 1937b).

The relation of auxin to cambial growth has also been studied by Brown and Cormack (1937), Söding (1940), Künning (1950), and others. Chowdhury and Tandan (1950), working with both evergreen and deciduous trees in India, report that buds burst in February or March and that growth in length continues until May. Not until the new leaves are fully expanded and length growth has ceased does cambial activity begin. It starts at the tip of the last year's shoot and proceeds down the tree and up into the new shoot. Growth in length begins again in the summer and is accompanied by cambial activity until both cease in the fall. The authors suggest that there are two types of substances operating here, one concerned with apical growth and one with cambial. Aspects of cambium physiology were discussed by Priestley in a series of papers (1930 and others).

A continuous cambium, laying down a solid ring of vascular tissue, is found in all woody gymnosperms and angiosperms and in many herbaceous forms. In other herbaceous stems the cambium ring is discontinuous and produces distinct vascular bundles. These may be separated by undifferentiated fundamental tissue. Across these gaps and connecting the cambium of one bundle with that of the next there is often an interfascicular cambium, probably a vestigial structure persisting from the time when the cylinder was continuous and the stem was woody. In many cases it consists of a row of cells with only a few tangential divisions. Under suitable conditions, as in the base of a stout herbaceous stem, the interfascicular cambium may become active and produce typical xylem and phloem. Its development offers some interesting morphogenetic problems.

The distribution of cambial activity over the axis in woody plants also deserves further investigation. The amount of wood produced by the two branches at a given fork of a stem, for example, bears a rather close ratio to the amount in the main axis below them, but this ratio will depend on the relative size of the two branches, the angle between them, and the orientation of the main axis itself (p. 108).

Another relatively unexplored field but one which may become of much interest for morphogenesis is that of anomalous secondary growth. In certain families the normal situation of a continuous cambial sheath is altered (Mullenders, 1947). An additional cambium may arise outside the phloem and start another vascular cylinder or series of bundles. There may be more than one of these. Such anomalous bundles may also appear in the pith. In other cases the surface of the cambium, instead of being circular in cross section, may be irregular so that radial lobes of secondary tissue are formed. In more extreme cases the cambium may become quite atypical and patches of secondary xylem and phloem may be intermingled in the vascular cylinder. Anomalous growth is often found in stems such as those of lianas or rhizomes which have other functions than support or conduction. It is frequently present in fleshy roots. One sometimes has difficulty in drawing a line between anomalous growth of this sort, which is really normal for a particular plant, and truly abnormal, or teratological, structures (Chap. 11).

The vascular cambium has been little explored from a morphogenetic viewpoint. Although it is much more difficult to study directly than are the apical meristems, its products, especially wood, are so firm and measurable that they offer attractive material for a quantitative study of many problems in growth relationships.

The Cork Cambium. The vascular cambium and the root and shoot apices are not the only localized embryonic regions in the plant. Increasing diameter of the axis necessarily results in the rupture of its outer layers, notably the cortex and the outer phloem. Infection and water loss would take place through these breaks in the tissue were it not for the formation of layers of suberized cells, the cork, or *phellem*. This is secondary tissue formed by a cork cambium, or *phellogen*. It has its origin in a row of cells, tangentially adjacent to each other, which divide periclinally and link up into a meristematic layer that produces a series of daughter cells on its outer side. There may be from one or two to many of these and their walls become suberized and impervious to water. On the inside are formed one or a few layers of daughter cells, the *phelloderm*, presumably vestigial in character.

The first phellogen usually arises just under the epidermis, but as axis diameter increases and outer tissues are ruptured, new phellogens appear in the deeper layers. Sometimes these form a single continuous layer of cork which may be peeled off. In other cases the phellogen arises as a localized, often slightly concave sheet which isolates a scale-like patch of tissue. In older stems these phellogens appear in the earlier and more or less crushed and functionless phloem. The phellogen cells obviously are alive and must originate in still living cells of this outer tissue. In many cases, corky cells arise beneath wounds in various regions. In the abscission of leaves and fruits a layer of cork is formed at the region of separation. In both these cases, growth substances (wound hormones or auxin) have been shown to be related to the origin of the cork cambium. Corky layers often show an unusual histological trait in having the new division walls in tangentially neighboring cells laid down directly opposite each other instead of being staggered, thus forming a characteristic stratified structure unlike that of most plant tissues (p. 195).

From a morphogenetic point of view the most interesting thing about cork-forming cambia is the way in which a continuous layer of such cells may suddenly arise in a mass of old and partially collapsed tissue. A host of dormant cells become embryonic again, link themselves up with neighboring cells, and form a cambial layer. In the typical rhytidome form of bark, this may be somewhat irregular in outline and often is not closely parallel to the surface of the organ or to the vascular cambium below. Where cork forms under a wound or just below the epidermis, its position may be explained by its location at a particular point in a physiological gradient, but in these more complex cases such an explanation is less satisfactory. Their origin resembles the way in which a pattern of wall thickenings or a net of fibers (p. 197), which transcends cellular boundaries, may become differentiated in a mass of tissue. The origin of such phellogen layers is a problem in differentiation which deserves more attention.

MERISTEMS IN DETERMINATE GROWTH

Potentially, the plant axis can grow indefinitely in length through the activity of its apical meristems and in width through the activity of the vascular cambium. Actually, of course, growth finally ceases for various reasons, but these axial meristems are essentially indeterminate in their activity.

The organs of the plant other than stem and root, however—the leaves, floral parts, and fruits—are structures of limited, or *determinate*, growth. They finally reach maturity and cease to enlarge. In this respect, one of them is much like an animal individual with a definite life cycle of its

own. Such organs provide an opportunity for a study of plant development which has been somewhat neglected in favor of the more sharply
limited meristems in apex and cambium. Because of the more diffuse
character of their growth, a study of these determinate organs will probably throw more light on the development of form than can be gained
from those of indeterminate growth.

How, we may ask, does a determinate organ grow? Is it through the
activity of localized groups of dividing cells, as in the axes, or by un-
localized, interstitial growth, as in most animals? The fact is that both
methods are usually employed.

The determinate organ which has been most extensively studied is the
leaf. The first step in its development is the appearance of a small swelling just below the dome of the shoot meristem. This grows into a leaf
primordium and finally, through a series of developmental steps, into a
mature leaf (p. 187). As to just how much of the meristematic tissue
actually takes part in forming a leaf primordium, there seems to be considerable variability among different groups of plants. Rösler (1928)
reports that in wheat only the outermost layer (dermatogen) is concerned. This pushes out and then pulls together from all sides to meet in
the center, like a collapsing glove finger, so that the whole leaf grows
from this one layer. Schwarz (1927), on the contrary, found that in
Plectranthus and *Ligustrum* the first *two* layers produced the entire leaf,
and this part of the meristem he termed the *phyllogen.* Most other
workers (see Foster, 1936) have found that tissue below the second layer
also contributes often to the formation of the young leaf, particularly the
veins. Whether this is simply tunica or both tunica and corpus depends
on the extent of layering and seems not to be important.

Critical evidence in this problem is provided by a study of leaf primordia formed by periclinal chimeras (p. 268). Here one or two of the
outer layers come from one of the graft partners and the rest from the
other. In chimeras between nightshade and tomato the tissues from each
can be distinguished by the fact that in nightshade the cells are much
larger. Here Lange (1927) was able to show that although a leaf primordium in this chimera was formed chiefly from the two outer layers the
third layer also contributed to it. In periclinal chimeras between forms of
Datura stramonium differing in number of chromosome sets (and thus in
cell size) Satina, Blakeslee, and Avery (1940) observed the same thing,
as did Dermen (1947*a*) in cranberry. In all these cases the third layer
gave rise to the vascular tissue of the leaf.

The way in which the primordium develops into the leaf also differs
considerably in different forms. In fern leaves, growth of the lamina is
largely determined by an apical cell resembling that in the shoot and
root (p. 58). In many higher plants the early growth of the primordium

in length is chiefly apical and seems to be governed by a group of cells at the tip, just under the epidermis—essentially a meristem. This produces the central tissues of the young primordial axis, or midrib, and growth of the epidermis keeps step with it. Such apical growth soon ceases, however, and later growth is diffuse.

The development of the tobacco leaf studied by Avery (1933) may be taken as a typical example of the growth of a determinate organ (Fig. 4-24). After the axis is about 1 mm. long and while still it is very narrow, growth of the lamina begins on both sides of this axis, pushing out like a wave of developing tissue. It increases faster in the middle than at either

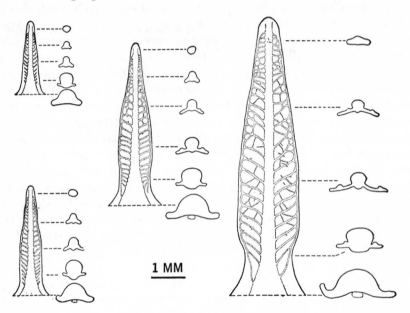

Fɪɢ. 4-24. Early developmental stages of a tobacco leaf, from a young primordium (upper left) to later ones where lamina and veins are being formed. (*From G. S. Avery.*)

end, and this produces the characteristic leaf shape. The rate of growth, as a result both of the division of the cells and of their increase in size, is greater in certain dimensions than in others. Avery contrasts the growth differences resulting from such polarized growth, primarily due to differences in plane of cell division, with localized differences in rate of division. Differences in cell shape due to differential cell expansion have little share in over-all shape changes in the organ as a whole. In most leaves, growth in the various dimensions of the blade, whatever its cellular basis, is unequal, so that blade form changes somewhat during development. These changes are under morphogenetic control, however, and show close allometric relationships (p. 105). The development of a few similar organs of determinate growth has been studied, such as the thorn shoots of *Gleditsia* (Blaser, 1956).

In leaves which do not show the usual dorsiventral character but various, more complex shapes, such as pitcher-like or peltate blades, the origin of these structures is by a system of localized meristems (Roth, 1957). These have not been studied extensively and present some important developmental problems.

The growth of other organs, such as perianth parts, ovaries, and fruits, resembles that of leaves in showing certain localized differences in rate and direction of growth, but growth is mainly diffuse and nothing comparable to a true localized meristem is operative save in exceptional cases. Not only are the different dimensions of such an organ clearly correlated in a progressively changing pattern but different parts of the organ, such as blade and petiole, and fruit and pedicel, although often growing at different rates, also keep in step with each other. Growth of certain structures, notably the fruit stalk, involves some cambial activity.

Whatever type of growth a plant organ may show, whether by apical meristems, cambium, or diffusely distributed embryonic activity, it is under strict developmental control. The problem of this control is somewhat more complex in a plant, where both diffuse and localized growth occur, than in an animal, where the latter is generally absent. The presence in a plant of these two somewhat different methods of growth offers certain advantages because of the possibility of studying in the same individual two different types of morphogenetic control. However growth occurs, its activities are correlated and not isolated events.

PART TWO

The Phenomena of Morphogenesis

CHAPTER 5

Correlation

The most significant fact about organic growth, as described in the preceding chapters, is that it is a process under definite control and thus leads to the development of bodies of definite form and size. This control is shown in the character of the growth cycle itself which, as we have seen, marches forward in an orderly fashion to the attainment of a specific size. It is shown even better in the distribution of this growth during development. If growth were equal in all parts and directions, organisms would be spherical. The remarkable variety of forms that living things display and that constitutes one of their important differences from most lifeless objects is due to the fact that the amount of growth in one region is different from that in another and that its rate in the various dimensions of a structure is unequal. These differences are not random ones, for if they were, a jumble of fantastic forms would result; they arise in an orderly sequence and progress in a regular fashion until a specific organic structure is developed. Something evidently guides the growth and differentiation of the organic mechanism. Occasionally this control is seriously disturbed and in such cases abnormal growths and monstrosities of various kinds appear (p. 275), but in the great majority of cases orderly development and the production of specifically formed structures take place. It is clear that in some fashion the parts of an organism are so related to each other that a change in one affects the rest and that the whole is thus integrated into an organized system.

All the phenomena of development which are to be discussed—polarity, symmetry, differentiation, regeneration, and the rest—are simply different aspects of this developmental relatedness, and the various factors concerned are those which have been found to affect it in one way or another. The fundamental causes of this integrated development are yet unknown. They are often attributed to *correlation,* a term which, because it is in most cases merely a name for our ignorance, has with many students of morphogenesis fallen into disrepute. Nevertheless correlation is a fact, explain it how we will, and no one can approach a study of the phenomena of morphogenesis without recognizing this. Therefore at the beginning of a discussion of these problems it will be useful to consider some typical examples of the ways in which growth of one part or dimension is related to growth elsewhere or to the plant's various activities. These will illustrate how plant forms arise and an integrated organism is produced and will serve as an introduction to the fundamental problem of morphogenesis, approached from many directions throughout this book —the problem of biological organization.

There have been many discussions of correlation in the literature of plant development, and for some of them the reader is referred to the works of East (1908), Harris (1909–1918), Love and Leighty (1914), Murneek (1926), Goebel (1928), Thimann (1954*b*), and others.

Correlations have been classified in many ways, as environmental, physical, morphological, physiological, genetic, compensatory, or meristic, depending on the characters and factors involved. For purposes of convenience in the present treatment, there will be grouped together, as *physiological*, those correlations for which a physiological mechanism— metabolic, hormonal, or other—seems to be operative and as *genetic*, those which seem to depend primarily upon the genetic constitution of the individual and its formative relationships and are thus produced by mechanisms more deeply seated and obscure than the ordinary physiological ones.

PHYSIOLOGICAL CORRELATIONS

Physiological relationships are of particular morphogenetic interest since through an analysis of them the mechanisms for other types of correlation may be discovered. The various factors concerned will be treated in later chapters. The particularly important role of growth substances in plant correlation has been discussed by Thimann (1954*b*).

It will be useful here to mention a few typical examples of physiological correlation and to formulate some of the problems that they present.

Nutritional Correlations. The simplest type of correlation is one which depends on nutrition. A region that does not produce or contain food must depend for its growth on one that does. Correlation of this sort between root and shoot must obviously occur. The root-shoot ratio is a favorable one in which to study correlation and the factors that modify it, and considerable attention has been given to the problem. Kny (1894) cut off part of the roots from growing seedlings and part of the shoot from others. When a considerable amount of reserve food was still available in the seed, loss of one part did not greatly affect the growth of the other. Pearsall (1923), Keeble, Nelson, and Snow (1930), and others found that removal of the seedling shoot sometimes actually stimulated growth of the root, presumably because of reduced competition for food stored in the seed. More commonly, however, in older plants and in cuttings, a rather close balance becomes established between root and shoot and is restored if altered experimentally.

This ratio is subject to change during development, for in most plants the shoot grows consistently faster than the root. Other factors also affect it. In poorly nourished plants the root is relatively large and in etiolated ones, relatively small. Crist and Stout (1929) found that in some plants it was affected by soil acidity, soil fertility, and day-length. Roberts and Struckmeyer (1946) observed that temperature and photoperiod modified the ratio but not in the same way in all plants. The top-root ratio was studied by Shank (1945) in maize inbreds with low and with high ratios, and in their hybrids, under different amounts of phosphorus, nitrogen, and water in the soil. Increase in each of these substances tended to increase this ratio. Richardson (1953) measured root growth microscopically in small maple seedlings growing in glass tubes under controlled conditions. Any change in the environment of the shoot which modified photosynthetic activity had a commensurate effect on rate of root growth. Correlations depending on nutrition are evidently rather susceptible to change by environmental factors.

The influence of shoot on root is not always nutritional but may result from the action of auxin, vitamins, or other growth-regulating substances. The nutritional influence of root on shoot is well shown by the horticultural practice of producing dwarf trees by grafting scions from normal-sized varieties on roots of genetically dwarf types in which the root system is too small to supply the growth requirements of a large tree.

Among other correlations which have their basis in nutritional factors are those between the size of a fruit and the amount of leaf area available for the support of its growth (Haller and Magness, 1925). There is also a close relation between the amount of foliage on a tree (the size of its crown) and the amount of stem growth. Young and Kramer (1952) and Labyak and Schumacher (1954) have studied this problem by reducing experimentally the size of the crown in pine through pruning and observing the effect on trunk growth. In apples, Murneek (1954) found a relationship between fruit size and leaf area (presumably nutritive) and also between fruit size and seed number per fruit (presumably stimulatory).

Because of its practical importance, many studies have been made of the relation between the size of seed planted and the size of the plant growing from it. If a positive correlation existed between these characters it would pay to use only large seeds in many agricultural operations. Agronomists have sought all such characters in fruit and seed that might be correlated with high yield but have had little success. Where such a relation has been found, in most cases it is simply between seed size and early plant size. Passmore (1934), working with reciprocal hybrids between large-seeded and small-seeded cucurbits, and Oexemann (1942), with several vegetables, observed that plants from large seeds have an initial advantage in size because of the larger amount of food stored in the seed but that this usually disappears after a time.

Similarly, in vegetative propagation the size of a "seed" piece in potatoes, though it may influence early sprout growth, has no effect on yield (Wakanker, 1944), though if the bigger pieces have more buds on them, sprout number will be larger and yield somewhat increased.

A positive correlation between the size of a fruit and of the seeds in it has often been found, as by Schander (1952) in apple and pear and by Simak (1953) for seed size and cone size in pine. In fruits and cones of the same size, however, seed size was inversely proportional to seed number. Both nutritional and compensatory correlations are probably involved here.

Ashby (1930) suggested that the larger plant size resulting from heterosis was due to greater size of the embryos that produce the heterotic plants, thus giving them an initial advantage which was maintained throughout growth. Present evidence, however, does not support this idea.

Compensatory Correlations. The nutritional factor in the relation between two parts of a plant may be evident in other ways than by transfer of food from one to another. Each growing part or organ constitutes what Goebel called an "attraction center" which under normal conditions draws to itself a specific amount of building material. This may be small or large, depending on its genetic constitution. In one of the higher plants, which has many similar growing parts such as leaves, flowers, and fruits, the number of these parts may be reduced by accident or experiment. In such cases there is often a compensatory increase in the growth of the remaining structures, so that a negative correlation results between the size and the number of parts (Lilleland and Brown, 1939). Thinning of fruits by mechanical or chemical means is sometimes practiced so that the remaining fruits will grow larger. In the same way, the removal of all buds but one in a certain type of chrysanthemum results in the development of this single flower head, through compensatory growth, to a size very much larger than normal.

The reverse of this relationship also may occur, for if many fruit are set, they will be small. In such cases, some may drop off. Thus in apples there usually occurs a "June drop" in which many of the young fruit, unable to attract to themselves a sufficient supply of food or auxin, stop growing and are cut off by abscission layers. In a somewhat similar way, the more seed developing in a tomato fruit and the more fruits in a cluster, the smaller will be the weight of each seed (Luckwill, 1939; Schander, 1952; and Simak, 1953).

Where flowering and fruiting are continuous, as in squashes, if a certain number of fruit are set, related to the food-producing capacity of the plant, the development of more flowers ceases and will not be resumed unless the growing fruits are removed. There is thus a continuous compensatory balance between the development of multiple plant organs and the amount of material or hormone available for their growth.

A balance also occurs between the vegetative and the reproductive phases of a plant (Murneek, 1926). Tomatoes in which fruits are allowed to form abundantly will soon cease vegetative growth, but if flowers and young fruits are continually removed, the plants will grow to a much greater size. A potato plant in which tuber formation is prevented will often bear a large crop of fruits, structures which normally fail to develop presumably because of the diversion of food to the tubers. Mirskaja (1926) removed all flower buds from plants of a number of species and found that this stimulated formation of lateral shoots and increased the size of leaf blades, tubers, and pith cells and the amount of lignified tissue.

Removing the axillary buds from *Coleus* plants was found by Jacobs and Bullwinkel (1953) to induce longer stems, larger leaves, and more rapid growth of the main shoot (Fig. 5-1). The ancient art of *topiary* is simply a manipulation of these compensatory correlations. The removal of certain buds stimulates the growth of others which would have remained dormant, and by this means the form of the plant can be altered.

Such correlations may perhaps be called competitive rather than compensatory. In certain hybrid cherries, for example, the embryos start their development but when partly grown they shrivel and die. Tukey (1933) and others were able to bring such embryos to normal maturity by removing them from the seed and growing them in culture. In normal plants the embryo may be thought of as competing successfully with maternal tissues for food during development, but in these unusual cases most of the food is drawn instead to maternal tissues, and the embryo dies. Release from such maternal competition allows it to grow.

Compensatory correlations are also to be observed in the development of individual organs. MacDougal (1903b), who has reviewed the early literature, described many examples of this, as did Goebel and others. In some plants, for example, if the blade is removed from the young and growing leaf, the stipules will become much enlarged. The building material available to the leaf is employed in its growth but the distribution of this material is not the usual one.

A good instance of compensation is reported by Johnston (1937) between the coleoptile and the first internode of *Avena*. Light stimulates the growth of the former but depresses the latter. Regardless of light, the total growth is much the same, reduction in one structure being compensated by increase in the other.

Stimulatory Correlations. Many correlations, however, do not depend upon the distribution of building materials but upon the operation of other factors which affect development, particularly the stimulatory and inhibitory action of auxin and other growth substances.

The stimulatory effect is well shown in the control of root growth. Van der Lek (1925) and others have found that in many cases cuttings

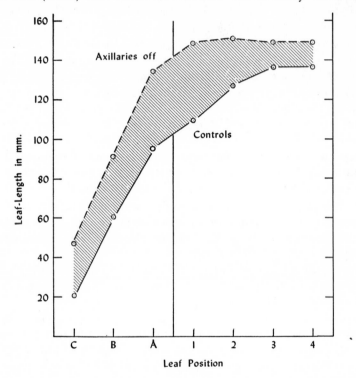

Fig. 5-1. Compensatory correlation in *Coleus*. Increase in leaf length in 27 days after removal of axillary buds and branches, as compared with controls. Leaves at left of vertical line had not unfolded from apical bud. (*From Jacobs and Bullwinkel.*)

on which buds are present will root much better than those without buds. This evidently is due to a root-stimulating substance produced by buds which passes down to the base of the cutting. The character of the buds may also be important, for O'Rourke (1942) has shown that blueberry cuttings root better if the buds on them are leaf buds than if they are flower buds.

The relation between a leaf and the development of a bud in its axil is a complex one. Felber (1948) observed that in apple the size of a vegetative bud at maturity is proportional to the size of its subtending leaf, suggesting a nutritional relation. Champagnat (1955 and other papers) presents evidence that there are several distinct stimulating or inhibiting influences that the leaf exerts on its bud. Snow and Snow (1942), on the basis of experiments at the meristem, believe that an axillary bud is determined by the primordium of the leaf that subtends it, particularly the basal part. If the primordium is partially isolated from the stem apex, its bud grows larger than it otherwise would.

Related structures often affect each other. The cotton boll and its seeds will not reach normal size if the involucre of the flower is removed (Kearney, 1929). Knapp (1930) reports that the perianth of a liverwort grows only if the archegonium that it covers is fertilized. The ovary in most plants will not grow into a fruit unless at least a number of ovules are forming seeds. These developing parts produce substances, apparently, that stimulate the ovary wall to grow. This stimulation can be imitated by the use of certain synthetic growth substances to produce parthenocarpic fruits (p. 378). In case of *metaxenia* (p. 407), where the male parent has a direct effect on the character of the fruits, this presumably results from something introduced through the pollen tube.

Inhibitory Correlations. There are many developmental relationships which are just the reverse of stimulatory and in which one part inhibits the growth of another by some other means than competition for food. These relations, like those of stimulation, commonly involve the action of auxin and related substances.

The best known case of such inhibition is the *dominance* by a terminal bud which prevents the growth of lateral buds below it (p. 386). Similarly, the epicotyl and its bud, in seedlings like those of beans, inhibit the growth of buds in the axils of the cotyledons. Often a leaf can be shown to inhibit the growth of the bud that it subtends, for if the inhibiting organ is removed, the bud will then grow. Sometimes physiological isolation has the same effect as removal. Child (1919, 1921) chilled a portion of a bean epicotyl and found that the cotyledonary buds then began to grow. Shading a leaf sometimes results in removing its inhibiting influence.

Preventing the growth of the apical bud by encasing it in plaster sometimes has the same effect as removing it. Many of the early studies in growth correlation involved this plaster technique (see Hering, 1896). For example, if the portion of pea epicotyl between the terminal bud and the cotyledons is so encased that it cannot grow in *width*, growth in *length* is much reduced as compared with the control.

Nutritional factors may have something to do with the inhibition of cotyledonary buds, for Moreland (1934) observed that in bean seedlings the growing foliage leaves have a greater inhibiting effect on these buds than does the epicotyledonary bud itself and believes that this is owing to the removal by these leaves of some food material necessary for bud growth.

Other structures may be inhibited. If root nodules and root tips are removed from roots of red clover inoculated with an effective strain of nodule bacteria, the number of nodules subsequently formed will be increased (Nutman, 1952). This is thought to be owing to the removal of inhibitory activity centered in the meristems of nodules and root.

Inhibition by terminal buds has various practical implications. Reed (1921) found that heavily pruned young pear trees have a greater growth of new shoots than do unpruned or lightly pruned ones and suggests that this results from the removal from them of much growth-inhibiting substance present in the buds near the tips of the branches.

Correlations of Position. Many parts of the plant can be shown to have the capacity for much more extensive growth than they normally display. If a leaf is removed and treated as a cutting, it will frequently grow to a greater size and live much longer than if it had remained a part of the plant (Mer, 1886; Riehm, 1905; Winkler, 1907; and others). Single cells, under suitable conditions of isolation and stimulation, will sometimes develop into whole plants. All parts of the plant tend thus to be *totipotent.* Why these potentialities are not realized when the part is a member of an organic whole is a problem. Not only is each part of this whole limited in its growth, but the particular way in which it develops depends on *where* it is. Driesch's famous dictum emphasizes the fact that an organism is an organic pattern in which every part develops in a specific relation to the rest. The correlations that these parts display with one another are simply manifestations of the control that this pattern exercises in development.

Experimental change of the position of a part in this pattern often effects marked alteration. Ward and Wetmore (1954) partially released young fern embryos from their contact with the prothallus and found their growth to be slower and somewhat abnormal. Wetmore asks the significant question as to why a spore and an egg should grow so differently. Each is a haploid cell and they presumably are identical genetically, but the surroundings under which they develop are very different. He suggests that perhaps the difference between sporophyte and gametophyte in ferns may be the result of this positional correlation.

Mason (1922) reports that the terminal bud from a cotton shoot that has stopped growing will grow vigorously if it is budded on a young plant. A flower bud inserted on a vegetative shoot where it would not normally occur often changes in its development and may produce a flower cluster which is gigantic or otherwise abnormal.

The operation of such a constantly regulated balance among activities is well shown in the formation of reaction wood (p. 356). This wood (in conifers) elongates faster than normal wood and thus tends to bend a branch away from the side on which it occurs. The branches have a specific angle of orientation to the main axis, or to gravity, which is maintained by the development of reaction wood on one side of the branch. If this normal orientation is experimentally altered, reaction wood will appear at the precise place and in the precise amount elsewhere which will tend to restore the normal branch pattern. The origin and character of this pattern are the essential problem. What happens to any component of it depends on the place that this occupies.

There are many other examples of the operation of such developmental patterns in the plant body. Among these are the studies of Dormer (1950) on the development of xylem in different internodes of the young plant of *Vicia;* of Friesner and Jones (1952) on the relation of primary and secondary branches in length growth; and of various workers on the structure of leaves borne at different levels on the stalk. Ashby and his colleagues (1948) have emphasized the structural and physiological differences among successive leaves along the axis and have related this to the problem of aging. Instances of positional differences shown in topophysis (p. 212) are particularly clear and may become irreversible.

The control that the organized whole exercises over its parts is sometimes termed "correlative inhibition." This term explains nothing but it emphasizes the fact that inhibitory action is certainly involved. In the physiology of development both inhibition and stimulation are important. A number of workers, among them Libbert (1954, 1955), have discussed the various interactions between substances which promote and those which check the growth of buds. Thimann (1956) has called attention to the fact that in most physiological processes there is a balance between reactions tending to promote the process and others tending to inhibit it. No single factor is solely responsible, but physiological activities, including those of development, are often under multiple control. Furthermore, certain factors such as auxin may stimulate under certain conditions and inhibit under others.

Some students of development are therefore inclined to look on the growing organism as the seat of constant competition between different and distinct processes, a state of equilibrium between opposing forces. This resembles the concept of the organism as a balance between distinct cellular individuals each with specific tendencies of its own. It also calls to mind the older idea of the "battle between the parts" as the basic fact in development. Analysis of the structures and the activities that go to make up an organism gives some support to this interpretation of development. The close correlations that are everywhere present in development, however, and particularly the persistent tendency toward regulatory action by which a specific norm or pattern of form and function is restored if disturbed, are difficult to explain on the basis of independent action by many variables. The organism more closely resembles an organized army under disciplined control than it does a mob where each individual acts competitively for himself.

The balance between stimulation and inhibition, however, is worth careful study by students of morphogenesis. In a few cases it has been investigated in the lower plants. In the coenocytic alga *Caulerpa*, for example, the "assimilators" (leaves) produce strong growth inhibition but the rhizoids have the opposite tendency (Dostál, 1945). The balance between the influences of these two sets of organs has an important effect on the character of the plant as a whole.

More favorable material for a study of this aspect of correlation is found in the over-all form of the plant body, especially in such higher plants as trees. A tree is a rather loose aggregation of axes which usually does not show as precise a form as does an individual organ such as a leaf or a flower but which, nevertheless, is characteristic and recognizable. This has been found to result from an interaction of factors in the terminal buds and in the growing tips of the branches. Some of these factors tend to push the branches down, in relation to the main axis, and others tend to lift them up. The relative length of branches and main axis is also similarly controlled, evidently by domination of the terminal bud over those of the lateral branches. Münch (1938) has discussed the diverse tendencies that govern such tree form in conifers and interprets these in terms of hormonal action, but he emphasizes the harmony and balance that exist among them. Others (Snow, 1945) have considered the problem. It is a basic one for morphogenesis since the form of the plant body as a whole, although relatively variable, is nevertheless a true organic one. Presumably the factors that govern it resemble those that bring about the much more constant and specific forms of the separate organs. The body is an aggregation of these parts, less tightly organized than are its individual organs, but clearly showing organization. The beginnings of organization and of the emergence of those correlations that determine form may profitably be studied in these plant bodies, which in a sense are intermediate between colonies of semi-independent parts and true organic individuals.

GENETIC CORRELATIONS

Organized bodily patterns, with their localized differences and specific characters, are examples of physiological correlation though the mechanisms involved are obscure. They doubtless have some genetic basis. Many other growth correlations, including those concerned in the form of plant parts, are more precise but are even further from a satisfactory biological explanation. They are inherited, but the genetic mechanisms involved have hardly begun to be explored. At present we can simply describe and classify these correlations.

The various structures in a growing organic system tend to increase together and thus to be correlated in size. In a given organ its dimensions are likewise correlated. Since growth usually is not uniform, as development proceeds, the relations between the parts of the system or between the dimensions of the organ may change progressively and thus produce differences in form. Growth is usually exponential in character, and therefore the relationship between the sizes of two structures growing at different rates may best be found by plotting the logarithms of their sizes against each other. If the rates are different but the *relation* between the two is constant, these values will fall along a straight line the slope of which measures the growth of one structure relative to that of the other. It is noteworthy that in most cases where two parts of the same growing system, or two dimensions of a growing organ, are compared, their *relative* rates are found to be constant, however different their absolute rates may be.

This relationship can be described simply by an equation. If y is the size of one variable, x that of the other, b the value of y when x is of some arbitrary size, and k the ratio of the growth rate of y to that of x, then

$$y = bx^k$$

or

$$\log y = \log b + k \log x$$

This phenomenon of constant relative growth (*heterauxesis*) has been observed by many biologists but was first widely emphasized by Julian Huxley (1932). He termed this type of growth *heterogony*, a term now replaced in much of the literature by *allometry*. The constant b measures differences in level, or at the beginning of growth, between two variables. The constant k provides a measure of relative growth rate and may sometimes offer a clue to the mechanisms involved. It may be used to express differences when these are based on genetic, environmental, embryological, biochemical, or even evolutionary factors. This method of analysis has proved useful in the study of many kinds of growth correlations.

Correlations of Part and Whole. Among the familiar growth correlations are those between an organ and the rest of the body or between members of a series of multiple parts and the structure that they constitute. In animals, large individuals typically have their organs correspondingly larger than those of small ones. In plants, however, with their lower level of organization, their often indeterminate growth, and their multiple organs, this relationship is not so simple. In beans, for example, Sinnott (1921) has shown that there is a positive correlation between size of leaf and size of entire plant up to a certain plant size. Beyond this the size of additional leaves is no greater even if leaf number and plant size may increase considerably (Fig. 5-2). Size of pod and of seed show a similar relationship to plant size. These facts suggest that organ size may depend on the size of the embryonic mass or the shoot meristem and that this may increase up to a certain point only, beyond which increase in total plant size involves only the addition of more units (internodes, leaves, and others).

In cucurbits and many other types, although organs on the same plant tend to be correlated in size (forms with large fruits also having large leaves, thick stems, and long internodes), there is a certain amount of flexibility in these relationships, depending on genetic constitution. Thus

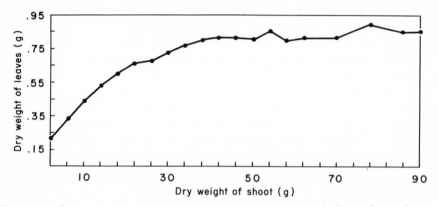

Fig. 5-2. Relation of size of leaf to size of shoot in progressively larger bean plants. For a while, leaf and shoot increase together, but after a certain point, shoot size increases without further increase of individual leaves. (*From Sinnott.*)

if a pumpkin type, which has all its parts large, is crossed with an egg gourd, where they are all small, the F_2 generation contains plants that show some differences in the relative size of their parts, but there are none that have the large fruit size of the pumpkin and the small vine type of the egg gourd. The general physiological correlation of parts within the same plant makes it impossible for sizes of individual organs to segregate independently in inheritance.

The size of the meristematic region bears some relation to that of plant and organ size. Crane and Finch (1930) have shown that the size of buds has an effect in determining the size of shoots that grow from them. In a comparative study of large-fruited and small-fruited races in *Cucurbita pepo*, von Maltzahn (1957) found that, although the dome-like undifferentiated meristem is essentially the same size in all types, the region just back of this and the primordia of flowers and leaves that originate there are considerably larger in the large-fruited type.

In this general category of correlations are many of those described by J. Arthur Harris. In *Nothoscordum* and *Allium* (1909), for example, he found that flower clusters with relatively large numbers of flowers are borne on relatively long peduncles. Size changes are not always proportional, however, for in *Ficaria* (1918) he found that flowers with a large number of sporophylls have relatively more pistils than stamens.

The relation between cell size and body size belongs to the part-to-whole category. This has been discussed in a previous chapter (p. 32) and is the basis of a very considerable literature. In a single organ there are often marked differences among the various tissues in the strength of the correlation between cell size and tissue size (Sinnott, 1930). In general, it is clear that body size usually does not depend on cell size but on cell number. In many cases, however, it has been shown that in organs of limited growth, such as fruits, large cell size is associated with large organ size, though the range of the former is much less than that of the latter.

Correlations between Different Parts. There are many genetic correlations which do not involve part-to-whole relationship but one between different parts and are thus less obvious as to origin. Sometimes these parts grow at the same rate but more frequently they do not.

One of the most conspicuous of such growth relationships in higher plants is that between the two main organ systems of the body, the root and the shoot. Its nutritional aspect has already been discussed. The relation is often so precise, however, as to suggest that it has a basis in the genetic constitution of the plant. Its value differs in different plants, at different stages of development, and under different environments. In most cases the root is relatively large in the seedling but grows less rapidly than the shoot. One increases at a rate which maintains a constant proportion to that of the other. Pearsall (1927) plotted the dry weight of the root against that of the shoot, both logarithmically, in a series of growing plants in various species. In most cases the allometric constant k was greater than 1, though its value differed in different species. In other words, the shoot grew more rapidly than the root. In etiolated plants, however, it was much greater than 1, and in those with storage roots, it was much less.

Tammes (1903) made a study of the growth relationships between an internode and the leaf above it. She found that removal of a leaf would shorten the length to which the internode below would grow but would not reduce the number of its cells. This relationship does not hold in climbing plants, where internode length is usually attained before the leaf above becomes very large. In *Ipomoea* the excision of leaves on the main shoot has a variety of effects on the shape of leaves produced later by the terminal bud and on the size and number of their cells (Njoku, 1956*b*).

The various parts of the shoot system also show growth correlations, and these are responsible for the form of the shoot. They are readily observable in coniferous trees where the growth of the terminal shoot, which will form the trunk, is usually greater than that of the branches. This leads to the spire-like form of many of these trees. There are also definite relationships between the members of a branch system. The new

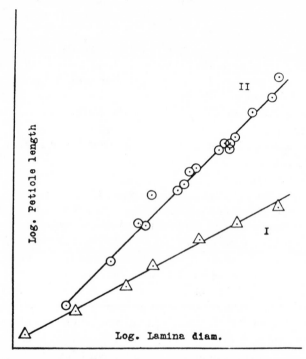

Fig. 5-3. Allometric relation between lamina and petiole in *Tropaeolum*. I, a series of growing leaves. II, mature leaves in shade. (*From Pearsall.*)

material added each year is distributed unequally but in regular fashion throughout the tree.

A somewhat different type of correlation is that between the volume of the shoot system or any part of it and the cross-sectional area of the stem that supports it. Murray (1927) analyzed this relationship in a number of trees and finds that it is constant and predictable and that as the tree grows larger the cross-sectional area of its trunk becomes relatively smaller. It has been shown that where a trunk branches the cross-sectional area of the two branches is larger than that of the united trunk below them but that the degree of this difference depends on the relative size of the two branches and on the angle between them. It is an expression of the polar tendency of the trunk.

There are also correlations between the parts of an organ. In leaves, for example, although the length of the petiole is much more variable

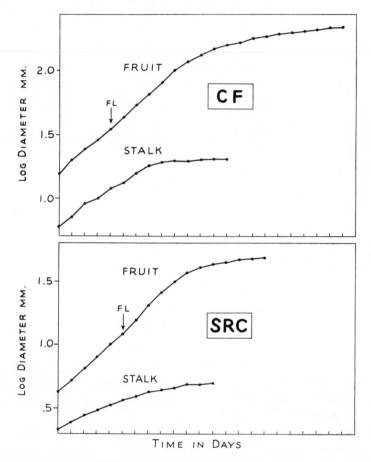

FIG. 5-4. Diameter of stalk plotted against diameter of fruit in a large-fruited race of *Cucurbita* (above) and a small one (below). Rate of growth is less for stalk than for fruit but at flowering the logarithmic distance between the two is approximately the same in both races. (*From Sinnott.*)

than the dimensions of the lamina, there is a relation between them. In *Tropaeolum,* Pearsall (1927) found that this was allometric, with lamina width growing faster than petiole length (Fig. 5-3). In *Acer* the volume of the leaf blade is much more closely correlated with the cross-sectional area of the petiole than with its length. In the runner bean the area of the lamina and the cross-sectional area of the petiolar xylem are related allometrically, but the xylem grows only about 0.6 as fast as the lamina (D. J. B. White, 1954). Alexandrov, Alexandrova, and Timofeev (1927) observed that in *Bryonia* the number of vessels in any given part of the stem is correlated with the dimensions of the leaves in that region. These various facts suggest that physiological factors are here involved and that the amount of water transpired from the blade is important in determining the conducting capacity of the petiole. This hypothesis will be discussed later (p. 332). In the light of other evidence, it is doubtful whether such a "functional stimulus" is actually operative.

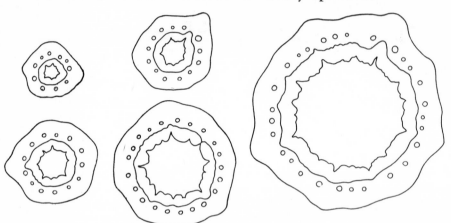

Fig. 5-5. Relation of pith diameter to diameter of shoot in young stems of *Pinus strobus* of different sizes, showing greater relative size of pith in larger stems. (*From Sinnott.*)

Somewhat similarly, the diameter of a growing cucurbit fruit and of the stalk that bears it are closely correlated in early growth, the fruit increasing more rapidly. Stalk growth ceases earlier than fruit growth, however (Sinnott, 1955; Fig. 5-4).

Some correlations between parts are due to the similar effect of a gene or group of genes on a series of morphologically related organs. Anderson and de Winton (1935) studied the effect of a number of mutant genes, in *Primula sinensis*, on the morphology of the leaf, bract, sepal, and petal. In several cases they had a very similar influence on development (producing lobing) in all four categories of organs. Such correlations are examples of what is sometimes called *homeosis*.

Many examples of growth correlation are found in internal structures. Thus Buchholz (1938) in *Sequoia* has shown that in stems of different sizes the vascular cylinder occupies a relatively larger portion, as measured in cross section, in large stems than it does in small ones. In pine stems of different size the pith is relatively larger in the large stems and the cortex relatively smaller (Sinnott, 1936a; Fig. 5-5).

Sometimes these size relationships are found to extend below the level of the organ. The relation of cell size to nuclear size has already been discussed (p. 27). Klieneberger (1918) measured this relationship in a large number of plants, and the subject has been reviewed by Trombetta (1942). Both Budde (1923) and Schratz (1927) found a rather close correlation between the total surface area of the plastids and the volume of the cell.

These relationships between structures have important evolutionary implications which cannot be discussed here. The increasing size of the leaf during the development of the pteropsid stock seems to have been correlated with the change from a protostelic to a siphonostelic stem structure (Wetmore, 1943). The association of the trilacunar leaf trace

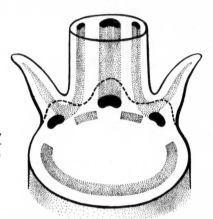

Fɪɢ. 5-6. Diagram of a trilacunar node, showing relation between stipules and lateral leaf traces. (*From Sinnott and Bailey.*)

with the presence of stipules (Sinnott and Bailey, 1914; Fig. 5-6) is another instance. This has been emphasized by the observation of Sensarma (1957) that when only one lateral trace branches only the stipule on that side develops. Another case is the relation of absolute size of the axis to its vascular development (p. 359). Among animals there are many examples of evolutionary allometry where increasing size of the organism results in a proportionally greater increase of certain organs.

Correlations between Dimensions. Correlations between part and whole or part and part evidently involve coordinating mechanisms that bind these parts into an integrated organism. The same sort of control is shown, though in a somewhat different manner, in the correlation between the various dimensions of an organ or other determinate structure. Here one is concerned with the very essence of form itself, with the way in which growth is distributed in one direction relative to that in another. This relative growth, like that between parts, is under definite control and proceeds in a regular and orderly fashion (Fig. 5-7). Since most plant organs are determinate structures, their forms are more constant and precise than are those of the whole plant body.

The origin of specific form in a plant or its organs may be studied in embryological development but more readily in the growth of organs that originate at the meristem, especially leaves, flowers, and fruits. In some cases the mature form or a close approximation to it is established very early, and from an examination of a tiny primordium, when its size may be only a fraction of a cubic millimeter, the final shape of the organ can be seen. The critical period in form determination here is evidently near the beginning of development. More frequently, however, the early primordium is simple, often nearly isodiametric, and the final form develops by differential growth.

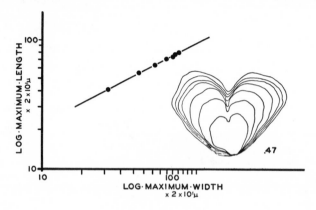

Fig. 5-7. Relative growth of length to width in developing fern prothallium. (*From Albaum.*)

Plant embryology in its widest sense is the record of such differential growth by which the complexity of organic form is attained. Most of our knowledge of the process is from verbal or pictorial descriptions, but in some cases it has been analyzed more precisely. The techniques of measuring allometric growth are as applicable in such cases as they are in the more frequently studied ones of part-to-part analysis. Richards and Kavanagh (1943) have extended the method further and show how it may be applied to three-dimensional growth. If this proves generally feasible, analysis of form development will become much more precise. Schüepp (1945, 1946) has used the methods of allometry to supplement others in a rather complex analysis of the development of leaf shape and of the origin of the leaf primordium at the meristem.

Sinnott (1936*b*) applied these methods to the study of form development in fruits of various races of cucurbits where form difference is due to differential growth rates in various dimensions (Fig. 5-8). In the long, narrow types, such as the "club" gourd, length increases faster than width but at a constant relative rate, the value of k being approximately 1.2. In other races, such as the "bottle" gourds, width increases faster than length, k being about 0.8. In the latter race, which has an upper sterile lobe and a lower fertile one with a constricted isthmus between, the ratios of the diameters of these to each other and to the polar diameter of the ovary are specific, so that, as the fruit grows, not only the ratio of length to width changes but the form of the organ as a whole undergoes

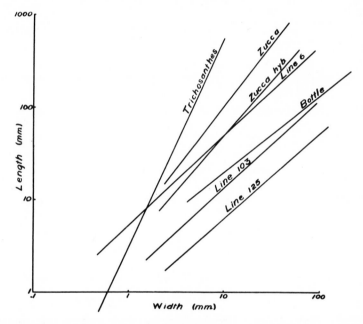

Fɪɢ. 5-8. Relative growth of length to width (plotted logarithmically) of developing fruits of several types of cucurbits. (*From Sinnott.*)

precise development (Fig. 5-9). An organic pattern results not from one or a few correlations between dimensions but from a complex of such correlations. In crosses between the two gourd types mentioned, the value of k has been found to segregate after crossing and at least in one case in a simple fashion, suggesting that this is what is under direct gene control (p. 423). Evidently the form of the mature fruit in such cases depends not only upon the relative rate of its dimensional growth but upon the total growth attained, so that the problem of the inheritance of form involves not only the genetic basis of relative growth but also that of size.

Dimensional relationships are not constant throughout the plant. Dif-

ferences in shape are often found between early and later fruits, or between leaves on different parts of the axis. Meijknecht (1955) has
analyzed some of these differences and concludes that this variation is
least when the structure occupies the position on the plant in which it
shows its "ideal" development, the expression of its typical specific character. This calls to mind a concept of the early "idealistic" morphology.

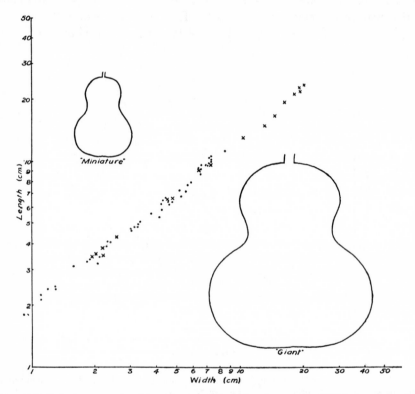

FIG. 5-9. Relative growth of length to width in bottle gourds. Width increases faster
than length, but the relative rate is the same in "miniature" (dots) and "giant"
(crosses), so that although the shape of the two races at maturity is different, their
genotype for shape is the same. The inherited difference between them is in size.
(*From Sinnott.*)

   The mechanism by which the control of relative growth is exercised
and growth correlation established is not known, but evidently cell
polarities are involved. Where growth is more rapid in one dimension
than in another, it has been shown (p. 51) that cell divisions are more
frequent in that direction. Whether the axis of the spindle or the cytoplasmic polarity by which this seems in certain cases to be preceded is
what is immediately involved in relative growth, or whether this is second-

ary to some more general form-determining mechanism, is a basic problem.

In this chapter there have been presented only a few of the great number of developmental, physiological, and genetic correlations that may be found throughout botanical literature, but these are representative of the rest and emphasize an important fact in plant development. A plant is typically a rather loosely organized system but every part of it is nevertheless affected to some degree by its relations with other parts. These correlations are not random ones but are simple expressions of that general organized interrelatedness that is the distinguishing character of an organism. What happens to the whole affects the parts and what happens to a part affects the whole. An organ removed from this correlative inhibition may have a very different fate from its normal one. A single cell, on isolation, will often regenerate an entire plant. That it did not do so in its original position is owing to this inhibition. The term "correlation" is simply a description of the facts and explains nothing. It is of value, however, in emphasizing that the results of any experiment with a portion of the plant body must be interpreted not as an isolated event but as taking place against the background of the whole organism. How each portion of this organism behaves under given conditions and what its developmental fate will be depend upon its position in the organized system of which it forms a part. The nature of this organized system is the fundamental problem that continually faces the student of morphogenesis in whatever part of the science he may be at work.

CHAPTER 6

Polarity

In plant development, growth does not proceed at random to the production of a formless mass of living stuff but is an orderly process that gives rise to specific three-dimensional *forms* of organ or body. The various correlations described in the preceding chapter are manifestations of this formative control, which knits the developing organism together so that growth in one region or dimension is related to growth in the others and the plant thus becomes an integrated individual. A notable feature of these bodily forms of plants (and animals) is the presence in them of an *axis* which establishes a longitudinal dimension for organ or organism. Along this axis, and symmetrically with reference to it, the lateral structures develop. The two ends or poles of the axis are usually different both as to structure and physiological activity. Thus a typical vascular plant has a major axis with the root at one end and the shoot at the other and with lateral appendages—leaves, branches, or lateral roots— disposed symmetrically around it. Growth is usually more rapid parallel to the axis than at right angles to it, so that an elongate form results, though this is by no means always the case. Single organs such as leaves, flowers, and fruits also show axiate patterns, as do the bodies of lower plants. These patterns appear very early in development as the result of differences in growth or in planes of cell division. This characteristic orientation of organisms, which is typically bipolar and axiate, is termed *polarity*.

Polarity may manifest itself in many ways. The structures at the two ends of an axis are unlike, as in the case of root and shoot, "stem end" and "blossom end" of fruits, and petiole and blade of leaves. In regeneration, the organs formed at one end are usually different from those formed at the other. Cells and tissues may show polar behavior in grafting experiments. The transportation of certain substances may take place in one direction along the axis but not in the other, thus manifesting polarity in physiological activity. Both in structure and in function there are gradients of all sorts. Individual cells show polar behavior in plane of division and in the different character of their two daughter cells.

It is important at the beginning to understand exactly what is meant by the term polarity. Sometimes this is regarded as an innate quality of an organism which makes its parts line up in a given direction, like iron filings in a magnetic field or opposite electrical charges at the two poles of an electrophoretic system. How far such polarizing factors operate in organisms we do not know. The term polarity as used most commonly, and certainly in the present discussion, implies much less than this and involves no assumption as to its causes. Polarity is simply *the specific orientation of activity in space*. It refers to the *fact* that a given biological event, such as the transfer of material through an organ or the plane in which a cell divides, is not a random process but tends to be oriented in a given direction. If this were not so, an organism would grow into a spherical mass of cells, like tissue in a shaken culture. This differential directiveness is responsible for organic *form*. What is the cause of it we do not know, but one often invokes it, although as an expression of ignorance, in attempting to account for a morphogenetic fact. Polar behavior is no more and no less mysterious than organic formativeness but is merely the simplest manifestation of this, the tendency to develop a major axis with lateral ones subordinate to it.

It is essential to realize, however, that polarity is not a trait that is originally and invariably present. There is good evidence that entirely undifferentiated cells, such as eggs in their early stages and other very simple ones, manifest no polarity at all. Within them, doubtless, there are polar molecules but these are arranged at random, like iron filings that are not in a magnetic field. Sooner or later a gradient is established in the cell which lines up these molecules in a specific orientation. This orientation originates in asymmetric factors in the outer environment, such as gravity, light, or the influence of adjacent cells, or perhaps within the cell from gene action. As a result, the various phenomena of polarity make their appearance, but not until a gradient has first been set up. Once a cell or a group of cells have thus become polarized, they will usually proceed to develop into an axiate system which then produces an organic form without necessity for further environmental induction.

The *tendency toward polar orientation*, which may be strong or weak or reversible and is differentially susceptible to outer influences, is the fundamental fact of polarity. It must be distinguished from the various *factors of induction* that call forth and make manifest this polar tendency. To say that light induces polarity in the egg of *Fucus* is to describe a morphogenetic fact, but a different problem is to explain the character of the cell that makes it capable of a specific polarization. An explanation of polarity in physical and chemical terms is difficult but a beginning at this task has already been made. In most biological discussions today, however, the term polarity is primarily a descriptive one.

Polarity is involved in many morphogenetic phenomena, and it will necessarily be referred to repeatedly in other chapters. Thus symmetry is the orderly distribution of structures in relation to a polar axis. Polar differences are the simplest aspect of differentiation. Regeneration is in most cases a polar process. Form results from a pattern of polarities set up in the developing plant. Polarity may be regarded as the framework, so to speak, on which organic form is built.

The polar behavior of plants has long attracted the attention of morphologists and physiologists, from whose work a great body of knowledge has accumulated. Theophrastus and other ancient writers described the abnormal behavior of plants grown in an inverted position. There are a number of other early observations, especially those on regeneration following the girdling of trees, by Agricola, Hales, and Duhamel du Monceau. The term *polarity* was used by Allman in 1864 in connection with phenomena of animal regeneration and is now generally employed by students of morphogenesis in both botany and zoology. Vöchting made extensive studies of polarity in plants in its relation to problems of regeneration, growth, and differentiation (1878, 1908, 1918). Important botanical work was also done by Goebel (1908), Janse (1906), Loeb (1924), and others. The theoretical aspects of polarity have been extensively discussed not only by Vöchting but by Sachs (1882), Pfeffer (1900–1906), Klebs (1903, 1904, 1913), Winkler (1900, 1933), Went and Thimann (1937), Lund (1947), Bünning (1952*b*), and others. Polarity in animals has been studied by many workers, notably Driesch, Roux, Morgan, and Harrison. Reviews of the field of plant polarity or parts of it have been written by Bloch (1943*a*), Gautheret (1944), and Bünning (1958). Polarity is important not only for theoretical problems of plant development but for many practices of horticulture and vegetative propagation (Priestley and Swingle, 1929).

The establishment of a morphological axis in which the two ends are different and along which there is a gradation from one pole to the other may be looked upon as the first step in the process of *differentiation,* an important aspect of morphogenesis. The expression of polarity differs considerably in different plants and under different environmental conditions and is thus open to a wide range of experimental investigation. This most conspicuous aspect of organic form will probably not be fully understood until the mechanism of orderly and correlated growth control is discovered. As a relatively simple manifestation of form, however, it provides a useful point of attack on morphogenetic problems.

Polar behavior in plants presents many problems. How far is it an inherited character, potentially present from the beginning of development, and how far induced by the action of various environmental factors or by intercellular correlation? Once established, can it be reversed? Are the physiological manifestations of polarity the cause or the results of morphological polarity? Is polarity an aspect of the whole organism or do individual cells possess it?

To present the various phenomena of polar behavior and the problems that they pose, it will be helpful to discuss the subject from several points of view and to describe its manifestations in external structure, internal structure, isolated cells and coenocytes, physiological activity, and the development of organic pattern.

POLARITY AS EXPRESSED IN EXTERNAL STRUCTURE

The most conspicuous expression of polarity is in external morphology. In higher plants the differences between root end and shoot end are determined very early, perhaps at the first division of the fertilized egg. This differentiation is not irreversible, however, for roots often appear on stems under favorable conditions and, less commonly, buds and shoots appear on roots. Polar behavior occurs in thallophytes and bryophytes, even in some very simple forms like those of many filamentous algae, though in such cases it is less sharply marked and more easily reversed than in vascular plants. Organisms without morphological polarity are rare. A few amoeboid forms have no axes in the vegetative stage but form polarized fruiting bodies. Algae like *Pleurococcus* are spherical and apparently apolar but may be induced to produce filaments, an expression of axiation. Forms like *Spirogyra,* desmids, and diatoms have an axis of symmetry but its two poles seem to be alike. In most filamentous types, however, a rhizoidal pole and a thallus pole can be distinguished.

Experimentally, polarity can best be demonstrated through its expression in regeneration, and it is here that most of our information about it has been gathered. Polar regeneration has long been known and manipulated in the horticultural practices of vegetative reproduction.

Vöchting (1878) cut twigs of willow and kept them under moist conditions. Some he left in their normal, upright orientation and others were inverted. Regardless of orientation, however, roots tended to be regenerated more vigorously from the morphologically basal end and shoots from buds at the original apical end. This is the classical example of polarity (Fig. 6-1). If such a shoot were cut into two or more parts transversely, each part regenerated roots and shoots in the same polar fashion. Even very short pieces of stem showed this polar character. Vöchting removed a ring of bark in the middle of a shoot and confirmed earlier observations that roots were formed above the ring and shoots below, just as if the stem had been cut in two. From these and similar experiments he concluded that polarity was a fixed and irreversible characteristic of the plant axis and that probably the individual cells of which the axis was formed themselves possessed a polar character.

Experiments like these have been carried out on many plants. A wide variety of results, often conflicting, have been reported and several

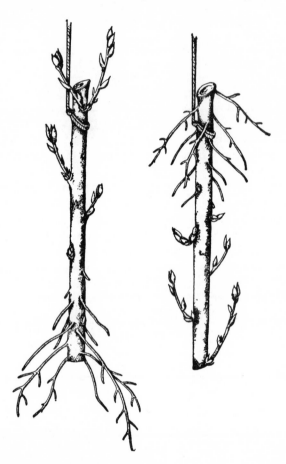

FIG. 6-1. Polarity in willow shoots. Left, portion of a stem suspended in moist air in its normal position and producing roots and shoots. Right, a stem similarly grown except in an inverted position. (*After Pfeffer.*)

theories to explain polarity proposed. Klebs (1903), for example, found that roots would grow at the apical end of an inverted shoot, that water stimulated root formation at any point on the twig, and that removal of the bark could reverse polarity. He believed that environmental conditions rather than innate polarity determined the place where buds and roots develop on a stem. Vöchting (1906) replied to these criticisms of the theory of polarity. The problem, however, is evidently not quite as simple as Vöchting at first thought.

Polar regeneration is also evident in the lower groups of the plant kingdom. If fern prothallia are sliced transversely, regeneration from their cut surfaces is polar (Albaum, 1938b; Fig. 6-2) and is related to physiological gradients, especially of osmotic concentration (Gratzy-Wardengg, 1929). In isolated primary leaves of ferns, polarity is evident, but both the character and the polar distribution of regenerated structures are somewhat diverse (Beyerle, 1932).

Fɪɢ. 6-2. Polar character of regeneration in fern prothallia from which pieces have been removed by transverse cuts. An apical portion restores a single heart-shaped structure, but from a basal one a group of small prothallia is formed. (*From Albaum.*)

In the regeneration of hepatics and mosses, polar behavior varies. The gemmae of *Marchantia* and *Lunularia* form rhizoids from either surface while they are young but only from one when they grow older (Haberlandt, 1914), indicating that embryonic tissue, as it proves to be in many other cases, is relatively unpolarized. Polarity here can be reversed by gravity, light, and other environmental factors (Fitting, 1938). Vöchting found relatively little polarity in the regeneration of the thallus of *Marchantia*. In the mosses, cuttings formed rhizoids at the lower end and protonemata at the upper one. This behavior could be reversed by inversion of the cuttings (Westerdijk, 1907), but regenerating structures were always more vigorous at the morphologically basal pole.

Polarity is evident in the sporophores of the higher fungi but here, also, it is not firmly fixed, for a segment of the pileus may be successfully grafted back to the same pileus in an inverted position (Lohwag, 1939).

In most algae there is a sharp distinction between the rhizoidal, or hold-fast, pole and the thallus, or shoot, pole. Especially in the simple forms and in early stages of the more complex ones, this polarity may be reversed by changed relations to gravity, light, or other factors (Wulff, 1910; Zimmermann, 1923). Studies on the egg of *Fucus* and on coenocytic algae are illuminating here (p. 135).

Manifestations of polar behavior in higher plants are much more uni-

form and fixed, presumably because of the higher level of organization
and differentiation among them. It must have its origin verv early in
embryonic development. Vöchting's conclusion, however, that every

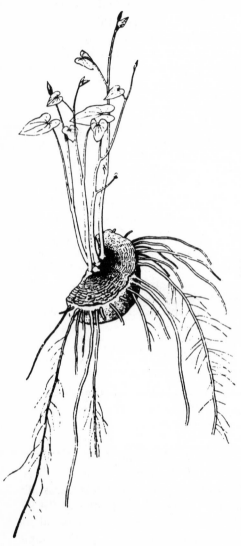

FIG. 6-3. Transverse polarity in *Dioscorea.*
Half slice of a tuber with regenerating
shoots next the core and roots on the
periphery. (*From Goebel.*)

cell is polarized has been challenged by those who point out that many
cells theoretically may become completely embryonic again and ultimately produce an entire plant and thus can have no fixed polar charac-

ter. Pfeffer and Klebs have emphasized the probability that the cells of the terminal growing points have no original polarity of their own, any more than does an egg cell. In older parts a more stable polarization results from the influence of conditions in the environment. Vöchting's idea of the irreversibility of polarity in these higher plants has also been disputed. Many investigations concerned with these problems cannot be judged critically because of insufficient evidence, particularly as to anatomical facts.

Polarity may be manifest in the transverse axis as well as in the longitudinal one. This is evident structurally in the transversely polar gradient often associated with regeneration. Thus Goebel (1908) found that in half slices of the root of *Dioscorea sinuata* shoots grew out from the central part of the axis and roots from the margin directly opposite to this (Fig. 6-3). Transverse polarity is also manifest in the flow of auxin in various tropisms (p. 384). The subject has been discussed in detail by Borgström (1939).

Stem Cuttings. In stem cuttings, polar regeneration of shoots and roots is clearly obvious in most higher plants, but there are considerable differences between species. Polar behavior may be obscured in various ways, as by the tendency of monocotyledons to form roots at nodes and by the influence in many cases of the age of the cutting upon the formation of root primordia. The specific polar reactivity of tissues from which buds and roots originate must be taken into account, as well as the fact that a different complex of conditions may control each of the successive processes in the development of these structures, such as the formation of primordia, their growth, their final differentiation into roots and shoots, or the formation of callus which may give rise to either roots or shoots.

Various modifications of polar behavior in regeneration from stem cuttings have been reported. Roots, for example, tend more characteristically to be limited to one pole in their growth than do shoots. Doposcheg-Uhlár (1911) observed this in *Begonia,* and Massart (1917) studied 30 species of plants, some of which showed strongly polar regeneration of both roots and shoots, some weakly polar regeneration, some only root polarity, and some only shoot polarity. Root polarity was related to the growth habit of the plant, for species with pendant branches rooted readily at their apical ends.

Polar tendency is also expressed in the manner of callus formation in cuttings, since in most cases callus tends to develop more vigorously at the basal pole than at the apical. From the basal callus, roots are usually formed, and shoots from the apical one. Simon (1908) noted certain anatomical differences between apical and basal calluses and made the observation that calluses from opposite poles may be made to fuse but not calluses from the same pole.

Various investigators (Klebs, 1903; Küster, 1904; Freund, 1910; and Ursprung, 1912) found that local differences in water or oxygen may affect root production and thus obscure the inherent polar tendency. Only Plett (1921), who studied phenomena of internode polarity in 410 species, has attempted to explain the variability in distribution of roots and shoots on the basis of the anatomy of the plant from which the cutting was taken. He found that shoots from axillary buds regenerate in a polar fashion, as do adventitious roots that arise endogenously. Adventitious buds growing from callus or superficial regions of the cortex, however, are generally distributed rather irregularly, a fact which suggests that the inner layers of the stem have stronger polar tendencies than do cortex and callus tissues.

Root Cuttings. Cuttings of roots behave in polar fashion. Dandelion, chicory, and sea kale have been studied most frequently in this regard. Shoots are commonly regenerated at the basal or proximal pole (the end next the shoot) and roots from the apical (distal) pole. This polarity is maintained even when the root cutting is grown in an inverted position (Fig. 6-4). Wiesner (1892c) made the observation, often confirmed since, that, in relatively short pieces of root, shoots regenerate at *both* ends. This was also seen by Neilson-Jones (1925) and, in stem cuttings, by Fischnich (1939). If the growing roots were continually trimmed off from the apical end, shoots finally appeared there. Czaja (1935) produced roots at both ends by trimming off tissue from the *basal* end. Centrifugation toward the shoot pole results in bud formation at the root pole, as does enclosing the base in sealing wax (Goebel, 1908). These results are now interpreted as due to the effect of auxin (p. 392), which tends to move toward the root apex. A high concentration of it tends to produce roots and a low one, shoots. This has been shown clearly by Warmke and Warmke (1950). Callus develops more vigorously at the proximal pole. As early as 1847 Trécul reported that, in root cuttings of *Maclura*, buds and roots showed polar distribution and were formed endogenously but that in *Ailanthus*, where the buds arose in the cortex, polarity was much less evident. This agrees with Plett's findings in stem cuttings and emphasizes the more intense polar behavior of the inner tissues.

Leaf Cuttings. Leaves when treated as cuttings behave quite differently from stems and roots and show a somewhat different type of polar behavior, evidently related to the fact that they are organs of determinate growth. In most cases, regeneration of both roots and shoots occurs at the leaf base near the cut end of the petiole. Hagemann (1931) performed inversion experiments on various species. In certain cases he found that wound stimulus or water affects regeneration. In *Achimenes*, shoots were thus obtained from the apical cut surface and roots from the base under certain conditions, but Hagemann concluded that, in general, polarity as expressed in the location of regenerating structures in leaves is determined by anatomical structure. Behre (1929) reports that regeneration in the leaves of *Drosera* is apolar.

There has been much discussion as to whether, in the higher plants, polarity once established can be reversed. It has been the common experience of botanists and horticulturalists that cuttings in which the apical end is put into the soil will not do as well as those with normal orientation. Some inverted cuttings are found to take root, however, and may

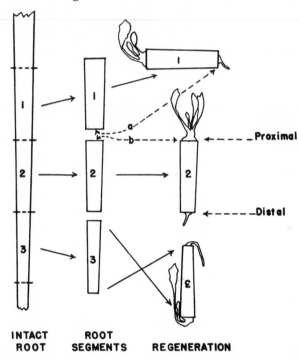

INTACT   ROOT
ROOT   SEGMENTS   REGENERATION

Fɪɢ. 6-4. Polarity of regeneration in root of *Taraxacum*. A root segment produces shoots at the proximal end (next the base of the plant) and roots at the distal end, whether the segment is normally oriented, horizontal, or inverted. Compare with Fig. 18-17. (*From Warmke and Warmke.*)

live thus for some time. Kny (1889) successfully grew cuttings of *Hedera* and *Ampelopsis* inverted for several years, and Graham, Hawkins, and Stewart (1934) did so with willow cuttings, which were still flourishing after 11 years. The tips of weeping willows will often root at the apex if they are dipping into water (Pont, 1934). Such inverted structures, however, often show external malformation and anatomical distortion. Growth may become normal again if the cutting is restored to its upright orientation and can form roots at the morphologically basal end. Lundegårdh

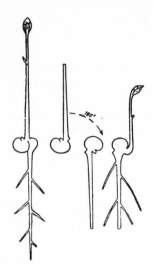

FIG. 6-5. "Inversion of polarity." Etiolated pea seedling with epicotyl decapitated, inverted, and placed in water. Roots now grow out from the epicotyl and a shoot from a cotyledonary bud. (*After Castan.*)

(1915) found that apparent reversal of polar behavior in *Coleus* was only temporary.

Reversal seems to be easier to accomplish in seedlings than in older plants. Castan (1940) cut off the epicotyl and the primary root from etiolated pea seedlings and inverted them. Roots then grew out from the originally apical end and shoots from the basal one (Fig. 6-5). Rathfelder (1955) confirmed this observation and believes that it is a real reversal.

Reversal of polarity is much easier to accomplish in the lower plants (p. 138).

POLARITY AS EXPRESSED IN INTERNAL STRUCTURE

Polar phenomena are manifest not only in external form but in internal structure. This is evident in many ways.

Embryonic Development. In vascular plants the first manifestation of polar behavior is in the division of the fertilized egg. This in most cases seems to be related to the polar character of the gametophyte. Wetter (1952), confirming earlier work of others, finds that in ferns the planes of division in the young embryo are related to the axis of the prothallium and that the segment that will form the first leaf is always directed toward the growing point (notch), a fact also evident later in the orientation of the young leaf itself. This relationship persists regardless of the direction of the incident light. In *Isoetes*, the first division of the fertilized egg is at right angles to the axis of the archegonium, and early embryo development is not affected by external factors (La Motte, 1937; Fig. 6-6).

In seed plants the embryo has a definite orientation in the ovule, the tip of the young radicle always being directed toward the micropyle and the plumular end toward the chalaza. This has its origin in the polar relation between embryo sac and ovule, since the archegonium, or egg apparatus, lies at the micropylar end of the sac. Even the group of four megaspores is polarized, and it is the one at the micropylar end that germinates into the female gametophyte. The planes of division of the proembryo are related to the axis of the ovule. In the young embryo as it develops at the end of the suspensors, the distinction between root and shoot begins very early, with the first transverse divisions. The direction of the polar axis is evidently impressed upon the embryo, as upon the egg, by the axial organization of the embryo sac and ovule, and once established this polar behavior persists and is apparently irreversible.

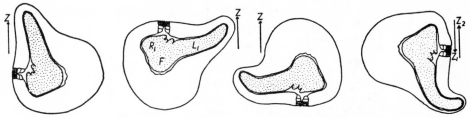

Fig. 6-6. Young embryos in the female gametophyte of *Isoetes* which have developed in the positions indicated. Early orientation is with reference to the polar axis of the archegonium, but when the leaf begins to push out it becomes negatively geotropic. Z, direction of zenith; R, root; F, foot; L, leaf. (*From La Motte.*)

Embryonic polarity, however, may arise in other ways than through this simple relationship to the ovulary axis. In cleavage polyembryony several embryos may arise from a single egg (p. 206), each showing typical polar character. Adventitious embryos are sometimes formed by growth of nucellar cells and not from fertilized eggs, and these grow into normal plants. Structures essentially like embryos sometimes occur elsewhere in the plant ("foliar embryos" of *Kalanchoe*, p. 254) and these show typical polar behavior. The first manifestation of differentiation in any embryo, whatever its origin, is the appearance of a polar axis.

A number of cases have been reported (Swamy, 1946) in which the polar character of the angiosperm embryo sac is reversed, an egg apparatus appearing at both ends, or even the antipodal cells at the micropylar end and the egg at the opposite one.

Tissue Reorganization. Various histological changes occur in cuttings grown in an inverted position, as described by Vöchting (1918) and others. Such plants are evidently abnormal in a number of respects. There is often a tendency in them to form swellings and tumors, particularly near the insertion of branches, which now tend to grow upward.

The cause of these swellings may lie in the fact that the original tissues cannot function properly under the changed orientation and that considerable cellular rearrangement must be brought about in the new tissue formed after inversion. These tumors resemble anatomically the "whorls" commonly found in wound wood and consist of parenchymatous, sclerenchymatous, and tracheidal elements. Vöchting here has described the structure of such tumors in *Salix fragilis* and other species and believes them to be due to the innate polar tendency of individual cells. On such an interpretation, the tissues are thought to twist about (Fig. 6-7) until finally those of the root and of the new shoot are connected by cells of the same polar orientation (Küster, 1925).

There has been considerable controversy as to this hypothesis. Mäule (1896) uses it to explain the behavior of cambium cells in wound wood.

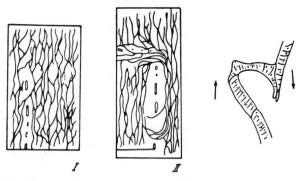

FIG. 6-7. Vessel polarity after budding. *I*, longitudinal anastomoses between vessels in normally oriented bud and stock. *II*, twisting of vessels when bud has been inserted upside down. At right, single vessel from the latter. (*From Vöchting.*)

Neeff (1922) made an extensive series of studies of the changing orientation of cambial cells in decapitated stems, finding that these tend to turn until they become parallel to the newly regenerating axis instead of to the old one (Figs. 6-8, 6-9), and he explains this in terms of the inherent polar behavior of the cells, which tends to conform to that of the functional axis. Both Jaccard (1910) and Küster, on the other hand, disagree with Vöchting's explanation and attribute the changing orientation of the cells mainly to mechanical factors. Twisting whorls may also appear in normal callus where mechanical factors can hardly be operative. More intensive studies are needed of the conditions that cause change in direction of cell growth. Altered direction of sap flow, for example, might affect the direction of cambial cell growth in Neeff's experiments. Similar changes in cellular orientation have been reported by MacDaniels and Curtis (1930) in spiral ringing wounds in apple, by Janse (1914) in bark strips left across a ringing wound in *Acalypha,* and by Tupper-

Carey (1930) in tissue bridges in *Acer* and *Laburnum*. Pressure, nutrient movements, and basipetal cambial activity have been suggested as causes. The results of Went (p. 384) with inverted cuttings of *Tagetes* indicate that the direction of auxin flow in them is ultimately reversed. It is clear that in some way histological changes are related to the new conditions under which an inverted cutting has to grow.

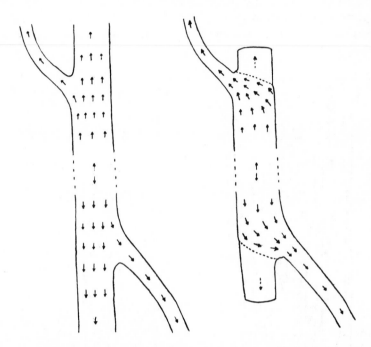

FIG. 6-8. Left, diagram showing direction of cambium cells (and their derivatives) in a normal shoot of *Tilia*, with a lateral root and lateral shoot growing from it. The cells are parallel to the particular axis of which they form a part. Right, change of direction of these cells when the main axis has been decapitated at both ends and the lateral axes are becoming the main ones. The direction of the cells in the original main axis has now turned to become parallel with the new ones. (*From Neeff.*)

The results of grafting provide a direct way of testing polar differences in tissues. Vöchting (1918) used the swollen stem of kohlrabi for a series of such experiments. If the top of a stem is sliced off transversely and a V-shaped cut made in its upper surface and if the lower portion of another stem is sharpened to fit this cut and inserted firmly into it, the tissues of the two stems will knit together. If, however, a piece is sliced off from the lower part of a kohlrabi stem and it is then *inverted*, and the surface now uppermost cut as before, and if a sharpened upper piece is inserted into this cut, the tissues will not knit. Furthermore, rootlets will begin to grow out from the upper piece into the lower one, as if growing in a foreign substratum. Thus a root pole will fuse with a shoot pole but two similar poles, when brought together, will not fuse. Vöchting also found that a square bit of tissue cut out from a beet root and put directly back will knit in its former place but will not do so if turned through 180° before being replaced there. These facts can be explained by assuming that the tissues of the plant, even such relatively undifferentiated parenchymatous ones, have definitely polar behavior. Bloch (1952), however, observed that tissues of the fruits of *Lagenaria* do not behave in this way but that plugs, cut out and replaced, will knit in any

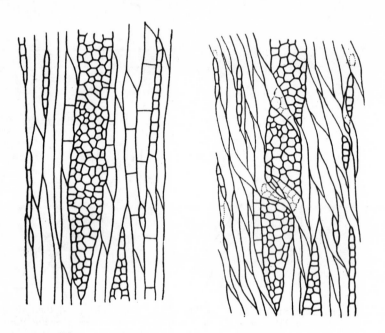

FIG. 6-9. Tangential sections through tissue of an axis like those in Fig. 6-8. Left, normal wood. Right, after decapitation, direction of cells changing to conform to the axis of the lateral root, now the main one. (*From Neeff.*)

orientation. Microscopic examination after a few days showed normal cellular fusion.

In horticultural practice it has long been recognized that buds must be placed in normal orientation on the stock if they are to knit well. Colquhoun (1929) removed buds and pieces of bark in *Casuarina* and reapplied them in an inverted position. Observation of the anatomical structure showed that the cells of the cambium joined freely and continued to grow regardless of orientation. Wood fibers and vessels, however, show the characteristic turns and twists reported by Vöchting. This suggests that the cambial cells are unpolarized or in a condition of unstable polarity and that, as wood elements differentiate, polarity is gradually impressed upon them. Cells inversely oriented are now unable to unite, and the translocation of materials in them, tending in each to follow the original direction of flow, is seriously disturbed. This gradual assumption of polarity is perhaps related to changes at the cell surface as the wall is formed or in the structure of the wall itself.

Another manifestation of polar activity in histological characters, perhaps related to the basipetal tendency in the renewal of cambial activity or to the polar flow of auxin (p. 384), may be observed in the reconstitution of severed vascular strands across the ground parenchyma of pith or cortex in herbaceous dicotyledons (Simon, 1908; Sinnott and Bloch, 1945; Jacobs, 1954). This always begins at the basal end of a severed strand and proceeds downward toward the apical end of the cut bundle or to uninjured ones.

Cell Polarity. To test Vöchting's contention that polar behavior of a tissue is the result of the polarity of its individual cells is not easy. The fact that very small tissue pieces retain their original polarity and that inversely grafted tissues do not fuse supports Vöchting. Many other facts can also be cited. The two daughter cells following a division are often unlike (p. 133). In these cases, each of the two types is found invariably on the same side, toward or away from the tip of the axis. Thus in many young roots the last division of the surface cells is unequal, the smaller daughter cell becoming a trichoblast and producing a root hair (p. 190). This cell is always on the side toward the tip of the root. Before division, the apical end of the mother cell is also more densely protoplasmic. In some cases (*Phleum*) the division is markedly unequal and polar. In others (*Sporobolus*) the two cells are more nearly equal and a root hair is not always formed (Fig. 6-10). Here the polar behavior is much less marked. In the leaf epidermis of monocotyledons some cells divide unequally, and the one toward the leaf tip becomes a stomatal mother cell. These facts suggest that the cells themselves have a polar orientation.

The tendency of cells to divide in specific directions is at the bottom of all form determination, since it is concerned with the plane of division and thus the direction of growth. In the growth of elongate gourd fruits, for example, divisions are predominantly at right angles to the axis of the fruit, but in isodiametric ones they are at all angles (p. 51). Whether polarity is a quality of the whole developing organ or simply of its component cells is still uncertain and is a problem involving the deeper one of the relation between cell and organism. Various examples of polarity in unequal cell divisions have been discussed and figured by Bünning (1957; Fig. 6-11).

Even when the cell does not divide, the difference between its two

ends is often evident. That the cytoplasm is the seat of this polar difference is shown by the fact that, when vacuolate cells divide, the first
indication of the plane of division, and thus of the polar axis, is the appearance of a cytoplasmic diaphragm in the position where the future
partition wall will be formed (p. 25). In such cells the direction of the
axis may be related to gradients in hormone concentration, oxygen, or
other factors. This polar difference may be visible in the contents of the
cell, for in *Enteromorpha* (Müller-Stoll, 1952), in *Isoetes* (Stewart, 1948),
and other plants the chromatophore is almost always on the side of the
cell away from the base of the thallus, or plant body. The distribution of
chloroplasts in higher plants is also sometimes polar.

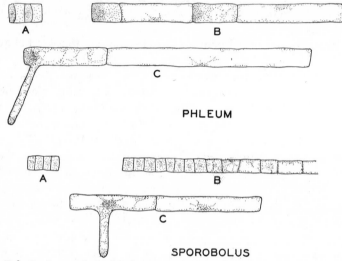

FIG. 6-10. Polarity in root-hair development. A, B, and C, successive stages, with root
apex toward left. In *Phleum,* the last division is unequal, and the cell toward the apex
forms a root hair. In *Sporobolus,* the division is essentially equal, and the cell toward
the apex does not always form a root hair. (*From Sinnott and Bloch.*)

The wall itself may show polar behavior, a fact which is of particular
importance in producing differences in cell shape. Most cells are nearly
isodiametric at the beginning, and if one at maturity is much longer than
wide, this is the result of more rapid growth in length. Such differential
growth, in turn, presumably comes from differences in the fine structure of the wall, which itself is ultimately dependent on factors in the
cytoplasm. Wilson (1955) has shown that in the wall of the large cells
of the alga *Valonia* there are two systems of orientation of cellulose
fibrils which converge to two poles at the ends of the cell. The complex
and remarkable shapes of many cells, both in simple organisms and
within the tissues of larger ones, are probably due to a complex pattern

of wall polarities that determine growth in a number of directions. How this is brought about is a morphogenetic problem at a different level from most of those here discussed, and its solution may provide suggestions for an approach to other problems of form.

It is sometimes possible to demonstrate the polarity of single cells experimentally even though their contents are homogeneous and both ends

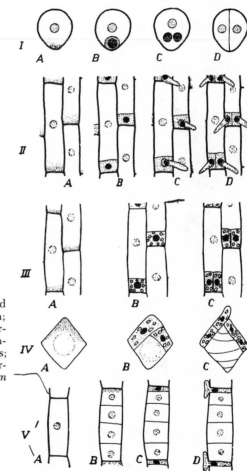

Fig. 6-11. Various types of unequal and polar cell divisions: *I*, in pollen grain; *II*, in differentiation of root hairs in certain monocotyledons; *III*, in differentiation of stomata in monocotyledons; *IV*, in leaf cells of *Sphagnum; V*, in formation of sclereids in *Monstera.* (*From Bünning.*)

appear to be alike. This can be done by isolating cells and observing the structures that regenerate from them. Miehe (1905) accomplished this in the filamentous alga *Cladophora*. Here polar organization is present but not conspicuous. At the basal end is a rhizoid which attaches to the substratum, and the rest of the filament or the thallus, a single row of cells, is undifferentiated. Miehe plasmolyzed the cells of a filament just enough to pull them away from the walls and break whatever connections there may have been with other cells, but without killing them. The plant was then deplasmolyzed. Each cell, now as effectively isolated as though it had actually been removed, began to enlarge, broke out of its wall, and proceeded to regenerate a new filament. The significant fact is that from the basal end of each cell a new rhizoid was formed and from the apical end, a new thallus. The polar character of the cells, otherwise impossible to demonstrate, could thus be established. These experiments were repeated and extended by Czaja (1930; Fig. 6-12). Borowikow (1914) succeeded in reversing the polarity of *Cladophora*

FIG. 6-12. Polarity in a single cell. A cell isolated from a filament of *Cladophora*, regenerating a thallus from its apical end and a rhizoid from its basal one. (*From Czaja.*)

cells by centrifugation, showing again the close relation between the distribution of material in the cytoplasm and the polarity of the cell.

In some filamentous algae, the plant's organization may disintegrate under certain circumstances and the individual cells thus become freed from their correlative inhibition. In *Griffithsia*, for example, Tobler (1904) observed such cells in culture and found that, when they began to regenerate, rhizoids grew from the basal end (distinguishable by its shape) and shoots from the apical one. Schechter (1935) centrifuged similar ones and found that their polarity could be altered by this means and that shoots always appeared at the centrifugal pole.

The rather loosely organized tissues of these simple algae provide excellent material for studies in cellular polarity even though their cells are not isolated. In bits of tissue cut from *Enteromorpha*, for example, Müller-Stoll (1952) found that the cells near the apical portion of the piece regenerate papilla-like structures but that the cells at the base form rhizoids.

To prove the existence of polar behavior in the cells of one of the higher plants is more difficult. Here it is sometimes possible to regenerate a new plant from a single cell or small group of cells, especially in the epidermis, but it is not easy to relate the polarity of the newly produced structure to that of the cell from which it grows.

POLARITY IN ISOLATED CELLS

In many cases, polarity may be studied in cells that are isolated in nature and not through experiment. The most notable example of this is the egg of the rockweed, *Fucus*, which is discharged into the water and there is fertilized and grows into a new plant. The *Fucus* egg is comparable to the eggs of certain animals that develop in water and that have proved such a rich source of knowledge of early embryology. More work has been done on this egg than on any other naturally isolated plant cell.

The unfertilized egg is naked, and its nucleus is at the center of the cell. It shows at the beginning no polarity whatever nor is there any visible differentiation in its cytoplasm. After fertilization, the egg falls to the bottom and in about 12 to 24 hours, under normal conditions, a protuberance appears on its lower surface. This develops into a rhizoid by which the young plant becomes anchored to the bottom. Soon the egg divides in a plane at right angles to the axis of the protuberance. The two cells that result are very different in shape and in their future development. The upper, rounded cell gives rise to the main portion of the thallus. The lower one forms little besides the rhizoid. The growth of the rhizoid and the first division of the egg establish a permanent polar axis in a system which at first is quite without one. Here is evidently one of the simplest expressions of polarity among plants.

Among earlier investigators of the *Fucus* egg were Kniep (1907), Nienburg (1922*a* and *b*), Lund (1923), and others. The more recent experiments of Whitaker and his colleagues have provided a large body of detailed information. Only the main facts will be presented here. This work has been reviewed by Whitaker (1940) and Bloch (1943).

Gravity seems not to be an important factor in the induction of the polar axis for, if the eggs are kept in the dark, the rhizoid develops in any direction. There is evidence that in eggs of the related *Cystosira barbata*, if reared in darkness, the rhizoid is formed at the point of entrance of the sperm (Knapp, 1931). Light is clearly a very important factor in *Fucus* (Hurd, 1920). In eggs lighted from one side by white light of a certain intensity (or light of particular wave lengths), the rhizoid always forms on the side opposite the source of light, and the first wall is laid down at right angles to this direction. Nienburg (1922*a*, *b*) showed more specifically that it is not the direction of light but the intensity gradient that is the determining factor.

Lund (1923) was able to prove that the first division wall in the *Fucus* egg was at right angles to the flow of an electric current and that the rhizoid grew toward the positive pole. Here the polar axis can evidently be determined electrically.

A peculiar phenomenon first noted by Rosenwinge (1889) but studied particularly by Whitaker is the so-called "group effect." If an egg of *Fucus* lies near a group of other eggs, its rhizoid will develop *toward* this group (Fig. 6-13). Whitaker observed that this occurs even when the eggs belong to different species. These results have been attributed to the

Fig. 6-13. The "group effect" in *Fucus* eggs. Where there is a cluster of these, the rhizoidal pole is typically on the side toward the other eggs. (*After Whitaker.*)

establishment, in the medium near the egg, of a concentration gradient of metabolic products from the other eggs, but Jaffe (1955) finds evidence that such a gradient, if it exists, does not involve H ion, CO_2, or O_2. Jaffe also found (1956) by exposing eggs to polarized light that the rhizoids tended to develop in the plane of polarization.

Whitaker (1937) subjected *Fucus* eggs to centrifugal force and showed that in such cases the rhizoid grows from the centrifugal pole. Polarity here seems to be dependent on the rearrangement of materials in the egg. Other factors, such as pH, temperature, auxin, and even the shape of the egg have also been shown by Whitaker to modify egg polarity.

Not many other cases of the induction of a polar axis in isolated algal cells are known, although in certain green algae the polarity of the young plants developing from swarm spores is determined by the way in which these spores become attached to the substratum (Kostrum, 1944).

The remarkable umbrella-shaped alga *Acetabularia* is really a single cell though it may be several centimeters tall. During its development it has only one large nucleus, situated usually at the base of the stalk. Here the rhizoids develop. At the summit of the stalk is the disk. If a nucleus is introduced into a plant or plant segment which lacks one, a new rhizoid system will arise wherever the new nucleus is placed and polar behavior of the plant may thus be modified or reversed (Hämmerling, 1955).

In the germination of a moss spore, the young protonema pushes out on the side of the spore toward the light, and the rhizoid forms at the opposite end, indicating that here, as in the *Fucus* egg, its polarity is determined by light. In several moss species, Fitting (1949) was able to reverse this polarity by reversing the direction of the light. In this way the young protonema becomes converted into a rhizoid.

Heitz (1940) prevented polar germination of *Funaria* spores by application of auxin. Cell division was also inhibited by this means and "giant" cells thus produced. D. von Wettstein (1953) confirmed this and found that vitamin B_1 and chloral hydrate destroyed polarity without preventing cell division. Such apolar growth continued for 50 cell generations, producing an undifferentiated, tumor-like body. Such a result emphasizes the importance of polar behavior for orderly development and the production of form.

How the polar axis is determined in the spores of vascular plants has been demonstrated in a few cases. In *Equisetum,* the spore of which shows no external or internal polarity, germination is followed by division into two cells. The division wall, as in *Fucus,* is laid down at right angles to the gradient of light absorption (Stahl, 1885). The more strongly illuminated daughter cell becomes the primary prothallial cell and the one on the darker side, the rhizoidal cell. Nienburg (1924) showed that this alignment of the mitotic figure parallel to the direction of the incidence of light does not occur until a redistribution of cytoplasmic material has taken place, especially an aggregation of chloroplasts on the illuminated side (Fig. 6-14).

In germinating fern spores, light modifies the polar behavior but this effect is different in different wave lengths (Mohr, 1956). Näf (1953), also working with ferns, found evidence that the spore of *Onoclea* has an inherent polarity but that this can be modified by light. He carried the study of polarity reversal much further by growing the young prothallia in a liquid culture which was constantly shaken. The prothallia thus developed in an environment where there were no environmental gradients and where the plant was exposed on all sides to equal stimulation by gravity, light, and other factors. The result was a spherical, tumor-like mass of tissue. Grown on agar and without movement, this tissue again formed structures much like the normal prothallia. The genetic basis for a normal prothallium, specific in character, is in the spore but such a prothallium will develop only where there is an environmental gradient by which its polar axis is established. Such results emphasize the fact that neither genetic constitution nor environment alone controls the development of organic form, but an interaction between them.

Polarity is also to be found in the microspores and pollen grains of higher plants, though here it is not easily open to experimental analysis. The spore axis, as indicated by the orientation of the division of the spore nucleus, has a constant relation to the planes of division of the pollen mother cell.

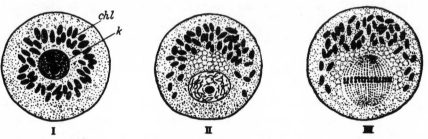

Fig. 6-14. Origin of polarity in a single cell. *I*, unpolarized spore of *Equisetum*. *II*, beginning of polarization as shown by changed positions of plastids (*chl*) and nucleus (*k*). *III*, first nuclear division. (*After Nienburg.*)

POLARITY IN PLASMODIA AND COENOCYTES

In larger and multinucleate protoplasmic units, notably coenocytic forms, polarity finds a somewhat different expression than in uninucleate protoplasts. Thus in the plasmodium of *Plasmodiophora brassicae*, as reported by Terby (1933), the axes of the many nuclear division figures lie parallel to one another, indicating that the whole mass of protoplasm has a uniform anisotropic orientation, though here without a polar axis. This parallelity is also found in the first sporogenic division but disappears at the second one. In most plasmodia, however, this simple sort of polar behavior seems not to be present.

True coenocytes show some remarkable examples of organized systems where there is pronounced differentiation of parts but no cellular partitions in the cytoplasmic body. Conspicuous among these are the algae *Bryopsis* and *Caulerpa*.

Bryopsis has an axis from which "leaves" come off in a pinnate arrangement above and rhizoids below. This polar organization can be completely reversed if the plant is held in an inverted position. The leaves then produce rhizoids and the rhizoids, leaves (Noll, 1888; Winkler, 1900; and others). It now seems probable that a different relation to light rather than to gravity is responsible for this reversal. Steinecke (1925) has shown that in these inverted plants there is a movement of the cytoplasm that was originally in the upper portion into the base, and vice versa. The easy reversal in such plants seems to be related to the fact that the cytoplasm can move readily throughout the whole body. The cellular organization of higher plants may contribute to the more fixed polarity that they display as well as to their higher degree of differentiation.

Caulerpa has a more complex structure than *Bryopsis*, for it possesses a horizontal "rhizome" from which "leaves" grow out above and rhizoids below. The leaves are negatively geotropic, the rhizoids positively so, and the rhizome is diageotropic. Regeneration in this plant has been studied by many workers (Wakker, 1886; Janse, 1906 and 1910; Dostál, 1926 and 1929; Zimmermann, 1929; and others). Its polar phenomena are rather complex. Zimmermann found that gravity determines the dorsiventrality of the rhizome and that this can be reversed. He also observed that in each portion of a cut leaf new rhizoids are formed below new leaves. An inverted leaf with its tip buried will produce leaves at its original base and rhizoids at its original apex, as in *Bryopsis*. Janse has shown, however, that rhizoids normally appear chiefly at the apical portions of cut leaves, and Dostál finds that, although regeneration is polar in young leaves, the new organs may be distributed over the entire surface of older ones. Polarity in *Caulerpa* is less stable than in higher plants and this, again, is probably because of the ease with which cytoplasmic movement may take place.

PHYSIOLOGICAL MANIFESTATIONS OF POLARITY

Differences in the external or internal structure of the plant body are almost invariably accompanied by physiological differences, though the latter are usually more difficult to demonstrate. Among these are the unidirectional flow commonly shown by auxin and often by other substances; the differences in bioelectric potential which can be demonstrated between different parts of the plant; and the many examples of physiological gradients in the plant body—in pH, rate of respiration, osmotic concentration, auxin concentration, and others. These are doubtless related to visible morphological polarities but the character of the relationship is obscure. Whether such physiological polarities control the morphological ones or whether both are determined by more deeply seated morphogenetic factors in the living material, which are physiological only in the broadest sense, is not known.

Electrical polarities are found in many organs and in the plant body as a whole. Unfortunately, any discussion of the significance of electrical potentials in relation to morphological polarity and polar regeneration must remain for the present rather hypothetical because of the uncertainties which still exist as to the nature and origin of the potential differences themselves (p. 361). The phenomena of organic polarities have so many similarities to electrical ones that it is tempting to explain the former entirely in terms of the latter, but there is insufficient evidence as yet for such a simple solution of the problem.

Physiological gradients of various kinds, particularly metabolic ones, and their significance have been extensively discussed by Child (1941). Such gradients are along the major axes of the organism, and indeed their existence is thought by some to establish these axes and to be a major factor in the origin of polarity. Child believed that they arise early in development as the result of some unilateral difference in the environment and that, once established, they persist. He points out that they often can be obliterated or redirected by external differentials and infers that they are of great importance in determining patterns of development. The inherent properties of protoplasm, unable alone to control development, produce their morphogenetic effects through specific reactions to such axial gradients. Prat (1948, 1951) has reviewed the relations between physiological and histological gradients.

Gradients in respiratory activity such as have so often been described in animal axes are found in plants (Wanner, 1944). Ball and Boell (1944), however, have shown that in some plants the rate of respiration at the meristematic tip is less rapid than in the zone immediately behind this (p. 73). Hurd-Karrer (1926) found that in corn stalks the minimal concentration of solutes is in the basal internodes and increases upward, a gradient reported by others for leaves at different levels in a tree. In plant exudates there is a concentration gradient with the highest values near the apex (Tingley, 1944). The proportion of ash to dry weight in herbaceous plants was shown by Edgecombe (1939) to increase toward the tip of the plant. Many other examples might be cited.

These gradients are often related to translocation of solutes and food and thus to localized and differential growth. Hicks (1928a, b) found that nitrogen tends to move toward the morphological tip of a stem and carbohydrates toward the base, even in inverted shoots, so that a gradient in C/N ratio results in the stem. She believes that this may be responsible for the phenomena of polarity, but this may be a parallelism rather than a causal relation.

The unidirectional flow of nutrients to particular "centers of attraction" in shoots, roots, leaves, and other structures has been emphasized by Goebel as of particular importance in regeneration and other phenomena of development. What causes the establishment of such centers and thus directs the location of growth is a question closely related to that of polarity. Simon (1920) has suggested that the polar character of regeneration in leaves is related to the basipetal movement of carbohydrates.

How much the direction of flow in the phloem is due to polar behavior in the strict sense and how much to other factors is not clear, but Schumacher (1933, 1936) has shown a polar flow of fluorescein there, basipetal in the petiole and in various directions in the stem. It seems clear that in most vegetative stems the flow of nutrients in the phloem is predominantly basal. Sax (1956 and earlier papers) removed a ring of bark in a young tree and then replaced it in an inverted position. Under these conditions phloem transport is markedly checked and the tree is much reduced in growth. This effect is not permanent, however, because the new bark regenerated at the seam permits phloem transport upward.

The clearest case of physiological polarity and the one most thoroughly studied is that of the flow of auxin (p. 384). In the *Avena* coleoptile it has been shown that auxin normally is produced at the tip and moves toward its base. If the coleoptile is cut off, decapitated, and auxin applied at the morphological apex it will move toward the other end, whether the coleoptile is normally oriented or inverted. If auxin is applied to the morphologically basal end, however, it will not move toward the tip even if the coleoptile is inverted and the auxin is placed at the end now uppermost. Auxin flow here is therefore strictly polar. The cause of this polarity is not clear, for there is no histological difference with which it is correlated. It seems to be characteristic of auxin transport generally, for this substance, commonly produced in buds, moves downward from them but not upward. Jacobs and others (p. 384), however, report that auxin may sometimes move acropetally, especially in weak concentrations.

Went (1941) has shown that the auxin flow continues to be morphologically basipetal in inverted cuttings of marigold but that after a time, presumably following the production of new and reoriented vascular bundles, the flow is reversed and auxin now moves downward toward the new root system. He suggested that auxin polarity is electrical in character, but this idea has encountered some difficulties (p. 360).

The significance of auxin polarity for many problems of plant development is great since this substance is so intimately related to both stimulation and inhibition of growth and to so many specific growth reactions, such as the initiation of shoots and roots (p. 390).

It is tempting to explain all structural polarity in the plant as due to this polar flow of auxin, but here again it may be that both are the result of some more deeply seated factor. No satisfactory solution of the problem has yet been found. It is surely a remarkable fact that a simple, relatively undifferentiated parenchyma cell of the oat coleoptile will allow auxin to pass through it in only one direction. An understanding of the mechanisms involved in this polar flow would doubtless contribute to the solution of many problems in physiology and development.

POLARITY AND DEVELOPMENTAL PATTERN

The chief significance of polarity for students of morphogenesis lies in the fact that it is the simplest expression of the general phenomenon of organic pattern. These patterns, which are exhibited in such profusion in the bodies of animals and plants, are each built around a polar axis which provides, so to speak, the theme or foundation upon which the whole develops. This, of course, is by no means the only expression of polarity in the plant. In a tree, for example, not only the main trunk but the many branches growing out from it may each have a polar axis of its own. The frequency and size of these branches and the angles which they make with the trunk produce the characteristic pattern of the tree's crown, one which is almost as specific as the pattern of its leaf. The character of this crown is due to the dominance of certain buds or branches over others and thus to a controlled localization of growth and a balance between the various axes of the tree. This, in turn, seems to be governed by a specific polar pattern of auxin distribution. It seems probable that the form and development of a leaf, which involve a pattern of major and minor vein polarities, have a similar basis. In such cases as these, organic form appears to be the expression of a series of interrelated polar axes.

Such a condition probably occurs also in forms in which the organic pattern is related to the polarity of individual cells. This is well shown in the development of shoots that grow by a large apical cell. Here the growth and differentiation of the axis are clearly associated with a precise series of divisions in various planes, both of the apical cell and of those cut off from it (p. 58). This pattern of diverse cell polarities is less easy to trace in other meristematic regions but is evidently operating there as well. In such a structure as the growing primordium of a young ovary, cell divisions are very abundant but occur in every direction, as though the planes of division were at random. That such divisions are all part of a definite organic pattern, however, is shown by the fact that the structure in which they occur shows a regular and progressive development toward its specific form. Each plane of division, presumably determined by the orientation of the cytoplasm, is related to the complex pattern of diverse polarities of which it forms a part (Sinnott, 1944).

The polar phenomena of coenocytes and other evidence support the contention that the basic fact in polarity is the orientation and polar behavior of the cytoplasm. Where this is confined within cell walls, more complex and stable patterns may be produced, but the fundamental problem everywhere seems to be the development of polar patterns in the whole cytoplasmic body of the organism, whether this is cut up into cells or not.

Polar patterns are not confined to organisms that have developed in the ordinary way by growth from a reproductive unit such as a spore or egg but are found in what are essentially organic communities. Thus in certain slime molds such as *Dictyostelium* (p. 223) the vegetative individual is a tiny myxamoeba. At the end of vegetative growth some thousands of

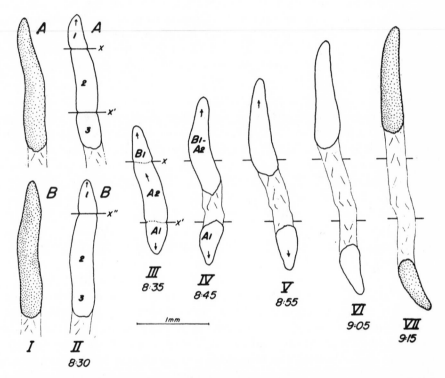

FIG. 6-15. Polarity in *Dictyostelium*. If an apical piece of a pseudoplasmodium is placed in close contact with the *apical* end of another, coalescence takes place. If it is placed next the basal end, either of the same plasmodium or of another, there is no coalescence, and the terminal piece moves off independently. (*From K. B. Raper.*)

these become aggregated into a pseudoplasmodium where each retains its individuality. This colonial structure shows a polar organization, for the terminal portion of it can be grafted to the decapitated apex of another pseudoplasmodium, though not to the base (Fig. 6-15). The tip is evidently the dominant region, for if grafted to the side of a pseudoplasmodium it will withdraw from it a group of individuals and start out as a new unit. The sorocarp that ultimately develops has a vertical polar axis and, in some species, lateral axes as well. Polarity in organisms like these appears to be a property not of the individual cells but of the aggregate that they form.

Three Aspects of Polarity. Polarity is evidently a complex phenomenon which is intimately related to the whole process of development. It may be broken down, for purposes of more detailed examination, into several different aspects or elements which may possibly involve different physiological or developmental processes.

First, one may recognize the *oriented behavior* of living substance, as distinct from axiation or bipolarity. This is evident in the differential growth of cells and tissues, where one dimension increases more rapidly than the others; in the controlled plane of cell division, in which the cytoplasm, as evident especially in vacuolate cells, sets up a pattern oriented in a definite direction; and in coenocytes and plasmodia where growth, movement, or direction of nuclear spindles is similarly oriented. The fundamental basis of this behavior is not known. There may be involved the orientation of micelles or other submicroscopic units, the paracrystalline properties of cytoplasm, the orientation of molecules at cell surfaces or interfaces, or the nature of the fine structure of the cell wall. It is reasonable to suggest that some sort of cytoplasmic anisotropy is concerned in this oriented behavior. Here is evidently a major problem for the student of the ultimate structure of protoplasm, a problem intimately related to the whole question of directed growth and thus of organic form. Whatever the basis of oriented behavior may be, in some cases it can evidently be changed in direction readily by environmental factors, but in others, when once established, it becomes firmly fixed.

A second aspect or element of polarity is *axiation*. The oriented behavior of living material most commonly, though not invariably, is expressed in cellular systems which develop symmetrically in relation to an axis or plane of symmetry parallel to the direction of orientation. Most cells and most multicellular structures possess an axis. Such structures as the cells and filaments of unattached filamentous algae may show no evident difference between the two ends of the axis, either in cell or filament, but they are clearly axiate. The problem of the symmetrical growth of a living system about this axis, so characteristic of almost all organic development, is an essential part of the general problem of pattern. Experimental attack upon this phenomenon of symmetry is promising, for its character can often be changed by modifying the environment.

The third aspect of polarity is *polar difference*, the appearance of dissimilarity between the two ends of the axis. This is regarded by many as the essential characteristic of all polarity and is present in the great majority of organic axes. In not a few cases, as we have seen, cytoplasm may show oriented behavior, or an axis of symmetry may develop, without any demonstrable evidence of difference between the two ends of the system.

Only where polar differences occur, however, with the resulting morphological and physiological gradients from one end of the axis to the other, can there develop the complex patterns characteristic of most living organisms.

The relation between these three aspects of polarity involves the problem of the origin of polarity itself. If they can be shown to form a progressive series, in phylogeny or ontogeny, this would indicate that polarity may increase in complexity. In free-floating algal filaments (as in *Spirogyra*) there is no evidence that the two poles are unlike. In filamentous forms like *Cladophora*, however, where one end is attached to the substratum, each individual cell displays a polar character in its regeneration. Here, and in many other cases where environmental factors are different at the two ends of the axis (as in the *Fucus* egg), it appears that this difference sets up an axial gradient in a system originally unpolarized, which results in the polar difference. Child and his school regard all polarity as having its origin in such environmentally induced gradients, which determine both the direction of the axis and the difference between its poles. On the other hand, since instances of similar poles are rare, it may be held that the two ends of every axis are fundamentally unlike and that in cases where they seem alike the difference is merely masked and difficult to demonstrate. If this view is correct, polarity may be due to something quite different from a gradient and may be comparable to, and perhaps result from, an inherent polar tendency, presumably electrical in character.

Whatever its origin, the direction of this bipolar axis is often continually changing but under definite control, and upon this fact depends the orderly development of organic patterns. Thus in a three-faced apical cell the polar axis must shift 120° between successive divisions. In more complex meristems the planes of cell division are equally orderly, though less evidently so. How such a system of changing polarities is controlled so that growth in one direction is precisely related to that in another is a part of the same problem of orderly development which the student of morphogenesis so often meets.

The ease with which polarity may be reversed in the simplest plants suggests that even in more complex ones it is not irrevocably fixed by genetic factors. Like any trait with a genetic basis, polarity is not a specific characteristic but a specific reaction to a specific environment. The environmental factor may be external, such as the direction of light, or internal, like the correlation between the axis of the young embryo and that of the archegonium, but unless there is an environment to which the organism can orient itself, the phenomena of polarity will rarely appear. Sometimes this environmental reaction is determined early and is later irreversible, as in cases where polarity becomes firmly fixed in the fertilized egg. In other instances polar behavior is subject to induction through environmental factors at all stages. Many cases of polarity are like this. Sometimes this polar plasticity persists indefinitely, as in *Caulerpa*. In other cases, like the egg of *Fucus*, it lasts only till the polar axis is determined and then remains unchanged, regardless of the environment. What is present in all living stuff seems to be a persistent tendency for the establishment of polar behavior. This, indeed, is an essential preliminary for the development of a formed and organized system.

The study of polarity has thus far raised more problems than it has solved. Most of these, however, are of a sort more amenable to analysis and experimental attack than are many others in organic development. Especially through subjecting each of the various aspects of polarity separately to experiment, aspects which may perhaps involve distinct developmental processes, is there hope of progress.

CHAPTER 7

Symmetry

The presence of an axis, so generally characteristic of the form of body or organ in animals and plants, is manifest not so much as an actual material structure but as an *axis of symmetry*, a geometrical core or plane around which or on the two sides of which the structures are symmetrically disposed. One of the most obvious manifestations of organic pattern in living things is this symmetrical arrangement of their parts.

Symmetry is evident in both external form and internal structure. Lateral roots arise from a primary root in two, three, four, or more equally spaced rows. Leaves are symmetrically disposed around the stem in a phyllotactic spiral. Floral diagrams, both transverse and longitudinal, also provide good examples of axial symmetry, though here the axis is usually much shortened.

Symmetry is equally conspicuous in internal structure. The cross section of almost any vertical plant axis shows symmetrical arrangement of its tissues, both primary and secondary. Even single cells, especially when they possess a considerable internal diversity like those of *Spirogyra*, are symmetrical.

In horizontal organs the simple *radial* type of symmetry characteristic of vertical axes is replaced by a *dorsiventral* one where the two halves on either side of a vertical plane of symmetry are alike. Many prostrate stems and most leaves are examples of such dorsiventrality. Sometimes one type of symmetry may be changed to the other by modifying the orientation of the structure to light or gravity. In other cases the pattern of symmetry is inherited and cannot be influenced by environmental factors.

Many structures are in themselves asymmetric. In leaves of *Begonia* and elm, for example, the portions on either side of the midrib are usually quite unlike; and there are marked internal asymmetries, as when two daughter cells are dissimilar. In most cases of this sort, however, the asymmetry proves to be part of a larger and more complex pattern which is symmetrical.

Symmetry is often more conspicuous in embryonic structures or meristematic regions than at maturity, and some of its most remarkable ex-

147

pressions are in soft and watery structures which seem to be a direct expression of protoplasmic configuration. Even though protoplasm is seemingly an amorphous and semiliquid material, these structures that it builds are far from formless, and the beautiful symmetries that they display seem clearly to be manifestations of the fundamentally symmetrical character of living stuff itself. Organic symmetry presents a basic problem for students of morphogenesis.

INORGANIC AND ORGANIC SYMMETRIES

There are many examples of symmetry among inorganic objects. These often resemble the symmetries of living things, but there are certain fundamental differences between them. What the relation between these two types may be and whether organic symmetries have their origin in those of the inorganic world are problems that have long been discussed but are still far from solution.

The arrangement of iron filings around the two poles of a magnet is a familiar example of symmetry, as are the lines of force in an electrostatic field. The least-surface configurations shown by liquids and especially by liquid film systems provide beautiful examples of symmetry. The resemblance of such systems to multicellular structures in plants and animals, particularly the more minute ones, has been observed by many biologists and is discussed at length by D'Arcy Thompson (1942), who has analyzed the various forms possible in a film system. The molecular forces that operate here, however, are probably not important in determining the symmetry of large organic bodies.

Much is now known, from X-ray studies and other sources, of the actual structure of molecules, and these are found to display symmetries, often very complex and specific ones. Whether such molecular forms have any relation to the bodily forms of plants and animals is a problem which has aroused much speculation but on which little evidence is available. Harrison (1945) has discussed some of the possibilities here.

Crystals provide the most familiar and remarkable examples of symmetry in the inorganic world. Their very specific forms are the reflection of the forms and relationships of the molecules that compose them. The study of crystal symmetry is a complex science in itself and has intimate relationship to geometry, chemistry, and mineralogy. Crystals possess axes and planes of symmetry, as do organic structures, but crystalline symmetry is a much more formalized and rigid phenomenon than organic. Many biologists have endeavored to find a relation between crystals and organisms in their form and symmetry, but this search, in general, has been a rather fruitless one. Organic symmetries can be described in the same geometrical language that we use for crystals, but whether there is any fundamental similarity between the two is uncertain. For a discussion of this problem the reader is referred to the work of Haeckel (1866) and others.

Although many symmetries in cells and minute multicellular structures resemble those in inorganic systems under the control of surface forces, organic symmetries are conspicuous in much larger bodies where these forces are not operative. Organic bodies are semiliquid systems which are subject to continual loss and replacement of material, as is shown by tagged isotopes and in other ways, and in this respect are unlike crystalline structures, which are usually fixed and static. This semiliquid character is also reflected in the almost universal presence of curved lines and surfaces in organic bodies as compared with the systems of straight lines and planes which distinguish molecular and crystalline forms. This is what makes possible the infinite number of similar planes of symmetry around an organic axis instead of the limited number of two, three, four, and six found in crystals.

Aside from these differences from the inorganic, the symmetries shown by living plant structures also possess two distinctive features of their own which provide the key to an understanding of their nature.

First, they are often expressed in *multiple* parts. A typical plant body consists of an indeterminate series of repeated, essentially similar parts, laterally dispersed along a continuous axis. These are leaves, branches, and lateral roots in higher plants and analogous repetitive structures in lower ones. The most conspicuous examples of organic symmetry are found in the relations of these repeated structures to the axis from which they arise. This is a type of symmetry unlike that found in most inorganic systems.

Second, many plant axes, particularly those of the aerial portions of the plant, have either a spiral twist or a spiral arrangement of their parts. This complicates the expression of symmetry and, in the case of phyllotaxy, has given rise to a great deal of speculation. Spirality seems to be a characteristic feature of protoplasmic behavior in many cases. The course of streaming is often spiral in a cell and thus may be reflected in the structure of the cell itself, as in the familiar cases of *Chara* and *Nitella*. Cell growth may be spiral, as has been shown by Castle (1936) in the hyphae of *Phycomyces*, and there are many other examples.

These two traits—multiple parts and spirality—make the symmetry of plant parts radically different, at least in external expression, from the symmetries of the inorganic world.

A few single-celled forms and some colonies like those of *Volvox* may be spherical and completely symmetrical around a point. This seems to be primarily an expression of surface forces, however, rather than of inherent symmetry. Most single-celled plants, however, like the desmids, and most protozoa, show axial symmetry, often complex in character; and all typical examples of symmetry in higher plants are those manifest around an axis or a longitudinal plane. Three general types of such symmetries are recognized: radial, bilateral, and dorsiventral. All the common patterns for the structure of plants and their organs are based on these symmetries.

RADIAL SYMMETRY

In this type there is an axis of rotation around which symmetry is uniform. There may be one or two evenly spaced longitudinal planes of symmetry, as in stems with distichous and with opposite-leaf arrangements, or these may be almost infinite in number in stems with spiral symmetry. Radial symmetry is present in vertically elongated axes such as those of the main stem and primary root and in many flowers and fruits. It is therefore much commoner in plants than in animals, since most of the latter show dorsiventrality, and it is regarded by many as the most primitive type of symmetry, at least in vascular plants, since their first axes were presumably vertical.

In Lower Plants. Individual cells often show radial symmetry regardless of their orientation, as in *Spirogyra* and *Chara*. Many plant bodies in the thallophytes have this type of symmetry, a familiar example of which is the "mushroom" form of sporophore in the fleshy fungi. Many red algae have radial thalli, as do some brown algae. Most true mosses also are radial.

In Roots. Almost all roots are radially symmetrical. This symmetry is shown in the straight and evenly spaced rows of lateral roots and in the characteristically radial primary vascular structures, in which arms of xylem typically alternate with bundles of phloem in a star-shaped pattern, with lateral roots arising opposite the xylem arms.

In two respects the expression of symmetry in the root is different from that in the stem. Roots, even horizontally growing ones, are usually strictly radial and (save for a few cases such as air roots of orchids) show no dorsiventrality, regardless of their orientation, whereas horizontal stems commonly do show this. Roots also have very little twisting or spirality in their internal or external structures, such as most stems display. These two differences emphasize again the fundamental diversity in developmental behavior of root and stem which is evident in many other respects. Whether these differences are inherent or are due to the radical differences in the environment in which roots and stems usually develop is an interesting morphogenetic problem.

In Shoots. The symmetry of shoots, and particularly that shown by the arrangement of leaves (*phyllotaxy*), has attracted more attention than any other aspect of the problem of organic symmetry. The external symmetry of an upright stem is typically radial and often very regularly so. In the simplest cases, as in certain mosses such as *Fontinalis*, this is related to the activity of a three-sided apical cell, the segments cut off from its three sides giving rise to three rows of leaves. In higher plants, however, leaf arrangement is not related to meristematic structure.

In stems with opposite leaves, at successive nodes the leaf pairs rotate through 90°. This *decussate* phyllotaxy thus shows four rows of leaves along the stem. More frequently, phyllotaxy shows a spiral character. Sometimes this is manifest, even in opposite-leaved types, by a twisting of the whole axis so that members of successive pairs are a little more than 90° apart. Spirality more commonly expresses itself, however, in the arrangement of so-called "alternate" leaves. These are rarely exactly alternate but are so dispersed that a line connecting the points of attachment of successive ones follows a regular spiral course around the stem. The fact of this spiral and the various types in which it is manifest have for many years attracted the interest of botanists and mathematicians. Many of the discussions and speculations that have centered about the phyllotactic spiral are of no great significance for morphogenesis. Some are highly theoretical or even almost mystical. The developmental origin of the various types of phyllotaxy, however, is an important morphogenetic problem, and a knowledge of the factors involved may contribute to an understanding of the origin of organic form.

Goethe was greatly attracted by the spirality of leaf arrangement and made it the basis of one of his theories. Charles Bonnet (1754) in the middle of the eighteenth century discussed the spiral structure of the pine cone. It was the work of Schimper (1836) and Braun (1831), however, that established the study of phyllotaxy on its modern basis. Various explanations of the origin and significance of spiral leaf arrangement have been proposed, and the literature of the subject is extensive. No comprehensive review of it is available, though the earlier literature has been surveyed by C. de Candolle (1881). For the more important ideas the reader is also referred to the works of the brothers Bravais (1837), Hofmeister (1868), Wright (1873), Schwendener (1878), Schoute (1913, 1914), Church (1920), Hirmer (1922), Crow (1928), Goebel (1928), Snow and Snow (1934), D'Arcy Thompson (1942), Plantefol (1948), Wardlaw (1949a), and Richards (1950).

Spiral phyllotaxy is not an example of symmetry in the strict sense since planes of symmetry, in the crystallographic meaning of the term, are absent. The leaves do have regular positions along the axis, however, with reference to each other, and these, under proper analysis, can be expressed in terms of geometrical symmetry. The spiral formed by the points of attachment of successive leaves—the *genetic* or *developmental* spiral—represents the order in which the leaf primordia are formed in the bud. Their positions in the spiral are not indefinite but commonly fall into a few precise categories, the relations of which have long excited the interest of morphologists. Simplest of all is the distichous, or truly alternate, arrangement, with successive leaves 180° apart around the stem. To pass from a leaf to one directly above it involves one circuit of the axis and two leaves, a condition which may be expressed by the fraction ½. In other types this spiral passes once around the axis but every third leaf is over one below it, a condition that may be represented by the fraction ⅓. Commoner than either of these is a spiral where in passing from a leaf to one above it two circuits of the axis are made and the fifth leaf is reached,

Fig. 7-1. Diagram showing ⅜ phyllotaxy.

the ⅖ type. Frequently observed in stems is a ⅜ phyllotaxy (Fig. 7-1) and less commonly that of $\frac{5}{13}$. In cones and other compact axes more complex phyllotaxies of $\frac{8}{21}$, $\frac{13}{34}$, and $\frac{21}{55}$ may be found. The series is thus ½, ⅓, ⅖, ⅜, $\frac{5}{13}$, $\frac{8}{21}$, $\frac{13}{34}$, $\frac{21}{55}$, $\frac{34}{89}$, and so on. Each obviously represents the fraction of the circumference of the axis, or the angle, traversed by the spiral in passing from one leaf to the next. The number in both numerator and denominator of each fraction is the sum of those in the two preceding fractions. This particular series is known as the Fibonacci series. The higher fractions become more and more uniform and approach as a limit the decimal fraction 0.38197, or the angle 137°30′28″, the so-called "ideal" angle. It has been shown by Wright (1873) that if successive leaves were formed at just this angular distance around the stem from each other no leaf would ever be directly over any below it. The advantage sometimes suggested for this arrangement, that it would distribute the leaves most evenly to the light and thus be most efficient in preventing shading, is open to many objections.

The fraction 0.38197 is of interest in another connection, for it designates the "golden mean," or *sectio aurea*, the distance from the end of a line at which, if the line is cut there, the smaller fraction of the line is to the larger as the larger is to the whole. Thus 0.38197 : 0.61803 = 0.61803 : 1.0. The golden mean has long been known and has received much attention from artists and mathematicians, and its significance in the geometry of symmetry may be considerable, but its biological importance seems negligible. One should also remember that there are other series of fractions which converge to the same limit.

This analysis of the genetic spiral assumes that, as it twists around the stem, a given leaf position on it is directly over one below, after passing 3, 5, 8, 13, etc., leaves on the spiral. Thus there should be vertical rows of leaves, relatively few in the simpler phyllotaxies but more numerous in the complex ones. These have been called *orthostichies* and mark the end points of each successive fraction into which the genetic spiral is divided. Their presence is essential if the mathematical analysis of this spiral, going back to the work of Schimper and Braun and elaborated by so many botanists since then, is to mean very much.

The existence of these orthostichies, however, has been challenged by more recent students of phyllotaxy, who have approached its problems not by an analysis of mature structures but by a more truly morphogenetic investigation of the way in which the leaves originate. The best place to study leaf arrangement, they maintain, is in the bud or at the apical meristem. Church (1920), one of the pioneers in this method of attack, discovered that in the arrangement of primordia as seen in a cross section of the bud there are no orthostichies at all, for no leaf primordium arises directly over one below. Thus doubt was cast on all the early conclusions based on the assumption that the genetic spiral could be divided into repeated portions.

But other relationships are more important than this. A study of leaf primordia packed into the bud, or of other cases such as pine cones and sunflower heads where there are a great many structures spirally arranged but crowded together, shows the existence of another series of spirals, resembling the genetic one in certain respects but reached in a different fashion. If one looks at the cross section of a bud, or the face view of a sunflower head in fruit, or the base of a pine cone, he will notice that the units are not packed uniformly together like the pores of a honeycomb. Instead, the various structures—leaves, primordia, fruits, or scales—form two sets of spiral curves, starting in the center and moving to the circumference, one going to the right (clockwise) and the other to the left (counterclockwise). The effect is something like that of a spinning pinwheel, or rather of two spinning in opposite directions. The inner members of each spiral are progressively smaller since they were formed later. We are looking down, in effect, on the top of a growing system, even though growth may have stopped. These spirals are logarithmic ones, since the radial distance to each successive unit on them increases geometrically and not arithmetically. The spirals are termed *parastichies*, or sometimes *contact parastichies* since each unit is usually somewhat flattened against its inner and outer neighbors in the spiral, a fact which

Fig. 7-2. A pine cone seen from below. The scales are in two sets of parastichies, 8 counterclockwise and 13 clockwise.

makes the spiral easy to trace (Fig. 7-2). The spirals intersect each other at an angle which is near to 90°.

In a bud or meristematic tip that will give rise to a shoot with a relatively low phyllotactic fraction (2/5 or 3/8), the units are fewer than in large structures like a cone. In a cross section of such a bud (Fig. 7-3) it is possible to distinguish by the relative sizes of the leaf primordia the order in which they were produced. The genetic spiral can thus be traced, compact and almost two-dimensional here although later it will be pulled out like a telescope when the shoot elongates. In a bud like this one can confirm the observation of Church, that orthostichies do not exist. Were they here, they would appear as radial rows made by every fifth, or eighth, or thirteenth primordium. These are not to be seen. Furthermore, if one carefully studies the angular divergence between successive primordia he finds (in the great majority of cases) that it is close to the "ideal" Fibonacci angle of 137.5° which the series of phyllotactic fractions approaches as a limit.

The number of clockwise and of counterclockwise parastichies in a given axis is not the same. In different types, however, their relative numbers are fixed and specific. These also fall into a characteristic series. Thus in the bud section shown in Fig. 7-3 one can count five parastichies turn-

Fig. 7-3. Cross section of apical bud of *Pinus pinea* showing absence of orthostichies. The primordia, numbered in succession, are separated by the Fibonacci angle. Five counterclockwise parastichies and eight clockwise ones are evident. (*From R. Snow, courtesy of Endeavour.*)

ing to the left and eight to the right. In simpler forms there may be three in one direction and five in the other. In more complex cases, such as many pine cones, there are 8 of one and 13 of the other, or 13 of one and 21 of the other. Some systems have 21 and 34. Most sunflower heads show 34 spirals in one direction and 55 in the other. Arranging these pairs of numbers in the form of fractions, as was done with the genetic spiral, one obtains the series $\frac{2}{3}$, $\frac{3}{5}$, $\frac{5}{8}$, $\frac{8}{13}$, $\frac{13}{21}$, $\frac{21}{34}$, $\frac{34}{55}$, $\frac{55}{89}$, and so on, though the higher fractions are rare. The numbers in numerators and denominators form a series, as in the genetic spiral, but here the denominator of one fraction forms the numerator of the next one instead of the next but one. The fraction which this series approaches as a limit is 0.61803, the larger one of the two which are separated by the golden mean. This fraction is thus the difference between 1.0 and 0.38197, the limit approached by the other series. The two spiral systems are evidently related but just how they are is a nice mathematical problem. It is no wonder, as D'Arcy Thompson says, that these various relationships have long appealed to mystics and to those who seek to square the circle or penetrate the secrets of the Great Pyramid!

Parastichies are present in shoots around which leaves are borne in a phyllotactic spiral, but because they are pulled out so far lengthwise they are much less conspicuous than when many structures are packed together. In elongate shoots orthostichies, though absent in buds, can usually be demonstrated. The tensions resulting from elongation apparently operate to straighten out the spirals and in many cases to bring the insertion of a leaf almost directly over one that is three or five or eight leaves below. Not much of a twist is needed to accomplish this and to produce an orthostichy. One should recognize, however, that such are secondary rather than primary phenomena of symmetry.

The problems of phyllotaxy were already involved enough when a French botanist, Lucien Plantefol (1948), added a further complexity. His theory has been extensively developed by others, particularly in his own country. It is based on a study of the insertion of the leaf traces on the stem. Plantefol does not regard the genetic spiral as significant. He traces two (sometimes more) *foliar helices* connecting the leaf bases in parallel spirals that wind up the stem, and he usually represents these helices as projected on a plane where their relationships can more easily be seen (Fig. 7-4). They originate in the traces of the two cotyledons, and the series remain distinct as they pass up into the bud. Here they terminate in a *generative center* of embryonic tissue just below the tip of the meristem (Fig. 7-5). In this the new primordia are differentiated. The position of each is determined, he believes, by stimulation from the foliar helices below, the relations being harmonized by an "organizer." Lance (1952) found in a number of cases a zone of abundant mitoses somewhat below the apex of the meristematic dome but few at the very tip. Crockett (1957) finds some evidence of the same thing in *Nicotiana*. Loiseau (1954) cut off the tip of the meristem in *Impatiens* and observed that in many instances this resulted in changing the number of helices. This he believes was due to a disturbance of the generative center. Popham (1958), on the other hand, in a census of mitoses at the apex of *Chrysanthemum*, found no evidence of a generative center nor of its necessary corollary, a region of few mitoses at the very tip. Newman (p. 60) made the same observation in living material. The problem has been discussed by Wardlaw (1957b), who concludes that, although there are various complexities in the shoot meristem, there is little good evidence from this source in support of Plantefol's theory.

Although this theory has received strong support from a number of French botanists, objections have been raised against it in other quarters. What are chosen as foliar helices are evidently one of the parastichies or spiral rows of leaf traces to be seen along the axis, but which of these is the true helix in any instance seems difficult to determine. The leaves on a helix must have some vascular connection with each other, according to the theory, but in most stems at least two different parastichies could be chosen which would fulfill this requirement. A figure in one

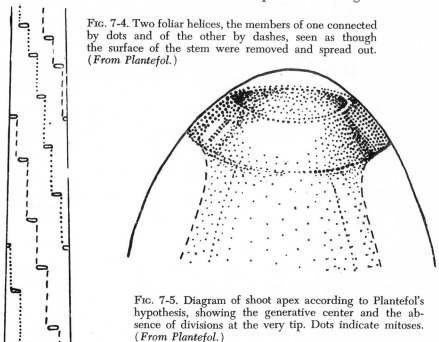

Fig. 7-4. Two foliar helices, the members of one connected by dots and of the other by dashes, seen as though the surface of the stem were removed and spread out. (*From Plantefol.*)

Fig. 7-5. Diagram of shoot apex according to Plantefol's hypothesis, showing the generative center and the absence of divisions at the very tip. Dots indicate mitoses. (*From Plantefol.*)

of Dr. Esau's papers (1943, Fig. 1), though it was not drawn to clarify the problems of phyllotaxy, makes these relationships evident (Fig. 7-6). This is a diagram of the primary vascular system of *Linum*. The genetic spiral is shown, with the leaves numbered along it. In the series 25–33–41, the bundle is continuous with a branch that passes laterally to the next in the series, and there are eight of these helices around the stem. In the series 28–33–38, the right-hand lateral of one is continuous with the left-hand lateral of the next, and there are five helices. Members of the series 30–33–36 have no direct vascular connection with one another but are in a definite row. Which of these spirals should be chosen as the foliar helix? One might determine the true one, perhaps,

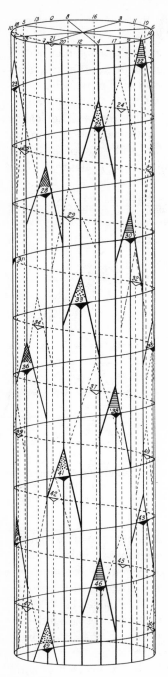

FIG. 7-6. Diagram of the primary vascular strands in the stem of *Linum perenne*. The numbers from 21 (above) to 49 (below) mark the positions of leaves in the generative spiral, indicated by a thin line. The bundles are shown by heavy lines for those on the nearer surface and by dotted ones for those behind. Various helices, in Plantefol's terminology, may be distinguished, such as 30-33-36, 28-33-38, and 25-33-41. There seems no certain way to determine which are the "true" ones. (*From Esau.*)

by tracing the system back to the cotyledonary node. Camefort (1956) has presented a full account of Plantefol's theory and has endeavored to reconcile it with the classical concepts of phyllotaxy and modern experimental studies.

The solution of these problems of leaf arrangement is evidently to be sought near the apical growing point where the leaf primordia actually originate, for their relations here will determine those between mature leaves on the elongated stem. This emphasis on the study of primordia is a return to the point of view of Schwendener (1878), who believed that mechanical contact and pressure exerted by the primordia on one another accounted for their distribution, and especially of Hofmeister (1868), who proposed the general rule that a new primordium arises in the largest space available to it. This conclusion is generally accepted, but the developmental basis for it is not clear. The essential morphogenetic problem beneath all this is what determines the origin of a particular primordium at a particular place and time.

An early idea was that a leaf-forming stimulus passes along the genetic spiral, but the significance of the spiral itself now seems rather slight. Church (1920), concerning himself chiefly with parastichies, believed that the point of intersection of the two major ones determined the point of origin of a primordium. This leaves undetermined the reason for the course of the parastichies themselves. Some workers are inclined to think that stimuli from previously formed leaves or primordia determine the position of new ones. Plantefol assumes that a foliar helix extends upward into the meristem to the generative center where the primordia are formed. Sterling (1945) finds that in *Sequoia* the procambial strands are always continuous with the older ones below and differentiate acropetally, pushing up into the apical meristem before the emergence of the primordia into which they will pass, and suggests that these procambial strands may influence the position of the primordia. Gunckel and Wetmore (1946) reach the same conclusion for *Ginkgo*. Opposed to this idea is some experimental evidence, chiefly derived from isolating part of the meristem from regions below it by incisions without disrupting normal phyllotactic arrangement, a result which suggests that the stimulus for the development of a primordium does not come from below. Perhaps in such cases as this it is incorrect to assume that a given development is the cause of another which succeeds it in time. A series of related structures and processes are part of the same organized whole and should be thought of as developing together rather than each step as inducing the one that follows it.

The problem of what determines the phyllotactic series is open to experimental attack, and much work has been done on it by various people, among them Wardlaw, Ball, and especially the Snows. They have been able to modify phyllotaxy operatively in a number of ways. Thus in *Epilobium hirsutum,* a species in which the leaf arrangement is decussate (opposite), the Snows (1935) split the apex diagonally and found that the two regenerating shoots had spiral phyllotaxy. They were also able (1937) to change the phyllotaxy in the same way by applying auxin to the shoot apex. There may be a rather delicate balance between decussate and spiral phyllotaxy in this plant, for in the group to which it belongs (and even in a single plant of this species) both types may occur. In other plants the direction of the phyllotactic spiral may be reversed in regenerating shoots after splitting the apex.

What determines the location of a given primordium is the basic problem here, and as to this there are two major hypotheses. One, first proposed by Schoute (1913), assumes that the presence of a primordium tends to inhibit the development of another one near it, presumably by the sort of inhibition by which one bud checks the growth of another through the agency of auxin. This is the same problem studied more recently by Bünning (p. 199), who has evidence that each stoma produces a substance that prevents the development of another stoma close to it, thus accounting for the regular spacing of these structures. Such a hypothesis is in harmony with physiological theory, but some experimental results seem to be opposed to it. For example, the Snows (1952) removed the youngest actual primordium in an apex of *Lupinus* and after 14 days determined the positions of the next three successive primordia that had appeared since this was done. In every case these later ones occupied the places in which they normally would have appeared, indicating that their positions in the series had not been affected by removal of a primordium and any inhibitory influence from it.

That the primordia develop independently of either stimulatory or inhibitory influences from neighboring ones is also shown by an experiment of Wardlaw's in which he isolated by radial cuts the areas presumably to be occupied by the next primordia in the series, thus effectively isolating them from physiological contact with primordia already formed. He found that these areas developed primordia normally.

Other factors than chemical ones may here be involved. Wardlaw (1948) finds that each primordium tends to produce a region of tangential tensile stress around it but that this is absent in the area where new primordia are to arise. He suggests that a primordium will develop where tensile stress is at a minimum.

The second hypothesis assumes that a primordium will not develop unless there is sufficient available free space for it. This is related to the ideas of Schwendener and Hofmeister and really comes down to the problem of the most efficient filling of the space on the surface of the meristem. It has been supported, in essence, by van Iterson (1907), and in recent years the Snows have brought forward evidence in its favor. Among other experiments (1952) they isolated by two radial cuts the larger part, but not the whole, of the area presumptively to be occupied by the next-but-one leaf primordium. In such a case none develops between the cuts, although this region grows and continues otherwise to be normal. They explain this result as due to the fact that the area now available was too small for a primordium to be formed.

These two hypotheses, though stressing different factors, are not diametrically opposed to each other. What is to be explained is the even distribution of primordia, equidistant from each other (in origin) and regularly arranged. This is the same problem posed by the distribution of multiple structures. Something regulates the differentiation of each of these structures in such a way that each occupies an area of its own and that these individual areas are of about the same size. In the case of leaf primordia the situation is complicated by the fact that these arise on a curved surface and in a progressive series in time. Although mechanical and chemical factors are doubtless involved in the distribution of primordia, as in all morphogenetic processes, it is perhaps too simple an explanation to regard the determination of each as due to crowding by its neighbors, to the presence of the "first available space," or to inhibition by other primordia. It seems more logical to regard the problem of the distribution of primordia at the growing point as another instance of a self-regulating biological pattern which may have its roots in genetic factors, the fine structure of protoplasm, or whatever else may be responsible for organic form.

On either hypothesis mentioned above, if primordia are to arise in a spiral around the axis each should be as far as possible from its immediate neighbors, those coming just before and just after it in origin. In opposite leaves each is placed as far away as possible, 180°. In spiral phyllotaxy this cannot be done. If primordium B, let us say, originates at an angle from A of 137.5° (the golden-mean fraction of the circumference), and if the next one, C, is placed at the same distance farther on (thus incidentally dividing the remainder of the circumference by the same ideal proportion), B is equidistant from A and C, and this is the maximum possible distance at which successive members can be placed from each other. If the distance A–B and B–C is less or greater than this ideal angle, C will not arise in the middle of the largest space available, as Hofmeister's postulate requires. What this means is that only if successive primordia are separated by this ideal angle will they fill the available space evenly and with the greatest economy. This is the property of golden-mean spacing that makes it significant in problems of this sort.

Richards (1948, 1950) has worked out some of the implications of this fact and has returned to methods of mathematical analysis in approaching the problem of the development of the primordia at the meristem. He emphasizes the importance of the plastochron ratio, the ratio of the radial distances from the center of the meristem to two consecutive primordia. Where this distance increases considerably in each plasto-

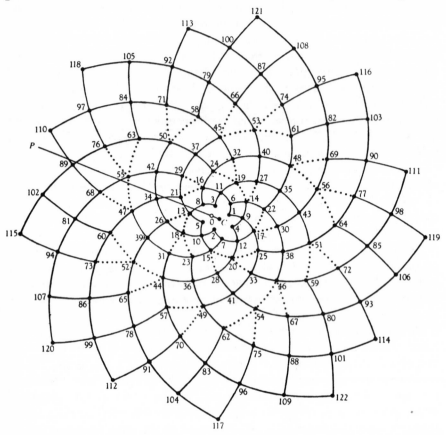

FIG. 7-7. Diagram showing a spiral succession of points, each separated from the next by the Fibonacci angle, or about 137.5°. Parastichies can be recognized by intersections of approximately 90° between them. At the center there are five counterclockwise ones and eight clockwise. The counterclockwise series soon shift from 5 to 13, and later the clockwise ones from 8 to 21. (*From F. J. Richards.*)

chron, both the genetic spiral and the spirals of the parastichies will open out rapidly. The meristem itself under these conditions will tend to be relatively steep, the primordia few and the parastichy numbers low. On the contrary, when the radial distance increases but little from one primordium to the next, the primordia are packed closely, the meristem is likely to be flatter (as in a cone or flat head), the primordia will be more numerous, and the parastichy fractions will have higher numbers.

Richards calls attention to the fact that the parastichies at a growing point are not limited to the two conspicuous "contact" ones emphasized by Church but that there may be a series of others though these are not obvious since they do not intersect each other at right angles. An advantage of this concept is that it makes clear how the parastichies shift from one pair of numbers to another, a problem that has troubled students of phyllotaxy. Richards (1948; Fig. 7-7) has constructed a diagram of a rather large meristem, something like a sunflower head, showing a series of primordial positions numbered along the genetic spiral in which each diverges from the last by the Fibonacci angle of 137.5°. In such a system one can readily trace parastichies. Near the center there are five counterclockwise ones crossing eight clockwise, the $\frac{5}{8}$ arrangement, which intersect at approximately right angles. To trace this series very far out becomes difficult since the angles of intersection diverge increasingly from 90°. As one moves out, therefore, the system seems to change and the five counterclockwise spirals shift to thirteen, giving the $\frac{8}{13}$ arrangements of spirals that now have more nearly right-angled intersections. Still farther out the eight clockwise spirals are less easy to trace, and 21 others become more conspicuous, now making the $\frac{13}{21}$ arrangement and restoring the steeper intersections. Thus in the more complex systems with large, flat meristems and little difference in radial distance between successive primordia, the parastichies, at least those that are conspicuous and easy to trace, may be seen to shift to progressively higher numbers. This does not happen in ordinary shoots where the meristem is steeper and the primordia are fewer and larger and increase rapidly in size at each plastochron but it may sometimes be seen even in such cases (Fig. 7-8). These changes involve no biological mystery, as Church was inclined to believe they do, but are simply the result of the unique properties of the Fibonacci angle.

Barthelmess (1954) has pointed out that the scheme proposed by Richards is essentially a two-dimensional one, whereas the meristematic region has three dimensions, a fact that must be taken into account. There are various other complications presented by an analysis of phyllotactic patterns. Bilhuber (1933) and others, for example, find that the situation in many of the cacti is often different from that in most families. These plants are essentially leafless and have angled stems so that in the apical regions one actually finds what look like orthostichies, which are related to the development of the angled pattern. *Bijugate* spirals (Hirmer, 1931; Snow, 1950) occur in some groups, where a $\frac{3}{5}$ pair of parastichies, for example, becomes split into a $\frac{6}{10}$. Here primordia occur in opposite pairs but the plane of each pair is not at right angles to the previous one. This produces two parallel spirals. For a discussion of other recondite aspects of spiral phyllotaxy the reader is referred to the work of Church, Hirmer, Richards, the Snows, and others who have gone deeply into these problems.

Of some morphogenetic interest is the *direction* of the genetic spiral itself. Observers generally agree that leaf positions around the stem are as likely to be in a clockwise as in a counterclockwise spiral. Beal (1873), studying cones of Norway spruce, found 224 cases of the former and 243 of the latter. Allard (1946) examined 23,507 tobacco plants and found that the two types were almost exactly equal. Direction of spirality was not inherited. How the direction is determined for a given plant is not known, but it is probably in some critical early cell division. This neutrality of the phyllotactic spiral is unlike the behavior of climbing plants,

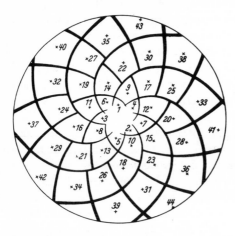

Fig. 7-8. Diagram of distribution of primordia at the shoot apex, each diverging from its predecessor by the Fibonacci angle. As the primordia increase in size, the recognizable contact parastichies shift from 5 + 8 near the center to 8 + 13 farther out. (*From Barthelmess.*)

in almost all of which a given species climbs in either a clockwise or a counterclockwise manner exclusively.

The difference in direction of the phyllotactic spiral, however, sometimes alters from one part of the plant to another in conformity to a general pattern of symmetry, much as in the case of floral structures (p. 167). In shoot growth of *Citrus*, for example, Schroeder (1953a) reports that there are successive "flushes" with a dormant period between them and that a regular alternation occurs between right and left spirality in successive shoots. Secondary shoots have spirality opposite from their parent one. Thorns develop to the left of the petiole in left-handed shoots and to the right in right-handed ones. The direction of spirality in axillary shoots of *Vicia* also takes place in a precise and alternating order which depends on their position (Dormer, 1954).

Spirality. Spiral phyllotaxy involves a number of problems as to the spacing and relative position of leaves which are not present in decussate (opposite-leaved) phyllotaxy. In the latter type the two primordia at a node are as far apart as they can be, and the position of each successive pair is at right angles to the pairs above and below. This more nearly fulfills the requirements for efficient spacing and maximum divergence than does the spiral arrangement. One therefore wonders why the latter is so much more common, particularly since the cotyledons and sometimes the first foliage leaves are opposite. The transformation of an opposite to a spiral phyllotaxy involves a radical rearrangement of the meristematic region. This seems to be an expression of an inherent tendency toward spirality which is evident in so many places in the structure and activity of plants and their parts. This inherent spirality, imposed on systems of different sizes and forms may, from the mere geometrical necessities of the case, result in the various systems of spiral phyllotaxy that we have been discussing. Physiological factors doubtless have an important role here—auxin, mechanical pressure, genetic determination of growth, and others—but the underlying spirality seems to be a phenomenon fundamental to all organisms. This may appear to be an oversimplification of a problem that has involved more diverse hypotheses than almost any other in plant morphology. If it proves possible, however, thus to get at the heart of this mass of facts and pick out one that underlies them all, we shall have come closer to an understanding of one aspect, at least, of the phenomenon of organic symmetry.

Spirality seems to be deeply seated in living stuff. It is evident in the spiral movements (nutations) seen in the growth of roots and shoots, particularly when this is speeded up by time-lapse photography. Tendrils coil spirally. Protoplasm streams in a spiral course. Molecules of DNA are spiral. Spiral threads (cytonemata) occur in cytoplasm (Strugger, 1957). Spiral grain has been found almost invariably in tree trunks (Northcott, 1957). In protoxylem the wall markings are in spirals, save in the earliest cells, and there are spiral markings in many other xylem cells. Whether these are all due to the same basic cause may perhaps be doubted, but one can find spirality almost everywhere in the plant body.

The simplest place to study it is in the cell itself and especially in the cell wall. Much now is known about the submicroscopic structure of this wall and of the system of microfibrils that compose it (Preston, 1952; Frey-Wyssling, 1953). The sporangiophore of the fungus *Phycomyces* is favorable material for this sort of work since, as it elongates, it twists spirally, as can be shown by following the course of marks placed on the cell surface (Castle, 1942). Spirality here seems to have its basis in the minute structure of the wall. Heyn (1939) believes that it is due to the fact that the chitin molecules which form the framework of the cell take up positions at angles of 13.5 or 27° from the long axis of the organ, these angles resulting from the character of the chitin molecule. Denham (1922) observed that in the cotton hair, at least, the spiral markings and striations on the wall coincide with the spiral path of the streaming nucleus and cytoplasm. Preston (1948) compares the growth of this cell to the pulling out of a flat, spiral spring which rotates as it extends, and he has suggested an explanation for this in mechanical terms; but Castle (1936) thinks that this does not determine the structure of the growing wall, though it may produce a spiral layering where the wall is not elongating. He points out that not only the structure of the wall but its elastic properties must be taken into account and believes (1953) that, although the growth of the wall is helical, its course is not absolutely fixed by its structure, since the angle of spiral growth can be reversed by a change of temperature. Frey-Wyssling (1954) calls attention to the fact that in certain polypeptid chains the divergence angles between the amino acid residues show the same regularities as are found in the Schimper-Braun phyllotactic spiral and suggests that the same geometric cause—the necessity for most efficient packing—may underlie both.

Green (1954) studied the growth of the long cells of *Nitella* which had been marked and found that these marks, as well as the two natural striations in the cell, showed a uniform dextral twist. Its regularity is maintained by growth processes evenly distributed through the whole cell and presumably resulting from changes in the fine structure of the cell wall.

The *spiral grain* found in the wood of many trees is another manifestation of spirality. This may be very conspicuous in some cases and seems to be most common in trees growing in exposed situations or under unfavorable conditions. The spiral may be right-handed or left-handed. This subject has been reviewed by Champion (1925). Preston (1949), using the data of Misra (1939), attempted to relate spiral grain to the spiral growth of single cambium initials and assumes that these twist or roll spirally. This would involve some slipping of cells past each other. From what is known of intercellular relationships, it is rather unlikely that such a change occurs. The essential fact in most cases of spiral grain is that vertical files of cells become tilted slightly to the right or to the left and that this results in a spiral course for the cells of the wood. Some slipping of the cells may be involved, but this might be accomplished by localized intrusive growth (p. 82) such as has been shown to take place at the tips of the cambial initials. The tilt seems to be related to a change in cell polarity. Neeff (p. 128) found that when a new polar axis was established the cambial cells gradually changed their direction until this became parallel to the new axis. That there may be a spiral polarity in the trunk itself is suggested by the work of Misra (1943), who reports that where there is eccentricity in the woody axis the position of maximum thickness in any eccentric ring follows a spiral course along the length of the axis. There is also a relation between this eccentricity and spiral grain, for the degree of both decreases upward in the trunk, and the direction of the spiral eccentricity (left or right) is the same as that of the spiral grain in any given axis.

Priestley (1945) distinguishes between true *spiral* grain, characteristic of hardwoods and resulting from a twist in the primary cambium cylinder, and *tilted* grain, characteristic of softwoods where the grain is always straight in the wood of the first year.

In Flowers and Inflorescences. Angiosperm flowers are apparently to be regarded, in an evolutionary sense, as shortened axes; and their parts, particularly the calyx and corolla, often show evidence of the same sort of spiral symmetry that exists between leaves. This can rarely be shown by the actual insertion of the parts, since they are at essentially the same level and might be regarded as a whorl, but is evident in the relation of their expanded portions to one another, particularly as visible in the bud. In flowers of dicotyledons there are usually in each circle five parts or a multiple of five. A very common relationship here (in the calyx, for example) is that two of the sepals have both edges *outside* the others, two have both edges *inside,* and one has one edge outside and one inside. This *quincuncial* arrangement can be interpreted through developmental evidence as a $\frac{2}{5}$ spiral, since the parts appear in the same order as leaves in $\frac{2}{5}$ phyllotaxy. Various modifications of this are found, but the typical dicotyledonous flower may be regarded in its symmetry as representing a $\frac{2}{5}$ spiral. The flower of monocotyledons, on the other hand, has its parts typically in threes and may be regarded as a $\frac{1}{3}$ spiral in symmetry. The problem of flower symmetry, particularly as expressed in transverse diagrams, has been the object of long study by floral morphologists and forms the basis of an extensive early literature (Eichler, 1875).

For students of morphogenesis the symmetry displayed by inflorescences provides a notable example of the orderly control of growth relationships. Matzke (1929) has described a particularly fine example of such symmetry in *Stellaria aquatica* (Fig. 7-9). Here the inflorescence is a cyme, and the first flower terminates the main axis. Just below this flower arise two buds in the axils of opposite bracts, and from these buds shoots arise, each of which is likewise terminated by a flower. Below each of these flowers, in turn, two shoots again arise, and so on. The flower in this species shows quincuncial arrangement of the sepals. These sepals may show a clockwise spiral or a counterclockwise one. As an observer looks down on a diagram of such an inflorescence, it is evident that, of the two flowers below the first, one is clockwise and the other

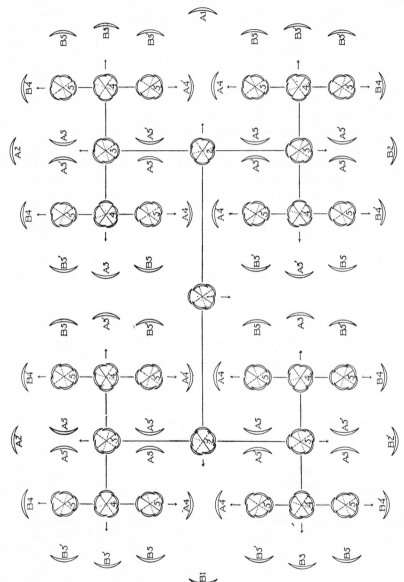

Fig. 7-9. A complex instance of symmetry. Diagram of an inflorescence of *Stellaria aquatica*, with the diagrams of its various flowers. In the center is the terminal flower. At its right and left are the two which arise just below it, and below each of these, in turn, are two others. Note the precise relationship between the plan of each flower and that of adjacent ones, particularly as to the "odd" sepal. (*From Matzke.*)

counterclockwise and that this holds for each succeeding pair. This relationship is not a random one, for the two types show a regular order as one progresses to successively later pairs so that the symmetry of each flower is predictable. Furthermore, the relative position in each flower of the "odd" sepal also changes with complete regularity. In one member of a given pair of flowers it has rotated 72° in a clockwise direction from the single flower next them, and in the other, 72° counterclockwise. The particular edge of the sepal which is inside also has a definite and predictable position. The whole inflorescence is thus a complex pattern of symmetries, each successive floral meristem fitting precisely into its place in this pattern. The factors that determine the symmetry of each flower are therefore not purely local ones but operate as members of a much larger system. Such a system, with its parts so widely separated and so easy of observation, offers a particularly good opportunity for the experimental study of symmetry.

BILATERAL SYMMETRY

This is a relatively rare type in which there are two planes of symmetry, so that front and back, and right and left sides, are similar. A bilaterally symmetrical organ resembles a radial one that has been compressed equally on two opposite sides.

This type occurs chiefly in vertically oriented structures in which, from one cause or another, one of the dimensions is smaller. Thus the stems of certain cacti such as *Opuntia* are bilaterally symmetrical, as are the still further flattened phylloclads of *Muehlenbeckia* and *Phyllocladus*. These have doubtless arisen from radial types. The leaves of *Iris* and similar plants are essentially bilateral but have probably come from dorsiventral structures. All plants, such as the grasses and some other monocotyledons, which are truly distichous (the leaves arising only on two opposite sides of the stem) may be regarded as bilaterally symmetrical. So may the flowers of the mustard family, Cruciferae, since two of the six stamens, directly opposite each other, are short and the other four long. A few of the simpler bryophytes have distichous leaves or leaf-like structures, as in *Schizostegia*, and are thus bilateral, as is the pinnate plant body of the coenocytic alga *Bryopsis*. The thallus of some of the larger algae, notably forms like *Fucus* and *Laminaria*, is flattened and shows this type of symmetry.

In a few cases, as in some of the algae, a transition from radial to bilateral symmetry may be seen, and in *Schizostegia* the apex is radial. Doubtless in many instances one type could be induced from the other experimentally. Certain abnormal structures, such as many fasciated stems, are bilaterally symmetrical.

DORSIVENTRAL SYMMETRY

In this type there is only one plane of symmetry, which extends vertically through one dimension of the structure. The two sides are alike but the front and back (or top and bottom) are not, thus distinguishing it from bilateral symmetry. It is characteristic of structures growing under an environment which is asymmetrical, as in the case of horizontal ones, of those exposed to light on one side only, and of those growing attached to some substratum. Among plants, creeping stems, rhizomes, most leaves, many thalli, a wide variety of flowers, and, in general, those structures which are not vertically oriented often show dorsiventral symmetry.

Dorsiventrality in plants is manifest in external form, in internal structure, and in physiological behavior. Single cells and coenocytes may show such symmetry. Dorsiventrality may be genetically determined and thus appear under various environments, or it may be directly induced by environmental factors. Thus a dorsiventral structure may sometimes become radial, and vice versa. In some cases the plant body may actually alternate between radial and dorsiventral symmetry, as in *Mnium undulatum* and *Cladonia verticillaris*.

Cases of dorsiventrality which are most obvious and easy to study are those in structures that are typically horizontal, either because they are weak and rest on the ground or because they are plagiotropic and tend to grow in a horizontal position.

In Thalli. Among lower plants many thalli are dorsiventral. The coenocytic plant body of the alga *Caulerpa* is typically horizontal and on its lower surface bears "rootlets" and on its upper surface, "leaves." The familiar heart-shaped prothallus of a fern is similarly dorsiventral, bearing sex organs and rhizoids on its lower surface only. This type of symmetry is characteristic of the plant body of many liverworts, both of the thalloid and the leafy types (Halbsguth, 1953). The factors which induce it in such plants have been studied by various workers (Fitting, 1935, 1950; Pfeffer, 1871; Bussmann, 1939; and others, p. 355). Fitting studied especially the gemmae of liverworts. These are roundish, notched plates of cells the dorsiventral orientation of which is determined by the balance between light, gravity, and stimuli from the substrate, acting on preformed meristems in the notch. Fern prothallia exposed to an environment without gradients (shaken or on a turntable, p. 137) lose their symmetry as well as their polarity.

In Roots. Dorsiventrality is much less evident in roots than in stems. Indeed, horizontally growing subterranean roots show little or no change from radial symmetry either externally or internally. A few forms, such as *Isoetes,* have roots that are not radial. In a number of orchids, the air roots are dorsiventral in symmetry (Janczewski, 1885; Goebel, 1915). This is especially conspicuous where the root is in contact with a substrate (Bloch, 1935*a*).

In Shoots. Horizontally growing stems and branches are often conspicuously dorsiventral. Notable examples of this are found among the conifers where the lateral shoots tend to branch in a single plane and thus form flat sprays (*amphitrophy*). This form may become so firmly fixed that it persists even in cuttings (p. 189). In some species of *Lycopodium* and especially *Selaginella,* these flattened branch systems look almost like much dissected compound leaves. Indeed, there is evidence that the large pinnately compound leaves of ferns may have evolved from such branch systems. In many horizontal shoots the leaves are usually horizontal in orientation and confined to the two sides. This may result from a torsion of the petioles which are actually inserted on the stem in a spiral or decussate fashion or, more rarely, from an actual modification of the phyllotaxy.

Aside from this tendency to form flattened systems of leaves and branches, the dorsiventral character of shoots is also conspicuous in the dissimilarity of the leaves borne on the two sides. Such differences, to which Wiesner gave the term *anisophylly* (1895), are common in many plants and have been much discussed (Figdor, 1909; Goebel, 1928).

Anisophylly is often induced by external factors, notably gravity and light. It is particularly conspicuous in woody plants with opposite, decussate leaves. In horizontal shoots of maple, for example, the upper member of a vertically oriented pair is much smaller than the lower; and in a horizontally oriented pair the upper half is smaller than the lower (Fig. 7-10). Experiment shows that in many cases if shoots which would normally be vertical are held in a horizontal position as they grow from winter buds they become anisophyllous. In horizontal branches twisted through 180° before their buds open, the new shoots show reversed anisophylly, the lower leaves (originally on the upper side) now becoming the larger.

Anisophylly of this sort is present in certain species of *Lycopodium* (such as the common ground pine, *L. complanatum*), where the creeping rootstock is radially symmetrical but the ultimate branches flattened and dorsiventral (though they are radial if grown in darkness, Fig. 7-11). These branches have four rows of leaves, one on the upper side, one much smaller on the lower, and two lateral ones, the lateral leaves being the largest. Transitions from radial to dorsiventral symmetry are common, and the differences between the two are clearly due to environmental factors. In conifers such as *Thuja* the ultimate branches are dorsiventral and anisophyllous and much resemble those of *Lycopodium* (all tending to grow horizontally).

There are other plants in which the occurrence of anisophylly seems much less directly dependent upon environmental factors and occurs throughout the plant. This "habitual" anisophylly, as Goebel calls it, is probably to be interpreted as a genetic tendency to develop in this way

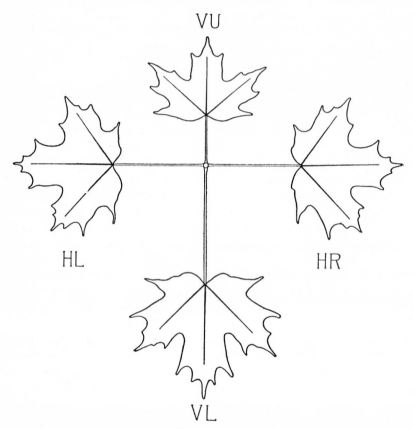

FIG. 7-10. Diagram of a horizontally grown branch of maple, showing anisophylly. The vertically oriented pair of leaves (VU, VL) differ greatly in size but are symmetrical. In the horizontally oriented pair (HL, HR), the lower half of each leaf is larger than the upper. (*From Sinnott.*)

under such a wide range of environments that it has become essentially an inherited trait. In many foliose liverworts, for example, the axis has three rows of leaves, two of them lateral and the third, the much reduced *amphigastria*, borne on the under side. Most species of *Selaginella* have four rows of leaves: two lateral and relatively large and the other two on the upper surface between these and somewhat smaller.

Among some families of angiosperms this same genetic or habitual
anisophylly occurs. Thus in *Pellionia* (Urticaceae), in *Centradenia*
(Melastomaceae, Fig. 7-12), and in *Columnea* (Gesneriaceae) one member of each pair is a large typical foliage leaf but the other, directly
opposite it, is a small bract-like structure. These differences are apparently unrelated to environmental conditions. It is noteworthy, how-

FIG. 7-11. Dorsiventral (flat) shoot of
Lycopodium. At right is a branch grown
in the dark, which is radially symmetrical. (*From Goebel.*)

FIG. 7-12. Anisophylly in *Centradenia.*
Leaves are opposite but one member of
each pair is much larger than the other.
Only the larger ones have axillary shoots.
(*From Goebel.*)

ever, that this anisophylly is most extreme in horizontal shoots of such
plants and is much reduced in those which grow more nearly vertically.

On flattened plagiotropic shoot systems there are often changes in the
pattern of symmetry that are more complex than anisophylly. In such
shoots, for example, many leaves are asymmetric, but in a regular and
predictable fashion (Fig. 7-13). Thus in horizontal branches of elm and
linden, the inner half of the leaf, directed toward the apex of the shoot,

is larger than the outer, and its blade often reaches farther down the midrib. In the beech, on the other hand, it is the outer part of the leaf which is the larger. Many cases of leaf asymmetry, notably the conspicuous examples in species of *Begonia,* are related to the position of the leaf on the stem, although here the stem is often short and inconspicuous.

Somewhat similar expressions of apparent asymmetry are evident in the branch pattern of plagiotropic shoots. In some cases, the branches which arise on lateral shoots are larger on the inside, toward the apex of the shoot, as in flat stems of *Thuja.* More commonly those on the outside, away from the axis, are larger, a phenomenon which Wiesner (1892*a*, 1895) has called *exotrophy* and which he explains as due to nutritional causes. Leaves on the outside of lateral shoots are often larger than those on the inside, a special type of anisophylly.

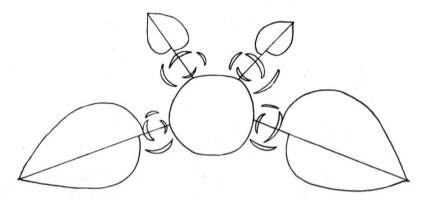

Fɪɢ. 7-13. Anisophylly in *Goldfussia.* Diagram of shoot from above. The leaves are opposite but the pairs are somewhat displaced. One member of each pair is larger than the other, and one side of each leaf is larger than the other side. In the axillary shoot, position with reference to the symmetry of the whole determines leaf size. (*From Goebel.*)

All such structures, which in a strict sense are asymmetric, are really complex patterns of symmetry induced when a fundamentally radial system becomes dorsiventral. What the factors are—whether nutritional, hormonal, or other—which determine these differences is not known. This is evidently the point where the relatively simple phenomenon of symmetry merges into the more complex one of organic pattern in general. In flat, dorsiventral shoots, which are essentially structures in two dimensions only, there is an excellent opportunity to analyze the problem of pattern in one of its simplest expressions.

The external dorsiventrality of stems is often accompanied by dorsiventrality of internal structure. Where the stem is flattened, the vascular cylinder is likely to be so as well. Sometimes the symmetry changes do not involve the whole cylinder. In the horizontal rhizome of *Pteridium*, for example, the outer ring of bundles is essentially circular in section, but the group of medullary bundles tend to be flattened dorsiventrally. In *Selaginella* the few bundles which form the vascular system also tend to be flattened in the same way. This flattening may even persist in those orthotropous shoots which have become radially symmetrical externally.

Examples of internal asymmetry in the stems of seed plants are found in the horizontally growing branches of woody plants. Here the branch itself is not flattened but its internal structure is excentric, the pith occupying a position some distance above the geometrical center of the branch in gymnosperms and below it in angiosperms. The nearer the branch approaches a vertical orientation, the less this excentricity is. There has been much discussion of the factors responsible for this internal dorsiventrality (p. 356). The problem is far from a simple one and seems to be involved with the specific pattern of branching characteristic of the plant.

In Leaves. All leaves are typically dorsiventral structures, but those of pteridophytes and seed plants are most characteristically so. A leaf, to perform its usual functions satisfactorily, must be relatively broad and thin and oriented with its major surface at right angles to incident light.

Dorsiventrality of leaves is especially evident in their histological structure. The stomata and spongy tissue tend to be confined to the lower part of the leaf, with the palisade layer and a continuous epidermis on the upper. Some vertically oriented leaves such as those of *Iris* are equifacial and show no dorsiventrality, either external or internal. Others, such as those of certain rushes, may actually be tubular and essentially radial in their symmetry.

The dorsiventrality of leaves in the higher vascular plants, however, is inherent in something more fundamental than the orientation of the blade. The vascular supply for each leaf is a segment, or group of segments, of the primary vascular ring with phloem outside and xylem inside. When this passes outward into the leaf as the leaf trace and finally becomes the vein system, the phloem therefore tends to be on the lower surface and the xylem on the upper, a characteristic dorsiventral orientation from the first. Even the leaf primordia become dorsiventral very early. There is evidence, however, that this is the result of induction from the meristematic apex, for if a region where a primordium is to form is isolated from the apex by an incision, the structure that emerges may be radially symmetrical (Sussex, 1955).

In Flowers. Floral structure provides many examples of dorsiventrality. The presumably primitive types of flowers are radially symmetrical, or *actinomorphic* (regular). In many families, however, such as the papilionaceous legumes, the figworts, the orchids, and others, especially those in which the flowers are borne laterally on an inflorescence, this radial symmetry has become dorsiventral and the flower is said to be *zygomorphic* (irregular; Fig. 7-14). The pea flower, with its standard, two wings, and keel is a familiar example, and the median plane of symmetry here is especially well marked. Flowers of this sort provide many of the notable adaptations for insect pollination. In most cases zygomorphy is

Fig. 7-14. Dorsiventrally symmetrical (zygomorphic) flower of *Linaria vulgaris.* (*Courtesy of Rutherford Platt.*)

evident from the beginning of development and is unaffected by the relation of the flower to gravity or other environmental factors. In other cases (such as *Epilobium, Friesia,* and *Digitalis*), if the flower develops in a vertical orientation or on a clinostat, it becomes radial, indicating that dorsiventrality here is directly affected by gravity (Fig. 7-15). In cases of *peloria* (p. 282) the flower of a species which is normally zygomorphic (as in *Linaria* or *Digitalis*) may become radially symmetrical. Most zygomorphic flowers are geotropic and will assume a definite position with relation to gravity.

In some cases certain flowers of an inflorescence are dorsiventral and others radial. This is true of the ray florets of Compositae and of certain Umbelliferae, where that part of the corolla directed toward the outside of the head is much larger than that directed toward its center. In such cases the entire inflorescence shows a radial symmetry. Here, again, the

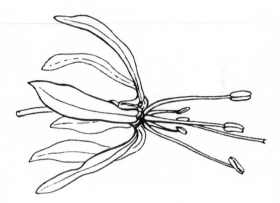

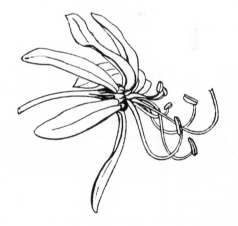

Fig. 7-15. Flower of *Asphodelus*. Below, under normal conditions. Above, after developing on a clinostat. (*From Vöchting.*)

whole pattern is symmetrical though certain of its elements are by themselves asymmetric. The situation may be still more complex. In some Compositae there are as many as five types of fruits, as to size and shape, formed on the head but showing symmetrical distribution (Pomplitz, 1956).

Most inflorescences (like that described for *Stellaria*, p. 167) are radially symmetrical, but some are definitely dorsiventral. A familiar example of this is the heliotrope and its allies, where the flower cluster is one-sided and constitutes a *scorpioid* cyme. The vetches and some other legumes are less extreme cases, and there are many others. The flowers of such dorsiventral inflorescences may themselves be radially symmetrical.

Physiological Dorsiventrality. Dorsiventrality is manifest in physiological activity as well as in structure, though usually not so obviously. Plagiotropic roots, shoots, and other organs assume this position presumably because of specific distribution of growth substances in the growing tip such that the pull of gravity is counteracted and growth maintains either a horizontal course or one at a given angle to a vertical axis. In cases where the first division of a cell sets apart two different daughter cells, as in the first division of the egg of *Fucus,* there is clearly a physiological difference between the upper and lower halves. Indeed, the differentiation of root and shoot in the embryonic axis, with the radical differences in activity of these two poles, may be looked upon as an example of physiological (and morphological) dorsiventrality.

In leaves of certain water plants, externally alike on both surfaces, Arens (1933) has presented evidence that the physiological activities at the two surfaces are unlike, materials from the environment entering through the lower surface and waste products (chiefly carbon dioxide) being given off from the upper. What the mechanism of such physiological dorsiventrality may be is not known, but bioelectrical differences (p. 361) are perhaps involved.

DEVELOPMENT OF SYMMETRY

The causes of organic symmetry are not well known, but in endeavoring to find them it is first necessary to determine how these relations actually arise in the process of development.

The Origin of Symmetry in Coenocytic and Colonial Systems. Symmetry is by no means confined to cellular structures. From the plasmodium of myxomycetes, formless and unsymmetrical, there arise specifically formed and radially symmetrical fruiting bodies of great variety. Here the morphogenetic process may be seen in one of its simplest expressions, as the sporangium is molded from the plasmodial mass.

Even more remarkable are those slime molds belonging to the Acrasiaceae (*Dictyostelium* and its allies, p. 223) where the vegetative body is a single myxamoeba. At the end of the vegetative period thousands of these come together into a pseudoplasmodium but do not fuse. This colony, after some migration, settles down and develops into a radially symmetrical stalked sorocarp.

More closely resembling the bodies of the higher plants but still without cellular boundaries are the coenocytic members of the algae and similar groups. Here there is no formless mass of protoplasm but, from the beginning, an organized system which grows at the tips of these branches that constitute the "rhizome," "leaves," and "roots." These systems are symmetrical, either radially as in *Bryopsis,* or dorsiventrally as in *Caulerpa.* In all these cases the origin of symmetry obviously is not related to planes of cell division or to other aspects of a multicellular system but is dependent upon the behavior of the entire protoplasmic system.

Origin of Symmetry in Cellular Systems. In cellular plants, the origin of symmetry can be traced more readily because it is expressed in the division, growth, and relationships of cells at meristematic regions.

In simple colonial forms like *Pediastrum* there is a regular sequence of cell divisions from which a symmetrical plate of cells arises. In many algae with an indeterminate thallus, growth is controlled by a large apical cell. The origin of branches and the whole pattern of symmetry are determined here. In simple two-dimensional thalli, the apical cell cuts off a daughter cell, first on the right-hand side and then on the left, to form the so-called *pendular* symmetry. In most leafy liverworts and mosses there is a pyramidal apical cell with three faces, and from each of these, in regular succession, a daughter cell is cut off. The origin of leaves is related to these faces, and in the simplest cases there are three rows of leaves produced directly by this apical cell.

In ferns and *Equisetum,* however, which also grow by a three-sided apical cell, there is usually no relation whatever between the phyllotaxy of the shoot and the configuration of this cell. In the seed plants there is no single apical cell and no evident relation between the spiral pattern of symmetry and any visible structures in the meristem. It seems clear that, in all except the simplest plants, the origin of spiral symmetry is not related to cellular configuration at the meristematic region but must have its basis in the entire embryonic mass.

Dorsiventral symmetry in most cases is not established at the meristem itself but has its origin in changes which arise later. Almost all meristems or terminal embryonic regions are radially symmetrical. Dorsiventrality may arise from these in the process of normal development. This is sometimes due to the influence of external factors such as light or gravity. It is sometimes the result of position in the general plant body, as when a branch becomes dorsiventral in symmetry. It is sometimes associated with particular stages in the life cycle. In plants that are dorsiventral throughout the mature plant body the seedlings are usually radial. In *Hedera,* the vegetative stage of the life cycle is dorsiventral but the flowering shoots are radially symmetrical (p. 213). Such changes are evidently due to alterations in the internal environment.

Such modifications of symmetry, particularly the change from the radial to the dorsiventral type, involve not local regions but the entire pattern, which may be deformed much in the fashion that D'Arcy Thompson has demonstrated (p. 424). This can be seen by comparing the dorsiventral maple shoot in Fig. 7-10 with one growing vertically.

SYMMETRY AND FORM

An analysis like this emphasizes the close relationship that exists between symmetry and organic form in general. Such form results from the *symmetrical distribution of material around an axis in a specific pattern.* An important part of this pattern lies in its symmetry. As we have seen, certain portions of the pattern (as the lateral leaves of the maple shoot in Fig. 7-10) appear by themselves to be asymmetrical, but they nevertheless constitute a part of a larger pattern of symmetry which may be modified in various ways. A second part of the pattern is polar axiation, affecting the lengthenings or shortenings of the axis and the steepness of gradients along it. A third is the tendency toward spirality already emphasized. Organic form results from the genetic and environmental modification of these three developmental tendencies.

CHAPTER 8

Differentiation

At the beginning of its development the young plant, as it grows from a fertilized egg or from some larger embryonic mass, is relatively simple and homogeneous. A characteristic feature of the developmental process, however, is the origin of differences in the amount, character, and location of growth which lead to differences between the various parts of an individual. Such structural or functional *differentiation* and its origin in development constitute one of the chief problems of morphogenesis.

Differentiation is the manifestation of that "division of labor" which is so conspicuous a characteristic of living things. Organs are differentiated. Tissues in their development become unlike each other. Cells grow very diverse in character. Even the contents of a single cell are divided into nucleus and cytoplasm, and each of these possesses a considerable diversity of its own. There is evidence that even the clearest cytoplasm possesses submicroscopic differentiation. Strictly speaking, there is probably no really undifferentiated structure in a plant. Protoplasm is an organized system, not a homogeneous material, and this implies a degree of physical and chemical diversity. Furthermore, because of the dynamic quality of protoplasm, differentiation in living cells can never be entirely stable but is subject to change under changing conditions.

Differentiation occurs wherever a true *development* is taking place and may be expressed in many ways. At a terminal meristem like that of a typical shoot, the primordia of leaves, buds, and flowers early become distinguishable. From cambium cells, uniform in character, there differentiate sieve tubes, fibers, tracheids, vessels, and other cell types. In the primordium of a fruit, where growth is diffuse and determinate, internal differences of many sorts begin to manifest themselves throughout the mass. In regenerative development a single cell or group of cells may dedifferentiate (p. 232) and become meristematic, and from this embryonic center a new series of structures then differentiates. Many differences have no visible expression in structure but involve physical, chemical, or physiological distinctions only. During ontogeny the course of dif-

181

ferentiation often changes, not only as to the structure of the parts developed but as to their reactivity and developmental potency.

An important aspect of the process of differentiation is that it seems not to involve genetic diversity. The regeneration of an entire normal plant is sometimes possible from a single cell, which may come from almost any of the parts of the plant body, and from various tissues (p. 253), a fact which suggests that every cell of the plant is totipotent and identical genetically with all the rest. This conclusion is supported by the common observation that the number and character of the chromosomes, and thus presumably of the genes, are the same in all cells, save for the occurrence of somatic polyploidy. Although the process of differentiation is doubtless under genetic control, this cannot operate, as Weismann and others once suggested, by a parceling out of genetic "determiners" during development. The conclusion seems obvious that in these processes that part of the cell must be involved which is *not* identical everywhere in the body, namely, the cytoplasm. The origin of structural diversity in the midst of genetic identity is the chief problem that faces students of differentiation.

GROWTH AND DIFFERENTIATION

Although growth and differentiation usually proceed together, they seem to be distinct processes, each more or less independent of the other. Growth may occur without differentiation by a simple multiplicative process, as in large parenchymatous masses such as the endosperm of a seed, in the tissue of an amorphous gall, or in tissue culture. In the early stages of many embryos, on the other hand, in the development of the female gametophyte in certain lower vascular plants, and in similar cases there is differentiation without growth. A notable example of this is furnished by the Acrasiaceae, a family of slime molds (p. 223). Here the entire vegetative growth occurs while the individuals are myxamoebae, and the elaborate differentiation of the colonial sorocarp does not begin until this vegetative phase is over. Animal embryology, particularly in the early cleavage stages from large eggs, provides many similar cases.

The independence of these two major developmental processes is further emphasized by the fact that conditions which favor one tend to be different from those which favor the other. In general, abundance of water and available nitrogen tend to induce growth, whereas abundance of accumulated carbohydrates, with less nitrogen and water, promotes differentiation (Loomis, 1932). Red rays of the spectrum tend to promote growth and blue rays differentiation (p. 313). Under one photoperiod a given species will produce nothing but vegetative growth whereas another photoperiod will stimulate the differentiation of reproductive structures (p. 315).

When the cycle of differentiation is complete, growth usually ceases. Thus, after the formation of reproductive organs in one of the higher plants has begun, growth of the plant as a whole is reduced and finally stops. When a fruit is fully differentiated, its growth in volume ceases, though dry weight may continue to increase for some time. The two processes of growth and differentiation may go on at different rates, and therefore their *relative* rates are important in determining differences in size. Where growth is relatively rapid, a large size will be attained before the completion of the cycle of differentiation stops; where it is slow, the cycle will be complete before much growth has occurred and the structure will be much smaller. This is well illustrated by the analyses of inherited size differences in gourd fruits (p. 20). The balance between these two major processes in development—the addition of new material and its differential distribution—is of much significance.

The process of differentiation and the problems it presents may be examined from several different points of view.

1. Differentiation may be studied in plant *structure*, for it is here that differences can most readily be seen. For purposes of convenience we may distinguish between external differentiation, which involves the outward structure and configuration of the plant, and internal differentiation, which involves the cells and tissue systems of which the plant body is composed.

2. Differentiation may be considered in its *ontogenetic* aspects. It is not a static process, evident in mature structures alone, but often changes its expression during development. Differentiation in a young plant is unlike that in a mature one, and these changes proceed in an orderly cycle of development both of the plant as a whole and of each of its components. Such differences are not in structure alone but in the reactivity and developmental potency of its parts.

3. What course differentiation will take is determined not only by the genetic constitution of the plant but by the particular *environment* in which development takes place. External factors of many sorts affect the character of the structures which arise in the process of differentiation.

4. The ultimate basis of differentiation must be in *physiological* changes in the living material itself. Most of these express themselves sooner or later in visible structural diversity, but there are many cases in which cells, structurally alike, can be shown to differ physically, chemically, or in physiological activity.

Examples of these four aspects of the process of differentiation, and the problems they involve, will be considered in the present chapter.

DIFFERENTIATION AS EXPRESSED IN STRUCTURE

External Differentiation

One of the most obvious examples of differentiation is that which arises between the ends of a polar axis (p. 116). In all but the simplest axes the structures that are developed at the two ends are quite unlike. The most familiar instance is the differentiation of the shoot and root in higher plants. These two systems are set apart very early, almost at the beginning of embryonic development, and are fundamentally unlike in structure, function, and method of growth. Roots frequently develop from shoots but shoots less commonly from roots. Berger and Witkus (1954) have reported that in *Xanthisma texanum* the cells of the root always have four pairs of chromosomes but in those of the shoot, some plants have four pairs and some have five. The two types of plants are morphologically indistinguishable. How this difference in chromosome number arises in development is not known, but it is present in young seedlings.

Another conspicuous instance of differentiation in structure is that between the vegetative and reproductive phases of the life cycle. In its early stages, the plant is becoming established. Its roots and leaves are formed or its vegetative thallus developed, and its career as a food-producing or food-acquiring organism is begun. Few plants, however, are permanently vegetative. When a certain stage is reached, growth no longer produces exclusively vegetative structures. Flower buds appear at the meristem, or in lower plants reproductive organs of various sorts begin to develop. These usually are formed as the result of internal metabolic changes in the plant, such as the accumulation of carbohydrates or the production of specific substances. The onset of the reproductive phase, however, is often closely related, as to time and extent, with certain environmental factors, notably light (p. 315). Short-day plants will flower only when the daily period of illumination is relatively short, and long-day ones only when it is longer. Some plants may never flower, and others may do so when they have hardly begun to develop. The balance between vegetation and reproduction may be tipped in various ways but the potency for reproduction is always present in the genetic constitution. This may not always be for sexual reproduction. In species which reproduce chiefly by vegetative means flowers may be present but fail to function (as in the potato), may be much reduced (as in the banana), or may even be quite absent. Reproduction of some sort obviously is necessary, and the alternation of vegetative and reproductive phases, each essential in the life of the plant, is an important manifestation of differentiation.

The difference between these two types of structure begins at the meristem and may often be recognized there by the presence of a large number of axillary buds which are destined to be flower buds. The development of the floral apex has been studied by many workers (p. 67). A single flower is a modified axis, and its parts arise from primordia which, although limited in number, are distributed in a precise pattern. The differentiation between them takes place early and produces sepals, petals, stamens, and carpels. The origin of these parts from particular layers of the meristem has been worked out, through the aid of chimeras, by Satina and Blakeslee (p. 272). In abnormal growth some floral organs may be so modified that they resemble others, as in the conversion, partial or complete, of petals to stamens or sepals to leaves (p. 277).

In many trees the differentiation of flower buds begins very early, usually in the season before the flowers are borne. This is an important matter for horticulturalists and has been extensively studied (Zeller, 1954, and others), since environmental conditions favoring flower production must be provided early. Whether a tree will flower (and fruit) well in a given season is often determined in June of the year before.

Implicit in the process of reproduction is the differentiation between the sexes. In plants with perfect flowers this is evident only in the difference between stamens and pistils. In monoecious plants, there are two kinds of flowers on the same plant and in dioecious ones these are on different plants. The significance of such differences lies in the various mechanisms that tend to accomplish pollination, in many cases cross-pollination. A genetic basis has been found for some of these and is doubtless present in others. Environmental factors of various sorts are also operative here, notably nutrition and light. It is sometimes possible, for example, to change a staminate into a pistillate plant by altering the photoperiod (p. 317). The existence of sexual reproduction itself, in contrast with the much less precarious method of vegetative reproduction, is based on the presumptive advantage of the higher variability that results from the recombination of genetic potencies following syngamy and meiosis.

Other traits are sometimes associated with the fundamental difference between the sexes, as observed in *Mercurialis annua* (Basarman, 1946), *Valeriana dioica* (Moewus, 1947), *Urtica dioica*, and *Rumex acetosa* (Umrath, 1953; Fig. 8-1). In general, the female plants are larger and are also different from the males in the size and shape of their leaves.

A conspicuous example of external differentiation, since it involves an entire plant body, is that between the gametophyte and the sporophyte. In many of the simpler plants the two generations are very much alike, but they are markedly different in bryophytes and vascular plants. The advantage of this differentiation into sexual and nonsexual plants may lie in the possibility of the extensive multiplication of the products of a single sexual union. Among flowering plants, where mechanisms for effecting fertilization are more efficient than in many lower ones, the differentiation into two generations has almost disappeared.

A gametophyte, coming from a spore produced by meiosis, typically has the haploid number of chromosomes, and the sporophyte has the diploid number. Many haploid plants are now known, however, which are undoubtedly sporophytes, and diploid gametophytes may readily be produced. Chromosome number is evidently not the cause of the difference between the two generations, but it is difficult to see why a haploid spore and a haploid egg (or diploids in each case) should pro-

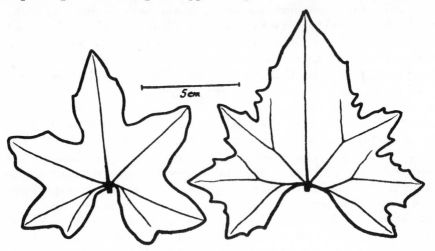

Fig. 8-1. *Bryonia alba.* Left, leaf from a shoot bearing male flowers; right, one from a shoot bearing female flowers. (*From Umrath.*)

duce two structures as unlike as the prothallus and the sporophyte of a fern. The difference is probably attributable to the very different environments in which these two cells develop.

Origin of Differences. In most cases the origin of an organ or part is first evident as a group of meristematic cells which, by growing more rapidly in certain dimensions than in others, produces a definite form. For an analysis of such specific differentiation, however, it is necessary to determine how such a developing organ originates and the successive steps by which it becomes distinct from others. Sometimes this is relatively easy. In leptosporangiate ferns, for example, the sporangium can be shown to arise from a single cell of the epidermis. In eusporangiate forms, like some of the ferns and all higher plants, the sporangium initial can be traced to a cell of the subepidermal layer. Analysis of differentiation in terms of cell lineage can often be carried further.

The development of larger organs involves more than a single cell lineage. It may be studied in the differentiation of lateral organs in the apical regions of both root and shoot. From the root there grow only lateral roots, which arise in the pericycle and push out through the cortex. The shoot meristem, however, is more complex (p. 89). At the base of the terminal dome of cells arises a series of minute protuberances, the early leaf primordia, arranged in a precise order.

The cause of the differentiation of these primordia from the rest of the apical meristem is not known. Schüepp (1952) suggested that, since cell division in the outer layer of the meristem is always anticlinal but in the tissue below may be in various directions, this surface layer will expand more rapidly than the surface of the underlying tissues and will thus tend to buckle or pucker, starting the formation of primordia. This would not explain the very regular pattern in which these arise, however, and it can also be shown that the initial bulge results from division in a group of cells just beneath the surface layer. Snow and Snow (1947) have submitted this theory to experimental test by making shallow incisions at the surface of the meristem. Instead of closing up, as they would do if the outer layers were under pressure, these gaps open, indicating that this region is actually under tension.

The fate of a small lateral primordium may not always be to grow into a leaf. Wardlaw and his students (p. 71) have performed various experiments on the meristems of ferns in which, by deep cuts, they were able to isolate from the apex a young primordium or a region that was about to develop into a primordium. In most cases this structure, instead of forming a dorsiventral leaf, developed into a radially symmetrical bud-like organ which, in culture, was capable of growing into a whole plant. Factors in the surrounding meristematic tissue evidently help determine into what sort of structure a given primordium will differentiate.

The growth of the leaf primordium into a mature leaf has been studied by many workers (p. 90, and Foster, 1936). In general, the upper and lower epidermis is continuous with the outer layer of the meristem, and what will later form the palisade and spongy layers is continuous with the subepidermal layer. The veins usually arise from a layer just below this. The differentiation of the leaf of tobacco has been described by Avery (1933) and of *Linum* by Girolami (1954; Fig. 8-2). Foster (1952) has reviewed the development of foliar venation. The mode of development and differentiation in certain leaves of unusual shape, as in *Podophyllum* and *Sarracenia,* is described by Roth (1957). The growth of a fern frond, at least for some time, takes place by the activity of an apical cell (Steeves and Briggs, and Briggs and Steeves, 1958).

An important morphogenetic problem here is how far the development of such a lateral structure depends on factors in the meristem from which it grew and how far it is independent. Steeves and Sussex (1957) removed primordia of several sizes and ages from the meristem of *Osmunda* and other ferns and grew them in sterile culture. These developed normally into mature leaves just as they would have done if attached to the plant, except for being smaller. Evidently after a certain stage is reached the control of development is within the leaf itself. This

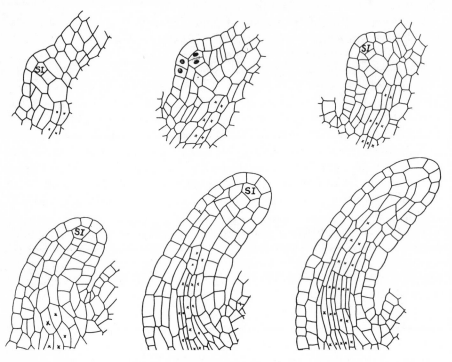

Fig. 8-2. Early stages in development of the leaf of *Linum*. *SI*, subapical initial; *x*, procambial elements. (*From Girolami.*)

self-differentiation has been found in other cases and shows that the organization of the plant is not as tight as it is in animals but that there is some degree of independent control of differentiation in individual organs.

A branch or secondary axis differentiates by the activity of a bud arising in the axil of a leaf primordium (Garrison, 1955). In herbaceous plants such a bud develops directly but in woody ones it has a dormant period and is covered by bud scales, or cataphylls. Bud development in pine has been studied by Sacher (1955) and in angiosperms by Foster

(1931). In inflorescences the leaves may be reduced to bracts. Foliage leaves, bracts, and cataphylls are presumably equivalent morphologically, and the development of a primordium into one or the other depends on its function. Primordia at a meristem are thus *multipotent* (Foster), since they may form several kinds of structures.

How a given structure differentiates is closely related to the position that it occupies in the developmental pattern. Not all morphologically equivalent organs develop alike. In *Ginkgo* the axis is differentiated into short shoots and long shoots (Gunckel and Wetmore, 1949). All buds form short shoots but some of these will grow into long ones. The ratio of the two affects the form of the tree. A somewhat similar situation occurs in *Cercidiphyllum* (Titman and Wetmore, 1955).

The vertical axis of a tree and the lateral axes (branches) that it bears also may differ markedly, the former being radially symmetrical and orthotropic, the latter more or less dorsiventral and plagiotropic. Coniferous trees offer familiar examples, where the lateral branches are much flattened and branches of the second order occur in two lateral ranks. In *Abies* and *Picea* this is evidently related to gravity, for if the terminal bud or branch is removed, a lateral branch will bend upward and replace it. In *Araucaria excelsa,* however, this difference is so deeply seated that if cuttings are made from the lateral branches, the flattened character now persists in the new plant even if the cutting is oriented vertically. Not only structure but physiological behavior may be permanently altered, for such lateral branches will grow horizontally in whatever position they may now be placed. Carvalho, Krug, and Mendes (1950) report a similar behavior in *Coffea.* There are many other examples of such topophysis (p. 212).

The differentiation of particular organs—root, stem, leaf, flower—during development is markedly influenced by growth substances of various sorts (Chap. 18).

Internal Differentiation

Visible differentiation involving external diversity in organs and their parts is accompanied in most plant structures by a high degree of internal diversity. This involves differentiation among various types of cells and tissues.

Histological differentiation presents two chief problems: (1) How do cells become different from one another and (2) what is the origin of the various tissue patterns found in the internal structure of plant organs?

Origin of Cellular Differences. Cells differ from each other in many ways. Frequently it is possible to determine the exact cell division at which such a difference becomes evident. In young roots of certain grasses

(p. 131), for example, the last division of many (sometimes of all) of the surface cells results in a small daughter cell at the apical end and a larger one at the basal end. This initial difference is intensified during the later development of these cells, for the smaller cell (a trichoblast) sends out from its surface an elongate sac which becomes a root hair. Such a structure is lacking in the larger cell (Cormack, 1949). The beginning of this difference may be seen even before the last division, for the cytoplasm at the apical end of the mother cell becomes much more dense than that at the basal end. Differentiation between the two daughter cells is thus related to the strongly polar character of the mother

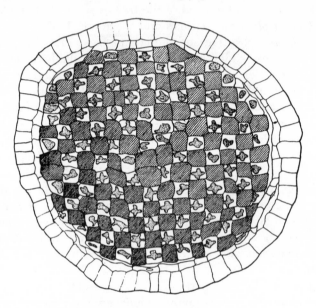

Fig. 8-3. Section through developing liverwort sporangium showing differentiation of alternating spores and elater cells. (*From Goebel.*)

cell. In *Phalaris* the epidermal cells contain a natural red pigment which is deeper in color in the prospective root-hair cells, and they can be distinguished early for this reason (Bloch, 1943*b*). In many plants the surface cells of the root are all potentially alike, and the differentiation of some cells into root hairs and others into hairless cells is not determined at a differential cell division but by environmental factors. The difference between these two types of root-hair determination may be related to anatomical characters (Cormack, 1947). A close relation exists between the distribution of cellulose-forming enzymes and the location of the root hair on a surface cell (Boysen-Jensen, 1950).

There are many somewhat similar cases of cellular differentiation. In

Ricinus the secretory cells are formed, in the young meristem or in later development, by differential cell division (Bloch, 1948), though conforming to no sharp pattern. Once formed, these cells continue to divide, producing rows of similar cells in a cell lineage. This may even persist in tissue culture.

The differentiation between chlorophyll-bearing and colorless cells in the leaf of *Sphagnum* results from a differential division, preceded by a polar movement of the cytoplasm (Zepf, 1952). The origin of elaters in

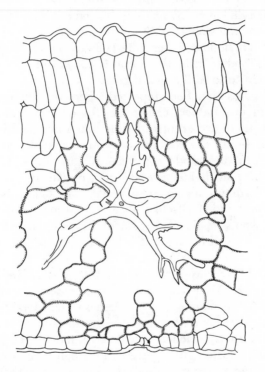

Fɪɢ. 8-4. *Trochodendron.* Section of leaf with a large branching sclereid. (*From Foster.*)

the capsule of liverworts is similar, a cell of the archesporial tissue dividing into a spore mother cell and an elater cell (Fig. 8-3).

Certain trichosclereids develop in much the same manner. These cells, which in *Monstera* become very long and thick-walled, are set apart at the last division of certain cells of the meristematic cortex. The smaller daughter cell (this time at the basal end), possessing a relatively larger nucleus, develops into the sclereid and the other into a typical parenchyma cell. Although the sclereid begins in this case as the smaller daughter cell, it soon sends out one or more processes which grow longitudinally between neighboring cells and often become very long (Bloch, 1946). A study of the origin of such *idioblasts* (cells distinctly different from their neighbors) (Fig. 8-4) may throw light on problems of cellular differentiation (Foster, 1956, and others).

Stomatal initials are set apart by differential cell divisions (Bünning and Biegert, 1953). A smaller, more densely cytoplasmic cell and a larger one are formed by a late division of a surface cell. The former divides again, this time equally and longitudinally, to form the guard cells, the contents of which soon become markedly different from those of the other epidermal cells. In monocotyledonous plants like this, where the cells are in regular longitudinal rows, the stomatal initials are cut off at the ends of elongate cells. In most dicotyledons, where the cells of the developing epidermis are more nearly isodiametric, the initial is cut out of a corner of the cell and divides again to form the guard cells.

A number of cases have been reported where the differentiation of one type of cell evidently induces changes in the character of adjacent ones. Thus in *Sedum* there are groups of cells that form tannin, and in these regions stomata do not differentiate (Sagromsky, 1949). In *Potamogeton* roots those cells of the exodermis that are just under the already differentiated trichocytes divide several times, unlike the other cells in this layer, and so form groups of small cells, one below each trichocyte (Tschermak-Woess and Hasitschka, 1953*b*). In a species of *Begonia* where there are silver spots on the leaf surface, there is a hair formed in each spot save the very small ones, and the larger the spot, the longer the hair (Neel, 1940).

Cell Size (p. 29). Some of the most conspicuous differences between cells are in their size. Meristematic cells in most cases are small, and after the final division the daughter cells increase considerably in size. The extent of this increase is determined by the time in development when division ceases in that particular cell lineage and by the position of the cell in the general histological pattern. Pith cells are usually large because they have had a long period of enlargement since their last division, and epidermal cells relatively small since division there lasted longest. Many size differences, however, such as those between the large vessels of ring-porous woods and the small elements around them, are due to local differential factors, since the cambial initials are alike.

One type of cellular differentiation is unlike all others in that it involves fundamental alteration of the cell itself. Many instances are now known in which mature cells, aroused to division by various agents, are found to have twice as many chromosomes (or more) as they did at their last preceding mitosis. During the differentiation of such a cell from meristematic condition to maturity a doubling of the chromosome complement must have taken place. Such a change, though not directly observable in the cell, is usually reflected in increased cell size and may be a factor in other changes which occur during differentiation. How important this factor is in cellular differentiation is not known. It may account for some of the diversity in cell size but probably has little to do with other aspects of differentiation (p. 441).

The Cell Wall. Some of the most distinctive ways in which cells differ are concerned with the cell wall. The wall is of much greater variety and significance in plant cells than in animal cells, and the key to cellular differentiation in plants is often to be found in it. Walls may differ greatly in thickness, chemical composition, and structure, depending upon the function of the cells of which they are parts. In certain tissues the cells die early, and only the thickened walls which they formed remain. The size and shape of the cell and the manner of its growth seem often to be dependent primarily upon the character of the wall. Studies of the chemistry and fine structure of the wall show how complex its constitution may be and make clear that any detailed analysis of cellular dif-ferentiation must pay attention to changes not only in the living material of the cell—the true protoplast—but in the wall that is the result of its activity (Bailey and Kerr, 1935; Frey-Wyssling, 1955).

In a few cases the origin of differentiation in the wall may be observed, especially where sculpturing occurs, as in the ringed, spiral, and reticulate cells of the xylem and in other tissues with similarly unequal wall thickening. Crüger (1855) and Dippel (1867) many years ago showed that the first indication of where such thickenings were to occur in developing cells was the accumulation of cytoplasm, more densely granular than the rest, in a definite pattern. The thickenings of the wall (rings, reticulations, or others) were laid down in close relation to this cytoplasmic pattern (Barkley, 1927). Strasburger (1882) observed streaming of cytoplasm along these strands. Large and vacuolate parenchyma cells that are being redifferentiated as reticulate xylem cells in regeneration are particularly good material in which to observe the cytoplasmic network upon which the wall reticulum is being built (Sinnott and Bloch, 1945; Fig. 8-5). Küster (1931) called attention to the similarity between such cytoplasmic configurations and Liesegang rings. Denham (p. 166) reports that in many cells the directions of cytoplasmic streaming has a definite relation to the micellar configuration of the wall.

Differentiation and Position. In all the cases of cellular differentiation here described, the position of the cell in the developing system is evidently closely concerned with the type of differentiation that it undergoes. A notable example is the formation of reaction wood, which differentiates in the precise position where it will tend to bring a terminal or lateral axis into a specific orientation in the pattern of the whole (p. 356).

We may distinguish position with reference to the external environment (light, oxygen, chemical stimuli, and many others), with reference to various factors in the internal environment (surfaces, air spaces, conducting strands, and cells previously differentiated), and with reference to the autogenously unfolding and genetically controlled pattern of development. To distinguish these aspects of position is often difficult or impossible. The important fact is that in the organized system specific parts are markedly unlike each other and that these differences, which in the aggregate distinguish the system, may arise from various causes.

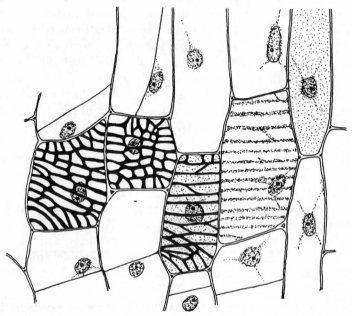

Fig. 8-5. Portion of a regenerating xylem strand in *Coleus,* showing pattern of wall thickenings laid down along bands of granular cytoplasm. Earlier stage at right. (*From Sinnott and Bloch.*)

Intracellular Differentiation. The parts of a single cell often show a high degree of diversity. The distinction between nucleus and cytoplasm is present even in embryonic cells, but as the differentiation of the cell takes place, the protoplast may exhibit a wide range of structures. Conspicuous among these are the plastids. In the algae (as *Spirogyra*), these may be represented by large and often complex chromatophores. Much more minute bodies, the mitochondria, occur and multiply (Sorokin, 1955; Hackett, 1955). Bodies similar to the Golgi apparatus of animal cells have been reported (Weier, 1932), but their general occurrence is doubtful.

The proportions of these intracellular structures often change during differentiation. Thus in moss protonemata the nucleus increases in size from the tip of the caulonema backward but the nucleolus decreases for the first few cells. The nucleus also gradually changes from a spherical to a spindle shape, and other changes are evident (Bopp, 1955). Intracellular diversity is particularly conspicuous in the differentiation of large coenocytic bodies, as in certain algae.

Differentiation of Histological Patterns. Differentiated cells rarely occur separately but are grouped into tissues. Endodermis, vascular tissues, and many others are familiar examples. These tissue patterns begin to appear in the embryo (Miller and Wetmore, 1945; Fig. 8-6; Spurr, 1949; Esau, 1954), grow more diverse in the seedling, and reach their maximum differentiation in the mature plant. Nowhere else are the complexities of differentiation so evident as in the development of these

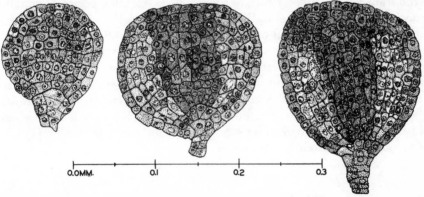

Fig. 8-6. Beginnings of differentiation in early embryo of *Phlox*. Successive stages, showing origin of central procambial core. (*From Miller and Wetmore*.)

histological patterns. Specialized as these may be, each constitutes an element in an integrated whole.

Wall Relationships. One of the basic elements in histological pattern is the relationship of cells to each other. This is determined primarily by the position of new walls in dividing cells relative to walls in adjacent cells. In most tissues a new wall is so placed that it does not come opposite a neighboring cell partition, and the cells are thus "staggered" in position, like bricks in a building (p. 47). In a few cases, however, walls in adjacent cells are exactly opposite, so that they extend in continuous lines across the tissue (Fig. 8-7). This is particularly evident in cork and in regenerating tissue at wounds. This arrangement lends itself well to the development of aerenchyma, since when such cells pull apart at their corners a larger volume of intercellular space results than if the walls were staggered. The two types of pattern may well be seen

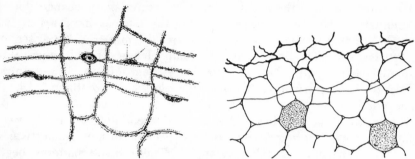

FIG. 8-7. Partition walls opposite adjacent ones. At left, dividing cells in tissue of wounded petiole of *Bryophyllum,* the walls being laid down directly opposite those in adjacent cells. At right, similar divisions in more mature tissue below wound surface. (*From Sinnott and Bloch.*)

in the transverse section of certain roots, where the inner cortex is radially concentric, with opposite walls, but the outer cortex shows the alternating arrangement typical of ordinary parenchyma (Fig. 8-8).

Endodermis. One of the simplest of these tissue patterns is shown by the endodermis. This is a single layer of cells differentiated in a specific way, as by special thickenings in the walls or the presence of a Casparian strip. It separates the vascular cylinder from the cortex. The position it occupies is usually a very definite one, and in such plants as *Equisetum* its particular pattern with reference to the bundles is specific enough to be valuable for taxonomic purposes.

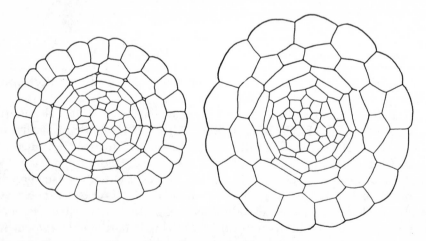

FIG. 8-8. Transverse sections of two roots. Left, *Sporobolus,* in which there are three layers of radially concentric cells in the cortex, the walls having been laid down directly opposite those in adjacent cells. Air spaces later appear at intersections. Right, *Agrostis,* in which the cell walls in the cortex always avoid adjacent ones. (*From Sinnott and Bloch.*)

The exact localization of the endodermis makes it of particular interest morphogenetically. Light is important in its development, for it is well differentiated in roots and etiolated stems and much more poorly developed in the light (Bond, 1935). Venning (1953), however, finds that factors other than light are responsible for the formation of a typical endodermis. Van Fleet in a series of papers has studied differentiation histochemically (1954a and b), with particular reference to the position of the endodermis on an oxidation-reduction gradient as well as to the distribution of various enzymes. He has stressed the importance of histochemical determination of enzyme distribution (1952) as a means of discovering chemical differentiation before it is evident in structure (Fig. 8-9).

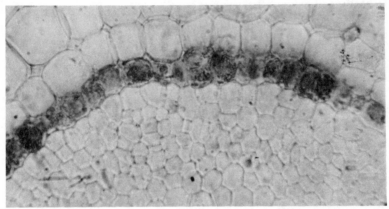

Fig. 8-9. Chemical differentiation of the endodermis. Its cells stain differently from those of adjacent tissues. (*From Van Fleet.*)

Fiber Patterns. An example of the differentiation of a somewhat more complex pattern but one consisting of a single type of cells is provided by the development of a system of fiber strands such as that found in the pericarp of the cucurbit fruit, and especially well developed in the "dishcloth" gourd, *Luffa* (Sinnott and Bloch, 1943). Here the pericarp tissue in the early ovary primordium consists of longitudinal rows of squarish parenchyma cells with most of the divisions at right angles to the axis of the young ovary or parallel to it. Here and there begin to occur divisions not in these two orientations but obliquely at various angles (Fig. 8-10). Parallel to each such division is a series of others so that in a given cell or its neighbors several elongate and parallel cells are cut out. This group becomes connected with other groups in a continuous series, though successive members of this series may arise at somewhat different angles. The result is that strands of cells are formed, twisting about through the original rectangular cellular system and connected in an interwoven pattern. These small elongate cells expand with the growth of their parenchymatous neighbors and develop into long sclerenchymatous cells aggregated into strands a fraction of a millimeter wide which are organized into the complex fibrous "sponge." This sponge is not a random mass of fibers but has an organization of its own, for the outer members of it are arranged in rows transverse to the axis of the fruit and most of the inner ones extend lengthwise. They are united into a continuous system. This system seems to be the expression of a histological pattern superposed upon the fundamentally different system of regularly arranged parenchyma cells of the early ovary. How the course of its interconnected but continuous strands is established is a baffling problem. In somewhat the same way as these sclerenchymatous strands develop, the young bundle initials of the veins arise in

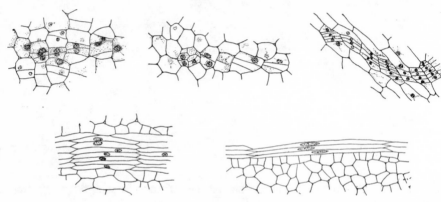

FIG. 8-10. Young ovary of *Luffa*. Successive early stages in the origin of a fiber strand differentiating in ground parenchyma. (*From Sinnott and Bloch.*)

the mesophyll of a developing leaf blade, as described by Meeuse (1938; Fig. 8-11).

Cambium. A familiar example of a complex pattern of differential development is that of the vascular cambium and its products (p. 84). The typical cambium consists of a continuous tangential layer of elongate initials in which most of the divisions are in the tangential plane. The cells cut off on the inside develop into tracheids, fibers, vessels, parenchyma, and ray cells of the xylem, and those on the outside into sieve tubes, companion cells, fibers, and other phloem cells. There are profound differences between a huge vessel element in oak wood and a small parenchyma cell beside it but both come from similar cambium cells.

There are a number of morphogenetic problems presented by a study of this development of **secondary vascular tissues.**

1. What determines the relative frequency of divisions on the inside of the cambial initials to those on the outside, the relative amount of xylem and phloem?

2. What determines how cambium derivatives differentiate into the widely diverse sorts of cells found in the mature tissues?

3. What maintains so perfectly the anatomical pattern of the xylem and phloem?

Bannan and others (p. 81) have shown that many radial files of cells are begun at the cambium and then die out and that many rays are initiated only to disappear, the net result being a very precise distribution of rays and vertical elements with reference to each other. The files of tracheids remain at a constant width, and the rays are evenly spaced with reference to each other, as can be seen in a tangential section of wood. These rela-

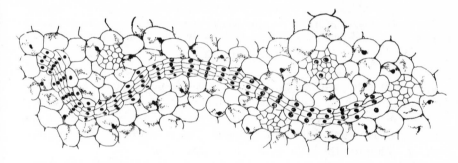

Fig. 8-11. Portion of transverse section of leaf of *Sanseviera*. Bundle of fibers beginning to differentiate in the midst of fundamental tissue. Compare with Fig. 8-10. (*From Meeuse.*)

tionships are so constant and specific that they are used as taxonomic characters.

This same problem of a specifically patterned distribution of structures meets us in many other places, such as in the spacing of bundles in cross sections of the stems of monocotyledons, of stomata in the leaf epidermis, of root hairs, or of developing sclereids in the cortex. Bünning has explored this problem (1948, pp. 173–179). He suggests that a specific developing structure prevents the differentiation of another like it within a certain distance of itself and cites some experimental evidence in support of this idea (Bünning and Sagromsky, 1948). In the cells immediately around a young stoma initial, the nuclei always lie on the side of the cell next to the initial, as if in response to a chemotactic stimulus (Fig. 8-12). A few cells farther out, they have normal positions. Bünning believes that a hormonal substance passes out from the young stomatal cells which stimulates cell division, as shown by the production of accessory

cells and others, and thus inhibits differentiation of stomata (and sometimes of hairs or glands). Near wounds, cell division occurs but stomata
are not differentiated. If auxin paste or juice from crushed tissue, presumably containing wound hormones (p. 402), is applied to the young

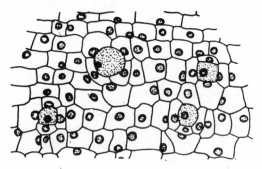

Fig. 8-12. Relation of nuclei to stomata. Nuclei of cells adjacent to stomatal initials,
in young and developing leaves, are pressed closely to these initials as if chemically
attracted to them. (*From Bünning and Sagromsky.*)

leaf, cell divisions are plentiful but stomata do not develop (Fig. 8-13).
This suggestion is of much interest in relation to the differentiation of
other evenly spaced structures, but it does not explain how the inhibiting
center itself is initiated in the first place. This is a promising point, however, at which to attack the problem of organic pattern.

In the histological pattern that originates back of the apical meristem,
Bünning (1952*a*) believes that the meristem itself inhibits differentiation
within a certain distance. Farther back, each bundle initial, which is in the

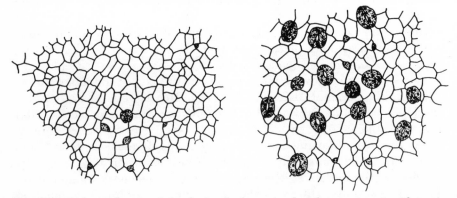

Fig. 8-13. Left, epidermis of developing leaf two weeks after treatment with auxin
paste. Stomata are almost absent. Right, epidermis of untreated half of the same
leaf. (*From Bünning and Sagromsky.*)

process of growth but is not part of the meristem proper and which he terms a *meristemoid,* inhibits the development of others near it.

The differentiation of tissues produced by the vascular cambium has been studied by Linnemann (1953), who observed that in beech the proportion of rays is greater in the wood of isolated trees than in dense stands but that it does not vary consistently with age or as between trunk and branches. Rays tend to increase in width during an annual ring and to be wider in the narrower rings.

The fact that vessel elements occur in longitudinal series to form a duct indicates the operation of a continuous stimulus longitudinally along the axis. Priestley, Scott, and Malins (1935) have shown that a single duct differentiates almost simultaneously throughout a long extent of trunk. A leaf trace passing down into a young stem exerts a considerable correlative influence upon vessel differentiation below it. Alexandrov and Abessadze (1934) found that there are fewer vessels in a segment just below a leaf trace and that they appear earliest next the rays that delimit the trace. The vessel-forming stimulus clearly moves downward, thus suggesting the operation of a hormonal control.

That auxin has a role in the initiation of the ring-porous condition is suggested by the work of Wareing (1951), and Chowdhury (1953) has analyzed some of the factors responsible for the transformation of diffuse-porous to ring-porous structure in *Gmelina.*

Continuity in differentiation of similar cells is also shown by the cork cambium, or phellogen (p. 88), in old cortex or phloem. Here it arises as a series of almost simultaneous divisions which, as seen in transverse section, somewhat resemble those described for the *Luffa* strands, since they are connected to one another in a series and often follow a somewhat irregular course through the tissue in which they arise. They form a continuous sheet of meristematic cells, often in localized patches, which cut off elements from their outer faces. Their cells suberize later, thus sealing off the outside tissues. The origin of these phellogens is the more interesting because they have their beginning in tissues where the cells are mature and intermixed with dead or necrotic ones. Their origin after wounding is related to the operation of wound hormones.

A notable example of the differentiation of a histological pattern is furnished by the system of lignified thickenings (the *"réseau de soutien"* of van Tieghem, 1888) in the air roots of certain orchids, which is presumably concerned with providing rigidity for tissue otherwise soft and easily collapsed. These arise as bands of lignified wall thickenings which surround individual cells. They may occasionally fork. It is noteworthy that the band in a given cell is directly contiguous to that in an adjacent cell, so that a continuous patterned network of thickened strands is established (Fig. 8-14). This reminds one of the way in which the ringed

thickenings in protoxylem and regenerating xylem cells are directly opposite those in adjacent ones.

In all these examples of the differentiation of histological pattern it
is evident that the pattern as a whole transcends cellular boundaries and
involves an extensive and correlated series of changes. This poses in most
direct fashion the problem of pattern in general.

More Complex Patterns. In most cases an anatomical pattern consists
of more than one type of tissue and thus is much more complex than
the ones just described. In plants that grow by a large apical cell at
the meristem, differentiation of the various tissues from particular cells
cut off from this apical cell may be traced. Thus in *Selaginella* (p. 58),

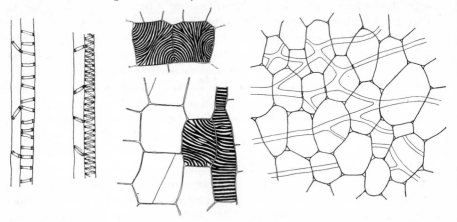

FIG. 8-14. Continuity in the differentiation of various wall thickenings. Left, rings
and spirals in protoxylem of *Zea*. Center, thickenings in reticulate vessel elements
that have developed from parenchyma cells in bundle regeneration. Right, lignified
bands (*réseau de soutien*) in cortex of air root of an orchid. In all these cases the
thickenings form a continuous pattern across cell boundaries. (*From Sinnott and
Bloch.*)

the apical cell, by an unequal division parallel to one of its faces, produces on its apical side a large cell, the continuing apical initial, and
on its basal one a cell which, seen in section, has parallel anticlinal walls
(Barclay, 1931; Fig. 4-4). This cell divides into two by a wall at right
angles to the first division. Each daughter cell divides again into two
in the same way. Thus a row of four cells is produced. Proceeding down
the shoot axis, in a longitudinal section, one can observe the fate of similar rows of four cells which had been cut off by previous divisions of the
apical cell. The outermost of the four becomes a cell of the epidermis.
The second (by later divisions) produces the cortex. Descendants of the
third and fourth form the innermost tissues. Thus the progress of differentiation can usually be followed in various lineages of cells. Specific

types of differentiation seem to be related to specific lineages, almost as though "determiners" were being parceled out at each division. The same type of differentiation has been described by Bartoo (1930) in *Schizaea*. In these cases differentiation is a true *development*, the unfolding of an internally directed pattern, with each division evidently related to the polarity of the cell. Cell division here seems a dominant factor in the determination of pattern. It should be noted, however, that there are often irregularities in this progression and that it is by no means always so precise.

In many other plants, especially those with large apical cells, differentiation also follows a rather regular course like that just described. *Chara*, *Fontinalis*, and some species of *Equisetum* (Fig. 4-3) are examples. In others, however, such precise relationship between a specific type of differentiation and cell lineage does not occur, for a particular tissue may sometimes have one cell ancestry and sometimes another. The origin of root, stem, leaf, and foot from the quadrants of a young fern embryo, for example, is not rigidly determined.

In higher vascular plants where an apical cell has been replaced by a mass of meristematic tissue, in most cases it becomes impossible to trace the origin of a group of differentiated cells from a single ancestor or to determine the precise divisions at which a fundamental difference between two cells (or their descendants) originates. Such divisions may occur, but in these there is no great difference between daughter cells nor is regularity of lineage usually observable. It is probably true that in very many instances differentiation is the result of factors of environment or position and is not related at all to differential cell division.

There is, however, a good deal of cellular differentiation to be seen in the apex of shoot and root, either as layers or zones (p. 62) and these often bear a close relation to the structures that develop from them. Thus in periclinal chimeras (p. 272) it is possible to determine with much accuracy the derivation of particular tissues from particular layers at the apex. Nevertheless, in forms without meristematic layering (as in some gymnosperms) differentiation of tissues takes place equally well. The problem of how the histogens become distinct from each other, in forms which show them, is one which for its solution must go back to the young embryo.

In the mass of relatively undifferentiated tissue below the apex arise the beginnings of vascular tissue. The distinction between the procambial or provascular cells (those which are to give rise to the primary vascular tissue) and the cells of the fundamental tissue begins to make its appearance early in development near the tip of the meristem. The first difference to be observed here often is not a structural one but a difference in the staining reaction of the cells. The earliest structural difference to be seen, in most cases, is the elongate form of the procambial cells in longitudinal section. This form is due either to fewer transverse divisions in these cells as compared with their neighbors or to more frequent longitudinal ones. From groups of these elongated provascular cells arise the vascular bundles of the stem. There is a close relation between the differentiation of these bundles and of the leaf primordia near the apex, for the young leaf traces that enter the base of each primordium are continuous with the differentiated vascular tissue below.

There has been some difference of opinion as to just how the pattern of vascular differentiation originates. It is now rather generally agreed (Esau, 1953*b*) that the procambial strands develop acropetally, continuous with the mature vascular tissue below and pushing up into the bases of the primordia themselves. In a transverse section of the axis, the procambium forms a ring which may be continuous or consist of a series of bundles. On the outside of a procambial strand the first phloem differentiates, and on the inside, the first xylem. The developmental history of these tissues is different, however. The phloem, like the procambium, develops continuously from the base toward the tip. The xylem, on the contrary, differentiates first in the base of the enlarging leaf primordium and then both upward and downward. In its downward course it meets the upward developing xylem in the axis below (Miller and Wetmore, 1946). Jacobs and Morrow (1957) traced the downward differentiating xylem strands and found that they did not always make connection with the normally opposite ones below. In the root, the procambium, phloem, and xylem all differentiate acropetally and continuously (Heimsch, 1951; Popham, 1955*b*).

The physiological significance of these facts is not clear, but morphogenetically they are concerned with the important question as to whether the course of initiation and development of structures at the apical meristem, notably the position of the leaf primordia and the pattern of internal differentiation, results from stimuli proceeding up from the mature structures below or whether in its development the tip is independent of what has gone before. This problem is discussed elsewhere in the light of some experimental results (p. 238). Torrey (1955), working with root tips cut off and grown in culture, presents evidence that the pattern of vascular differentiation (triarch, diarch, or monarch) just back of the tip is not induced by the tissue farther back but is related to the dimensions of the apical meristem at the time the cylinder is differentiated.

Much work has been done on this problem of differentiation at the apical meristems, and it is well covered by Esau (1953*b*). Among other recent publications are an extensive review by Esau (1954) and papers by Rathfelder (1954), Young (1954), Wetmore and Sorokin (1955), McGahan (1955), and Jacobs and Morrow (1957).

DIFFERENTIATION DURING ONTOGENY

Differentiation, like most problems of morphogenesis, must be studied not only as it is found in the structure of the mature plant but as it arises during development. The mature plant is obviously very different from the embryo and the seedling, but an important question, still far from settlement, is whether the changes that take place here are simply the result of increased size and the effects of environment or are internal modifications arising during development and becoming manifest in the progressive differentiation of the individual as its life cycle unfolds.

It is obvious that environment is of great importance in determining the differences that arise, and most of the experimental work in morphogenesis is concerned with a manipulation of environmental factors. It is also clear that the specific response to an environment depends on the innate genetic constitution of the individual. What is not so evident, however, is whether this response always remains the same or changes as the organism grows older.

There is a good deal of evidence that changes in the plant, independent of environmental conditions, do indeed occur as development proceeds. Juvenile stages are often very different from adult ones. That these are real and often irreversible differences is proved by the fact that they can be perpetuated by cuttings. Progressive changes in the shape and character of organs, especially leaves, at successive points along the stem have often been observed and by some biologists are attributed to advancing maturity or physiological aging. The onset of actual senescence has been reported in some cases. A considerable school of physiologists believe that the life history of a plant, particularly up to the time of flowering, consists of a series of successive phases, each the necessary precursor of the next but independent of the amount of growth attained. This concept has come in part from the idea of vernalization (p. 339).

In such phasic development the major change is the onset of the reproductive period after one of purely vegetative development. This apparently begins by a physiological change, the "ripeness to flower," as Klebs called it. Only after this has begun do the floral primordia appear at the meristem. They may not be the first visible evidence of the onset of reproduction. Roberts and Struckmeyer (1948 and other papers) have shown that the induction of the flowering phase is very early indicated by a number of anatomical changes. Root growth is much reduced, cambial activity almost ceases, and the vascular tissues tend rapidly to complete their full differentiation. In other words, the plant structures become mature. Reproduction is a sign of maturity, and these anatomical changes are evidence of a more general one that is about to take place. Many factors are involved here, either as causes or concomitants. There seems to be a major physiological change involved in this shift from vegetation to reproduction. An important problem in both physiology and morphogenesis is to find what is involved in this shift. To solve it would throw light on one of the major formative processes in the plant.

Embryology and Juvenile Stages. The science of embryology in the higher plants, in the sense in which it has been developed in animals, can hardly be said to exist. The early embryo is relatively inaccessible and is simple in structure. The divisions immediately following fertilization have been studied for many plants by Souèges (1939) and Johansen (1950; Fig. 8-15) and show differences in certain groups, but little as precise as the early stages in animal embryology is to be seen. Toward the micropylar end of the ovule the young radicle begins to differentiate and forms an apical meristem at its tip. At the other pole, in gymnosperms and dicotyledons, arise the cotyledons, with the first bud between them. The monocotyledons have a somewhat more complex structure here but it follows the same general course.

Especially important to students of morphogenesis is Wardlaw's book on Embryogenesis (1955a), which discusses embryogeny throughout the plant kingdom, with particular emphasis on the factors that determine development. Maheshwari (1950) has written a general survey of angiosperm embryology, including a useful discussion of experimental embryo culture. The ability to take embryos out of the ovule at a very early stage and grow them in culture has opened up a wide field of investigation which should be fruitful for morphogenesis.

Several facts of significance, particularly for regeneration, have come from a study of plant embryos. In a number of cases the young embryo may spontaneously divide into several parts each of which apparently has the capacity to develop into a whole plant. Such *cleavage polyembryony* has been studied by Buchholz and others (p. 235). In certain plants, notably some members of the citrus family, embryos may arise not only through a sexual process but by budding from the tissues of the nucellus. Such *nucellar embryos* are important for genetics as well as for morphogenesis.

Of particular interest, however, are those forms in which the early structures are markedly different from later ones and in which characteristic "juvenile" stages can be seen. This type of development has been termed *heteroblastic* by Goebel in contrast to the more gradual *homoblastic* type. The difference is particularly conspicuous in the character of the leaves, which in the seedling are often quite unlike those of the mature plant. The first pair of leaves in the *Eucalyptus* seedling, for example, are horizontally oriented and dorsiventral in structure though all later foliage is characteristically pendulous and bifacial. The juvenile leaves of *Acacia*

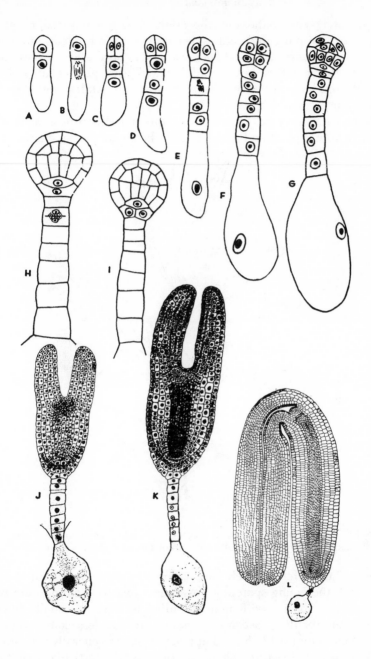

Fig. 8-15. Development of the embryo of *Capsella bursa-pastoris* from the first division of the fertilized egg to the mature embryo. (*From Johansen, after Souèges and Schaffner.*)

207

are pinnately compound but the adult ones are reduced to phyllodes (Fig. 8-16). In pine, the seedling leaves are not in fascicles but are borne singly. The young plant of *Phyllocladus* has needle-like leaves, common in most other conifers, but the adult plant bears phylloclads only. Seedlings of cacti have leaves but these are absent in adult plants. Many more such examples could be cited (Jackson, 1899).

There are some cases in which the *internal* structure is markedly different in young plant and adult, usually being simpler in character in the

FIG. 8-16. Juvenile leaves of *Acacia* seedling (pinnately compound) contrasted with the flattened phyllodes that constitute the adult foliage. (*After Velenovsky.*)

former. Thus in ferns which have a complex vascular system in the mature plant, the young sporeling possesses a relatively simple protostele or siphonostele. Species with many-bundled leaf traces usually have only three in the seedling. Secondary tissues are also less complex in young plants. Schramm (1912) finds that juvenile leaves generally resemble adult shade leaves in structure. There are differences, particularly as to venation, between the early, deeply pinnatifid leaves of *Lacunaria* and the simple mature type (Foster, 1951). Röbbelen (1957) finds that in chlorophyll-defective mutants the juvenile form of leaf is retained later than normally and has a relatively small meristem. Normal leaves are not produced until the meristem reaches a diameter of 80 to 90 μ.

Schaffalitzky de Muckadell (1954) has reviewed the literature on juvenile stages.

Juvenile traits often resemble those of plant types presumably ancestral for the stock in question (Sahni, 1925, and others). This seems evident in many of the examples cited. Most Leguminosae other than *Acacia* have leaves and not phyllodes, and most Myrtaceae other than *Eucalyptus* have dorsiventral leaves. These facts suggest that the seedling repeats or recapitulates ancestral traits, much as the animal embryo has

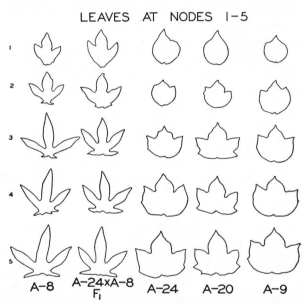

LEAVES AT NODES 1−5

A-8   A-24xA-8   A-24   A-20   A-9
            F₁

Fɪɢ. 8-17. Changes in leaf shape in cotton at five successive nodes above the cotyledons, in four varieties of cotton and an F₁. (*From Dorothy Hammond.*)

been thought to do. There is much doubt in many cases, however, as to what the course of evolution actually has been and so much variation in early ontogeny in many plants that it is impossible to establish the doctrine of recapitulation as an invariably useful guide to phylogeny.

Progressive Developmental Changes. More common than these conspicuous cases of differentiated juvenile stages are those where there is not a sharp distinction between juvenile and later forms but a gradual change from the younger part of the plant to older ones. Many examples of this are reported in the literature. Goebel (1896) described eight successive leaf types in the climbing aroid *Anadendrum medium* which occurred at different levels and showed an increasing degree of complexity. Hammond (1941; Fig. 8-17) and Stephens (1944) have described similar changes in leaf shape in cotton, and Montfort and Müller (1951) in mistletoe. Von Maltzahn (1957; Fig. 8-18) has compared leaf characters throughout plant development in large and small races of *Cucurbita* and the hybrid between them.

Similar alterations have also been found in reproductive structures. In *Chamaecyparis* there is a gradient of sexuality in the branches, the tips being sterile, with female cones below and male ones still farther back (Courtot and Baillaud, 1955). There is a flower bud in the axil of each leaf of *Cucurbita pepo* but the type of flower produced by it tends to vary with the position of the leaf on the plant, in the following sequence: underdeveloped male, normal male, normal female, inhibited male, and parthenocarpic female (Fig. 8-19). The order of these steps in progressive feminization is constant but the length of each is affected by temperature

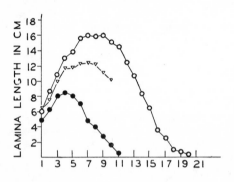

Fig. 8-18. Change of leaf size during plant growth. Lamina length of successive leaves in cucurbit plants of small-fruited and large-fruited types and the F_1 between them. (*From von Maltzahn.*)

and day-length, high temperatures and long days extending the male phase and delaying the female one (Nitsch, Kurtz, Liverman, and Went, 1952).

Leaves are especially good material in which to study such changes, and Ashby (1948b, 1950a, and Ashby and Wangermann, 1950) has made a thorough investigation of the changing character of the leaves in *Ipomoea*, describing the progressive differences in their size and shape and in the size and number of their cells from lower nodes to upper ones (Fig. 8-20). He presents evidence that these changes are not primarily due to environmental factors (although such are operative) but to alteration of inner conditions. In his 1948 papers Ashby reviews this field and discusses at some length Krenke's theory (1940) that such changes are due to the physiological age of the plant, as contrasted to its age in time. Krenke regards aging as progress toward maturity, particularly reproductive maturity, which is sometimes followed by further changes, in a cycle. At points along this progression rejuvenescence may occur, as on shoots grown from lateral buds. Successive nodes are units in a developmental scale, and the form of the leaf is a quantitative criterion of physiological age. In cotton, maximum lobing of the leaf is reached at flowering, earlier and later leaves being less lobed. The cyclical change proceeds more rapidly in early-flowering than in late-flowering types, and conditions that hasten flowering hasten lobing. Krenke believes that rate of change in leaf shape is inherited and that early-maturing varieties may thus be distinguished in the seedling stage.

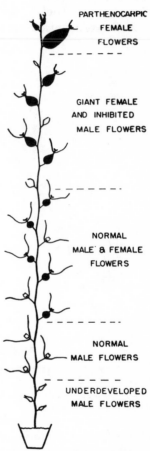

PARTHENOCARPIC
FEMALE
FLOWERS

GIANT FEMALE
AND INHIBITED
MALE FLOWERS

NORMAL
MALE & FEMALE
FLOWERS

NORMAL
MALE FLOWERS

UNDERDEVELOPED
MALE FLOWERS

Fig. 8-19. *Cucurbita*. Sequence of flower types on a plant of the acorn squash. (*From Nitsch, Kurtz, Liverman, and Went.*)

Ashby has confirmed some of Krenke's conclusions but finds others very doubtful. The possibility, however, of relating successive morphological changes to physiological ones has important implications for the problem of form determination. One may question Krenke's assertion that his hypothesis is based on dialectical materialism, but the hypothesis itself should be explored as one hopeful approach to morphogenetic problems.

The bearing of Krenke's ideas on the problem of senescence is of interest. Attention has already been called (p. 38) to Benedict's work on progressive reduction in size of structural units (cells and vein islets) in vegetatively propagated clones as they grow older, presumably the result of loss of vigor. This conclusion is still open to doubt, however.

Topophysis. The changes so far discussed have been either juvenile ones or those distributed through most of the life cycle. In many plants, however, the contrast in differentiation does not come until the onset of reproductive maturity. Diels (1906) observed that environmental factors which promote flowering also hasten the transition from juvenile to adult foliage.

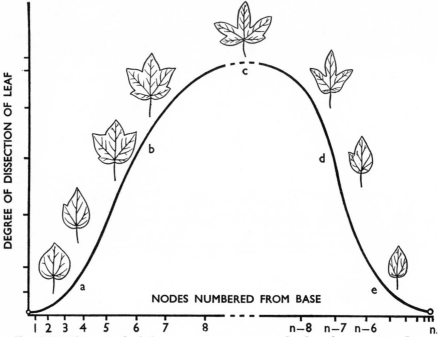

Fig. 8-20. Change in leaf shape at successive internodes from base to tip in *Ipomoea caerulea*. (*From Ashby.*)

The reproductive stage is marked by characteristic changes at the meristem, especially in the shape of its terminal dome. In the vegetative phase this is typically low and rounded, but when flower buds are to be differentiated it assumes a much steeper and more elongate form. The production of reproductive organs marks for most plants a radical reorganization of their developmental processes (p. 184) and is often accompanied by changes so profound that they are irreversible. This is of especial morphogenetic significance.

In most cases these changes have little effect on the character of the vegetative organs, but such cases are sometimes found. In the conifer

Dacrydium cupressinum, for example, needle-like foliage (resembling that of seedlings in many species with scaly leaves) occurs not only in the seedling but throughout the early life of the tree. Only when it begins to bear reproductive organs, at the age of 20 years or more, does the foliage assume the scale-like character which then continues throughout the rest of its life. This may be interpreted as the persistence of a juvenile condition until the period of reproduction.

A more conspicuous example and one which has been widely studied is that of the English ivy, *Hedera helix* (Fig. 8-21). The vegetative phase of this plant is a vine with five-lobed leaves climbing by adventitious roots

Fig. 8-21. *Hedera helix.* Flowering shoot with ovate, entire leaves, and a single leaf of the vegetative "juvenile" region. (*From Goebel.*)

and flattened against its support and often is the only form of this species to be seen. After some time and under conditions favorable for reproduction, however, flower-bearing shoots arise and will grow for many years. Their tropistic behavior is changed, for they no longer climb but grow directly outward toward the light and away from their support. Their structure is also much altered, for the leaves are now oval rather than lobed and are spirally arranged. The lobed climbing form may be regarded as a persistent juvenile condition.

The reorganization of the pattern of differentiation in the transition from seedling to adult or from the vegetative to the reproductive phase of the ontogenetic cycle is usually reversible in the sense that cuttings taken from any part of the shoot system or at any stage of development will, by regeneration, produce a normal plant. In some cases, however, changes at the growing point have been so great that the newly developed structures seem to have undergone irreversible modification. A notable example of this is the English ivy described in the preceding paragraph, for in this plant cuttings made from the flowering shoot rarely revert to the climbing form but instead produce upright, radially symmetrical plants, the variety *arborea* of horticulture. These are often used as dwarf, tree-like ornamentals but usually die after a few years. No genetic change is involved here, for seeds produce the climbing, lobed form again. There has been a good deal of debate as to the complete irreversibility of this change (Bruhn, 1910; Furlani, 1914), but the usual behavior is the one just described. Kranz (1931), however, finds that the transition from juvenile to adult foliage is often not a sudden one but that the five-lobed type gives place to a three-lobed one before the mature, ovate leaves are formed. Robbins (1957) was able to change the adult form of foliage to the juvenile one by treatment with gibberellic acid.

A somewhat similar case is the persistence of juvenile structures which can sometimes be induced by growing cuttings from the seedling stem. The most notable example of this is found in certain of the cypress-like conifers, where the seedling leaves are needle-like but are soon followed by the scale-like foliage characteristic of the species. If cuttings are made from the lateral branches arising just above the cotyledons in *Thuja*, for example, they will produce plants, often growing to small trees, which bear nothing but the needle-like juvenile foliage, the horticultural variety "*Retinospora*" (Beissner, 1930). Such plants do not flower and are relatively short-lived. In some way, severance of the juvenile shoot from its roots seems to have prevented completion of the normal ontogenetic cycle. Other cases have been reported in which seedlings used as cuttings grow very differently from those which are left on their own roots (M. R. Jacobs, 1939). Beissner's results were challenged by Woycicki (1954), who grew cuttings from seedlings of *Thuja, Chamaecyparis,* and *Biota* but found that the juvenile foliage did *not* persist. He believes that the *Retinospora* forms arose by spontaneous mutations in seedlings or young shoots.

Whatever the facts in this case may be, others have been reported in which it is certain that cuttings taken from various parts of the plant produce individuals different from the normal type and like the part of the plant from which they came and in which these differences persist during the life of the cutting, or at least for a long time, but do not involve genetic change. This phenomenon Molisch (1930) termed *topophysis*. A familiar example occurs in *Araucaria* (p. 189), where the flattened, dorsiventral character of the lateral branches persists in cuttings made from these branches. All these cases of persistent differentiation are of particular interest in providing material for a study of the cause and character of differential change.

The origin of differences arising at different *times* in a repeated cycle, rather than at a different *place* on the plant, Seeliger (1924) has termed *cyclophysis*.

DIFFERENTIATION IN RELATION TO ENVIRONMENT

Most of the examples of differentiation thus far cited seem to be primarily the expression of a developmental pattern controlled by the genetic constitution of the individual. Obviously such a constitution cannot operate except in an environment of some sort, for genes control specific differences in reaction to specific environmental factors. It is therefore to be expected that differentiation should be greatly influenced by the environment, both internal and external.

The basis for differentiation itself is provided by the environment, for the most important contribution that the physical environment makes, morphogenetically, is to set up a *gradient* in the organism. This cannot be done unless the environment itself displays a gradient in direction or intensity. Fern prothallia, for example, grown in culture on a shaking machine, and thus exposed equally to gravity on all sides, or on a revolving table, and thus exposed equally to light on all sides (p. 137), are in a homogeneous environment which has no gradients, no single direction of gravity or light. As a consequence the organism produces an amorphous mass of tissue for it is without a polar axis, the basis for its differentiation. Such an axis must be induced, at least at the very start, by an asymmetrical environment.

Environment and External Differentiation. The most obvious relation between environment and differentiation is in the effect that external factors have on the form and character of plant organs. Most of the final part of this book will be concerned with the morphogenetic effects of such factors. Light influences the differentiation of reproductive and other structures by its intensity, its wave length, and the duration of its photoperiod. The amount of available water is important in the induction of xeromorphic structures. Temperature, particularly in early development, seems to affect the rate of certain processes that are precursors to flowering. Chemical agents, notably growth substances, have a marked influence on differentiation of all sorts. The discussion of these problems must wait until later pages. There are a few conspicuous instances, however, where differentiation obviously is dependent on environmental factors which can best be described here.

One is the general phenomenon of *heterophylly*, where two or more widely different types of leaves, usually without intermediate forms, may occur on the same plant. This difference is most commonly, though not always, associated with the plant's ability to live either submersed in water or rooted in the ground with its shoots in the air (Glück, 1924, and p. 330). This may be interpreted as a case of heteroblastic development in which the manifestations are reversible. It is related to the problems of juvenile stages and progressive development discussed in the preceding section.

In many species of the pondweeds (*Potamogeton*) the floating leaves, which rest on the surface of the water, are relatively broad and have an internal structure not unlike ordinary herbaceous foliage, whereas the leaves borne under water are long, narrow, and membranous, thus being adapted to live as submerged organs. Somewhat similar differences may be seen in various "amphibious" plants (p. 332), such as the water buttercup (*Ranunculus aquatilis*) and the mermaid weed (*Proserpinaca palustris*). These species live in environments where part of their foliage grows in air and part is submersed under water. Under the former condition, the leaves are relatively broad and well provided with stomata and intercellular air chambers. In the latter they are much dissected and thinner. These effects of the environment on water buttercup were observed by Lamarck and played an important part in the development of his theory of evolution. The relation of differences between the "water" and "land" forms in such plants to those between juvenile and adult stages has been discussed by various workers. Burns (1904) believes that the "water" form of *Proserpinaca* is the juvenile stage, associated with unfavorable conditions, and the "land" form the adult type and associated with flowering. He found that only the broad, entire leaves were formed in the flowering season and only the dissected ones in the winter. Whether all such cases of heterophylly may thus be interpreted is a question. Vischer (1915) has called attention to the close relation between certain environmental factors (such as removal of leaves, weak light, damp air, depletion of carbohydrate reserves, and increased soil fertility) and the production of juvenile foliage (see also p. 206). Factors which favor reproduction tend to produce adult foliage. Under certain conditions a return to the juvenile condition may be induced (Woltereck, 1928). There is no evidence that the ribbon-like submersed leaves of *Potamogeton* are juvenile in type, however. Arber (1919) points out that in *Sagittaria* (another "amphibious" plant) the first leaves are thin and ribbon-like even when the plant is growing out of the water and that they appear at maturity whenever the plant grows weakly. She believes that an aquatic environment is not responsible for heterophylly but that the occurrence of heterophylly is a necessary prerequisite for the ability of a plant to live in both aquatic and terrestrial habitats.

Pearsall and Hanby (1925) have evidence that leaf variation in *Potamogeton* is due, at least in part, to chemical differences in the soil, and Gessner (1940) and Bauer (1952) relate it to rate of metabolism in the buds. McCallum (1902) thought that in *Proserpinaca* the water type of leaf arose primarily because of reduction in transpiration. H. Jones (1955) has made extensive studies of the differences in development of the primordia that produce the linear and the ovate leaves of *Callitriche* and the conditions under which these are formed.

There are many instances where, instead of the permanent induction of structures at certain ontogenetic levels, there may be reversion to earlier stages under certain environmental conditions. This is especially frequent in those cases where juvenile stages are adapted to different environments than are the adult ones. A commonly cited example is that of *Campanula rotundifolia*, which has rounded juvenile leaves adapted to weak light, although the mature leaves are linear. A mature plant grown in low illumination will often revert to the juvenile type of foliage. Seedlings, even in strong light, however, bear nothing but juvenile foliage. Often wounding will bring about such reversion, as in shoots growing from injured regions of certain pines, which for a time bear foliage like that of the seedling. With many perennials there is a partial return to the juvenile stage at the beginning of each growing season.

Frank and Renner (1956) found that in *Hedera helix* chemical treatments of various sorts did not induce reversion to the juvenile state but that cold shocks and X irradiation did so. De Zeeuw and Leopold (1956) were able to induce flowering by auxin treatment in juvenile plants that otherwise would not have flowered. They suggest that the completion of the juvenile phase may be due to the accumulation of a sufficient auxin level. Robbins (1957) has shown the effectiveness of gibberellin in juvenile reversion. Allsopp (1955) attributes heteroblastic differentiation in general to changes, chiefly of size, in the shoot apex following alteration of the water balance (p. 332).

Environment and Internal Differentiation. Internal differentiation, also, may be greatly affected by environmental factors. It is important to recognize that changes that take place in this process are part of an underlying pattern of relationships among the cells and between them and the environment.

This fact is made clear whenever such relationships are disturbed. If tissue like the cortex, for example, is exposed to the outside air by removal of the outer cell layers, structures tend to differentiate at the new surface which are characteristic for such a position. Thus when Vöchting

(1908) sliced off a portion of a kohlrabi tuber, the living cells at the new surface differentiated into a rather typical epidermis in which even stomata were formed. In roots of the Araceae and air roots of orchids, where there is no cell division after an injury, parenchyma cells near a newly exposed surface redifferentiate into thick-walled ones essentially like those of a normal hypodermis.

Even more complex patterns may be reconstituted under the influence of a different environment. In the roots of *Philodendron Glaziovii* there is a row of brachysclereids a few cell layers below the surface. After the experimental removal of the outer tissues, a similar row of thick-walled cells differentiates at about the same distance below the new surface (Bloch, 1926). In the air root of *Monstera*, the cells of the cortex normally remain undifferentiated for a considerable distance back from the tip.

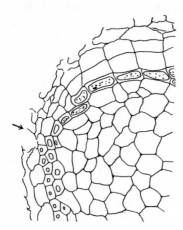

Fig. 8-22. Air root of *Philodendron*. Below arrow, normal hypodermal tissue pattern, with layer of brachysclereids. Above, regeneration of similar layer below wound. (*From Bloch.*)

At this point, however, the four or five cell rows next the outside often form thick, lignified walls and develop into brachysclereids. The difference between these cells and their unlignified neighbors is not evident at the last cell division nor can it be traced through any cell lineage. It arises as these two types of cells become mature. The occurrence of lignification is apparently related to the position of cells with reference to the surface of the root and thus probably to such an environmental factor as an oxygen or water gradient. When a root of *Monstera* is wounded in such a manner that the parenchyma cells of the inner cortex are now exposed to a new, artificially produced surface, they become thick-walled brachysclereids (Bloch, 1944; Fig. 8-22). When Wardlaw isolated the central core of the shoot meristem by vertical incisions, he observed that the cylinder of vascular tissue regenerating inside the core developed at a constant distance from the new surface made by the cuts (p. 238).

In a few instances where the normal ontogeny may be completed under a given environment, exceptionally favorable conditions will enable the plant to realize developmental potencies which it never would display otherwise. Thus Bloch (1935*b*) has shown that in *Tradescantia fluminensis,* which typically has bundle sheaths with only thin-walled cells, wounding may so stimulate differentiation that thick-walled sheath cells, similar to those in related species of *Tradescantia,* may be formed. Here the ontogenetic cycle has been extended beyond its normal course, either in reversion to a former evolutionary level or toward the realization of developmental potencies not yet normally expressed by this species, though common in related ones.

Often the whole histological pattern may be affected. In air roots of orchids growing freely, adventitious roots are produced on all sides; but if the root is in contact with a support, these lateral roots are formed only next the support, presumably because of differences in moisture or other factors on the two sides (Bloch, 1935*a*). Anatomical differences are also evident in these two root sectors.

In differentiation, the role of specific substances, particularly growth substances, is important (p. 390). Root-forming substances, shoot-forming substances, flower-forming substances, and others have been postulated. That a substance by itself has a specific organ-forming character is probably too naive a conception, but certainly auxin and various other hormones and growth substances are effective as stimuli which call forth specific morphogenetic responses in the plant. Auxin influences the growth of cambium, the development of vessels, and other histological processes. It also inhibits certain activities. Beneath epidermal cells that regenerate new shoots (p. 245) vascular tissue often differentiates, presumably because of a substance coming from the young bud, which thus is able to establish a connection with the main vascular system. Camus has shown that buds grafted to pieces of fleshy root in tissue culture induce the differentiation of vascular tissue in parenchyma cells beneath them, and Wetmore found that auxin alone does the same thing (p. 405).

In general, environmental factors seem chiefly to affect the later stages in cellular differentiation and especially the character of the cell wall. The fundamental pattern of a structure is less affected than are its quantitative expression and the size and character of the cells that compose it.

What a cell or tissue will do depends in part upon its innate genetic potentialities and in part upon the environment in which it happens to be. Cells possess different degrees of reactivity to environmental differences. In some, this is small, and the fate of the cell is therefore rather fixed and limited, regardless of its environment. In others its developmental repertoire is much wider, and it may be greatly influenced by the conditions which surround it. It should be remembered that the degree of a cell's reactivity is not constant but that it may vary with the position that the cell occupies in the whole developmental pattern and in the ontogeny of the individual and especially that it depends upon the point that the cell has reached in its own cycle of maturity. The developmental expression of the genetic constitution of a plant and of its various parts is therefore not fixed and constant but is continually changing.

PHYSIOLOGICAL DIFFERENTIATION

All differentiation, of course, has its basis in the physiological activities of living substance, but it can usually be recognized most readily when these activities result in the production of visible differences in structure. It is such differences that have chiefly been considered in the preceding pages. Physiological differentiation itself, however, can often be demonstrated, and experiments in this field offer hope for the solution of many developmental problems. A few typical examples will be discussed briefly here and others in later pages.

The diversities in structure between root and shoot are doubtless the expressions of fundamental physiological differences. One of the most conspicuous of these is in vitamin synthesis. By culture methods it is possible to grow roots indefinitely from a bit of root tip. Such root cultures must be provided with the necessary mineral salts and also with a source of carbohydrates (usually sucrose). These alone prove to be not enough to secure indefinite growth, and they must be supplemented by small amounts of certain vitamins, in most cases thiamin. It is clear, therefore, that such roots are unable to synthesize this vitamin. Since thiamin is known to be present in the shoots of plants, this is evidently the region in which it is produced. In nature, roots must obtain their supply from the shoots. Just when this physiological differentiation first occurs is not known, but it is probably at the time when root and shoot are set apart in early embryology.

It has been shown that root and shoot also differ in their ability to synthesize certain alkaloids. Tobacco shoots can be grafted onto tomato roots, and leaves and stems of such shoots are free from nicotine (Dawson, 1942). If tomato shoots are grafted on tobacco roots, however, the tomato tissues contain large quantities of this alkaloid. It is therefore obvious that in such cases the capacity to synthesize nicotine is confined to the tobacco *root* and is not possessed by its leaves, as has commonly been assumed. Certain other alkaloids (as quinine) can be shown by such experiments to be synthesized in both roots and shoots. The fact that a substance occurs in a certain part of the plant is evidently no proof that it is formed there. This technique of reciprocal grafting provides a useful tool for the demonstration of physiological differentiation of this sort.

Studies of geotropic reaction of typical roots and stems show that they are also different in their response to auxin, the growth of roots being inhibited by concentrations which stimulate growth of stems, a fact which explains the geotropic reactions characteristic of these two organs. They differ physiologically in other respects, for Collander (1941) has shown that certain cations may be differentially distributed between root and shoot, sodium and manganese being more abundant in the former and calcium, strontium, and lithium in the latter.

Differences between vegetative and reproductive phases of the life cycle are sometimes physiological as well as structural. Many early workers (Sachs, 1880, 1882) noticed the difference between "blind" and "flowering" stems, the former when used as cuttings producing vegetative growth only and the latter, flowering shoots. This difference has now been shown to be related to the presence of some substance or substances which induce flowering (p. 397). Torrey (1953) reports that three synthetic substances which inhibit root elongation have specific effects on the acceleration or retardation of the differentiation of xylem and of phloem.

Physiological differentiation must evidently be important in sex determination, and chemical differences between the sexes have been found by several workers. By the Manoilov reaction, for example, staminate and pistillate plants of poplar can be distinguished, as well as "plus" and "minus" strains of *Mucor* (Satina and Blakeslee, 1926). Stanfield (1944) has described chemical differences between staminate and pistillate plants of *Lychnis dioica*. Aitchison (1953) found that in several genera the sexes were unlike in oxidase activity, this being greater in some cases in males and in others in females. Hoxmeier (1953), working with *Cannabis* and *Spinacia*, reports that the tissue fluids of staminate plants are more acid than those of pistillate ones. In *Cannabis*, Cheuvart (1954) observed differences between the sexes in chlorophyll content, especially in the rate at which this is reduced at the time of flowering. Reinders-Gouwentak and van der Veen (1953) found that in poplar the female catkins tended to stimulate wood formation on the stem below them whereas males did not, suggesting a difference between the sexes here in the production of a growth substance.

Regular changes in the physiological activity of the series of successive leaves on a plant, related to both position and age, have been observed by various workers. Dormer (1951) determined the dry weight per unit of length in successive internodes of *Vicia* from the apex downward and found that during the unfolding of the ninth leaf there was a sudden change in the distribution of the dry-weight increment. The nutritional history of an internode thus seems to be a function of its position in the stem. The developing seedling has also been shown to change in its physiological character. Rietsma, Satina, and Blakeslee (1953a), by growing *Datura* embryos in tissue culture, have shown that the minimal sucrose requirement falls steadily from the earliest stages to the mature embryo.

A notable example of physiological ontogeny has been reported by Wetmore (1954). In the developing fern sporeling the first leaves are two-lobed. These are followed by three-lobed ones and finally by pinnate leaves in which an apical cell has appeared. Shoot apices from small fern sporelings, cultured in mineral nutrients and various concentrations of sucrose, grew into whole plants. Where the concentration was low, only two-lobed leaves were formed. Higher concentrations produced three-lobed ones and still higher, pinnate ones. The normal ontogenetic progression here thus seems to be related to an increasing supply of sucrose.

Metabolic gradients are marked by various physiological differences, especially as to the rates of reactions. Prévot (1940) observed that respiration in the apical region of the root of several genera was greater than in the more distal regions. This is not always the case, however, in shoot meristems (p. 73).

Wardlaw (1952c) has found that the nutritional status of the apical region in ferns has an important effect on the size and character of the leaves and stelar structure. Apices that normally produce large and complex leaves and an elaborate vascular system, if reduced in size by poor nutrition, will form "juvenile" leaves and simpler stelar patterns.

Biochemical differences of many sorts, presumably indicating physiological diversity, can be shown in cells and tissues. Differential staining reactions are familiar examples of this. Differences in hydrogen-ion concentration between cells visibly alike can be shown by the use of indicators. Blakeslee (1921) demonstrated the presence of two chemically different areas of cells in the petals of certain races of *Rudbeckia* with solid petal color by dipping the petals into phenolphthalein. Sometimes differentiation is shown by the occurrence of natural pigments, as in the root tips of *Phalaris arundinacea* where the trichoblasts are pigmented but the cells that are not to produce root hairs are colorless. Van Fleet's work on the histochemical differentiation of the developing endodermis has been mentioned (p. 197). Microchemical tests of various sorts being out differences between many kinds of cells, even in early development, such as tannin cells, crystal cells, and latex ducts. Spectrometric demonstration of differences in distribution of the nucleic acids are among notable recent examples of this sort of analysis.

Less work has been done in demonstrating physical differences between cells. In fern prothallia Akdik (1938) and Gratzy-Wardengg (p. 121) found a definite pattern of differences in osmotic concentration over the surface of the prothallus, and this seems to be related to differences in behavior of these regions in regeneration. In iris leaves Weber (1941) showed that the first indication of differentiation of stomatal mother cells is a difference in osmotic concentration.

Much cellular differentiation is due to changes in the cell wall. Boysen-Jensen (1957) in a series of papers has demonstrated various wall changes in the differentiation of root hairs with particular references to the action of enzymes.

These and many other observations show that morphological differentiation has its physiological concomitants. To explain how these arise during development is a major task of the student of differentiation.

DIFFERENTIATION WITHOUT GROWTH

There are a number of instances among the fungi where development of the fruiting structures does not take place until the vegetative phase of the life cycle has ended and no more food is absorbed from the environment. Growth, in the broader sense of the term, is therefore completed before differentiation begins, and the latter process can be studied without the complications that are usually involved when growth accompanies it. One of the .most notable examples of this is furnished by the Acrasiaceae, a family of the slime molds.

The vegetative individual in these plants is a single amoeboid cell, or *myxamoeba*. These multiply profusely by simple division and live chiefly on several species of bacteria. They can readily be grown in culture. After vegetative life has gone on for some time and when external conditions are favorable, a large number of these myxamoebae, in a group of from several thousand to about 150,000, begin to move toward a center of aggregation, streaming in from all sides and piling up into a mass of cells, the *pseudoplasmodium* (Fig. 8-23). This is a millimeter or two in length, is elongate in form, and somewhat resembles a small grub. It is surrounded by a thin sheet of slime. By the time that this aggregation begins, all vegetative growth has ceased, so that in the life cycle of these plants growth (in the sense of increase by assimilation) and differentiation are separate from each other in time.

The process of aggregation seems to be controlled by the production of a chemotactically active substance, *acrasin*. The timing and mechanism of this process have been discussed by Shaffer (1957). As to what determines the origin of these centers of aggregation, however, there is some difference of opinion. Sussman (1952) believes that a few *initiator cells* appear in the population and attract their neighbors into a many-celled aggregate.

Wilson (1952) presents evidence that aggregation has its origin in a sexual process, two myxamoebae fusing early in aggregation and establishing a center. Other fusions occur later and are followed by meiosis. The zygotes can be distinguished by their greater size.

In the pseudoplasmodium the myxamoebae do not fuse but each circulates freely among its neighbors, and the whole mass moves over the surface of the substratum by means that are not yet clearly understood. This body of separate cells, however, is not without some degree of differentiation. It is elongated in the direction of its movement, which is toward the light. The apical end is slightly pointed and lifted above the rest and is richer in acrasin than the other regions. It is the part of the mass that is

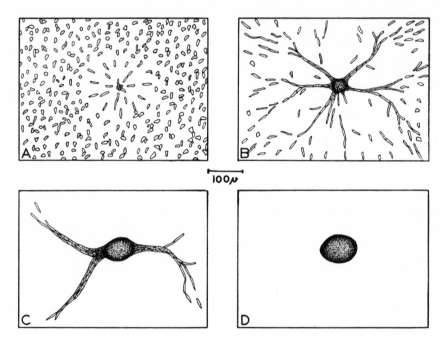

Fig. 8-23. *Dictyostelium.* Stages in aggregation of myxamoebae into a pseudoplasmodium. (*From J. T. Bonner.*)

sensitive to the stimulation of light and seems to serve as a directive center for the whole. A pseudoplasmodium from which the apex has been removed will stop its motion and settle down at once to form a fruiting body.

Two groups of cells may be distinguished in the pseudoplasmodium. Those near the apex and destined to form the stalk of the sorocarp are somewhat larger than the ones in the posterior region, which will later form spores. The proportion between these two types is maintained by a regulatory process irrespective of the size of the whole mass. Some cell division continues in the pseudoplasmodium but the rate is different in its two regions. If the apical and the basal halves of the pseudoplasmodium are experimentally separated, each will form a sorocarp, but the one from the apical half produces the larger spores. Despite these evidences of the beginning of differentiation, cells in one group can be changed to resemble those of the other, and every cell apparently is totipotent. If a few cells are removed from the mass they are no longer subject to its organizing control, and if food is present, they will become vegetative cells again and proceed to multiply.

That the pseudoplasmodial axis is polarized is shown not only by the difference in structure of its two ends but by their behavior. K. Raper (1940*b*) performed a series of grafting experiments between plasmodia that could be distinguished by their color, one group having fed on red bacteria. The apex, if cut off and placed at the rear of another plasmo-

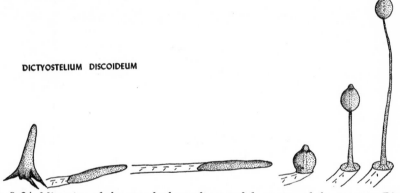

DICTYOSTELIUM DISCOIDEUM

FIG. 8–24. Migration of the pseudoplasmodium and formation of the sorus in *Dictyostelium discoideum*. (*From J. T. Bonner.*)

dium, will not fuse with this one but will start off by itself. It fuses with the apical end of a decapitated plasmodium (Fig. 6-15). If an apex is cut off and placed next the side of an intact plasmodial mass it will attach itself there and finally draw off a considerable mass of cells and establish a separate plasmodium. The tip of the mass sometimes splits, and in this case two are formed. If two happen to come together, they may fuse into a single one of double size.

Morphogenetically the most significant part of the life history is the formation of the stalked fruiting body, or sorocarp. After a few hours of migration, or when a pseudoplasmodium reaches drier surroundings, it stops moving and attaches itself firmly to the substratum by a disk of differentiated cells (Fig. 8-24). The cells of the apical region, from which the stalk is to be formed, become large and vacuolate and each is enclosed in a cellulose sheath. As this is happening, they are pushed down into the pseudoplasmodium by other prestalk cells climbing up around them which in turn become stalk cells (Fig. 8-25). As Bonner describes it, "The process is the reverse of a fountain; the cells pour up the outside to become trapped and solidified in the central core which is the stalk. In so doing the whole structure rises into the air until all the prestalk cells have been used up." This description applies to the species most commonly studied, *Dictyostelium discoideum*. In *D. mucoroides* and *D. purpureum*, however, the stalk begins to be formed during the brief migration of the pseudoplasmodium.

About 10 per cent of the myxamoebae take part in the formation of disk and stalk. The others, still moving freely over one another, follow the growing tip of the stalk upward in a body and (in *Dictyostelium*)

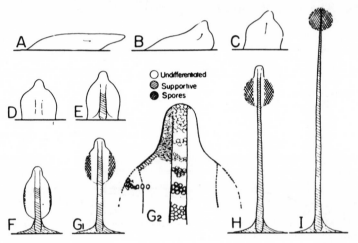

Fig. 8-25. *Dictyostelium discoideum*. Diagram of sorocarp formation. A, B, migrating pseudoplasmodium. (*From J. T. Bonner.*)

form a spherical mass of cells, the sorus, at its summit. Here each myxamoeba rounds up to make a dry spore, and these spores are later carried away by air currents, each now capable of developing into a myxamoeba. Wilson presents evidence that some mitotic division occurs before spore formation.

In the genus *Polysphondylium* there is not only an apical sorus but several whorls of lateral stalks along the main one, each terminating in a smaller sorus, so that the sorocarp becomes a structure of considerable complexity.

These plants, though so unlike higher ones, have constant generic and specific differences (Fig. 8-26). If myxamoebae belonging to two species grow intermingled in the same culture or if pseudoplasmodia of two species are crushed and experimentally mixed, the cells in time sort them-

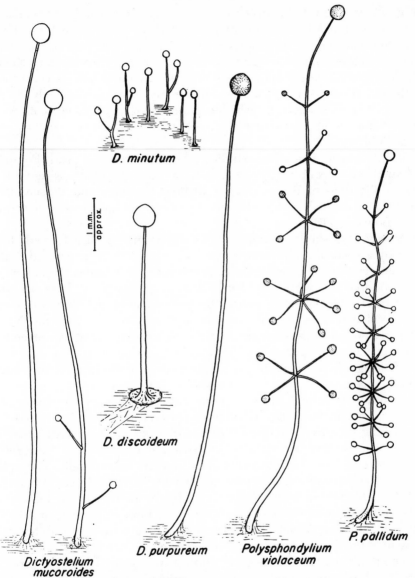

Fɪɢ. 8-26. Sorocarps of various members of the Acrasiaceae. (*From K. B. Raper.*)

selves out and form sorocarps typical of each species. The specific character of the sorocarp can be shown to be carried by its spores.

Sussman (1955) has found a number of mutants of *Dictyostelium discoideum* in which the aggregating groups, and consequently the size of the sorocarps they form, is much smaller than normal. In some of these the fruiting body consists of as few as 12 cells but it still retains the form, proportions, and cellular structure of the larger ones, surely a remarkable example of the inherent formativeness of these cells. Here form determination finds one of its simplest expressions. The behavior of the myxamoebae in the Acrasiaceae reminds one of the well-known instance among the sponges where the entire body may be separated into its constituent cells and these later will come together and re-form the body of the sponge. The mechanism by which such morphogenetic movements occur in the slime molds and sponges presents some of the most baffling problems in biology.

The Acrasiaceae have been studied intensively in recent years. For more detailed accounts of experimental work on them the reader is referred to the publications of Bonner, Raper, Shaffer, Sussman, and Wilson, some of which are listed in the bibliography. The field has been reviewed by J. T. Bonner (1959).

A somewhat similar example of the differentiation of a formed structure by a mass of undifferentiated cells is shown by a specialized family of bacteria, the Myxobacteriaceae. This is a group in which the individual is a rod-like cell which divides by transverse fission. it lives on other bacteria. In the vegetative period these cells may be distributed throughout a colonial mass or may occur in radiating strands or ridges. Myxobacteria do not possess flagella, but their gliding or creeping movements are in some way associated with the abundant slime that they secrete. In the fruiting phase the individuals aggregate into masses, probably under the chemotactic influence of an acrasin-like substance, but no true pseudoplasmodium is formed. In simple types the aggregates are merely rounded mounds, but in forms like *Chondromyces crocatus* complex stalked and branching systems are formed. Here, as the rods move upward, piling on top of one another, the mass is constricted at the base and the layer of slime secreted by the advancing rods hardens into a stalk. The apical mass of cells continues to move upward and divides to form branches which culminate in multicellular cysts. In the production of these complex fruiting structures by the migration of individual cells, and in the specific character which these structures display, the Myxobacteriaceae resemble the Acrasiaceae, though the groups are not closely related. The same morphogenetic problem as to how a specifically formed structure is produced by independent and undifferentiated cells is presented by both groups of plants.

A general account of the Myxobacteriaceae has been written by Quinlan and Raper for Volume XV of the "Encyclopedia of Plant Physiology."

Another case resembling these but involving much larger size and a higher level of organization is to be found in the development of the fruiting body in the fleshy fungi, such as the common mushroom, *Agaricus campestris*. The vegetative body here is a much branched mycelium which absorbs food from the organic matter in the soil. When it has a good supply of this, and other conditions are also favorable, the mycelial material is mobilized into a rounded mass just below the surface of the ground. This develops into a "button" and then into the familiar mushroom fructification, with its high degree of differentiation. This is composed not of a mass of cells that are attached in a firm tissue, as in the higher plants, but of a body of tangled hyphae, free to slide past each other. As the stalk increases in length, these hyphae tend to be oriented parallel to its axis, though at the base and in the pileus ("umbrella") they remain much tangled. Growth takes place primarily by elongation of the cells of the hyphae and is entirely at the expense of food already available in the mycelium. How, from such an apparent chaos of snarled threads, the very precisely formed fruiting body of the fungus grows and differentiates poses the same difficult problem as does the development of the sorocarp in the Acrasiaceae, and one lying at the heart of the morphogenetic process. Bonner, Kane, and Levey (1956) have reexamined the development of *Agaricus* and confirmed and extended the results of the classic studies of de Bary, Atkinson, and Magnus, but the problem has attracted relatively little attention in recent years. The development of these fungus fruiting bodies, however, offers to the student of the problems of differentiation and form determination some of the most promising material available for his work.

CHAPTER 9

Regeneration

In the preceding chapters there have been considered those morphogenetic phenomena which manifest themselves in normal development. Polarity, symmetry, differentiation, and the wide variety of correlative manifestations evident as the plant and its parts progress from embryo to maturity are all indications of the orderly control of growth processes which is the visible aspect of biological organization. But the progress of development is not always unimpeded. Accident and injuries of various sorts may happen to the growing plant which remove a part of its tissues or divide it into two or more incomplete portions. In nature this may result from the attacks of fungi, insects, or higher animals; from mechanical injuries of many sorts; or from unfavorable conditions which impede the functions of its organs. The changes that follow such injuries, losses, or functional disturbances often throw much light on morphogenetic activities, and one of the most fruitful methods of studying developmental processes has been to observe the consequences which follow their experimental disturbance. Indeed, this is the only way at present by which many of these processes can be investigated at all.

This field of morphogenetic research is not as active today as it was in earlier years, and many of the most important papers in it go back to some decades ago. For a review of the earlier literature the student is referred to McCallum (1905), Kupfer (1907), and Goebel (1908). Bünning (1955) has discussed some of the recent work.

An important fact which such studies reveal is that the organism shows a tendency to restore or replace parts that have been removed and thus *to produce again a complete individual.* To this general process, which includes a wide range of developmental phenomena, the term *regeneration* is commonly applied. Regenerative activities are much more common in plants, with their less highly organized bodies, than in animals and can often be subjected to a more complete developmental analysis.

Regeneration can be brought about not only by the removal of a part but by isolating it physiologically from the rest of the plant. In a young bean plant, for example, if the epicotyl is decapitated the buds in the axils of the cotyledons will grow into shoots, thus replacing the leafy shoot that would have grown from the epicotyl; but these buds may also be induced to grow by chilling a portion of the epicotyledonary stem and thus preventing the interchange of stimuli or substances between it and the tissues below (Child and Bellamy, 1919).

In general, the more simple and undifferentiated a plant is, the more completely will it restore missing parts; and the more specialized and differentiated it is, the less regenerative capacity it will show. Early developmental stages are thus more likely to regenerate readily than later ones, and groups lower in the phylogenetic scale than those of higher position. Ability to regenerate is often completely lost.

The origin of regenerative powers in plants and animals is sometimes explained as the result of natural selection, much as in the case of other traits. That a long process of competition and selection conferred the ability to repair almost every type of injury seems unlikely. However this may be, the developmental activities in regeneration are not essentially different in their origin and control from those which occur in normal development. In both, the production of a single, complete individual is the final result. The factors involved in regeneration seem neither more nor less difficult to understand than those in normal ontogeny, nor do they require a fundamentally different explanation. Both are manifestations of general developmental control, a fundamental self-regulation in the individual. Both seem to be the result of the same formative process.

Regeneration is a term that has been variously defined. The author proposes to use it here in the broadest sense, as *the tendency shown by a developing organism to restore any part of it which has been removed or physiologically isolated and thus to produce a complete whole.* This covers processes from wound-healing to the reproduction of adventive structures and vegetative multiplication, in which many different activities are involved.

In general, the method of restoration of lost parts is different in plants and in animals. Animal tissues are composed of thin-walled cells, usually able to divide and often to migrate. Most plant cells at maturity are relatively thick-walled and ordinarily do not divide or grow further, though it has been shown that many retain the power to do so. Regeneration in animals, therefore, consists largely in a reorganization of the remaining portion of the organ or body. In plants, on the contrary, this type of regeneration is limited to meristematic or rapidly growing regions or to the relatively rare cases where cells become embryonic again. Much more commonly, at least in the higher types, replacement of lost parts results from the growth of dormant buds or primordia or the development of new ones. Such primordia arise from cells in the plant body which remain alive and are potentially meristematic. These primordia, often very numerous, remain dormant under ordinary conditions.

This fact raises the question of what it is, if these primordia are capable of growing and forming new organs, that prevents them from doing so. The concept of the organism as a balance between stimulatory and inhibitory factors suggests itself here, but the problem remains as to what localizes and correlates the activity of these factors so that a specific organic system is established, maintained, and restored, and what stops the regenerative process when this has been accomplished.

It should be remembered that, in spite of modifications acquired during the process of differentiation, all the cells are probably identical genetically, save for occasional polyploidy. The potentially meristematic cells thus serve, so to speak, as a "germ plasm" or genetic reserve which can direct the processes of regeneration and further development. Each cell, at least in theory, is capable of producing an entire individual.

In regeneration, mature or nearly mature cells may sometimes become embryonic again and then undergo changes that restore a disturbed tissue pattern. How this is accomplished is of much interest for morphogenesis. In it the first visible step is usually a marked increase in the amount of cytoplasm and in the size of the nucleus and an acceleration of metabolic activity. The wall also tends to become thinner. This process, commonly termed *dedifferentiation,* has been described and the literature reviewed by Buvat (1944, 1945, 1950). Dedifferentiated cells assume the character of meristematic ones and can divide and grow. The tissue thus formed may then differentiate again in conformity with its new function or position in the regenerated structure.

REGENERATION IN THE LOWER PLANTS

Among the thallophytes and bryophytes, with their simpler bodies and lower level of organization, regeneration is relatively common. It will be discussed briefly in these groups before taking up the more complex aspects of it that vascular plants display.

In most of the lower plants single cells or groups of cells have the ability to develop readily into a whole plant, and in many instances they do so regularly as a means of vegetative reproduction. Extreme instances of this are the conversion of vegetative cells into specialized nonsexual reproductive cells such as zoospores and others.

Even when not thus differentiated for reproduction, the cells of many algae are readily separable from the loosely organized thallus and grow into new plants, as in *Callithamnion* (Weide, 1938) and *Cladophora* (Schoser, 1956). In the last genus the cells may be separated from one another by plasmolysis, and each then grows into a new plant. Among simpler fungi almost any adult cell on isolation will give rise to a new mycelium. Kerl (1937) found that single cells from the surface of *Pyronema confluens* would do this. Such instances could be multiplied almost indefinitely.

Individual cells, if injured, will often restore themselves, especially large ones like those of *Vaucheria* (Weissenböck, 1939), *Dasycladus* (Figdor, 1910), and *Acetabularia* (Hämmerling, 1936) or the coenocytes of *Bryopsis* and *Caulerpa* (Janse, 1910; Winkler, 1900; Dostál, 1926). In such algae as *Sphacelaria*, which grow by an apical cell, this cell may be replaced, if injured, by the cell next below it, which first undergoes considerable reorganization (Zimmermann, 1923). Other cases have been described. Höfler (1934) observed in the filamentous alga *Griffithsia* that, if a cell dies, the one above it will send a tube either through it or around it which makes connection with the cell below and thus restores the continuity of the living filament.

In the early development of certain animal embryos, if one of the first two blastomeres is killed, the other develops into an entire organism. A somewhat similar instance in plants occurs in *Fucus*. Here, after the fertilized egg has formed two cells, an apical and a basal (rhizoidal) one, the apical cell will produce a new rhizoid at the basal pole if the first is destroyed (Kniep, 1907). Setchell (1905) in his studies of the kelps describes the way in which a stipe, if the blade is cut off from its tip, will regenerate a new one from the cut surface. This commonly happens in nature where these plants are buffeted by the waves, for there has developed an intercalary meristem near the leaf base which becomes active when the blade is removed. Killian (1911) describes the way in which an injured stem is reconstituted in *Laminaria digitata*.

Some of the most remarkable cases of regeneration occur in the fruiting bodies of the fleshy fungi—toadstools, mushrooms, bracket fungi, and similar types. These are formed from masses of tangled hyphae which do not adhere to their neighbors as do cells in higher plants but are merely packed together in a weft of tangled threads. Even so, they tend, if injured, to restore the missing portions and produce a normal sporophore. This has been observed in *Stereum* by Goebel (1908), in *Agaricus* by Magnus (1906), and in other fleshy fungi. Under favorable conditions almost any part of one of these fruiting bodies will restore portions of its tissues that are removed. Such structures provide promising material for studies in regeneration. Brefeld and Weir maintain that every cell of *Coprinus* has the potentiality of producing an entire sporophore.

Among bryophytes, the hepatics regenerate with particular readiness. Early work with these plants has been reviewed by Correns (1899). The process here is a common means of reproduction. In *Sphaerocarpos*, Rickett (1920) found that regeneration occurs from single cells (or sometimes groups of adjacent cells) from almost anywhere on the thallus. At first the mass of cells is globular, cylindrical, or ribbon-like but it soon develops into a typical thallus much as does a germinating spore.

In a study of vegetative reproduction in *Metzgeria*, Evans (1910) observed that certain cells on the thallus dedifferentiate and that each then grows into a gemma from which a new plant arises. The distribution of these regenerative cells is not a random one, however. A robust thallus produces no gemmae, and they are fewer in plants that bear sex organs. If the apical region is very active, there are no gemmae near it. If a piece of thallus is isolated, however, gemmae arise in it abundantly. Evidently there are factors in this plant that tend to inhibit regeneration by its cells.

Plantlets are frequently produced from single cells in the leaves of Jungermanniales, and here they often, though not always, develop much as spores do. It is sometimes difficult to tell whether they come from ordinary vegetative cells or from ones that are predisposed to produce them. Fulford (1944, 1954) has described many cases of reproductive regeneration in these plants.

Many mosses also regenerate readily. The early work here has been reviewed by Heald (1898). Protonemata and, from these, new plants arise on the stem of some mosses but rarely from the leaves unless the latter are detached (Gemmell, 1953). Here they grow chiefly from the surface cells of the midrib.

Morphogenetically, the most significant aspect of moss regeneration is that under appropriate conditions protonemata develop not only from the gametophyte but from sporophyte tissue, both seta and capsule, and thus are diploid. From these diploid gametophytes, tetraploid sporophytes can be produced. This possibility was first discovered by the Marchal brothers (1907–1911) and opened up a wide field for exploration. Its genetic and physiological aspects have been explored by F. von Wettstein (1924) and his students (p. 437). In several cases (as by Springer, 1935, with *Phascum*) sporogonia have been observed to develop directly and apogamously from diploid gametophytes without a sexual process. Still more remarkable, Bauer (1956) observed that diploid protonemata of another moss, *Georgia pellucida*, under certain conditions form buds which do not develop into leafy gametophytes, as ordinarily happens in such cases, but produce sporogonia directly. Spores in these develop rarely, but when they do they germinate into normal haploid protonemata.

Regeneration of diploid gametophytes from sporophytes of *Anthoceros* was accomplished by Rink (1935) through cutting away portions of the sporophyte. Here the diploid thalli are smaller and more irregular in shape than the haploid ones.

REGENERATION IN THE HIGHER PLANTS

Among vascular plants there is a much higher degree of differentiation than in lower forms and as a consequence the processes of regeneration are more complex. In these plants we may recognize, for convenience, three rather different types of regenerative activities. *Reconstitution*, or regeneration proper, includes those cases in which, as in animal regeneration, there is a reorganization of the embryonic tissue by which its original structure is re-formed. This is usually limited to truly embryonic regions, such as growing points and young embryos, and to structures where there is a reorganization of the tissue pattern by dedifferentiation and subsequent redifferentiation. *Restoration* describes the wide range of cases where missing tissues or organs are replaced through meristematic activity arising in adjacent regions. This may result from the activation of dormant buds or primordia already present or in the formation of new ones such as occurs in the origin of new roots and shoots in the familiar processes of vegetative propagation. *Reproductive regeneration*, or vegetative reproduction, involves the separation, by natural means, of a part of the vegetative body from the rest and its establishment as a new plant, a process which often occurs in the lower groups. Similar cases are those where plantlets develop on the leaves and drop off to form new individuals. These are all specialized instances of the ability of the plant, under favorable conditions, to produce a new whole from a part of its body, an ability that comes from the totipotency of its various members.

Reconstitution

This process, the reorganization of living material by which the normal structure is restored when disturbed by outer circumstances, is relatively uncommon in plants, since truly embryonic conditions persist in them for only a relatively short time before changing into a mature state where reorganization is difficult. Such reconstitution as does occur is of two sorts. In one, truly embryonic or meristematic tissues may be reshaped into a new whole. In the other, tissue already well along toward maturity may undergo a certain degree of dedifferentiation and redifferentiation so that its structure is reorganized and the original pattern, at least in part, reconstituted.

Meristematic Reconstitution. Among the simplest cases, and one which not infrequently occurs in nature, is cleavage polyembryony. In many conifers (Buchholz, 1926), though less commonly in angiosperms, the early embryo rudiment, carried down into the endosperm at the tip of the suspensors and still consisting of only a few cells, divides and develops into two or more parts (Fig. 9-1). These all grow for a time but usually only one survives and develops into the embryo of the seed. A portion of the original embryo thus reconstitutes a complete whole. This recalls the not infrequent cases among animals where one fertilized egg produces two or more individuals (as in identical twins) or where a single blastomere, experimentally isolated, will form a whole.

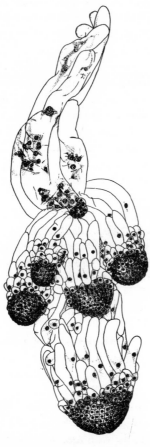

FIG. 9-1. Cleavage polyembryony in *Torreya.* This group of young embryos have all come from a single fertilized egg by cleavage. (*From Buchholz.*)

It is with the terminal meristems of the older plant axis, however, that most of the experimental work on regeneration has been carried on. In roots it is generally agreed by observers that if only the extreme tip is removed, about ½ to ¾ mm., a new growing point will regenerate directly at the wound surface from the underlying tissue of the plerome. If a little more is cut off, regeneration is only partial and chiefly by the formation of new growing centers in the outer portion of the root. If still more is removed, true reconstitution ceases and a callus is formed with adventitious roots growing out from it. The early papers of Prantl (1874) and Simon (1904) on angiosperms and of Stingl (1905) on gymnosperms present the basic facts, which have been reviewed by Nemec (1905).

More recently Torrey (1957*b*) has studied the regeneration of decapitated roots grown in culture media and as affected by auxin. If an abundance of auxin was present, the vascular cylinder of the new roots was hexarch instead of the normal triarch. Such a root reverted to triarch again if returned to the usual medium. Torrey interprets these changes as due to the direct effect of auxin on the size of the meristematic tip, the structure of which evidently is not determined by the mature tissue farther back.

If the young root is split lengthwise, scar tissue forms on the inner portion of the cut surface but each tip will become reorganized into a new and complete meristem and will finally reconstitute a normal root (Lopriore, 1892). This argues against the idea that there is a single apical cell in the root. Ball (1956) split the hypocotyl tip of a *Ginkgo* embryo and found that the effect of this was evident for some distance upward in the epicotyl in the differentiation there of a divided vascular cylinder.

In the shoot meristem the situation is complicated by the presence of leaf primordia. Only the terminal dome, about 80 μ back of the actual tip, will be regenerated if it is removed. The earlier workers believed that a new apex was formed here, as in the root, by direct growth from the cut surface, and more recently Mirskaja (1929) has reported that this occurs in *Tradescantia*. Most observers, however, have found that scar tissue forms over the wound and that one or more new meristems arise at the edges of this.

Several plants have marked powers of meristematic reconstitution. In the much reduced aquatic *Podostemon ceratophyllum*, if the tip of the shoot is cut off a new one arises from a group of cells just back of the cut surface in or around a vascular bundle. A decapitated root is reconstituted in much the same way (Hammond, 1936). In *Zamia*, a new shoot will often grow out directly from the stump of an old one, usually from the region of the central cylinder (Coulter and Chrysler, 1904). Such simple and direct regeneration in plants is rare.

Karzel (1924) and others split growing shoot tips and found that each half regenerated more or less completely, depending on the species. Pilkington (1929) split simply the terminal meristem itself and observed the same result. From the tissue of dodder which remains within the host plant after the external portion of the parasite has been experimentally removed, Truscott (1958) observed the regeneration of a shoot meristem which pushed out through the surface and developed into a normal dodder shoot.

Much experimental work on the regeneration of the shoot apex has been done by Ball in *Lupinus* and *Tropaeolum* and by Wardlaw in *Primula* and several ferns. Ball (1948, 1952*a*) went still further than Pilkington and was able to split the meristematic apex into four, and later even into six, strips (each still connected basally with the axis) and found that each was able to reconstitute a whole shoot unless its tip had been reduced below a minimal size. Vascular tissue tended to be poorly developed in it until leaves were formed by the new shoot.

Both Ball (1952*b*) and Wardlaw (1950) isolated the central core of the shoot meristem from the rest of the axis by three or four longitudinal incisions (Fig. 4-14), thus leaving the meristematic dome (or the apical cell and its neighbors) connected with the vascular tissues below only by a plug of pith tissue. Both investigators found that this isolated tip continued to grow and in time produced procambial tissue independent of that in the axis below. In the flowering plants studied this differentiated basipetally and finally joined the vascular system of the main axis. In the ferns, however, it did not do so. At the apex of the isolated core new primordia were formed and (except in ferns) if this core was not below a minimal size, it finally developed into a normal leafy shoot. Wardlaw observed that the phyllotaxy of the new shoot in *Primula* was continuous with that of the original axis but in Ball's material it was independent and often showed reversal of the earlier spiral. Wardlaw observed that the vascular tissue developing in the central core followed the outline of the cut piece and differentiated at a rather constant distance from the cut surface, suggesting that its position was dependent on a gradient of some sort (Fig. 9-2).

These experiments are of morphogenetic interest since they show that the apical meristem is a self-determining region which can produce a normal shoot without any connection, other than through undifferentiated pith cells, with the tissues below. Furthermore, Ball (1946) and others have shown that small meristem tips, growing in tissue culture, will produce entire plants. All this is not surprising, however, since many cases are known where a single cell (p. 253), without any vascular connection with other tissues at first, develops into a fully differentiated plant. It is to be expected that an active terminal meristem would do the same. Although the differentiated tissues below the meristem may not be necessary for its growth, they contribute to the character of its development, for through them come water, nutrients, and various morphogenetically important substances. The terminal meristem seems neither to be completely self-determining nor completely under the control of the rest of the plant, but the two together act as an integrated system.

Reconstitution of parts other than the meristems of the axis has often been reported. In a number of ferns such as *Gleichenia*, the leaf grows at the tip by a terminal meristem, thus perhaps harking back to the time when the leaf was a lateral branch of indeterminate growth. In most fern leaves, unlike those of angiosperms, growth continues longest at the tip and in some species the leaves root readily there. It is thus to be expected that fern leaves should sometimes reconstitute new tips if the old ones are injured or removed. Goebel (1908) with *Polypodium* and Figdor (1906) with *Scolopendrium* cut away a small bit of tissue from the growing leaf tip and found that this meristematic region was reconstituted but that a double or forked lamina was produced.

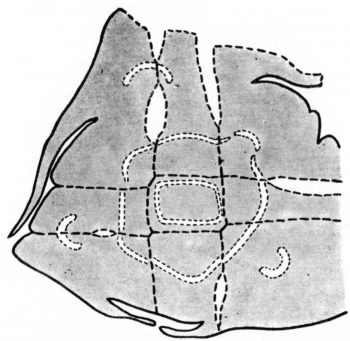

FIG. 9-2. Diagram of transverse section of apex of *Primula* in which a central plug of pith was isolated by four vertical incisions (broken lines). In this plug a new vascular cylinder has been regenerated at a constant distance from the surface. (*From Wardlaw.*)

Among higher plants, leaves of some of the Gesneriaceae are easily regenerated. In *Saintpaulia* and some species of *Streptocarpus*, Figdor (1907) split a young leaf nearly to the base along the midrib and found that a considerable amount of new lamina was regenerated from the basal part of the cut surface, which is the latest to mature. If the blade is removed from a young primary leaf of *Cyclamen*, two new blades regenerate by reconstitution of the meristematic region at the sides of the petiole apex (Winkler, 1902). Figdor also reported (1926) that if the terminal leaflet of the pinnately compound leaf of *Bryophyllum* (*Kalanchoe*) was cut off when the leaf was very small, it was partially regenerated. Other cases of such regeneration have been reported, but the leaf, doubtless because of its generally determinate growth, shows meristematic reconstitution much less readily than does root or stem.

Gametophytes sometimes display this type of regeneration. Albaum (1938*a*), confirming earlier workers, found that if the ordinary prothallium of certain ferns is cut transversely the anterior portion, near the meristematic notch, will re-form the typical heart-shaped structure again. In the posterior region this does not happen, but new adventive prothallia are produced from the cut surfaces (p. 121). Meyer (1953) reports that the meristematic region in the notch of the prothallus, and particularly its apical cell, seems to inhibit the formation of other apical cells; for if the prothallus is divided lengthwise into three parts, the central one, which includes the apical cell, will regenerate its lost portions whereas the two lateral pieces will each first produce a new apical cell and then proceed to develop into typical prothallia. True reconstitution of a meristematic region thus seems to be limited to very early developmental stages. In later ones, even though the tissue may still be meristematic, it has lost some of its morphogenetic potencies and injury will result either in simply a wound reaction or in the production of new adventitious growing points rather than in a remolding of the old one.

Reconstitution of Tissue Patterns. A somewhat different type of reconstitution occurs where the structure that is removed is not a meristem but a part already differentiated, at least to some degree. To restore the disturbed tissue pattern involves a more complex process and is rarely as complete as the reconstitution that occurs in a meristem. Where mature or nearly mature cells are part of this pattern, some of these cells must evidently become embryonic again and assume a new function in the reorganized system. There are some remarkable examples of this which provide particularly interesting morphogenetic problems.

The first step in such a reconstitution is healing of the wound itself. Wound reactions differ with the type of plant and the conditions. Cells near the wound surface generally become more active and soon, under the influence of wound hormones, cell division is initiated parallel to the surface. A phellogen here develops which forms a layer of protective cork over the wound. In many cases this is all that happens. Sometimes a callus is formed here and from it primordia of roots and shoots may develop. The phenomena of wound reactions have been reviewed by Bloch (1941, 1952). Fourcroy (1938) has discussed the same subject and particularly emphasizes the accelerating influence of wounding on differentiation and its effects on vascular anatomy.

In many plants, however, the tissues under the wound may be reorganized to some degree. This is especially true of the epidermis. In kohlrabi Vöchting (1908) observed that when the layer of wound cork was sloughed off an epidermis had developed under it which was essentially identical with that of the normal tuber and in which typical stomata were present. Cells destined to be cortical in character had been radically altered to form a tissue appropriate for their new position in the system.

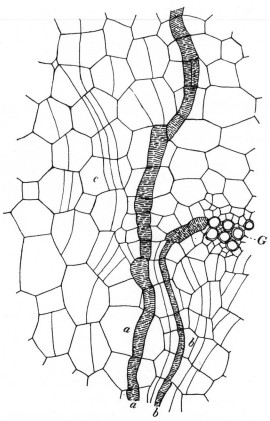

Fig. 9-3. Vascular strands *a* and *b* regenerating in parenchymatous tissue to connect strand *G* with others; *c*, an earlier stage in this process, where procambial strands are being differentiated. (*From S. Simon.*)

Such reconstitution has been reported by others. The cuticle of epidermal cells may also be regenerated if it has been sliced off (Fritz, 1935).

More deeply seated tissues may be regenerated by the redifferentiation of others, as is the exodermis in air roots of orchids (Küster, 1899; Bloch, 1926, 1935b) and hypodermal sclerenchyma (p. 218) in air roots of palms and Araceae (Bloch, 1937, 1944). In every case these newly developed tissues are appropriate in character for the place where they now are and are much like those normally present in such regions.

Somewhat more complex is the redifferentiation of vascular bundles in places where these have been severed. Simon (1908; Fig. 9-3), Nemec (1905), Sinnott and Bloch (1945), and Jacobs (1952) have studied this in various herbaceous stems. If a bundle or group of bundles is severed by a lateral incision and the region examined in longitudinal section after a week or two, a new vascular strand can be seen developing behind the incision and connecting the severed upper and lower ends of the bundle (p. 193). This strand is formed by the conversion of large, squarish parenchyma cells of the pith into xylem cells with reticulate lignified thicken-

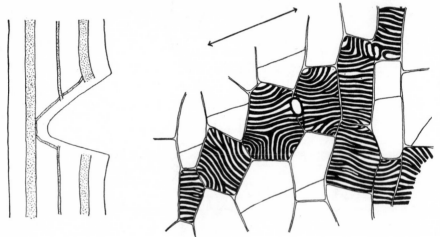

Fig. 9-4. Left, regeneration of connection between severed vascular bundles in stem of *Coleus*. Right, differentiation of parenchyma cells into reticulate xylem cells in the development of this strand. Arrow shows the direction of its development. Note new walls parallel to it. (*From Sinnott and Bloch.*)

ings (p. 194 and Fig. 9-4). Differentiation seems always to be basipetal, suggesting the downward passage of a morphogenetic substance, presumably auxin, from the upper bundle toward the lower. The regenerated strand is not directly at the cut surface but about the same distance behind it that the normal bundles are from the uninjured surface. Jost (1942) caused the plant to form these vascular bridges in many ways and finds that, although their general course is basipetal, they may develop acropetally for a while in passing around an obstacle. They do not always take the shortest route. The position of the strand seems to be determined by a gradient of some sort from the wound surface inward. It is significant that the conversion of parenchyma to xylem is an "all or none" reaction, with no cells intermediate in character.

A somewhat similar regeneration of vascular strands is to be seen in leaves where some of the veins have been cut. New strands are differentiated in the mesophyll cells which connect the severed ends. Freundlich (1908) studied the origin of these xylem strands, and Kaan-Albest (1934) followed the differentiation of new sieve tubes (Fig. 9-5). The latter do not arise, as do those of the xylem, by conversion of whole parenchyma cells, but small cells are cut out of the sides of these larger elements and join up with one another, end to end, from one cell to the next. These

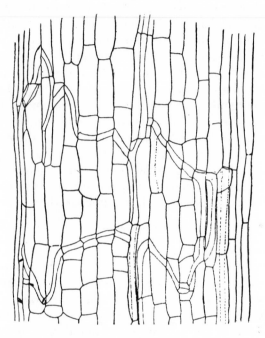

Fɪɢ. 9-5. *Impatiens.* Sieve-tube connections developing between phloem bundles, one of which has been severed. (*From Kaan-Albest.*)

phloem strands in their development suggest the fiber strands of *Luffa* (p. 197).

What are the factors, one may ask, that impel the redifferentiation of a vascular system when intercommunication among its parts has been interrupted? Auxin may be diffusing from the end of a cut bundle, but how this operates to convert a series of parenchyma cells into a vascular strand is difficult to understand. Here is differentiation in very simple expression. Doubtless the same general factors are involved as in normal development but the process takes place here on a greatly enlarged scale where it can be more readily studied than in the very small-celled tissues near the meristem. Regenerative tissues of this sort are particularly promising material for a study of cytological differentiation.

These are examples of the relatively simple reconstitution of a tissue pattern. A much more involved one is that described by Vöchting (1908) in his classic studies of regeneration in kohlrabi. If a young and growing tuber of this plant was cut transversely at about half way from the tip to base, care being taken not to injure the leaves on the basal portion, the cut surface of this portion soon began to swell and by the end of the season had developed a convex, rounded structure which in some cases restored the general form of the normal tuber except that no leaves developed on its surface. Internally, however, the complex system of bundle connections in the reconstituted half was hardly to be distinguished from that of the original portion. This provides the most remarkable example so far described of a structure already well differentiated internally which proceeded to reorganize itself and reconstitute, in almost its original form, a large mass of tissue. There was meristematic activity here, following the dedifferentiation of much of the structure near the cut surface, but it was diffuse meristematic activity like that of a leaf or fruit rather than that of a localized growing point. Studies on regeneration in this very promising material have been largely neglected in the half century since Vöchting's description of his work was published.

Restoration

Most regeneration in plants is not due to the reorganization of embryonic regions but to the onset of meristematic activity in regions adjacent to the place where loss has occurred. This leads to the production of substitute structures that restore the original whole by indirect means.

These processes are examples of compensatory correlation (p. 98) in which the balance of the organism is restored after being disturbed. As redifferentiation after injury often throws light on the problems of differentiation and tissue pattern, a study of the restoration of lost structures offers a useful means of analysis of developmental potencies and the processes of correlation.

In many cases, as the result of wounding, a callus is produced (p. 288) at the cut end of a stem or root. This often originates from the cambium but may come from other tissues. From such calluses primordia of roots and shoots commonly arise. This is the most frequent type of regeneration in the higher plants and underlies the horticultural arts of multiplication by vegetative propagation, chiefly the rooting of cuttings. This field has been reviewed from the botanical point of view by Priestley and Swingle (1929) and Swingle (1940, 1952).

Almost every plant organ has been used as a cutting—stem, root, leaf, hypocotyl, floral axis, and flowers—and all have been found to have some ability to restore lost parts. The axial organs—stem and root—are the ones most commonly employed in the practices of propagation and have been most thoroughly studied.

Stem Cuttings. In stem cuttings of dicotyledons buds develop most frequently at the apical end and roots from the basal one (p. 119) but this polarity varies considerably. The buds may be the usual axillary ones, many of which would not normally develop, or they may be accessory buds. If these are absent, dormant primordia may grow. Carlson (1950) has described the origin and distribution of dormant root initials on willow shoots. Primordia may also develop anew, from callus or from the normal tissues of the stem. Adventitious roots in young stems usually come from the pericycle but in older ones they may have a deeper origin in the vascular cambium (Plett, 1921). Mahlstede and Watson (1952) found that adventitious roots in blueberry originate in cambium or phloem and push out through vascular tissue, cortex, and epidermis. Priestley (1926a) stated a general rule that, of the two lateral meristematic regions of the axis, the phellogen is more likely to produce buds and the vascular cambium to produce roots. Morphogenetic problems here involved concern the causes of the differentiation of dormant or "reserve" primordia in particular places and especially the factors that first keep them dormant and then stimulate their development in regeneration.

Bud formation is frequent on hypocotyls and has been studied particularly by Rauh (1937). In a few species these buds normally develop into shoots. In other cases they may be present but do not develop and in still others they may be induced only by the stimulus of regeneration, after the decapitation of the hypocotyl. In *Linum usitatissimum*, the origin of these buds has been traced, in decapitated hypocotyls, to single cells of the epidermis (Crooks, 1933; Link and Eggers, 1946a) in which divisions begin to appear. A group of cells is thus produced which develops into a bud initial and finally into a shoot. Several buds may begin to grow, only one of which becomes dominant. In undecapitated hypocotyls a few epidermal cells may divide but they rarely produce buds. Bud development is induced more readily in young hypocotyls than in older ones. After a bud begins to grow, vascular strands differentiate which connect it with the main vascular cylinder (Fig. 9-6). Van Tieghem (1887) described similar bud development in the hypocotyl of *Linaria*, as did Bain (1940) in cranberry. Such hypocotyls offer a good opportunity for the study of cellular totipotency and the redifferentiation of vascular tissue.

So-called "adventitious leaves" (really reduced shoots, Rauh believes) are produced abundantly on the decapitated hypocotyl, or seedling tuber, of *Cyclamen* (Boodle, 1920; Rauh, 1937) and develop there from subepidermal cells. There are transitions here from simple leaves to fully developed buds. The great number of these buds normally produced suggests that this is a case of reproductive regeneration rather than of restoration.

The stems of most monocotyledons lack a cambium, and this somewhat limits the possibilities of regeneration of lost parts in them. Axillary buds are often present, however, and the nodes and bases of leaves remain somewhat meristematic. New roots commonly arise in these regions. Methods of regeneration and of vegetative reproduction are generally very specialized. Some members of the Juncaceae and Cyperaceae reproduce vegetatively from tips or nodes of culms, as in *Eleocharis rostellata*, where buds grow from the sterile culm tips (La Rue, 1935).

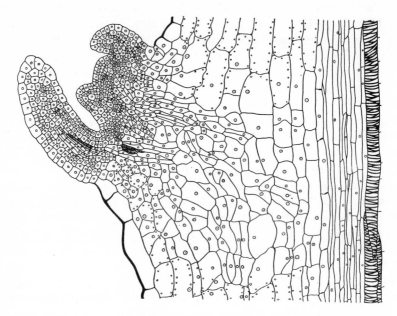

Fig. 9-6. A young adventitious bud which has grown from epidermal cells on a decapitated hypocotyl of flax. Note the cell divisions in the cortex which will give rise to a vascular connection with the stele. (*From Crooks.*)

Factors in the rooting of conifer cuttings have been discussed by Deuber (1940).

The physiological basis of such regenerative processes has been widely investigated. Gardner (1929) observed that, in both deciduous and evergreen trees, cuttings from 1-year-old stems rooted more readily than those from older ones. The influence of auxin and of various synthetic growth substances has been much emphasized (p. 391), particularly in root formation. Van der Lek (1925) found that cuttings rooted better if there were buds on them, presumably because of the production of root-stimulating substances by the buds. Discovery of the effectiveness of various organic acids in root formation has made "root hormones" of importance in horti-culture.

Bud formation, also, is influenced by physiological conditions. Miller and Skoog (1953) report that tobacco-stem segments, in sterile culture, form buds much more readily if adenine is present and that indoleacetic acid reduces their development. Both results, presumably, are due to effects on nucleic acid metabolism. Ruge (1952) and a number of earlier workers observed that a functioning chlorophyll apparatus is necessary for the successful rooting of most cuttings. Shoots with variegated leaves or in the dark root poorly. Whether this is owing to the production by the leaves of food or of a growth substance is not clear, but van Overbeek, Gordon, and Gregory (1946*b*) believe that the main function of leaves in the rooting of cuttings is simply to supply nutrition.

Hereditary tendencies may also influence the character of regeneration, as in the conversion of axillary buds into tubers in the potato (Isbell, 1931).

Root Cuttings. Under natural conditions shoots are produced by roots rather infrequently and chiefly in woody plants. In many cases roots may be used as cuttings, however. Here the restoration of lost structures by the production of adventitious roots or shoots occurs much as in the stem, shoots tending to be restored at the basal (proximal) end and roots at the apical (distal) one. Most growth is from callus. Roots show a greater tendency to form adventitious buds than do stems. Naylor (1941) finds that both structures arise from meristematic tissue produced by paren-chyma cells in the younger phloem and not from the cambium. The polar development of regenerating structures on fleshy roots has been studied by various workers (p. 124).

Way (1954) investigated regeneration on apple roots of different sizes. In some varieties the larger ones (8 to 12 mm. in diameter) produced only shoots and the smaller (3 mm.) only roots. When both were formed, the zone of shoot production (at the proximal end) extended farther distally in the wider roots, and that of root production (at the distal end) ex-tended farther proximally in the narrower ones. Way interprets these dif-ferences as due to auxin gradients, with different concentrations in large and small roots.

Buds on roots are usually endogenous in origin. In *Bryophyllum* they arise from the subepidermal layer (Ossenbeck, 1927), and Rauh finds them originating at the scars of the delicate branch roots. In *Aristolochia* and the Podostemaceae they grow from the cortex. Carlson (1938) reports that in the orchid *Pogonia* an adventitious shoot arises by enlargement and division of the surface and cortical cells at the tips of lateral roots. This forms a swelling in which a bud develops.

An important morphogenetic question concerned with regeneration from roots and one which has been rather widely discussed is whether the early primordia of new organs are "indifferent" in nature and may produce *either* buds or roots, or whether they are determined from the first to form one or the other. A bud is a young shoot and has the rudiments of leaves, which the root primordium does not have, and it should therefore presumably be easy to tell one from the other. This seems often to be difficult, however, in the very early stages, and many instances where root primordia have been reported to change into shoots, and vice versa, may be due to erroneous observation. Dore (1955) has studied the origin of young primordia in the regeneration of horseradish roots and finds that these are produced as organized meristems in close association with the scars of lateral roots and that they originate in the phellogen of the main root. He is certain that at the beginning they are capable of developing into either roots or shoots. That this is so is suggested by the fact that the ratio of buds to roots, where they can be definitely distinguished, is not constant but varies with conditions, as though neutral primordia were being tipped in one direction or the other. If this should finally prove to be the case and the existence of truly indifferent primordia be established, useful material would be provided in which to examine the very early stages in the differentiation of these two structures which soon become so dissimilar. This reminds one of the case in *Selaginella* reported by Williams (1937). Here an "angle meristem" near the tip will normally produce a rhizophore, a structure somewhat intermediate between root and shoot and which finally grows downward and forms typical roots. If the main axis of the shoot is decapitated, however, the young primordium which would have produced a rhizophore will now grow upward into a typical shoot. Mention has been made earlier (p. 71) of cases where a young leaf primordium, if isolated by deep cuts from the meristem tip, will grow into a bud-like structure.

Cuttings from Other Parts. A variety of phenomena of regeneration has been described in typical leaves and in cotyledons, scales, and carpels, as well as in inflorescences, flowers, and fruits. In contrast to the axial portion of the plant, leaves are organs of determinate growth, and the restoration of lost parts by them is thus somewhat different from the process in axial structures. It is especially common in succulent leaves.

The restoration of roots or shoots on leaves detached from the plant and with petiole placed in soil has often been observed (Stingl, 1908; and Yarwood, 1946). In such cases, after adventive roots and buds have been formed on lamina or petiole, various anatomical changes may be observed, especially a marked increase in the vascular tissue of the petiole. Furthermore, instead of being disposed in an arc, as in normal petioles, this tissue often enlarges to form a complete vascular ring. The petiole thus becomes structurally as well as functionally a stem. Winkler (1907a) reviewed cases of such conversion and studied a particularly good example of it in *Torenia asiatica.* He believed that increased transpiration is the cause of the change. Simon (1929) found essentially the same thing in *Begonia* and noted that the bundles from the young roots induced new vascular tissue only in that part of the petiole just below them, suggesting the polar distribution of a hormone. Similar results were obtained by Doyle (1915) through grafting buds onto the petioles of rooted leaves.

In leaf cuttings, adventitious structures are formed predominantly at the leaf base. Hagemann (1931), in an extensive survey of the regenerative ability of leaves, investigated 1,204 species of gymnosperms, dicoty-

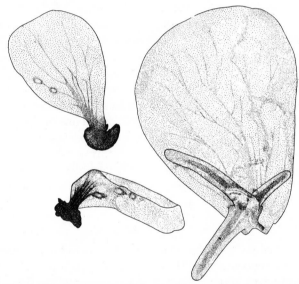

Fig. 9-7. Petals of *Epilobium angustifolium* which produced roots when cultured on nutrient agar. (*From La Rue.*)

ledons, and monocotyledons. He found that some of these showed no restoration, a very few formed shoots or both roots and shoots, and the largest proportion roots only. Schwarz (1933) examined many other species. The location of the regenerated structures is determined mainly by the anatomy of the leaf. It is noteworthy that in a number of species, predominantly though not always succulents, restoration and vegetative reproduction occur in other parts of the leaf than the base, as in species of *Drosera, Achimenes, Begonia, Torenia,* and the Crassulaceae. In *Utricularia* Goebel (1908) found adventive shoots formed by the leaf tips.

Restoration of organs may also occur from isolated cotyledons. Küster (1903*b*) obtained both roots and shoots from cotyledons of *Cucumis* and

Luffa, Kowalewska (1927) shoots from *Phaseolus* and *Pisum*, and Carlson (1953) only roots from *Raphanus* and *Brassica*. La Rue (1933) reviewed work on this subject and reports his own success in obtaining roots on excised cotyledons of 19 species and shoots on those of 22 species.

Several investigators have studied regeneration in inflorescences. If this structure is cut off and treated as a cutting, root formation and subsequent vegetative development of the inflorescence often follow. Bormann (1939) reviewed the literature and made extensive investigations himself, finding that, of 391 species studied in 65 genera and 45 families, the conversion of an inflorescence into a vegetative shoot by treating it as a cutting occurred in about 17 per cent of all the species.

Flower cuttings of Cactaceae, where the stem is incorporated into the fruit, have been found to form roots and develop dormant buds (Goebel, 1908). The ovary of *Jussiaea* as well as immature fruits of *Lecythis* react in the same way. Carrière (1877) describes the rooting of the capsule of *Lilium speciosum* and Kupfer (1907) that of pods of *Phaseolus*.

La Rue (1942) found that, under favorable cultural conditions that provide both moisture and food, many flowers or their parts may be induced to root (Fig. 9-7), and by this means he obtained roots on flowers of three genera of monocotyledons and 22 genera of dicotyledons. He went further and was able to induce regeneration even in gametophytes. Female gametophytes of *Zamia* in sterile culture not only increased in size markedly but in a few cases developed small roots and buds. The latter produced leaves resembling miniature seedling ones. He later obtained similar results with *Cycas* (1954).

Reproductive Regeneration

The ability of a part of the plant to restore missing structures and thus regenerate a whole is essentially the ability to reproduce. Regeneration is a reproductive process, and it is understandable that during the course of evolution many plants should have developed means to use the totipotency of their individual cells and tissues as means for vegetative reproduction. In many cases this has become a normal and spontaneous process, as in the formation of foliar embryos on the leaves of many Crassulaceae or of bulbils in other forms. Isolation or injury may stimulate the growth of similar structures, and this process thus grades over into regeneration. In many cases it is difficult to distinguish between the two.

This type of reproduction has been described most commonly in leaves and leaf cuttings (Fig. 9-8). Many cases have been studied in both dicotyledons and monocotyledons. Goebel cites a variety of these from the earlier literature. In some cases plantlets occur naturally on leaves and drop off to form new individuals (*gemmipary*). In others these appear only when the leaf is removed from the plant or its vigor reduced. Instead of actual plantlets, bulbils or bulblets may be formed, modified buds which drop from the plant and produce new individuals.

Many plantlets develop from preformed meristematic cells or cell aggregates and thus are clearly to be regarded as reproductive structures even though in some cases they are induced only by rather abnormal conditions. Others arise from unspecialized cells, usually epidermal or subepidermal ones, much as do the shoots on the hypocotyls previously described. When these are frequently formed in nature they are usually to be regarded as reproductive rather than regenerative structures. Only a few typical examples can be mentioned here.

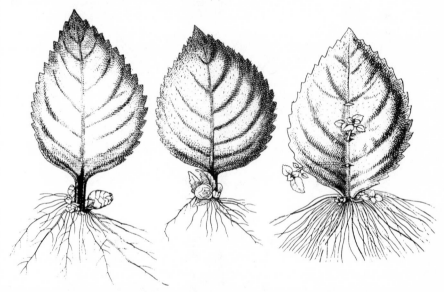

FIG. 9-8. Leaves of *Achimenes*, used as cuttings, regenerating roots and bulbils from the base and producing plantlets where veins have been cut. (*From Goebel.*)

A familiar one is that of *Tolmiea menziesii* (Yarbrough, 1936*a*), in which a plantlet regularly is formed at the junction of petiole and blade from a preformed bud at that point. This readily separates from the parent plant and forms a new one. In *Cardamine pratensis* (Goebel, 1908) adventitious shoots or plantlets grow in the autumn or under special conditions from the axils of the leaflets by the activity of groups of meristematic cells. At the junctions of the larger veins occur slight swellings and these may also develop into plantlets (Fig. 9-9). In such forms there are evidently many cells that can easily be induced to become meristematic and form plantlets. How such cells differ physiologically from others it is important to discover.

Some species of *Drosera* may also readily be induced to form shoots on their leaves (Behre, 1929). These develop from single epidermal cells on the morphologically upper side of the lamina, at the base of a tentacle, on the petiole adjacent to stomata or trichomes, or in young inflorescences adjacent to glands. In *Drosera binata,* a species with linear leaves, the young plants thus produced have roundish blades much like those of our

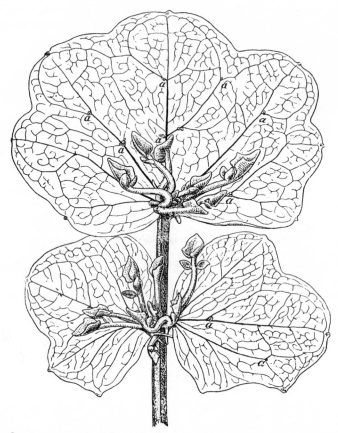

Fig. 9-9. *Cardamine pratensis.* After a leaf is removed, plantlets develop on it from preformed embryonic areas (*a*). (*From Goebel.*)

own common *Drosera rotundifolia.* It would be interesting to find whether this fact has any phylogenetic implications.

In *Begonia rex* and some other varieties of begonia, shoots may be induced very readily on petiole and blade by removing the growing points of the shoot. Prévot (1938, 1939) found that these arose from epidermal cells, but only after they had reached a certain stage of maturity. Hartsema (1926) has described the changes that such cells undergo at the start of shoot development (strong protoplasmic streaming, migration of the nucleus, and increase in cytoplasm). Here and in a good many other plants, shoots will appear on the blade if one or more of the veins are cut (Fig. 9-10), thus perhaps preventing the access of inhibiting substances. Prévot was able to induce bud formation on begonia leaves by the application of various substances and by growing the plants in the absence of oxygen. He also found that strips of epidermis removed from the leaf would form buds. Not all begonias have high regenerative ability, and this seems to be an inherited character when various types are crossed.

Much like these cases is the development of young plants on the leaves of *Saintpaulia ionantha*. This species is often reproduced in cultivation by plantlets formed on leaves that have been cut off and placed in a humid atmosphere. From individual cells of the upper epidermis shoots

FIG. 9-10. Propagation of rex begonia. If a leaf is removed and placed on moist sand and certain of its major veins severed, plantlets will regenerate at these cuts. (*From Avery and Johnson.*)

develop, and roots originate from parenchymatous cells near the boundary between xylem and phloem in the veins (Naylor and Johnson, 1937; Fig. 9-11).

Torenia asiatica behaves in much the same way (Winkler, 1903). In leaf cuttings, numerous shoot primordia begin to develop over the surface of the blade, each from an epidermal cell above a vein. Only a few of these primordia grow into shoots, and a single leaf thus shows a wide range of stages in shoot development. The shoots that form come to flowering very quickly, sometimes when they have only one well-developed leaf, and should thus make excellent material for a study of the factors that induce flowering.

Many members of the family Gesneriaceae, to which these plants belong, regenerate readily. Leaf cuttings of *Achimenes* produce clusters of bulblets at the base of the petiole and shoots from the blade if the veins are severed (Doposcheg-Uhlár, 1911). *Streptocarpus* (Goebel, 1908) illustrates most types of regeneration.

The most familiar examples of reproductive regeneration are provided by members of the Crassulaceae. In *Kalanchoe pinnatum* (*Bryophyllum calycinum*), plantlets develop from the marginal notches of the fleshy leaves. This may sometimes take place while the leaf is attached to the plant but is more common after it has fallen to the ground. In each notch is a preformed *foliar embryo* (Fig. 9-12), long ago described by Berge (1877) and more recently by Yarbrough (1932) and Naylor (1932). This is more than a mass of meristematic cells, for it has already taken the first steps toward organization of a plantlet and shows the minute beginnings of root, stem, and leaf. In other species the degree

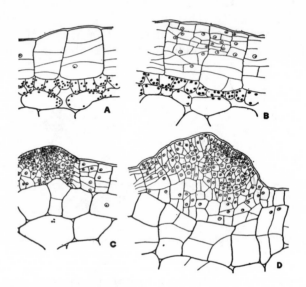

FIG. 9-11. Development of an adventitious bud from cells of the leaf epidermis of *Saintpaulia*. (*From Naylor and Johnson.*)

of differentiation of the foliar embryos varies (Stoudt, 1938). In *K. daigremontana* and *K. tubiflora* the plantlets attain appreciable size before the parent leaf has reached maturity. In *K. rotundifolia* there is a residual meristem on the axial surface of the petiole which develops a bud, but root primordia do not become differentiated until after the leaf has fallen from the plant.

The factors that induce the foliar embryos to develop into plantlets have been actively discussed. Loeb (1920), who made an extensive study of regeneration in this genus, believed that a hormonal mechanism inhibited their growth as long as the leaf was attached to the plant. Reed (1923) attributed their behavior to the metabolic condition of the leaf and showed that they tend to grow if the lamina loses vigor. Ossenbeck

(1927) regards the mechanical or physiological conduction between the leaf and the growing points of stem and root as important factors in inducing their development. Mehrlich (1931) exposed plants to a wide range of environmental factors in an attempt to solve the problem. In the activity of certain enzymes and in the relative amounts of carbohydrates, he noticed a difference between leaves in which the foliar embryos grew out and those where they did not. Varietal differences were also evident. Götz (1953) finds that plantlets grow out readily in long days but that short days tend to inhibit them. They are accelerated if the

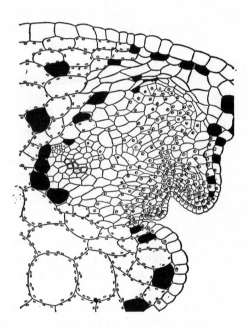

Fig. 9-12. Section through a notch on the leaf of *Kalanchoe,* showing a preformed "foliar embryo" with two leaf primordia below and a root primordium above, buried in the tissue. (*From E. E. Naylor.*)

vessels between lamina and petiole are cut or if auxin levels are low (Vardar and Acarer, 1957).

Other Crassulaceae differ in some respects from *Kalanchoe.* In *Byrnesia weinbergii,* Stoudt (1934) found that the foliar meristem from which a plantlet comes is at the base of the blade, not the margin. It is quite undifferentiated and will not develop until the leaf is removed from the plant. In *Sedum* (Yarbrough, 1936c) there are no preformed meristems at all, but these arise after the leaf is detached.

In *Crassula multicava* (McVeigh, 1938) a still different condition occurs and one reminiscent of *Begonia* and *Saintpaulia,* for here, after a leaf has been kept for a time in a moist chamber, plantlets begin to develop. Entire plants—not the shoot alone, as in many other cases—have their origin in single epidermal cells. These cells are not only presumably but demonstrably totipotent.

In a considerable number of forms the reproductive structures arising in regeneration are not plantlets, already differentiated and ready to start growth, but dormant, almost seed-like structures. In *Lilium tigrinum*, for example, in the axils of the upper leaves there are, instead of buds, hard black bulbils which fall off and produce new plants. Detached scale leaves in a number of the Liliaceae form adventive buds or bulbils from their bases. On leaves of *Hyacinthus*, removed from the plant, similar structures may be formed, but Naylor (1940) has shown that in this case they do not come from preformed meristematic tissue but develop from epidermal and subepidermal cells.

In many ferns vegetative cells of the prothallus may produce sporophytes by apogamy. Aposporous gametophytes are also frequently formed, especially on isolated juvenile leaves. Lawton (1932, 1936) was able to induce apospory in 13 species of ferns and obtained from them tetraploid sporophytes by methods similar to those used in mosses. Aposporous structures are often strictly gametophytic, but Beyerle (1932) found adventive structures in 34 fern species to include sporophytic buds, undifferentiated structures, prothallia, and bodies intermediate between sporophytes and prothallia (reviews by Du Buy and Neurnbergk, 1938, and Steil, 1939, 1951).

Regeneration in the fern sporophyte often results in the production of new plants. Buds may be formed on leaves and roots, and foliar embryos resembling those of higher plants may be produced, as in *Camptosorus* (McVeigh, 1934; Yarbrough, 1936*b*). A review of reproductive regeneration in ferns, covering 35 genera and 197 species, has been made by McVeigh (1937).

There should also be mentioned a special kind of reproductive regeneration that occurs in vegetative tissues of the embryo sac and ovule, by which embryos develop from synergids, antipodal cells, or cells of the nucellus and not only from the fertilized egg (Lebèque, 1952). Strasburger (1877) called this *adventive polyembryony* (as opposed to cleavage polyembryony, p. 235). Examples of this are known in *Funkia, Coelebogyne, Citrus,* and others (review by Webber, 1940). The embryos here formed somewhat resemble the foliar embryos of the Crassulaceae and similar plants. Though sometimes started in their development by a regenerative stimulus, these are cases of specific reproductive processes made possible by the totipotence of cells in various vegetative portions of the plant and which in a way are comparable to asexual propagation by spores.

In recent years experimental work on morphogenetic problems has been concerned primarily with the effects of environmental factors, particularly light and physiologically active substances. There is still opportunity for fruitful investigation through an experimental manipulation of the developmental process itself, especially by work on problems of regeneration such as have been discussed in this chapter. The significant results of earlier botanical workers in this field, now cultivated somewhat less actively than in the past, could be extended very profitably by supplementing the older methods with the advantages of modern techniques.

CHAPTER 10

Tissue Mixtures

In animal bodies such combinations of genetically unlike tissues as grafts, mosaics, and chimeras are rare in nature and rather difficult to bring about experimentally, but in plants these are much commoner and easier to produce. This is presumably due, in large measure, to the presence of localized growing points in plants, which knit together readily. The arts of grafting and budding have long been known to horticulturalists and provide means for combining two or more varieties of related plants and especially for vegetative multiplication of types that cannot be propagated by seeds or in which cuttings do not easily root.

In chimeras and in localized genetic changes, tissue mixtures may be much more intimate than in ordinary grafting and provide opportunities for a study of organization and tissue relationships which are not available in homogeneous plant bodies.

STOCK-SCION INTERRELATIONS

In the practice of grafting, a small branch or shoot, the *scion*, is inserted into a larger rooted portion, the *stock*, by means of a cleft or other opening in such a way that meristematic regions of the two come into contact. The same result is achieved in a somewhat simpler fashion by budding. Here a bud from one type is slipped under a cut in the bark of another so that the two cambia are in contact, the bud later growing into a shoot. A third piece, in "double-worked" trees, is sometimes inserted as an intermediate between stock and scion. In practice, these methods are used chiefly in woody plants and are the means by which most horticultural varieties of trees and shrubs are propagated. The problems in these plants will therefore be discussed first.

A question of much importance both practically and theoretically concerns the effects produced by the stock on the scion or the scion on the stock. What substances can, and what cannot, pass from one to the other across a graft union? Do the two graft partners remain in complete physiological isolation save for the passage of water and solutes

from stock to scion, or in a mutual exchange between the two do the specific qualities of one become transferred, in any measure, to the other? There has been much disagreement about these matters in the past, and final answers are not yet available.

There are several means by which the two graft partners may affect each other. Of most importance, probably, is nutrition. If a root into which a scion is grafted has less capacity to absorb, store, or utilize nutrients than do the roots of the plant from which the scion was taken, reduction of size and vigor of the shoot system produced by the scion will result. Many cases have been found where there are such physiological differences between stock and scion clones which modify the effect of one on the other, particularly of root on scion. Second, there may be differences between the two partners in the ease with which they translocate water and nutrients. The wood of dwarf rootstocks usually has a much smaller proportion of vessels than normal roots. Differences in phloem transport are probably even more important, as is shown by the dwarfing effect of inverted rings of bark and in other ways. Finally, there may be differences between partners in the amount of auxin in each or in the rate at which it is inactivated. In several herbaceous plants it has been shown that dwarf types are relatively poor in auxin. This may be the case in woody forms, for dwarf types of fruit trees are much branched, an indication that auxin-induced bud inhibition is weak in them. Other growth substances may pass from one partner to the other.

It is clear that water and salts from the soil pass from stock to scion and that carbohydrates also pass across a graft union, and in either direction. Certain nutritional changes are thus produced by one on the other. A common practice in producing dwarf fruit trees is to graft scions of standard varieties on stocks which are genetically small and thus have small roots. This reduces the amount of top growth. Most of this dwarfing results from the reduced water supply available from the roots (Colby, 1935), and dwarfing rootstocks also tends to cause earlier cessation of growth in the fall (Swarbrick, 1928). Dwarfing may be produced in other ways than by reduction in root size. Tukey and Brase (1933) found that where a dwarf variety was used either as a rootstock, intermediate stem piece, or top scion its effect was to dwarf the whole plant. Some dwarfing may also be attributed to defective graft unions and the consequent failure to transfer materials readily (Bradford and Sitton, 1929). Dickson and Samuels (1956) have studied translocation across a graft union by means of radioactive tracers and find that there is a high concentration of the isotope at the junction of stock and scion, suggesting that the dwarfing effect may be due to a block in the flow of nutrients to the roots.

But there seem also to be more subtle factors involved. A special kind of dwarfing is that produced in some plants by growth from seeds that have not been afterripened. A case of this sort in the peach where the dwarfs retained their dwarf character when grafted on normal plants was studied by Flemion and Waterbury (1945). The roots of such dwarfs were able to support normal shoot growth, so that the seat of the dwarfing seems to be in the shoot. There is no evidence of a stimulating substance produced in the normal plant or of an inhibiting one in the dwarf.

Some varieties are incompatible in grafting and so do not thrive together even though the graft union between them may be good or a variety compatible to both is inserted as an interstock (Sax, 1953, 1954). Tukey and Brase present evidence that not only the character of stock and scion and their compatibility are important in determining tree size but also the effect of environmental factors on each partner and on their combination.

Aside from purely quantitative effects of stock on scion in horticultural plants, other traits have been reported to be transmitted from one to the other. McClintock (1937) found that leaves of the Grimes apple grafted on Virginia crab stock have a greater green weight and are physiologically different in some respects from those of the same variety on other stocks. Blair (1938) grafted Bramley Seedling apple on French crab but in a number of cases inserted between stock and scion a 9-in. piece of one of three other varieties, Malling II, IX, and XIII. Even though here stock and scion were the same, the effect of these middle pieces on the tree that grew out of them was markedly different in each case, as shown in leaf poise, general habit of branching, leaf color, and time of defoliation. The effect of the various middle pieces on the root was also evident. Rogers, Beakbane, and Field (1939), however, found that intermediate pieces from different sources had relatively little effect on the rootstocks. By grafting apple scions from various sources on roots, Swarbrick and Roberts (1927) found that the character of the root tended to be like that of the variety which contributed the piece of stem just above it, whether this was scion or middle piece. Amos, Hatton, and Hoblyn (1930) dispute this conclusion and believe that the effect of scion on root is simply quantitative.

In citrus fruits Halma (1934) reports that Eureka lemon scions grafted on sour-orange roots greatly modify the form and color of the latter. In the reciprocal graft, only the color of the root was changed. These changes were observed in grafted but not in budded trees.

Early work on the stock-scion relationship is reviewed by Swarbrick (1930), and Garner (1949) has presented the subject from a practical point of view.

The mixture of tissues by grafting and the relation between the graft partners pose problems of wider interest than for horticulture alone. It has long been known, for example, that successful grafts are usually limited to closely related plants, either between those of the same species or between species close together taxonomically. In exceptional cases grafts can be made between genera and very rarely between families. Simon (1930), for example, has grafted *Solanum* and *Iresine*, belonging to the widely separated families Solanaceae and Amaranthaceae. Nickell (1948) grafted white sweet clover on sunflower, and the plants continued to grow with normal vigor for 5 months. Silberschmidt (1935) studied 550 grafts between plants of the same species, of related species, and of unrelated species. Anatomical fusion in some cases occurred in grafts of unrelated species but here union was slower and less extensive, passage of nitrogen from scion to stock was reduced, and proteolytic activity of stock juices increased. The last fact is presumably concerned with the failure of unrelated grafts.

Schröter (1955) reports that *Zinnia elegans,* one of the Compositae, can be grafted to tobacco, although not on some plants in the same family as tobacco. He attributes the successful *Zinnia* grafts to the presence of nicotine in this plant. Mothes and Romeike (1955) grafted scions of tomato, petunia, belladonna, and tobacco on tobacco stocks of varying nicotine content and found that the richer the stock was in nicotine, the poorer was the development of the grafted scion.

The passage of nicotine from tobacco roots to tomato scions has been described (p. 220). Hieke (1942) found that in grafts between *Lycopersicon, Nicotiana, Atropa,* and *Datura* the alkaloids found in the scion were those characteristic of the root to which this was grafted.

Kostoff (1929) presented evidence from grafts between various plant types that immunity, as tested by the precipitin reaction, can be acquired by plants much as in animals. Chester and his colleagues, however, in a series of papers (1932 and others) showed that the precipitates reported are not the result of a true precipitin reaction but are simply calcium oxalate, a widespread substance in plants.

Monocotyledonous plants have been found more difficult to graft than dicotyledonous ones, presumably because they lack a cambium. Muzik and La Rue (1954), however, grafted a number of species of grasses, including some belonging to different genera.

The closer to the embryonic condition a tissue is, the more readily it can be grafted. The smallest successful graft of this sort seems to be one made by Gulline and Walker (1957) in which a shoot tip containing only about 600 cells and with a volume of less than $\frac{1}{1000}$ cu. mm. was grafted back on the apex from which it had been cut. Later development was normal.

As to the reciprocal relations of stock and scion in nonwoody plants, many conflicting results have been reported. Daniel described various instances of a marked qualitative effect of stock on scion or scion on stock. The production of tubers, for example, he believed could be transferred by grafting from the Jerusalem artichoke to the common sunflower, which normally bears no tubers. In one of his last papers (1929) Daniel maintains that these induced changes have sometimes become transmissible through seed for several generations and regards this as proof of the inheritance of an acquired character.

This is essentially the position taken by Lysenko and his Russian colleagues. One of them, Avakian (1941), reported marked reciprocal effects, on fruit color and other characters, of red-fruited, yellow-fruited, and white-fruited tomatoes when grafted together in various ways. Similar experiments were repeated in this country by Wilson and Withner (1946), who were unable to confirm these results in any respect. Böhme (1954) also found that no inheritable effects were produced by grafting between varieties of tomatoes.

There are a number of well-authenticated cases, however, of the transmission, between graft partners, of factors that determine qualitative and not simply quantitative and nutritional differences. These present some important problems both for morphogenesis and for physiology. Conspicuous among them are the numerous instances where a flowering stimulus, from a plant which has been induced to flower by a particular photoperiod, can be transferred by grafting to a nonflowering plant and cause it to flower (p. 396). Evidently some substance is transmitted across the graft that stimulates flowering.

The effect of this stimulus may be modified in various ways. Haupt (1954), using a late-bearing variety of peas, grafted terminal shoots of different ages on stocks of different ages. If scions of young plants are grafted on older ones, flowering takes place up to six nodes earlier than in controls grafted to stocks of their own age. Evidently the substance concerned with flower development is not formed in the first stages of the plant's growth but can be effective then if introduced from older plants.

The production of flowers after grafting may be due to other factors than a specific flower-inducing substance. The Jersey type of sweet potato rarely flowers in this country but can be made to do so by grafting it to another species of *Ipomoea* that does not form storage roots (Kehr, Ting, and Miller, 1953). These authors believe that flowering results from the accumulation of carbohydrates in the shoots after grafting.

The tendency to form tubers in potato may be transmitted by grafting. If the shoot of a variety that produces tubers under a long day is grafted to a short-day variety and grown under long days, the short-day variety will now produce earlier and larger tubers than it would have done by itself (Howard, 1949). This effect was not transmitted through these tubers when they were used as seed. Somewhat similar results are reported by Gregory (1956), who also found that the tuber-forming stimulus could be transmitted from all parts of the shoot by grafting.

Some recent experiments on the graft transmission, or lack of transmission, of plant traits are the following:

In English ivy (*Hedera helix*) Doorenbos (1954) grafted scions from the juvenile type (with lobed leaves) onto the adult, upright, flowering form and found that the latter often lost its ability to flower and showed other juvenile traits.

Popesco (1949) reports that when *Sophora japonica*, a woody perennial leguminous plant, is grafted to the common bean, the bean flowers 15 to 20 days later than it otherwise would and becomes perennial in habit.

Hybrids between *Meliotus alba* and *M. dentata* are deficient in chlorophyll because of some gene interaction and die in a few days. If such hybrids are grafted to sweet clover, however, they grow well, flower, and bear seed (W. K. Smith, 1943).

In spruce (*Picea abies*), Müller-Stoll (1947*a*) examined grafts of shoots from the tops of old trees on young seedlings. After 3 years these flowered abundantly, far earlier than they would have done otherwise. Only female cones were produced, presumably because the branches used as scions were from the top of the tree, which bears chiefly female cones. This localization the author interprets as an instance of topophysis.

Many cases have been described of the effect of stock on fruit size in the scion. Bitters and Batchelor (1951) report such a case in the orange, where Washington navel oranges were grafted on 32 different rootstocks and Valencia on 26. Differences were found between stocks in their effects on fruit size in the scion. These differences are not related to those in tree size or in number of fruits.

An incompatible graft is reported in cucurbits by Wellensiek (1949). Grafts of muskmelon on *Cucurbita ficifolia* grew for a time and then suddenly wilted and died. Muskmelon as an interstock between cucumber and *C. ficifolia* has the same effect. If a few leaves are left on the latter, however, the graft with muskmelon is successful. The reciprocal graft thrives, so that incompatibility is in only one direction. The author believes that muskmelon fails to give the stock of *C. ficifolia* a substance necessary for its growth and that this is provided if a few leaves are left on it.

Yampolsky (1957), in the dioecious *Mercurialis annua*, grafted male and female plants together in a variety of ways but found no alteration in the sexual character of either.

Of particular interest for genetics are those cases where there is a known genetic difference between scion and stock. *Hyoscyamus niger*, the black henbane, has an annual variety and a biennial one, the annual forming a flower stalk and flowers in a single season but the biennial remaining in the rosette stage for the first year unless experimentally exposed to low temperature. This difference is due to a single gene, with the biennial character almost completely dominant. Melchers (1937) grafted a scion from the annual variety (and also scions from *Petunia, Nicotiana,* and other related annual plants) into the rosettes of the biennial variety in its first year and by this means induced the biennial to flower in the same season. Melchers attributes this to the passage across the graft union of a nonspecific flower-forming substance. The genetic difference between the annual and the biennial varieties seemed to be due to the ability of the former to produce a flower-forming hormone without previous exposure to low winter temperature. Melchers later (1938) found that if a short-day variety of tobacco, grown under long-day conditions and thus unable to flower, was grafted into biennial *Hyoscyamus* in its first season, the latter soon produced flowers. The gene in *Hyoscyamus* may thus control the ability to respond to the flower-inducing substance rather than to form it.

In *Petunia nyctaginiflora* von Wettstein and Pirschle (1938) found a gene *d* which differed from the normal *D* in producing plants that are smaller and have fewer branches, smaller and more rounded leaves, and a marked chlorophyll deficiency. Scions of *dd* grafted on *DD* stocks had slightly larger leaves and stems and more branches but were not much different from ungrafted *dd*. Scions of *DD* on *dd* showed general reduction in size and a chlorophyll deficiency, which was greatest next the graft union and decreased in intensity above this. The authors believed that a substance was produced in the mutant that passes into normal scions and there either inhibits chlorophyll formation or causes chlorophyll degradation. Pirschle later (1939) presented evidence that *dd* lacks a hormone, present in *DD*, that stimulates growth in size but does not affect the shape of leaves or flowers. Objection may be raised that these are nutritional and not hormonal effects.

When tobacco and tomato are grafted with the *dd* mutant of *Petunia*, their leaves show chlorophyll deficiency when the *dd* plant is used as a stock and to a lesser degree where it is used as a scion (Pirschle, 1940). The gene-produced *d* substance is clearly not species-specific. The possibility cannot be disregarded that the supposed *d* mutant is actually a virus infection, although its clear genetic segregation from *D* would suggest that it is not.

The single-gene mutants *nana* of *Antirrhinum siculum* and *sterilis* of *Solanum lycopersicon* were produced by radium irradiations and have been studied by Stein (1939). The former has a single unbranched main stalk (unlike *A. siculum*); is flowerless; and has larger, thicker, and darker leaves. When grafted as a scion on *A. siculum* stock, the stem is somewhat.shorter and bears abnormal flowers but is otherwise unchanged. The tomato mutant is dwarf, has scanty chlorophyll, and lacks branches and flowers. When grafted as a scion on tomato stock its chlorophyll remained deficient but its growth became approximately normal as to height, branching, and flower development. The particular interest of these cases lies in the fact that the various effects of a gene here seem to be separated, some of them passing across the graft union and others not doing so. Such material offers a favorable opportunity for the study of gene action.

Rick (1952) found a tomato mutant, wilty dwarf (*wd*), which differed from normal in having fewer and shorter internodes, smaller leaves, thinner stems, blue-gray leaf color, and a tendency to wilt in summer. This was grafted in various ways on homozygous normal (+) lines differing from *wd* in only this one gene. Control grafts of *wd* on *wd* and of + on + showed no modification. Reciprocal grafts of + on *wd* and *wd* on + had their leaf dimensions and stem lengths shifted markedly toward the character of the stock. In double graft combinations, *wd*/+/*wd* and +/*wd*/+, the top scion was unaltered but the middle piece was changed in the direction of the stock. The author concludes that the effect of stock on scion here is not due to factors in the stem or leaves but in the root system of the stock.

Kostoff (1930*b*) observed irregular meioses in the pollen cells of tobacco grafted to other genera, and such scions produced much abortive pollen. If flowers on them were selfed, various chromosomal aberrants appeared in the progeny but none in the controls.

In *Petunia*, Frankel (1956) grafted fertile scions to stock showing cytoplasmic male sterility and found sterility in the offspring of such scions, suggesting that cytoplasmic sterility determinants had passed from stock to scion. The author recognizes the possibility that nutritional changes induced by grafting may have been responsible for these effects.

Wagenbreth (1956) made grafts between a number of species of legumes and found by inoculation experiments that, although bacteria specific for the stock would produce nodules in such plants, bacteria specific for the scion would not.

Common experience has shown that strictly qualitative characters such as shape are usually gene-controlled and not influenced by grafting, despite early claims to the contrary. A few pieces of positive evidence, however, have been reported in recent years. Heinicke (1935) observed that McIntosh apples borne on defoliated scions grafted into Northern Spy, and thus grown from material produced by Northern Spy leaves, tended to be modified in the direction of the latter variety. Southwick

(1937) also found that Malling stock had some influence on the form and size of McIntosh apples grown on it. These cases need confirmation.

In general, from the mass of literature available, one may conclude that stock can influence scion in producing differences in plant size, size of leaves and fruits, plant habit, flowering time, life span, content of inorganic and certain organic substances and growth substances, and to some extent in fertility and resistance to disease. Influence of scion on stock is much less marked. Most of these effects definitely have a chemical or nutritional basis, and few cases of strictly qualitative changes are known. It should be recognized, however, that a purely quantitative difference, as in fruit or leaf size, may influence shape by allometric correlation (p. 105). Truly morphogenetic effects rarely—perhaps never—pass across a graft union. The great preponderance of evidence also supports the conclusion that no permanent genetic change is induced by one graft partner on the other.

Stock-scion relationships have been reviewed by Rogers and Beakbane (1957). Much of the literature on grafting (and many other things) is summarized in Krenke's (1933) monumental work. The theoretical aspects of grafting have been reviewed by Roberts (1949).

CHIMERAS

The instances of tissue mixture just described have been by the artificial union of two genetically different plants. These types remain sharply separated, each branch or other unit of the plant belonging definitely to one or to the other. There are tissue mixtures, however, where the fusion is much more intimate than this and where an organ such as a stem, leaf, or root is not homogeneous but is made up of two or more tissues that are genetically unlike. This difference may arise by somatic mutation, the mutated cells multiplying and forming a part of the whole, or it may be the result of a mixture of meristematic tissues at a graft union. The important fact, morphogenetically, is that these diverse groups of cells do not each form an organism or produce developmental abnormalities but that they coexist as parts of the same organized system. What is produced is a normal, whole plant. Here the organizing capacity of living stuff and the self-regulatory quality of the organism are particularly conspicuous.

Mixtures of tissues that come from different sources are called *chimeras,* a term proposed by Winkler (1907*b*) from the analogy between such plants and the chimeras of mythology which were part lion, part goat, and part dragon. A number of types of chimeras are recognized, depending on the relationship of their components.

The work on chimeras has been reviewed by Swingle (1927), Weiss (1930), Neilson-Jones (1934, 1937), and Cramer (1954).

In the so-called *mixed* chimeras the two kinds of tissue are mingled irregularly together. This mixture may persist but it is often a temporary stage and succeeded by one of the more regular types as the meristem becomes better organized. In *mericlinal* chimeras, often derived from mixed ones, one type of tissue forms a thin layer over a part of the surface of the other.

The other types show a more regular relation between their two components. In *sectorial* chimeras, a definite sector of a radially symmetrical structure such as a root, stem, or fruit is of one type and the

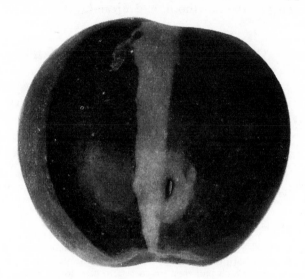

Fig. 10-1. Sectorial chimera in apple. (*From Zundel.*)

rest is of the other (Fig. 10-1). It is not uncommon to find in fruits such as apple or orange a sector in which the color or texture of the skin is different from that of the rest and which sometimes can be traced into the axis of the fruit. Such a sector may be distinguished in the stem, also, and the line between the two components sometimes runs out through the blade of a leaf. The term sectorial chimera may be used more broadly for a type in which there are large masses of diverse tissue adjacent to each other, regardless of whether the boundary line has any relation to the axis of symmetry. Thus an apple in which the terminal portion is of one type and the basal another, with an irregular boundary between, has been called a sectorial chimera. Sectorial chimeras are often found in shoots that arise from the vicinity of a graft union. Some of them may really be mericlinal ones, with one member covering a sector but only skin deep. Sectorial chimeras may sometimes be discovered by a study of their internal structure (Brumfield, 1943, p. 76, and Fig. 10-2).

Of most interest to morphogenesis, however, are *periclinal* chimeras. In these remarkable plants the outer cell layers are derived from one graft partner and the entire inner portion of the plant from the other. "Graft hybrids," which have long been a puzzle to horticulturalists, prove to be periclinal chimeras. They arise from grafted plants and partake of certain of the characters of each, but their own characters cannot be transmitted through seed. One of the familiar forms is *Crataegomespilus*, originating from a graft between two rosaceous genera: *Crataegus*, the hawthorn, and *Mespilus*, the medlar. Another is

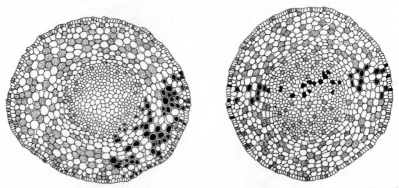

Fig. 10-2. Sectors of a root of *Vicia* after previous exposure to X radiation. Stippled cells are those in which observed mitoses showed that the chromosomes were unchanged. Black cells are those where a chromosomal change could be observed. These cells presumably are descended from a cell at the very tip in which a change had been induced and which had then given rise to a sector or wedge of similar cells. (*From Brumfield.*)

Cytisus-laburnum, coming from a graft between these two leguminous genera.

Plants of this sort were first experimentally produced and carefully studied by Winkler (1907*b*, and later papers). He grafted two closely related species, the nightshade, *Solanum nigrum,* and the tomato, *Solanum lycopersicon.* After union, most of the scion was cut off, and from adventitious buds arising near the point of union plants developed which sometimes showed mixtures of the two types of tissue. Most of these were sectorial chimeras. Occasionally, however, Winkler found a plant that showed no obvious separation into two types of tissue but was clearly intermediate in character between nightshade and tomato. Several distinguishably different types of such "graft hybrids" appeared in these experiments, were maintained by vegetative propagation, and bore flowers, fruits, and seed. Whether these were really mixtures of tissue, or, in some cases at least, were actual vegetative hybrids, was not clear at first. Baur's (1909) analysis of a *Pelargonium* with white-margined leaves showed that in this plant both the epidermis and the layer beneath it lacked chlorophyll. This conception of a continuous layer of one type of cells covering a core of another type was applied to Winkler's chimeras, and the latter proved to be periclinal ones. Such forms apparently arise at a place where there is a thin layer of one tissue over the other. A growing point, originating in the deeper tissue, pushes up and carries on its surface one or two cell layers of the other type. From this layered meristem a new shoot is formed. Mericlinal chimeras may thus be converted into periclinal ones. Jorgensen and Crane (1927) repeated Winkler's experiments, using five species of *Solanum*, and observed in more detail the origin of chimeras.

In the tomato-nightshade chimeras four different forms were recognized, propagated, and even given Latin names. In one there was a single layer of tomato over a core of nightshade; in another, two layers; in a third, one layer of nightshade over tomato; and in a fourth, two layers of nightshade. The reason that there are rarely more than two layers of the outer component is presumably because a new growing point always arises near the surface.

In Winkler's material it was relatively easy to distinguish the two components of the chimera cytologically, since tomato has 24 chromosomes ($2n$) and nightshade 72. When chromosome counts could not be made, the size of the cells (much larger in nightshade) was almost as good a criterion. It was found that the layers could be distinguished at the apical meristem and that they maintained their specific character throughout the life of the plant. When the outermost layer at the growing point was from one partner (tomato, for example) only the epidermis of the plant was of that type. When the second layer of the meristem, as well, was from tomato, the two outer layers of the plant were of this type. Occasionally in certain tissues of the mature plant these layers would become somewhat thicker by periclinal divisions and thus include more cells, but this was relatively uncommon.

In periclinal chimeras (as in all seed plants) the genetic character of the plant is determined by the cell layer just beneath the epidermis. From this layer the sporogenous tissue is formed. The offspring of a chimera, by seed, is therefore identical with the graft partner that contributes the subepidermal layer of cells.

Winkler maintained that two other types of chimeras that he obtained from grafts were true *burdos*, or vegetative hybrids, in which one layer had arisen by an actual nuclear fusion between cells of the two component species. The aberrant chromosome counts (cells with neither 24 nor 72 chromosomes) can probably be explained in other ways. Brabec (1954) repeated Winkler's work and found cells with varying and irregular chromosome numbers but attributed this fact to the origin of the new shoot from highly polyploid cells. Pith cells, as has been shown by various workers, are often polyploid, and when chimeras come from such tissue the chromosome situation is often complicated. The genetics and cytology of the *Solanum* chimeras have been studied by Gunther (1957). Present evidence is against the occurrence of vegetative hybridization and the existence of burdos. In the light of recent knowledge of periclinal chimeras, Bergann (1956) has reinvestigated the *Crataegomespili*.

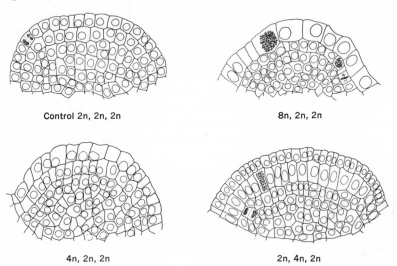

Control 2n, 2n, 2n   8n, 2n, 2n

4n, 2n, 2n   2n, 4n, 2n

Fig. 10-3. Apical meristems of four periclinal chimeras in *Datura* consisting of 2n, 4n, and 8n layers. Labels refer to the first two layers and the core. (*From Satina, Blakeslee, and Avery.*)

In leaf and fruit, the tomato and the nightshade are very different. Each of the four periclinal chimeras produced by Winkler by grafts between them shows distinctive combinations of these traits so that it is possible to determine the effects of one and of two cell layers of each type when it covers a core of the other. Such chimeras provide an excellent opportunity to study the morphogenetic influence of the various meristematic layers and the developmental origin of shape differences and of tissues.

The most complete and thoroughly analyzed series of periclinal chimeras are those studied by Satina and Blakeslee in *Datura* (1941, 1943, 1944, 1945; Fig. 10-3). By soaking seeds of *Datura stramonium* in colchicine solution, polyploidy was induced in certain cells of the shoot meristem in 68 plants. The first cell layer (L I), the second (L II), and the third (L III, including everything below the first two) were often affected independently. L I was changed most often and L II least. These layers retained their specific chromosome complement throughout the structure of the plant that developed from this meristem. These plants are periclinal chimeras, not obtained from graft unions but by chemical induction. Unlike the tomato-nightshade forms and similar ones, here there may be three genetically different layers ($2n$, $4n$, and $8n$) instead of two, and these three were found to occur in almost any order from without inward. In the first report there were the following distributions of polyploidy among the layers: $2n$, $2n$, $4n$; $2n$, $4n$, $2n$; $2n$, $4n$, $4n$; $2n$, $8n$, $4n$; $4n$, $2n$, $2n$; $4n$, $2n$, $4n$; $4n$, $8n$, $4n$; $8n$, $2n$, $2n$; $8n$, $4n$, $4n$. Other combinations were found later.

There is little difficulty here in distinguishing the layers since cell size is approximately proportional to chromosome number and the $2n$, $4n$, and $8n$ cells are thus markedly different. Since plants belonging to the polyploid series differ little except in size, morphological combinations of characters, as in the tomato-nightshade chimeras and others where the partners are so unlike, cannot be seen.

An understanding of periclinal chimeras has aided in the solution of a number of horticultural and morphological problems. Not only have the classical examples of the "graft hybrids" been given a satisfactory interpretation but other facts discovered in vegetatively propagated plants are now explained. Bateson (1921), for example, found that in a variety of *Bouvardia* with pinkish-white flowers root cuttings produced plants with red flowers. Here it is probable that the core of the plant was of a red-flowered variety and only the outer layers were genetically pink. Since lateral roots arise from the vascular cylinder (here genetically red) and push out through the cortex and epidermis, buds from these lateral roots would be expected to form red flowers. Asseyeva (1927) observed in the varieties of potatoes arising by bud mutation that if the buds are removed from the seed tuber the new ones which now arise from the deeper tissues form plants like those from which the mutant variety had come. Zimmerman (1951a) reports a similar case in roses. Such vegetatively propagated plants are probably periclinal chimeras with only the outer layer or layers of cells belonging to the mutant type.

Other horticultural plants prove on examination to be chimeras. Einset and his colleagues at the Geneva (N.Y.) Experiment Station have found that six large-fruited sports of several apple varieties are really periclinal chimeras. The core tissues of the meristem are tetraploid, and these are covered by one, two, or rarely three layers of diploid cells (Einset, Blaser, and Imhofe, 1947; Blaser and Einset, 1948).

Dermen has worked extensively with polyploid chimeras. In apples he found some types in which (like those examined by Einset) the layers are 2n, 2n, 4n. In others, these are 2n, 4n, 2n, the whole core being diploid (Dermen, 1951). He has also studied chimeras in the cranberry (1947a). Einset and Lamb (1951) conclude that most of the so-called tetraploid grapes are actually diploid-tetraploid periclinal chimeras, as in apples.

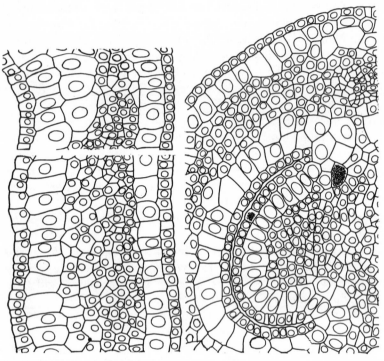

Fig. 10-4. Portion of carpel wall and placenta of *Datura* in a periclinal chimera that was 2n, 8n, 2n in constitution. In material like this it is possible to trace the origin of tissues from specific layers at the meristem. (*From Satina and Blakeslee.*)

Kerns and Collins (1947) obtained chimeras in pineapple with colchicine. Some had a 2n epidermis with all the other tissue 4n, and these resembled the completely tetraploid plants. Some had a 4n epidermis and the rest 2n and resembled completely diploid plants. These authors believe that there are only two "germ layers" in the pineapple.

Periclinal chimeras have made an important contribution both to morphology and morphogenesis by making it possible to trace the continuity between the regions of the meristem and the structures of the mature plant, since when the cells of the components of a chimera are distinguishable, their descendants can be traced throughout development (Fig. 10-4). This is particularly true in the polyploid chimeras. The work on *Datura* by Satina and Blakeslee has provided much information here, and Dermen (1953) presented similar evidence for the peach. There seems to be no invariable rule as to just what mature structures are produced by different layers at the meristem. The particular tissues contributed by *L* II and *L* III are not only different among species but between large and small individuals of the same species (Dermen, 1951).

It is significant that in the root, where a root cap is present and continuous layers of cells do not cover the tip of the meristem, periclinal chimeras do not occur. Sectorial chimeras, however, have been observed in roots (p. 76).

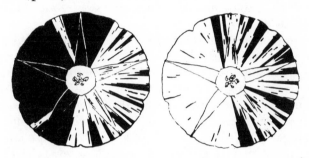

Fɪɢ. 10-5. Somatic mutation. Sectors of cells in corolla of *Pharbitis* resulting from mutation from colorless to colored sap. The wider the sector, the earlier was the origin of the mutation in the development of the flower. (*From Imai and Tobuchi.*)

SOMATIC MUTATIONS

Mixtures of various types of tissue may appear not as a result of grafting or experimental treatment but spontaneously. Mutations in vegetative cells are not uncommon in some plants. Where a mutant cell is distinguishable, by color or in other ways, its descendants form a spot or stripe of tissue unlike the rest (Fig. 10-5). The earlier the mutation occurs, the larger the mass of tissue that will be produced. In annual *Delphinium*, Demerec (1931) found a gene that mutated frequently in petal cells, changing their color from rose to purple. An early mutation altered a large part of the plant but later ones formed only small spots on the petals. Some cases of variegation, as in maize pericarp (Anderson and Brink, 1952), are due to mutable genes of this sort though most color patterns in plants result from differentiation during development and not from a mixture of genetically different tissues. Some genetically variegated plants become chimeras, and Dermen (1947*b*) has been able to determine the specific meristematic layer (*L* I, *L* II, or *L* III) in which the mutation took place.

McClintock (1929) reported a case in maize where the microsporocytes had 19 chromosomes but the root tips 20, suggesting that a chromosome had been lost during the development of the upper part of the plant.

A number of instances are known in hybrid plants where twin stripes or spots occur, differing from each other and from the background color. These have been interpreted as the result of crossing over in somatic cells. Thus in *Phaseolus* the F_1 of a cross between plants with violet and with lilac flowers produced a form with light violet flowers. In one of these there were two stripes, side by side, one of them violet and one lilac (Prakken, 1938). A sectorial chimera presumably due to such vegetative segregation was reported for a pear fruit by Gardner, Crist, and Gibson (1933). Twin spots, also apparently caused by somatic crossing-over or chromosome translocation, are frequent in maize pericarp (Jones, 1938).

Huskins and others (Huskins, 1948; Huskins and Cheng, 1950) reported numerous instances where, as the result of low temperature or of various chemical treatments, somatic mitoses occur in which the number of chromosomes is reduced, as it is in meiosis. Wilson and Cheng (1949) found that in such cases members of homologous pairs separated much oftener than they would have done by chance, indicating a true genetic segregation in the body cells of a heterozygous plant.

In all these instances of genetic alteration in a few cells, the difference between these cells and the normal type is usually not very great, and there is less to be learned morphogenetically than in grafts and chimeras. Whenever genetically different tissues from any source are present together in the same individual, however, their coexistence in a single whole is evidence of the organizing capacity of living stuff.

CHAPTER 11

Abnormal Growth

The basic problem of morphogenesis, as stated frequently in the preceding chapters, is posed by the fact that every organism is an organized system that in its development tends to produce forms and structures of specific character. Within each organism there seems to be a norm toward which its development conforms. The expression of this norm, however, may vary greatly as the result of a wide range of environmental factors. Such variation is familiar and to be expected. There are many cases, however, where divergence from the norm is so great that we usually speak of them as "abnormal" or "atypical." Just what do we mean by these terms?

Every organism, and doubtless every cell, has a far wider range of development potencies than it generally displays. When conditions are different from the usual ones, the expression of its norm is also different, but the norm is just as specific as before and the organism still persistently regulates its development in such a way that the characteristic form for that environment is produced. Norms of the individuals in a given species are much the same. The basis of each is the genetic constitution of the organism. It is well understood by geneticists, however, that what a particular gene determines is not a particular character but a particular reaction to a particular environment, external or internal. In many cases it requires very special environmental factors, such as wounding, irradiation, application of growth substances, or deposition of an insect egg to bring to expression developmental potencies which would otherwise remain latent.

Under such unusual conditions, or from genotypes which are markedly different from those of most members of the species, individuals sometimes develop which are so unlike ordinary ones that they are called "abnormal." This does not mean that they are exceptions to the general biological determination that controls the growth of all living things. Neither do they constitute a sharply defined group set apart from all others, for every gradation between normal and abnormal may be found. One may be uncertain, for example, as to whether the occasional production of different forms of leaves on the same plant or the growth of plantlets on the leaf margins or many structures appearing during the process of regeneration are normal or not. What seems at first to be abnormal may prove to be simply an intensified or exaggerated manifestation of developmental potency. The degree of divergence from the average is the basis on which we term a structure or an individual abnormal, and biologists often disagree as to how divergent an organism must be to warrant this designation. "Abnormalities" in animals and plants are recognized largely as a matter of convenience in order not to complicate still further an already difficult taxonomic and morphological situation.

Thus there are two concepts of what a norm is and therefore of what is abnormal. One is a developmental concept: the norm or standard, based on a specific protoplasmic pattern, to which the organism tends persistently to conform. The existence of this norm is the basic fact in biological organization. Its expression may vary greatly as the environment changes but it always remains as the core of the morphogenetic process. In this sense, *nothing* is abnormal. The other concept of the norm is a purely statistical or taxonomic one. In most species the developmental norms of its individuals do not vary widely in their expression since these individuals are genetically very similar and have been exposed to a relatively narrow range of environmental influences. This rather constant developmental expression may for convenience be regarded as a norm, and everything that differs from it substantially may be called abnormal. It is in this statistical sense that the term "abnormal growth" is generally employed.

The student of morphogenesis, however, does not put aside these instances of abnormal growth and development as unimportant for his purpose. Such may well prove to be more enlightening than most "normal" individuals. They are exceptions, extreme cases, and from exceptions like these often come clues to the solution of particularly difficult problems. Furthermore, in many cases of abnormal growth certain levels of the very quality that we associate with life—organization—have disappeared. Tissue cultures and many tumors and galls are formless, largely unorganized masses of cells which no longer produce the beautifully coordinated structures called organisms. Individual cells here must still retain a basic, vital organization in their living stuff, for otherwise they would die, but the higher levels of organization have now broken down. In other types of abnormal growth quite the opposite change has occurred and entirely *new* structures, specifically formed and well organized though on a different plan, are produced, as in many insect galls.

The subject of abnormal growth is therefore a promising one for students of plant morphogenesis since by the study of these unusual structures development may be examined at various levels and degrees of organization. Relatively little work has been done in this field, however, and most of the results are descriptive and relate to mature structures. In the few cases, such as crown gall, where many experimental and developmental studies have been made, these have proved to be very rewarding.

There is some confusion between the concepts of "pathological" and "abnormal" growth. Pathology is concerned with questions about the health and survival of the organism when it is attacked by parasites or subjected to unfavorable conditions. Abnormal growth is often produced by this means though here, again, it is difficult to draw the line. One would hardly call the aecium of wheat rust an abnormal growth, but a crown gall certainly is one. There are many cases of abnormal growth, on the other hand, which clearly are not pathological, such as inherited fasciations or the root tubercles of legumes. A student of abnormal growth is not concerned with the health of the plant, nor does a pathologist examine primarily the ways in which the plants with which he deals diverge from the norm. Historically, however, the two fields have been close together, and Küster's (1925) classic book on abnormal growth is entitled "Pathological Plant Anatomy."

There is no very obvious way in which to organize the widely various phenomena of abnormal growth. It will be most logical, perhaps, to proceed from cases where divergence from the norm is relatively slight and move to those where it is more extreme. In the present chapter there will be discussed (1) the abnormal development of organs belonging to the usual categories, (2) the production of new types of organized structures, and (3) the production of amorphous structures. The whole field has been briefly reviewed by Bloch (1954).

ABNORMAL DEVELOPMENT OF ORGANS

In many cases structures still recognizable as leaves, stems, roots, flowers, or other organs have been modified in many ways, sometimes very radically. This is the field of *teratology,* the study of malformations, freaks, and monstrosities, which has long excited the curiosity of botanists (Moquin-Tandon, 1841; Masters, 1869; Worsdell, 1915; Penzig, 1921; and Heslop-Harrison, 1952). Little but descriptive work has been done on most of them. For a long time their scientific value was chiefly to morphologists, who looked to malformations for evidence as to the morphological nature of certain organs. Thus the "metamorphosis" of petals and sepals into leaf-like structures (*phyllody;* Fig. 11-1) suggests that they are really leaves but have been modified in function during evolution. Heslop-Harrison lists three causes for such phenomena: abnormalities in *growth,* of little morphological significance; abnormalities in *development,* owing to failure of hormonal systems or other form-

Fig. 11-1. Sepal phyllody. Sepal of a rose flower showing abnormal development into a structure much like a foliage leaf. (*From T. E. T. Bond.*)

determining factors; and minor abnormalities arising from genetic or environmental causes. Some teratological changes may be reversionary and some progressive.

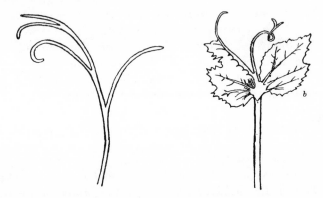

Fig. 11-2. Left, normal tendril of *Cucurbita.* Right, abnormal structure intermediate between a tendril and a foliage leaf. (*From Worsdell.*)

There are various categories of these abnormal structures, or *teratomata* (Figs. 11-2, 11-3), which are only loosely related to each other. About certain of them a considerable literature has grown up. In many cases the causal agent is known, but often it is not. Little developmental work has been done on most of them.

Organoid Galls. Under this term Küster (1910) included many cases of abnormal development or distribution of organs which are clearly the result of parasitism, nutritional disturbances, or other known causes and which often show little constancy of form or structure. Such galls may appear at some distance from the site of the stimulating agent. With these are usually included similar types of abnormalities even if their causal factors are unknown.

In some of these galls it is chiefly the form that is abnormal. In the leaves of various species of *Juncus* parasitized by *Livia juncorum,* for example, the sheath reaches extraordinary size while the lamina remains small or atrophied. In *Populus tremula* small stipules turn into large, leaf-like structures. *Eriophyces* also produces floral abnormalities in which

Fig. 11-3. Abnormal flower of gloxinia, with extra petal-like structures on the outer surface of the corolla and an increase over the normal number of corolla lobes. (*From Worsdell.*)

stamens or carpels become petal-like. Flower buds that have been grafted in a place where leaf buds would normally be sometimes produce unusually large and abnormal flowers, evidently because of nutritional changes.

Some of these changes are comparable to those occurring in regeneration. Thus in vigorously regenerating shoots of *Symphoricarpos* simple leaves become pinnately cut, and in regenerating stalks of *Sambucus,* stipules may be converted into leaves. The removal of the main shoot in the seedling of *Vicia faba* results in the formation of primary leaves or transitional ones instead of those of mature type. It is well known that decapitation, defoliation, and similar injuries lead to various changes. Goebel (1882) thus obtained leaves instead of bud scales in *Prunus padus,* and Blaringhem (1908) reported many morphological abnormalities due to wounding. The formation of cups or aecidia on leaves seems often to be due to nutritional disturbances. Bond (1945) found that sepal phyllody in roses is an effect of hormones that control the vigor of growth and the balance between reproductive and vegetative tendencies. This and other transformations of one sort of floral organ into another may be compared to changes in sex expression that have been found to occur after hormone treatment (Löve and Löve, 1946) or as the result of photoperiodic change.

In other organoid galls, abnormality consists in the formation of structures in places where they do not ordinarily occur. Thus ovaries may appear in normally staminate flowers, stamens within an ovary, or ovules on its surface. In the well-known case of *Lychnis vespertina* attacked by the smut fungus *Ustilago antherorum*, stamens are produced in the female flower (Strasburger, 1900). Flowers and cones may proliferate into vegetative shoots after attack by mites or for other reasons. *Cecidomyia* causes the formation of rootlets on the stalk nodes of *Poa* (Beyerinck, 1885) and *Eriophyces fraxini* small, shortened shoots on the leaves of *Fraxinus*. The attack by mites sometimes results in the growing out (*enation*) of small leaves on large ones or the formation of extra perianths.

Familiar examples of abnormal development which may also be classed as organoid galls are "witches'-brooms" (Fig. 11-4), dense clusters of small, much-branched shoots, chiefly on woody plants and resulting from excessive production of buds which grow immediately into shoots. Attacks by mites and various fungi, especially Exoascaceae and Uredineae, are often the causal agents, though in many instances no parasites are known to be involved. The physiological basis for the development of such structures has been thought to be the accumulation of nutrients, though doubtless there are other factors.

A rather extensive literature has grown up about the character and causation of witches'-brooms, for which the reader is referred to Solereder (1905) and Liernur (1927). Liernur cites 96 instances the causes of which are known, occurring on 49 species of plants in 19 families, and 51 cases of unknown origin. They differ in morphology, anatomy, and etiology but resemble each other in their general character of copious, compact branching. As compared with normal structures, the tissues of their leaves and branches tend to be somewhat less highly differentiated, thus approaching cataplasmatic galls, though mechanical elements are often well developed.

Fasciations. A special type of abnormalities of a rather distinct kind and which may be classed with organoid galls are *fasciations*. These are cases where a normally cylindrical or radially symmetrical plant part becomes flattened and elliptical in cross section to form ribbon-like or sometimes ring-like structures. The origin of fasciation has attracted a good deal of attention among morphologists. Much of the literature is reviewed in the papers of Schoute (1936), Bausor (1937), and O. E. White (1948).

The term fasciation, like others in the field of abnormal growth, has been applied to a rather wide variety of phenomena which probably have different origins even though the final result in all of them is a flattened structure. Frank (1880) distinguished between fasciations that arise by a gradual expansion of the growing point in one plane and others that come from lateral fusion or *connation* between two or more separate

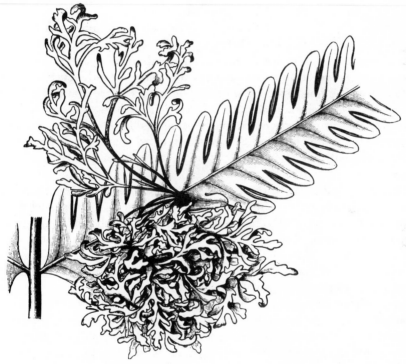

Fig. 11-4. "Witches'-broom" on a fern leaf. (*After Giesenhagen.*)

structures, in natural self-grafting. Schoute believes that the term fasciation should be limited to Frank's first category, and this is now the commonest practice. The difference between the two concepts can be determined only by developmental studies. Johansen (1930) has shown that the genesis of fasciation may be recognized even in early embryogeny.

Fasciation is most conspicuous in the main-shoot axis but occurs also in roots (Schenck, 1916) and may be found in almost all parts of the plant. It may vary from one part to another. Many abnormalities resembling fasciation are to be seen in leaves, such as "double" leaves and others.

Certain instances of fasciation have received special study. It has long been observed that if the epicotyl of a seedling of *Phaseolus multiflorus* is cut off and the buds in the axils of the cotyledons are then allowed to grow they will produce flattened shoots. These later revert to a cylindrical form and produce normal branches. This is an unstable kind of fasciation, and the factors responsible for it are not yet clear (Sachs, 1859; Klebs, 1906; Georgescu, 1927; Bausor, 1937).

Fasciations resulting from other types of mutilations and from wounds are discussed by Blaringhem (1908). They frequently follow pruning in *Salix, Populus, Robinia, Tilia,* and *Corylus.*

Various other factors, both external and internal, have been found to produce fasciation. Growth substances applied in high concentration may induce such vigorous local growth that ribbon-like structures result (Bloch, 1938). In strawberry varieties that have a tendency toward fasciation, this is emphasized by short day-lengths (Darrow and Borthwick, 1954). It has been suggested that fasciation is due to a high level of nutrition, to insufficient nutrition, to changes in correlation produced by growth substances, and to various factors that have been shown, in both normal and regenerative growth, to induce correlative disturbances.

Of especial interest are those instances where fasciation, or a tendency toward it, is inherited. The best known of these is in the cockscomb, *Celosia cristata,* where the inflorescence is often much flattened. Hereditary fasciation has also been found in *Nicotiana* (O. E. White, 1916), *Pharbitis* (Imai and Kanna, 1934), and *Phlox drummondii* (Kelly, 1927). The large-fruited varieties of tomato with more than two carpels may be regarded as examples of genetic fasciation.

Fasciation is found in all groups of vascular plants. Penzig (1921) has reported it for *Psilotum* and *Lycopodium*; Kienholz (1932) for *Pinus,* and Schenck (1916) for other gymnosperms. It is widespread in angiosperms, both dicotyledonous and monocotyledonous, and many instances are cited by Masters. It is particularly frequent in *Taraxacum, Antirrhinum,* and *Delphinium* and has even been found in the giant cactus, *Carnegiea gigantea.*

Pelory. Pelory (or peloria) is a type of floral abnormality, quite different from the others that have been mentioned, in which dorsiventrally symmetrical (bilabiate) flowers become radially symmetrical. It was first discovered by Linnaeus in *Linaria vulgaris,* where it may frequently be found in nature, and has been studied by Sirks (1915) and others (Fig. 11-5). In this species peloric flowers, where they occur, are found at the base of the inflorescence and may show a transition to normal ones at the top. This is perhaps another instance of phasic development. Peloric flowers have also been investigated in *Linaria spuria, Antirrhinum majus,* and *Digitalis purpurea.* Pelory is frequent in Labiatae, where it usually occurs at the top of the inflorescence.

As to the cause of pelory, opinion is divided. In cases such as *Digitalis* the difference between the bilabiate and the radial condition is clearly induced by gravity for it can be reversed experimentally. Peyritsch found that in Labiatae it may be induced by strong illumination. Sachs believed that physiological factors are operative in causing it. There are many cases, however, reported by Vrolik, Darwin, de Vries, Baur, Lotsy, and others, where this type of abnormality, or at least a tendency to produce it, is inherited.

FIG. 11-5. Peloric flower of *Linaria vulgaris,* almost radially symmetrical. (*From Goebel.*)

PRODUCTION OF NEW TYPES OF ORGANIZED STRUCTURES

In organoid galls and similar types of abnormalities that have been discussed, structures recognizable as those found in normal plants are present, though their size, form, and arrangement may be altered and the general pattern of organization distorted. In the group now to be considered the structures produced are entirely novel and cannot be placed in any such morphological category as leaves or stems. They can hardly be regarded as organs, but they are much more than tissue abnormalities for they have a constant and specific form, size, and structure and a very considerable amount of histological differentiation. They result from the attack of parasites. In most cases they undergo a definite period of development, or life cycle, correlated with that of the parasite and thus are different from the cataplasmatic abnormalities to be discussed later. In Küster's terminology they are *prosoplasmatic* galls. There is no sharp line between these and the simpler gall types but their large number and definite forms set them apart as a rather distinct group. The majority are zoocecidia (galls formed by animals). The most conspicuous and best known owe their origin to parasitism by the gall wasps or cynipids, a family of the Hymenoptera. Others are produced by flies of the gall midges and simpler ones by mites. A few are the result of fungus parasites.

Prosoplasmatic galls are so numerous and so remarkable in many respects that they have received much attention and are the basis of an extensive literature. They are discussed in many papers and books by Beyerinck (1883), Molliard (1895), Magnus (1914), Thompson (1915), Felt (1917), Kostoff and Kendall (1929), Küster (1930, 1949), Ross (1932), Carter (1939, 1952), and others. A typical example has been described in detail by Hough (1953).

The small galls produced by some of the rusts or by *Synchytrium pilificum* on the leaves of *Potentilla* may perhaps be included among prosoplasmatic galls, as may those formed on the petioles of *Populus* by *Pemphigus bursarius*. Here the gall is simply a mass of expanded epidermal and cortical cells which have divided anticlinally.

Fɪɢ. 11-6. Insect galls on leaf of rose. (*From Wells.*)

There is a higher degree of organization in cynipid galls, and they have received much more attention than any others (Fig. 11-6). In these the female wasp deposits an egg in the body of the plant, where the larva develops, and the gall results from the reaction of plant tissues to stimulation from the egg and the developing larva. Such galls possess a concentric type of organization. The histology of these structures is as varied as their form (Figs. 11-7, 11-8). Some are relatively simple but others consist of three, four, or even five different types of tissue. Some of these tissues show adaptation to specific functions such as mechanical support, storage, and aeration. The mechanical tissues are of particular interest because of their relation to the position of the larva within the gall and the means of its escape.

The special morphogenetic significance of these galls is that in them a specific modification of the tissue pattern of the host plant is caused by the presence in it of an egg and larva of the parasite. A given cynipid will always produce the same kind of gall on a given plant species, and the galls induced by different wasps on the same plant are quite dissimilar. On *Celtis occidentalis*, Carter found 17 different sorts of galls formed by 17 species of wasps. Each type of gall is related to the character of the larva that develops within it.

Doubtless the formation of these formed galls results from a specific stimulus coming from the wasp or the growing larva and a specific response by the tissues of the host plant, but how such a subtle control of

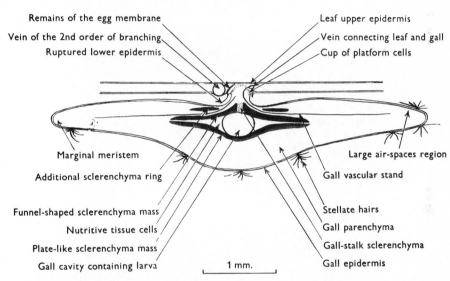

FIG. 11–7. Diagram of a longitudinal section through a cynipid gall on the leaf of oak, showing its specific form and considerable structural differentiation. (*From Hough.*)

the morphogenetic potencies of the host cells is exerted by the parasite is unknown. Various theories have been proposed and many experiments performed to throw light on this problem. It has been suggested that the gall-inducing stimulus is a mechanical one, but this seems rather unlikely, and most workers now believe that the stimulus is chemical in nature, perhaps an enzyme or a specific formative substance.

Many investigators have tried to extract the gall-forming agent from the insect, inject it into a plant, and thus produce a gall artificially, but earlier attempts all failed. Recent ones have been more successful. Parr (1940) and Plumb (1953) injected extracts from the salivary glands of coccids and an aphid into young needles of Norway spruce and induced the formation of galls much like those normally produced by these insects.

K. M. Smith (1920) had shown that the damage to leaves of apple by capsid bugs was caused by secretions of the salivary glands, and this suggested the possibility that the glands of the gall-producing larva secrete an enzyme which calls forth a specific growth reaction in the host tissue. Parr demonstrated the presence of enzymes in the gland extract but found that these did not stimulate gall formation when sterilized. Martin

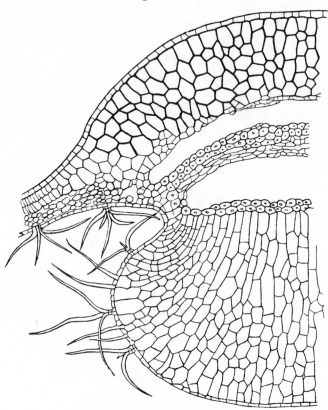

FIG. 11-8. Section through portion of an insect gall showing modification of normal leaf structure (left). The larval chamber is surrounded by mechanical tissue. (*From Küster.*)

(1942), however, produced abnormal growth in sugar cane with sterilized extracts.

Substances produced by the growing larva rather than those injected with the egg are probably most important in gall formation. Little is known about these substances, however, or the place and manner in which they are introduced into the tissues of the plant (Kostoff and Kendall, 1929).

A morphological problem of some interest is whether these galls and the tissues that compose them are really to be considered as "new" structures, morphologically different from the familiar categories. Certainly they have cells and tissues unlike any normally found in their host plants. Such are the various hairy projections on the surface of certain galls, the opening mechanisms, the mechanical tissues, and others concerned with nutrition and aeration. As to whether these are "new" or not depends on our definition of that term. A given morphological category, such as the leaf, presumably has a continuous evolutionary history beginning with early vascular plants. It is part of the norm of plant structure. In this sense such galls are certainly new. They have arisen, however, because of a novel factor in the plant's environment—the gall wasp. It seems probable that if such wasps had existed in the Paleozoic they would have induced galls in the vascular plants of that era. Gall-making ability on the part of the wasp is advantageous to it and doubtless has been developed by selection, but the gall response by the plant to the parasite is not. Presumably the capacity for producing these galls has long been among the developmental potencies of plants. It can be regarded as new historically but not morphologically.

From the morphogenetic point of view the most important fact about these prosoplasmatic galls is that they are highly organized and specifically formed structures induced by an outside stimulus. Here we can see the process of form determination manifest in a simpler fashion than in normal development, for here the inducing agent is not a part of the developmental mechanism but is introduced into the organism. If we understood exactly how these galls are formed, we should doubtless gain some important clues as to the morphogenetic process generally. Something more is involved here than partial loss of organization, the change that takes place in most other galls. Here is operating a constructive, not a degenerative, process.

AMORPHOUS STRUCTURES

In the two previously discussed categories of abnormal growth the original organization was either present in altered form or something entirely different from the normal was produced. There is a third group in which organization at its highest level, with the production of specifically formed structures, is inoperative to a large degree, and only formless, or amorphous, structures are developed. Within these structures there may be some histological differentiation but it is much less than in normal tissue. The cells remain alive, however, and perform many normal physiological activities. They must still possess a certain amount of organization, evident in regulatory action. If this were not so, death would ensue.

There are various sorts of amorphous structures which are not easy to distinguish from each other, but a number of categories may be recognized, such as intumescences, callus, tumors, and galls. The terms "gall" and "tumor" have no very precise meanings, but a gall is most commonly regarded as an anomalous growth due to an attack by a parasite and a tumor as one which results from other causes, though there are many exceptions to these definitions.

Intumescences. The simplest sort of amorphous abnormal growth is one in which a group of cells at the surface of an organ expands into a wart or pustule. These are termed *intumescences* (Sorauer, 1899) and result from various causes (Wallace, 1928). Sometimes, as on the leaf of cabbage (Von Schrenk, 1905), they are groups of watery (hyperhydric) cells, swollen by excessive absorption of water resulting from contact with spray materials or other substances. In woody plants intumescences usually are formed by proliferation of cork cells, sometimes from lenticels and sometimes elsewhere. Such intumescences involve an increase in the cell number (hyperplasia) as contrasted with an increase in cell size (hypertrophy) as in the cabbage leaf. They may result from exposure to ethylene gas and other substances. Intumescences often resemble naturally occurring corky spots on certain plants, especially at lenticels.

Callus. As a result of wounding, a layer of cork cells is usually produced over the wound surface through the action of wound hormones (p. 402). This perhaps is not to be called "abnormal" tissue in the ordinary sense, since it is very common and indeed accompanies bark formation in trees, where new cork layers cover the breaks resulting from expansion of the axis. In many cases, however, these do not occur in the intact, uninjured plant and may best be included among abnormal structures.

In cases of more serious wounds, as where a cutting is removed for rooting, something more complex than a few layers of cork cells is formed at the surface. Here often develops *callus*, an amorphous mass of rather large-celled, loosely arranged parenchymatous tissue, produced by cell division in the ground tissue or more commonly from cambium (Fig. 11-9). Its elements show relatively little differentiation, but there may be some meristematic growth near the surface. For its nutrition, callus depends on food from the normal tissues beneath it.

A callus may reach considerable size but its mass has no definite form and there is little morphogenetic control over its growth. In its later stages, callus may undergo various types of development depending on the kind of plant, the location of the wound, and the external conditions. Often some differentiation appears in it, and cells are produced resembling those of normal tissue. Isolated nests of single cells or groups of cells may develop into tracheid-like elements, usually with reticulate pitting. Sclereids are formed in the same way. These irregular nests have a characteristic appearance, and their presence often indicates the origin of a meristem in the callus.

The structure and arrangement of the cells in such wound tissue as callus are often atypical, especially near the wound itself. The cells twist and turn, and so-called "whorls" thus formed have been described by Mäule (1896), Neeff (1914), and others. Krieg (1908) observed several concentric circles of cambium in the pith of ringed branches of *Vitis* adjacent to a wound. In the outer ring, development was inverted, phloem being formed toward the inside and xylem toward the outside.

Fig. 11-9. Callus on cut stem of *Cleome* produced by application of growth substance. (*Courtesy Boyce Thompson Institute.*)

Save under particular conditions, a callus does not remain callus indefinitely but tends to produce normally organized structures again. This it does by means of new apical meristems, both of shoots and roots, which frequently appear in it. Such meristems arise in several ways. Cells abutting on nests of tracheids may produce a meristem in the form of a hollow sphere. Others may appear elsewhere in the callus or where it is in contact with the pith, cambium, or cortex. These meristems may form secondary wood or phloem. Meristems of roots tend to arise well below the surface and those of shoots either at or just below the surface. From such meristems typical organs may be regenerated in any region of the callus, thus showing that there have been no fundamental changes in the genetic character of the callus cells themselves. Their potencies to produce typically organized structures have been masked but not lost.

Structures much like calluses may be induced by other factors than wounding, especially by various chemical substances. Among these substances are ether, chloroform, camphor, ethylene gas, liquid paraffin, and especially various growth substances (p. 407). Many are nonspecific in their action, and it is to be assumed that their effect is primarily one of injury to the tissues, which produces changes in the cells and thus leads rather indirectly to atypical growth reactions. Others, especially the growth substances, produce rather specific reactions.

One of the properties of the synthetic growth substances (such as indoleacetic, indolebutyric, and naphthaleneacetic acids and paraffin) is their action in stimulating an increase in the number and the size of cells to which they are applied. Sizable overgrowths and calluses may thus be formed on various plant organs if sufficiently high concentrations of these agents are applied; and if this treatment is repeated, tumor-like masses are produced (Schilling, 1915; Brown and Gardner, 1936; Kisser, 1939; Levine, 1940; and others). These often resemble the ones associated with certain bacterial infections.

Callus-like overgrowths are more readily obtained if the paste in which the inducing substances are carried is applied to the more sensitive regions such as those near the shoot tips, particularly after decapitation. Many experiments have been performed, especially on herbaceous dicotyledons, to test the effects of various growth substances on development (see especially the publications from the Boyce Thompson Institute and those of E. J. Kraus and his colleagues at the University of Chicago, p. 405). Differences have been found among the growth substances in the character and extent of abnormal growth they induce, and their effects are also related to the kind of plant, its age, and the region treated. Histological study of these tumors shows that they resemble other calluses and wound tissues, especially in the absence of a constant form or size, the presence of some cellular differentiation as the tumor ages, and the development on them of root and shoot primordia.

Amorphous Galls Produced by Parasites. Amorphous structures which in certain respects resemble intumescences, calluses, and chemically induced tumors are caused by various parasites such as nematodes, mites, insects, fungi, and especially bacteria. Even viruses are now known to be involved in their production (Black, 1949). There is a great variety of these, from small, simple structures to large and relatively complex forms. Some of the huge burls on trees are due to parasites but others apparently are caused by mechanical or other nonparasitic factors. Many amorphous galls have a somewhat more highly organized character than others but they show little constancy in size or form and their histology is less regular and their differentiation simpler than in normal structures. Küster describes and figures many of these (1903a, 1911, 1925). He gave them the name by which they are now commonly known, *cataplasmatic* galls.

Crown Gall. Here belongs the gall that has been studied more intensively than any other, crown gall (Fig. 11-10). This is produced on a wide variety of plants, at least 142 genera in 61 families, by the bacterium

FIG. 11-10. A crown gall on sunflower. (*Courtesy Department of Plant Pathology, University of Wisconsin.*)

Agrobacterium tumefaciens. There are reviews of work on such galls by Levine (1936); Riker, Spoerl, and Gutsche (1946); de Ropp (1951*a*); Klein and Link (1955); and Braun and Stonier (1958). Crown gall has been investigated by Erwin F. Smith and his colleagues (1911, 1917, and many others) and later by various botanists among whom Braun,

Gautheret, Levine, Riker, de Ropp, and P. R. White have been especially active.

The inception of a crown gall seems always to come by means of a wound. In the early stages of this infection the reactions of the host cells produced either directly or indirectly by the parasite are much like wound reactions, but in the young gall the new cell walls soon lose the regular arrangement found in wound tissues. Reparative wound calluses and those formed at grafts often resemble the early stages of crown gall, but as the gall develops, rapid cell division occurs in the outer layers and a large mass of callus is formed. The great difference between crown gall and ordinary callus, however, is that the latter is self-limiting and soon becomes quiescent whereas gall tissue is capable of indefinite and amorphous growth. This is a fact of particular morphogenetic significance. There is now good evidence that the cells of crown gall have undergone a permanent change in character. This seems to involve an acquirement of the capacity for autonomous growth, which may result, Braun (1958) believes, from the permanent activation of a series of systems by which growth substances are synthesized. In normal cells these systems are precisely regulated and growth ultimately stops. Normal cells in culture require auxin from an outside source but crown-gall cells do not. Crown gall thus differs from most other galls, which are self-limiting and do not grow indefinitely. In some cases the crown gall matures, stops enlarging, and undergoes some histological differentiation. Nests of vascular cells, chiefly xylem, appear in it (Fig. 11-11), and the primordia of roots and shoots may develop. The cytological and histological changes in the development of a typical crown gall have been described by Therman (1956) and Kupila (1958).

The process of conversion of normal cells into tumor cells is a gradual one. Its inception depends both on a wound stimulus and on the presence of an auxin (Braun and Stonier, 1958). Tumors differ in appearance, in the degree of their organization, and in their capacity for growth. These differences may be the result of their location on the plant, the virulence of the strain of infecting bacteria, or other factors. Crown-gall tissues can be grafted into normal ones, and these may be carried through an indefinite series of graft transfers. There is no good evidence that they induce adjacent normal tissue to form tumor cells, though temporary alterations may take place there. Gall tissues can readily be grown in culture and can then be grafted back to normal ones and form galls. In all these cases their cells remain unchanged.

In a few plants *secondary* tumors may develop, often at some distance from the original gall or primary tumor. In certain cases this results from an infection near the apical meristem and a subsequent separation of the secondary from the primary gall by growth. Sometimes, however, secondary galls develop after growth in length is over but always in close association with the xylem, as though the latter were the pathway of induction. Secondary tumors behave much like primary ones in grafts and in culture, and there seems to be no very fundamental difference between the two.

Remarkably enough, many crown galls, particularly secondary ones, seem to be free from bacteria. There is evidence, however, that bacteria must always be present at the very beginning of tumor growth but that they soon disappear. Braun and White (1943) made *Vinca rosea*

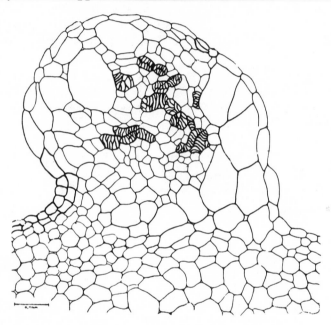

Fig. 11-11. Section of a young crown gall on *Pelargonium,* showing a nest of vascular cells. (*From Noël.*)

galls free of bacteria by heat treatment. Such tissues retained their gall-producing properties when grafted into healthy plants (White, 1945). Although bacteria are required for the inception of crown gall, once the change is induced they no longer seem necessary for the growth of gall tissue.

Crown gall (and presumably other amorphous galls of this general type) does not result from a single cause but involves a series of factors. Klein and Link (1955) discuss this in their extensive account of the etiology of crown gall (Fig. 11-12). There is first a *conditioning* phase, perhaps induced by wounding and involving wound hormones. This makes the cells susceptible to conversion into tumor cells. It is possible that the activation process in ordinary wound healing and in the inception of tumors may be the same. This is followed by an *induction* phase in which a tumor-inducing substance of some sort enters the host from the bacterium. A heat-labile product of virulent crown-gall bacteria has been found to alter conditioned cells into incipient tumor cells. How this is done is not clear. The substance may itself be the agent of change, possibly a virus or a macromolecule of DNA or even a gene or a hereditary agent in the cytoplasm; or it may induce the change by causing gene mutation or the production of permanent, self-reproducing bodies, sometimes called plasmoids. Finally, in the *promotion* phase the gall grows to completion. Here auxin is involved, in the promotion of an incipient into a primary tumor cell, in the multiplication and per-

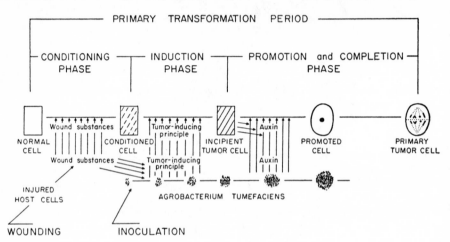

FIG. 11-12. Diagram of probable interrelations of various factors in the transformation of a normal cell into a primary tumor cell. (*From Klein and Link.*)

haps the differentiation of tumor cells, and in causing various host effects which accompany tumor formation. The physiology of crown-gall formation has been further discussed by Klein (1958).

A question often raised is whether crown gall and its derivatives are really plant cancers, as Smith vigorously maintained they were, or if something different from true cancer is here involved. This question has been discussed by Levine (1936), White and Braun (1942), and others. It should be remembered that such a condition as malignancy is difficult to define in the same terms in organisms as different in structure and organization as plants and animals. The unrestrained, invasive type of growth characteristic of animal cancer, with its metastases and lethal quality, could hardly be expected in a plant, which has no true circulatory system and lacks the high degree of organization that makes animals so vulnerable. The animal cancer cell has lost its specificity and become, so to speak, an independent parasitic entity of unlimited growth. What this change involves and what causes it are still not understood. Crown-gall tumor cells are certainly in this same category for they grow indefinitely and do not depend on the continual presence of the factors that induced them. The true cell invasions and metastases, in which bits of cancer tissue are carried away to other parts of the body and there develop new centers of malignancy, are absent in plants, but transfer of gall tissue from place to place by grafting is readily accomplished. Many students of the problem are inclined to regard crown-gall tumors as basically no different from animal cancers. It is obvious that these examples of abnormal growth provide some of the best material known for a study of the way in which the higher levels of organization in the plant are broken down. For students of morphogenesis they long have had a particular interest.

Root Nodules. Another type of cataplasmatic galls rather different in character from the others here described and of much practical importance to man are the nodules formed on the roots of leguminous plants from the invasion of their cortical tissues by species of *Rhizobium.* They are an example of what has been called "controlled parasitism," for the relation between this bacterium and the plant may better be regarded as symbiosis rather than parasitism since the host plant obtains an advantage because of the atmospheric nitrogen fixed by the bacteria. These nodules have a higher degree of organization and produce more specialized structures than do most cataplasmatic galls and perhaps should be included under prosoplasmatic ones (Allen and Allen, 1953). The particular character of the nodule depends upon the host plant and the species of bacterium that invades it. As in crown gall, auxin action may here be involved.

Abnormal Growth Due to Other Causes. Many cases have been reported of abnormalities due to other factors than parasitism or chemical stimulation. X rays may produce them (Sankewitsch, 1953), as may ionizing radiations (Gunckel and Sparrow, 1954). Some resulted from the A-bomb tests in the Pacific (Biddulph and Biddulph, 1953).

In some plants tumors arise from no recognizable cause and are presumably due to somatic mutations or to a modification of organized development by other genetic factors. The best known case is that of the tumors occurring spontaneously in hybrids between *Nicotiana glauca* and *N. Langsdorfii* (Kostoff, 1930a; Kehr and Smith, 1954). These are small amorphous structures appearing on stems and branches, and histologically resembling wound callus and crown gall. Kostoff believes that they are due to a disturbed growth balance, either in nucleus or cytoplasm, between these two particular species. These tumors, removed from the plant, are the ones used by P. R. White in his first tissue cultures (1939). He found later that they retained their specific properties in culture for years and continued to grow as tumors when grafted into young stems of *Nicotiana glauca* (1944). Satina, Rappaport, and Blakeslee (1950) studied the development of somewhat similar tumors appearing in fertilized ovules from incompatible crosses in *Datura*.

Changes in cellular character are sometimes associated with abnormal growth. Prothallia of some ferns, when grown in culture, often produce various types of proliferations (Partanen, Sussex, and Steeves, 1955). Some of these remain essentially prothallial in character and show no fundamental deviation from normal. Their cells are still able to regenerate normal prothallia again. Certain tumor-like forms, however, are modified much further, for they have lost this ability. This loss is accompanied by a modification in cellular character, visible as an increase in chromosome number from $1n$ to $3n$ or $4n$. Such forms may be comparable in a sense to crown gall. White and Millington (1954) have described a woody, nonbacterial tumor in spruce which begins in a single cambium cell. This has been altered, physiologically or genetically, and forms a mass of abnormal tissue. The plant becomes what is essentially a sectorial chimera.

Various aspects of the problem of plant tumors have been discussed by P. R. White (1951), de Ropp (1951a), Klein and Link (1955), and others.

Tissue Cultures. Tissue cultures can hardly be called tumors or galls, but in them the normal organization of the plant has disappeared to a greater extent than in any other case here discussed. A book on morphogenesis is not the place to consider this subject in any detail but it does have some important morphogenetic implications that should be mentioned. So-called tissue cultures of plant material on sterile media have been studied actively in recent years, and for an account of them the reader is referred to the publications of the pioneers in this field, especially P. R. White, Robbins, Gautheret, and Nobécourt.

Animal tissues have been cultured for half a century but it was much more recently that this was done successfully with plants. The problems involved were first clearly stated by Haberlandt, who himself failed to grow isolated cells from higher plants in artificial media. A necessary prerequisite for the success later attained was the development of satisfactory media consisting of pure substances of known chemical character, including salts, carbohydrates, organic nitrogenous materials, vitamins, and growth substances. The media developed by the early plant workers were superior to the sera and other complex and little understood ones previously used by tissue culturists.

The first plant cultures were not tissue cultures in the strict sense that they consisted of only one kind of cells, as in many animal cultures. Most were really organ cultures. Those grown from root tips can be carried through an indefinite number of subcultures and produce large masses of root tissue. Shoot axes may be cultured in the same way from apical meristems, and Nitsch (1951) and others have succeeded in growing fruits from small primordia. Leaves can be grown to maturity in the same way (Steeves and Sussex, 1957), as also can ovules (Maheshwari, 1958). These organ cultures have given much information on the nutritional requirements of various parts of the plant and have

FIG. 11-13. Culture of stem callus of tobacco on nutrient agar, six weeks after transfer to new medium. (*Courtesy Department of Plant Pathology, University of Wisconsin.*)

been of importance for an understanding of their physiology. Wetmore (p. 222) grew fern plants from shoot apices in culture and found pronounced morphological effects of differences in the medium, a result of much morphogenetic significance.

Something closer to a true culture can be attained by growing calluses, tumors, parenchyma, and bits of tissue from the cambial region (Fig. 11-13). Structures much like amorphous tumors and galls result. In these the strict morphogenetic control is relaxed and the explanted material may be grown in unlimited quantities by subculturing. Such cultures have been made of spontaneous tumors and of secondary crown gall.

Gautheret (1945) showed that with ordinary plant material, as in carrot, endive, and various woody plants, a callus must first be allowed to develop from an excised piece and that this callus could then be cultured.

There are many differences between species and between different parts of the same plant as to growth and structure of the culture produced. Pieces of tissue from the cambial region, for example, which retain some degree of organization for a time, gradually lose it in successive transfers. Some cultures finally become essentially homogeneous masses of parenchyma. In a few cases, however, patches and whorls of tracheid-like tissue appear in these, as do meristems of roots and shoots. The conditions under which this differentiation occurs vary, depending in part on the source of the material and especially on the character of the nutrient medium and the age of the culture.

It is now possible to produce plant cultures where the cells are not united into masses but grow and divide as individual cells, much as they do in certain animal cultures. This may be thought of as representing the lowest level of plant organization, the loss of all relationships above the single cell. Among those who have done pioneer work in this field are Muir, Hildebrandt, and Riker (1954, 1958); de Ropp (1955); Nickell (1956); Reinert (1956); Torrey (1957a); and Tulecke (1957).

Of particular interest for morphogenesis is the culture work of Steward and his collaborators (1958 and p. 75). Using a basic liquid culture medium supplemented by coconut milk and continually rotated, they grew small explants of carrot tissue taken from the phloem of the root. Single cells here often became separated and floated freely, dividing very irregularly and growing into small cell aggregates. When these reached a certain size, the cells at the middle of the aggregate began to show differences from the rest, and some developed as tracheid-like structures, surrounded by a ring or sheath of cambium-like cells. From this center, one or more root meristems developed. When such an aggregate is grown on the surface of an agar medium it produces a shoot meristem and in time a carrot plant. So far, a whole plant has not been produced directly from a single cell but only by way of a cell aggregate. It is significant that although bits of carrot phloem tissue, placed directly in culture with coconut milk, may form large masses of callus-like tissue, they much less readily produce roots and shoots, perhaps because of inhibiting substances still present in them.

Radical though the changes are which plant tissues display when cultured, there is no evidence that any permanent or genetic effect is produced in them or any new developmental potencies induced. A considerable degree of morphogenetic control has been relaxed, just as it has been in amorphous galls.

It is evident that there is an immense amount of information available about abnormal growth but that students of morphogenesis have not as yet made very much use of it for their purposes. Three facts, however, which emerge from a study of this subject have already proved to be of much morphogenetic significance:

1. The actual developmental potencies of most plant cells are far wider than ever come to expression in normal development.

2. It is possible to break down the organization of the plant body into a series of successively lower levels and then to restore normal organization again.

3. This can be done without modifying the genetic character of the cells.

A continued study of these facts, and of others in this field, will certainly prove very fruitful. Abnormal development is only development under unusual conditions, and the wider spectrum of morphogenetic information thus made available provides the student of development with a powerful tool for the study of some of his most difficult problems.

PART THREE

Morphogenetic Factors

CHAPTER 12

Introduction to Factors

In earlier chapters various morphogenetic phenomena were discussed, but relatively little was said as to the factors that produced them. There now remains the task of relating these phenomena to changes in the outer or inner environment of the plant and attempting to account for their origin. This is really a part of the broader field of plant physiology, and no sharp line can be drawn between the two. Much of physiology, particularly those parts of it that deal with the various metabolic processes, is not of primary interest for morphogenesis. Other parts of it, however, such as photoperiodism, vernalization, auxin action, water relations, and the carbohydrate-nitrogen ratio, for example, have much significance for the morphogenetic phenomena of polarity, differentiation, regeneration, and others. To present these morphogenetic implications adequately would mean going more deeply into plant physiology and its vast literature than can be attempted in the present volume. No discussion of the problems of plant morphogenesis would be complete, however, without some mention of the physiological factors which influence development so powerfully. The purpose of this final section of the book is to introduce the reader to the more important of these factors and to provide him with an entry into the literature of the subject. No attempt will be made to discuss them thoroughly from the point of view of plant physiology.

It is first necessary to consider the relation between the two chief sorts of factors—environmental and genetic. A living plant is an organized system maintaining itself in a complex and changing environment. Its genetic constitution (or *genotype*) remains unaltered save for occasional doubling of the chromosomes in local areas or the rare occurrence of somatic mutations. Despite this, the plant does not remain unchanged. Its appearance (or *phenotype*) is often greatly modified as the environment is altered, and we commonly say that this change is the result of an environmental factor. So, in a sense, it is, but there is often difficulty in disentangling the effects of heredity and environment in morphogenetic changes. One should remember that *both* are always operating. A visible trait is the developmental reaction of a specific (and constant) genetic constitution to a specific environment. Every trait is therefore inherited since it will always be produced if the environment is of a certain sort. In some traits the expression of the genetic constitution is essentially the same under a wide range of environments. The relative position of the floral parts, for example, the arrangement of the leaves, or the character of the pitting on the side walls of the vessels in the wood is usually quite unchanged under various conditions of light, moisture, temperature, or auxin concentration. Such traits, for this reason, are especially useful in taxonomy. Others, such as the height of the plant, the thickness of the cuticle on its leaves, and whether it flowers or not, may be very different under different conditions of nutrition, water supply, and photoperiod. Such traits are usually said to be determined by environmental factors. Actually, both types of traits are inherited and both are environmentally determined. In the former, the repertoire of responses of the genetic constitution to changes in the environment is relatively meagre whereas in the latter it may be very wide. Under a given length of day, for example, salvia plants will flower but lettuce plants remain entirely vegetative. What promotes or inhibits flowering is not simply the day-length but the different inherited responses of these two plants to this day-length.

Where the developmental response of a plant varies widely under different environments as it often does when such factors as light or water or auxin concentration are changed, the obvious way to study the morphogenetic processes concerned is to use genetically uniform material but to change one or another of the environmental conditions under experimental control. This method has proved very successful and has yielded a great body of information as to the relations of environment to plant development. This has been by far the most fruitful method of morphogenetic analysis since it lends itself so readily to experimental attack.

Traits in which environmental changes have little effect on the developmental expression of the genetic constitution can be studied by the usual techniques of genetics. These consist primarily in maintaining a constant environment, crossing genetically pure stocks that show different aspects of the trait to be studied, and analyzing the results in subsequent generations. There is much less opportunity here to modify the variables, for the genes themselves can be altered only with great difficulty and in an unpredictable fashion. The rise of biochemical genetics, however, is providing a much wider basis for experiment here.

A question often raised in the discussion of these environmentally induced characters is whether they are adaptations and thus may serve to maintain the life of the plant. Many structural traits, such as the much reduced leaf size of microphyllous xerophytes, the nectaries in many flowers, or the wound cork produced on an injured surface, are present under almost all environments and are so deeply embedded in the genotype, so to speak, that the only way they may be changed is through genetic mutation. They have doubtless arisen by means of natural selection, and their adaptive character is due to this fact.

Other traits, such as the shape and structure of the leaf blade in heterophyllous plants, the degree of development of vascular tissue in the stem, or the place of origin of roots and shoots along a regenerating axis, are often subject to very wide differences, depending on light, water, auxin concentration, mechanical stresses, and other factors. Though they can be greatly modified experimentally, these changes seem in most cases clearly advantageous under natural conditions and are thus to be regarded as adaptations. The adaptation here (doubtless also the result of natural selection) is not a specific and unchanging structure but the tendency to react developmentally in a favorable way as conditions change.

It seems clear, however, that in many other cases, where there is a wide range of developmental differences induced by changes in the environment, these are not adaptive or favorable for survival but are neutral in this respect. The degree of lobing in a leaf as affected by temperature, the relative abundance of male and female flowers as affected by nutritional factors, or the shape of the fruit as affected by the size to which it is able to grow seem none of them to have significance for survival. Such traits appear to be simply accidental developmental results of the interaction between genetic constitution and environment. Among these, particularly the ones induced by extreme environmental changes, are some of the most interesting for morphogenesis. It is therefore necessary to divorce completely the problem of adaptation, which is an evolutionary one, from that of the environmental induction of characters, which is a morphogenetic one.

In studying the various factors that are important in plant development, emphasis in some cases is put on changes in the environment—external and internal—and in others on changes in the genetic constitution. This is purely an arbitrary classification, however, and simply for convenience. In the present treatment of the subject morphogenetic factors will be discussed in several general groups. Some, such as light, temperature, gravity, and some mechanical factors, originate chiefly in the external environment though their effects, of course, are produced internally. They may be grouped together as physical factors. Among these is included water, since its morphogenetic effects (as opposed to its physiological ones) are due not so much to its chemical composition as to the physical processes of its absorption and evaporation.

A second group are the chemical factors, which derive their importance primarily from their participation in the chemical processes going on in the plant. Some substances, notably those in mineral nutrition, come into the plant from the outside, but many originate internally as products of the plant's metabolism. Especially important in morphogenesis are the various growth substances.

A third group of factors, the genetic ones, may also be regarded as part of the internal environment. Here are to be considered the genes, permanent and self-perpetuating; the chromosomes, which may have certain morphogenetic effects apart from the genes they contain; and the cytoplasm, the intermediary between genes and developmental processes. These factors, though doubtless effective because of their physical or chemical character, are difficult at present to reduce to such terms and are best considered by themselves.

The effects of these various factors on development are complicated by the fact that they are operating on an organized living system which tends to regulate its activities in conformity to a specific norm. Three consequences of this should be borne in mind:

First, a given factor does not lead directly to a given result but serves instead as a stimulus or evocator that sets off a reaction in the organism. What this will be depends on the state of the system at the time. The effect of light on a photographic plate is easily predictable, but its effect on a plant depends on the part of the plant concerned, the age of the plant, and its physiological condition.

Second, the effect of one factor may be greatly modified by another. The photoperiodic effect of light, for example, may depend in a given case on the temperature of the environment, so that one factor may sometimes be substituted for another. Although the essence of good experimental work is to deal with only one variable at a time, this often is impossible in morphogenetic experiments (and in biology generally) for no one factor can be studied entirely independently of the others. What it will do depends on the rest of the environment and on the state of the organism.

Third, the organized system is not a constant one but tends to change in character from one phase in its life cycle to the next and from one region of the body to another. The *potency* of a cell (the repertoire of developmental possibilities open to it), high at first, is reduced as the cell grows older. Doors continually close behind it, so to speak. The *reactivity* of a cell (the response it will make to a given environmental change) also is different at successive developmental stages. Both potency and reactivity may be unlike in different parts of the organism.

An investigation of the effects of various factors on plant development, particularly environmental ones, though not as simple as might at first appear, may still be very fruitful. It is often possible to examine the effects of changes in one factor without serious complications from others, and the organism does remain essentially constant over short periods. The very considerable knowledge now available as to the factors that modify plant development has proved most important for an understanding of the problems of morphogenesis, and there are wide possibilities for extending it much further. The next seven chapters are devoted to a brief consideration of the operation of these factors.

CHAPTER 13

Light

Light is a powerful factor in determining the course of development in plants and has a much more important morphogenetic effect on them than it does on animals. This is to be expected, since light is necessary for photosynthesis and thus for the production of food. Experiment has made it clear, however, that the morphogenetic influence of light is much more subtle and indirect than this and results from its control not only of food production but of various physiological activities in the plant by which this food is distributed in the processes of growth and differentiation. The role of light in plant development has been studied actively for many years and is the basis of an extensive literature. Among the more inclusive reviews of this field are those by MacDougal (1903*a*), Burkholder (1936), and Parker and Borthwick (1950).

Many of the early results are invalid because of the impossibility in those days of exact control of light, as to its intensity and quality, in experimental work, but most of these difficulties have now been overcome, and light in a plant's environment can be manipulated with relative ease.

It is a matter of common observation that plants reach their greatest size and vigor in good light and that insufficient illumination results in weak and spindly growth even if water, soil nutrients, and temperature are at their optimum levels. Most of the experimental work with light has involved not merely differences between light and darkness but measured differences in the light stimulus itself. Three of these are of chief importance: the *intensity*, the *quality*, and the *duration* of the light. Intensity is the brightness of the illumination, the actual energy of the radiation. Quality concerns the wave length of the light. Duration refers to the relative lengths of the alternating periods of light and darkness to which the plant is exposed. These differences are not always sharply separable, and one often modifies the effects of another.

308

INTENSITY OF LIGHT

Since rate of photosynthesis increases with light intensity, up to a certain point, the growth and vigor of a plant are generally proportional, within limits, to the brightness of the light to which it is exposed. Shirley (1929) grew a variety of plants in different intensities of daylight and found that at low ones dry weight was directly proportional to intensity but that at higher ones growth was relatively less. He observed that intensity also affected certain qualitative traits, such as ratio of root to shoot, strength of stem, thickness of leaves, and development of vascular tissue.

It has frequently been observed that plants grown in shade have relatively small root systems. In general it may be said that stem elongation varies inversely with light intensity but that width varies with it directly (Popp, 1926). The effect of light may be different on different parts of the plant and at different stages of development. Some morphological effects of light may be quite specific though the mechanisms involved are unknown. Some herbaceous stems, for example, have zig-zag form in the light but are straight if grown in the dark. Plants that twine in the light usually lose this ability in darkness.

Light is also important morphogenetically for some plants lacking chlorophyll. In certain mushrooms, for example, the fruiting body will not develop normally in complete darkness although the whole vegetative mycelium is subterranean (Borriss, 1934*b*).

Etiolation. The most conspicuous effect of differences in light intensity on plant structure is to be seen in the phenomenon of *etiolation*. It is a familiar fact that green plants growing in darkness or relatively weak light tend to be tall and spindly, with small, pale leaves, weak roots, and poorly developed vascular tissues. Such plants soon die unless considerable reserve food is available in seeds or other storage organs, in which case etiolated growth may continue for some time. The early work of Kraus (1869) showed that etiolation involves a considerable increase in cell length, though in most cases this is accompanied by some increase in cell number in the longitudinal dimension.

Different parts of the plant and different species differ considerably in their manifestations of etiolation. Only shoots etiolate and not roots, flowers, or fruits. Avery, Burkholder, and Creighton (1937*a*) observed marked differences between the first internode and the coleoptile as to their elongation in various light intensities. Intensity may also affect the proportions of parts. In *Tropaeolum* plants, for example, which are growing in weak light the ratio of petiole length to lamina width becomes progressively greater as the leaves develop, whereas under normal illumination the two dimensions grow at about the same rate (Pearsall, 1927).

As to the causes of etiolation there has been much discussion but no final agreement. Auxin is undoubtedly involved, for it is well known that sensitivity to it increases in darkness. Wave length of light is also important here, for etiolation may be very different in red light and in blue. The two processes of leaf growth and stem elongation may be affected differently.

Priestley (1926*b*) called attention to the fact that in etiolated stems the endodermis tends to be well developed and to have thick-walled cells. An etiolated stem is thus somewhat like a root in structure. He suggests that for this reason water and nutrients, coming from the roots

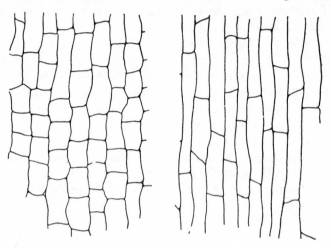

Fig. 13-1. Effect of etiolation on cell shape. Longitudinal section of cortical parenchyma of the stem of *Vicia faba* when grown in light (left) and in darkness (right). (*After Kolda.*)

into the vascular cylinder, may be confined there and prevented from passing outward. This would tend to accelerate growth at the tip of the shoot and to check the development of leaves.

The relation of light to normal and etiolated growth evidently involves the problems of cell division and cell enlargement. In beans Brotherton and Bartlett (1918) found that in the epidermis about a third of the added growth in length of etiolated as compared with normal plants was due to more cells and about two-thirds to longer cells, the rate of both processes of division and enlargement being inversely proportional to light intensity. Cell elongation has been shown in many other cases to increase with diminished light intensity (Fig. 13-1). This is evident not only in green plants but in fungi (Castle and Honeyman, 1935).

Whether light produces its effect on cell size by changing osmotic concentration, permeability of cell membranes, attraction of protoplasm for water, character of the cell wall, or other processes is not clear. It is significant that not merely is cell size increased in low light intensity but size along the polar axis of the cell.

Meier (1934) studied the effects of the intensity of light on cell division in the unicellular alga *Stichococcus bacillaris* and found that its multiplication in culture is proportional to the intensity of illumination up to a certain point but that high intensities check it.

Thomson (1954) grew seedlings of oats and of peas with different amounts of light and reports that light accelerates whatever growth processes are going on while it acts, its effect depending on the stage of development of the tissues concerned. Exposure early in the course of either the cell-division phase or that of cell elongation hastens the

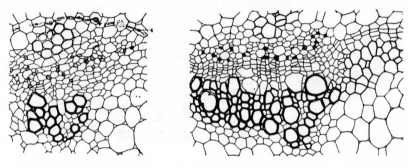

Fig. 13-2. Light and vascular development. Portion of the vascular cylinder of the stem of *Vicia faba* grown in darkness (left) and in the light (right). (*From Borgström.*)

completion of that phase of growth, but after it is under way light hastens the transition to the next phase and thus reduces the final number or length of cells.

Shape traits may be modified by light. Smirnov and Zhelochovtsev (1931) found that in *Tropaeolum* leaves the reduction of blade expansion in weak light modified the fundamental growth pattern. Njoku (1956a) reports that differences in light intensity change the leaf shape in *Ipomoea*.

Anatomical characters are also affected. Penfound (1931) observed that stems of *Helianthus* and *Polygonum* growing in full sunlight have a much greater amount of xylem and more and thicker-walled cells in the mechanical tissue than those in shade. The much reduced vascular tissue of etiolated plants is well known (Fig. 13-2). Bond and others have found that as light intensity is reduced the development of the endodermis increases in the stem, where it normally is weak or absent. That this tissue is much better developed in roots than in stems may be related to the fact that roots normally grow in darkness and stems in light.

Leaf structure is often different in different light intensities. It has long been known (for example, Nordhausen, 1903) that in many cases leaves on the south side of the tree ("sun leaves") are thicker and better differentiated than those on the north side or the interior of the crown ("shade leaves"; Fig. 13-3). This has been discussed by Lundegårdh (1931) and others. A particularly striking case is described by Cormack (1955). The question has been raised (p. 327) as to whether this effect is actually due to light intensity or to differences in water relations, par-

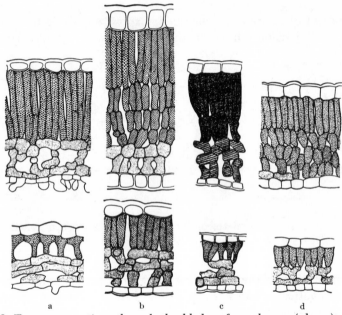

a   b   c   d

FIG. 13-3. Transverse sections through the blades of sun leaves (above) and shade leaves (below) of a, *Acer;* b, *Quercus;* c, *Fagus;* and d, *Tilia.* (*After Schramm.*)

ticularly rate of transpiration, for sun leaves tend to be xeromorphic in character. Talbert and Holch (1957) studied the leaves of 37 species and found that sun leaves usually had smaller laminar area, shorter blade perimeter, deeper lobes, more pronounced veining and marginal serrations, more hairy surfaces, and shorter petioles than shade leaves.

Anderson (1955) studied the development of sun and shade leaves in *Cornus* and *Viburnum* and finds that in the latter the large leaf size is the result of earlier and more rapid growth. The greater thickness of sun leaves is due to greater cell elongation. Differentiation takes place earlier in shade leaves.

QUALITY OF LIGHT

Much work has been done on the effects of different wave lengths (colors) of light. Many of the early results here are of doubtful value since it was often difficult to change the wave length without at the same time modifying intensity. There are many well-established facts, however, from which conclusions can be drawn.

It seems clear, for example, that the longer wave lengths, notably those in the red, promote a marked elongation of cells and thus of tissues, whereas the blue rays (and white light) check this effect and tend to prevent elongation. Teodoresco (1929) describes many examples of this, especially from less highly organized forms such as young plants of liverworts or fern prothallia growing from spores. In these cases where white or blue light is used, a rather compact group of cells develops from the spore, but in red light a much elongated, spindly cell. The same effects are evident in fungi. An important fact is that the plane of cell division is usually controlled by the light. Mohr (1956) finds that in young fern prothallia in red light cell division tends to be at right angles to the polar axis of the structure so that filaments of elongate cells are formed, whereas in blue light division is in various planes, so that a plate of cells develops. In a normal and growing fern prothallium transferred to red light, many of the cells grow out to form filaments.

The same effects are to be seen in the more complex higher plants. Thus Teodoresco finds that blue light checks petiole elongation but increases blade area, and Vince (1956) that in many plants, when grown under lights of equal energy levels, total stem length, internode length, and leaf length increase with increase in the wave length. Not all plants react alike, however. Whether the mechanism by which the red rays promote elongation is like that by which low light intensity does so is not clear, but presumably the same processes are affected by both factors. Wassink and Stolwijk (1952) used equipment by which it was possible to grow plants in various wave lengths of monochromatic light, and under these conditions there was strong elongation of the stem and curling of leaves and petioles in green, yellow, and red light but essentially normal growth in blue. Fortanier (1954), however, observed that only at high light intensities is stem elongation greatest in red, yellow, and green. At low ones it is greatest in blue. Leaf number was not affected by wave length.

Quality of light also affects flowering. Curry and Wassink (1956), working with annual *Hyoscyamus niger*, found that flowers were produced in blue and infrared-plus-red radiation but that neither stem elongation nor flower-bud formation occurred in green or red light.

The relation of wave length to auxin production and other problems of photomorphogenesis have been discussed by Stolwijk (1954).

Other developmental traits are affected by light quality. Thus Funke (1931) observed that in heterophyllous water plants, where the juvenile immersed leaves are ribbon-like, these never develop into anything else if the plants are grown in red or in green light. In blue or white, however, normal mature foliage is produced. This change may be reversed by changing the wave length of the light. In root cultures of peas, red light inhibits the formation of lateral roots more effectively than blue or green, perhaps by inactivating substances necessary for root growth (Torrey, 1952). Many other instances of the effects of light of different wave length on development in higher plants have been reported.

Less work has been done with lower plants. Meier (1936), again with the alga *Stichococcus,* found that in cell culture the individual cells in a given time multiplied fourfold in white light, threefold in blue, but only twofold in yellow and red. Green light proved to be destructive to them.

In the slime mold *Didynium nigripes,* light is necessary for the development of sporangia (Straub, 1954). Green light has no effect but red and blue have. If plasmodia treated with these wave lengths are killed by freezing and fed to living plasmodia, the latter produce sporangia after a briefer exposure to light and much more rapidly than control plasmodia which had been fed untreated ones. Evidently a substance conducive to sporangium production is formed by the action of light of certain wave lengths. Gray (1953), using the slime mold *Physarum polycephalum,* found that continuous irradiation with monochromatic light in the blue and green and a narrow band in the yellow induced fruiting bodies, the rate of their formation being inverse to the wave length of the light used. He suggests that a changed acidity resulting from the irradiation may be responsible for the production of sporangia.

There are general discussions of the morphogenetic effects of different wave lengths of light by Parker and Borthwick (1950) and Wassink and Stolwijk (1956).

DURATION OF LIGHT

One might expect that the longer a plant is exposed to light favorable for photosynthesis, the more it would grow and the more vigorous it would be. Keeping plants in continuous light, however, is often found to result in less vigor and in a disturbance of the normal reproductive cycle. It is evident that the production of flowers and fruits is not something that inevitably occurs but rather that it will happen only when environmental factors are favorable for it. In 1920 Garner and Allard published the results of their pioneer observations which showed that flowering is not determined by the intensity or the quality of light alone but by the length of daily exposure to light, or the *photoperiod*. What essentially is involved is the relative length of the alternating light and dark periods, or, perhaps more accurately, the length of the dark period for some plants and of the light period for others. This phenomenon of *photoperiodism* has now been subjected to intensive study. A history of the work on it until 1948 was written by Murneek (1948). Other surveys of the subject or particular aspects of it are those by Garner (1937), Burkholder (1936), Hamner (1944), Leopold (1951), and Naylor (1953).

All plants do not respond alike to photoperiodic stimulation. In the so-called short-day forms, flowering is induced by relatively short periods of daily illumination (and thus longer dark periods). Such plants flower naturally in fall or early spring. Long-day plants require a longer period of light and in nature are summer-flowering forms (Fig. 13-4). Many plants, such as the tomato, are day-neutral and will flower under long or short photoperiods or continuous illumination.

This classification is not a very exact one, for different steps in the reproductive process may each have their optimal photoperiod. Thus most strawberries flower under a relatively short day but fruit under a long one, and *Phlox* is a long-day plant for flowering but is day-neutral for fruiting. The optimal period for the formation of flower primordia at a growing point may be different from the one determining the later growth and opening of the flowers. These relationships have been discussed by Roberts (1954).

There is a close relation between temperature and photoperiodism which has been studied by a number of workers, among them Purvis (1953) and Vlitos and Meudt (1955). High temperature will sometimes induce flowering even when day-length is not favorable for it. In vernalization (p. 339) it is necessary not only to expose the germinating seeds to low temperature but to provide the proper photoperiod for later growth. Schwabe (1951) concludes, from experiments with vernalized short-day and long-day *Chrysanthemum* cuttings, that the effects of vernalization and of day-length in this plant are operative at different stages in the train of reactions leading to flower initiation. Sometimes a high level of nutrition, especially of nitrogen, may be substituted for day-length. Short-day soy plants have a higher concentration of nitrogen than do long-day ones. In many cases an exposure for a few days to a photoperiod favorable for flower production will result in flowering regardless of the one to which the plant is later exposed. Plants vary in their sensitivity to this *photoperiodic induction*.

Plant parts affected by photoperiodic stimulation in most cases are the

FIG. 13-4. Above, long-day plant, *Nicotiana sylvestris*. Below, short-day plant, *Nicotiana tabacum*, var. Maryland Mammoth. At left, under long days; at right, under short days. (*From Melchers and Lang.*)

young but fully developed leaves. Evidence indicates that a flower-forming substance is produced in these which then diffuses through living cells to the meristem and there stimulates the formation and growth of floral primordia (p. 397). This substance can be transmitted by grafting from a plant in flower to one which is not, and the latter plant, even though kept under a photoperiod unfavorable for flowering, will then flower. The age of the plant may change its photoperiodic response. In *Kalanchoe*, for example, young plants 3 months old flower only in short days, but after 5 months they have become day-neutral (Harder and von Witsch, 1940*a*).

Even though the initiation of floral primordia has begun under a given photoperiod, the later differentiation of the various structures can be greatly altered by changing the length of the period. Thus in the staminate inflorescence of maize, after the initiation of primordia, later growth under longer photoperiods will cause the flowers to be infertile and even to show progressive changes toward a vegetative condition. The glumes develop ligules and the lemmas differentiate into blade, ligule, and sheath until the spikelet becomes much like a vegetative shoot and can be propagated as such (Galinat and Naylor, 1951). When transferred to a photoperiod unfavorable for flowering, buds which would have produced flowers will sometimes grow into abnormal vegetative shoots (*phyllody*), as reported by Behrens (1949) and others. Skok and Scully (1955) present evidence that floral development is associated with a dark-dependent mechanism and the elongation of the main axis with quite a different and light-dependent one.

The length of the photoperiod may affect the differentiation of the sexes. This is well shown by the work of Schaffner (1931) on sex reversal in staminate plants of hemp, *Mercurialis annua* (Fig. 13-5). He planted seeds in the greenhouse every 2 weeks from July 15 until May 15 and found that in the beginning, when days were long, the flowers were all staminate but that the percentage of pistillate ones steadily increased up to the plantings of Nov. 1 and 15 (which came to flower during the shortest days) and that the percentage of these flowers gradually decreased after this until in the long days of spring the plants were all staminate again. Long days obviously favor the production of staminate, and short days, of pistillate, flowers. Similar results were obtained by others, as by Jones (1947) in *Ambrosia*.

In *Cannabis sativa* under a 16-hour day flowering takes place in from 4 to 6 weeks, the leaves become more complex (with up to nine leaflets), and the plants are about half males and half females. Under 8-hour days, however, development is more rapid, flowering is reached in 3 or 4 weeks, and the plants are about half hermaphrodites and half females (Petit, 1952).

Day-length also affects reproduction in the lower plants. In the alga *Vaucheria sessilis* (League and Greulach, 1955) the production of sex organs was earlier and more abundant under 18-hour days than under 8-hour ones. Addition of glucose and peptose to the culture medium hastened their formation under short days. Sex organs were not produced unless there was a high concentration of fat globules near the point of origin. These authors believe that this is not a case of true photoperiodism but that the low production under short days results from a limited availability of food.

Klein (1948) reports that in the fungus *Pilobolus* there is a definite cycle of asexual reproduction caused by periods of light and darkness,

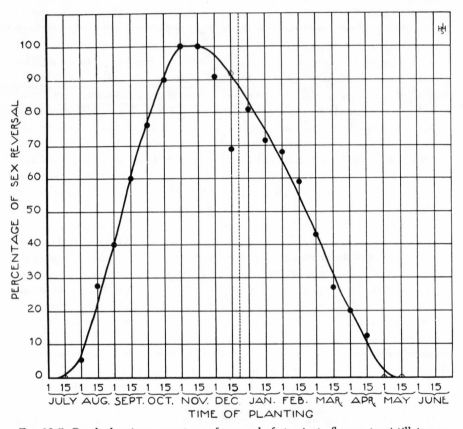

Fɪɢ. 13-5. Graph showing percentage of reversal of staminate flowers to pistillate ones in genetically staminate plants of *Mercurialis annua* planted at different dates. Day-length markedly affects sex expression. (*From Schaffner.*)

sporangiophores maturing at the end of a dark period and new ones remaining immature at the end of the light one. Light is essential to growth, but a dark period seems necessary to establish a periodicity of growth and maturation of the fruiting bodies. Periodicities other than those found in nature could be established in this plant by artificial illumination. Among these were light-dark cycles (in hours) not only of 12-12 but 16-16, 15-9, and 9-15. The 16-16 period was quite consistent and evidently had been acquired by the plant.

The physiology of photoperiodism presents many problems which are too complex to be discussed here. One hypothesis proposes that in the light a substance is produced which persists in the subsequent dark period. In the latter another is formed which is destroyed by a very brief exposure to light. These substances interact to make a flower-forming substance. In the short-day species *Kalanchoe Blossfeldiana*, which has been studied intensively (Harder, 1948), a single leaf borne at the tip of the plant (those above it having been removed) if exposed to a long day will almost completely prevent flowering in the plant below. Harder, Westphal, and Behrens (1949) conclude that in it is formed a substance which inactivates the flower-forming hormone before this reaches the floral primordium. Auxin presumably is involved in some of these processes. This has been discussed by various workers, among them Konishi (1956).

In some cases the photoperiodic reaction can be changed. Working with an early-blooming variety of peas which is day-neutral, Haupt (1957) reduced flowering by removing the cotyledons and modifying the soil nutrients. The plants now reacted as though they were long-day and late-blooming types. He found that a true late-blooming variety which is normally a long-day plant lost its photoperiodic reaction and bloomed early if a scion from a blooming plant was grafted into it.

Earliness of blooming may be due to other factors than day-length. Thus in an early-blooming and a late-blooming variety of *Chrysanthemum*, both grown under short days, Doorenbos and Kofranek (1953) found that the initiation of the florets took place at the same rate, but the time from the end of this stage until the date of blooming was 28 days in the early variety and 42 days in the late one.

Photoperiodism has been studied chiefly in relation to the differentiation of reproductive structures, but it has a pronounced effect on others also. Among instances of this are the following:

Pfeiffer (1926) grew buckwheat with daily illuminations of 5, 7, 12, 17, 19, and 24 hours and found that maximum stem length and diameter were produced in the 17-hour day.

The effect of the photoperiod is different on different parts of the plant and under different conditions. Hall (1949) grew gherkins under greenhouse conditions from seedling to maturity. At high nitrogen levels, plants given a 16-hour day had larger stems than those under 8 hours but at low nitrogen levels this was reversed and plants under the shorter days grew larger. Under the 8-hour photoperiod more nodes and leaves were produced but the total leaf area was smaller and there were fewer roots.

Deats (1925), studying tomato and pepper, found that the amounts of both phloem and xylem varied directly with the length of day.

Garner and Allard (1923) made the significant observation that as the photoperiod becomes less favorable for vegetative growth the structure of the plant becomes somewhat xeromorphic—the stem tends to become more branched, underground parts to enlarge, pubescence to increase, abscission layers to cause leaf fall, and flowers to appear.

In a study of heterosis in beans, Malinowski (1934) crossed two races and grew them and their hybrids under long and short days. In long days the F_1 plants were larger in every way than the parents. In short days they were about the size of the parents and flowered 6 weeks earlier than under long days. This acceleration of flowering seems to have cut down their vegetative growth and reduced heterotic vigor.

MacVicar and Struckmeyer (1946) grew soybeans with a deficiency of boron in different photoperiods. The deficiency symptoms were much more severe under long-day treatment than under short. The boron content of all the plants was much the same, and these authors believe that the effect of day-length was to alter the boron requirement of the plants.

The relative size of the leafy shoot to roots or tubers is markedly influenced by day-length. Radish, for example, grown under short days, as in a greenhouse in the winter, forms a very large root and a small shoot, but in the longer days of spring the root is relatively much smaller. Other plants with storage roots behave in the same way, as do potatoes in the ratio of tops to tubers (Pohjakallio, 1953). Zimmerman and Hitchcock (1929) observed that in dahlias short days produce heavy, fleshy root systems but long days, fibrous ones. These workers also found (1936) that growing Jerusalem artichokes under short days stimulated tuber production but that the same result was obtained by subjecting only the tip of the stem to short days by capping it part of the time with black cloth. This indicates that the control of tuberization by day-length is centered in the growing tip and its young leaves. In general, the growth of underground storage regions is stimulated by day-lengths different from those favorable for the vegetative growth of the shoot. Where the photoperiod is such that the shoot in its growth is unable to use carbohydrate beyond a certain amount, this accumulates in storage regions. Jenkins (1954) reports that long days and relatively high temperatures are necessary for bulb formation in shallots. In *Poa*, long days favor the growth of bulbils and short days of ears (Schwarzenbach, 1956).

In potatoes (Chapman, 1958), short photoperiods induce tuber formation. A tuber-forming stimulus is produced near the growing points of the plant and moves basipetally. It is able to cross a graft union and produce tubers in a noninduced plant. In plants with forked stems, one half was given short periods and the other long. Tubers were produced on that part of the stolon below the short-day branch.

Reduction of growth of the axis, with the formation of leafy rosettes, is favored by relatively short days. Thus *Oenothera* forms rosettes in the fall and tall flowering stems in the next spring. Lettuce makes compact heads in the short days of early spring but shoots upward in the longer ones of June.

In strawberries, long days increase leaf size and cell number (Arney, 1956). Ashby (1950*b*) reports that day-length also affects leaf shape in *Ipomoea*. In 16-hour days, plants begin to flower at the fifteenth or sixteenth node and lobing begins at the fifth to seventh node. Under 8-hour days, however, flowering begins at the first node and lobing is almost entirely suppressed.

Götz (1953) has made an intensive study of the effect of day-length on the formation of plantlets on the leaves of three species of *Bryophyllum*. In short days neither plantlets nor their primordia are formed nor are flowers produced, and the leaves become somewhat more succulent. Under long days, however, plantlets appear in abundance. The effect of different day-lengths on plantlet production can be studied in different leaves on the same plant. Neither grafting a scion from a long-day plantlet-producing plant into a short-day plant, or injecting sap from one, will induce the formation of these structures.

The photoperiod also affects rooting of cuttings. Some species root best under long days and others under short (Stoutemyer and Close, 1946). The photoperiod under which the stock plant has been growing actually affects the rooting of cuttings taken from it more than does that under which the cuttings themselves are grown (Pridham, 1942).

As to leaf structure, Gümmer (1949) found that in *Kalanchoe* a change in the photoperiod affects the thickness of the epidermal cell walls, the size of the vein islets, and the form, size, and number of mesophyll cells but that the number of stomata responds more slowly and the size and form of the epidermal cells are unaffected. In the ten species she studied, plants grown under short days had thicker leaves than under long ones, and this was almost entirely because of greater size of the mesophyll cells, which elongate at right angles to the surface of the lamina. They also increase somewhat in width. If a single leaf on a *Kalanchoe* plant growing under long days is itself exposed to short days, it grows considerably thicker and changes its form somewhat. It is significant that these changes are transmitted to other leaves directly above this one, suggesting that a morphogenetic substance is involved. Detached and rooted leaves respond to day-length by the same changes in form and structure as do those that remain attached to the plant (Schwabe, 1958).

In many woody plants studied, both flowering and vegetative growth are markedly affected by the photoperiod (Wareing, 1956; Downs and Borthwick, 1956). In general, short days induce dormancy and long ones prolong growth. Marked ecotypes as to photoperiod have been found in a number of species.

Cellular characters are also affected. Von Witsch and Flügel (1952) found that in leaves of *Kalanchoe Blossfeldiana* ($2n = 34$) formed in long days the mesophyll cells have chromosome numbers between 128 and 135. Under short days these cells are much larger and the degree of polyploidy is increased, the chromosome number going up to about 540. In tetraploid plants of *Hyoscyamus niger* produced by colchicine, the critical day-length for flowering and the time preceding the elongation of the internodes were both shortened, the number of leaves was reduced, and the time of flowering delayed, as compared with diploid plants (Lang, 1947).

The problems of photoperiodism are complicated by the fact, emphasized by Bünning (1956) and others, that there are endogenous rhythms in certain of the physiological processes of the plant. It has been found, for example, that a light period of 12 hours alternating with 12 hours of darkness gives in many plants a different result from an alternation of 6 hours of light and 6 hours of darkness and thus two cycles in a day. The total amount of light and darkness are the same but their effects are not. There is evidently a changing sensitivity in the reaction of the plant during the day to various environmental factors. This fact is of much importance for plant physiology but its significance for morphogenesis has as yet not been very fully considered. The existence of innate rhythms may account for the conflicting results obtained in experiments on the morphogenetic effects of various environmental factors.

RELATION TO OTHER FACTORS

The various morphogenetic effects of light provide an excellent example of the complexity of interaction of factors in plant development. Light powerfully influences flowering, but so do temperature, growth substances, nutrition, and genes, and in some cases water supply and gravity. They often have parallel effects on vegetative structures as well. These factors frequently can be interchanged to some extent and produce the same result, as when temperature is substituted for photoperiod, and vice versa. Auxin is closely concerned with many of the traits that light affects, but the exact relation between light and auxin is not clear. Sometimes light seems to destroy it and sometimes to stimulate its production. Specific photoperiodic reactions have been found to be gene-controlled. The morphogenetic effects of bright light and of limited water supply are sometimes hard to disentangle. It is difficult, as has been said before, to separate any one factor sharply from the others and to study it in isolation. All are concerned with the entire organized system that is the plant.

CHAPTER 14

Water

Water is closely involved with many activities of the plant, especially photosynthesis and transpiration. It fills the cell vacuoles and constitutes the bulk of protoplasm. It maintains the turgidity of the tissues and thus is an important factor in growth. Botanists still are very far from explaining the complex problems of the water relations of plants. These have been discussed in an extensive physiological literature (see Crafts, Currier, and Stocking, 1949; Kramer, 1945, 1955; Meyer, 1938; and Walter, 1955).

Xeromorphy. Water is also of significance in problems of plant structure and thus for morphogenesis. Where it is relatively scarce or the amount that can be absorbed is limited for other reasons (as in saline soils) or where evaporation is excessive, plants display characteristic structural features. Such *xerophytes* tend to have reduced leaf surfaces, heavy cuticle, small and thick-walled cells, high stomatal frequency, abundant mechanical tissue, and large root systems, and they often are spiny or succulent. These traits, collectively termed *xeromorphy*, have been regarded as adaptations which increase absorption or reduce transpiration and thus maintain a sufficient water supply under dry conditions. Xerophytes may show other adaptations such as hairy surfaces, rolled leaf blades, and stomata sunken in pits or otherwise protected against undue exposure to evaporation. The characteristic structures of xerophytic plants have long attracted the interest of ecologists and provide much of the subject matter for the science of ecological anatomy.

Such traits presumably have arisen through the action of natural selection and are thus not ultimately attributable to the direct effect of the environment. Many plants, however, if grown under conditions where water is scarce or transpiration high, have been observed to assume some degree of xeromorphism. Leaf surfaces will tend to be somewhat reduced, cells smaller and thicker-walled, and mechanical tissue more abundant. Such structural changes are clearly the result of an environmental factor—a reduction in amount of available water. What is inherited here is this specific response to the environment.

There has been considerable controversy, however, as to whether or not such changes are adaptive and are advantageous to the plant. That they should be so is a plausible conclusion, and for such traits as heavy cuticle it may be correct. Its general validity has been challenged by a number of people, notably Maximov, who has reviewed the problem comprehensively (1929, 1931), especially as to the physiological basis of drought resistance. Maximov called attention to the earlier work of Zalenski (1904), published (chiefly in Russian) a quarter of a century before and largely neglected outside the country of its origin. Zalenski observed that the veining of the leaves in plants growing in dry, open spaces was much more abundant than in the leaves of those in the shade or in protected spots. These observations he then extended to a comparative study of the structure of leaves on the same tree. Here he found that, as a rule, leaf structure changed with the level of insertion on the tree, the structure being more xeromorphic with increasing distance from the root. The progressively higher leaves had smaller cells throughout, smaller stomata and more of them per unit of area, greater vein length per unit of area, thicker and less sinuous walls in the epidermal cells, a greater contrast between palisade and spongy layers, less intercellular space, and better developed mechanical tissue. These relationships were later called "Zalenski's law" and were independently discovered by others, among them Yapp (1912). Zalenski's results are evident in herbaceous as well as in woody plants. Some data that he presents for *Dactylis glomerata* are shown in Table 14-1. Salisbury (1927)

Table 14-1. Variations in Anatomical Elements of Leaves of Different Tiers in *Dactylis glomerata* *

Tier	1	2	3	4	5
Height of insertion (cm.)	0	10.2	25.2	37.0	51.0
Length of leaf (cm.)	7.1	10.3	18.5	18.0	13.2
Breadth of leaf (cm.)	0.30	0.35	0.54	0.52	0.45
Length of vascular bundles (mm./sq. cm. of leaf surface)	371	511	557	625	626
Mean diameter of cells of upper epidermis (mm.)	0.0418	0.0294	0.0272	0.0217	0.0189
Number of stomata in field	34	42	61	80	64
Length of stomata (mm.)	0.0434	0.0415	0.0403	0.0356	0.0384

* From Maximov (1929), after Zalenski.

found that stomatal frequency per unit area increases with the height at which the leaf is borne but that the stomatal *index* (ratio of stomata to epidermal cells in the same region) changes relatively little. This is a necessary implication of Zalenski's observations.

These structural characters are among those regarded as typically xeromorphic. Zalenski, Yapp, and others, however, have explained them without relating them to water conservation but simply as direct or indirect results of decreasing cell size with progressively higher leaf insertion. Small cell size, in turn, grows out of the greater difficulty with which water is obtained by the higher leaves, since they have to lift it farther and against the competition of the lower ones. It follows that at the critical period of rapid leaf growth, which results primarily from cell expansion through the absorption of water, the cells of the upper leaves cannot attain the size of the lower ones. The other structural traits are a consequence of this basic difference. That such a conclusion is correct is indicated by other evidence, such as the fact that if lower leaves are removed while the upper ones are still growing the latter will resemble in structure leaves that would normally be lower on the stem.

Xeromorphy in these upper leaves therefore seems unlikely to be an adaptation for reducing water loss. Indeed, it was later shown that upper leaves may transpire *more* rapidly than the lower ones. These results have cast doubt on the adaptive character of the traits of xerophytes in general. Maximov calls attention to the fact that when water is abundant many xerophytes transpire more rapidly than mesophytes and it is only under drought conditions that their water loss is markedly cut. He attributes this, and therefore the quality of drought resistance in general, not to any structural traits but to protoplasmic characters, notably osmotic concentration and changes in cell colloids that would enable the plant to conserve its water supply and thus endure dry conditions better than other plants. Eckardt (1953) agrees with this conclusion. The physiology of drought resistance has been reviewed by Iljin (1957).

In earlier years a number of Russian investigators, assuming that types with small cells were more resistant to drought than those with large cells, determined for various cereal varieties their "anatomical coefficients" (chiefly cell size), hoping to find a means of identifying resistant types by direct inspection. This possibility was not supported by the work of Maximov. More recently, however, Lal and Mehrotra (1949), working with sugar cane, have found that some cell characters, notably small size, seem in certain cases to be associated with drought resistance.

Farkas and Rajháthy (1955) reexamined anatomical gradients in some herbaceous plants, particularly tomato, and found that cell size in leaves decreases from below upward and that number of stomata per unit area increases, thus again confirming Zalenski (Fig. 14-1). Under dry conditions this gradient is much steeper. They found several other physiological gradients some of which may be explained as dependent on that for water. In others the relation to the latter is not clear. Stage of development of the leaves also complicates the problem here.

Shields (1950), who has reviewed the whole subject of xeromorphy, agrees in general with Zalenski, Maximov, and Yapp that this type of structure has little significance as an adaptation in drought resistance. She also emphasizes the importance of physiological factors in relation to water loss. Many of the structural characteristics of xerophytes, she suggests, may be the result of physiological differences. Thick cell walls and abundance of mechanical tissue may result from active photosynthesis in a plant where all its products cannot be used in growth because of the shortage of water.

Ashby (1948*b*), however, presents evidence that the relative xeromorphy of the upper leaves, at least as indicated by cell size, is not due to com-

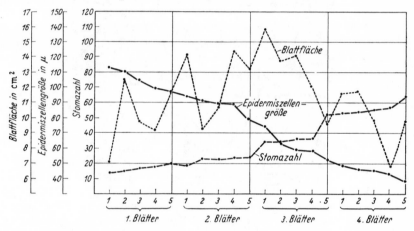

Fig. 14-1. Gradient of cell size in tomato leaves. Graph showing stomatal number (in a given microscopic field), epidermal cell size (in microns), and leaf surface (in square centimeters) for the first four leaves of five young tomato plants. These are arranged in each case according to the ascending order of stomatal number for each leaf class. (*From Farkas and Rajháthy.*)

petition for water but to the influence of immature leaves on those above them, an influence which may be hormonal in character.

Leaves on the outside, and particularly the south side, of the crown of a tree (sun leaves, p. 312) are often considerably thicker and more xeromorphic in appearance than those in the center (shade leaves). This has been attributed to the direct action of light. This difference may be due in part to water relations, for Hanson (1917) showed that, on the outside of the crown, conditions favored much more rapid evaporation than in the interior. He found that leaves on the outside are smaller, more deeply lobed, and lower in water content and that they transpire faster per unit of area (Fig. 14-2). This has frequently been confirmed. Huber (1926) agrees that sun leaves result from a water deficit. Söding

(1934) grew trees in pots and found that, by adding a small amount of salt to the soil, leaves like sun leaves were formed by the plant. Light, however, probably has a share in the production of xeromorphy, for

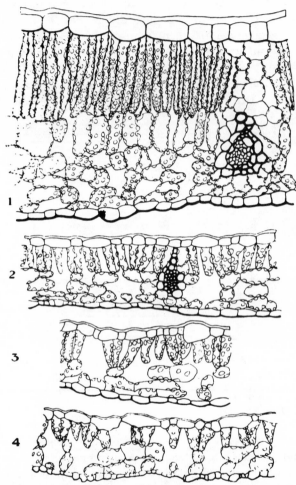

Fig. 14-2. Effect of environment on leaf structure. Sections of leaves of *Acer saccharum* from 1, south periphery of the tree; 2, center of crown; 3 and 4, base of crown. Various factors are doubtless involved in these changes, but differences in rate of transpiration (higher in exposed leaves than in the others) seem especially important. (*From Hanson.*)

bright light has been shown to reduce leaf area and to increase blade thickness. The xeromorphy observable in many tropical plants may check the harmful effects of too intense insolation.

Still other factors are probably involved in the development of this sort of leaf structure. Müller-Stoll (1947*b*) has evidence that xeromorphy of plants in peat bogs is due to a deficiency of nitrogen rather than of water. He fertilized such plants and observed a marked increase in leaf area and cell size and a decrease in stomatal frequency, cell-wall thickness, and venation. Lack of nitrogen and lack of water thus seem to produce similar structural changes. These two factors are associated in other morphogenetic phenomena.

Experimental Work. Many experiments have been performed to determine directly the effect on plant structure of varying amounts of water in the soil or in the air. Only a few of these can be mentioned here.

Rippel (1919) studied white mustard growing in moist and in dry soil. Vein length per unit area of leaf surface was considerably greater in dry soil. In both, it increased progressively from the first leaf to the fifth, and this gradient was steeper in dry soil than in wet.

Penfound (1931) paid particular attention to stem anatomy and found that, although increased soil moisture reduced xeromorphic traits, it increased the relative amount of xylem in the stem.

Cain and Potzger (1940) brought *Gaylussacia* plants into the greenhouse. They varied the amount of available water and also grew some of the plants in front of a fan. Though dry air and fan induced some xeromorphy, the mesophyll was considerably thicker in plants in the moister soil, contrary to most earlier observations.

Simonis (1952) studied four genera grown in soils of high and low water content. In all, the leaf surface was reduced under water deficit, but the morphological responses of different plants were somewhat different. Water content tended to be unchanged under dry conditions, or sometimes even was increased, and succulence was generally greater.

Simons (1956) grew year-old apple seedlings in greenhouse pot culture in moist and dry soil. Reduction in water supply affected leaf area and also thickness and size of cells in epidermis, palisade, and xylem.

Fewer experiments have been done on the morphogenetic effects of differences in the humidity of the air. Eberhardt (1903) grew a wide variety of plants under bell jars, maintaining light and temperature the same in all but changing the humidity. Dry air tended to produce the ordinary xeromorphic traits and also an increase in hairiness (Figs. 14-3 and 14-4). The results of Lebedincev (1927) and Rettig (1929) were much the same. The effects of dry air were more pronounced when the soil was also dry.

At the opposite extreme from xeromorphy, produced by water deficit, are those changes that result from submersion in water. As a rule, the roots of such plants are small or lacking, the vascular and mechanical tissues poorly developed, the leaves thin and often much dissected, the stomata vestigial or absent, and the cell walls thin. These traits are generally regarded as adaptations to an aquatic habitat. A few heterophyllous water plants (p. 216) can live either submersed or growing in the air with

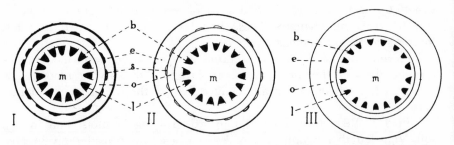

Fig. 14-3. Diagram of cross sections of stems of *Achyranthes*, showing relative development of tissues in air which is dry (I), normal (II), and humid (III). b, xylem; l, phloem; s, sclerenchyma; m, pith. Dry air tends to reduce size of pith and cortex and to increase development of xylem and sclerenchyma. (*From Eberhardt.*)

their roots in soil. Among these are *Polygonum amphibium* and the water buttercup, *Ranunculus aquatilis*. In these plants the land form, essentially mesophytic in structure, is very different from the water form

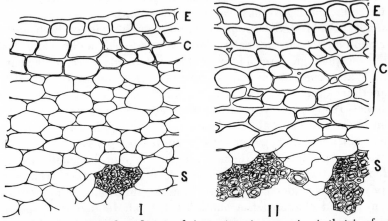

Fig. 14-4. Outer cortex and epidermis of *Aster sinensis* grown in air that is of normal humidity (I) and that is dry (II). The latter shows greater wall thickness in collenchyma and larger bundles of sclerenchyma. E, epidermis; C, cortex; S, sclerenchyma. (*From Eberhardt.*)

and in some cases was not at first recognized as belonging to the same species. Occasionally, as in the buttercup, foliage transitional from one to the other may be found. In plants like the mermaid weed, *Proserpinaca palustris*, leaves borne in the air are broad and little-lobed

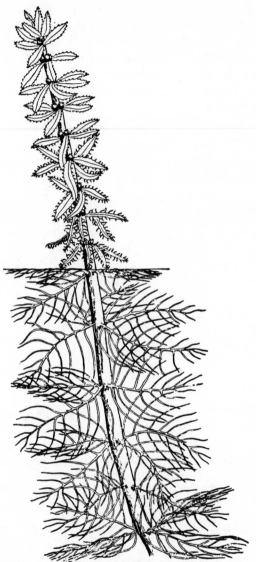

FIG. 14.5. A species of *Myriophyllum,* an "amphibious" plant, showing differences between leaves grown in water and in air. (*From Fassett.*)

whereas the submersed ones are much dissected (Fig. 14-5). *Potamogeton* and similar forms are entirely aquatic but in some species there are both broad floating leaves, exposed on their upper surfaces to the air, and delicate submersed ones.

Various explanations have been proposed (p. 216) for the differencs between shoots grown in water and in air, especially in *Proserpinaca*. Transpiration, seasonal differences, and reversion to juvenile stages may be involved. Combes (1947) found that in *Oenanthe* low temperature is effective in producing deeply incised leaves. Allsopp (1955) has studied the water fern, *Marsilea*, grown under various conditions, and has discussed the general problem of the structure of water plants. The land form of leaf has four leaflets, and there are stomata on both surfaces, but the water form is merely lobed and lacks stomata in the lower epidermis (Fig. 14-6). Raising the osmotic concentration of the culture

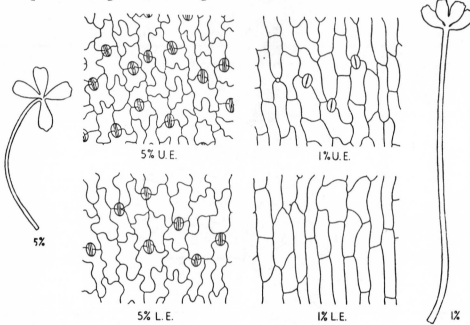

Fig. 14-6. Comparable sporeling leaves of *Marsilea Drummondii*, an "amphibious" plant. Form of leaf and structure of upper and lower epidermis in leaves grown in media containing 5 per cent glucose (left) and 1 per cent (right). The former resemble typical land forms and the latter, water forms. (*From Allsopp.*)

medium by adding glucose produces the land type of leaf. Whether this is an osmotic or a nutritional effect is not certain. Allsopp concludes that it is the water balance of the developing tissues, determined by the osmotic pressure of the surrounding liquid, and the relative humidity of the air or, in general, the diffusion pressure deficit of the water of the environment, which produce the structural features distinctive of land or water forms. Here, again, the morphogenetic problem involves much more than the direct effect of a single environmental factor.

Effect of Transpiration Stream. Another aspect of the problem of the morphogenetic effects of water involves the influence of water supply and transpiration rate on the development of vascular tissue. Does a strong transpiration stream stimulate the formation of conducting cells and thus serve as a "functional stimulus"?

There is clearly a quantitative relation between a transpiring surface and the vascular tissue supplying it. D. J. B. White (1954), in a study of the relation of laminar area to petiolar xylem in the bean leaf, found that there is an allometric developmental correlation between the two, the cross-sectional area of xylem growing about two-thirds as fast as laminar area (Fig. 14-7). There have also been a good many measurements of the amount of vascular tissue at different levels in the stem, both absolutely and in proportion to the area of leaf lamina above. Reliable

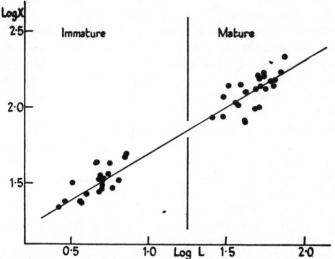

Fig. 14-7. Relative growth of area of lamina (L) and cross-sectional area of petiolar xylem (X) in immature leaves of bean. (*From D. J. B. White.*)

data as to the amount of transpiration in relation to cross section of vascular tissue are difficult to obtain. Rübel (1920) measured the xylem area at different levels on a sunflower plant and the total leaf area above each level. In plants grown in a normally sunny situation there was about 0.21 sq. mm. of vascular tissue per square decimeter of leaf area, as compared with 0.10 sq. mm. in shaded plants. Since there is more transpiration in the sun, there is evidently a relation here between transpiration and the amount of conducting tissue. In the lowest stem levels there was from ¼ to ⅓ sq. mm. of cross section of conducting tissue to every gram of dry weight of leaves above it, but in young and vigorous leafy plants this increased to ½ sq. mm., again showing a presumptive relation to transpiration. The proportion of wood to phloem decreased at upper levels. The leaves at different levels transpired at about the same rate.

Alexandrov, Alexandrova, and Timofeev (1927) observed that in *Bryonia* (a running vine) the number of vessels in any part of the stem varies with the dimensions of the leaves in that region. The size of the vascular tissue in a petiole is also related to the area of its lamina.

In fir, spruce, and beech, Huber (1928) found that the *relative conducting surface* (the ratio of the area of conducting tissue to the fresh weight of leaves above it) increases from base to apex in the stem. In lateral branches this ratio was smaller than in the main stem, a fact presumably related to the dominance of the latter. The relative conducting surface and the amount of transpiration were determined for various plants by Huber and the rate of flow of water through the vascular system calculated. This was found to be relatively high for herbaceous plants, low for conifers and xerophytes, and intermediate for broad-leaved trees, thus seeming to be related to the amount of transpiration. Huber also observed (1924) that in oak branches growing in bright sunlight a square decimeter of leaf area transpired 75 mg./hour and was supplied through a cross-sectional area of 0.42 sq. mm. of vascular tissue. In branches growing in shade there were 46 mg. of water transpired through a vascular cross section of 0.20 sq. mm. In other words, the greater the transpiration stream passing through the vascular system, the larger this system was. He believes, however, that the amount of water carried upward depends primarily on the osmotic pull exerted by the leaves and the resistance to flow in the vascular tissues rather than solely on the size of the vascular tissue itself.

These various facts show that there is a definite correlation between the amount of water passing through the vascular tissue and the amount of such tissue that is developed. This, consequently, suggests that the transpiration stream itself acts as a formative stimulus for the differentiation of vascular tissue. Doubt as to the correctness of such a conclusion, however, is raised by some remarkable results reported by Werner (1931) in maize. He was able to grow a plant of almost normal size (suspended in the air in a transpiration experiment) that was connected to its root system in the soil by only a single extremely thin root about 10 cm. long. The entire water supply for this plant, the stem of which was several centimeters wide, passed through a vascular strand only about 0.5 mm. in diameter. Here, at least, there is little evidence that a heavy transpiration flow stimulates a proportionate development of vascular tissue. Similarly, in a frond of *Osmunda*, all the water transpired by a large blade area is drawn through a leaf trace which is very small as it leaves the stele. At the base of the frond this expands into a ring of large bundles.

In such cases as these, one is forced to conclude that much more vascular tissue is normally developed than is required to carry the normal transpiration stream. The relation so frequently observed between area of transpiring surface and cross-sectional area of conducting tissue may therefore be simply another instance of developmental correlation, of one tissue keeping step with another (p. 107), and may be without causal significance for the differentiation of vascular tissue.

There are other ways in which water may have morphogenetic significance. Positive hydrostatic pressures often occur at the time of early and rapid leaf growth, and leaves developing then tend to be large and to have shallow lobes. A little later, when sap pressure is lower or absent, the leaves are smaller and the lobes deeper. Experiments of Pearsall

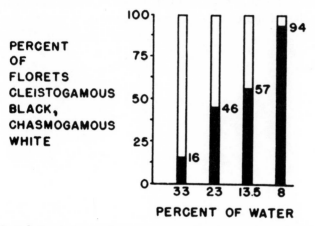

FIG. 14-8. Relation between the percentage of water in the soil and the percentage of cleistogamous florets in *Stipa*. (*From W. V. Brown.*)

and Hanby (1926) tend to confirm this, since when they applied considerable hydrostatic pressure to stems while the leaves were developing, the lobes were shallow, but they were deeper under less pressure. The angle at which the lateral veins go off in palmate leaves seems to affect their ability to deliver water. Where this angle is more than 90° the flow of water under pressure is reduced. This fact may be related to the determination of leaf shape.

Osmotic pressure has important morphogenetic effects since it is one of the factors determining the amount of cell enlargement. Various circumstances affect the osmotic concentration of the cell sap. One of these is chromosome number, for Becker (p. 40) observed that in a polyploid series of moss cells the concentration varied inversely with the degree of polyploidy. Schlösser (1935) found in tomato that maternally inherited differences in osmotic concentration in the cytoplasm, as well as in the environment, affected the expression of genes for plant height. The character of growth may also be influenced. If the alga *Stigeoclonium* is grown in relatively high osmotic concentrations, its cells round up and divide in all planes to form a so-called palmella colony. In weaker solutions vegetative activity is increased and the cells become cylindrical, divide in only one plane, and form filaments (Livingston, 1900).

Water may also affect differentiation in other ways, such as the increased proportion of cleistogamous flowers formed as soil moisture decreases (W. V. Brown, 1952; Fig. 14-8).

A study of the water relations of plants, and especially of the formative effects of water on plant growth, has recently been somewhat neglected. These relations provide a promising opportunity, however, to approach some of the problems of plant morphogenesis from a direction different from that of most experimental work today.

CHAPTER 15

Temperature

Temperature is obviously of much importance for the physiological activities of a plant since the rate of metabolic processes is markedly affected by it. Though its chief significance is in physiology, it also influences development in various ways. These have been summarized by Went (1953).

Both light and temperature apparently produce their morphogenetic effects by speeding up or slowing down particular physiological processes. What the effect in a given case will be evidently depends on the sensitivity of the plant to these stimuli in a particular part of its body or on a particular phase of its development. The effect of temperature is especially important on rate of growth. The optimum temperature for this may be different in different regions of the plant, at different stages of development, or even at different times of day. This may result in a change in proportions of various parts and thus of form and structure. Bünning (1935), for example, observed that the later in the season the seeds of beans mature, the shorter is the epicotyl of seed and seedling and the quicker do the primary leaves reach maturity. This he found to be a temperature effect, for high temperature during the 5 weeks preceding seed maturity produces longer epicotyls and a slower development of primary leaves.

In *Ipomoea*, Njoku (1957) found that the higher the night temperature (with a good level of mineral nutrition) the less deeply lobed were the leaves (Fig. 15-1). Here what temperature seems to affect directly is the rate of production of leaves at the growing point, and this, in turn, is correlated with depth of lobing. Many other cases have been found where temperature thus exerts an indirect effect on form and structure because of the fact that different parts are differently susceptible to its influence.

Thermoperiodism. There is often a daily rhythm in reaction to temperature as there is to light. At any temperature that is constant throughout the 24 hours many plants will grow less rapidly than if their environment is relatively cool at night and warm during the day. The optimum temperature for growth may therefore be different under different conditions. This *thermoperiodism* affects growth in various ways (Went, 1944, 1945, 1948). Went found in tomato, for example, that if the greenhouse temperature is held constant the optimum is about 26.5°C, at which there is a steady growth in length of 23 mm. per day. At all other temperatures, growth is less (Fig. 15-2). Plants kept warm (26.5°) during the day, however, but cooler at night (17 to 20°) grow still better, about 27 mm. per day. It is significant that this low temperature is effective only if it is applied during the *dark* period of daily growth. The same thermoperiodism is evident in fruit development, the best fruit set occurring when the night temperatures are 15 to 20°. Evidently two different

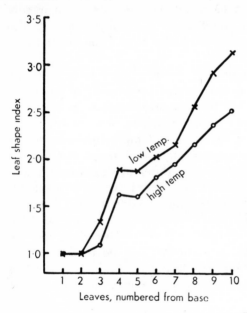

Fig. 15-1. The effect of low and of high night temperature on shape of successive leaves in *Ipomoea caerulea*. Shape index measures degree of lobing. (*From Njoku.*)

processes are involved, one going on in the light and the other in the dark, and with different temperature optima. Plants differ considerably in their response to thermoperiodism (Knapp, 1956). Sproston and Pease (1957) have shown that thermoperiodism is related to the production of the sexual stage in the fungus *Sclerotinia*.

There is a close relation between temperature and photoperiodism, for it has frequently been shown that a particular temperature can be substituted for day-length in determining the balance between vegetative growth and flowering. Thus in *Rudbeckia*, a long-day plant, flowers are produced in shorter days if the temperature is kept high (Murneek, 1940). Flowering in beets can be controlled by manipulating the relation between temperature and the photoperiod (Owen, Carsner, and Stout, 1940), a technique which has been termed *photothermal induction.*

The problem of dormancy, of why plants or parts of them fail to grow until particular conditions are satisfied, has implications for morphogenesis, particularly in relation to buds, since there are usually very many buds on a plant that do not develop. Whatever determines the particular ones that are to grow has an important influence on the form of the plant. Factors that inhibit or stimulate growth of these meristematic regions have been studied chiefly in connection with growth substances (p. 386), but others are involved. Among them temperature has an important place. It is well known that low temperature is one of the most effective means for breaking the dormancy of seeds, buds, and other plant parts. The

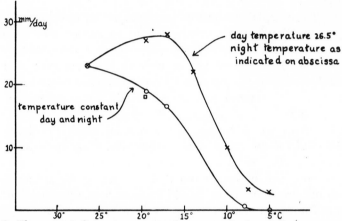

Fig. 15-2. Thermoperiodicity in tomato. Stem growth (in millimeters per day) in plants kept constantly at the indicated temperature (lower curve) and for 8 hours during the day at 26.5°C but at night at the temperature indicated (upper curve). (*From Went.*)

influence of temperature on bud growth has been widely studied by horticulturists because of its practical importance (see Chandler et al., 1937).

Vernalization. A more significant effect of temperature for morphogenetic problems is evident in the processes of *vernalization,* by which flowering is accelerated through the application of low temperature at a particular stage of development. Horticulturists have known for many years that the chilling of seeds or seedlings will in many cases force plants into bloom earlier than would otherwise occur. Scientific study of this effect, however, began in comparatively recent years and at first was explored chiefly by Russian plant physiologists, especially Lysenko. A conspicuous example of the effect of vernalization is the speeding up of flowering in some of the cereal grains so that "winter" varieties, superior in certain respects, can be treated like "spring" varieties. A winter race of rye, for example, is normally sown in the fall and flowers and fruits the next season. If planted in the spring it will produce abundant vegetative growth but no flowers. A spring race sown in the spring will fruit in that growing season. If seed of winter rye is soaked in water, however, and is then exposed to low temperature (0 to 10°C or thereabouts) for a few hours or days, it can be sown in the spring and will bear flowers and fruit just as rapidly as spring rye does. Grain germinated at 1°C and then planted will produce rye that flowers in 68 days, but if germinated at 18°C, flowering does not take place for 150 days (Gregory and Purvis, 1938). The vernalized seed may be kept dormant for some time or even dried and it will still grow like spring rye when it is planted.

These facts are explained on the assumption that development is to a great extent independent of growth, that in an annual seed plant there is a specific series of developmental stages, each a necessary precursor to the next, and that these stages require for their completion different environmental conditions, especially as to temperature and light. This is an aspect of the general concept of phasic development previously discussed (p. 205).

In these cereals the first stage is the one in which the floral initials are formed, and for this process low temperatures are necessary. Winter rye sown in the fall will produce these initials because it is exposed to the low temperatures of winter but if it is sown in the spring the temperature is not low enough for this to happen. Vernalization thus acts as a substitute for winter temperature.

The next stage, the development of the flowers themselves, usually requires higher temperatures but also relatively long days. Flowering will be delayed indefinitely if plants at this stage are exposed to short light periods. In the long, warm days of spring, both winter and spring varieties will thus come into flower. The difference between them is that spring varieties will form floral primordia in these warm days and winter varieties will not do so without treatment.

In certain plants a definite number of primordial structures are formed at the growing point of the embryo, and it can be shown that the fate of some of these has not been determined in the seed but that leaves or flowers will form from them, depending on environmental conditions. Thus in winter rye there are usually 25 embryonic primordia. The first seven will always develop into leaves. The next 18 are indeterminate, and the lower the temperature to which they are exposed, the more of them will develop flowers. At high spring temperatures, none of them will do so unless previously chilled.

Different plants respond very differently to vernalization, and in some it is without effect (Kondratenko, 1940). Vernalized plants may be devernalized, usually by high temperature following the cold treatment, and they may sometimes even be revernalized (Lang and Melchers, 1947).

The induction of flowering by low temperature is by no means limited to the cereal grains or to seed treatment. Young plants beyond the seedling stage may be vernalized and thus forced into flower, and some biennial varieties will flower in their first season if subjected to cold. The growing stem tip is the region sensitive to the vernalizing influence. Low-temperature effects on growing plants, particularly as to flowering, have been widely investigated. This work is reviewed by Thompson (1953).

The exact way in which low temperature produces its effects in vernalization is not clearly known but in some cases it has been thought to influence the production and distribution of auxin and perhaps also of substances that stimulate flowering (p. 397). Hatcher (1945), however, finds that the auxin content of grains of winter and spring races of cereals is the same and that there is no detectable amount of auxin in the embryos either at normal or low temperatures. He concludes that it is not concerned in the process of vernalization.

Although the most conspicuous effect of vernalization is the acceleration of flower development, vegetative characters may also be affected, such as leaf size. Hänsel (1953) found that early leaves were longer if germination temperatures were slightly below 0°C than if they were slightly above this (Fig. 15-3). Internal differentiation is also affected (Roberts and Struckmeyer, 1948).

The literature of vernalization and of its relation to photoperiodism and phasic development is extensive. The history of research in this general field has been reviewed by McKinney (1940) and Whyte (1948). The latter is one of a series of papers on this general subject brought together by Murneek and Whyte (1948). Among other related publications are those of Gregory and Purvis (1938), and Whyte (1939).

Other Temperature Effects. There are many other instances where morphogenetic effects of temperature have been observed. Some typical examples of recent investigation in this field are the following:

Burström (1956) finds that under higher temperatures the final length of cells in roots is reduced because of the shorter period of cell elongation. Cell-wall plasticity and calcium requirement are also reduced.

Schwabe (1954), working with *Chrysanthemum*, limited low-temperature treatment to the growing tip and confirmed earlier conclusions that this is the region where the stimulus of vernalization is perceived. The stimulus did not pass across a graft union but it was translocated to lateral buds that were distant from the one that was chilled and had formed some time after it was treated.

Wittwer and Teubner (1957) observed that in tomato low-temperature treatment of seeds had no effect, but exposure of very young seedlings to low night temperatures (10 to 13°C) for 2 or 3 weeks induced earlier flowering and more flowers in the first cluster, in contrast to those grown at higher temperatures (18 to 21°C). Cold treatment of older seedlings increased the number of flowers in later clusters. Other factors, especially

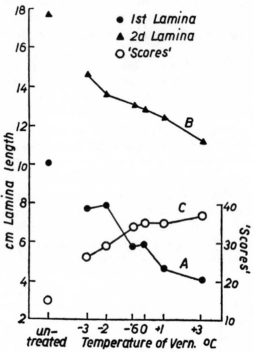

Fig. 15-3. Effect of vernalizing temperatures on length of lamina of first (A) and second (B) leaves in winter rye, and on stage of differentiation of spike as measured by an arbitrary scale of "scores." Controls at left. (*From Hänsel.*)

nitrogen nutrition, also affect flower formation and complicate the problem of studying it.

Hall (1950) compared buckwheat plants in culture with their roots and shoots at different temperatures with others where the entire plant was grown at either high or low temperature. Development was more normal under the latter condition. High temperature for the shoot checked vegetative growth and hastened flowering, maturity, and senescence, and low air temperature there prolonged ontogeny. Increase in duration of the vegetative phase, however, did not result in the production of more plant material.

L. D. Tukey (1952) subjected bearing branches of sour cherry to several different night temperatures and found that higher temperatures accelerated development during stages I and II (early growth and stone formation) but checked it in stage III (fleshy pericarp growth) (Fig. 2-5).

Leopold and Guernsey (1954) treated germinating peas with various growth substances and followed this with low temperature. The combination of chemical with temperature stimulation they termed *chemical vernalization*. It hastened flowering, but only if carbon dioxide was later present. Changes in day-length had no effect. They conclude that there are two stages in the growth of young pea plants which are affected, the first requiring auxin and low temperature and the second requiring carbon dioxide. The function of carbon dioxide here is not understood.

Chaudri, Bünning, and Haupt (1956) observed that the exposure of young onion plants to 3 hours of low temperature during the dark portion of the photoperiod hastened the development of bulbs. This effect was greatest when the low temperature was applied during the latter part of the dark period.

Fisher (1954) worked with a trifoliate New Zealand species of *Ranunculus* in which the juvenile leaves are undivided. Sometimes the adult ones show a partial reversion to this juvenile form. He grew plants under controlled conditions and found that when the temperature was relatively high (20°C in the daytime and 15°C at night) there was a complete reversion to the undivided juvenile leaf shape but that at lower temperatures (10 and 5°) the adult form persisted.

Steinberg (1953) studied Mammoth Rustica tobacco, a type which came originally from a cross between *Nicotiana rustica* and *N. tabacum*. This is indeterminate in growth and very rarely flowers, but it can readily be made to do so if the night temperatures are dropped to 50 or 60°F, regardless of day-length. In this respect it is unlike Maryland Mammoth (p. 316), which also is indeterminate in growth but flowers only in short days, regardless of temperature. The indeterminate character of growth in both is due to the fact that flowering is prevented, in one type by high temperature and in the other by long days. Steinberg suggests that there may be a separate genetic basis for the two types of reaction.

Benson-Evans and Hughes (1955) observed that in the liverwort *Lunularia cruciata*, which is world-wide in distribution but rarely reproduces sexually except in a "Mediterranean" type of climate, the induction of archegoniophores requires subjection to low temperature, later followed by higher temperature and long days, thus fitting it to its particular ecological distribution.

Margalef (1953) found that in cultures of the green alga *Scenedesmus obliquus* low temperatures cause cell size to increase, although other factors have a minor effect on it. Since cells in this species grow faster in length than in width, large cells have a more slender shape than small ones, so that temperature indirectly affects cell shape.

CHAPTER 16

Various Physical Factors

There are a number of other morphogenetic factors which may be grouped together as physical ones in a general sense, notably such clearly mechanical factors as external compression, tension, bending and swaying; gravity and inner tissue tension, together with absolute size and bioelectrical factors, each with its bearing on development.

Those factors which may be called mechanical in the strict sense are relatively simple in character in comparison with light, electricity, and many chemical ones and evidently produce most of their morphogenetic effects indirectly through modifying physiological processes in the living cells. Much of the early work in this field was done by Schwendener (1878, 1898). Among other problems, he emphasized the importance of such factors in determining the arrangement of leaf primordia at the apical meristem.

Mechanical effects are in many cases much like the ones produced by other factors, suggesting that both are acting upon the same protoplasmic mechanisms. Such parallel effects are familiar to the student of morphogenesis and emphasize again the importance of the complex reacting system rather than that of the relatively simple stimulus or evocator. There has been a good deal of disagreement as to experimental results in this field, much of which is probably due to the fact that the reactivity of the plant is very different at different stages of its development and under different environmental conditions.

In studying these effects it is sometimes difficult to separate various plant movements and tropisms from more strictly form-producing and morphogenetic phenomena. Changes in the positions of parts, as in the leaves of *Mimosa*, the fly-traps of *Dionaea*, the stamens of various plants, and other structures, are due chiefly to changes in turgor brought about by specific substances. This is essentially a problem in plant physiology and offers opportunity to study the mechanisms of stimulus and response, with their various chemical and electrical correlates.

Tropistic responses to gravity and light, however, are usually due to more rapid cell elongation on one side of the axis than on the other and are thus, in part, growth reactions. The various thigmotropisms, or responses to contact, involve more definitely morphogenetic changes. When the tip of a tendril is lightly touched on one side, as by a small branch or wire, the tendril will coil around it and thus tend to anchor the plant to a support. This coiling results from the more rapid growth of that side of the tendril not touching the support. There is evidence that the stimulus of contact tends to produce a substance that checks growth, although the mechanism which makes a tendril react thus, and later contract in a coil, pulling the plant toward a support, is not well understood.

Mechanical factors are also concerned in other growth reactions. Bünning and his colleagues (1941, 1948, 1954), working with *Mimosa, Sinapis,* and *Vicia,* have found that mechanical stimulation (stroking with paper or agitating on a shaking machine) checks the lengthening of stems in darkness (etiolation) in much the same way that light does. The internal structure of stems grown in darkness but mechanically stimulated is quite different from that of etiolated stems and hardly to be distinguished from ones growing in the light (Fig. 16-1). He suggests that both mechanical stimulation and light partially inactivate auxin action. Both stimuli are more effective if repeated at intervals than if applied continuously, a fact which may be due to a refractive stage following the stimulus.

Borriss (1934b) showed that *Coprinus* fruiting bodies which would not have matured in the darkness will do so, at least partially, if mechanically stimulated, and Stiefel (1952) finds that the stipe of the fruiting body of *Coprinus* responds to mechanical stimulation and to light just as do the stems of higher plants, both stimuli tending to check elongation.

Mechanical pressure may have an important morphogenetic effect by determining the plane of cell division in meristematic tissue (p. 49), the plane of division tending to be parallel to the direction of the pressure.

It is with the more specifically morphogenetic effects of mechanical stimuli, however, that we are particularly concerned here. Chief among these are tension, compression, bending, swaying, and the omnipresent stimulus of gravity.

Tension. Much work has been done on this problem, especially in earlier years, but the results are often contradictory. Hegler (1893) stretched seedlings of sunflower and petioles of *Helleborus* by attaching weights to them. After a 2-day application of 150 gm., it required a pull of 350 gm. to break these structures as compared with only 160 gm. in the controls. Traction seemed to have increased the tensile strength, and Hegler found that traction had increased the cell-wall thickness and the amount of collenchyma.

Newcombe (1895) reviewed the very considerable amount of early literature in this field. His own work confirmed Hegler's. He also found that if stem bases were enclosed in plaster and thus relieved of mechanical strain they produced less mechanical tissue.

Ball (1904), however, repeated Hegler's experiments, using pulleys and carefully comparing stretched plants with their controls, but found no difference between them in structure or tensile strength. Hibbard (1907) confirmed Ball. Still later Bordner (1909) studied the problem again and confirmed Hegler's results, using similar material. In stretched plants the amount of vascular tissue and the tensile strength were in-

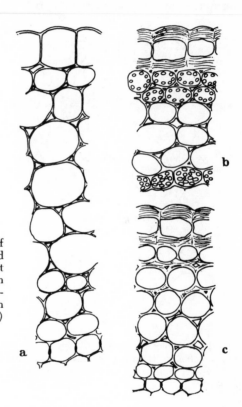

Fig. 16-1. *Vicia faba.* Outer portions of transverse sections through the second internode. a, grown in darkness without shaking; b, grown in light; c, grown in darkness and shaken. Mechanical stimulation has much the same effect on growth as does light. (*From Bünning.*)

creased. He found that no effects were produced unless the plants were growing, a fact that may help explain the conflicting results of these various workers.

Flaskämper (1910) and others subjected flower and fruit stalks to additional weighting but found no change in histological structure. Wiedersheim (1903) hung weights on branches of a weeping variety of beech and reported that these grew less rapidly and had shorter cells but formed no additional vascular tissue.

In all this early work on mechanical factors the suggestion was natural that the plant would tend to react in such a way as to oppose the effect of the factor and, in the cases here discussed, to develop more mechanical tissue which would resist traction and prevent breakage of the plant. Vöchting (1878), with his versatile interest in all such problems, asked the practical question as to whether plant axes, subject to different tensile strains in nature, showed structural differences as a result. He compared the pedicels of squash fruits hanging from trellises with similar ones growing on the ground and found more vascular tissue in the former. However, when such a fruit was supported on a platform beside

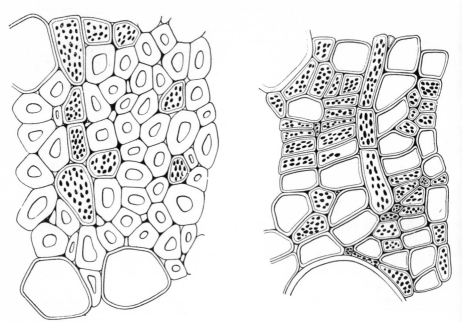

FIG. 16-2. Effect of tension on wood structure. Left, transverse section of wood of *Fagus sylvatica* from a root grown under strong tension; right, section of root of the same species not under tension. Note generally thicker cell walls in the former. (*From Jaccard.*)

a freely hanging one, he found the same amount of vascular tissue in the stalks of both. Vöchting suggested that the differences first observed were due to differences in the amount of transpiration rather than to tension. He also tried to induce mechanical tissue by traction in weak, poorly vascularized plants, but without success. However, he grafted a normal shoot on such a weak one and observed the development in the latter of a marked increase of vascular tissue.

It might be objected that stems are not usually subject to tension but that roots are, and it was evidently important to study these organs as well. Wildt (1906) fastened the seedling stem and the adjacent part of its root in plaster and pulled gently. The soft central tissue disappeared and a solid vascular core resulted. Flaskämper, who repeated and confirmed this, found that roots which had been subjected to traction had somewhat *less* tensile strength than the controls. Newcombe (1895) stretched roots of sunflower and squash and observed that they grew somewhat stouter and were definitely stronger than the controls. Jaccard (1914) studied some experiments of nature in this field, notably cases where a small root crosses a larger one and is stretched by the growth in diameter of the latter. In the root under tension the cell walls of the wood were thicker than in the control (Fig. 16-2). The amount of mechanical tissue was less, however.

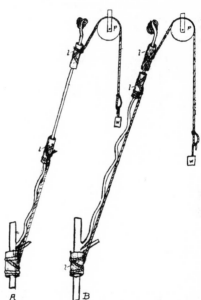

Fig. 16-3. Effect of tension on a tendril. Device for subjecting part of a tendril to tension by weight over pulley (A) and for relieving the other part by having a cord bear all the tension (B). Stimulus of contact is the same in both. (*From Brush.*)

Among the organs of a plant most commonly subject to tension in nature are tendrils. Many experiments have been undertaken with them to determine whether traction (pulling) affects their structure. Much difficulty was found by early workers in separating the effects of contact (to which stimulus tendrils are particularly susceptible) from traction. Brush (1912) placed a tendril in lengthwise contact with a thread to the free end of which, thrown over a pulley, weights were attached. In the control, this thread was continuous and sustained all the pull. In the experimental one the thread was interrupted in the middle so that the tendril itself bore all the pull. Each tendril was thus in contact with the thread through all, or almost all, its length, but one was under tension and the other was not (Fig. 16-3). In both, there was more xylem than in tendrils having no stimulus of contact, but in the one under traction the walls of the fundamental tissue cells were markedly thicker than in the other tendrils.

Compression. Because of technical difficulties, not as many attempts have been made to produce the opposite sort of mechanical stimulation, compression in the lengthwise direction.

Pennington (1910) hung weights on woody and herbaceous stems of various sorts as they were growing in height but found no appreciable effect on structure or mechanical strength. Himmel (1927) used more

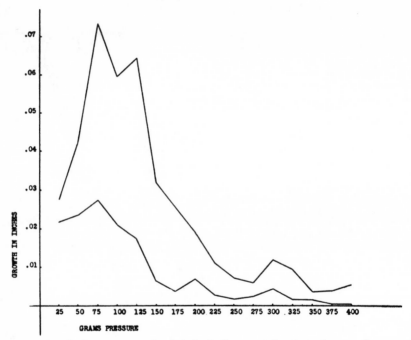

Fig. 16-4. Graph showing growth of *Podophyllum* petioles, in inches per hour, under lengthwise pressure from various weights. Upper curve, control; lower, experiment. Growth is markedly reduced by pressure. (*From Himmel.*)

favorable material, the growing petioles of the large, umbrella-like leaves of *Podophyllum*. On the apices of these petioles he hung weights which were periodically increased as growth continued. He found that growth rate in the weighted petioles was less than in the controls but that growth in the former finally equalled that in the latter (Fig. 16-4). The rigidity of the petioles was somewhat increased.

Rasdorsky (1925), working with sunflower and marigold, approached the problem in another way. He held up the plant by a gently stretched thread attached to the upper part of its stem and thus relieved it from supporting its own weight. Plants thus treated were definitely weaker than the controls. No structural changes are reported. The upward pull, weak as it was, may have stimulated growth in length and thus tended to make the plant top-heavy.

Newcombe (1895) supported the base of the stem in young sunflower and squash plants by encasing it in plaster, thus relieving it of mechanical strain. In that part of the stem under the cast much less mechanical tissue was formed, although this developed rapidly when the cast was removed. Other effects of such treatment, especially on respiration, might account for the results obtained.

The studies on experimental traction and compression are contradictory and indecisive, and many factors other than mechanical ones may well be involved. Little work has been done in this field in recent years. Schwarz (1930) subjected the problem of mechanical factors in development to critical review and concluded that they have little effect and that the results attributed to them may well be due to nutritional influences and transpiration. Rasdorsky (1931), however, took issue with him strongly.

Bending and Swaying. There is much more agreement as to the effect of bending and swaying plant organs. Most workers find that, when growing herbaceous stems are bent, the cells (especially collenchyma and bast fibers) on the *convex* side are smaller in cross section and thicker-walled than corresponding ones on the concave side. The same results are evident in plants grown on a clinostat, showing that gravity is not involved.

A good discussion of this problem is presented by Bücher (1906). To this result of bending he gave the name *camptotrophism.* Since cells on the convex side of the bend are evidently under tension and those on the concave side under compression, the histological differences observed seem related to the type of mechanical strain involved. These effects agree with the ones from the experiments just reported where tension seems to increase wall thickness and reduce cell size, and compression produces the opposite result. Bücher obtained more direct evidence in support of this conclusion. He enclosed in plaster most of the lower portion of a growing hypocotyl of *Ricinus.* The upper part was enclosed in another casing of plaster, leaving a short portion of hypocotyl unenclosed between the two. The weight of the upper layer of plaster was supported by the hypocotyl, which was thus subjected, particularly in its free portion, to considerable lengthwise compression (Fig. 16-5). In the control plants the hypocotyl had relatively small and thick-walled cells. In the compressed hypocotyls, however, the cells were much larger and had very thin walls. This sort of experiment seems worth repeating with modern techniques of analysis. What, for example, would

the electron microscope show as to the character of such cell walls laid
down under pressure?

Bücher found that when a growing shoot, negatively geotropic, is
forcibly kept horizontal the cells of the upper side are smaller and
thicker-walled than those of the lower. This phenomenon he called
geotrophism and explained it on the assumption that since the lower
side grows more rapidly (tending to bend the stem upward) it must
be under compression and the upper side under tension. To test the
relative effects of gravity and bending, he inverted a plant of *Ricinus*
and held its tip bent at 90° to the axis (and thus horizontal). Camptotrophism and geotrophism should thus be brought into opposition. Actu-

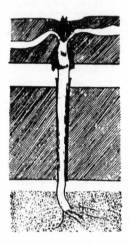
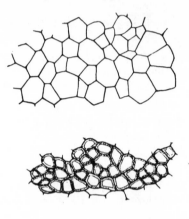

FIG. 16-5. Effect of vertical compression on hypocotyl of *Ricinus*. At left, young
seedling, protected by sheath and cotton plug, held in two blocks of plaster and there
subjected to compression from weight of plaster. At right, bast bundle from upper part
of such a hypocotyl (above, under compression) and from the normal control (below), showing increase in cell size and reduction in wall thickness as a result of compression. (*From Bücher.*)

ally, the plant reacted as it would to gravity, with smaller cells on the
upper, concave side. Perhaps in such a case it is the difference in degree
of tension that determines the result.

Vöchting (1908) placed the stem of a potted plant in a horizontal position and put a support under it at some distance from the pot. On the
free end he hung weights and observed a considerable increase in the
cross section of the stem, especially of its vascular system. This was most
marked near the point of support, where the strain was greatest, and on
the upper and lower sides. Growth of the stem in length had ceased,
so that these changes resulting from mechanical stimulation were evidently in the secondary tissues. Haerdtl (1927) found similar results.

Many experiments have been conducted, beginning with Knight (1811), on the effect of continually swaying plants as they grow. The swaying was done by clockwork and pendulum, water wheel, or motor. Observers are generally agreed that the cross section of the axis tends to be elliptical under these conditions, with its wider dimension in the plane of sway (Fig. 16-6), and that more vascular and mechanical tissue is developed than in the controls (Rasdorsky, 1925; Burns, 1920).

It may be objected that in these swaying experiments conditions are so abnormal that results may be due to other factors than purely mechanical ones. The experiments of M. R. Jacobs (1954) are significant here. He supported the trunk of a young pine tree with guy wires attached about

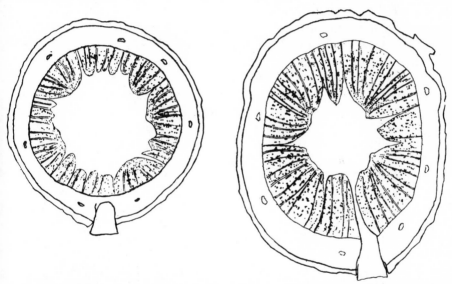

Fig. 16-6. Effect of swaying on sunflower stem, cross sections. At left, control. At right, stem swayed for 3 weeks in the vertical plane of the figure. (*From Rasdorsky.*)

20 feet from the ground so that lateral movement below this point was prevented although the trunk above the point of attachment was subject to ordinary wind sway. This portion increased normally in thickness but the unswayed lower portion grew much less rapidly than the upper or than the unsupported controls. When the guy wires were removed, this part grew rapidly in thickness until its normal diameter had been attained. Evidently in such cases swaying stimulates cambial activity. This may be a factor in producing the relatively slender trunks of trees in a forest as compared with those grown in the open.

A somewhat similar case has been reported by Venning (1949) for celery, an herbaceous plant. One series of seedlings was grown in constant wind and another in a windless environment. The former developed 50 per cent more volume of collenchymatous tissue than the latter. In all such cases, however, it is difficult to separate mechanical effects from those caused by increased water loss.

Ultrasonics. The morphogenetic effect of a quite different mechanical factor, intense ultrasonic vibration, has been reported by several workers. Takashima and others (1951) found that in germinating radish seedlings exposed for 16 minutes the shoots were much deformed. In peas similarly exposed, length of root and shoot was increased through increased cell size.

Gravity. Gravity is unlike the mechanical factors just discussed in that it is continuous, unchanging in intensity, and constant in direction. It is one of the most important formative factors, for plants must continually regulate their growth to it. The upright position of main-shoot axes, the downward growth of primary roots, and the various intermediate orientations of leaves and lateral branches and roots are manifestations of geotropic growth reactions. The general growth pattern of the plant body is a specific reaction to gravity. The problem of tropisms is primarily one for plant physiology but the student of morphogenesis should not lose sight of the fact that these tropisms, whether reactions to gravity, light, or other stimuli, are continually molding the pattern of the plant.

One can distinguish between the tropistic effects of gravity in the strict sense, which involve the orientation of parts, and its truly formative ones. Conspicuous among the latter are the modifications of symmetry from radial to dorsiventral or vice versa (p. 176). Many years ago Wiesner (1868) and others studied the dorsiventral symmetry of plant structures, especially leaves, when the axis on which they were borne was horizontal instead of vertical, and succeeded in inducing form changes in them experimentally. For such a difference in form between the upper and the lower leaves of a horizontal branch or between the upper and lower sides of such leaves, Wiesner proposed the term *anisophylly* (p. 171). Goebel later distinguished between anisophyllous forms which are constant and hereditary and those which can be reversed by changing the relation of the growing structures to gravity.

Gravity has been found to modify internal structure also. Brain (1939) grew various plants horizontally on a clinostat and found that this modified the cells somewhat, those on the clinostat being generally shorter and wider, presumably because of the greater extensibility of their cell walls. Larsen (1953) found that gravity has little effect on rate of cell elongation when acting on roots growing in the normal direction but checks such elongation when acting in the opposite direction or at right angles to it. Imamura (1931) was able to change the position of palisade and spongy parenchyma by reversing the orientation of *Iris japonica* leaves to gravity. Kreh (1925) examined changes in the fruiting bodies of the fungus *Lenzites* which had been turned through an angle of 180° with relation to gravity and found that in new growth the original dorsiventral structure was restored. Many other cases of the effect of gravity on structure have been reported.

It is often difficult to distinguish the effects of gravity from those of light, since a change in the relation to one usually produces a change in the relation to the other unless experimental conditions are carefully controlled. Wiesner (1892c) in a later paper recognized that his earlier results in anisophylly were due to light as well as to gravity, and Bussmann (1939, 1941) found the same to be true of induced dorsiventrality in fern prothallia.

Gravity presumably does not modify plant structure directly but acts through its influence on other factors. It produces tension and compression of tissues with consequent effects on cell division and expansion. The reaction of woody plants in developing stem tissues strong enough to resist bending and wind sway has been mentioned, and there must be the same regulatory control of growth to resist weight of trunk (Esser, 1946). In this sense, gravity acts as a mechanical factor. Opatowski (1946) explains the oblique growth of trees under the action of prevailing winds as a mechanical response, based on the concept of maximum strength.

Equally important is the role of gravity in the distribution of growth substances. Just how this occurs is not clear, but differential distribution of substances under the stimulus of gravity must be involved (p. 380; Brauner, 1927). This presumably affects the form of structures when symmetry is changed from radial to dorsiventral, for example. It also has less direct effects. Van Overbeek and Cruzado (1948) and Fisher (1957) have shown that flower formation is geotropically stimulated in horizontally placed pineapple and soybean plants, presumably by alteration in the distribution of growth substances. Other phenomena of differentiation may perhaps be explained in the same way.

Gravity serves as the frame of reference to which the whole pattern of plant growth is regulated. A plant develops under the constant and uniform stimulus of gravity, and its tropistic and morphogenetic responses—hardly to be distinguished from each other here—are such that a specific bodily form is produced. Without this regulation to a steady orienting directive, the general pattern of the plant body would doubtless be much less specific and might even fail to be developed. Because of their being anchored in one spot, plants are much more sensitive of such gravitational form control than are animals.

Reaction Wood. The example of such control that has been worked out most fully is one which was first observed in the development of reaction wood of conifers and later in similar tissue in angiosperms. Students of wood structure have long noticed that horizontal branches of coniferous trees are excentric in cross section (p. 175), with the pith nearer the upper side than the lower. Below the pith is a wedge-shaped sector of wood, reddish in color when freshly cut, and hence often called "rotholz." Since the lower side of a branch is obviously under compression, this was long regarded as the cause for the development of this sort of structure, and it was called "compression wood." Its cells are somewhat shorter than those of normal wood, and the micellae in their walls are less steeply pitched. Such wood is absent, save exceptionally, in vertical axes and thus in the main trunk but develops wherever such an axis is forced to grow at an angle from the vertical, as in a tree bent partly over. Such wood grows somewhat more in length than does normal wood and thus produces considerable longitudinal compression. If a tree grown in an oblique position is sawn across, beginning on the lower side, the saw therefore tends to bind.

This tissue has now been shown not to be the result of growth under compression but to have a nature and function of much morphogenetic significance. It is now more correctly called *reaction wood*. Together with the corresponding tissue in angiosperms, it has been studied by various wood anatomists, especially Hartmann (1932, 1942, 1943), whose work has been extended somewhat by Sinnott (1952). In young conifers, especially pines, before the growing season began, these workers tied some of the lateral branches downward and others upward. They also tied the tip of the main axis into a position out of the vertical, sometimes even in a loop. When new shoots of the current year developed from the terminal buds of these various axes, these new shoots tended to have the same direction of growth that they would have had if the shoot out of which they grew had not been fixed in an atypical position (Fig. 16-7). The main axis bent around so that it again grew upward. The lateral branches (in white pine) grew out at an angle of about 70° from the main trunk and thus from the directional pull of gravity. In other words, there was, in a sense, a regeneration of the normal growth pattern of the tree.

In this process the reaction wood performs an essential function, for it always occurs in such a place that its greater lengthwise growth will tend to bend the new shoot (and the free portion of the old shoot) into a direction which would be normal for it. If a lateral branch has been bent upward, for example, the reaction wood will be on the *upper* side, for this will push the branch down. Such a change continues until the orientation of the shoot is normal, when reaction wood again develops on the lower side, as in ordinary branches. Its function here seems to be to counteract, by its upward push, the downward pull caused by the weight of the branch. A bent-over terminal shoot develops reaction wood on its lower side and thus pushes the axis up to vertical. If the terminal shoot is removed, an excess of reaction wood begins to develop on the under side of the lateral branches just below the tip and one of them is finally pushed up to the vertical and becomes a new "leader." Sometimes two share this leadership, neither becoming quite vertical.

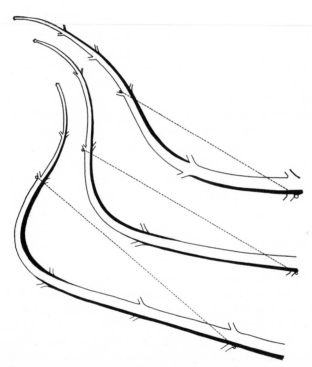

Fig. 16-7. Development of reaction wood in pine in three branches which had been bent upward artificially. Reaction wood normally is formed on the lower side but in the new growth on these branches it develops on the upper side after bending and thus tends to push them back to their normal orientation. (*From Sinnott.*)

Angiosperm branching is regulated in much the same way except that the reaction wood here is normally on the upper side of a branch and acts by producing tension rather than compression, thus pulling the branches into place instead of pushing them. Wardrop (1956) believes that the distribution of tension (reaction) wood in *Eucalyptus* is regulatory and operates to maintain normal tree form much as reaction wood does in the conifers.

That compression itself is not responsible for the formation of this wood is shown by the fact that when a terminal shoot is bent around and tied in a vertical loop, reaction wood is formed on the under side of both the upper and lower parts of the loop. In the former, the wood is under compression but in the latter under tension. That gravity is not directly responsible is shown by the appearance of reaction wood on the *upper* sides of branches which are being pushed down. In every case the development of this wood is such that it will bring back the normal pattern.

The reaction of each part of the plant seems to be a specific orientation to the direction of gravitational pull. This reaction is different in different parts of the growth pattern of the tree. In herbaceous material (branches of *Aster*) the author has found that a lateral branch tied out of position will tend to assume its normal angle to gravity rather than its normal angle to the main axis of the plant. When gravity is replaced experimentally by centrifugal force, reaction wood is also produced (Scott and Preston, 1955).

Auxin has been shown to be responsible for the relation between a terminal bud and lateral ones below it (p. 386), and it is presumably concerned with the production of reaction wood (Wershing and Bailey, 1942). The problem of morphogenetic significance is why there is just enough auxin (and thus enough reaction wood) at just the right place and time to produce such a specific pattern of branching that this can be used as a diagnostic character for the species. Here is the problem of organic form in one of its simplest but most puzzling manifestations.

Spurr and Hyvärinen (1954*a*) have reviewed the literature of reaction wood in the conifers.

Tissue Tension. Another factor, mechanical in its nature, which may be of some morphogenetic importance is tissue tension. Not all the cells in a tissue are equally turgid, and cell walls differ in their elasticity and their plasticity. Tissues also grow at different rates. These differences often cause tensions between cells or groups of cells which, since plant cells adhere firmly to each other, cannot be reduced by cellular readjustments in position.

In an early and thorough paper Gregor Kraus (1867) examined this problem. He measured the length of a piece of growing herbaceous internode and then sliced it into longitudinal strips, each consisting of only one tissue (pith, wood, cortex, or epidermis). When he measured the length of these, he found that the outer ones had shrunk in comparison with their original length before isolation but that the inner ones had expanded. Evidently there was considerable tension between them in the intact internode, the outer tissues being stretched and the inner ones compressed.

The degree of tissue tension is not constant but is usually low in young internodes, increases farther back, and finally decreases in most cases to zero as growth finally ceases. The distribution of tension among the tissues also changes. Schüepp (1917) found that there was tension in the growing point but that here it was opposite in its distribution from that in tissue which was extending. Schneider (1926) found no tension in the growing point itself but saw it first in the leaf primordia, which for this reason tend to bend inward.

What bearing tissue tension may have on differentiation or on the development of form is not clear but it may be of some importance. In young ovaries, however, where presumably form and structure are being determined, there seems to be little tension though this increases in later stages of development. A remarkable instance of tension in dead, dry wood has been reported by M. R. Jacobs (1945), who found that if a board which includes the whole width of the log is sawed at one end part way down by a series of parallel longitudinal cuts the strips thus separated tend to spread apart fanwise, indicating the existence of a very considerable degree of tension between the inner and the outer parts of the log.

Absolute Size. Another morphogenetic factor, which in a sense may be regarded as physical, is absolute size itself. It is clear, as Galileo long ago pointed out in his principle of similitude, that as any body increases in size its volume enlarges as the cube of the diameter but its surface only as the square. Thus the ratio of surface to volume will progressively decrease. In a living organism, where physiological activity is often limited by the amount of available surface for interchange of material between organism and environment, or between one tissue and another, the surface-volume relationship is of much importance and is obviously related to changes in shape and structure.

This shows most simply in the increased elaboration of bodily form as size increases. Among algae, for example, the smaller types are relatively simple and compact but the larger ones, through branching or surface convolution, have a much more elaborate conformation, with the result that the ratio of surface to volume is not very different in the two. A good example of the same thing is the difference between the small, rounded chloroplasts of higher plants and the very much larger chromatophores of some of the lower ones, which are elaborately branched and dissected. Internal anatomy displays the same tendency, for in the sporeling of a fern the vascular cylinder is a solid rod but as the plant grows this soon opens out to form a hollow tube. It may later be broken up into a ring of bundles or even a series of concentric rings or tubes. The radial thickness of each strand thus tends to be approximately the same, with the result that the surface of contact between xylem and phloem, so important in the physiology of the plant, remains relatively constant. Every unit mass of phloem tissue has essentially the same "frontier" on the xylem as every other one, and none is limited in its water supply. Similarly, as roots increase in size, the number of radial arms increases, with the result that the xylem-phloem surface remains relatively constant.

There are many examples of this correlation between absolute size and complexity of conformation, a fact which Bower (1930) was the

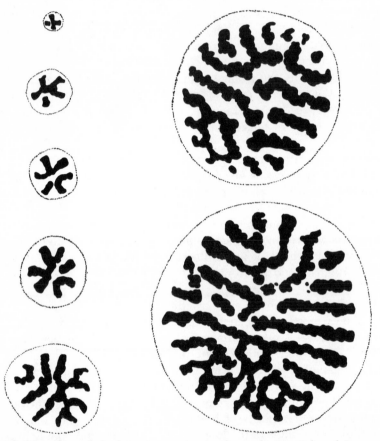

FIG. 16-8. The effect of absolute size on structural complexity. Steles of *Lycopodium scariosum* of seven progressively larger sizes showing the increase in complexity that accompanies increased size. (*From Bower.*)

first to bring forcefully to the attention of botanists (Fig. 16-8). Although the advantage of such a correlation is obvious, the problem of how it is brought about morphogenetically is not clear. The advantage is not effective physiologically until the structures are mature and functioning but the pattern is laid down in the meristem. It may be that this is simply a case of inheritance of a particularly advantageous developmental pattern which has arisen through natural selection, as have other embryonic characters.

The relation between size and form here seems to be too immediate, however, to be accounted for in this long-range fashion. An inherited pattern ought to be evident in a small and stunted as well as in a large individual, but the effect of size seems to be more direct. One is tempted to see here another example of the regular spacing of structures to which attention has earlier been called (p. 199). In the same way there may be maintained a constant ratio between primary xylem and phloem, a ratio which originates within the tissues of the primary meristem. This morphogenetic problem, which has an important bearing on the origin of differentiation and of structure in general, seems especially favorable for biochemical and perhaps even mathematical attack.

Bioelectrical Factors. For many years the possibility that electricity, in one way or another, might affect the physiological and developmental activities of plants has interested botanists, and there is a very considerable literature on the subject. Unfortunately, this is a field that is theoretically and technically so complex that few workers are qualified to obtain dependable results in it, and much of the published work is therefore of doubtful value. The present writer is certainly not competent to review it critically.

Students of tropisms have discussed the possibility that differences in electrical potential may be involved in these activities. Went (1932) suggested that the polar flow of auxin is an electrophoretic process. Clark (1938) raised doubt as to this idea and pointed out that it is possible by certain chemical treatments to abolish the polarity of auxin transport without changing the electrical polarity, protoplasmic streaming, or other characters of the system (p. 385). Schrank, however, who has discussed the problem in some detail (1957), has shown that in the transverse distribution of auxin in the *Avena* coleoptile, a transverse electrical polarity precedes the movement of auxin, thus tending to support Went's theory. The early work on the electrical control of polarity was reviewed by Thomas (1939).

Morphogenetically the most significant result of the work with electricity is the evidence that in many organisms there are continuous bioelectrical currents and a distribution of electrical potential differences so constant that a bioelectrical field is set up in the organism. By the use of a very delicate micropotentiometer Burr was able to demonstrate the existence of such a field in amphibian eggs (1941). Even in the young ovaries of cucurbits such relations between the form of the ovary and the bioelectrical pattern could be shown (1944). Burr and Northrop (1939) have discussed the general problem of electrodynamic fields in living organisms. Lund (1931 and others) carried out a series of studies on electrical potential differences in trees, as related to the phenomena of polarity, dominance, and correlation in them.

If bioelectrical fields are actually concerned with the specific character of development, it would seem possible to change them by applying other electrical fields externally and thus perhaps to modify organic form. This turns out to be very difficult to accomplish, however. Nevertheless, Lund (1945) was able to inhibit completely the growth in length of an onion root by passing an electric current upward through it, although the same current passing downward produced little or no inhibition.

It is tempting to explain all form differences as results of these constant bioelectric fields, and they may well be concerned with the control of organic development. Such fields are doubtless related to the fine structure of protoplasm and the complex pattern of surfaces which this presents. Whether the fields are the cause of developmental changes or are themselves the result of chemical or physical factors is an important theoretical question. The problem of bioelectric factors is too complex for easy solution, but it should certainly continue to be attacked vigorously by those who are qualified to do so.

The volume by Lund and his collaborators (1947) presents a good account of the problem of bioelectrical fields and their implications for morphogenesis. Rosene has gathered for it a bibliography of 1,406 titles.

CHAPTER 17

Chemical Factors in General

Chemical factors are of paramount importance for metabolism and for physiology generally, but they also have an important part in the determination of form and structure. Physical factors—light, water, temperature, gravity—produce their effects on development chiefly through the external environment, but chemical ones operate morphogenetically both from inside and outside the organism, and in studying them it is necessary to recognize this fact. Nitrogen, for example, by its presence in the soil, markedly affects the growth and development of a plant rooted there, but it does so because of what happens after it has entered the living system of the plant. Here it may be moved from place to place and, as a constituent of protoplasm, it affects the course of development in many ways. The student of morphogenesis concerns himself, therefore, not only with the visible effects of changing amounts of nitrogen in the soil but with the history of this element as a part of the organic mechanism. This is true for other chemical substances, whether taken in from the outside or synthesized within the plant. Much of differentiation results from differential distribution of substances throughout the plant body.

Many effects of these substances are *local*. In studying them experimentally it is therefore not enough to examine their effects upon the plant as a whole but to discover what happens in particular parts of the plant as their concentration in these parts is altered. The most important discoveries in the field of growth substances, for example, have been made by studying their local effects on a developing root or leaf or ovary.

The role of chemical substances in development also changes with *time*, for the life of the plant is a life history and this history consists of specific progressive changes. These are reflected not only in alterations in structure, as between juvenile and adult foliage, but in physiological changes that go on within the plant. Some of these are gradual but others are more sharply marked. Such is the transition from the vegetative to the flowering state (p. 184), in which meristematic activity shifts from one region and one type to others that are quite different and where there is often a radical redistribution of substances in the plant body. The plant's life history is composed of such progressive steps. This concept is of importance for morphogenesis and perhaps especially for its chemical aspects.

The subject of chemical factors in plant life, and particularly of the biochemistry of metabolism, is one of the chief concerns of physiology, but the only aspect of this field germane to the science of morphogenesis is the somewhat limited portion of it which deals directly with the relation of chemical substances to development. The present discussion will necessarily treat this subject in nothing more than a very brief and general fashion. One chapter will be devoted to the role of the elements and the compounds that are primarily significant for their role in nutrition rather than in morphogenesis. A second chapter will deal with those substances that, even in very minute amounts, have been found to exert profound effects on growth and development and are commonly called growth substances.

ELEMENTS

It has long been known that only a few of the chemical elements are essential for plant life. These, in addition to carbon, oxygen, hydrogen, and nitrogen, are sulfur, phosphorus, calcium, magnesium, potassium, and iron, together with a number of others, notably boron, zinc, copper, manganese, cobalt, and a few others which, in very small amounts, are essential for the nutrition of most plants and are known as *trace elements*.

Several of the elements, or simple compounds of them, have been found to have some effect on development and are thus of morphogenetic importance, though except for nitrogen this is relatively minor.

Nitrogen. This element is of outstanding significance in many ways. It is an essential constituent of all proteins and thus of protoplasm, and from its presence in the nucleoproteins it is concerned in the production of new living stuff and thus in all growth and reproduction.

That nitrogen tends to increase the vegetative growth of plants has long been known, but it may also have certain specific effects on their structure. Burkholder and McVeigh (1940) grew maize (both inbred and hybrid) with varying applications of nitrogen in sand culture. Where nitrogen was abundant, as compared with plants where this was limited, meristems were better developed, length and diameter of stem were greater, cell size and cell number increased as did the size and number of the bundles, there was greater differentiation especially in the phloem, and both sieve tubes and vessels increased in diameter (Fig. 17-1).

Plants growing with little available nitrogen tend to be woody and to have thick cell walls, presumably because much of the carbohydrate is deposited in these structures, whereas if nitrogen were abundant it would be used in protein synthesis. Shields and Mangum (1954) studied the content of total and of amino nitrogen in the leaves of 40 species of plants and found it highest in thin, mesophytic herbaceous leaves, next in small xeromorphic dicotyledons, and least in monocotyledons with much mechanical tissue.

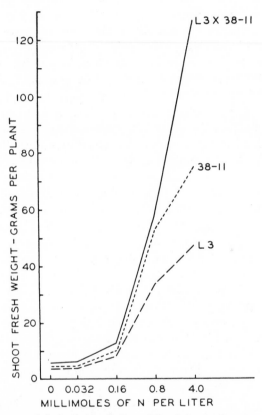

Fig. 17-1. Nitrogen and hybrid vigor. Two inbred lines of maize and their hybrid grown in sand culture with various amounts of nitrogen. The increase in size with added nitrogen is much greater in the hybrid than in either parent. (*From*ʼ*Burk-holder and McVeigh.*)

Nitrogen supply may be related to the differentiation between male and female sex organs, for Kocher (1941), studying the dioecious species *Melandrium album,* found markedly more nitrogen (as percentage of dry weight) in leaves of female plants than of male. This difference was slight in seedlings, rose until flowering took place, and then disappeared.

There may be interaction between nitrogen and other factors. In onion, for example, Scully, Parker, and Borthwick (1945) observed that, with plants grown at photoperiods longer than necessary for bulb production, variations in nitrogen had little effect, but when the photoperiod was close to the critical one for bulbs, bulb development was considerably greater at low nitrogen levels than at high ones.

Cohen (1953) reports the effect of a nitrogen compound, ammonia, on the development of the slime molds *Dictyostelium* and *Polysphondylium*, two members of the Acrasiaceae (p. 223). Treatment with a low concentration of ammonia greatly simplifies the morphogenetic expression of these forms and reduces the degree of their differentiation. The sorocarps produced resemble those of the genera *Guttulina* and *Guttulinopsis*.

Carbohydrate-Nitrogen Ratio. Many other instances of the developmental effects of nitrogen could be cited. More widespread than these changes produced by nitrogen directly, however, are the ones that result from the balance between nitrogen and carbohydrates. Horticulturists know that nitrogen stimulates vegetative growth, that weakly vegetative plants tend to flower early, and that in vigorously vegetative ones flowering is either scanty or does not occur until the amount of available nitrogen is reduced. This problem was first studied intensively by Kraus and Kraybill (1918) in tomatoes. They found that in strongly vegetative plants bearing few flowers or fruit the C/N ratio was low. Those producing fruit abundantly had a high C/N ratio but had been given a good supply of nitrogen at the beginning of their growth. They interpret these facts to mean that when nitrogen is abundant all the carbohydrate produced by the plant will be used in forming new vegetative tissue. If nitrogen is in short supply, however, carbohydrates will tend to accumulate, and when the C/N ratio becomes high enough, the development of reproductive structures will be stimulated. This happens early in weakly vegetative individuals, but such plants are too small to produce a large crop of fruit. Maximum yield results from an abundant supply of nitrogen at first and an active production of carbohydrates later by the fully grown vegetative structures. This is what normally happens under favorable conditions. The important morphogenetic aspect of this hypothesis is that it maintains that the differentiation of reproductive organs is dependent on the accumulation of carbohydrate in the plant. Until this happens, vegetative structures take priority over reproductive ones in the use of available carbohydrate.

In general, the younger the tissue, the lower is the C/N ratio. From a low point in the seedling it increases as foliage develops and as the ratio of top to root grows larger until it reaches the point where reproductive structures are formed. This would explain why flowering normally is deferred until the plant has reached a considerable vegetative development.

The relation of the C/N ratio to flowering is evident in many ways. In biennially bearing apple trees, for example, it is high in the bearing years and low in the "off" ones. In fruit spurs where the buds are developing into flower buds, starch content tends to be high and nitrogen low, whereas in barren spurs the opposite is true. Potter and Phillips (1927), however, found that flower-bud formation in fruit spurs was more closely related to the amount of nitrogen than to any ratio between this element and carbohydrates.

Loomis (1932) has emphasized the fact that the effect of water on development resembles that of nitrogen, both tending to stimulate vegetative growth. He believes that the balance is not so much between carbohydrate and nitrogen as between the factors that tend to produce growth and those that tend to induce differentiation. The former include both water and nitrogen together with any other factors, such as temperature, that favor the synthesis of new protoplasm. Differentiation, on the other hand, requires an excess of available carbohydrate. Why this is so is by no means clear, though there may be a selective advantage in a mechanism which tends to defer the development of reproductive structures until a plant has reached the size where it is large enough to produce fruit abundantly.

The carbohydrate-nitrogen ratio is related to other structures than reproductive ones, notably the shoot-root ratio. In general, the higher the C/N ratio, the larger is the relative size of the root. When nitrogen is abundantly available in the soil, the increased growth tends to occur in the shoot more than in the root. Hicks (1928b) found that in willow cuttings the carbohydrates pass downward and the nitrogen upward so that the C/N ratio is higher at the base, where roots develop, than at the tip, where shoots are formed. Davies (1931) also observed that in willow cuttings roots develop in regions where nitrogen, as a percentage of dry weight, is low and shoots where it is high. These facts obviously have a bearing on the problem of polarity in regeneration (p. 119).

Reid (1924) made stem cuttings from tomato plants that were high in C/N ratio and from others that were low and found that the former made better roots than the latter. She also observed (1929) that the relative development of the root in seedlings of various species was related to the proportion of carbohydrate to nitrogen in the seed from which they grew. Where this was high the seedlings had stronger roots than where it was low.

Despite the evident relation between the C/N ratio, as observable in the chemical composition of the plant, and the processes of flowering and root formation, there is now a good deal of evidence that this ratio may not be the cause but rather an accompaniment of these activities. In a number of instances, such as the soybean (Murneek, 1937) and wheat

(Polster, 1938), floral initiation begins some time before the change from low to high C/N ratio takes place. In various plants that have been brought to flowering by other means, such as chemical or photoperiodic stimulation, the increase in C/N is much less conspicuous than under natural conditions. In many cases, also, there is no precise ratio that may be counted upon to induce flowering. Both in carbohydrates and compounds of nitrogen there are many different chemical forms, and it is a matter of doubt whether the ratio should regard total, soluble, or easily available carbohydrate, on the one hand, and total, protein, or soluble nitrogen on the other.

Despite these criticisms, the general concept that in the living plant there is at any particular stage a balance between various chemical constituents and that a shift in this balance is related to a change in the activities of the plant is an important one. The organism tends to maintain a homeostatic equilibrium among its various processes but this is not a static condition, for the equilibrium changes progressively as the organism develops from one phase to the next. This is so complex that the ratio between any two chemical substances will usually give only an incomplete picture of it. A study of the C/N ratio, whether this be cause or effect of the onset of the reproductive phase, will doubtless continue to provide information about this major step in the life history of the plant.

Other Elements. Much of what is known about the morphogenetic effects of the other essential elements comes from observation of changes in development produced when each is deficient in amount. These changes are usually differences from the normal amount of growth or are abnormalities of various sorts, "hunger signs" resulting from insufficient nutrition. The literature of physiology and pathology is full of such instances. Venning (1953) has described the developmental effects of deficiencies in sulfur, calcium, nitrogen, potassium, phosphorus, and iron. The effects of the various trace elements have been reviewed by several workers, among them Brenchley (1947) and Wallace (1950).

A few of the effects of various elements are of morphogenetic interest.

Phosphorus is of much importance in physiology and genetics because it is a constituent of the nucleic acids. Morphogenetically it is significant in relation to mitosis. Phosphate promotes cell division in roots but has little effect on cell elongation, whereas nitrate promotes elongation but not division.

Stanfield (1944) analyzed roots and tops of staminate and pistillate plants of *Lychnis dioica* and found that the staminate had a higher percentage of phosphorus than the latter in both vegetative and early flowering phases.

Pierce (1937) observed that in violet plants grown in nutrient solutions without calcium the chromosomes in root-tip cells were markedly smaller than when grown in complete nutrient. When phosphorus was in excess, however, the chromosomes were about twice normal size. These differences were also reflected in the size of the nucleus.

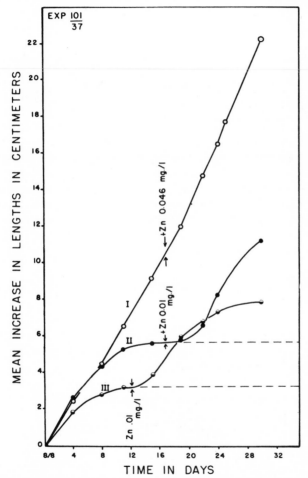

FIG. 17-2. Effect of zinc on tomato plants grown in nutrient solution. Curve I, plants to which zinc was applied from the start; Curves II and III, plants in which zinc was added to the medium at the times indicated by arrows. Dash lines show growth without further addition of zinc. (*From Skoog.*)

There is a good deal of evidence that phosphate fertilizers increase the growth of roots as compared with tops, particularly in root crops.

Calcium is closely connected with the formation of the cell wall. When it is deficient in amount the cytoplasm tends to break down, the walls to fall apart, and meristems to degenerate. Calcium itself does not enter into the composition of the wall but produces its effects through changes in the cytoplasm (Sorokin and Sommer, 1929).

More conspicuous effects of calcium have sometimes been observed. Pearsall and Hanby (1925), for example, found that in *Potamogeton*

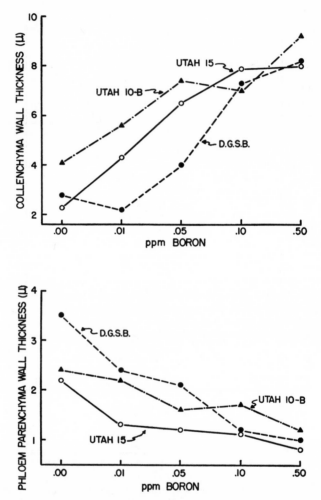

FIG. 17-3. Relation of boron to cell-wall thickness in three varieties of celery. (*From A. R. Spurr.*)

excess calcium made the leaves broader and their cells more numerous.

In field plots abundantly fertilized with potassium, plants of flax, ramie, oats, and willow showed marked increase in number and size of bast fibers (Tobler, 1929). Hemp was but slightly affected.

Robbins and his colleagues (1929) have observed a shape difference related to potassium. Sweet potato plants grown with little potassium have longer and more slender roots as compared with "chunkier" ones on plants grown where this element is abundant. The difference seems to be due to the greater cambial activity in the well-nourished plants as a result of increased protein synthesis resulting from an abundance of potassium.

Zinc has indirect morphogenetic importance since it seems to be necessary for the maintenance of auxin in an active state (Skoog, 1940; Fig. 17-2).

Boron evidently is concerned with the development of the cell wall and affects the process of carbohydrate condensation into wall material (Spurr, 1957; Fig. 17-3). Reduction in amount of boron produces hyper-

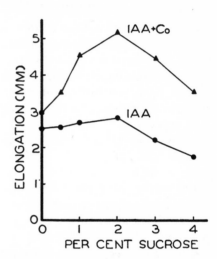

Fig. 17-4. Effect of cobalt on etiolated pea stem segments supplied with auxin alone (below) and auxin plus cobalt (above). (*From Miller.*)

trophy and hyperplasia of tissues, especially the cambium, in tomato, turnip, and cotton and affects the number and the maturation of the fibers (Palser and McIlrath, 1956). MacVicar and Struckmeyer (p. 320) observed that day-length altered the boron requirement of soybeans.

Cobalt has been found by several workers to increase the size of cells, particularly in association with sucrose. Miller (1954) reports that in etiolated pea stems cobalt salts plus auxin produced only slight elongation. Sucrose alone had the same effect, though it considerably increased fresh weight (Fig. 17-4). When sucrose and cobalt were applied together to the pea stem there was greatly increased elongation. He believes that water uptake and wall growth are separate processes and suggests that sucrose tends to increase cell volume but that cobalt promotes the ability of the cell to enlarge its surface.

Lyon and Garcia (1944) studied the effects of anions and cations on stem anatomy of tomato plants in over 40 nutrient solutions varying in the relative proportion of nitrogen, sulfur, and phosphorus, and of calcium, potassium, and magnesium. Differences in stem diameter and in relative amounts of phloem, xylem, and pith, as well as cellular differences in parenchyma of pith and cortex, vessels, fibers, phloem cells, and pericycle fibers, were correlated with specific differences in the nutrients.

Makarova (1943) examined the relation of various nutrient elements to traits described by Maximov as xeromorphic and found that, in general, such traits were intensified by phosphorus, boron, and manganese and diminished by potassium and iron. These effects chiefly concern cell size.

MORE COMPLEX SUBSTANCES

Sucrose itself may have certain morphogenetic effects. Yates and Curtis (1949) found that the root-shoot ratio in orchid seedlings growing in nutrient media is not related to the C/N ratio, as in so many cases, but to the concentration of sucrose alone, the optimum concentration for root growth being markedly higher than for shoot growth. At the best concentration for root growth, shoot growth was reduced.

In sporelings of *Marsilea* grown with varying concentrations of glucose, Allsopp (1954) observed that in low concentrations the plants showed many of the traits of the water forms of amphibious plants, and those at higher concentrations resembled land forms. This presumably is not owing, however, to the specific morphogenetic effect of glucose but to the fact that in the lower concentrations water is more available osmotically and conditions therefore to some extent simulate aquatic ones (p. 332).

By using glycogen, soluble starch, or dextrin as a carbon source instead of sugar, Nickerson and Mankowski (1953) were able to convert the normal budding yeast type, in *Candida albicans,* to a filamentous mycelial type.

Sossountzov (1954) tried various amino acids instead of inorganic nitrogen as nitrogen sources in the culture of fern prothallia and found that under these conditions they tended to be atypical but that in most cases the proportion of filamentous prothallia to cordate ones was considerably increased.

Hammett and Walp (1943) studied 10,000 fertilized *Fucus* eggs, half of which were exposed to proline and half were not, and observed that proline increased differentiation here (as measured by the production and growth of rhizoids) much as it has been shown to do in animals. Barghoorn (1942), however, found no definite evidence that proline stimulates the differentiation of protoxylem in roots of cotton and beans.

By adding certain chemical substances to the medium, Tatum, Barratt, and Cutter (1949) produced various nonheritable morphological changes in *Neurospora* and *Syncephalastrum* which they termed *paramorphs*. Anionic surface-active agents such as Aerosol induced the formation of compact colonial paramorphs. Sorbose proved to be the most effective paramorphogen. Discovery of the mechanisms by which these substances cause the production of such specific forms in these very simple organisms might yield important information on the origin of forms at higher levels.

There is a considerable group of chemical substances, the vitamins, which are of great importance in animal nutrition. Many of them are synthesized by plants, and some are now known to be essential for the growth of certain plants or plant structures. Vitamin B_1 (thiamin), for example, can be shown to be necessary for the growth of excised roots in culture, but it is synthesized in the shoots. Nicotinic acid also seems to be essential for root growth, but what other vitamins may also be necessary for the life of plants is not certainly known. All the vitamins are effective in extremely small concentrations.

The morphogenetic importance of the vitamins for plants seems not to be very great. Reid (1941) has evidence that vitamin C affects cell size in the meristematic region, and there are a few similar instances. Schopfer (1950) has reviewed the problem of the vitamins in morphogenesis.

CHAPTER 18

Growth Substances

The chemical substances discussed in the previous chapter are primarily important in the nutrition of the plant, and most of them are required in relatively large amounts since they contribute to the composition of protoplasm. In relatively few cases, however, have they been shown to be of any very great morphogenetic significance.

There is another group of physiologically active substances which are not concerned with nutrition and which, although present in most cases in very low concentrations, are of great importance for the growth, development, and differentiation of plants. They have been given various names—hormones, inductors, *Wuchsstoffe*, activators, evocators, growth regulators, and growth substances. They were first studied in animal physiology but in recent decades they have assumed major importance for an understanding of the development of plants as well. They are diverse in character and effect and are the chemical means by which many morphogenetic processes are controlled. Among these processes are growth, tropisms, many correlations, and the determination and differentiation of specific organs and structures in the plant body. Indeed, as our knowledge of these substances increases, more and more of the activities in development and differentiation are found to be affected by them, and, in interaction with the genes, they seem to be the chief agents in morphogenesis. It must not be forgotten, however, that they are agents merely and that the ultimate control of development lies in the factors that determine the concentration, distribution, and interaction of these and other chemical and physical mechanisms. Here lies the ultimate problem.

Many of these substances, in great diversity, are produced and controlled by the plant itself and are thus of particular interest in normal morphogenesis. It has been shown, however, that a large number of synthetic compounds have effects comparable to naturally occurring ones, and this has greatly extended the means for experimental attack on developmental problems (Zimmerman and Wilcoxon, 1935; Zimmerman, 1951*b;* and an extensive series of other papers).

The literature in this active field is large, and in a brief space little more than a very general introduction to it can be made. The student may be referred to a number of books, symposium volumes, and reviews, among which are the following: Boysen-Jensen (1936); Went and Thimann (1937); Avery and Johnson (1947); Thimann (1948); Skoog (1951); Söding (1952); Audus (1953); Leopold (1955); Wain and Wightman (1956); and the Eleventh Symposium of the Society for Experimental Biology (1957).

The term *hormone* was first used by Starling in 1904 with reference to secretin, a substance important in animal physiology. Such hormones are regarded as "chemical messengers" since they are produced in one part of the body and carried to some other part, where they affect development and various physiological processes. Their discovery marked a great advance in an understanding of the chemical control of growth and differentiation.

With the demonstration that there are substances in plants which are physiologically active in similarly small amounts, the term hormone was carried over into plant physiology by Fitting (1909) in relation to a substance in orchid pollen which produced swelling of the ovary. Various *phytohormones* are now recognized. This word is not a particularly happy one, however, for plants lack the efficient circulatory system of animals. Indeed, many of these substances exert their effects in the region where they are produced and thus are not "messengers" at all. The most important natural plant hormones, the auxins, also differ from typical animal ones in being relatively nonspecific and involved in a great variety of growth processes rather than in particular ones. Huxley (1935) discussed the relationship of these various substances, in animals and plants, and suggested a classification and terminology for them. Evidently there are many compounds and processes involved, and for plants, at least, it seems preferable to use for all such morphogenetically active materials the relatively noncommittal term *growth substances.* This will be employed in the present discussion to refer to those substances of whatever sort or activity that, in low concentration, are involved in the control of growth, development, and differentiation. It should be recognized that some of these substances are effective in retarding these processes rather than in their stimulation.

The history of the work on growth substances has been reviewed by a number of authors (Leopold, 1955, Chap. 1; Went, 1951*a;* and Audus, 1953). Most of it dates from about the beginning of the second quarter of the present century and was largely confined, at the start, to workers in continental Europe. Among early students of the subject were Boysen-

Jensen, Cholodny, Dolk, Fitting, Kögl, Laibach, Paal, and Went. The modern understanding of auxin was established by an important paper by the last-named botanist in 1928.

Growth substances have been shown to be present in many species and throughout the plant kingdom, in algae, mosses, ferns, and a great variety of seed plants. They have relatively less effect on the growth of fungi.

TYPES OF GROWTH SUBSTANCES

There are many growth substances but the best known and those apparently of the greatest general importance are the ones that occur naturally in plants and are usually termed the *auxins*. These were identified first in the oat coleoptile but are now known to be present in almost all plants and to be concerned in a great variety of developmental processes. There has been a good deal of discussion as to how many auxins there are, but one of them, identified by Kögl and his colleagues (1933) as 3-indoleacetic acid, seems to be of primary importance, and all known auxins are related to it chemically. In the present discussion the term "auxin" will be generally limited to this and chemically similar compounds.

Our knowledge of indoleacetic acid (IAA) is now very substantial but there are a considerable number of other naturally occurring growth substances, or substances which have been thought by many to exist in plants, which are unrelated to this chemically but are important in various ways. About these we know much less. Here belong the wound hormones (traumatins); the various flower-forming substances (florigens); the so-called root-forming, stem-forming, and leaf-forming substances or calines; the gibberellins; the hormones concerned with the determination of sex; various substances that amplify or antagonize the effects of auxin; and others. About the chemical nature of most of these little is known, and the very existence of some of them is in doubt. The conception of "organ-forming substances," in the narrow sense, is far from being established and has been involved in the general discussion of determination. It is clear, however, that there are a great many compounds, some of them very specific in their influence, which in minute amounts have important effects on one or another of almost all phases of plant development. An understanding of their nature and mode of action is proving of much importance for the solution of morphogenetic problems.

It should again be emphasized that most growth substances in plants are much less specific in their effects than are the hormones of animals. Thus IAA is concerned in cell expansion, cell division, cambial activity, abscission, parthenocarpy, tumor formation, root production, dominance relationships among buds, nastic responses, and tropisms generally. The effect in each case must evidently be a function of the specificity of the responding system, including other biologically active compounds, rather than of a particular evocating substance.

The developmental effects of growth substances are chiefly of three sorts: on growth in general (defined as permanent increase in volume), on the correlations of growth, and on development and differentiation of specific structures. These may involve very different problems.

GROWTH SUBSTANCES AND PLANT GROWTH

Growth of the plant as a whole may be controlled by various growth substances. Van Overbeek (1935) showed that in genetically dwarf races

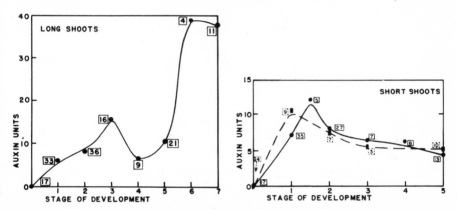

FIG. 18-1. Yield of diffusible auxin from long shoots (left) and short shoots (right) at successive stages in development in *Ginkgo*. (*From Gunckel and Thimann.*)

of maize there was much less auxin than in plants of normal height, indicating that auxin was associated with growth in stem length. The dwarfing gene here effects a more rapid destruction of auxin rather than a lesser production of it. Von Abrams (1953) sprayed IAA on etiolated plants of dwarf and tall varieties of peas. The dwarf increased 30 per cent in height but the tall one was slightly reduced, an instance of the frequently observed fact that the effect of auxin is different with different material. In a number of other cases the dwarfing of plants has been shown to be related to a deficiency of auxin.

Auxin particularly affects growth in length, especially of the stem, and in many cases has been found to be the factor that determines length growth of the internodes. Gunckel and Thimann (1949) compared the amount of auxin in developing short shoots and long shoots of *Ginkgo* and found that elongation of the latter was associated with a sharp rise in auxin content (Fig. 18-1).

Auxin is also involved in the growth of fruits (Fig. 18-2), though not all the steps in the process are yet well understood (Murneek, 1954; Lund, 1956). There are reviews by Nitsch (1952) and Luckwill (1957). An increase in auxin content often occurs at pollination, again at fertiliza-

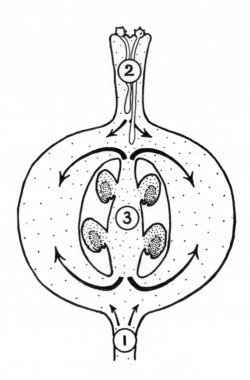

Fig. 18-2. Centers of origin of auxin in the development of a fruit. 1, from mother plant; 2, from pollen; 3, from developing ovules. (*From Nitsch.*)

tion, and usually during endosperm growth and the development of the seeds. This increase of auxin in the ovary is often followed by its increase in the pedicel and adjacent regions.

That fruit development is stimulated by growth substances is made clear by the occurrence of *parthenocarpy*, or growth of fruits without fertilization and seed development (Fig. 18-3). Gustafson (1936) induced parthenocarpy in cucurbits by applying synthetic growth substances to the pistil, and this has now been done frequently with other plants. He also showed that fruits which are naturally parthenocarpic have a much higher concentration of auxin than do seed-bearing ones. In some cases parthenocarpy does not require application of a growth substance to the unfertilized ovary but simply the presence in the air of the greenhouse of vapor of a specific substance. Induction of parthenocarpy is by no means universally possible and has been found more frequently in members of the Solanaceae and Cucurbitaceae than in other families. The subject has been reviewed by Vazart (1955).

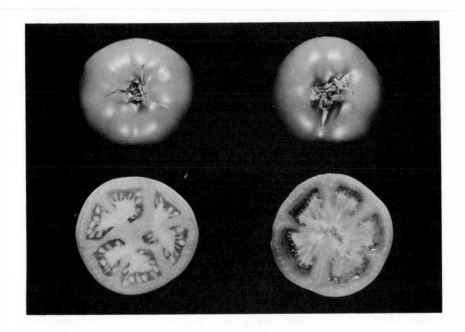

FIG. 18-3. Parthenocarpy. Left, normally pollinated tomato fruit with many seeds. Right, parthenocarpic fruit produced by treatment with synthetic growth substance. (*Courtesy Boyce Thompson Institute.*)

Davidson (1950) found that several marine algae were stimulated in their growth by synthetic substances in the sea water (Fig. 18-4). Although auxin seems rarely to be concerned with the growth of fungi, Fraser (1953) reports that indoleacetic acid stimulates growth in the common mushroom.

Cell Enlargement. The primary effect of auxin on plant growth seems to be its promotion of increase in cell size, especially in the stem and in its longitudinal dimension. In phototropism the side of the axis away from the light grows faster than the lighted one, and Went (1928) and others showed that auxin is more abundant on this shaded side. Avery and Burkholder (p. 30) found that the more rapid elongation here was the result of increase in cell length rather than in cell number.

Most tropisms have now been shown to be due to greater growth on the convex side because of longer cells there (Fig. 18-5). In both phototropism and geotropism, however, the role of auxin is different in root and shoot. If a young plant, for example, is placed in a horizontal position, auxin can be shown to accumulate on the lower side, though how this occurs is not well understood. In the stem, this results in a bending *upward* of the axis. The young primary root, however, will bend *down-*

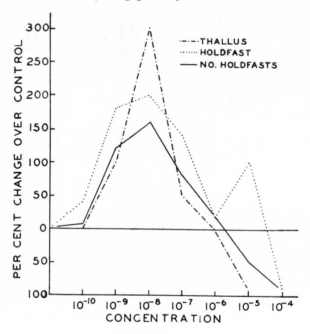

Fig. 18-4. Effect of different concentrations of indoleacetic acid on the growth of *Fucus*, as measured by length of thallus and length and number of holdfasts, in comparison with untreated controls. (*From Davidson.*)

ward, the cells elongating faster on its upper side. Evidently the same concentration which stimulates cell elongation in the stem checks it in the root, another example of the difference in the effect of auxin under different conditions. Geiger-Huber and Huber (1945) found that by continually decapitating a root its auxin content was markedly reduced and that it now bent upward instead of downward.

How much of the difference in cell size among the various tissues of the plant is due to auxin it is hard to say but, directly or indirectly, this substance is probably involved in most of the differences in degree of cell enlargement that occur between the meristematic condition and maturity. Gibberellin acts in a similar manner.

Cell Division. Growth substances are also associated often with cell division and with meristematic activity generally. Buds, especially as they begin to expand, are rich in auxin. Cambial activity is closely related to the presence of auxin (Snow, 1935; Fig. 18-6; Söding, 1936), and the progressive awakening of the cambium in the spring from the stem tips downward is accompanied by a progressive increase in auxin concentration (Avery, Burkholder, and Creighton, 1937*b;* Fig. 18-7; Gouwentak and Maas, 1940).

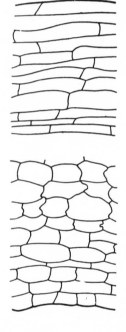

FIG. 18-5. Cell size in geotropic curvature. Lengthwise section through the convex side (upper) and the concave one (lower) of a root of *Zea* bending down geotropically. Bending is produced by the greater elongation of the cells on the upper side resulting from a relatively weak concentration of auxin there. (*After MacDougal.*)

Various synthetic growth substances have been found to stimulate cell division even in tissues which are mature or nearly so. Such a substance, applied to a young stem, will often produce there a callus-like mass of cells, so that it is easy to see why growth substances are associated with the formation of galls and tumors. This ability to produce cell division in older tissues has often been used for the determination of chromosome numbers in their cells, since it is now possible to observe mitotic figures there.

The various wound hormones produce their effect by increasing the division of cells below wound surfaces.

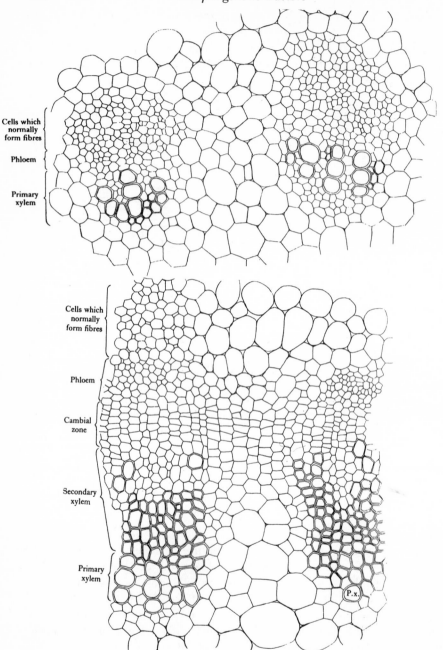

Fɪɢ. 18-6. Stimulation of cambial activity by auxin. Above, two bundles from control plant, decapitated but no auxin applied. Below, a similar region from a plant in which auxin had been applied to the decapitated tip. Cambial growth is markedly stimulated by the auxin. (*From Snow.*)

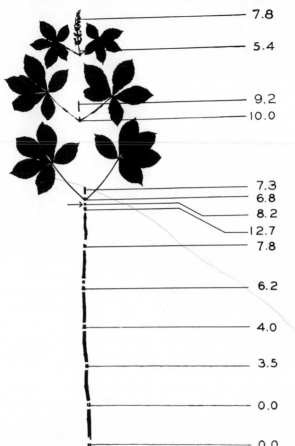

Fig. 18-7. Concentration gradient of growth hormone (in terms of *Avena* curvature) at various levels in a twig of *Aesculus* on May 16, when the growth of the current year (above arrow) was just completed. (*From Avery, Burkholder, and Creighton.*)

GROWTH SUBSTANCES AND CORRELATION

Of much significance for morphogenesis is the role of growth substances in the correlation of growth (Thimann, 1954b). Here is involved the whole problem of organized development. These substances seem to be the agents by which many such correlations are achieved, but one should hesitate to call them "growth regulators" since the actual regulation must go further back, to the mechanism that controls their distribution and local concentration and binds the parts and processes into an organism.

Differential Movement. An important fact about auxin is that in living cells it does not move in all directions but has a definitely polar flow, going from the more apical regions of the plant downward (p. 141). This was first observed in the oat coleoptile, where auxin is formed at the tip and then passes basipetally, regardless of how the axis is oriented. If a portion of the coleoptile is cut off and inverted and auxin is then applied to the end now uppermost, it will not move downward, though auxin placed at the other end will move up, in the original polar direction. Such polar transport is also shown in the stem axis, in which auxin moves down through the phloem. Inverted stems, after some time and apparently after the development of some new vascular tissues, may gain the ability to transport auxin in the opposite direction from the original one (Went, 1941).

Auxin transport may not invariably be polar, for Jacobs (1954) has reported that, if relatively weak concentrations are used instead of the strong ones commonly employed in experiments, there is a good deal of upward translocation. In a young internode of *Coleus* he found that about one-third as much auxin moved upward as downward. He also observed that in young bean hypocotyls, although auxin transport was always basipetal, the ability to transport it at all was lacking in very young seedlings but increased as they grew older. It was greatest in the upper portion of the hypocotyl and decreased toward the base. Oserkowsky (1942) concluded that where auxin moves only basipetally it is carried in living cells but that transport in both directions may result from diffusion through dead cells or cell walls. Leopold and Guernsey (1953*a*) showed that in *Coleus* the flow was clearly basipetal in the shoot and in the opposite direction in the root (Fig. 18-8) and that flowering stems transport auxin in both directions. Haupt (1956), however, reports that polar transport of auxin is as clear in the floral structures he studied as it is in vegetative shoots. Niedergang-Kamien and Skoog (1956) were able to reduce or inhibit polar flow by triiodobenzoic acid (Fig. 18-9) and suggest that the reported effect of this substance on growth correlations is due to this fact.

Nevertheless, polar transport of auxin seems to be a general phenomenon and is obviously of much morphogenetic importance since it underlies the marked structural differentiation between the two ends of the plant axis. It is probably involved in the polar character of regeneration (p. 119) and in many other developmental events.

Auxin flow may show a transverse as well as a longitudinal polarity, notably in geotropic movements. The accumulation of auxin in the lower half of a horizontally placed axis, although doubtless a response to the stimulus of gravity, is not simply a downward diffusion but is made possible by differential and unidirectional changes in the permeability of the cells. Such transverse polarities have been emphasized by de

Haan (1936), who reexamined the fact earlier noted by Noll that when primary roots are bent, lateral roots grow chiefly from their *convex* sides (Fig. 18-10). He observed that in such cases the root primordia, pushing out through the cortex, bend toward what is at that point the convex side of the root (Fig. 18-11), and he interprets this as the result of a transverse polar gradient in a root-forming hormone. Such transverse reactions of plants are extensively discussed by Borgström (1939), who shows their importance in many structural and physiological characters of plants.

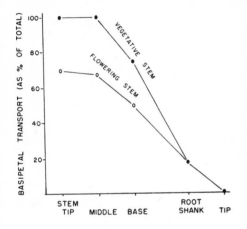

FIG. 18-8. Relative amount of basipetal transport of auxin in various regions of the vegetative and of the flowering axis of *Coleus* (*From Leopold and Guernsey.*)

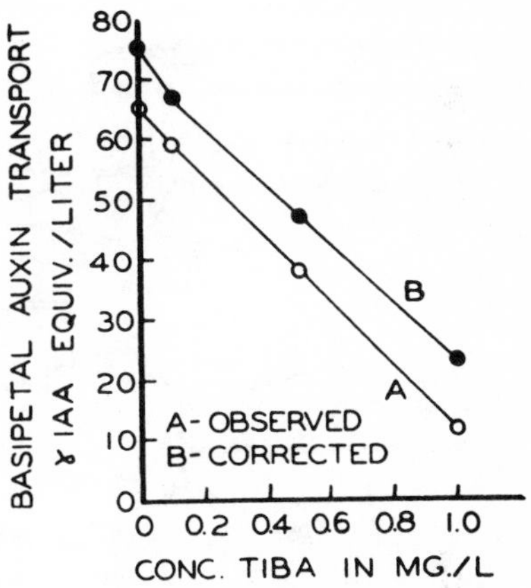

FIG. 18-9. Effect of 2,3,5-triiodobenzoic acid on polar transport of auxin. Graph showing reduction in amount of auxin transported basipetally in sunflower epicotyl cylinders which had been pretreated for 2½ hours with various concentrations of TIBA. (*From Niedergang-Kamien and Skoog.*)

No satisfactory explanation of polar auxin transport is available (p. 361). The suggestion of Went (1932) that electrophoretic diffusion might account for it has been shown by Clark (1938) to be doubtful, since the polar transport of auxin can be abolished by the application of sodium glycocholate without producing any change in the electrical polarity. Schrank, however, in a series of papers (1957 and others) presents evidence that electrical polarity is the essential basis for the polar transport of auxin. The question of auxin transport is part of the more general one as to why many substances move about the plant in certain directions more than in others. Auxin is doubtless important in the development of growth patterns, and an understanding of the mechanism of its differential movement would clear up many morphogenetic problems.

Dominance, Inhibition, and Stimulation. Whatever the mechanism for the differential distribution of growth substances may be, there is no question that it has much to do with the effect of one part on another and thus with growth correlation in general (Chap. 4).

Meristematic regions are commonly centers of auxin production, and from them this substance moves to others where it may either stimulate or inhibit growth. The most familiar example of this is the so-called *dominance* of apical buds. It is well known that in most cases, if such a

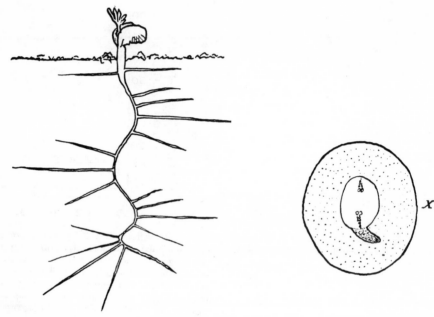

Fig. 18-10. Curved primary root of a lupine seedling, showing lateral roots growing from convex sides only. (*After Noll.*)

Fig. 18-11. Cross section of a curved root like that in Fig. 18-10, showing that the lateral root, in its course through the cortex, bends toward the convex side, X. (*After Noll.*)

bud is present, the buds below it will not grow but that they will do so if the apical bud is removed. Thimann and Skoog (1934) showed that if this apical bud is cut off and paste containing indoleacetic acid placed on the stump the lower buds will not develop, though in the controls, with paste alone, they do so. Such a result has been confirmed many times and has led to the widely held view that auxin inhibits growth of the lower buds and thus produces the dominance of the apical one.

Snow, in a series of papers (1937, 1940, and others), calls attention to some facts that are not easily explained on this hypothesis. He finds that buds farthest from the apex are most inhibited, which does not seem logical if auxin from the terminal bud is the inhibitor. Furthermore, inhibition may sometimes pass upward, although auxin typically passes downward. Snow believes that auxin is either changed into an inhibiting substance (for which Libbert, 1955, has evidence) or stimulates the production of one and that the greater the distance from the apex, the greater the amount of the inhibitor. Such a substance is not polar in movement and can thus pass into lateral buds as auxin presumably cannot.

Champagnat (1955 and others) has studied especially the effects upon bud growth of the cotyledons or leaves that subtend them and comes to the conclusion that both inhibitory and stimulatory substances are involved.

Thimann (1954b) is inclined to think that auxin itself is the major inhibiting influence and that the various apparent objections to this hypothesis may be met by assuming that auxin may sometimes move in an apolar direction and that its effects may be different under different circumstances. He does not rule out the possibility of the existence of other and specifically inhibiting substances.

Meanwhile other workers have emphasized the importance of nutrition in apical dominance. Van Overbeek (1938) observed that after removal of the terminal bud the auxin content of the stem decreases. He believes that in some way auxin blocks the passage of nutrients to the lateral buds, which have only a poor vascular connection with the main cylinder. When the amount of auxin is reduced a better connection is established, nutrients enter the buds, and they begin to develop.

The nutrient theory of apical dominance is strongly supported by Gregory and Veale (1957). They suggest that the degree of dominance is proportional to the supply of available carbohydrate and nitrogen and that competition among the various buds explains the difference in relative bud growth. Auxin is concerned in this competition since a high auxin content prevents the formation of the vascular connections between bud and vascular cylinder.

The underlying mechanism in such an apparently simple phenomenon as bud dominance is still by no means clear. The general fact of dominance is established, however, and helps toward an understanding of some of the differences among plants in their bodily patterns, for whatever determines bud growth determines the shape of the plant. There are usually a great number of potential growing points on an axis but most of them do not develop into shoots, apparently because of inhibitory action mediated in one way or another by growth substances. Plants differ in the degree of this inhibition. For example, in *Aster novaeangliae* there is one main stem with only a few floral branches at the top. *Aster multiflorus,* on the other hand, is much branched and bushy. Delisle (1937) found that in the former species the concentration of auxin at the tip was high (Fig. 18-12). In the latter it was much lower, suggesting that the copious branching resulted from weak inhibition. After removal of the apex in the young plant, *A. novaeangliae* became much branched, and application of auxin to the tip of *A. multiflorus* resulted in the growth of a main stem with relatively small branches. Thus an important taxonomic character is related to the amount of auxin present in the plant.

Many of the effects of growth substance in correlation are stimulatory rather than inhibitory. There is a close relation, for example, between the presence of growing seeds and the development of a fruit, the seeds producing the auxin necessary for fruit growth. In some cases, as has been

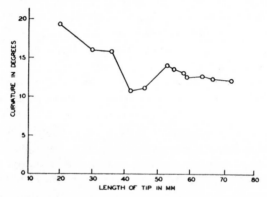

Fig. 18-12. Effect of auxin on inhibition of branching in *Aster.* Auxin concentrations at successive distances from apex in *A. novaeangliae,* an unbranched species. The amount of auxin in *A. multiflorus,* which is more branched, is considerably less. (*From Delisle.*)

mentioned, synthetic growth substances may be substituted for the natural auxin and seedless fruits produced. Growth of the receptacle may also be related to seed production. When Nitsch (1950) removed the growing achenes from a strawberry, the fleshy portion stopped growing, but if synthetic growth substance replaced the achenes, the normal development of the strawberry was resumed (Figs. 18-13, 18-14). If only some of the achenes were removed, the weight of the mature ripe fruit was proportional to the number of achenes remaining. Nitsch found that the achenes contained a large amount of auxin but that this was absent from the receptacle.

Galston (1948) has described an example of competitive correlation in asparagus. Root primordia, stimulated by auxin, are formed during a period of minimum stem growth, but once they are laid down, stem growth again accelerates. Compensatory correlations (p. 98) of various sorts also have their basis in auxin action. Removal of the root tip almost always stimulates growth of lateral roots below it, somewhat as in

FIG. 18-13. Relation of presence of achenes to growth of strawberry. All achenes have been removed early in development except three vertical rows (left) or three horizontal ones (right). Growth of the receptacle is limited to the region in contact with the achenes. (*From Nitsch.*)

Mar., 1950]

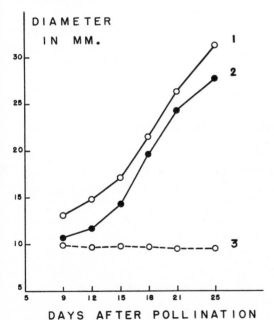

DAYS AFTER POLLINATION

FIG. 18-14. Auxin and growth of the strawberry. Curve 1, control. Curve 2, growth of fruit from which all achenes were removed and auxin in lanolin paste substituted. Curve 3, like 2 but without the auxin. (*From Nitsch.*)

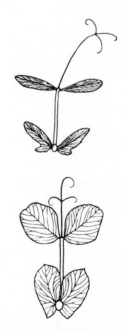

FIG. 18-15. Effect of 2,4-D on leaf shape. Below, leaf of untreated plant of *Pisum sativum*. Above, plant treated with 2,4-D paste. (*From Wenck.*)

apical-bud dominance. Active growth of lateral roots may also inhibit apical growth (Street and Roberts, 1952).

Correlations of position may be the result of auxin activity in many cases. Thus where an upright terminal shoot of a coniferous tree is removed, one of the lateral branches will swing up from its nearly horizontal position to a vertical one and replace the lost leader, evidently in response to the absence of auxin previously produced by the apical bud. In woody plants the orientation of branches with reference to the main axis and to gravity also seems to be due to auxin action since it is regulated by the production of reaction wood (p. 356), which seems to result from the presence of auxin. The precise amount of auxin (and thus of reaction wood formed) determines the angle that a given branch will assume and thus the branching pattern and form of the whole tree.

The form of individual organs, ultimately the result of dimensional correlations, may be affected by growth substances, particularly in leaves (von Denffer, 1951; Linser and others, 1955; Wenck, 1952; Fig. 18-15).

Such correlating activities are doubtless present in the lower plants as well. Moner (1954) describes the action of a substance, as yet unidentified, which is concerned with the development of the precisely formed colonies of the alga *Pediastrum.*

Much evidence is therefore available that the correlated and integrated character of the plant, whatever its final cause may be, is the immediate result of specific amounts of growth substances at specific places and times. What controls this precise production and distribution of these substances is a more difficult problem.

GROWTH SUBSTANCES AND THE DETERMINATION
OF STRUCTURE

The effect of growth substances on the specific form and structure of plants has attracted more attention than any other of their morphogenetic activities.

Tropisms and other auxin-mediated orientations of plant parts to certain factors in the environment, notably gravity and light, account for many features of external form, though the familiar patterns of plant growth are produced by interaction between these tropisms and certain specific inner factors. Sometimes a simple tropism may produce such a profound change in plant form as to be significant morphogenetically. In "lazy" maize (van Overbeek, 1936), for example, the stalk grows flat on the ground, not through mechanical weakness but because of the characteristic distribution of auxin in it. Tropisms are primarily the concern of physiology, however, and there is no room here to consider the extensive literature in which they are discussed.

The arrangement of structures in a radially symmetrical pattern doubt-less involves differential distribution of auxin, but little is known about this. When such radially symmetrical structures are placed in a horizontal position they often tend to become dorsiventral, as in certain flowers and stems. Since most such direct effects of gravity seem to be produced by differential distribution of auxin, as in the well-known cases of geotropism, auxin presumably is involved in structural dorsi-ventrality as well. Its role here in young liverwort plants has been described by Kohlenbach (1957).

Of wider morphogenetic interest are the effects of growth substances on the determination of specific structures. From his study of flower production Sachs (1882) suggested that organ-forming substances are operative in plants, especially in the determination of flowers and roots. The growth of knowledge of morphogenetically effective substances revived interest in this hypothesis, and it has stimulated a wide range of experiments which have thrown much light on the mechanisms of de-velopment. Organ-forming substances of many types have been postu-lated in the formation of roots, stems, leaves, flowers, galls, sexual struc-tures, and others. Just how such substances produce their effects is not known, and the actual existence of some of them is not yet proved, but the theoretical, and also the practical, importance of these problems is great. The most obvious way to account for development is to postulate the operation of a series of such substances. The difficulties of this con-ception, however, are obvious, for a very large number of them would be necessary. The tendency today is to assume the activity of a relatively small number and to explain the variety and specificity of their effects through their interactions and in other ways.

Root Formation. Van der Lek (1925) observed that a piece of stem (used as a cutting), on which there was a bud or young leaf, formed roots at its base, whereas a naked stem piece did so much less readily or not at all. This suggested that there was a substance, formed in buds and leaves, that moved downward and stimulated root production. Went (1929) demonstrated this by showing that an extract from the leaves of *Acalypha*, applied to the apex of a cutting, promoted root formation at its base. Several workers soon discovered that auxin and various natural and synthetic substances also have this effect and that cuttings could be made to root by the application of such substances.

In 1935 Laibach and Fischnich described a technique by which indole-acetic acid in lanolin paste applied to a stem would promote root for-mation. In the same year Zimmerman and Wilcoxon (1935) reported that several synthetic substances such as indolebutyric, indolepropionic, phenylacetic, and naphthaleneacetic acids had this effect and could be used in horticultural practice to hasten the rooting of cuttings when this was otherwise slow or difficult. The root-forming activity of 2,4-dichlorophyenoxyacetic acid, 2,4-D (Zimmerman and Hitchcock, 1942), was especially conspicuous. By their application in paste or other means under favorable conditions root initials may be produced almost anywhere on the plant. These substances are not equally active, and some of them which have less value in root formation show other morphogenetic effects. "Root-forming hormones" are now familiar aids in plant propagation (Fig. 18-16). These substances are chiefly effective in the production of root primordia and in most cases they actually check the later growth of the roots. Because of their great theoretical and practical interest, much work has been done on the root-forming effects of growth

Fig. 18-16. Effect of "root hormones" on cuttings of holly. At left, controls. At right, plants treated with mixture of indolebutyric and naphthaleneacetic acid. (*Courtesy Boyce Thompson Institute.*)

substances. There are a number of general reviews of this work, among them Pearse, 1939; Thimann and Behnke, 1947; and Avery and Johnson, 1947.

The movement of synthetic substances, like that of natural auxin, is polar except when their concentration is high. If applied at the apical end of a cutting, they tend to pass downward and to stimulate root formation at the base. If applied basally, they form roots there. The experiments of Czaja and others have previously been described (p. 124) in which regeneration in pieces of root is also polar in character, shoot buds forming on the upper end and root primordia on the lower. This is evidently owing to the accumulation of auxin at the lower (distal) end and its consequent relatively low concentration at the upper one, a low concentration being related to shoot growth and a higher one to root growth

(Fig. 18-17). When slices were repeatedly trimmed off from the lower surface, shoot primordia began to appear there, presumably because of the removal of auxin and the consequent reduction in its concentration.

When concentrations of growth substances are much higher than in natural conditions, they tend to have a local effect and to produce a downward bending of the leaves (hyponasty) and the formation of callus. Upon the latter, root primordia often appear. Growth substances applied to the soil may be absorbed, carried up in the transpiration stream, and affect the structure of the growing plant.

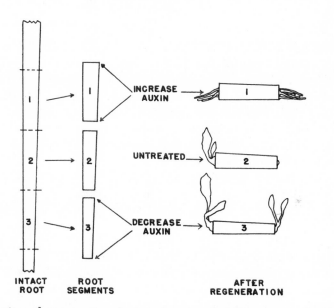

INTACT ROOT   ROOT SEGMENTS   AFTER REGENERATION

FIG. 18-17. Auxin and regeneration. In a root segment of *Taraxacum*, placed horizontally (2), regeneration is normally polar, shoots developing at the proximal end and roots at the distal one (see Fig. 6-4). When the amount of auxin is increased at the proximal end, roots are produced there (1). When it is decreased at the distal end, shoots develop there (3). (*From Warmke and Warmke.*)

It is recognized that growth substances are not the only factors concerned in root formation. A supply of sugar is necessary. Indeed, the stimulating effect of leaves on root formation may be due in part to their production of nutrients. In grafting experiments between rooting and nonrooting varieties of *Hibiscus,* van Overbeek and Gregory (1945) found that something formed in the leaves, in combination with auxin, is required for root growth, and van Overbeek, Gordon, and Gregory (1946) showed that this is not a hormone since it can be replaced by sucrose or nitrogenous substances. The importance of a high carbohydrate-nitrogen ratio in root determination has already been discussed

(p. 367). Torrey (1950) observed that pea root tips transferred directly to a culture medium provided with IAA produce lateral roots at once but that tips transferred after growing a week in culture do not do so for some time. A substance (not auxin) stimulating lateral root formation seems to originate in the lower part of the root and moves upward, producing laterals in acropetal succession.

It has been observed that the rooting response is often altered (generally increased) when two different substances, such as indoleacetic acid and naphthaleneacetic acid, are combined. Went (1939) applied different substances successively rather than in mixtures and found that cuttings of etiolated pea seedlings, which do not root after treatment with auxin alone, will do so if phenylacetic acid is first used, though this substance by itself is ineffective. He believes root formation results from the interaction of two factors and suggests that phenylacetic acid may act to mobilize or activate a specific root-forming factor, *rhizocaline* (Bouillenne and Went, 1933; Bouillenne, 1950; Libbert, 1956). The question of the existence of such a specific factor has been studied by a number of workers. Evidence for it is largely indirect, and rhizocaline has not been isolated; but auxin is evidently not the only factor operative in the initiating of root primordia.

It must not be concluded that growth substances can produce roots anywhere on the plant. They are often formed, to be sure, in unusual places, as along the surface of the stem. Even in such instances, however, the initiation of root primordia does not take place anywhere and indiscriminately but only in certain cells or at certain zones that are potentially capable of forming them. At such points roots may be formed under the stimulus of other factors such as ethylene, carbon monoxide, wounding, or abnormal nutrition. The nature and location of such regions are variable and depend on the general growth pattern of the plant treated. There is a difference, for example, between monocotyledons and dicotyledons as to rooting response. Treatment with growth substances is one of the methods by which knowledge may be gained as to the potentialities of various cells and tissues, not only for root formation but for other developmental activities.

Auxin and Rhizoids. Auxin is present in the coenocytic alga *Bryopsis* and is most abundant in that part of the plant where rhizoids are commonest. Jacobs (1951) finds that an application of indoleacetic acid stimulates rhizoid formation in the region where these are least abundant. He regards this as analogous to the effect of auxin on root initiation in higher plants.

Leaf Formation. Attempts have been made to find substances which might be involved specifically in the development and growth of the leaf blade. In some cases leaf growth is dependent on the presence of a factor coming from the cotyledons. Pilet (1952) observed that *Semper-vivum* leaves parasitized by *Endophyllum sempervivi* contain much more auxin than normal ones and, presumably for this reason, are accelerated in their development. The effectiveness of adenine in leaf formation has been observed by various workers (D. Bonner and Haagen-Smit, 1939). Auxin does not seem to promote the growth of the blade as a whole,

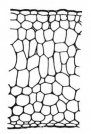

Fig. 18-18. Section through leaf blades of *Kalanchoe Blossfeldiana*. At left, from a plant grown under long days. At right, from one grown under short days. The difference in thickness is entirely due to cell size. (*From Harder and von Witsch.*)

however, although when embryonic leaves are treated with it, various changes may be produced (Laibach and Fischnich, 1936; Zimmerman, 1951*b*; Applegate and Hamner, 1957). These are probably to be looked upon as injuries rather than formative effects. Wenck (1952) has studied the stimulatory and inhibitory effects of auxin and of various auxin antagonists on leaf growth in a number of species.

Went (1938) here postulated a *phyllocaline,* analogous to rhizocaline. Later (1951*b*) he extended his concept of the calines more fully into the details of leaf form and structure. He calls attention to the importance of adenine for mesophyll growth and shows that vein tissue, on the other hand, can be increased by auxin without affecting mesophyll development. There are thus two morphogenetic tendencies in leaf development: one toward the formation of veins and induced by auxin and the other of mesophyll, induced by adenine. Whatever factor induces the former (as well as the stem and petiole) may be called a *caulocaline* and the latter a phyllocaline, whatever their chemical nature may turn out to be. Leaf shape is affected by the balance between the two. Leaves with a dominance of phyllocaline will tend to be palmate for they will have an excess of mesophyll, whereas those with more caulocaline will tend to be pinnate or parallel-veined, since they will have relatively more vein tissue. One may question, however, whether the problem of organic form can be solved quite as simply as this.

Harder (1948) observed that in certain succulents, such as *Kalanchoe Blossfeldiana,* variations in leaf shape and structure depend on the day-length. Plants grown under short days have short, apetiolate, and markedly succulent leaves (Fig. 18-18). A single leaf subjected to short days will transmit this "short-day shape" to the immature leaves above it which are developing under a long day-length. This effect Harder and von Witsch (1940*b*) attribute to a growth substance they call *metaplasin,* which is not identical with either auxin or florigen.

Stem Formation. It has proved difficult to demonstrate any substances specifically related to the growth of the stem. Went (1938) decapitated pea seedlings and measured the length of the secondary lateral branches. He gives evidence that stem growth here depended on the roots, not on the cotyledons, and suggests that it was due to caulocaline in conjunction with auxin. In later experiments neither auxin from the apex nor water supply from the root appeared to control stem growth, and Went again attributed this to caulocaline coming from the stem base and the root system.

Flower Formation. The existence of flower-forming substances has a firmer foundation. They were postulated by Sachs, who held them responsible for changing a plant from a vegetative to a reproductive state. The demonstration that such a change could be induced by altering the carbohydrate-nitrogen ratio (p. 366) and by photoperiodism (p. 315) cast doubt upon this idea. More recent work, however, has come to its support. Kuijper and Wiersum (1936), for example, found that if a soybean plant is brought to a flowering state by exposure to short day-lengths and another kept flowerless by long days a shoot of the former grafted into the latter causes the flowerless plant to form flowers abundantly. Hamner and Bonner (1938) reported that this effect could be produced in *Xanthium* through a barrier of lens paper without actual union of tissues. Withrow and Withrow (1943), however, failed to confirm this and showed that where transmission of the flowering stimulus had occurred there had been a slight fusion between cells which had grown through the lens paper. Nevertheless, in grafting experiments like these, a substance evidently passes from scion to stock across the graft union and induces flowering. To such a substance the name *florigen* has been applied.

Other experiments in photoperiodism also suggest the operation of such a flower-forming substance. Cajlachjan (1938), by localizing the reception of the photoperiodic stimulus, showed that this was received by the leaves but was effective in flower induction at growing points considerably distant and had therefore apparently passed, as a specific substance, down the petiole, along the stem, and into a lateral branch. Borthwick, Parker, and Heinze (1941) with soybeans found similar results. Harder (1948) observed that in *Kalanchoe* this substance passes directly down the stem from the site of induction but does not cross it, so that one side of the plant flowers but the opposite one does not.

Unlike auxin, the movement of which is usually polar, the flower-inducing agent seems able to travel in any direction in the plant. Since local applications of cold, heat, or narcotics reduce or inhibit the transport of such substances from centers of production to those of action, it seems probable that living tissue is involved, a conclusion supported by girdling experiments of Galston (1949) and others, who showed that the floral stimulus cannot pass across a water gap.

From the leaf of a unifoliate species of *Streptocarpus* that was ready to flower, Oehlkers (1955) made a series of cuttings. Those from the base of the leaf produced flowers at once, those from a little farther up produced them soon, and cuttings from near the tip formed only vegetative shoots. Oehlkers believes this was because of the differential distribution of a flower-forming substance.

Genic differences may also be involved. One variety of *Hyoscyamus niger* (henbane) is biennial and does not flower until its second year. Another variety is annual. If from the annual form a flowering scion, or leaf from one, is grafted into a plant of the biennial race during its first year, the latter will flower in this season (p. 264). It was also shown that the substance here concerned was not limited in action to this species for a flowering scion of tobacco or petunia (genera in the same family) has the same effect on biennial *Hyoscyamus*.

This nonspecificity of the flowering stimulus is also evident in certain host-parasite relationships. *Orobanche minor* (one of the broomrapes), when parasitizing clover, flowers only when the host plant flowers (Holdsworth and Nutman, 1947). *Cuscuta Gronovii* (dodder) flowers only in a long day if it is parasitic on the long-day plant *Calendula*, but in a short day if it is parasitic on the short-day plant *Cosmos* (von Denffer, 1948).

These various lines of evidence, about which a great body of facts has now been gathered, suggest that there are one or more specifically flower-forming substances. None of these florigens has yet been isolated nor is there any knowledge as to their chemical nature. Some substance that under certain conditions stimulates flowering is certainly able to pass across a graft union and thus seems hormonal in character. This substance is evidently closely involved with photoperiodism, though what it does depends to a great extent on the amount of auxin or other growth substances present. Thus J. Bonner and Thurlow (1949) completely prevented flowering in the short-day plant *Xanthium canadense*, grown under short days, by spraying it with auxin, and leaves thus treated did not transmit the flowering stimulus by grafting. Substances that antagonize auxin action, such as triiodobenzoic acid, increased flowering in soybeans (Galston, 1947). De Zeeuw and Leopold (1956) report that low auxin concentrations applied to two short-day species promoted floral initiation if applied before the induction period but are less effective afterward. In a *Xanthium* plant defoliated to a single leaf, Salisbury (1955) found that auxin inhibited flowering if applied before the flowering stimulus (produced by photoperiodic induction) had been completely translocated from the leaf but promoted it if applied afterward. Leopold and Guernsey (1953*b*), using the position of the first flower in peas as a measure of flower initiation, observed that a number of substances, notably sucrose, malic acid, and arginine, tended to inhibit flowering but that this inhibition was removed by auxin. Although flowering is usually an "all or none" reaction, structures intermediate between flowers and vegetative shoots sometimes occur. Such phyllody has been produced through manipulation of the flowering stimulus by Harder and his colleagues (1947). Gibberellin is often effective in flower induction (Lang, 1957).

The pineapple (Clark and Kerns, 1942) produces flowers abundantly if naphthaleneacetic acid or certain other growth substances are applied by spray to the center of the plant. Van Overbeek (1946*a*) has shown that plants thus treated will flower under long days, which ordinarily inhibit flowering in pineapple. In the sweet potato, also, Howell and Wittwer (1955) reported that flowering can be induced experimentally by a growth substance.

The problem of the relation of growth substances to flowering is evidently a complex one. It is the basis of a considerable literature, much of which can be found in Melchers and Lang (1948), Lang (1952), Bonner and Liverman (1953), and Liverman (1955).

Something analogous to the control of flowering by specific substances is even to be found in the algae, for von Denffer and Hustede (1955) were able to shift the sexual phase of *Vaucheria sessilis* to the vegetative one by treatment with indoleacetic acid (Fig. 18-19).

Sex Determination. Both in the determination of the sex of individual plants and in the development of the sex organs, growth substances of various sorts seem to be effective.

In the dioecious species *Cannabis sativa* (hemp) it is possible to distinguish genetically male from genetically female plants before they flower. Heslop-Harrison (1956) grew plants under controlled photoperiodic conditions and during the period of differentiation of flower buds applied naphthaleneacetic acid to leaves at the third and fourth nodes. In genetically male plants, female flowers were produced, sug-

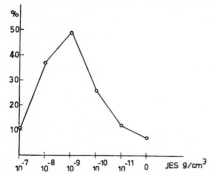

Fig. 18-19. Effect of different concentrations of IAA on the proliferation of antheridial primordia in *Vaucheria*. (*From von Denffer and Hustede.*)

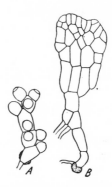

Fig. 18-20. Young prothallia of *Pteridium aquilinum* 11 days after spore germination. *A*, grown on agar to which a water extract of prothallia was added. *B*, grown on ordinary agar. The extract stimulates early development of antheridia. (*From Döpp.*)

gesting that sexuality is determined by the concentration of native auxin during the period of primordium differentiation and that femaleness is associated with a relatively high auxin level. In *Mercurialis ambigua* he found (1957) that carbon monoxide much reduced the number of male flowers in genetically monoecious types, presumably by its effect on auxin. Laibach and Kribben (1951) painted the lower surfaces of the leaves of cucumber, a monoecious plant, with naphthaleneacetic acid in lanolin and caused an increase in the proportion of female flowers, sometimes altogether suppressing the differentiation of males. Indoleacetic acid they found to be less effective and 2,4-D more so. Extending his work to other plants, Laibach concludes (1953) that, in general, female flowers or female parts of flowers tend to differentiate under higher concentrations of growth substances than do male flowers or parts.

It has been suggested that hormones comparable to those of the animal body may influence sex in higher plants. Löve and Löve (1946) found that in *Melandrium dioicum* sex expression is influenced by various animal sex hormones applied in lanolin to the axils of leaves in which flower buds are to develop. Crystalline estrone, estradiol, and estradiol benzoate shifted the sex of the flowers toward femaleness, whereas testosterone and its propionate promoted maleness. In general, hormones promoting maleness or femaleness in animals have the same tendency in *Melandrium*. Some doubt has been cast on these conclusions by Kuhn (1941), who studied dioecious species of *Cannabis* and *Mercurialis*. There is no evidence that substances identical with animal sex hormones are formed by plants. If sex in dioecious plants is determined by specific substances, these have not been isolated nor can they be passed from one plant to another of opposite sex by grafting (Yampolsky, 1957).

Maleness in ferns seems to be related to specific substances. Döpp (1950) made a water extract of the prothallia of the bracken fern which stimulated the production of antheridia in sporelings 4 to 8 weeks earlier than in untreated prothallia (Fig. 18-20). This can be carried in agar media. Näf (1956) confirmed this and was further able to induce antheridium formation on a variety of other related ferns even though these did not normally produce them in culture. The extract from prothallia of types of ferns that form antheridia under the conditions of culture used was several thousand times more effective than were extracts from types that do not form antheridia under these conditions. Such experiments suggest that in the prothallia of all polypodiaceous ferns there is a substance that stimulates the formation of male sex organs.

Sex hormones have also been found in all the thallophytes except the red algae and the basidiomycetes. Burgeff (1924) reported that in nonaquatic types such as *Mucor mucedo*, the hyphae of two different sexes ("plus" and "minus" races) influence each other by means of diffusible substances. Köhler (1935) confirmed these results, and Plempel (1957) has reported the activity of four substances in sexual interactions in this species. Köhler found that in *Phycomyces Blakesleeanus* two diffusible substances are produced by each sex. Krafczyk (1931) showed that in *Pilobolus crystallinus* at least three different processes are chemically controlled: the characteristic swelling and branching of the hyphae, the growth of hyphae toward each other, and the delimitation of the gametangia. Machlis (1958) has found in the water mold *Allomyces* a hormone, *sirenin,* excreted during female gametogenesis that attracts the male gametes to the female ones.

Similar processes have been more fully studied in the water mold *Achlya* by J. Raper (1939–1957), especially in *A. bisexualis* and *A. ambisexualis* (Fig. 18-21). Experiments involving the transfer of mycelia into water where plants of the opposite sex had been growing, and the use of cellophane membranes, gave evidence that in the very regular sequence of the sexual process four diffusible substances are concerned.

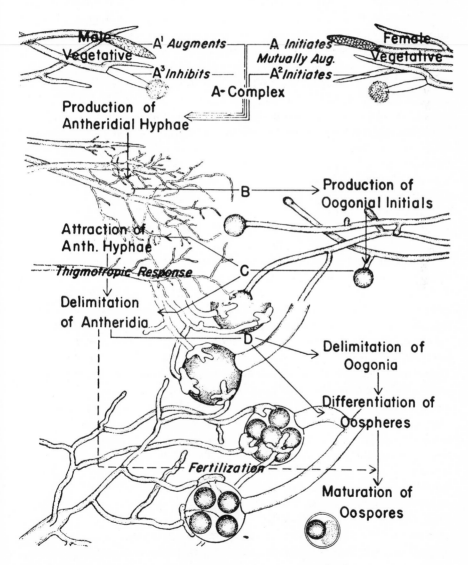

Fig. 18-21. Sex hormones in *Achlya*. Specific activities of substances A, B, C, and D in the development and function of the sex organs. (*From J. Raper.*)

In the male mycelium antheridial branches are first induced by hormone A, produced by the female mycelium. The antheridial branches then form hormone B, which induces the production of oögonial initials in the female plant. These structures now form hormone C, which causes the antheridial branches to grow chemotropically toward the oögonial initials. Lastly, it appears that hormone D, presumably formed in the antheridia, causes the oögonial initials to delimit the oögonia from their stalks. The chemical nature of these substances is still unknown.

The most complex examples of the effects of specific substances in sexual reproduction and sex determination in the lower plants are those described by Moewus (1940 and many other papers) in the unicellular green alga *Chlamydomonas eugametos,* in which the biochemical and the genetic basis of the various hormonal mechanisms were subjected to detailed analysis. A thorough reexamination of this work indicates that many of the facts and conclusions of Moewus are not well founded and that the contributions of the *Chlamydomonas* work to our understanding of sexuality in the lower plants are much less considerable than they were once thought to be.

Work on the sexual processes and substances in thallophytes has been reviewed by J. Raper (1952, 1957). Hawker (1957) has reviewed the whole field of reproduction in the fungi.

Wound Hormones. The substances first proved to have a determining effect on morphogenetic processes were the wound hormones, or necrohormones. It has long been observed that in the vicinity of dying and necrotic cells there occur divisions in other cells which under ordinary conditions would not have shown such division. These have a definite relation, both in distribution and orientation, to the accumulation of decomposition products released by the injured cells. Wound meristems are thus developed which produce layers of cork that cut off the injured region and protect the healthy tissue underneath.

Haberlandt (1921, 1922) was the first to attack this problem directly. He found that if the cut surface of a potato tuber is washed and the contents of the injured cells thus removed only a few cell divisions occur. It might be thought that in such cases the reduced access of oxygen to the flooded tissues would account for the reduction in metabolic activity and thus of cell division. The action of a definite substance, however, is strongly indicated by later experiments of Haberlandt and others in which the juice, debris, or extracts of tissues produced an effect on cell division much exceeding that from mere wounding (Fig. 18-22). When sap from crushed tissue was injected into small intercellular spaces, active cell division, presumably from wound hormones, was found to occur (Reiche, 1924). These substances are not species-specific, for those from one species will produce this effect in quite unrelated ones.

Much work has been done in isolating wound hormones and determining their chemical nature. Standard material for estimating relative effects of hormone activity was first sought. Wehnelt (1927) used the layer of parenchyma cells which lines the immature pod of the common snap bean. Such tissue responds sensitively to various types of stimulation by abundant cell division and the formation of intumescences, the size of which provides a rough measure of the intensity of the stimulus. This "bean test" has been used by many students of wound hormones (Jost, 1935; Umrath and Soltys, 1936). On such pod surfaces Bonner and English (1938) placed droplets of extract from crushed tissue

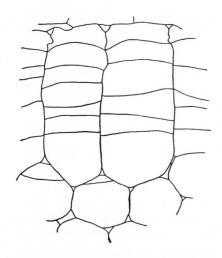

FIG. 18-22. Effect of wound hormones. Section of internode of *Kalanchoe* below a wound, showing how cortex cells have been induced to divide frequently, and parallel to the wound surface. (*From Sinnott and Bloch.*)

(chiefly bean pods) and found that the height of the intumescence which developed after 48 hours was proportional to the concentration of the wound hormone present in the extract. These proliferations are usually higher than the ones induced by other chemical or physical means.

Considerable progress has been made toward a knowledge of the chemical nature of these wound hormones. Bonner and English isolated from bean-pod juice a substance which in low concentration was very active in the bean test and named it *traumatin*. English, Bonner, and Haagen-Smit later (1939) purified from the same source a crystalline dibasic acid similar in its effects. Traumatin appears to be active on only a few types of cells, such as those of the potato tuber and the bean pod.

To understand wound reactions in any plant, organ, or tissue, account must be taken of many internal and external factors as yet imperfectly known (Bloch, 1941). Workers have often been puzzled by differences between cells in their response to wounding or wound hormones. Such cells evidently differ in character and reactivity. Thus the root pericycle and the vascular cambium respond to injuries by the production of wound tissue much more readily than do adjacent cells of the ground parenchyma. Auxin may be one factor which produces such specific reactivity. In *Populus balsamifera,* Brown (1937) found that the cambium was stimulated to active growth both by wound hormones released from dead cells and by a substance, presumably auxin, coming from buds and leaves distal to the wound. Application of auxin above the wound considerably increases a local wound reaction (Brown and Cormack, 1937). Other observations confirm this (Bloch, 1941).

GROWTH SUBSTANCES AND INTERNAL DIFFERENTIATION

Numerous instances have been reported where specific changes in internal structure are related to the action of auxin or one of the synthetic growth substances.

In the regeneration of buds on the decapitated hypocotyl of flax (p. 245), Link and Eggers (1946b) found that this was largely prevented if indoleacetic acid in lanolin was applied to the cut surface. Even the transverse division of epidermal cells, the first visible step in bud primordium differentiation, was usually inhibited.

Nysterakis and Quintin (1955) report that application of 2,4-D to growing stems of *Araucaria excelsa* reduced the length of the tracheids by more than half and changed the pitting from circular to scalariform.

Jacobs (1956) finds that the regeneration of severed xylem strands and the distribution of auxin proceed together, and from this and other evidence he concludes that auxin is usually the limiting factor in the differentiation of xylem. The chief distinction of xylem cells is their thick secondary wall. The facts that auxin is effective only in plants—organisms with cellulose walls—and that the only plant group where auxin seems to have little effect on growth is the fungi, which have chitinous rather than cellulose walls, both suggest that auxin acts on the cell wall.

Native auxin and synthetic growth substances have been shown to be effective in preventing the abscission of leaves and fruits. If a leaf blade is removed but the petiole left, this will soon drop off by abscission. If one of several growth substances is placed on the cut petiole stump, however, abscission will not take place. Presumably when the leaf is intact auxin is continually moving down the petiole and inhibits the differentiation of an abscission layer at the base. The use of sprays of various growth substances to prevent the fall of leaves or fruits under certain conditions is now a common horticultural practice. What the mechanism is by which the abscission layer is produced or inhibited is not known.

Sprays of this sort are also used to stimulate rather than inhibit abscission, notably for the purpose of thinning young fruits when too many have been set. How, one may ask, does the same substance act in two such different ways? Evidently a normal growing and functioning organ will produce enough auxin to prevent its abscission. When this production ceases, the organ will drop off unless a fresh supply is available through external application. Anything which checks or deranges normal growth, however, will tend to check auxin production and thus lead to abscission. Sprays of some substances and in certain concentrations will tend to do this, and hence their usefulness in the thinning of fruit. An answer to the problem of this double effect has been proposed by Jacobs (1955), who has shown that in addition to the inhibiting effect of auxin on abscission there may be a *speeding* effect produced by auxin formed in young nearby leaves. This stimulates the abscission of a petiole whenever the flow of auxin from its leaf blade is reduced. Abscission is thus controlled by an "auxin-auxin balance."

The differentiation of more specialized tissues may be stimulated by auxin. Camus (1949) grafted buds of *Cichorium* to pieces of storage tissue and found that vascular strands began to differentiate just below the bud and continued to develop until they established connection with the vascular tissue beneath. Buds encased in cellophane and inserted into tissues cultivated *in vitro* produced the same effect, indicating that a diffusible substance, possibly auxin, was involved (Fig. 18-23).

Of significance here is the work of Wetmore (1956) on the induction of xylem in callus tissues. Into homogeneous callus maintained in culture from parenchyma cells in the cambial region of lilac, a growing lilac stem apex was grafted by inserting it into a V-shaped cut. After tissue union was effected, strands of xylem began to differentiate into the homogeneous callus tissue below the graft. That auxin was the factor responsible for this is suggested by the fact that when the cut was filled with agar containing auxin but without a stem tip vascular tissue appeared below it in the same way, the distribution of the strands depending on the concentration of the auxin. It is significant that only xylem tissue was thus differentiated and not phloem. This was also the case in the regeneration of severed vascular strands in the stem of coleus (p. 242). It may be that the factors which stimulate xylem development are different from the ones involved in phloem production.

More profound effects of growth substances on the anatomy of plants have been described. Much of the work here has been done by Kraus and his colleagues at the University of Chicago, who have tried a variety of substances in different concentrations and on many plants. Their general conclusions are that most of the changes produced are in the abnormal distribution and proportions of tissues rather than in the production of new structures. Important factors in these changes are nutrition and the age and state of the tissues when treated. Marked differences in reaction to various substances were found, and morphogenetic processes may thus in part be manipulated. A review of this work has been made by Beal (1951).

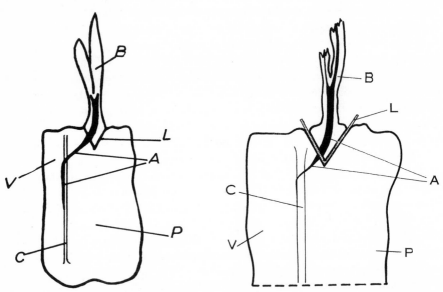

FIG. 18-23. At left, effect of a bud grafted to the phloem region of a piece of chicory root in culture. The bud stimulates the development of vascular tissue below it, presumably because of a growth substance it produces. At right, a similar experiment except that a sheet of cellophane, CL, has been placed between the bud and the tissue below. The same effect is produced, indicating that organic continuity is not necessary. B, bud; P, phloem; V, vascular parenchyma; C, cambium; A, histologically altered tissue; L, line of contact between bud and stock. (*From Gautheret, after Camus.*)

OTHER FORMATIVE EFFECTS

Various other substances of morphogenetic significance have been postulated, but little is known about them. Thus in *Dictyostelium*, the remarkable life cycle of which has been described earlier (p. 223), the factor controlling the aggregation of the myxamoebae into a pseudoplasmodium appears to be chemical in nature and diffusible (J. T. Bonner, 1949). To this substance Bonner has given the name *acrasin*.

In a few traits, such as time of fruit ripening in dates (Swingle, 1928) and staple length in cotton (Harrison, 1931), pollen seems to have a direct effect not only on the embryo but on the tissues of the ovary itself, tending to make these somewhat resemble ones of the paternal parent. This *metaxenia* must evidently be due to gene-produced chemical factors introduced through the pollen tube and modifying the development of such maternal tissues as the pericarp and the seed coat.

The development of galls with specific external and internal structures (p. 285) produced by fungi or insects seems to be dependent on various chemical substances. In insect galls these may be injected into the plant by the insect but more probably they result from secretions from the growing larva.

In other galls, particularly the one most actively studied—crown gall—auxin is clearly involved (p. 294). Experiments with tissue cultures have shown that cells of normal tissue in many cases are unable to grow unless supplied with auxin. Cells of bacteria-free crown-gall tissue, however, can do so. This fact suggests that the change from normal to tumor tissue may result from the acquirement by tumor cells of the ability to synthesize auxin. It is probable, however, that the problem is more complex and that changes in the ability to form other growth substances are also involved. Thus Braun and Näf (1954) have extracted from crown gall a biologically active substance which is not auxin but which, in association with auxin, produces active proliferation of tobacco-pith tissue in culture. Neither this nor auxin alone has a growth-stimulating effect of this sort. The question of the relation of auxin to crown-gall formation has been actively investigated. The subject has been reviewed by Braun and Stonier (1958).

Growth substances are also involved in the production of other gall-like structures. Swellings and malformations somewhat resembling typical root nodules associated with nitrogen-fixing bacteria have been induced by application of synthetic growth substance on the roots of several types of leguminous plants (Allen, Allen, and Newman, 1953).

A number of other growth substances deserve mention here. Adenine, for example, has been found to possess significant properties, especially for leaf growth, and the balance between it and auxin seems to determine the character of development in some cases (p. 414, and Skoog and Tsui, 1951).

The synthetic growth substances are too numerous to be discussed here. Of particular note is 2,4-dichlorophenoxyacetic acid (2,4-D), important because of its wide use as a herbicide. It produces such profound growth abnormalities that death usually ensues (Kaufmann, 1955; Fig. 18-24). For some unknown reason it has relatively little effect on monocotyledonous plants. Work with it has been reviewed by Woodford, Holly, and McCready (1958).

Maleic hydrazide is important in that it inhibits growth in a wide variety of plants without causing obvious morphological abnormalities. Plants treated with it tend to lose dominance in their apical buds and show certain other effects (Naylor and Davis, 1950). It seems to inhibit

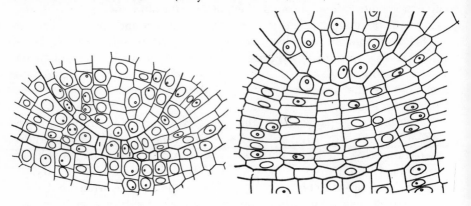

FIG. 18-24. Median longitudinal section of young adventitious root apices in rice. Left, of untreated plant. Right, of plant treated with 2,4-D. There is a great increase of periclinal divisions in the latter, which produces massive, abnormal roots. (*From Kaufman.*)

mitosis (Greulach and Atchison, 1953) and also checks the formation of flower primordia in both long-day and short-day plants (Klein and Leopold, 1953; Fig. 18-25).

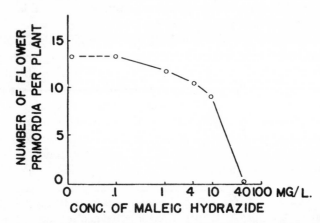

FIG. 18-25. The effect of maleic hydrazide on the total number of flower primordia at the first five nodes of soybeans. (*From Klein and Leopold.*)

Substances such as triiodobenzoic acid and coumarin under some conditions increase the effect of auxin and under others markedly inhibit growth. A number of substances occur that inhibit or antagonize auxin action (J. Bonner, 1949) and have been termed *antiauxins* (Fig. 18-26).

Some gases have been found to exert strong formative effects on plants and thus deserve to be included among the growth substances, although chemically they are very different from the rest. In studying the effects of illuminating gas and its constituents on greenhouse plants, workers at the Boyce Thompson Institute found that in tomato plants exposed under bell jars to atmospheres containing 1 per cent of carbon monoxide the stems became covered after a few days with an abundant growth of roots. Other gases produced similar effects. Carbon monoxide was found to induce rooting in many other plants (Zimmerman, Crocker, and Hitchcock, 1933). These results led to the investigation of the effects of ethylene, acetylene, and propylene (Zimmerman and Hitchcock, 1933). All were found to induce rooting and root-hair formation, leaf

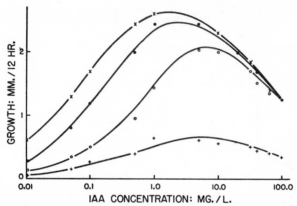

Fig. 18-26. Growth of *Avena* coleoptile (upper curve) induced by various concentrations of indoleacetic acid. The degree of inhibition of this growth by an auxin antagonist (4-chlorophenoxyisobutyric acid) at concentrations of 1, 10, and 50 mg./liter is shown in the three successively lower curves. (*From Foster, McRae, and Bonner.*)

epinasty, proliferation of callus-like masses of tissue, and abscission of leaves, flowers, and fruits. These gases, however, do not stimulate growth in the absence of auxin. The relation of ethylene to auxin has been discussed by Michener (1938).

In Puerto Rico Rodríguez (1932) discovered that ethylene induces flowering in the pineapple, and in Hawaii it was found soon afterward that acetylene will accomplish the same result (Lewcock, 1937). The effect of these gases on pineapple is much like that of the synthetic growth substances which induce flowering (p. 398).

In addition to the growth substances which have here been discussed—auxin, various other naturally occurring substances, and the synthetic compounds—another is now being actively studied and is assuming an important place in morphogenetic problems. This is *gibberellin*.

In a disease of rice produced by the fungus *Gibberella fujikuroi*, it was observed some years ago that many of the infected plants grew taller than uninfected ones (Kurosawa, 1926). Young and uninfected rice plants treated with culture filtrates of this fungus grew unusually tall. A similar increase in growth was observed when this filtrate was applied to some other plants, both monocotyledons and dicotyledons. Several different but related substances were purified from *Gibberella* and are now commonly termed the gibberellins. Their nomenclature is still somewhat confused but they may be named gibberellin A_1, A_2, and A_3, the last being the best known and often called gibberellic acid.

Gibberellin commonly produces a very marked increase in stem elongation (Fig. 18-27). This is particularly conspicuous in certain dwarf

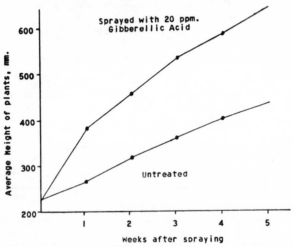

Fig. 18-27. Relation between concentration of gibberellic acid and plant height in bean plants. (*From Gray.*)

plants, notably peas. Brian and Hemming (1955) induced a fivefold increase in height in such plants, bringing them up to the size of tall races, by applying a little of this substance to one of the leaves. It had no effect on plants of the tall races. The length but not the number of internodes was increased. The so-called "slender" mutants of peas, which are tall but spindly, showed no effects of gibberellin treatment. Phinney (1956) found that gibberellin caused some dwarf mutants in maize to grow as tall as the normal plants from which they had been derived but some other dwarf races showed little response. Tall plants were unaffected. The relation of gibberellin to dwarfing is evidently a complex one. Most of the elongating effect is caused by increase in cell length rather than in cell number. There are a few cases, however, where cell division as well as cell elongation has been stimulated.

Leaf growth is affected by gibberellin and is often, though not always, increased. Radish leaves floated on a gibberellin solution in the dark grew larger than the controls. It is perhaps significant that kinetin has much the same effect and that when both substances are applied the increase in growth is equal to the sum of their separate effects.

Although gibberellin and auxin are similar in some respects, notably in stimulating cell elongation, they differ chemically and in other important ways. Gibberellin fails to produce typical epinasty nor does it induce callus formation, both of which usually result from auxin action. It also fails to show the polar transport within the plant so characteristic of auxin. It does not inhibit the growth of lateral buds but tends instead to stimulate their development. It does not check leaf abscission. It inhibits rather than promotes root initiation but does not inhibit root growth.

Gibberellin evidently has some relation in its effects on development to those produced by light, though this relation is not clear. Lang (1957) found that it induced biennial *Hyoscyamus* to flower the first season, regardless of day-length. The usual inhibition of growth produced by red light is removed by treatment with gibberellin. The effects of this substance much resemble etiolation but are independent of light. This is unlike the effect of auxin.

In its influence on dwarf plants, which seems to be its diagnostic feature, gibberellin perhaps substitutes for some essential factor that is normally present and which may have been lost by mutation. No effects of gibberellin have as yet been found in any of the lower forms. Substances essentially like it have now been extracted from several higher plants (Radley, 1958), and it is probably widely spread in the plant kingdom.

The literature in this field has been reviewed by Stowe and Yamaki (1957). Further study of gibberellin should yield important information on the factors governing plant development.

MECHANISM OF ACTION

Relatively little is known chemically about most of the growth substances. Some of them, like the calines, are little more than inferences. The existence of others, such as florigen, can be proved by experiment, though they have not been isolated. Others can be isolated, at least partially, but their chemical nature is not well known. As to auxin, gibberellin, and traumatic acid, fairly complete chemical information is now available.

Many attempts have been made to find some common features of chemical structure among these substances which have formative effects and thus to gain a clue as to how these effects are produced. These substances vary considerably. Having studied many such compounds, Koepfli, Thimann, and Went (1938) concluded that the minimal structural requirement for a substance to stimulate growth, at least in the pea test for auxin, is to possess an unsaturated ring system with a side chain adjacent to a double bond in the ring, and with a carboxyl group in the chain separated from the ring by a carbon atom. Thimann (1957) points out that there are a considerable number of biologically active compounds which do not have this structure and at least one that does not even contain a ring. It seems doubtful that an understanding of the mechanism of action, either of auxin or similar synthetic substances, will be gained by a knowledge of their chemical structure without an equal knowledge of the reacting systems that they stimulate. The general question of the chemistry and mode of action of plant growth substances was discussed at the Wye College symposium (Wain and Wightman, 1956).

Just how growth substances produce their morphogenetic effects is not well understood. The first visible result of auxin action is a speeding up of protoplasmic streaming, indicating that some aspect of metabolism is being accelerated. The marked influence of auxin on growth also suggests this, since growth requires the release of energy. Some physiologists believe that auxin acts as a respiratory coenzyme and thus has an important share in the respiratory cycle. No enzyme has yet been found, however, that can be activated by auxin in physiological concentrations.

Since what appears to be the primary effect of auxin is cell enlargement, it seems plausible to conclude that water uptake is controlled by it, and there is some evidence for this. The suggestion has been made that auxin increases the osmotic concentration of the cell sap and thus increases cell size. Cell growth may take place, however, even with a decreasing osmotic concentration. Burström (p. 41) believes that cell enlargement is not primarily caused by water uptake.

Interest at first focused on auxin-induced changes in the cell wall as related to growth, and Heyn (1940) has reviewed the evidence that auxin directly increases the plasticity of the wall and thus its irreversible extensibility. Some workers believed that the effect of auxin was indirect and only through its influence on the cytoplasm. Recent studies, however, support Heyn's view. Thus Cleland and Bonner (1956) present evidence that auxin directly induces a loosening of the cell-wall structure and thus a relaxing of wall pressure, which makes possible an expansion of the cell. The effect of auxin is independent of cell expansion. Auxin may affect the wall by altering pectin metabolism.

The relation of growth to protoplasmic viscosity and to the swelling capacity of cell colloids suggests that auxin may have something to do with these qualities. Northen (1942) observed that auxin usually decreases viscosity of protoplasm. He regards protoplasm as a "reversibly dissociable-associable system," in which auxin (and other agents) cause dissociation of cellular proteins and increased swelling pressure. As the result of such action, it is thought that components of the fine structure of the cell may undergo reorientation and the reactivity of the cell may be changed.

Of greater morphogenetic interest is the direct relation of growth substances to the development of organs or structures. The situation here is even less clear than in the control of growth. In a number of cases one is faced with a curious antithesis between the action of auxin in different situations. For example, at a given concentration it stimulates the growth of stem tissue but inhibits that of the primary root, with the result that differential geotropic bending occurs. It stimulates the development of root primordia and hence is useful in the rooting of cuttings, but it checks the elongation of the roots after their emergence. In some cases its effect is to accelerate flowering and in others to inhibit it. Sometimes it prevents bud growth and sometimes it stimulates this. In certain cases its effect is to stimulate the growth of roots rather than buds but in other cases it has just the opposite influence.

In this confusing situation the hypothesis of specific organ-forming substances appeals to many, especially those who seek direct and primarily chemical solutions to morphogenetic problems. To be sure, development often does seem to be the result of the action of such substances, as in the formation of roots, flowers, and abscission layers. But where, one may ask, does this specificity end? In the flower, are there separate substances for sepals, petals, stamens, and ovaries, for anther and filament, style and stigma? Does each tissue and each type of cell have its appropriate "caline"? It is easy to reduce to absurdity the more naive statements of this hypothesis.

To what, then, can one attribute the highly specific results of plant development? One answer is that the specificity lies in the protoplasmic system rather than in the growth substance and that the latter serves primarily as a trigger or evocator that calls out a specific response. We should remember that auxin, the substance about which most is known, is markedly nonspecific. A few such biologically active substances, stimulating responses from a highly organized protoplasmic system, might account for development. A dime, it has been said, will open a turnstile, activate a dial telephone, or bring a tune from a juke box, but the dime, like a molecule of auxin, is identical in every case. The difference lies in the complexities of the responding mechanism. The answer to morphogenetic problems is more difficult to come by on this conception than on that of specific formative substances since it involves an understanding of the whole protoplasmic system. This is a far goal, but, as Thimann (1957) has remarked, "It begins to look as though the whole cell were necessary to auxin activity."

But part of the living system in a plant evidently includes other biologically active substances. A good deal is known about several of these, and although they may not be "organ-forming" in the earlier sense of the word, their share in the control of developmental processes is more important than that of most other chemical compounds. A hopeful method of attack on morphogenetic problems is to study the *relationship* between these substances. It is now well known that there are compounds which enhance or which inhibit the effects of auxin. Still more promising are results such as those of Skoog and Miller (1957) on the relationships between auxin and adenine (or its derivative, kinetin). The presence of *both* seems to be necessary for vigorous growth, at least of tobacco callus in culture. If the proportions of the two are changed, however, the *character* of the growth is different. Relatively high levels of auxin and low ones of kinetin, either in cultures of tobacco callus or in cuttings, will tend to produce good root growth but little bud development, whereas high kinetin and low auxin levels favor growth of buds instead of roots. To be sure, kinetin is a substance which has not yet been found in the living plant, and its balance with auxin has been demonstrated in only a few cases, but the picture this balance presents of the possible control of differentiation through alteration in proportions within a relatively simple chemical situation opens up encouraging possibilities.

Other factors are doubtless concerned in these cases, and the problem must involve more than a simple two-compound interaction, but the idea that there may be a relatively small number of active but nonspecific substances, with the possibilities for complex interactions among them that this offers, makes understandable how an essentially infinite number of different structures might be produced without the necessity of postulating the activity of substances specific for each of them. Only 12 different kinds of chessmen can produce, by their various relationships, an almost limitless number of combinations on the board.

The study of plant growth substances has been of great significance and stimulation for morphogenesis, but it has done little more as yet than pose a series of deeper problems. Chief among these are three:

1. What is it that controls the distribution of growth substances as to space, time, and concentration?
2. What is it that determines the specific response which a given cell or tissue makes to them?
3. How do they interact in their control of development?

These problems are part of the deeper one of biological organization.

CHAPTER 19

Genetic Factors

The factors discussed thus far are effective chiefly through the environment of the plant, either its external surroundings or its inner physiological processes, which are open to relatively simple analysis. It is obvious, however, that these factors alone are not enough to explain all morphogenetic phenomena. There are also inborn differences, rooted in the specific constitution of each individual organism, which powerfully affect what it is and does. These differences are inherited, and it has been the great service of genetics to biology since the turn of the century to show that their physical basis is primarily in the genes, located in the chromosomes of the nucleus.

GENES

The various environmental factors exert their effects against this specific genetic background, the entire system of genes in the plant. Genes are sometimes thought of as though these bodies, known to be independent in inheritance to a certain degree, were also independent in development. This evidently is not true, however, for in their control of growth and differentiation the action of all the genes must be closely coordinated, in space and time, if an organism is to be produced. How these distinct entities are thus so precisely correlated in their action is a major problem for both genetics and morphogenesis. It is also clear that a gene does not produce its effect by determining a precise series of steps leading to the development of a specific trait, for the same genotype may have a very different effect if the environment is different. A gene simply determines a specific response to a specific environment. The genetic constitution that distinguishes a tall plant from a short one, for example, will not produce this difference unless the conditions of temperature, moisture, and soil fertility are such as to make vigorous growth possible.

The problem of gene action, of how a gene or group of genes produces its effects, is now one of the central concerns of genetics and is being

415

actively investigated. The role of genes in the synthesis of enzymes and other substances and thus in the determination of successive steps in metabolic processes is yielding much information as to the relations between genetics and physiology. Increasing knowledge of those remarkable compounds, the nucleic acids, is leading to an understanding of the chemistry of the gene and of the manner in which it reproduces itself. Indeed, desoxyribonucleic acid (DNA) has such significant properties that some biologists hopefully believe that it will finally produce answers for most of the basic problems of their science. All this, however, has as yet thrown little light on how it is that genetic factors affect the size, shape, and structure of plants and their parts. This is a much more difficult problem than working out the biochemical steps in the synthesis of an organic compound produced in plant metabolism. How a single pair of genes can determine, for example, whether a tomato plant will have the familiar deeply lobed leaves or the unlobed "potato-leaf" type is very difficult to see. Here something more than a series of chemical steps seems to be concerned. Growth *relationships* are being controlled, and at present we must admit that very little is known about how such control is exercised. A solution of this problem must start with a knowledge of what actually happens in the inheritance of form and structure. To make such a descriptive analysis and at the same time seek hopefully for clues that will lead to a knowledge of the mechanisms involved is the chief task at present of the student of morphogenesis who is interested in the genetic aspects of his science.

Genes and Growth. The underlying problem in growth is the increase of living substance, due ultimately to the reduplication of genes. How this is accomplished and how the DNA molecule divides into two new ones like itself are now beginning to be understood. Traits of size, either of body or organ, are markedly affected by environmental factors, but there is also a genetic basis for most of them. Since the pioneer work of East and Nilsson-Ehle it has been recognized that most quantitative traits depend not on single genes but on a series of multiple factors or polygenes, cumulative in their effect and in most cases without dominance. Such traits are difficult to analyze genetically since it is rare that the effect of individual genes can be followed, though there are statistical methods for determining the number of genes by which two individuals differ for a given trait. That polygenes are operative in quantitative inheritance is indicated by the fact that the variability of the F_2 is markedly higher than that of the parents or the F_1, as would happen if segregation were taking place. There is now a substantial body of evidence that confirms the multiple-factor hypothesis.

In a few cases the inheritance of size is not so complex, and the effect of individual genes can be traced. One of these, vine height in peas, was found by Mendel himself and is due to a single pair of genes, tall being dominant over short and segregating clearly in the F_2. De Haan (1927, 1930) has shown that in addition to this gene there are two (perhaps four) others that tend to inhibit growth. In this case a group of several genes, all modifying the same trait, can be recognized and their individual effects distinguished. In a considerable number of other cases it can be shown that two, three, four, or more pairs of genes are concerned in the inheritance of a size trait. Thus Quinby and Karper (1954) have evidence that in cultivated sorghum varieties, ranging from 2 to 15 ft. in height, four pairs of genes are operative.

Genes of this sort are cumulative in their effect. Sinnott (1937), Powers (1939), Charles and Smith (1939), and others have shown that this additive effect is geometric rather than arithmetic, each gene

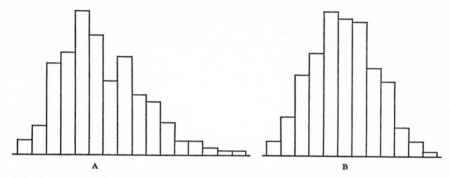

Fig. 19-1. Geometric action of genes determining size. A, graph of fruit weight of an F_2 population of cucurbit fruits consisting of 244 individuals plotted in arithmetically equal classes. B, the same population plotted in classes equal logarithmically. The first population is skewed, the second nearly symmetrical. (*From Sinnott.*)

contributing not a certain definite amount of height or weight but a certain percentage increase of the effect of the rest. This is shown by the fact that the F_1 is closer to the geometric average of the parents than to their arithmetic average and is thus somewhat nearer to the smaller parent in size. Furthermore, if a segregating F_2 is plotted in classes that are arithmetically equal, it skews toward the upper side, whereas if the scale is a logarithmic one, the F_2 population is symmetrically distributed around the geometric mean (Fig. 19-1).

A developmental study of inherited size differences shows that some are attained by differences in rate of growth and some in its duration. The size differences between plants showing hybrid vigor and their parent inbreds are related to a more rapid rate of growth, and some other size differences also have their basis in genetically controlled growth rates. In other cases the difference in size is due to longer duration of growth.

Large pumpkins differ from small gourds, for example, simply because they grow for a longer time (Sinnott, 1945*b*, and p. 16). The actual growth rate of these two varieties in terms of compound-interest growth is the same.

Inherited size differences are also related to cellular characters (p. 34). Most of them are due to differences in number rather than size of cells, large size being the result of more cell divisions during development. Less frequently the period of cell expansion is more extensive in the larger forms and their cells are consequently larger, though usually not in proportion to body size.

In the many cases where there are inherited differences in cell size, it is usually not the size of the meristematic cells that is different but the amount of increase that occurs after division ceases. Thus the fruits of large races of pumpkins have much larger cells than do small gourds, but this difference is not evident at the meristem. Some of it appears in the growth of the young ovary but most of it during the enlargement of the ovary in fruit development (Sinnott, 1939). Sugar beets have much larger cells (and leaves) than do table beets, but only in their mature structures. The meristematic cells are much the same size in both.

Many cases have been found in which there is not a gradation between large and small types but the small ones are so markedly different as to be regarded as somewhat abnormal dwarfs. In most such plants there is a single gene difference from normal which seems to control one important growth factor. A number of these occur in maize, and the auxin relations of some have been worked out (p. 377). Some dwarfs are small-celled but a few have cells larger than those of normal plants. There are also a number of *gigas* forms which are due to gene differences. Large and small types are also frequently related to chromosome number (p. 438).

Differences in height may result from mutations that alter a determinate type of growth to indeterminate. These have been found, for example, in tobacco (Jones, 1921) and maize (Singleton, 1946). Each shows single-gene segregation with normal determinate plants. The difference between bush and climbing varieties of beans, also due to a single gene, is really a difference between determinate and indeterminate growth.

Another important effect of genes on size is to be seen in cases of hybrid vigor or heterosis. The F_1 plants, in crosses between parents that are homozygous or essentially so, are often much larger and more vigorous than either parent (Fig. 17-1), and this fact has wide economic application, especially in maize. The difference is closely associated with heterozygosity and disappears with inbreeding. Various suggestions have been made to account for it—the stimulating effect of the heterozygous condition, the dominance of linked genes, increased embryo size, and others—but no ·satisfactory explanation has yet been reached. Gene action in heterosis has been discussed by Jones (1957), and there is a wide literature in this field (Sprague, 1953).

Genes and Form. The chief morphogenetic significance of genetic factors, however, is in their relation to the development of organic *form*. Here it is not the total amount but the distribution of growth that is important. Genes must in some way control *relative* growth—the amount of growth in one dimension as compared with that in each of the others so that specific shapes are produced. Many instances could be cited where the shape of leaf or flower or fruit is certainly inherited and where differences in it segregate and can be analyzed in mendelian terms, at least to some degree. Only a few can be mentioned here.

Leaf shape in cotton has had particular attention. In one of the earliest analyses of shape inheritance, Leake (1911) found that in crosses between broad-lobed and narrow-lobed forms the F_1 was intermediate and the F_2 showed segregation into $\frac{1}{4}$ narrow, $\frac{1}{2}$ intermediate, and $\frac{1}{4}$ broad. Peebles and Kearney (1928) crossed shallow-lobed and deep-lobed types and found F_1 to be intermediate and a ratio of 1:2:1 in F_2. In some varieties of cotton the genetic situation is much more complex. Both Hutchinson (1934 and others) and Silow (1939) postulate a series of multiple alleles, chiefly affecting lobing. They believe that the genes are "compound" and vary qualitatively as well as quantitatively. Hammond (1941) showed the importance of developmental analyses of shape in individual leaves and of changes of leaf shape along the stem. This method was carried further by Stephens (1944).

In the Japanese morning glory, *Pharbitis,* Imai (1930) and a number of other Japanese geneticists have studied the complex situation presented by the inheritance of leaf shape in crosses among its many varieties.

Among other traits of form the inheritance of which has been analyzed in mendelian terms are fruit shape in *Bursa* (Shull, 1914), root shape in radish (Uphof, 1924), and leaf lobing in *Tropaeolum* (Whaley, 1939).

Evidence for the Existence of Genes for Shape. The problem underlying all these instances of the inheritance of form is to find the method by which genes determine what the form is to be. The fact that such traits show segregation suggests that genes control them directly, but it is difficult to see how this is done. Some geneticists have tried to simplify the problem by assuming the operation of genes for individual dimensions only, as in the case of vine length in peas. Thus in tobacco flowers Anderson (1939) studied the inheritance of tube length and limb width in crosses between *Nicotiana Langsdorfii* and *N. alata,* species which differ in corolla shape. He observed that in F_2 there was much sharper segregation for length than for width, suggesting that fewer genes were operative in the former character than in the latter. There was by no means free recombination of length and width in F_2, however, as independent assortment would require. The combinations that did occur were only a narrow segment of those theoretically expected. When length was plotted against width in F_2, these were confined to a narrow segment of the total, running from combinations rather like one parent to those like the other through others resembling the F_1. He suggests that factors hindering free recombination might be gametic elimination, zygotic elimination, pleiotropism, and linkage. He believes that all of these may here be operative and suggests that *all* quantitative characters of an organism may be tightly linked, surely a radical conclusion. An extreme instance of the hypothesis that shape is the result of genes determining dimensions has been proposed by Frets (1947), who postulates that in the inheritance of seed shape in beans there are a series of independent genes for length, breadth, and thickness, respectively.

H. H. Smith (1950) studied a cross much like that made by Anderson and comes to the conclusion that there is a developmental restriction to free recombination but that this is due to a "correlated growth pattern." In simpler words, there are genes that control shape *directly* rather than through individual dimensions.

Evidence for the existence of such genes has been presented by Sinnott (1935), chiefly from studies of the inheritance of fruit shape in the Cucurbitaceae. This evidence is of several types, as follows:

1. If a race with flattened, disk-shaped fruits is crossed with a spherical one, the F_1 shows complete dominance of the disk shape and in the F_2 there is sharp segregation into $\frac{3}{4}$ disk and $\frac{1}{4}$ sphere. In another case, two different types of spheres, when crossed, show evidence of the action of complementary genes, for the F_1 is disk-shaped and in the F_2 there is dihybrid segregation into $\frac{9}{16}$ disk, $\frac{6}{16}$ sphere, and $\frac{1}{16}$ elongate. Other shape differences can be analyzed in equally simple mendelian terms, though more genes are usually involved.

2. In the disk-sphere cross, F_2 segregation for shape index (ratio of length to width) is sharp but those for length and for breadth are much less so, suggesting that the segregating genes control shape directly and not through dimensions.

3. In one disk-sphere cross, the fruits of the disk parent were considerably larger than those of the sphere. The size of the F_1 was close to the geometric mean between the two parental sizes, and the means of the segregating F_2 disks and spheres were essentially similar to each other and close to that of the F_1. This can be explained by assuming that size is determined by a series of genes but that the gene for shape is independent of these and molds into a particular form the material made available by the genes for size.

4. In a considerable series of crosses between races genetically more complex and differing in both the size and the shape of their fruits, a *positive* correlation was observed in each case between fruit length and fruit width in the parents and the F_1 (where presumably all size differences are caused by environmental factors) but a *negative* one in F_2 where segregation occurs. This again can be explained by assuming that shape is inherited independently of size. A certain amount of material is genetically available for every fruit, and if its shape genotype tends to produce an elongate one, this will be relatively narrow, and hence the negative correlation. Maximum parental length is never combined in F_2 with maximum width, or minimum length with minimum width, as they should be if dimensions are directly determined genetically and recombined independently.

5. In the F_2 the coefficient of variation for length is twice as large as that for width, which is to be expected in a radially symmetrical organ where shape and size are genetically independent, for if the amount of material for growth is fixed, a unitary change in width (equatorial diameter) should produce a much greater change in length, since volume is essentially width $\times$ width $\times$ length.

Further evidence that genes for shape are actually operative is found in the fact that in a number of plants, such as the tomato (Lindstrom, 1928; Butler, 1952), genes for fruit shape are linked with others and can be definitely located on chromosome maps (Fig. 19-2). If it were dimensions that are directly controlled, presumably their genes would occupy different loci.

If genes determining shape actually exist, the difficult problem arises as to how they produce their effects. The ultimate mechanisms are by no means clear but the visible steps in the process can be described. In some cases the shape of an organ, such as a fruit, is established when it is a very small primordium. After this, growth rates in the various dimensions are equal, and as the structure grows its shape remains constant. The critical step in establishing growth relationships here is taken very early. This is what happens in fruits of pepper, tomato, some races of *Cucurbita pepo*, and various other plants. It is usual in organs that are nearly isodiametric at maturity.

In many fruits and in most leaves, especially where the dimensions are markedly unlike, the primordium is a roundish mass of cells and the shape of the organ is produced by differential growth among the dimensions (Sinnott, 1936b). In various races of the gourd, *Lagenaria siceraria*, for example, mature fruit shape varies from long and narrow through round to flattish. All are alike in early primordia. In elongate types (like the "Hercules club") length increases faster than width and as the organ grows in size it becomes progressively more elongate. Conversely, the

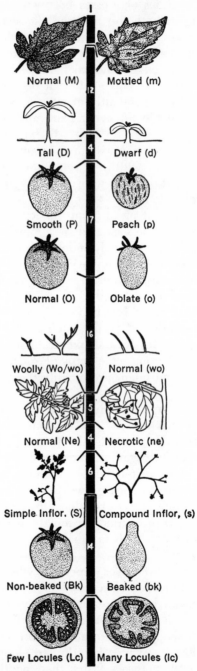

Fig. 19-2. Map of chromosome 1 of tomato. Two genes for fruit shape, and genes for other structural characters, have places on it. (*From Butler.*)

flattish types grow more rapidly in width. In all such instances, form changes as size increases. Where a particular race is genetically small, its fruit shape at maturity will be different from one which is genetically larger but has the same shape genotype. This fact complicates a study of the inheritance of shape in cases where the parents differ in both shape and size.

In types where shape changes during development the dimensional relations, if plotted logarithmically, are allometric, the points falling along a straight line the slope of which measures the relative growth rate of the two dimensions (Fig. 5-8). It is this *relative* rate which the genes control, for if two races of *Lagenaria* differing in the slope of this line

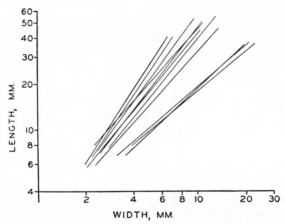

Fig. 19-3. Segregation of relative growth rates. Allometric growth of length to width of fruits in an F_2 from a cross between a rather elongate and a rather flat variety of cucurbits. The two F_2 classes resemble in general the parental forms. The F_1 was like the elongate type. What is segregating is the character of the relative-growth line. (*From Sinnott.*)

are crossed, the trait which segregates in F_2 is the steepness of this slope (Fig. 19-3), the value of k in the allometric equation (p. 105; Sinnott, 1958).

It should be remembered that what is being controlled is not simply the relationship between *two* dimensions but between all the dimensions that make up the organic pattern. In the "bottle" gourd, for example, the length of the axis during growth is related to the width of the upper, sterile lobe; of the isthmus; and of the lower, fertile lobe. Relative to the axis, the lower lobe grows fastest, the upper next, and the isthmus least. The form of the whole structure thus changes in a precise and predictable fashion.

This concept of shape inheritance may be illustrated most simply by inscribing the lengthwise profile of an organic form like that of a fruit in a series of rectangular coordinates, as D'Arcy Thompson (1942) has done with various structures, and then seeing how other forms may be derived from it by deforming these coordinates in a particular fashion (Fig. 19-4). A change such as might be produced by a single gene difference is evidently not a localized one but involves, at least to some degree, the pattern as a whole.

The objection may be raised that in some cases a single dimension does seem to be inherited, as in vine height in peas. In a strongly polarized organ like the stem, height may be changed with little reference to stem diameter. In such cases height seems to be a direct expression of size in

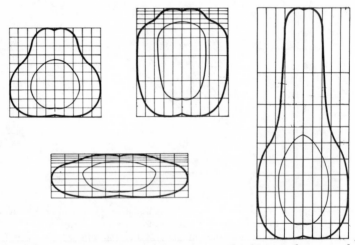

Fɪɢ. 19-4. Geometric modification of fruit shape. The fruit at the upper left has its longitudinal profile inscribed in a grid of equal coordinates. This may be changed to various other shapes by changing these coordinates. (*From Sinnott.*)

which the major effect of the genes is channeled in one particular dimension, that of the polar axis. Ear length in maize, one of the first characters to be analyzed in terms of multiple genes, is the major dimension of a polarized organ and thus strongly affected by any genes that control total amount of growth. Here, however, ear width is also involved to some extent, and there are differences in the relation of length to width in various races. Such a case may perhaps be regarded as intermediate in genetic control between one in which genes for shape express themselves in a weakly polarized structure (like a fruit), thus producing a wide range of patterns, and one in which growth is essentially limited to the polar dimension.

The evidence therefore favors the view that in most cases, certainly, genes control form directly. How this is done poses one of the most difficult problems of genetics and morphogenesis and one closely involved with that of biological organization itself. Most of the work on gene action has indicated that genes control the production of specific *substances;* but how, one may ask, does a substance control the development of a specific *form?* This involves the control of relationships, like that between length and width in a developing fruit, and not only single relationships but a whole series of them organized into a pattern. The amount of growth in one dimension is related precisely to the amounts in all the others. For a specific substance to do this involves the old question of organizers and organ-forming substances which are so easy to postulate and so difficult to picture in physical terms. These gene-produced substances seem rather to act as evocators, calling out or modifying formative potentialities in the living stuff of the organism. We need to assume the immanent presence in protoplasm of something that, for want of a better simile, can be compared to a system of coordinates in three dimensions.

A specific substance may be thought of as bending or otherwise modifying these coordinates in a particular way and thus regulating growth in such a fashion that a specific pattern is produced. The problem remains as to the nature of this underlying formativeness. It may be thought of, perhaps, as a molecular pattern in the cytoplasm (p. 455). To call it a "field" is to give it a name but not an explanation. It is evidently involved in the nature of the living, organized system that an organism is. To recognize that it exists, even though one cannot yet explain it, is a step in advance and may save us from a too naive conception of the nature of gene action in development.

Other Structural Traits. Aside from pure forms in the geometrical sense, various other structural characters are under gene control, or at least show mendelian segregation after crossing. Thus the zigzag stem that appeared in descendants of a certain cross between Tom Thumb popcorn and Missouri dent (Eyster, 1922) behaves as a double recessive to normal stem. "Corn grass," a mutation in maize with narrow leaves, many tillers, and few male flowers, is a single-gene dominant (Singleton, 1951). In peas, relatively long distance between first and second flowers as compared with the total length of the inflorescence was found by Lamprecht (1949) to be the result of three genes. Abnormalities of various sorts have also been shown to have a genetic basis. Among them are double flowers in many plants, as for example *Tropaeolum* (Eyster and Burpee, 1936), where doubleness is recessive but where a dominant "super-double" strain appeared, female sterile and with about 135 petals. Peloria in *Linaria vulgaris* and *Digitalis purpurea* has been shown by various workers to differ in some types by a single gene from normal flower. Fasciation is a single-gene recessive to normal in *Nicotiana* (O. E. White, 1916). In both peloria and fasciation individuals are found which are usually normal but occasionally produce these abnormalities, presumably because of some genetic predisposition in this direction. These should be of particular interest in studies of the basis of gene action.

There are two traits in the nature of abnormalities ("tufted" and "polycladous"), presumably gene-determined, in the liverwort *Sphaerocarpos* (Allen, 1924, 1925) which are of particular interest in that they occur in the haploid gametophyte generation so that the effects of a single gene are directly visible, unmodified by the influence of its allele.

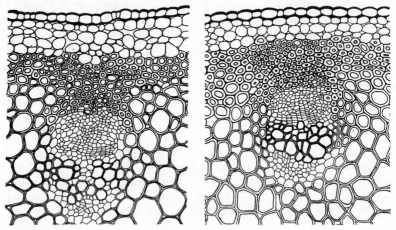

Fig. 19-5. Cross section of the stem of *Aquilegia*. Left, normal plant. Right, mutant with thicker cell walls. (*From Anderson and Abbe.*)

Anatomical characters have also been shown to be directly affected by genes. In *Aquilegia canadense* a dwarf race with bushy, compact growth and stiff, brittle branches has been shown by Anderson and Abbe (1933; Fig. 19-5) to differ from normal by a single gene. The direct effect of this gene is to cause precocious secondary thickening of the cell walls, from which all the other differences follow. Platt, Darroch, and Kemp (1941) report that in wheat, solid stem differs from normal hollow stem by three or four pairs of recessive genes.

In all these cases where the form or structure of a particular plant part has been found to be controlled by a gene or group of genes, much valuable information as to the method of control may be gained by a study of the development of this structure. In a few cases this has been done, as in cotton leaves and cucurbit fruits described above; in dwarf mutants in maize by Stephens (1948); in structure and growth rates of inbred and hybrid maize by Weaver (1946), Heimsch, Rabideau, and Whaley (1950), and Stein (1956); in a leaf mutant in maize by Mericle (1950); and in the leaves of two species of *Tropaeolum* and their hybrid by Whaley and Whaley (1942). In this last piece of work it was found that the pattern was essentially determined by early differential cell division in certain regions, the final form being attained by uniform cell expansion. Much more work of this sort, even at the purely descriptive level, needs to be done, for it will doubtless pose more sharply the problems which have to be solved and may suggest new methods of attacking them.

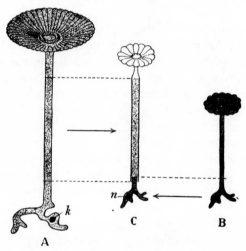

Fig. 19-6. *Acetabularia*. A, *A. mediterranea*. B, *A. wettsteinii*. C, a stalk piece (shaded) of the former species grafted to a rhizoid of the latter, which contains the nucleus. The regenerating "hat" resembles that of *A. wettsteinii* and thus seems to be determined by the nucleus. (*After Hämmerling.*)

Acetabularia. In a few cases more direct proof of gene control over form characters has been obtained. One of the most notable of these is presented by the coenocytic marine green alga *Acetabularia* (p. 136). This plant has a branching, rhizoidal base from which rises a stalk several centimeters high, surmounted by a "hat" something like the "umbrella" of a mushroom. At most stages of its life history, *Acetabularia* has but a single, large nucleus, located in one of the basal rhizoids. Two species of the genus differ in size and especially in the form of the hat. If a long piece of the stalk of the taller species (*A. mediterranea*) is cut out and grafted to a decapitated basal portion of the other (*A. wettsteinii*), which contains the nucleus, a new hat will be regenerated at the apex of the grafted stalk. At first this hat will resemble that of the species which contributed the stalk but at length it comes to be like that of the species at the base and thus like the one to which the nucleus belongs. Evidently the nucleus, with its genes, determines the form of the hat (Fig. 19-6). The delay in expressing this determination is thought to be due to the persistence for a time of specific substances in the cytoplasm of the stalk, produced previously by the nucleus of the species from which it came. *Acetabularia* has provided material for many experiments important for genetics and physiology as well as for morphogenesis, most of them by Hämmerling (see, for example, 1946).

Genes and Sex Structures. A particularly complex problem in genetics and one of much importance in morphogenesis is the inheritance of sex and the determination of the structures in which sexual differences are expressed.

In animals most individuals definitely belong to one sex or the other, and the production of both male and female gametes by the same organism is rare. In plants, however, it is much commoner than the unisexual condition. Among higher forms, staminate and pistillate flowers may be separate but on the same individual (the monoecious condition) or the flowers may be perfect and hermaphroditic. There are a considerable number of cases, however, where the two types of sexual structures are borne on different individuals (the dioecious condition). Such forms are strictly comparable to unisexual animals.

In determining just what the sexual character of a plant will be, however, the environment has a much greater effect than it does in animals. Sex reversal or the production of one sort of sexual structures rather than another due to physiological or environmental changes is rare in animals but in plants this is relatively easy to accomplish. In monoecious angiosperms the ratio of staminate and pistillate flowers to each other or to the perfect flowers which sometimes occur on such plants may be determined by light or by growth substances, or it may be an aspect of the general phasic development of the plant (as in cucurbit flowers; Nitsch, Kurtz, Liverman, and Went, 1952). The problem of sex expression in plants is therefore in large measure a developmental rather than a genetic one. Although there is a definite genetic basis for most of the sexual differences, this wide variability in its expression makes genetic analysis particularly difficult. There is a large literature on this subject only a very small part of which can be mentioned here.

With the rediscovery of Mendel's law there were many attempts to analyze sexual differences in dioecious plants in mendelian terms. Among the early workers were Correns (1907), Bateson (1909), and Shull (1910). The plants on which they first worked were *Melandrium* (*Lychnis*) and *Bryonia*. Correns concluded from his experiments that in *Melandrium* the egg cells all carry a tendency toward femaleness and that the male is heterozygous for sex, half the male gametes bearing female tendency and half male. This plant could therefore be regarded as having the XY type of sex inheritance and to be comparable to *Drosophila*. The later discovery by Blackburn (1923) of an unequal pair of chromosomes in *Melandrium* strongly supported this conclusion, and it is now generally accepted. It has been strengthened by the fact that definitely sex-linked traits have been found here, notably a difference in leaf shape (Fig. 19-7).

Sex chromosomes are not confined to vascular plants. In the liverwort *Sphaerocarpos Donnellii* Allen (1919) reported that the four spores of each tetrad produce two male and two female gametophytes. The females have a very large chromosome, apparently the X, and the males its much smaller homolog, apparently the Y (Fig. 19-8). This is the XY type of

Fig. 19-7. A sex-linked trait in *Melandrium*. At left, normal plant. At right, a narrow-leaved mutant, the gene for which is located in the X chromosome. (*From Shull.*)

sex determination but expressed in the gametophyte generation. A good many other dioecious liverworts and mosses have been found to possess a similar pair of sex chromosomes. It is significant that when such gametophytes are made diploid they become monoecious, evidently because they now possess both types of chromosomes, though in such cases the gametes usually fail to function. The genetics of bryophytes has been reviewed by Allen (1935, 1945).

There are a number of complications in the chromosome theory of sex determination in the higher plants, however. *Bryonia*, which, like *Melandrium*, is clearly male-heterozygous on breeding evidence, has no unequal chromosome pair, and it turns out that visibly unequal chromosomes, presumably sex chromosomes, are present in only about half the genera of dioecious plants. In some cases, also, like *Dioscorea*, the female is XX and the male XO, with one chromosome less than the female.

In others, like the dioecious species of the strawberry, *Fragaria,* it is the female that is the heterozygous sex and all male gametes are alike. Other difficulties appear. In *Rumex,* for example, the female has two X chromosomes and the male one, but the male has *two different* Y chromosomes. In *Humulus lupulus,* hops, the female apparently has two pairs of *different* X chromosomes and the male has one of each of these plus two different Y chromosomes.

The situation is so complex and the results reported often so conflicting that some botanists, among them Schaffner and Yampolsky, have entirely repudiated the chromosome theory of sex, particularly since in some cases, notably in *Cannabis,* sex can readily be reversed by various environmental factors, as Schaffner was able to do by altering the

Fig. 19-8. Chromosomes of *Sphaerocarpos.* From female gametophyte, above, showing X chromosome, and from male, below, showing Y. (*From C. E. Allen.*)

photoperiod (p. 317). McPhee (1924) obtained similar results. He showed that this does not invalidate the genetic basis for sex but simply demonstrates that the range of expression for the genotype in hemp in response to the environment is very wide.

The early ideas that two X chromosomes produce a female and one X a male are clearly too simple. The modern view of sex determination conceives of a balance between several, probably many, genes of which some are in the so-called sex chromosomes and others may be in the autosomes. This theory of balance is well shown by the results of several workers (Warmke and Blakeslee, 1940; Westergaard, 1940; and Warmke, 1946) with a dioecious race of *Melandrium* which had been made tetraploid by colchicine treatment. Here the female had four X chromosomes and four sets of autosomes, 4A + XXXX, and the male 4A + XXYY. By crosses among these and with diploids, the investigators were able to produce types with one or with two Y chromosomes combined with two, three, or four X's, the number of autosomes being kept the same in each combination. The Y was thus the only variable. They also combined one, two, three, and four X chromosomes with one Y, again with the same number of autosomes, so that the number of X chromosomes was the variable. The results as to male, female, and hermaphrodite flowers led to the conclusion that the autosomes have little sexual tendency (as they do have in *Drosophila*), that the Y contains strong male-determining genes, and the X, weaker female-determining ones. The ratio of X to Y chromosomes determines what the sex will be. It can also be shown that there are at least three genes for maleness in the Y chromosome.

Experiments like these support the hypothesis that genes with tendencies to produce male structures or female ones are carried by the X, the Y, or the autosomes and that the balance between them determines the particular expression of sex. These genes may be present in chromosomes where there is no morphological difference between members of the pair, and such difference is obviously not significant for sex determination. The sharp distinctions between maleness and femaleness in animals and the relative scarcity of intersexual forms among them make genetic analysis of sex much less difficult there than in plants.

Aside from the determination of sex in individuals as a whole, the degree of sex expression within the individual has also been shown to be under gene control. Typical illustrations of this are the following: In several cucurbits the monoecious condition is dominant over the andromonoecious (where some flowers are hermaphroditic and some staminate), and a single gene is involved (Rosa, 1928). Poole and Grimball (1939) extended this for *Cucumis* by demonstrating a two-factor difference between hermaphroditic and monoecious, since a cross between these types gave in F_2 nine monoecious: three gynomonoecious: three andromonoecious: one hermaphroditic. In *Carica*, Hofmeyr (1938) reports that three alleles, M_1, M_2, and m, are responsible for maleness, hermaphroditism, and femaleness, respectively (M_1m is staminate; M_2m, hermaphroditic; and mm, pistillate). Homozygous M_1 or M_2 are lethal. Janick and Stevenson (1955) find that the monoecious character in spinach is allelic to the XY pair of genes concerned in sex determination.

A notable example of the effect of genes on sex determination which could lead directly to the production of a dioecious condition from a monoecious one was demonstrated by Jones (1934) with maize. In this plant there are several recessive genes for tassel seed (ts) on chromosome 1, in which the staminate florets are replaced by pistillate ones and the plant is thus essentially female. The recessive silkless gene (sk) in chromosome 2 sterilizes the female flowers and thus produces a plant essentially male. The silkless gene has no effect in the presence of tassel seed and the double recessive *sksk tsts* is thus female. If this is crossed with a plant *sksk Tsts*, which is male, half the offspring are *Tsts* (male) and half *tsts* (female). Interbreeding such plants, which are incapable of self-fertilization, will continue to produce offspring of which half are staminate and half pistillate, so that these plants, if prevented from crossing with other types of maize, will constitute a dioecious race. In this case chromosome 1, on which tassel seed is located, functions as a sex chromosome although no morphological difference is visible.

A detailed review of the genetic basis for sex expression in flowering plants has been written by Allen (1940).

Genes and Growth Substances. Since growth substances so powerfully affect growth and development it is natural to expect that in many cases gene action will involve the production and distribution of these substances, and in a considerable number of cases this has proved to be the case. Thus in the profound changes in growth habit of "lazy" maize (p. 390) the character is due to the fact that auxin, instead of accumulating on the lower side of a horizontal stem, remains evenly distributed so that the stem does not turn upward. Its failure to do so is not the result of mechanical weakness but of abnormal auxin relations.

Mention has already been made (p. 264) of the single-gene difference between the annual and the biennial varieties of *Hyoscyamus niger* and the fact that this is apparently due to a growth substance which can be transmitted by grafting, to make the biennial form flower in its first season. It is probable that a growth substance may also be operative in other similar cases, like those of beets and white sweet clover, where the difference between annual and biennial forms has been shown to be due to a single gene. In the single-gene mutants reported by Stein (p. 265) which were grafted to normal stock, some of the effects of the gene seemed able to cross the graft union but others did not.

A particularly interesting case is reported by Scheibe (1956) for peas, where a recessive fasciated mutant, differing from normal by a single gene, has a higher concentration of natural auxin than the normal. Furthermore, fasciation can be produced in the normal type by application of indoleacetic or naphthaleneacetic acid. Here the difference between the two genes seems to be in their ability to produce a growth substance.

Genes are also concerned with photoperiodic response. The Mammoth mutant of tobacco differs from most strains by a single gene which, among other effects, has changed the normal day-neutral type to one that flowers only under short day-lengths. Chandraratna (1955) has shown that, in rice, races sensitive to photoperiod differ from day-neutral types by a single gene.

Goodwin (1944) crossed several races of a short-day species of *Solidago* differing in flowering time and found that a considerable number of genes were involved in the determination of this character, probably distributed among all nine chromosome pairs.

Since developmental traits involve reaction of the genetic constitution of the organism to various other environmental factors—water, temperature, light, mechanical factors, and others—it is obvious that genes or their combinations must take part in these reactions, and although there are not yet many cases in which the action of individual genes has yet been analyzed as successfully here as it has in the biochemical genetics of lower organisms, this will doubtless be accomplished and will give information of value for the solution of the problems of development. This knowledge will be second in significance only to that which may be gained as to the mechanisms by which these innumerable gene reactions are so organized in the growth and activity of the individual that it becomes an organism.

CYTOPLASM

The fact that an entire and normal plant may be produced by regeneration from a single cell (p. 253) or a group of similar cells in different regions and from different tissues is evidence that all the cells of the plant are genetically alike. This implies that all the nuclei are similar, a conclusion supported by the fact that in all cells (save in cases of polysomaty) the number and structure of the chromosomes are constant.

If this conclusion is valid, the basis of differentiation would appear to lie in the extranuclear portion of the cell, the cytoplasm. Much less is known about the cytoplasm than about the nucleus, and events in it are not as dramatic and easily observed. It is clear, however, that beneath its relatively homogeneous superficial appearance there must be a high degree of chemical and physical diversity, an understanding of which is necessary before the problems of differentiation can be mastered. The basis for cytoplasmic differentiation is doubtless at the submicroscopic level. Weiss (1956), Schmitt (1956), and some others have shown that the elements of the macromolecular pattern are markedly different from one another in size and distribution (see also Tartar, p. 455). A wide field of research at this level is now developing.

There are a few cases where the cytoplasm can be shown to be immediately concerned in determination of structural characters. This is particularly true of the cell wall, which is directly produced by the cytoplasm and is a primary element in many differences between cells. Examples of this are seen in the regenerative conversion of thin-walled parenchyma cells into xylem cells with reticulate lignified walls. The pattern of these lignified thickenings is preceded in development by an identical pattern of granular cytoplasmic strands on which the thickenings are laid down (p. 193). Other markings in the cell wall have also been traced to cytoplasmic differences.

The cytoplasm may be concerned in the development of characters above the cellular level. In the cells of air roots of orchids, the bands of wall thickening (p. 201) that keep these cells from collapsing are laid down by the cytoplasm in each cell. They are not isolated structures in single cells, however, but a thickening in one cell is directly adjacent to one in the next, so that a continuous system is produced extending from cell to cell and forming a histological pattern over a considerable mass of tissue. The differential fiber patterns in *Luffa* (p. 197) and similar cases doubtless originate in the cytoplasm.

The distribution and configuration of the cytoplasm probably have a more deeply seated relation to development, however, than in these examples of cellular patterns. The plane in which a cell divides, at least in vacuolate cells, is foreshadowed by the orientation of a cytoplasmic plate some time before the axis of the spindle is established (p. 25), a fact which suggests that cell polarity, and thus the direction of growth and ultimately organic form itself, may have their immediate basis in the distribution and patterning of the cytoplasmic body.

The relation of cytoplasm to such differences in form may be well seen in the coenocytic bodies of many red algae, notably the genus *Caulerpa*. Here there are no cellular barriers to the passage of cytoplasm from one part of the plant to another, and much streaming takes place. Differences may be observed in various parts of the plant body as to the character of the cytoplasm, part of which is fixed to the inner wall and does not stream. In such plants the differential distribution of the cytoplasm seems to be related to the differentiation of the plant body, though the mechanisms involved are unknown. The disadvantage in such organisms and the probable reason why they have never been able to develop very highly differentiated bodies is their difficulty in keeping the various components of their living material sufficiently isolated so that physiological differences can be maintained effectively and a high degree of organization thus made possible.

Even in multicellular plants visible differences in distribution of cytoplasm are related to differentiation. This is especially evident in cases of unequal cell division, as in the formation of trichoblasts in many roots (p. 190). In the mother cell, which is to divide unequally to form a small trichoblast and a larger hairless cell, much of the cytoplasm (and the nucleus) moves toward the end at which the trichoblast will be cut off, so that even before division there is a difference in cytoplasmic distribution. The formation of the new wall finally separates two regions which had already become cytoplasmically different. In the formation of stomatal mother cells, initials of trichosclereids, and many other examples of unequal cell division the same differential distribution of cytoplasm, before division, is evident.

In such cases, unlike the coenocytes, the differences which arise in the cytoplasm cannot become distributed beyond the limits of the original mother cell. If in each cell division, however, there were a quantitatively or qualitatively unequal distribution of cytoplasm between the two daughter cells, cellular differentiation would result. It seems reasonable to suppose that many cell divisions are thus cytoplasmically unequal even though the differences are not visible and may be at the submicroscopic or chemical level. Such inequality would provide the necessary cytoplasmic basis for differentiation.

If differentiation proves to be primarily a matter of cytoplasmic distribution, the mechanism by which this distribution is controlled must evidently be one of the major problems of morphogenesis. In some cases the cause may be ascribed to polarity. Certainly polarity is involved, as we have seen, in many axes other than the major one of the plant body and is evident in many developmental patterns. It may be that the mechanisms which are effective in the extreme and conspicuous cases of unequal and polar cell division may also be involved in all differential divisions (Bünning, 1958).

That the cytoplasm contributes to the determination of developmental processes through inheritance is clear from a number of facts, particularly in cases where the offspring of reciprocal crosses are unlike. Where the offspring tends to resemble the maternal parent this difference is evidently due to that which only this parent contributes to it, the cytoplasm. In traits where plastid differences are involved the influence of the cytoplasm is clear, since the plastid primordia are carried in it. In other cases it is more difficult to see what the mechanism of transmission is.

Crosses in *Epilobium*, where reciprocal hybrids are often markedly different in size, have been studied intensively. Lehmann (1936) showed that in such cases the smaller hybrids have a lower concentration of auxin than the larger ones. When Schlenker and Mittmann (1936) applied auxin to the smaller plants their size was considerably increased. These facts suggest that something carried in the cytoplasm stimulates the synthesis of auxin. It may be, as has sometimes been suggested, that sensitivity to auxin is determined by the genes but that auxin synthesis is carried on in the cytoplasm. Michaelis (1938) disagrees with Lehmann and believes that the facts can be explained by specific interactions between genes and cytoplasm. This *Epilobium* work, however, and the great body of evidence obtained by von Wettstein (1924) and his colleagues in experiments with mosses show that the genes are not independent in their effects but that what they do is determined to a considerable degree by the cytoplasm with which they are associated. Whether the specificity of the cytoplasm results from self-perpetuating bodies such as the often postulated plasmagenes or from persisting effects of genes on the cytoplasm (Mather, 1948) has not been determined. This question is primarily of genetic rather than of morphogenetic importance.

When a knowledge of the cytoplasm is more complete, that part of the cell, somewhat neglected by genetic investigations in the past, will doubtless contribute much more significantly to our understanding of development and differentiation. What has been called *protoplasmatic plant anatomy* is concerned with some of these problems. Its contributions have been summarized by Reuter (1955).

CHROMOSOMES

The control of development and form lies chiefly with the genes and their reaction to the environment, but it must also be recognized that differences in the number and character of the chromosomes, apart from the genes they contain, may be of considerable morphogenetic significance.

Polyploidy. Most plants in the sporophyte generation are diploid, the cells containing two sets of chromosomes, one coming from the male parent and one from the female, each chromosome belonging to a pair of homologous ones. In some plants, however, the number of sets has been multiplied so that every chromosome is represented by more than two homologs. Such plants are *polyploids*. There are many cases where the number of sets is doubled, to form tetraploids. Hexaploids, octoploids, and many other polyploid types are known, though polyploidy cannot be increased indefinitely throughout the plant because of loss of vigor in higher members of the series. Individual cells, however, or groups of cells may become very highly polyploid.

Polyploids are often found in nature, many species belonging to so-called polyploid series where each species has a particular multiple of a basic number of chromosomes.

Various ways of producing tetraploids artificially are known, and many polyploids used in experimental work have arisen in this way. One effective means is treatment with colchicine or certain other chemicals which check mitosis after chromosome division but before the new nuclear membrane is formed, so that the two daughter cells have the double chromosome number. Colchicine may be applied to seeds or to the whole plant. Growth after the latter treatment, as compared with normal development, has been described for cranberry by Dermen (1944). Many large cells in normal plants are polyploid, and a bud developing in such a tissue will be a tetraploid or higher (Jorgensen, 1928). In mosses and ferns gametophytes may be regenerated from diploid tissue under favorable conditions (p. 234) and are thus diploid in character. From them tetraploid sporophytes may arise. Haploid sporophytes in higher plants have been produced by various chemical and physical treatments and sometimes occur in twin seedlings (Christensen and Bamford, 1943). These cases prove that the differentiation into sporophyte and gametophyte does not result simply from difference in chromosome number.

The primary effect of a multiplication of chromosome number is an increase in the volume of the nucleus and the cell. Most other distinctive traits of polyploids follow from this one. The relationship between number of chromosome sets and cell size is not always a simple proportionality, however. A study of such a series as that in *Datura stramonium* (Sinnott, Houghtaling, and Blakeslee, 1934), for example, where $1n$, $2n$, $3n$, and $4n$ plants can be compared directly, shows that the increase in cell size is different in different tissues. In epidermal cells it is not far from $1:2:4:8$. In xylem cells the increase is a little greater, but in the parenchymatous cells of the fundamental tissue in the petiole, the tetraploid is usually much more than eight times the diploid.

In such cases, each added chromosome complement does not simply add an amount proportional to the increase in chromosome number but multiplies cell size by a certain amount. In other words, the addition is geometric rather than arithmetic. This is evident to some degree in the pedicel cells of *Datura* but particularly in the large ones of the petiole. It is well seen in mosses, where von Wettstein (1924) produced diploid gametophytes by regeneration of protonemata from sporophyte ($2n$) tissue so that haploid and diploid gametophytes could be directly compared. When this was done, Tobler (1931) found that the increase in cell size of diploid over haploid was different for different races and that in crosses between them it was a character which seemed to segregate. The effect of polyploidy may be different in related species (H. H. Smith, 1943).

In some polyploid series, like that reported by Harriet E. Smith (1946) for races of *Sedum pulchellum* with two, four, and six chromosome sets, cell size increased with number of sets. In many cases, however, members of such a polyploid series in nature do not differ appreciably in cell size. An observation of von Wettstein's (1938) may indicate the reason for this. He grew a diploid race of *Bryum*, which he named *Bryum corrensii*, from a regenerated diploid protonema. It had large leaves and cells about twice the haploid size and was quite sterile. Under vegetative propagation its size gradually became reduced until after 11 years it had returned to a practically normal condition as to leaf and cell size and fertility, although its chromosome number was still diploid. This suggests that regulation to a physiologically optimum cell size had taken place. In polyploid series in the higher plants it may be that regulation, through natural selection or otherwise, has produced an optimum cell size even with widely different numbers of chromosomes. In polyploid series of recent origin, however, such as those produced by colchi-

FIG. 19-9. Flower of diploid (left) and tetraploid (right) in *Antirrhinum majus*. (*Courtesy W. Atlee Burpee Co.*)

cine, there is almost always a close relationship between chromosome number and cell size.

The increased cell size of polyploids may be reflected in larger plant size (Fig. 19-9). *Oenothera gigas,* which proved to be a tetraploid, was named for its size, and "gigas" tetraploids of many species are now known. Frequently, however, the tetraploid plant is little larger than the diploid, and it may even be smaller. It usually has stouter stems and thicker leaves, and its flowers are larger. Haploid plants are universally smaller than diploid ones. Triploids may be intermediate between tetraploids and diploids but are often indistinguishable from the latter.

Genetic differences may sometimes determine the effect of polyploidy on plant size. Flax (*Linum usitatissimum*) has been selected commercially in two directions, toward the production of linseed oil and of flax fiber. Pandey (1956) compared the tetraploid with the diploid forms of both types of plants in this species and found that in the linseed type the 4n is a gigas form whereas in the flax type it is actually smaller than the 2n. The linseed tetraploid grows faster than its diploid but the flax tetraploid grows more slowly. The two tetraploids also show certain morphological differences.

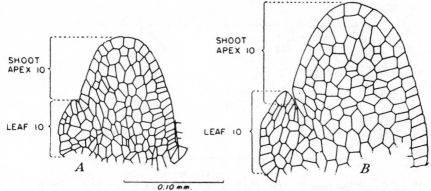

Fig. 19-10. Shoot apex and leaf primordium in *Zea mays*. Left, diploid; right, tetraploid. Difference in size is due entirely to larger cells of the tetraploid. (*From Randolph, Abbe, and Einset.*)

The origin of size differences in members of a polyploid series has been studied developmentally in a few cases. The apical meristem of the tetraploid is always broader than that of the diploid. Sometimes it is relatively flat, as in *Vinca rosea* (Cross and Johnson, 1941), or it may be the same shape as the diploid but doubled in size, as in maize (Randolph, Abbe, and Einset, 1944; Fig. 19-10). In the development of the cucurbit fruit, Sinnott and Franklin (1943) found that the ovary, from primordium to the time of flowering, was almost twice the volume in 4n as in 2n and thus was proportional to the volume of its cells (Fig. 19-11). In these plants, growth of the ovary into the fruit is chiefly by cell expansion. This second phase of growth is much less extensive in 4n than in 2n, so that the mature fruit is almost the same size in both, as are the cells of which it is composed. In these cases the flower is "gigas" but the fruit is not.

Members of a polyploid series often differ in other respects than size. There is a general tendency in tetraploids for organs to be relatively shorter and wider than in diploids. This difference is well shown in the series of capsules in *Datura* from 1*n* to 4*n* (Blakeslee, 1934). The haploid has a slender capsule and becomes progressively flatter in the upper members of the series. Fruits of tetraploid cucurbits produced by colchicine were in every case changed toward a flatter, or at least a less elongate, form. The leaves of tetraploid varieties of most plants show the same shape changes in comparison with the diploid. Straub (1940) observed that flower size changes in the same way, flowers from higher members of a polyploid series being relatively wider. In *Torenia* the position of the anthers with reference to the corolla is changed in the octaploid.

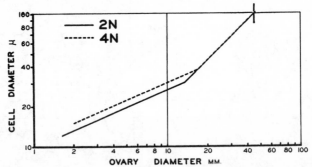

Fig. 19-11. Graph showing general relations between cell size and ovary size in developing fruits of diploid and tetraploid cucurbits. In early stages the 4N is larger in both respects but after flowering the growth of the 2N is greater and at fruit maturity (vertical bar) the two are essentially alike. (*From Sinnott and Franklin.*)

This shape difference probably originates at the meristem itself. Cross and Johnson found that in *Vinca rosea* the tetraploid apex was considerably wider but no deeper and that the increase in size of its component cells was also chiefly in width. Rüdiger (1952) has shown that in various plants the cells of the tetraploid are somewhat shorter and wider than those of the diploid. Organ shape may thus be a reflection of cell shape, though in other cases cell shape seems not to be markedly different in 4*n* and 2*n*. Why there should be such a shape difference, either in cell or organ, is not clear. Cell size alone is not enough to account for it, for there are large-celled races which do not differ in shape from small-celled ones of the same species.

Certain more general biological facts are related to polyploidy. Stebbins (1938), for example, has studied polyploidy in a large number of woody and herbaceous genera and finds that polyploid series are more abundant in perennial herbs than in annuals or woody plants (Fig. 19-12). The basic chromosome numbers, however, are significantly higher in woody genera.

Much work on polyploidy has been done by students of ecology and plant distribution (Müntzing, 1936), though most of this has little direct concern with morphogenesis. In general, polyploids can endure extremes of climate better than diploids. The distribution of polyploids as to latitude has been discussed and the literature reviewed by Löve and Löve (1949).

Polyploids are of importance for evolution not only in matters of selection and distribution but from the fact that by their means sterile hybrids can become fertile and genetic lines, separated by incom-

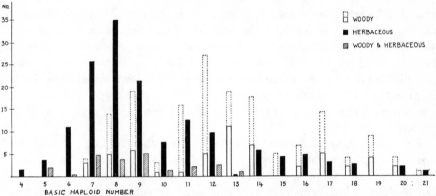

Fig. 19-12. Distribution of basic chromosome numbers in herbaceous and woody genera of dicotyledons. Dotted lines indicate genera known only tentatively. Herbaceous types tend to have smaller numbers. (*From Stebbins.*)

patibilities, thus be brought together. Many species will hybridize but the offspring are usually sterile. If their chromosome number is doubled (to form an allopolyploid), as sometimes happens in nature, fertility is restored since there are now pairs of homologous chromosomes and normal meiosis can take place.

Somatic Polyploidy (Polysomaty). Polyploidy is concerned with an important aspect of differentiation, for investigation has shown that many somatic cells, particularly the larger or physiologically more active ones, are polyploid and often to a rather high degree. This condition is termed *polysomaty*. In some cases, such as the meristematic region of the root of spinach (Gentcheff and Gustafsson, 1939; Berger, 1941), chromosomes of certain of the dividing cells, particularly in the periblem, are twice, or sometimes four times, the normal diploid number. This seems to be the result of an additional doubling in the prophase before the mitotic figure is formed. Polysomaty of this type has been reported in other cases, as in *Cucumis* (Ervin, 1941).

In many instances it has been shown that a process of *endomitosis* takes place in certain cells by which the chromosome number is doubled (or further multiplied) even though the cell is mature, the nuclear membrane intact, and no mitotic figure has been formed (Geitler, 1949). That this doubling has taken place is indicated by the fact that the number of visible chromocenters, presumably corresponding to the chromosomes, is doubled. The chromosome number may be definitely determined by inducing these cells to go into typical mitosis, either through wounding or by application of growth substances. Under such conditions the chromosomes can readily be counted. Grafl (1939) was thus able to prove that among mature and normally differentiated cells of *Sauromatum guttatum* some were tetraploid, some octaploid, and some 16-ploid. This situation has now been found in many other cases. D'Amato (1950), by the use of 2,4-D, observed it in roots of a number of monocotyledons, and Holzer (1952), by treatment with indoleacetic acid, in the roots of 27 species of angiosperms. Holzer found that the distribution of these polyploid cells was not at random but formed a pattern which was similar in groups of related plants. Often it is not the number of chromosomes (or chromosome centers) that increases but the number of strands per chromosome.

The connection between polyploidy and the volume of cell and nucleus has important morphogenetic implications. In certain animal tissues, among them the cells of the developing salivary glands of *Drosophila*, it has been observed that nuclear volume falls into definite classes, each approximately twice the volume of the one next below it. Such "rhythmic" distribution was observed in plants by Monschau (1930). The relation between polysomaty and nuclear volume has now become well established (Bradley, 1954, and others). This makes it possible to determine with some accuracy the degree of polyploidy in a mature and differentiated cell by measuring the volume of its nucleus or even of the cell itself, in comparison with related cells and ultimately with those in which the chromosome number can be determined directly. Thus in various angiosperm species, Tschermak-Woess and Hasitschka (1953a) have estimated the degree of polyploidy of certain cells in a tissue as various multiples of the basic number, up to 256-ploid (Fig. 19-13). Somatic polyploidy, as estimated either by direct count or by nuclear size, commonly increases with distance from the apical meristem (Fig. 19-14) and with age (Fig. 19-15).

All this obviously has a very important bearing on the problem of differentiation. Wipf and Cooper (1940) for example, found a close relation between the presence of naturally occurring tetraploid cells and the

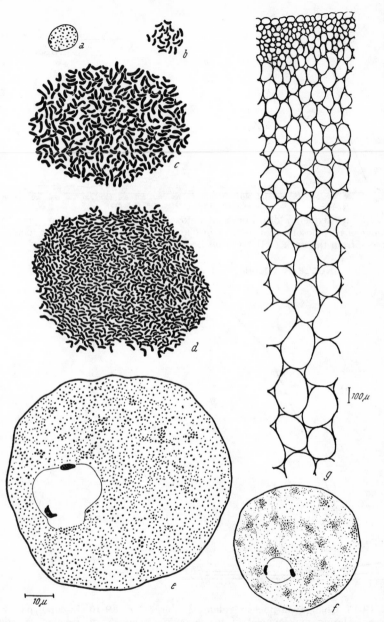

Fig. 19-13. *Cereus spachianus.* Cells showing increasing chromosome numbers during development. *a* and *b*, 2n; *c*, 32n; *d*, 64n; *e*, highly polyploid resting nucleus from an older portion of the cortex; *f*, young polyploid resting nucleus with chromocenters, 2 to 3 mm. behind the shoot apex; *g*, a part of the differentiated cortex showing marked differences in cell size, presumably because of somatic polyploidy. (*From Fenzl and Tschermak-Woess.*)

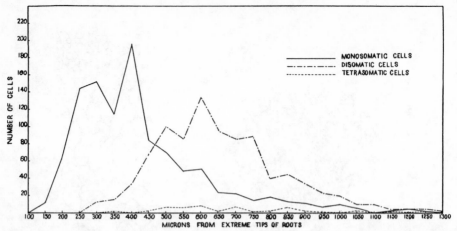

FIG. 19-14. Frequency distribution of mitoses with one, two, or four times the basic number of chromosomes, in the root of *Cucumis*. Chromosome number increases with distance from the apex (left.) (*From Ervin.*)

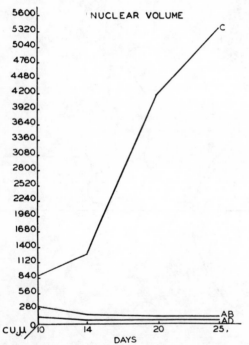

FIG. 19-15. Changes in nuclear volume (cubic microns) during development of maize endosperm. C, central region. AB and AD, surface layers. Nuclear growth here is due to endomitosis, with increase in number and size of strands per chromosome. Number of chromosomes presumably does not increase. (*From Duncan and Ross.*)

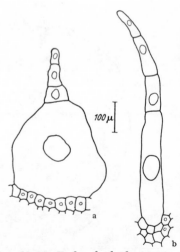

FIG. 19-16. Endopolyploidy in trichomes of *Bryonia*. a, glandular hair with basal cell 256-ploid; b, hair of filament, the basal cell 128-ploid, and others 16-ploid. The epidermis is diploid. (*From Tschermak-Woess and Hasitschka.*)

444

origin of root nodules in legumes. Von Witsch and Flügel (1952) found that meristematic tissue of *Kalanchoe Blossfeldiana* was diploid but that as the leaves differentiated the mesophyll became polyploid, as could be shown by wounding and observing mitoses in the wound callus. Incidentally, the mesophyll was only 8-ploid if the leaf had developed under long days but 32-ploid under short-day conditions. Steffen (1956) estimated from nuclear volume that chalazal haustoria in *Pedicularis* were 96-ploid and micropylar ones 384-ploid. An illuminating study of endomitotic polyploidy in the differentiation of the trichomes of angiosperms has been made by Tschermak-Woess and Hasitschka (1954; Fig. 19-16).

Somatic polyploidy has now been shown to be so frequent as to make it probable that much of the differentiation of plant cells, so far as cell size is concerned, is related to it, cell size being roughly proportional to the degree of polyploidy. Exceptions have been found to this relationship, and no firm generalization about it can yet be made. Obviously, too, there is much more to differentiation than change in size. However, the possibility certainly exists of learning much about the mechanism of cellular differentiation and of developing what has been called "karyological plant anatomy," a subject outlined in some detail by Tschermak-Woess (1956). D'Amato (1952) has also reviewed the field of polyploidy in differentiation, and Geitler's book (1953) discusses endomitosis more fully.

Other Effects of Chromosome Differences. There is sometimes a relation between cell size and total chromosome bulk. In 13 species of *Crepis* differing in number and length of chromosomes Navashin (1931) measured total chromosome length at a comparable stage of mitosis, using this as an indication of chromatin mass. In each species he plotted this against the volume of comparable cells in the root meristem and found a close correlation between the two, suggesting that the total bulk of chromosome material affects the size of the cell (Fig. 19-17). In some cases, notably in mutants of *Primula* and *Phragmites* (p. 35), both chromosomes and cells are markedly larger than normal, and this is also reflected in the size of the plant itself. Neither of these types is polyploid. In some plants there are "accessory" chromosomes which seem to have little or no genetic effect, but Müntzing and Akdik (1948) find that their presence causes an increase in the size of stomatal cells.

The influence of extra chromosomes was studied in *Crepis tectorum* by Schkwarnikow (1934). This species has four pairs of chromosomes called A, B, C, and D, and four races were available in each of which one of these chromosomes was represented by three instead of two members. Plants in which B or C was present as a trisome had cells larger than the normal diploid. Those in which A or D were the extra ones, however, had smaller cells than normal. Here evidently something more than bulk

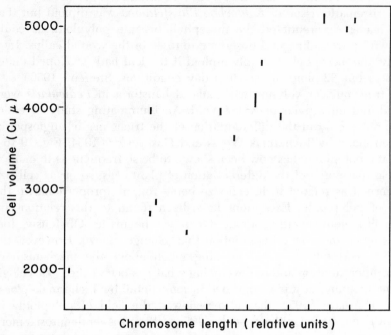

FIG. 19-17. Correlation between average cell volume (of dermatogen cells in root tip) and average total chromosome length (chromatin mass) in 13 species of *Crepis*. The length of bar for each species indicates the probable error for that determination. (*Redrawn from Navashin.*)

of chromosomes was concerned with cell size. This presumably was determined by the genes the chromosomes carried (Table 19-1).

Table 19-1. Average Cross-sectional Area (in Square Microns) of Primary Dermatogen Cells in Root of Diploid *Crepis tectorum* and in Four of Its Trisomics [*]

Diploid . . . . 260.0 ± 5.3
Trisomic A . . . . 235.5 ± 3.6
Trisomic B . . . . 282.6 ± 4.0
Trisomic C . . . . 271.0 ± 2.4
Trisomic D . . . . 228.5 ± 5.5

[*] From Schkwarnikow (1934).

A somewhat similar result was found by Sinnott, Houghtaling, and Blakeslee (1934) in the primary chromosome mutants of *Datura stramonium*. This species has 12 pairs of chromosomes, and in each mutant race there are three representatives of one of these chromosomes. The 12 trisomic races differed very considerably from one another, both externally and internally. In some the cells in certain tissues were larger and in some smaller than in the diploid. Such traits as the size of the bundles, the amount of internal phloem, and the development of pericycle fibers differed among the mutants. It is significant that for each trait the diploid was approximately the *average* of the 12 mutants, a good

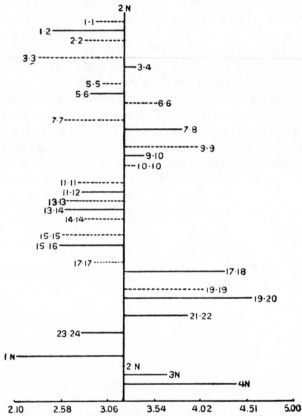

FIG. 19-18. Genic balance in *Datura stramonium*. Cross-sectional area of flower stalk in various chromosomal types (in square millimeters). Vertical line marks normal value for the diploid. Areas larger or smaller than this are shown by the lengths of the horizontal lines for each type. 1N, 3N, and 4N are below. Above, the primary mutants have solid lines, the secondaries dotted ones. Each chromosome is numbered by its two ends, the primaries being 1.2, 3.4, etc., and the secondaries 2.2, 3.3, etc. The geometrical mean of the primaries is almost exactly the value for the diploid. (*From Sinnott, Houghtaling, and Blakeslee.*)

example of genic balance (Fig. 19-18). Evidently each chromosome contributed something to the character of the plant, and when this chromosome was represented by three instead of two, this contribution was increased. Such a result seems clearly to be due to the genes which the chromosome carries, however, rather than to something specific in the chromosomes as such. It may be that all the effects now attributed to chromosomes may ultimately be found to be due to their genes.

It must regretfully be admitted that not very much of substantial importance has yet been contributed by genetic analysis to a solution of the problems of morphogenesis. Its most significant addition to our knowledge of development thus far is perhaps the discovery of the relation between the size of a cell and the degree of its internal polyploidy, with the bearing this fact has on the control of histological differentiation. Behind the other problems of morphogenesis still lurks the unanswered question of how genes control the development of form and structure and thus the orderly and integrated growth of an individual as an *organism*. Environmental factors have an important influence on the character of this organism, but the organizing process itself seems to be centered in protoplasm and thus to be under the control of the directive and self-multiplying elements in protoplasm, the genes. It is to this general problem of organization that attention in our final chapter is directed.

CHAPTER 20

Organization

Underlying the various phenomena of morphogenesis that have here been discussed stands a single basic problem: how a mass of living stuff is organized into a system, so well termed an organism. Organization is evident in various ways but most vividly in the development of *form* in living things. Form is not simply a trait to be described and classified. It is also the visible expression of a self-regulatory equilibrium which tends to be attained in development, maintained during life, and restored when disturbed. Every individual has a specific equilibrium of this sort, a morphogenetic norm, so to speak, to which it tends to conform. This is the unifying factor that gives continuity to an organism. It is a pattern for development in which every part, in its growth and activity, is related to all the others and by which the fate of each is determined by its position in the organized whole.

The manifestations of a given norm are various. It is not constant in expression but may change, in a precise and regular fashion, from embryo to maturity. It may produce very different results under different environmental conditions. Its basis is established in the genetic constitution of the individual. The nature of this norm, how it is modified in expression by factors inside and outside the organism, and how development is regulated in conformity to it are the basic questions with which the science of morphogenesis must deal.

To attack this problem hopefully one should break it down, if possible, into simpler components. These have already been discussed in earlier pages, but it will be useful here to bring them briefly together into focus on the main problem.

One of these components is *polarity*. All plants, at least at certain stages, are organized around an axis which provides a basis along which development takes place and in relation to which the lateral organs are formed. The two poles of this axis (save in rare cases) are unlike. The axis may be vertical or horizontal, and if lateral axes arise from it, these often have specific orientations, so that the plant body is really a pattern of polarities. In many cases transverse as well as longitudinal ones may be seen. Polarity is manifest in physiological activities as well as in structure.

The universal presence of polar phenomena in plants suggests that there is in living stuff an innate tendency toward polarization, although most eggs and undifferentiated cells at first are unpolarized. This provides a concrete point of attack on developmental problems. The suggestion is obvious that organic polarities may be related to those evident in the inorganic world, and especially to chemical and electrical ones, but this has proved somewhat difficult to establish experimentally. Polarity has been shown in some cases to be modified by specific factors in the environment.

Not only are the two ends of the polar axis unlike but other differences appear in graded series backward from each apex. These *gradients* are evident in the rate of various metabolic processes and in the form and structure of lateral organs arising successively at the growing point. Here is a simple place to study the origin of differentiation. One school of biologists regards these axial gradients as the most important factors in development.

The polar axis is not only a gradient axis but an axis of *symmetry*. Indeed, the symmetrical arrangement of parts around it is a conspicuous aspect of axiation. Organic symmetry, an expression of the basic regularity in the arrangement of plant structures, is manifest at every level from the internal structure of a cell to the configuration of a tree. It is obviously an important element in the orderly formativeness that living organisms display.

Radial symmetry—the regular spiral distribution of lateral structures around an axis—is best displayed in vertical plant axes where the stimuli of gravity and light affect all sides of the axis almost equally. Under these conditions, the symmetrical arrangement of the lateral organs seems to be traceable to an inherent *spirality* in living stuff itself. This has as yet received little experimental study, but its widespread occurrence in phyllotaxy, the spiral grain of wood, the spiral character of the cell wall and of protoplasmic streaming, and the spiral movements of the plant body suggest that spirality is another basic fact in organization.

Spirality is masked to a considerable extent in those axes which are horizontal and thus exposed differentially to gravity and light, but the dorsiventral symmetry of these structures provides good material for a study of the interaction of polarity, spirality, and environmental factors in the development of plant form.

We may therefore recognize several components in the general phenomenon of plant organization: polarity, differential gradients, symmetry, and spirality. These seem to be distinct characteristics and may have different bases in protoplasm. They certainly can be investigated separately.

All of them, or their rudiments, seem to be present in all plants. They provide the basic ingredients, so to speak, out of which the developmental norm is produced. Just what a specific norm will be depends on the interaction between these inherent protoplasmic traits and two other factors: the genetic constitution of the individual and the environment in which it develops.

The genetic constitution is the complement of genes in the organism. These act on the protoplasmic traits just mentioned to produce the form characteristic of that organism. This form, however, is not a specific pattern of polarities, gradients, spiralities, and symmetries but results from a specific reaction to a specific environment. Neither genes nor environment alone determines what an organism is, for their action is complementary and one cannot be separated from the other. In practical experimental work, however, much can be learned by studying the effects of different genotypes under the same environment or of the same genotype in different environments. The latter method has so far been much more fruitful, as is shown by the vast literature in the fields of the morphogenetic effects of light, water, temperature, mechanical factors, and various chemical substances. There is still opportunity for much fruitful work in all these fields. A study of gene action, on the other hand, although actively pursued, has thus far been concerned chiefly with the effects of genes on metabolic processes or on the synthesis of specific substances. How genes control developmental *relationships*, and thus the production of organic form, is almost unexplored territory.

In a given individual, therefore, through the interaction of its genotype and the particular environment in which it lives, both acting on the basic tendencies toward polarization, gradients, symmetry, and spirality, there is at any given stage of its development a norm to which it conforms. This involves more than a mere interaction between organism and environment. What emerges from the developmental process is an organized *system* in which the various parts are related and mutually interdependent and which controls its own development by a process of self-regulation. This is to be seen most clearly in the familiar phenomena of growth. A plant or animal exists in an environment of which the chemical constituents (atoms, molecules, or larger particles) are a heterogeneous mass and dispersed at random. When these particles are drawn into the organism they lose this randomness and each now comes to occupy a particular place in the living system. By some means this orderly disposition of new material into an organized whole is controlled. When death ensues, the control disappears and the dispersive tendencies of lifeless matter break down the system. This system is specific and is different in every individual. The mass of data now accumulated from studies of regeneration suggests that all the cells, at least at their beginnings, are totipotent and that the basis for the norm of the organism is present in the living stuff of every cell.

The omnipresence of the developmental norm is suggested by that quality in development termed by Driesch *equifinality*, the attainment of the same developmental goal in very different ways. There is no *single* or linear progression of steps by which a structure is formed, but the organism may shift its course of development according to circumstances. This is much more difficult to explain than is a linear step-by-step series of changes, each a precursor of the next. A regulatory mechanism of some sort must be involved. What gives unity to the individual is not so much its unchanging genetic constitution, important as this is, but rather this developmental norm, immanent in the organism from the first and often reached over different routes.

It should be emphasized that what is involved here is not inherent adaptability by which an organism naturally reacts in a favorable way to environmental changes, for a given norm may hinder survival. The "lazy" mutation in maize, for example, which causes the plant to grow flat on the ground, would not persist in nature. Most normative reactions of plants evident today tend to be favorable since they are the ones that have survived in the winnowing process of natural selection, but the fact of normativeness has no relation to adaptability.

The self-regulatory character of living things has often been observed and discussed. In bodily activities it is the basis of the homeostatic reactions so evident in physiology. Its most conspicuous manifestations, however, are structural and are seen in those cases where a portion of an organism is experimentally isolated from the rest and then proceeds to restore its missing parts so that a single whole is produced. Each of the first two cells from a *Fucus* egg, or the first two blastomeres in a frog embryo, if isolated, will develop not into half an organism but into a whole one. Single cells from the epidermis of a plant, under appropriate conditions, will develop into whole individuals. Cuttings restore lost roots. Missing shoots are replaced by others. Severed vascular strands are united by the growth of connecting bundles. The literature of plant regeneration is full of such examples. Many of these were brought together by Ungerer (1926), but botanists have in general been less concerned with this problem than have zoologists. Regeneration is such a dramatic fact that many attempts have been made to account for it. Actually, however, regenerative development is no more and no less difficult to explain than normal development. The real problem is not regeneration but self-regulatory, normative development.

Many suggestions have been made to explain this central enigma of morphogenesis, but it must be admitted that none has yet been proposed which is generally acceptable. The problem is enormously difficult and doubtless cannot be solved by any simple or single hypothesis. It is essentially one of synthesis, in which evidence from many sources must be coordinated. For discussions of it the reader is referred to the publications of Agar (1951), von Bertalanffy (1952), Child (1941), Driesch (1937), Holmes (1948), Lillie (1945), Meyer (1935), Needham (1936), Reinke (1922), E. S. Russell (1933), Smuts (1926), Troll (1928), Ungerer (1926), Wardlaw (1955c), Weiss (1950), Whyte (1954), and Woodger (1929). Woodger's discussion of the concept of organism (1930, 1931) is particularly useful.

The position that a biologist assumes toward this problem will usually be determined more by his attitudes and predilections than by the conflicting and inconclusive evidence that is now available. To those who assume that all organic traits must have been produced by natural selection, both normal and regenerative development will be regarded as the result of a long-continued selective process. Holmes (1948) and others have supported this view, and it is probably held by a majority of biologists who have considered the matter. Aside from the general presumption in its favor, there is some positive evidence for this position in the fact that organized, regulatory development is not invariable but sometimes breaks down. There are many examples of this in the various types of abnormal growth. Sometimes, as in teratological structures, only the last developmental stages become confused and irregular, but when the breakdown is more complete, tumors, galls, and other amorphous structures are produced. Finally, in tissue culture, all traces of multicellular organization seem to have vanished. There evidently are various levels of organization, and it is reasonable to suggest that the more complex ones have gradually evolved from the simpler because of the presumptive advantages that a highly organized system has.

There are some difficulties with this hypothesis, however. In the breakdown of visible regulation the organizing capacity itself has not been lost, for such abnormal structures as fasciations may revert to normal growth again, and in amorphous galls and tissue cultures growing points may appear which develop into typical plants. Single cells from a tissue culture may produce normal organisms. There is no necessary connection between the genetic constitution of the individual (which is what is presumably modified by natural selection·) and the appearance, or lack of it, of a visible state of organization. Furthermore, it must be remembered that even where gross visible organization has broken down, the living cells themselves are small organized systems with a complex though often submicroscopic structure and with a very considerable degree of physiological self-regulation. Indeed, if all organization disappears, death ensues. Organization seems to be a fundamental quality of living things, explain it in whatever way we can, rather than a simple trait comparable to those upon which natural selection is effective. One cannot discount the possibility, of course, that in the very beginning this regulatory normativeness may have arisen by a selective process and later became established as a general characteristic of all life.

An essential aspect of organization and of the organic forms that result from it is that these involve much more than a series of successive chemical steps, for form is concerned with *relationships*. In an earlier chapter evidence has been presented that relationships, and thus form, are genetically determined, but how genes act to produce this trait is far from clear. An organized system is a complex pattern of such relationships and one that is not static but changes during development and restores itself if altered. Whatever its origin, the problem still remains as to how, in terms of protoplasmic activity, such a self-regulating, patterned system is produced.

One of the simplest explanations is that proposed by Child (1941) and others who point out that an organized system does not develop unless a polar axis is first established in originally homogeneous material by the influence of an environment that differs on the two sides and that a gradient arises along this axis. The essential importance, at least at the beginning of development, of an asymmetric environment must not be forgotten, an environment which, so to speak, "lines up" the undifferentiated egg or mass of tissue in one direction and so orients it that it can then organize its developmental pattern in an orderly fashion. Gravity and unilateral light are the commonest asymmetric environmental factors for plants. They make one side of the structure different from the other and thus begin the continuing process of differentiation. Plants grown where these factors are uniform on all sides are usually amorphous (p. 137). The interaction between the polar gradient and the genes of the organism is an important factor in producing a specific form. For some biologists this explanation is sufficient to account for organic form, but it does not give a clear picture of how such interaction works nor does it explain the complex correlations that occur during development.

Among other suggested explanations one of the most promising is the concept of a biological "field" in conformity to which development takes place. Gurwitsch (1923) assumes such a field to be present around a developing organic structure, but this is difficult to describe in physical terms. In Gurwitsch's hands it acquires an almost mystical character and seems to resemble nothing so much as an astral body immanent in and around the growing organism. Where such a beautifully precise structure as a fungus fruiting body molds itself out of a complex and intertwining tangle of sliding hyphae, or where from a throng of individual myxamoebae a specifically fashioned sorocarp develops through their interaction, we must assume that in the mass of living stuff there is a formative factor of some sort, but it should be possible to describe this in more precise terms than does Gurwitsch.

Fields of various sorts have often been postulated in animal development, but in a somewhat more descriptive sense, as the developmental influence of a given region over structures in it. If the rudiment of a young and growing amphibian tail, for example, is transplanted at an early age into the region of a leg it will grow into a leg since it is now in a leg field. If it is somewhat older before transplanting it will become a tail, since its own tail field is now operative. This conception of a morphogenetic field recognizes the formative influence acting within a given region or throughout the embryo but offers little explanation of this action. Fields have been discussed by Weiss (1950), Raven (1943), and many other experimental embryologists. In botanical morphogenesis the field concept has been employed by the Snows and Wardlaw to account for the localized development of lateral structures at the apical meristem.

More specific is the suggestion of Burr and others (1932) that the morphogenetic field is a bioelectric one. Burr has found that around a developing structure, such as a fertilized egg in animals or a developing ovary primordium in plants, a micropotentiometer will reveal an orderly pattern of potential differences that is a correlate of the form which will develop from them. Burr and Northrop (1935) support the view that the primary entities in nature are fields and not particles and that the former determine the activities of the latter instead of the other way around. Both physical and biological phenomena certainly are electrical in their ultimate nature, but Burr's theory goes much further than that in assuming the organized biological pattern, manifest to our eyes, to be the visible expression of an underlying bioelectrical pattern. The origin of such a pattern and what determines the changes in it are yet unknown.

One of the difficulties in accounting for an organic pattern is to see how it can arise in a semifluid and formless protoplasmic system. How, one asks, can such a flowing and unstable material as protoplasm produce the very specific forms which come out of it? It is obvious that protoplasm, homogeneous though it seems to be, must have a structure of some sort. The electron microscope is beginning to show what this structure, at the macromolecular level, actually is (Weiss, 1956; Frey-Wyssling, 1953). The organized pattern which we see emerging from living stuff seems to be rooted in these submicroscopic configurations of molecules. The developmental norm or pattern must in some way be prefigured in the specific constitution of an organism's protoplasm. The possibility that there may be a persisting pattern in the cytoplasm is suggested by the work of Tartar (1956) on the ciliate protozoan *Stentor*, where such a pattern is passed from one generation to the next in the ectoplasmic striping, which is divided between the daughter cells. Tartar concludes that "it is possible that the complex activities of the cyto-architecture of stentor may forecast an appreciation that some homologous cytoplasmic pattern is common to all cells and is as important in its way as the chromosomal nucleus which also has its orderly arrangements."

How such configurations originate is not clear, but some biologists, among them Needham (1936), look for suggestions to the paracrystalline state of matter ("liquid crystals"). The molecular solutes in most solutions are distributed at random but in some it can be shown that these dissolved particles are arranged in a very regular fashion. This may determine such cellular events as differential growth and plane of division and thus provide a basis for organic orderliness.

A number of workers, among them Baitsell (1940), have gone still further and endeavor to translate molecular pattern into cellular pattern. The molecule is a specific and organized structure. Perhaps, so goes the argument, the forces that pull the atoms together into the orderly configuration shown by a large and complex protein molecule, for example, are of the same nature as those that bind together a vast number of such molecules into the system which is a living cell, the unitary structure of all organisms. On such a hypothesis the cell is to be looked upon as an enormous molecule. If this concept is carried one step further, the whole organism might be regarded as a single molecule and integrated by the same forces that organize simpler ones.

A promising hypothesis has come from Turing (1952), who suggests that a homogeneous system of substances which react on each other and are diffusing through a tissue may become unstable because of random disturbances in it and may thus produce a pattern. Turing analyzes a hypothetical example mathematically and shows that six different forms may result from a simple "diffusion-reaction" system of this sort. He seeks a mechanism by which genes determine structure and suggests that well-known physical laws, with their mathematical implications for development, are enough to account for many of the phenomena of organic form. Wardlaw (1953a, 1955c) has written a constructive discussion of Turing's rather involved theory and its applications to morphogenetic problems in plants.

Rashevsky in a series of papers (1944, 1955, 1958, and others) has approached the problems of biology from a physical and especially a mathematical point of view and in particular has endeavored to interpret biological processes in terms of position and relation.

The problems of growth and form have been discussed by Sir D'Arcy Thompson in his classic volume by that name (1942) already mentioned frequently in this book. He marshals evidence from physics, chemistry, and mathematics in considering such diverse questions of botanical interest as growth, surface-volume relations, size and form, phyllotaxy, cell shape, least-surface configurations, growing points, spiral growth, and the theory of transformations in biology. Perhaps his most important contribution is what seems a very simple one: the demonstration that, if a given organic form is inscribed in a series of rectangular coordinates, endless modifications of it may be derived by deforming these coordinates in various ways. This method is particularly useful in evolutionary studies by showing the progressive changes by which a structure has been modified. Its significance for development is also important in the demonstration that change of form is not a localized and particulate process but that a given form is an integrated pattern and changes as a whole, so that alterations in one region affect many others. This method of analysis somewhat resembles that of allometry in expressing relationships mathematically. If allometry could be extended to three dimensions, as Richards and Kavanagh suggest (1943), it could be used to make a more precise statement of developmental relations than D'Arcy Thompson has done. By these means the changes in a growing organic form may be described graphically and expressed in mathematical terms, surely an important advance; but they provide no clue as to what the protoplasmic basis of such a form may be.

In this impasse we grope for clues wherever they may be found. The science of cybernetics, for example, points to the resemblance between the giant electronic calculators, with their "feedback" mechanisms, and the nervous system, in which the brain is continually receiving reports from the peripheral organs and sending back messages to them. There well may be more than a curious resemblance between these complex machines and a living organism, and in seeking to understand biological organization we should not neglect the feedback principle. The fact that there is no differentiated nervous system in plants need not mean that this principle is not operative in them, for in plants the functions of the nervous system seem to be performed by unspecialized protoplasm.

From other sources which at first seem very unlikely to offer any help in this problem, clues may come. Information theory, with its systems of coding, which has been found useful in so many fields, may not be without significance for problems of development. In living stuff itself there may perhaps be "coded," so to speak, a mass of data on which the developing organism may draw and which may even be the basis of the morphogenetic norm that has here been discussed.

Since organization exists at other levels than the living organism, suggestions as to the mechanism for it there may come from simpler types of systems. In Whitehead's philosophy, the concept of organism holds a key position, from atoms to man. He has called physics the science which deals with very small organisms (atoms and molecules) and biology the one which deals with much larger ones. We know that the atom, far from being simple, is itself a system with many kinds of particles within it, bound together into a complex whole. Pauli has shown that the basis of this may reside in the fact that two electrons cannot occupy the same orbit and that the orbit of one is related to the orbit of another. This fact may perhaps be regarded as the germ of other organizational relationships higher in the scale.

In an exploration of the problem of organic form the obvious hypothesis, and the simplest one with which to work, is that there are formative *substances*. The quest for these has resulted in a vast deal of useful experimental work on various "organ-forming substances": chemical compounds that make roots or shoots or flowers; calines, organizers, hormones, growth substances, and other chemical bodies that are supposed to produce specific structures directly. All such ideas, if carried far enough, face the serious problem of how it is possible for a substance to become translated into a form. This was the difficulty on which Spemann's "organizer" came to grief. Today it seems much more likely that these various substances, the effects of which undoubtedly result in the production of form changes, act rather as evocators, releasers, or triggers which call forth specific responses by the organized living system.

The problem of organic form seems to be centered in the patterned character of protoplasmic structure rather than in its specific chemical constitution. Here are manifest those basic tendencies mentioned at the beginning of this chapter: polarity, spirality, and symmetry. It will be noted that almost all the suggested explanations of organic formativeness discussed in earlier paragraphs involve physical rather than chemical factors, relationships rather than substantiveness. To be sure, these are ultimately not easy to distinguish from each other; but for the immediate future it seems more likely that morphogenesis will find new, constructive ideas if it explores the many possibilities of biophysics rather than relying as exclusively on those of biochemistry as it tends to do today.

The fact is that we have as yet no idea of what the physical basis of biological organization really is. This problem is closely concerned with the origin and nature of life. Biochemists and biophysicists are beginning to make some shrewd guesses as to how simple organic molecules may have been synthesized in earth's primeval seas and even how such a complex entity as a virus particle was put together. A knowledge of the nucleic acids makes it possible to see how genes multiply. What happens in gene mutation is also fairly well understood. All this has led many to the optimistic belief that we now know how life originated, how it reproduces itself, and how it evolves. An essential trait of every living thing, however—its self-regulatory organization—must still be explained before we claim that we know what life is. This may well involve principles, still undiscovered, which are distinctively biological and different from the presently understood ones of the physical sciences. This is the position taken by men like Delbruck (1949) and Schrödinger (1945). The line between the physical and the biological sciences steadily grows less distinct, but this does not necessarily mean that biology is simply a specialized kind of physics and chemistry. Says Prof. Wald (1958): "If biology ever is 'reduced' to chemistry and physics, it will be only because the latter have grown up to biology. At this point it will be hard to say which is which."

Here the problem touches deeper questions of philosophy which lead us away from purely scientific ideas. That biology, and perhaps especially morphogenesis, is bound to have important philosophical implications cannot be denied, but these questions are beyond the purpose of the present discussion. It is important, however, for a student of the life sciences to remember that back of all the phenomena of genetics, biochemistry, and physiology stands the important fact that a living thing is an *organism*, that there is an interrelationship among its parts, which is manifest in development, and that if this system is disturbed it tends, by a process of self-regulation, to restore itself. The most evident expression of this organization is the form of the organism and its structures. Morphogenesis, the study of the origin of form, thus assumes a central position in the biological sciences.

Bibliography

Abbe, E. C., and B. O. Phinney. 1951a. The growth of the shoot apex in maize: External features. *Amer. Jour. Bot.* 38:737–744.

———, ———, and D. F. Baer. 1951b. The growth of the shoot apex in maize: Internal features. *Amer. Jour. Bot.* 38:744–751.

——— and O. L. Stein. 1954. The growth of the shoot apex in maize: Embryogeny. *Amer. Jour. Bot.* 41:285–293.

Abbe, Lucy B. 1936. The histological background for dwarfism in *Zea mays*. *Proc. Amer. Phil. Soc.* 76:743–747.

Abele, K. 1936. Zur Kenntnis der Zell- und Kernteilung in dem primären Meristem. *Protoplasma* 25:92–114.

Abrams, G. J. von. 1953. Auxin relations of a dwarf pea. *Plant Physiol.* 28:443–456.

Agar, W. E. 1951. *A contribution to the theory of the living organism.* 2d ed. Melbourne University Press. 235 pp.

Aitchison, J. A. 1953. Correlations between oxidase activity and dioecism in phanerogams. *Proc. Iowa Acad. Sci.* 60:74–81.

Akdik, Sara. 1938. Regenerationsversüche an Gametophyten von *Polypodium aureum tetraploideum*. *Rev. Fac. Sci. Univ. Istanbul, Ser. B., Sci. Nat.* 3:373–394.

Albaum, H. G. 1938a. Normal growth, regeneration and adventitious outgrowth formation in fern prothallia. *Amer. Jour. Bot.* 25:37–44.

———. 1938b. Inhibitions due to growth hormones in fern prothallia and sporophytes. *Amer. Jour. Bot.* 25:124–133.

Alexandrov, W. G., O. G. Alexandrova, and A. S. Timofeev. 1927. Versuch einer Grössenberechnung der Wasserleitungssysteme des Stengels und der Blattstiele. Materialien zur Kenntnis der Dynamik im Bau des Leitungssystem. *Planta* 3:60–76.

——— and K. J. Abessadze. 1934. Beiträge zur Feststellung der Gesetzmässigkeiten in der Gefässbildung des Leitbündels der Dikotylen. *Beitr. Biol. Pflanzen* 22:225–234.

Allard, H. A. 1946. Clockwise and counterclockwise spirality in the phyllotaxy of tobacco. *Jour. Agr. Res.* 73:237–242.

Allen, C. E. 1919. The basis of sex inheritance in *Sphaerocarpos*. *Proc. Amer. Phil. Soc.* 58:289–316.

———. 1924. Gametophytic inheritance in *Sphaerocarpos*. I. Intraclonal variation, and the inheritance of the tufted character. *Genetics* 9:530–587.

———. 1925. Gametophytic inheritance in *Sphaerocarpos*. II. The polycladous character. *Genetics* 10:1–16.

———. 1935, 1945. The genetics of bryophytes. I and II. *Bot. Rev.* 1:269–291; 11:260–287.

———. 1940. The genotypic basis of sex-expression in angiosperms. *Bot. Rev.* 6:227–300.

461

Allen, Ethel K., O. N. Allen, and A. S. Newman. 1953. Pseudonodulation of leguminous plants induced by 2-bromo-3,5-dichlorobenzoic acid. *Amer. Jour. Bot.* 40:429–435.

Allen, O. M., and Ethel K. Allen. 1954. Morphogenesis of the leguminous root nodule. *Brookhaven Symposia in Biol.* 6:209–232.

Allen, G. S. 1947. Embryogeny and the development of the apical meristems of *Pseudotsuga.* V. Late embryogeny. *Amer. Jour. Bot.* 34:73–79.

Allman, G. J. 1864. Report on the present state of our knowledge of the reproductive system in the Hydroida. *Rept. British Assoc. Adv. Sci. 1863.* Pp. 351–426.

Allsopp, A. 1954. Investigations on *Marsilea.* 4. Anatomical effects of changes in sugar concentration. *Ann. Bot.,* n.s. 18:449–461.

———. 1955. Investigations on *Marsilea.* 5. Culture conditions and morphogenesis, with special reference to the origin of land and water forms. *Ann. Bot.,* n.s. 19:247–264.

Amelung, E. 1893. Über mittlere Zellengrössen. *Flora* 77:176–207.

Amos, J., R. G. Hatton, and T. N. Hoblyn. 1930. The effect of scion on root. II. Stem-worked apples. *Jour. Pomol. and Hort. Sci.* 8:248–258.

Anderson, E., and Lucy B. Abbe. 1933. A comparative anatomical study of a mutant *Aquilegia. Amer. Nat.* 67:380–384.

——— and Dorothea de Winton. 1935. The genetics of *Primula sinensis.* IV. Indications as to the ontogenetic relationship of leaf and inflorescence. *Ann. Bot.* 49:671–687.

———. 1939. Recombination in species crosses. *Genetics* 24:668–698.

Anderson, R. E., and R. A. Brink. 1952. Kernel pattern in variegated pericarp maize and the frequency of self-colored offspring. *Amer. Jour. Bot.* 39:637–644.

Anderson, Y. G. 1955. Seasonal development in sun and shade leaves. *Ecology* 36:430–439.

Applegate, H. G., and C. L. Hamner. 1957. Effect of foliar application of substituted benzoic acid on leaf development in *Zinnia elegans. New Phytol.* 56:301–304.

Arber, Agnes. 1919. On heterophylly in water plants. *Amer. Nat.* 53:272–278.

Arens, K. 1933. Physiologisch polarisierter Massenaustausch und Photosynthese bei submersen Wasserpflanzen. I. *Planta* 20:621–658.

Arney, S. E. 1956. Studies of growth and development in the genus *Fragaria.* VI. The effect of photoperiod and temperature on leaf size. *Jour. Exper. Bot.* 7:65–79.

Ashby, E. 1930. Studies in the inheritance of physiological characters. I. A physiological investigation of the nature of hybrid vigour in maize. *Ann Bot.* 44:457–467.

———. 1948a. Studies in the morphogenesis of leaves. I. An essay on leaf shape. *New Phytol.* 47:153–176.

———. 1948b. The area, cell size and cell number of leaves of *Ipomoea* in relation to their position on the plant. *New Phytol.* 47:177–195.

———. 1950a. Leaf morphology and physiological age. *Sci. Progress* 38:678–685.

———. 1950b. Some effects of length of day upon leaf shape in *Ipomoea caerulea. New Phytol.* 49:375–387.

——— and Elisabeth Wangermann. 1950. Further observations on area, cell size and cell number of leaves of *Ipomoea* in relation to their position on the shoot. *New Phytol.* 49:23–35.

Askenasy, E. 1880. Über eine neue Methode, um die Vertheilung der Wachstumsintensität in wachsenden Pflanzentheilung zu bestimmen. *Verhandl. Naturh.-medic. Vereins zu Heidelberg* 2:70–153.

Asseyeva, T. 1927. Bud mutations in the potato and their chimerical nature. *Jour. Genet.* 19:1–26.

Audus, L. J. 1953. *Plant growth substances.* Leonard Hill, London. 465 pp.

Avakian, A. A., and M. G. Jastreb. 1941. (Hybridization by grafting.) *Iarovizatsiia* 1:50–77.

Avery, G. S., Jr. 1933. Structure and development of the tobacco leaf. *Amer. Jour. Bot.* 20:565–592.

———. 1934. Structural responses to the practice of topping tobacco plants: A study of cell size, cell number, leaf size and veinage of leaves at different levels on the stalk. *Bot. Gaz.* 96:314–329.

———. 1935. Differential distribution of a phytohormone in the developing leaf of *Nicotiana,* and its relation to polarized growth. *Bull. Torrey Bot. Club* 62:313–330.

——— and P. R. Burkholder. 1936. Polarized growth and cell studies on the *Avena* coleoptile, phytohormone test object. *Bull. Torrey Bot. Club* 63:1–15.

———, ———, and Harriet B. Creighton. 1937a. Polarized growth and cell studies in the first internode and coleoptile of *Avena* in relation to light and darkness. *Bot. Gaz.* 99:125–143.

———, ———, and ———. 1937b. Production and distribution of growth hormone in shoots of *Aesculus* and *Malus,* and its probable role in stimulating cambial activity. *Amer. Jour. Bot.* 24:51–58.

——— and Elizabeth B. Johnson. 1947. *Hormones and horticulture.* McGraw-Hill, New York. 326 pp.

Bailey, I. W., and H. B. Shepard. 1915. Sanio's laws for the variation in size of coniferous tracheids. *Bot. Gaz.* 60:66–71.

———. 1920a. The formation of the cell plate in the cambium of the higher plants. *Proc. Natl. Acad. Sci.* 6:197–200.

———. 1920b. The cambium and its derivative tissues. II. Size variations of cambial initials in gymnosperms and angiosperms. *Amer. Jour. Bot.* 7:355–367.

———. 1920c. The cambium and its derivative tissues. III. A reconnaissance of cytological phenomena in the cambium. *Amer. Jour. Bot.* 7:417–434.

——— and T. Kerr. 1935. The visible structure of the secondary wall and its significance in physical and chemical investigations of tracheary cells and fibers. *Jour. Arnold Arboretum* 16:273–300.

———. 1952. Biological processes in the formation of wood. *Science* 115:255–259.

Bailey, P. C. 1954. Temperature effects upon the rate of nuclear division in root tips of *Trillium sessile* L. *Bull. Torrey Bot. Club* 81:414–421.

Bain, H. F. 1940. Origin of adventitious shoots in decapitated cranberry seedlings. *Bot. Gaz.* 101:872–880.

Baitsell, G. A. 1940. A modern concept of the cell as a structural unit. *Amer. Nat.* 74:5–24.

Ball, E. 1944. The effects of growth substances on the shoot apex of *Tropaeolum majus* L. *Amer. Jour. Bot.* 31:316–327.

——— and E. J. Boell. 1944. Respiratory rates of the shoot tips and maturing tissues in *Lupinus albus* and *Tropaeolum majus.* *Proc. Natl. Acad. Sci.* 30:45–50.

Ball, E. 1946. Development in sterile culture of stem tips and subjacent regions of *Tropaeolum majus* and of *Lupinus albus*. *Amer. Jour. Bot.* 33:301–318.

————. 1948. Differentiation in the primary shoots of *Lupinus albus* L. and of *Tropaeolum majus* L. *Soc. Exper. Biol. Symposium* II:246–262.

————. 1952a. Experimental division of the shoot apex of *Lupinus albus* L. *Growth* 16:151–174.

————. 1952b. Morphogenesis of shoots after isolation of the shoot apex of *Lupinus albus*. *Amer. Jour. Bot.* 39:167–191.

————. 1956. Growth of the embryo of *Ginkgo biloba* under experimental conditions. II. Effects of a longitudinal split in the tip of the hypocotyl. *Amer. Jour. Bot.* 43:802–810.

Ball, O. M. 1904. Der Einfluss von Zug auf die Ausbildung von Festigungsgewebe. *Jahrb. Wiss. Bot.* 39:305–341.

Bannan, M. W. 1934. Origin and cellular character of xylem rays in gymnosperms. *Bot. Gaz.* 96:260–281.

———— and Barbara E. Whalley. 1950. The elongation of fusiform cambial cells in *Chamaecyparis*. *Canadian Jour. Res., Bot. Sci.* 28:341–355.

————. 1951. The annual cycle of size changes in the fusiform cambial cells of *Chamaecyparis* and *Thuja*. *Canadian Jour. Bot.* 29:421–437.

————. 1953. Further observations on the reduction of fusiform cambial cells in *Thuja occidentalis* L. *Canadian Jour. Bot.* 31:63–74.

————. 1954. Ring width, tracheid size and ray volume in stem wood of *Thuja occidentalis* L. *Canadian Jour. Bot.* 32:466–479.

————. 1955. The vascular cambium and radial growth in *Thuja occidentalis*. L. *Canadian Jour. Bot.* 33:113–138.

———— and Isabel L. Bayly. 1956. Cell size and survival in conifer cambium. *Canadian Jour. Bot.* 34:769–776.

Barclay, B. D. 1931. Origin and development of tissues in stem of *Selaginella Wildenovii*. *Bot. Gaz.* 91:452–461.

Barghoorn, E. S., Jr. 1940a. Origin and development of the uniseriate ray in the Coniferae. *Bull. Torrey Bot. Club* 67:303–328.

————. 1940b. The ontogenetic development and phylogenetic specialization of rays in the xylem of dicotyledons. I. The primitive ray structure. *Amer. Jour. Bot.* 27:918–928.

————. 1942. The effect of l-proline on proliferation of cells and differentiation of protoxylem in roots of cotton and bean. *Growth* 6:23–31.

Barkley, Grace. 1927. Differentiation of vascular bundle of *Trichosanthes anguina*. *Bot. Gaz.* 83:173–184.

Barthelmess, A. 1954. Über Musterbildung am Sprossscheitel der Phanerogamen. *Planta* 43:393–410.

Bartoo, D. R. 1930. Origin of tissues of *Schizaea pusilla*. *Bot. Gaz.* 89:137–153.

Basarman, M. 1946. La transpiration, facteur influent dans la proportion des sexes de *Mercurialis annua* L. *Rev. Fac. Sci. Univ. Istanbul, Ser. B, Sci. Nat.* 11:38–60.

Bateson, W. 1909. *Mendel's principles of heredity*. Cambridge University Press.

————. 1921. Root-cuttings and chimeras. *Jour. Genet.* 11:91–97.

Bauer, L. 1952. Studien zum Heterophyllieproblem. I Mitteilung. *Planta* 40:515–528.

————. 1956. Über vegetative Sporogonbildung bei einer diploiden Sippe von *Georgia pellucida*. *Planta* 46:604–618.

Baur, E. 1909. Das Wesen und die Erblichkeitsverhältnisse der "Varietates albomarginatae Hort." von *Pelargonium zonale. Zeitschr. Ind. Abst. Vererb.* 1:330–351.

Bausor, S. C. 1937. Fasciation and its relation to problems of growth. I. Shape changes in the shoot. *Bull. Torrey Bot. Club* 64:383–400; 445–475.

Beadle, G. W. 1931. A gene in maize for supernumerary cell divisions following meiosis. *Cornell Agr. Exp. Sta. Mem. 135.* 12 pp.

Beal, J. M. 1951. Histological responses to growth-regulating substances. In F. Skoog (ed.), *Plant growth substances.* Pp. 155–174.

Beal, W. J. 1873. Phyllotaxis of cones. *Amer. Nat.* 7:449–453.

Beatty, A. V. 1946. Oxygen consumption and cell division in the leaves of *Ligustrum lucidum* and *Hedera helix. Amer. Jour. Bot.* 33:145–148.

Becker, G. 1931. Experimentelle Analyse der Genom- und Plasmonwirkung bei Moosen. III. Osmotischer Wert heteroploider Pflanzen. *Zeitschr. Ind. Abst. Vererb.* 60:17–38.

Behre, K. 1929. Physiologische und zytologische Untersuchungen über *Drosera. Planta* 7:208–306.

Behrens, Gertrud. 1949. Blüten- und Gestaltsbildung bei *Chrysanthemum* und *Sempervivum* unter photoperiodischen Einflüssen. *Biol. Zentralbl.* 68:1–32.

Beissner, L. 1930. *Handbuch der Nadelholzkunde.* 3d ed. Paul Parey, Berlin. 765 pp.

Benedict, H. M. 1915. Senile changes in leaves of *Vitis vulpina* and certain other plants. *Cornell Agr. Exp. Sta. Mem.* 7:271–368.

Benson-Evans, K., and J. G. Hughes. 1955. The physiology of sexual reproduction in *Lunularia cruciata* (L.) Dum. *Trans. British Bryol. Soc.* 2:513–522.

Bergamaschi, Maria. 1926. Nuove richerche sui caratteri di senilita nelle piante. *Atti Inst. Bot. Univ. Pavia* 1926:115–145.

Bergann, F. 1956. Untersuchungen an den Blüten und Früchten der *Crataegomespili* und ihrer Eltern. *Flora* 143:219–268.

Berge, H. 1877. *Beiträge zur Entwicklungsgeschichte von Bryophyllum calycinum.* Zurich.

Berger, C. A. 1941. Reinvestigation of polysomaty in *Spinacia. Bot. Gaz.* 102:759–769.

——and E. R. Witkus. 1954. The cytology of *Xanthisma texanum* D.C. I. Differences in the chromosome number of root and shoot. *Bull. Torrey Bot. Club* 81:489–491.

Bertalanffy, L. von. 1952. *Problems of life. An evaluation of modern biological thought.* Wiley, New York. 216 pp.

Berthold, G. 1866. *Studien über Protoplasmamechanik.* Felix, Leipzig. 332 pp.

Beyerinck, M. W. 1883. Beobachtungen über die ersten Entwicklungsphasen einiger Cynipidengallen. *Verhandl. K. Akad. Amsterdam* 22:1–98.

——. 1885. Die Galle von *Cecidomyia poae* an *Poa nemoralis.* Entstehung normaler Wurzeln infolge der Wirkung eines Gallentieres. *Bot. Zeit.* 43: 305–316; 321–332.

Beyerle, R. 1932. Untersuchungen über die Regeneration von Farnprimärblättern. *Planta* 16:622–665.

Biddulph, Susan F., and O. Biddulph. 1953. Tumors in *Ipomoea tuba* from the atom-bomb test sites on Eniwetok Atoll. *U.S. Atomic Energy Comm. AECD-3446.* 24 pp.

Bilhuber, E. 1933. Beiträge zur Kenntnis der Organstellungen im Pflanzenreich. *Bot. Archiv* 35:188–250.

Bindloss, Elizabeth. 1942. A developmental analysis of cell length as related to stem length. *Amer. Jour. Bot.* 29:179–188.

Bissett, I. J. W., H. E. Dadswell, and A. B. Wardrop. 1951. Factors influencing tracheid length in conifer stems. *Australian For.* 15:17–30.

Bitters, W. P., and L. D. Batchelor. 1951. Effect of rootstocks on the size of orange fruits. *Proc. Amer. Soc. Hort. Sci.* 57:133–141.

Black, L. M. 1949. Virus tumors. *Survey Biol. Progress* 1:155–231.

Blackburn, Kathleen B. 1923. Sex chromosomes in plants. *Nature* 112:687–688.

Blackman, V. H. 1919. The compound interest law and plant growth. *Ann. Bot.* 33:353–360.

Blair, D. S. 1938. Rootstock and scion relationship in apple trees. *Sci. Agr.* (*Ottawa*) 19:85–94.

Blakeslee, A. F. 1921. A chemical method of distinguishing genetic types of yellow cones in *Rudbeckia*. *Zeitschr. Ind. Abst. Vererb.* 25:211–221.

———. 1934. New Jimson Weeds from old chromosomes. *Jour. Hered.* 25:80–108.

Blaringhem, L. 1908. *Mutation et traumatismes. Étude sur l'évolution des formes végétales*. Alcan, Paris. 248 pp.

Blaser, H. W., and J. Einset. 1948. Leaf development in six periclinal chromosomal chimeras of apple varieties. *Amer. Jour. Bot.* 35:473–482.

———. 1956. Morphology of the determinate thornshoots of *Gleditsia*. *Amer. Jour. Bot.* 43:22–28.

Bloch, R. 1926. Umdifferenzierungen an Wurzelgeweben nach Verwundung. *Ber. Deutsch. Bot. Ges.* 44:308–316.

———. 1935a. Observations on the relation of adventitious root formation to the structure of air roots of orchids. *Proc. Leeds Phil. Soc., Sci. Sect.,* 3:92–101.

———. 1935b. Wound healing in *Tradescantia fluminensis*. *Ann. Bot.* 49:651–670.

———. 1937. Wound healing and necrosis in air roots of *Phoenix reclinata* and leaves of *Araucaria imbricata*. *Amer. Jour. Bot.* 24:279–287.

———. 1938. Anatomical changes in *Tradescantia fluminensis* Vell. after treatment with growth substances. *Contrib. Boyce Thompson Inst.* 9:439–454.

———. 1941, 1952. Wound healing in higher plants. *Bot. Rev.* 7:110–146; 18:655–679.

———. 1943a. Polarity in plants. *Bot. Rev.* 9:261–310.

———. 1943b. Differentiation in red root tips of *Phalaris arundinacea*. *Bull. Torrey Bot. Club* 70:182–183.

———. 1944. Developmental potency, differentiation and pattern in meristems of *Monstera deliciosa*. *Amer. Jour. Bot.* 31:71–77.

———. 1946. Differentiation and pattern in *Monstera deliciosa*. The idioblastic development of the trichosclereids in the air root. *Amer. Jour. Bot.* 33:544–551.

———. 1948. The development of the secretory cells of *Ricinus* and the problem of cellular differentiation. *Growth* 12:271–284.

———. 1954. Abnormal plant growth. *Brookhaven Symposia in Biol.* 6:41–54.

Böhme, H. 1954. Untersuchungen zum Problem der genetischen Bedeutung von Pfropfungen zwischen genotypisch verschiedenen Pflanzen. *Zeitschr. Pflanzenzuchtung* 33:367–418.

Boke, N. H. 1955. Development of the vegetative shoot in *Rhipsalis cassytha*. *Amer. Jour. Bot.* 42:1–10.

Bond, G. 1935. The endodermis in light-grown and etiolated shoots of the Leguminosae: a contribution to the causal study of differentiation in the plant. *Trans. Roy. Soc. Edinburgh* 58:409–425.

Bond, T. E. T. 1945. On sepal phyllody in roses and some related phenomena. Experimental data and a quantitative interpretation. *New Phytol.* 44:220–230.

Bonner, D. M., and A. J. Haagen-Smit. 1939. The activity of pure substances in leaf growth. *Proc. Natl. Acad. Sci.* 25:184–188.

Bonner, James, and J. English, Jr. 1938. A chemical and physiological study of traumatin, a plant wound hormone. *Plant Physiol.* 13:331–348.

———. 1949. Limiting factors and growth inhibitors in the growth of the *Avena* coleoptile. *Amer. Jour. Bot.* 36:323–332.

——— and J. Thurlow. 1949. Inhibition of photoperiodic induction in *Xanthium* by applied auxin. *Bot. Gaz.* 110:613–624.

——— and J. Liverman. 1953. Hormonal control of flower initiation. In W. E. Loomis (ed.), *Growth and differentiation in plants.* Pp. 283–303.

Bonner, John T. 1944. A descriptive study of the development of the slime mold *Dictyostelium discoideum. Amer. Jour. Bot.* 31:175–182.

———. 1947. Evidence for the formation of cell aggregates by chemotaxis in the development of the slime mold *Dictyostelium discoideum. Jour. Exper. Zool.* 106:1–26.

———. 1949. The demonstration of acrasin in the later stages of the development of the slime mold *Dictyostelium discoideum. Jour. Exper. Zool.* 110:259–271.

———. 1952a. *Morphogenesis: An essay on development.* Princeton University Press, Princeton, N.J. 296 pp.

———. 1952b. The pattern of differentiation in amoeboid slime molds. *Amer. Nat.* 86:79–89.

———, K. K. Kane, and R. H. Levey. 1956. Studies on the mechanics of growth in the common mushroom, *Agaricus campestris. Mycologia* 48:13–19.

———. 1957. A theory of the control of differentiation in the cellular slime molds. *Quart. Rev. Biol.* 32:232–246.

———. 1959. *The cellular slime molds.* Princeton University Press, Princeton, N.J. 150 pp.

Bonnet, C. 1754. *Recherches sur l'usage des feuilles dans les plantes.* Göttingen and Leiden.

Boodle, L. A. 1920. The mode of origin and the vascular supply of the adventitious leaves of *Cyclamen. Ann. Bot.* 34:431–437.

Bopp, M. 1954. Ein Beitrag zur Differenzierung im Moosprotonema. *Ber. Deutsch. Bot. Ges.* 67:176–183.

———. 1955. Die Entwicklung von Zelle und Kern im Protonema von *Funaria hygrometrica* Sibth. *Planta* 45:573–590.

Bordner, J. S. 1909. The influence of traction on the formation of mechanical tissue in stems. *Bot. Gaz.* 48:251–274.

Borgström, G. 1939. *The transverse reactions of plants: Outlines of a new interpretation of the significance of growth hormones for life processes in plants.* Gleerup, Lund. 230 pp.

Bormann, J. 1939. Untersuchungen über die künstliche Umwandlung von Blütenständen in Laubsprosse. *Planta* 29:679–741.

Borowikow, G. A. 1914. La polarité renverse chez le *Cladophora glomerata. Bull. Jard. Bot. Pierre Grand* 14:475–481. (In Russian with French résumé.)

Borriss, H. 1934a. Beiträge zur Wachstums- und Entwicklungsphysiologie der Früchtkörper von *Coprinus lagopus. Planta* 22:28–69.

———. 1934b. Über den Einfluss äusserer Faktoren auf Wachstum und Entwicklung der Früchtkörper von *Coprinus lagopus. Planta* 22:644–684.

Borthwick, H. A., M. W. Parker, and P. H. Heinze. 1941. Influence of localized low temperature on Biloxi soybean during photoperiodic induction. *Bot. Gaz.* 102:792–800.

Bosshatd, H. H. 1951. Variabilität der Elemente des Eschenholzes in Funktion von der Kambiumtätigkeit. *Schweiz. Zeitschr. Forstw.* 102:648–665.

Bouillenne, R., and F. W. Went. 1933. Recherches expérimentales sur la néoformation des racines dans les plantules et les boutures des plantes supérieures. *Ann. Jard. Bot. Buitenzorg* 43:25–202.

———. 1950. La rhizogenèse. *L'Année Biol.* 26:597–628.

Bouygues, H. 1930. La pression de la zone cambiale proprement dite de la tige a-t-elle une influence sur l'orientation des cloisons de l'assise phellogénique? *Bull. Soc. Bot. France* 77:374–383.

Bower, F. O. 1930. *Size and form in plants.* Macmillan, London, 232 pp.

Boysen-Jensen, P. 1936. *Growth hormones in plants.* (Tr. by Avery and Burkholder.) McGraw-Hill, New York. 268 pp.

———. 1950. Untersuchungen über Determination und Differenzierung. 1. Über der Nachweis der Zellulosenbildner und über das Vorkommen und die Lage derselben in Wurzelhaaren und Trichoblasten. *Biol. Medd. Danske Vid. Selsk.* 18:1–18.

———. 1957. Untersuchungen über Determination und Differenzierung. 4. Über den aufbau des Zellwandgerüstes der Pflanzen und die Determination desselben. *Biol. Medd. Danske Vid. Selsk.* 23:1–47.

Brabec, F. 1954. Untersuchungen über die Natur der Winklerschen Burdonen auf Grund neuen experimentellen Materials. *Planta* 44:562–606.

Bradford, F. C., and B. G. Sitton. 1929. Defective graft unions in the apple and the pear. *Michigan Agr. Exp. Sta. Tech. Bull.* 99. 106 pp.

Bradley, Muriel V. 1954. Cell and nuclear size in relation to polysomaty and the nuclear cycle. *Amer. Jour. Bot.* 41:398–402.

Brain, E. D. 1939. Studies in the effects of prolonged rotation of plants on a horizontal klinostat. II. Anatomical structure. *New Phytol.* 38:240–256.

Braun, A. 1831. Vergleichende Untersuchung über die Ordnung der Schuppen an den Tannenzapfen. *Nova Acta Acad. Car. Leop.* 15:195–401.

Braun, A. C. 1941. Development of secondary tumors and tumor strands in the crown gall of sunflowers. *Phytopathology* 31:135–149.

——— and P. R. White. 1943. Bacteriological sterility of tissues derived from secondary crown-gall tumors. *Phytopathology* 33:85–100.

———. 1952. Conditioning of the host cell as a factor in the transformation process in crown gall. *Growth* 16:65–74.

——— and U. Näf. 1954. A nonauxinic growth-promoting factor present in crown-gall tumor tissue. *Proc. Soc. Exper. Biol. Med.* 86:212–214.

———. 1957. A physiological study of the nature of autonomous growth in neoplastic plant cells. *Soc. Exper. Biol. Symposium* XI:132–142.

———. 1958. A physiological basis for autonomous growth of the crown-gall tumor cell. *Proc. Natl. Acad. Sci.* 44:344–349.

——— and T. Stonier. 1958. Morphology and physiology of plant tumors. *Protoplasmatologia* 10:1–93.

Brauner, L. 1927. Untersuchungen über das geoelectrische Phänomen. *Jahrb. Wiss. Bot.* 66:381–428.

Bravais, L., and A. Bravais. 1837. Essai sur la disposition des feuilles curvisériées. *Ann. Sci. Nat. Bot.* II, 7:42–109.

Brenchley, Winifred E. 1947. The essential nature of certain minor elements for plant nutrition. II. *Bot. Rev.* 13:169–193.

Brian, P. W., and H. G. Hemming. 1955. The effect of gibberellic acid on shoot growth of pea seedlings. *Physiol. Plantarum* 8:669–681.

Briggs, W. R., and T. A. Steeves. 1958. Morphogenetic studies on *Osmunda cinnamomea* L. The expansion and maturation of vegetative fronds. *Phytomorphology* 8:234–248.

Brotherton, W., Jr., and H. H. Bartlett. 1918. Cell measurement as an aid in the analysis of variation. *Amer. Jour. Bot.* 5:192–206.

Brown, A. B. 1937. Activity of the vascular cambium in relation to wounding in the balsam poplar, *Populus balsamifera. Canadian Jour. Res.* 15:7–31.

——— and R. G. H. Cormack. 1937. Stimulation of cambial activity locally in the region of application and at a distance in relation to a wound by means of heteroauxin. *Canadian Jour. Res.* 15:433–441.

Brown, Nellie A., and F. E. Gardner. 1936. Galls produced by plant hormones, including a hormone extracted from *Bacterium tumefaciens. Phytopathology* 26:708–713.

Brown, R., and P. Rickless. 1949. A new method for the study of cell division and cell extension with some preliminary observations on the effect of temperature and of nutrients. *Proc. Roy. Soc. London, B,* 136:110–125.

——— and D. Broadbent. 1950. The development of cells in the growing zones of the root. *Jour. Exper. Bot.* 1:249–263.

———, W. S. Reith, and E. Robinson. 1952. The mechanism of plant cell growth. *Soc. Exper. Biol. Symposium* VI:329–347.

——— and F. Wightman. 1952. The influence of mature tissue on division in the meristem of the root. *Jour. Exper. Bot.* 3:253–263.

Brown, W. V. 1952. The relation of soil moisture to cleistogamy in *Stipa leucotricha. Bot. Gaz.* 113:438–444.

Bruhn, W. 1910. Beiträge zur experimentellen Morphologie, zur Biologie und Anatomie der Luftwurzeln. *Flora* 101:98–166.

Brumfield, R. T. 1942. Cell growth and division in living root meristems. *Amer. Jour. Bot.* 29:533–543.

———. 1943. Cell-lineage studies in root meristems by means of chromosome rearrangements induced by X-rays. *Amer. Jour. Bot.* 30:101–110.

Brush, W. D. 1912. The formation of mechanical tissue in the tendrils of *Passiflora caerulea* as influenced by tension and contact. *Bot. Gaz.* 53:453–477.

Bücher, H. 1906. Anatomische Veränderungen bei gewaltsamer Krümmung und geotropischer Induktion. *Jahrb. Wiss. Bot.* 43:271–360.

Buchholz, J. T. 1926. Origin of cleavage polyembryony in conifers. *Bot. Gaz.* 81:55–71.

———. 1938. Cone formation in *Sequoia gigantea.* I. The relation of stem size and tissue development to cone formation. II. The history of the seed cone. *Amer. Jour. Bot.* 25:296–305.

Budde, H. 1923. Beiträge zur Anatomie und Physiologie des Blattes auf Grund volumetrischer Messungen. *Bot. Archiv* 4:443–487.

Bünning, E. 1935. Über die Wirkung der Aussenbedingungen auf reifende Samen von *Phaseolus multiflorus. Flora* 29:120–139.

———. 1941. Über die Verhinderung des Etiolements. *Ber. Deutsch. Bot. Ges.* 59:2–9.

———. 1948. *Entwicklungs- und Bewegungsphysiologie der Pflanze.* Springer, Berlin. 464 pp.

——— and Herta Sagromsky. 1948. Die Bildung des Spaltöffnungsmusters in der Blattepidermis. *Zeitschr. Naturforsch.* 3b:203–216.

Bünning, E., Liselotte Haag, and G. Timmermann. 1948. Weitere Untersuchungen über die formative Wirkung des Lichtes und mechanischer Reize auf Pflanzen. *Planta* 36:178–187.

——. 1952a. Weitere Untersuchungen über die Differenzierungsvorgänge in Wurzeln. *Zeitschr. Bot.* 40:385–406.

——. 1952b. Morphogenesis in plants. *Survey Biol. Progress* 2:105–140.

—— and F. Biegert. 1953. Die Bildung der Spaltöffnungsinitialen bie *Allium cepa. Zeitschr. Bot.* 41:17–39.

—— and Christa Lemppenau. 1954. Über die Wirkung mechanischer und photischer Reize auf die Gewebe- und Organbildung von *Mimosa pudica, Ber. Deutsch. Bot. Ges.* 67:10–18.

——. 1955. Regenerationen bei Pflanzen. In *Handbuch der allgemeinen Pathologie* 6:383–404. Springer, Berlin.

——. 1956. Endogenous rhythms in plants. *Ann Rev. Plant Physiol.* 7:71–90.

——. 1958. Polarität und inaequale Teilung des pflanzlichen Protoplasten. *Handbuch Protoplasmaforschung VIII.* Vienna. 86 pp.

Burgeff, H. 1924. Untersuchungen über Sexualität und Parasitismus bei Mucorineen. *Bot. Abhandl.* 4:5–135.

Burkholder, P. R. 1936. The influence of light upon growth and differentiation. *Bot. Rev.* 2:97–172.

—— and Ilda McVeigh. 1940. Growth and differentiation of maize in relation to nitrogen supply. *Amer. Jour. Bot.* 27:414–424.

Burns, G. P. 1904. Heterophylly in *Proserpinaca palustris. Ann. Bot.* 18:579–587.

——. 1920. Eccentric growth and the formation of redwood in the main stem of conifers. *Vermont Agr. Exp. Sta. Publ.* 219:1–16.

Burr, H. S. 1932. An electro-dynamic theory of development suggested by studies of proliferation rates in the brain of *Amblystoma. Jour. Comp. Neurol.* 56:347–371.

—— and F. S. C. Northrop. 1935. The electro-dynamic theory of life. *Quart. Rev. Biol.* 10:322–333.

—— and ——. 1939. Evidence for the existence of an electro-dynamic field in living organisms. *Proc. Natl. Acad. Sci.* 25:284–288.

——. 1941. Field properties of the developing frog's egg. *Proc. Natl. Acad. Sci.* 27:276–281.

—— and E. W. Sinnott. 1944. Electrical correlates of form in cucurbit fruits. *Amer. Jour. Bot.* 31:249–253.

Burström, H. 1956. Temperature and root cell elongation. *Physiol. Plantarum* 9:682–692.

——. 1957. Auxin and the mechanism of root growth. *Soc. Exper. Biol. Symposium* XI:44–62.

Bussmann, K. 1939. Untersuchungen über die Induktion der Dorsiventralität bei den Farnprothallien. *Jahrb. Wiss. Bot.* 87:565–624.

——. 1941. Untersuchungen über die Induktion der Dorsiventralität bei apogamen Farnprothallien. *Jahrb. Wiss. Bot.* 89:615–636.

Butler, L. 1952. The linkage map of the tomato. *Jour. Hered.* 43:25–35.

Buvat, R. 1944, 1945. Recherches sur la dédifférentiation des cellules végétales. I. Plantes entières et boutures. II. Cultures de tissus et tumeurs. *Ann. Sci. Nat. Bot.* XI, 5:1–130; 6:1–119.

————. 1950. La dédifférentiation des cellules végétales. *L'Année Biol.* 26:399–412.

————. 1952. Structure, évolution et fonctionnement du méristème apical de quelques Dicotylédones. *Ann. Sci. Nat. Bot.* XI, 13:199–300.

Cain, S. A., and J. E. Potzger. 1940. A comparison of leaf tissues of *Gaylussacia baccata* grown under different conditions. *Amer. Midland Nat.* 24:444–462.

Cajlachjan, M. C. 1938. Motion of blossom hormone in girdled and grafted plants. *Compt. Rend. (Doklady) Acad. Sci. USSR* 18:607–612.

Camefort, H. 1956. Étude de la structure du point végétatif et des variations phyllotaxiques chez quelques gymnospermes. *Ann. Sci. Nat. Bot.* XI, 17:1–185.

Camus, G. 1944. Action différenciatrice des bourgeons d'endive sur les tissus sous-jacents. *Compt. Rend. Acad. Sci. Paris* 219:34–36.

————. 1949. Recherches sur le rôle des bourgeons dans les phénomènes de morphogénèse. *Rev. Cyt. Biol. Vég.* 11:1–195.

Carlson, Margery C. 1938. Origin and development of shoots from the tips of roots of *Pogonia ophioglossoides. Bot. Gaz.* 100:215–225.

————. 1950. Nodal adventitious roots in willow stems of different ages. *Amer. Jour. Bot.* 37:555–561.

————. 1953. Root formation in isolated cotyledons of *Brassica napus* and *Raphanus sativus. Amer. Jour. Bot.* 40:233–238.

Carrière, E. A. 1877. Un fruit qui s'enracine. *Rev. Hort.* 49:207.

Carter, W. 1939, 1952. Injuries to plants caused by insect toxins. *Bot. Rev.* 5:273–326; 18:680–721.

Carvalho, A., C. A. Krug, and J. E. T. Mendes. 1950. O dimorfismo dos ramos em *Coffea arabica* L. *Bragantia* 10:151–159.

Castan, R. 1940. Sur le rôle des hormones animales et végétales dans la développement et l'organogénèse des plantes vasculaires: Les "organisateurs" végétaux. *Rev. Gén. Bot.* 52:192–208; 234–255; 285–304; 333–352.

Castle, E. S., and A. J. M. Honeyman. 1935. The light-growth response and the growth system of *Phycomyces. Jour. Gen. Physiol.* 18:385–397.

————. 1936. The influence of certain external factors on the spiral growth of single plant cells in relation to protoplasmic streaming. *Jour. Cell. and Comp. Physiol.* 7:445–454.

————. 1942. Spiral growth and reversal of spiraling in *Phycomyces* and their bearing on primary wall structure. *Amer. Jour. Bot.* 29:664–672.

————. 1953. Problems of growth and structure in *Phycomyces. Quart. Rev. Biol.* 28:364–372.

————. 1958. The topography of tip growth in a plant cell. *Jour. Gen. Physiol.* 41:913–926.

Chalk, L., and M. Margaret Chattaway. 1935. Factors affecting dimensional variations of vessel members. *Tropical Woods* 41:17–37.

————, E. B. Marstrand, and J. P. de C. Walsh. 1955. Fibre length in storeyed hardwoods. *Acta Bot. Neerl.* 4:339–347.

Champagnat, P. 1955. Les corrélations entre feuilles et bourgeons de la pousse herbacée du lilas. *Rev. Gén. Bot.* 62:325–372.

Champion, H. G. 1925. Contributions towards a knowledge of twisted fiber in trees. *Indian For. Rec.* 11:1–70.

Chandler, W. H., and others. 1937. Chilling requirements for opening of buds on deciduous orchard trees and some other plants in California. *Univ. California Agr. Exp. Sta. Bull. 611.* 63 pp.

Chandraratna, M. F. 1955. Genetics of photoperiod sensitivity in rice. *Jour. Genet.* 53:215–223.

Chao, Marian D. 1947. Growth of the dandelion scape. *Plant Physiol.* 22:393–406.

Chapman, H. W. 1958. Tuberization in the potato plant. *Physiol. Plantarum* 11:215–224.

Charles, D. R., and H. H. Smith. 1939. Distinguishing between two types of gene action in quantitative inheritance. *Genetics* 24:34–48.

Chattaway, M. Margaret. 1936. Relation between fibre and cambial initial length in dicotyledonous woods. *Tropical Woods* 46:16–20.

Chaudri, J. J., E. Bünning, and W. Haupt. 1956. Über die thermoperiodische Beeinflussung der Zwiebelbildung bei *Allium cepa. Beitr. Biol. Pflanzen* 32:219–224.

Chester, K. S. 1932. Studies on the precipitin reaction in plants. II. Preliminary report on the nature of the "normal precipitin reaction." *Jour. Arnold Arboretum* 13:285–296.

Cheuvart, C. 1954. Expériences sur le développement de *Cannabis sativa* (sexualité et pigments foliaires) à température constante et sous différents régimes de photopériodisme. *Bull. Acad. Roy. Belgique* (Cl. Sci.) 1954:1152–1168.

Child, C. M., and A. W. Bellamy. 1919. Physiological isolation by low temperature in *Bryophyllum* and other plants. *Science* 50:362–365.

———. 1921. Certain aspects of the problem of physiological correlation. *Amer. Jour. Bot.* 8:286–295.

———. 1941. *Patterns and problems of development.* University of Chicago Press, Chicago. 811 pp.

Chowdhury, K. A., and K. N. Tandan. 1950. Extension and radial growth in trees. *Nature* 165:732–733.

———. 1953. The role of initial parenchyma in the transformation of the structure diffuse-porous to ring-porous in the secondary xylem of the genus *Gmelina. Proc. Natl. Inst. Sci. India* 19:361–369.

Christensen, Hilde M., and R. Bamford. 1943. Haploids in twin seedlings of pepper, *Capsicum annuum* L. *Jour. Hered.* 34:98–104.

Church, A. H. 1920. On the interpretation of phenomena of phyllotaxis. *Bot. Mem. Oxford Univ. 6.* 58 pp.

Clark, H. E., and K. R. Kerns. 1942. Control of flowering with phytohormones. *Science* 95:536–537.

Clark, W. G. 1938. Electrical polarity and auxin transport. *Plant Physiol.* 13:529–552.

Cleland, R., and J. Bonner. 1956. The residual effect of auxin on the cell wall. *Plant Physiol.* 31:350–354.

Clowes, F. A. L. 1950. Root apical meristems of *Fagus sylvatica. New Phytol.* 49:248–268.

———. 1954. The promeristem and the minimal constructional centre in grass root apices. *New Phytol.* 53:108–116.

———. 1956. Localization of nucleic acid synthesis in root meristems. *Jour. Exper. Bot.* 7:307–312.

———. 1958. Protein synthesis in root meristems. *Jour. Exper. Bot.* 9:229–238.

Cockerham, G. 1930. Some observations on cambial activity and seasonal starch content in sycamore (*Acer pseudoplatanus*). *Proc. Leeds Phil. and Lit. Soc.* 2:64–80.

Cohen, A. L. 1953. The effect of ammonia on morphogenesis in the Acrasieae. *Proc. Natl. Acad. Sci.* 39:68–74.

Colby, H. L. 1935. Stock-scion chemistry and the fruiting relationships in apple trees. *Plant Physiol.* 10:483–498.

Collander, R. 1941. The distribution of different cations between root and shoot. *Acta Bot. Fennica* 29:1–12.

Colquhoun, T. T. 1929. Polarity in *Casuarina paludosa*. *Trans. and Proc. Roy. Soc. South Australia* 53:353–358.

Combes, R. 1947. Le mécanisme de l'action du milieu aquatique sur les végétaux. Rôle du facteur température. *Rev. Gén. Bot.* 54:249–270.

Cormack, R. G. H. 1947. A comparative study of developing epidermal cells in white mustard and tomato roots. *Amer. Jour. Bot.* 34:310–314.

———. 1949. The development of root hairs in angiosperms. *Bot. Rev.* 15:583–612.

———. 1955. The effect of extreme shade upon leaf form and structure in *Vicia americana*. *Canadian Jour. Bot.* 33:293–297.

Correns, C. 1899. *Untersuchungen über die Vermehrung der Laubmoose durch Brutorgane und Stecklinge*. G. Fischer, Jena. 472 pp.

———. 1907. *Die Bestimmung und Vererbung des Geschlechtes nach neuen Versuchen mit höheren Pflanzen*. Berlin.

Coulter, J. M., and M. A. Chrysler. 1904. Regeneration in *Zamia*. *Bot. Gaz.* 38:452–458.

Courtot, Y., and L. Baillaud. 1955. Sur la répartition des sexes chez un *Chamaecyparis*. *Ann. Sci. Univ., Besançon Bot. Ser.* II, 1:75–81.

Crafts, A. S., H. B. Currier, and C. R. Stocking. 1949. *Water in the physiology of plants*. Chronica Botanica, Waltham, Mass. 240 pp.

Cramer, P. J. S. 1954. Chimeras. *Bibliogr. Genetica* 16:193–381.

Crane, H. L., and A. L. Finch. 1930. Growth character, leaf size and bud development in the pecan. *Proc. Amer. Soc. Hort. Sci.* 27:440–443.

Crist, J. W., and G. J. Stout. 1929. Relation between top and root size in herbaceous plants. *Plant Physiol.* 4:63–85.

Crockett, L. J. 1957. A study of the tunica, corpus and anneau initial of irradiated and normal stem apices of *Nicotiana tabacum* L. *Bull. Torrey Bot. Club* 84:229–236.

Crooks, D. M. 1933. Histological and regenerative studies on the flax seedling. *Bot. Gaz.* 95:209–239.

Cross, G. L., and T. J. Johnson. 1941. Structural features of the shoot apices of diploid and colchicine-induced tetraploid strains of *Vinca rosea* L. *Bull. Torrey Bot. Club* 68:618–635.

Crow, W. B. 1928. Symmetry in organisms. *Amer. Nat.* 62:207–227.

Crüger, H. 1855. Zur Entwickelungsgeschichte der Zellenwand. *Bot. Zeit.* 13:601–613; 617–629.

Curry, G. M., and E. C. Wassink. 1956. Photoperiodic and formative effects of various wavelength regions in *Hyoscyamus niger* as influenced by gibberellic acid. *Mededeel. Landbouwhoogesch. Wageningen* 56:1–8.

Cutter, Elizabeth. 1955. Anatomical studies on the shoot apices of some parasitic and saprophytic angiosperms. *Phytomorphology* 5:231–247.

———. 1956. The experimental induction of buds from leaf primordia in *Dryopteris aristata* Druce. *Ann. Bot.*, n.s. 20:143–165.

Cutler, Elizabeth. 1958. Studies of morphogenesis in the Nymphaeaceae. III. Surgical experiments on leaf and bud formation. *Phytomorphology* 8:74–95.

Czaja, A. T. 1930. Zellphysiologische Untersuchungen an *Cladophora glomerata*. Isolierung, Regeneration und Polarität. *Protoplasma* 11:601–627.

———. 1935. Polarität und Wuchsstoff. *Ber. Deutsch. Bot. Ges.* 53:197–220.

D'Amato, F. 1950. Differenziazione istologica per endopoliploidia nelle radici di alcune monocotiledoni. *Caryologia* 3:11–26.

———. 1952. Polyploidy in the differentiation and function of tissues and cells in plants. *Caryologia* 4:311–358.

Daniel, L. 1929. The inheritance of acquired characters in grafted plants. *Proc. Internat. Congr. Plant Sci.* 2:1024–1044. Ithaca, N.Y., 1926.

Darrow, G. M., and H. A. Borthwick. 1954. Fasciation in the strawberry. Inheritance and the relationship of photoperiodism. *Jour. Hered.* 45:298–304.

Davidson, F. F. 1950. The effects of auxins on the growth of marine algae. *Amer. Jour. Bot.* 37:502–510.

Davies, P. A. 1931. Distribution of total nitrogen in regeneration of the willow. *Bot. Gaz.* 91:320–326.

Dawson, R. F. 1942. Accumulation of nicotine in reciprocal grafts of tomato and tobacco. *Amer. Jour. Bot.* 29:66–71.

Deats, M. E. 1925. The effect on plants of the increase and decrease of the period of illumination over that of the normal day period. *Amer. Jour. Bot.* 12:384–392.

De Candolle, Casimir. 1881. *Considérations sur l'étude de la phyllotaxie.* Geneva.

Delbruck, M. 1949. A physicist looks at biology. *Trans. Connecticut Acad. Arts and Sci.* 38:73–190.

Delisle, A. L. 1937. The influence of auxin on secondary branching in two species of *Aster*. *Amer. Jour. Bot.* 24:159–167.

Demerec, M. 1931. Behavior of two mutable genes on *Delphinium ajacis. Jour. Genet.* 24:179–193.

Denffer, D. von. 1948. Über die Bedeutung des Blühtermins der Wirtspflanzen von *Cuscuta Gronovii* Willd. für die Blütenbildung des Schmarotzers. *Biol. Zentralbl.* 67:175–189.

———. 1951. Durch die Behandlung mit 2,3,5-trijodbenzoesäure hervorgerufene Gamophyllien. *Ber. Deutsch. Bot. Ges.* 64:269–274.

——— and H. Hustede. 1955. Wuchsstoffbedingte Umstimmung von der sexuellen zur vegetativen Entwicklung bei *Vaucheria sessilis. Flora* 142:489–492.

Denham, H. J. 1922. The structure of the cotton hair and its botanical aspects. *Jour. Textile Inst.* 13:99–112.

Dermen, H., and H. F. Bain. 1944. A general cytohistological study of colchicine polyploidy in cranberry. *Amer. Jour. Bot.* 31:451–463.

———. 1947a. Periclinal cytochimeras and histogenesis in cranberry. *Amer. Jour. Bot.* 34:32–43.

———. 1947b. Histogenesis of some bud sports and variegations. *Proc. Amer. Soc. Hort. Sci.* 50:51–73.

———. 1951. Ontogeny of tissues in stem and leaf of cytochimeral apples. *Amer. Jour. Bot.* 38:753–760.

———. 1953. Periclinal chimeras and origin of tissues in stem and leaf of peach. *Amer. Jour. Bot.* 40:154–168.

Desch, H. E. 1932. Anatomical variation in the wood of some dicotyledonous trees. *New Phytol.* 31:73–118.

Deuber, C. G. 1940. Vegetative propagation of conifers. *Trans. Connecticut Acad. Arts and Sci.* 34:1–83.

Dickson, A. G., and E. W. Samuels. 1956. The mechanism of controlled growth of dwarf apple trees. *Jour. Arnold Arboretum* 37:307–313.

Diels, L. 1906. *Jugendformen und Blütenreife im Pflanzenreich*. Berlin.

Dippel, L. 1867. Die Entstehung der wandständigen Protoplasmaströmchen. *Abhandl. Naturforsch. Ges. Halle* 10:53–68.

Dobbs, C. G. 1953. A study of growth rings in trees. III. *Forestry* 26:97–110.

Doorenbos, J., and A. M. Kofranek. 1953. Inflorescence initiation and development in an early and late *Chrysanthemum* variety. *Proc. Amer. Soc. Hort. Sci.* 61:555–558.

———. 1954. "Rejuvenation" of *Hedera helix* in graft combinations. *Proc. K. Néerl. Akad. Wetenschap., Ser. C* 57:99–102.

Doposcheg-Uhlár, J. 1911. Studien zur Regeneration und Polarität der Pflanzen. *Flora* 102:24–86.

Döpp, W. 1950. Eine die Antheridienbildung bei Farnen fördernde Substanz in den Prothallien von *Pteridium aquilinum* (L.) Kuhn. *Ber. Deutsch. Bot. Ges.* 63:139–147.

Dore, J. 1955. Studies in the regeneration of horseradish. *Ann. Bot.*, n.s. 19:127–137.

Dormer, K. J. 1950. A quantitative study of shoot development in *Vicia faba*. I. The xylem of the plumule. *Ann. Bot.*, n.s. 14:421–434.

———. 1951. A quantitative study of shoot development in *Vicia faba*. III. The dry weights of the plumular internodes. *Ann. Bot.*, n.s. 15:289–303.

———. 1954. Observations on the symmetry of the shoot of *Vacia faba* and some allied species, and on the transmission of some morphogenetic impulses. *Ann. Bot.*, n.s. 18:55–70.

Dörries-Rüger, Kate. 1929. Experimentelle Analyse der Genom und Plasmonwirkung bei Moosen. *Zeitschr. Ind. Abst. Vererb.* 52:390–405.

Dostál, R. 1926. Zur Kenntnis der inneren Gestaltungsfaktoren bei *Caulerpa prolifera*. *Ber. Deutsch. Bot. Ges.* 44:56–66.

———. 1929. Untersuchungen über Protoplasmamobilisation bei *Caulerpa prolifera*. *Jahrb. Wiss. Bot.* 71:596–667.

———. 1945. Morphogenetic studies on *Caulerpa prolifera*. *Bull. Internat. Cl. Sci. Math. Nat. Med. Acad. Tchèque Sci.* 46:133–149.

Downs, R. J., and H. A. Borthwick. 1956. Effects of photoperiod on growth of trees. *Bot. Gaz.* 117:310–326.

Doyle, J. 1915. On the change of the petiole into a stem by means of grafting. *Sci. Proc. Roy. Dublin Soc.* 14:405–444.

Driesch, H. 1937. Studien zur Theorie der organischen Formbildung. *Acta Biotheoretica* 3:51–80.

DuBuy, H. G., and E. L. Neurnbergk. 1938. Growth, tropisms and other movements. In Verdoorn, *Manual of pteridology*. M. Nijhoff, The Hague. Pp. 303–346.

Duncan, R. E., and J. T. Curtis. 1942. Intermittent growth of fruits of *Phalaenopsis*. A correlation of the growth phases of an orchid fruit with internal development. *Bull. Torrey Bot. Club* 69:167–183.

East, E. M. 1908. Organic correlations. *Rept. Amer. Breeders Assoc.* 4:332–343.

Eberhardt, P. 1903. Influence de l'air sec et de l'air humide sur la forme et sur la structure des végétaux. *Ann. Sci. Nat. Bot.* VIII, 18:61–153.

Echols, R. M. 1955. Linear relation of fibrillar angle to tracheid length, and genetic control of tracheid length in slash pine. *Tropical Woods* 102:11–22.

Eckardt, F. 1953. Transpiration et photosynthèse chez un xérophyte mésomorphe. *Physiol. Plantarum* 6:253–261.

Edgecombe, A. E. 1939. Differential distribution of ash in stems of herbaceous plants from base to tip. *Amer. Jour. Bot.* 26:324–328.

Eichler, A. W. 1875. *Blüthendiagramme*. W. Engelmann, Leipzig. 348 pp.

Einset, J., H. W. Blaser, and Barbara Imhofe. 1947. Chimeral sports of apples. *Jour. Hered.* 38:371–376.

—— and Barbara Lamb. 1951. Chimeral sports in grapes. Alleged tetraploid varieties have diploid "skin." *Jour. Hered.* 42:158–162.

Elliott, J. H. 1935. Seasonal changes in the development of the phloem of the sycamore, *Acer pseudoplatanus* L. *Proc. Leeds Phil. Soc.* 3:55–67.

English, J., Jr., J. Bonner, and A. J. Haagen-Smit. 1939. The wound hormones of plants. II. The isolation of a crystalline active substance. *Proc. Natl. Acad. Sci.* 25:323–329.

Ensign, M. R. 1921. Area of vein-islets in leaves of certain plants as an age determinant. *Amer. Jour. Bot.* 8:433–441.

Erickson, R. O., and D. R. Goddard. 1951. An analysis of root growth in cellular and biochemical terms. *Tenth Growth Symposium. Growth* 15(Suppl.):89–116.

—— and Katharine B. Sax. 1956. Rates of cell division and cell elongation in the growth of the primary root of *Zea mays*. *Proc. Amer. Phil. Soc.* 100:499–514.

—— and F. J. Michelini. 1957. The plastochron index. *Amer. Jour. Bot.* 44:297–305.

Eriksson, J. 1878. Über das Urmeristem der Dikotylen-Wurzeln. *Jahrb. Wiss. Bot.* 11:380–436.

Errera, L. 1888. Über Zellformen und Seifenblasen. *Bot. Centralbl.* 34:395–398.

Ervin, C. D. 1941. A study of polysomaty in *Cucumis melo*. *Amer. Jour. Bot.* 28:113–124.

Esau, Katharine. 1943. Vascular differentiation in the vegetative shoot of *Linum*. II. The first phloem and xylem. *Amer. Jour. Bot.* 30:248–255.

——. 1953a. Anatomical differentiation in root and shoot axes. In W. E. Loomis (ed.), *Growth and differentiation in plants*. Pp. 69–100.

——. 1953b. *Plant anatomy*. Wiley, New York. 735 pp.

——. 1954. Primary vascular differentiation in plants. *Biol. Rev.* 29:46–86.

Esser, M. H. M. 1946. Tree trunks and branches as optimum mechanical supports of the crown. I. The trunk. *Bull. Math. Biophys.* 8:65–74.

Evans, A. W. 1910. Vegetative reproduction in *Metzgeria*. *Ann. Bot.* 24:271–303.

Ewart, A. J. 1906. The influence of correlation upon the size of leaves. *Ann. Bot.* 20:79–82.

Eyster, W. H. 1922. Inheritance of zigzag culms in maize. *Genetics* 7:559–567.

—— and D. Burpee. 1936. Inheritance of doubleness in the flowers of the nasturtium. *Jour. Hered.* 27:50–60.

Farkas, G. L., and T. Rajháthy. 1955. Untersuchungen über die xeromorphischen Gradienten einiger Kulturpflanzen. *Planta* 45:535–548.

Felber, Irma M. 1948. Growth potentialities of vegetative buds on apple trees. *Jour. Agr. Res.* 77:239–252.

Felt, E. P. 1918. Key to American insect galls. *New York State Museum Bull.* 200. 310 pp.

———. 1940. *Plant galls and gall makers.* Comstock, Ithaca, N.Y. 364 pp.

Figdor, W. 1906. Über Regeneration der Blattspreite bei *Scolopendrium Scolopendrium. Ber. Deutsch. Bot. Ges.* 24:13–16.

———. 1907. Über Restitutionserscheinungen an Blättern von Gesneriaceen. *Jahrb. Wiss. Bot.* 44:41–56.

———. 1909. *Die Erscheinung der Anisophyllie. Eine morphologisch-physiologische Studie.* Deuticke, Leipzig and Vienna. 174 pp.

———. 1910. Über Restitutionserscheinungen bei *Dasycladus clavaeformis. Ber. Deutsch. Bot. Ges.* 28:224–227.

———. 1926. Über das Restitutionsvermögen der Blätter von *Bryophyllum calycinum* Salisb. *Planta* 2:424–428.

Fischnich, O. 1939. Weitere Versuche über die Bedeutung des Wuchsstoffes für die Adventivspross- und Wurzelbildung. *Ber. Deutsch. Bot. Ges.* 57:122–134.

Fisher, F. J. F. 1954. Effect of temperature on leaf shape in *Ranunculus. Nature* 173:406–407.

Fisher, J. E. 1957. Effect of gravity on flowering of soybeans. *Science* 125:396.

Fitting, H. 1909. Die Beeinflussung der Orchideenblüten durch die Bestaubung und durch andere Umstände. *Zeitschr. Bot.* 1:1–86.

———. 1935. Untersuchungen über die Induktion der Dorsiventralität bei den keimenden Brutkörpen von *Marchantia* und *Lunularia.* I. Die Induktoren und ihre Wirkungen. *Jahrb. Wiss. Bot.* 82:333–376.

———. 1938. V. Die Umkehrbarkeit der durch Aussenfaktoren induzierten Dorsiventralität. *Jahrb. Wiss. Bot.* 86:107–227.

———. 1949. Über die Umkehrung der Polarität in den Sporenkeimlingen einiger Laubmoose. *Planta* 37:635–696.

Flahault, C. 1878. Recherches sur l'accroissement terminal de la racine chez les Phanérogames. *Ann. Sci. Nat. Bot.* VI, 6:1–168.

Flaskämper, P. 1910. Untersuchungen über die Abhängigkeit der Gefäss- und Sklerenchymbildung von äusseren Faktoren nebst einigen Bemerkungen über die angebliche Heterorhizie bei Dikotylen. *Flora* 101:181–219.

Flemion, Florence, and Elizabeth Waterbury. 1945. Further studies with dwarf seedlings of non-after-ripened peach seeds. *Contrib. Boyce Thompson Inst.* 13:415–422.

Fortanier, E. J. 1954. Some observations on the influence of spectral regions of light on stem elongation, flower bud elongation, flower bud opening and leaf movement in *Arachis hypogea. Mededeel. Landbouwhoogesch, Wageningen* 54:103–114.

Foster, A. S. 1931. Phylogenetic and ontogenetic interpretations of the cataphyll. *Amer. Jour. Bot.* 18:243–249.

———. 1936. Leaf differentiation in angiosperms. *Bot. Rev.* 2:349–372.

———. 1939. Problems of structure, growth and evolution in the shoot apex of seed plants. *Bot. Rev.* 5:454–470.

———. 1943. Zonal structure and growth of the shoot apex in *Microcycas calocoma* (Miq.) A.DC. *Amer. Jour. Bot.* 30:56–73.

———. 1949. *Practical plant anatomy.* Van Nostrand, Princeton, N.J. 228 pp.

———. 1951. Heterophylly and foliar venation in *Lacunaria. Bull. Torrey Bot. Club* 78:382–400.

Foster, A. S. 1952. Foliar venation in angiosperms from an ontogenetic stand-point. *Amer. Jour. Bot.* 39:752–766.

———. 1955. Structure and ontogeny of terminal sclereids in *Boronia ser-rulata. Amer. Jour. Bot.* 42:551–560.

———. 1956. Plant idioblasts: remarkable examples of cell specialization. *Protoplasma* 46:184–193.

Fourcroy, Madeleine. 1938. Influence de divers traumatismes sur la structure des organes végétaux à évolution vasculaire complète. *Ann. Sci. Nat. Bot.* X, 20:1–240.

Frank, A. D. 1880. *Die Krankheiten der Pflanzen.* Breslau. 671 pp.

Frank, H., and O. Renner. 1956. Über Verjüngung bei *Hedera helix* L. *Planta* 47:105–114.

Frankel, R. 1956. Graft-induced transmission to progeny of cytoplasmic male sterility in *Petunia. Science* 124:684–685.

Fraser, I. M. 1953. The growth-promoting effect of indole-3-acetic acid on the common cultivated mushroom, *Psalliota hortensis. Australian Jour. Biol. Sci.* 6:379–395.

Frets, G. P. 1947. (The mendelian interpretation of heredity by polymeric fac-tors and its value for determining the measure of independence of the dimensions of the seeds of *Phaseolus vulgaris.*) In Dutch. *Proc. K. Ned. Akad. Wetenschap. Amsterdam* 50:798–806.

Freund, Y. 1910. Untersuchungen über Polarität bei Pflanzen. *Flora* 101:290–308.

Freundlich, H. F. 1908. Entwicklung und Regeneration von Gefässbundeln in Blattgebilden. *Jahrb. Wiss. Bot.* 46:137–206.

Frey-Wyssling, A. 1953. *Submicroscopic morphology of protoplasm.* 2d Eng. ed. Elsevier, Amsterdam. 411 pp.

———. 1954. Divergence in helical polypeptid chains and in phyllotaxis. *Nature* 173:596.

———. 1955. Die submikroskopische Struktur des Cytoplasmas. In *Handbuch der Protoplasmaforschung.* Springer, Vienna. 244 pp.

Friesner, R. C., and J. Johanna Jones. 1952. Correlation of elongation in primary and secondary branches of *Pinus resinosa. Butler Univ. Bot. Studies* 10:119–128.

Fritz, F. 1935. Über die Kutikula von *Aloë* und Gasteriaarten. *Jahrb. Wiss. Bot.* 81:718–746.

Fulford, Margaret. 1944. Sporelings and vegetative reproduction in the genus *Ceratolejeunea. Bull. Torrey Bot. Club* 71:638–654.

———. 1954. Sporeling patterns in the leafy Hepaticae. VIIIe *Congr. Internat. Bot., Rapp. et Comm. Sect.,* 16:55–64.

Funke, G. L. 1931. On the influence of light of different wave-lengths on the growth of plants. *Rec. Trav. Bot. Néerl.* 28:431–485.

———. 1937–1939. Observations on the growth of water plants. I, II, and III. *Biologisch. Jaarboek* 4:316–344; 5:382–403; 6:334–350.

Furlani, J. 1914. Zur Heterophyllie von *Hedera helix* L. *Oesterr. Bot. Zeitschr.* 64:153–169.

Galinat, W. C., and A. W. Naylor. 1951. Relation of photoperiod to inflores-cence proliferation in *Zea mays* L. *Amer. Jour. Bot.* 38:38–47.

Galston, A. W. 1947. The effect of 2,3,5-triiodobenzoic acid on the growth and flowering of soybeans. *Amer. Jour. Bot.* 34:356–360.

———. 1948. On the physiology of root initiation in excised asparagus stem tips. *Amer. Jour. Bot.* 35:281–287.

————. 1949. Transmission of the floral stimulus in soybean. *Bot. Gaz.* 110:495–501.

————, Rosamond S. Baker, and J. W. King. 1953. Benzimidazole and the geometry of cell growth. *Physiol. Plantarum* 6:863–872.

Gardner, F. E. 1929. The relationship between tree age and the rooting of cuttings. *Proc. Amer. Soc. Hort. Sci.* 26:101–104.

Gardner, V. R., J. W. Crist, and R. E. Gibson. 1933. Somatic segregation in a sectorial chimera of the Bartlett pear. *Jour. Agr. Res.* 46:1047–1057.

Garner, R. J. 1949. *The grafter's handbook.* Oxford University Press. 223 pp.

Garner, W. W., and H. A. Allard. 1920. Effect of the relative length of day and night and other factors of the environment on growth and reproduction in plants. *Jour. Agr. Res.* 18:553–606.

———— and ————. 1923. Further studies in photoperiodism, the response of the plant to relative length of day and night. *Jour. Agr. Res.* 23:871–920.

————. 1937. Recent work on photoperiodism. *Bot. Rev.* 3:259–275.

Garrison, Rhoda. 1955. Studies in the development of axillary buds. *Amer. Jour. Bot.* 42:257–266.

Gauchery, P. 1899. Recherches sur le nanisme végétal. *Ann. Sci. Nat. Bot.* VIII, 9:61–156.

Gautheret, R. J. 1944. Recherches sur la polarité des tissus végétaux. *Rev. Cyt. et Cytophysiol. Vég.* 7:45–217.

————. 1945. *La culture des tissus.* Gallimard, Paris. 202 pp.

Geiger-Huber, M., and H. Huber. 1945. Über die Ursache der gegensätzlichen geotropischen Verhaltens von Spross und Wurzel. *Experientia* 1:26–28.

Geitler, L. 1940. Kernwachstum und Kernbau bei zwei Blütenpflanzen. *Chromosoma* 1:474–485.

————. 1949. Ergebnisse und Probleme der Endomitoseforschung. *Oesterr. Bot. Zeitschr.* 95:277–299.

————. 1951. Über rechtwinkelige Schneidung von Scheidewänden und dreidimensionale Zellverbände. *Oesterr. Bot. Zeitschr.* 98:171–186.

————. 1953. *Endomitose und endomitotische Polyploidisierung.* Springer, Vienna. 89 pp.

Gemmell, A. R. 1953. Regeneration from the leaf of *Atrichum undulatum* (Hedw.) P. Beauv. *Trans. British Bryol. Soc.* 2:203–213.

Gentcheff, G., and Ä. Gustafsson. 1939. The double chromosome reproduction in *Spinachia* and its causes. *Hereditas* 25:349–358.

Georgescu, C. C. 1927. Beiträge zur Kenntnis der Verbänderung und einiger verwandter teratologischer Erscheinungen. In Goebel, *Bot. Abhandl.* 11:7–120. G. Fischer, Jena.

Gessner, F. 1940. Beiträge zur Biologie amphibischer Pflanzen. *Ber. Deutsch. Bot. Ges.* 58:2–22.

Giese, A. C. 1947. Radiations and cell division. *Quart. Rev. Biol.* 22:253–282.

Giesenhagen, K. 1905. *Studien über die Zelltheilung im Pflanzenreich. Ein Beitrag zur Entwicklungsmechanik vegetabilischer Gewebe.* Stuttgart. 90 pp.

————. 1909. Die Richtung der Teilungswand in Pflanzenzellen. *Flora* 99:355–369.

Gifford, E. M., Jr. 1954. The shoot apex in angiosperms. *Bot. Rev.* 20:477–529.

———— and R. H. Wetmore. 1957. Apical meristems of vegetative shoots and strobili in certain gymnosperms. *Proc. Natl. Acad. Sci.* 43:571–576.

Girolami, G. 1954. Leaf histogenesis in *Linum usitatissimum*. *Amer. Jour. Bot.* 41:264–273.

Glock, W. S. 1955. Tree growth. II. Growth rings and climate. *Bot. Rev.* 21:73–188.

Glück, H. 1924. *Biologische und morphologische Untersuchungen über Wasser und Sumpfgewächse*. Pt. 4. G. Fischer, Jena. 746 pp.

Goebel, K. 1882. Beiträge zur Morphologie und Physiologie des Blattes. Über die Anordnung der Staubblätter in einigen Blüten. *Bot. Zeit.* 40:353–364.

———. 1896. Über Jugendformen von Pflanzen und deren künstliche Wiederhervorrufen. *Sitz. K. Bayer. Akad. Wiss., Math. Phys. Cl.*, 26:447–497.

———. 1908. *Einleitung in die experimentelle Morphologie der Pflanzen*. Teubner, Leipzig and Berlin. 260 pp.

———. 1915. Induzierte oder autonome Dorsiventralität bei Orchideenluftwurzeln? *Biol. Zentralbl.* 35:209–225.

———. 1928. *Organographie der Pflanzen*. 3d ed. G. Fischer, Jena. 642 pp.

Golub, S. J., and R. H. Wetmore. 1948. Studies of development in the vegetative shoot of *Equisetum arvense*. I. The shoot apex. II. The mature shoot. *Amer. Jour. Bot.* 35:755–781.

Goodwin, R. H. 1944. The inheritance of flowering time in a short-day species, *Solidago sempervirens* L. *Genetics* 29:503–519.

——— and W. Stepka. 1945. Growth and differentiation in the root tip of *Phleum pratense*. *Amer. Jour. Bot.* 32:36–46.

——— and Charlotte J. Avers. 1956. Studies on roots. III. An analysis of root growth in *Phleum pratense* using photomicrographic records. *Amer. Jour. Bot.* 43:479–487.

Götz, O. 1953. Über die Brutknospenentwicklung der Gattung *Bryophyllum* im Langtag und Kurztag. *Zeitschr. Bot.* 41:445–482.

Gouwentak, Cornelia, and A. L. Maas. 1940. Kambiumtätigkeit und Wuchsstoff. *Mededeel. Landbouwhoogesch. Wageningen* 44:3–16.

Grafl, Ina. 1939. Kernwachstum durch Chromosomenvermehrung als regelmässiger Vorgang bei der pflanzlichen Gewebedifferenzierung. *Chromosoma* 1:265–275.

Graham, R. J. D., Kate H. Hawkins, and L. B. Stewart. 1934. An inverted willow cutting (*Salix alba*). *Trans. and Proc. Bot. Soc. Edinburgh* 31:343–344.

Gratzy-Wardengg, S. A. Elfriede. 1929. Osmotische Untersuchungen an Farnprothallien. *Planta* 7:307–339.

Gray, W. D. 1953. Further studies on the fruiting of *Physarum polycephalum*. *Mycologia* 45:817–824.

Green, P. B. 1954. The spiral growth pattern of the cell wall in *Nitella axillaris*. *Amer. Jour. Bot.* 41:403–409.

———. 1958. Concerning the site of the addition of new wall substances to the elongating *Nitella* cell wall. *Amer. Jour. Bot.* 45:111–116.

Grégoire, V. 1938. La Morphogénèse et l'autonomie morphologique de l'appareil floral. I. Le carpelle. *Cellule* 47:287–452.

Gregory, F. G., and O. N. Purvis. 1938. Studies in vernalisation of cereals. II. The vernalisation of excised mature embryos, and of developing ears. III. The use of anaerobic conditions in the analysis of the vernalising effect of low temperature during germination. *Ann. Bot.*, n.s. 2:237–251; 753–764.

Gregory, L. E. 1956. Some factors for tuberization in the potato plant. *Amer. Jour. Bot.* 43:281–288.

———— and J. A. Veale. 1957. A reassessment of the problem of apical dominance. *Soc. Exper. Biol. Symposium* XI:1–20.

Greulach, V. A., and Earlene Atchison. 1953. Inhibition of mitosis in bean buds by maleic hydrazide. *Bot. Gaz.* 114:478–479.

Grossenbacher, J. G. 1914. Gliding growth and the bars of Sanio. *Amer. Jour. Bot.* 1:522–530.

Grundmann, E., and H. Marquardt. 1953. Untersuchungen an Interphasekernen von *Vicia Faba*. I. Mitteilung. Desoxyribosenukleinsäure-Gehalt und Grösse der Kerne. *Chromosoma* 6:115–134.

Gulline, Heather F., and Rona Walker. 1957. The regeneration of severed pea apices. *Australian Jour. Bot.* 5:129–136.

Gümmer, Gertrud. 1949. Einfluss der Tageslänge auf den Habitus, vor allem auf die Blattstruktur, einiger Langtags- und Kurztagspflanzen (Besonders von *Kalanchoë Blossfeldiana*). *Planta* 36:439–465.

Gunckel, J. E., and R. H. Wetmore. 1946. Studies of development in long shoots and short shoots of *Ginkgo biloba* L. II. Phyllotaxis and the organization of the primary vascular system; primary phloem and primary xylem. *Amer. Jour. Bot.* 33:532–543.

———— and K. V. Thimann. 1949. Studies of development in long shoots and short shoots of *Ginkgo biloba* L. III. Auxin production in shoot growth. *Amer. Jour. Bot.* 36:145–151.

————, K. V. Thimann, and R. H. Wetmore. 1949. Studies of development in long shoots and short shoots of *Ginkgo biloba* L. IV. Growth habit, shoot expression and the mechanism of its control. *Amer. Jour. Bot.* 36:309–316.

———— and A. H. Sparrow. 1954. Aberrant growth in plants induced by ionizing radiation. *Brookhaven Symposia in Biol.* 6:252–277.

Günther, Elisabeth. 1957. Die Nachkommenschaft von Solanaceen-Chimären. *Flora* 144:497–517.

Gurwitsch, A. 1923. Versuch einer synthetischen Biologie. *Abhandl. Theoret. Biol.* 17:1–83.

————. 1926. *Das Problem der Zellteilung physiologisch betrachtet*. Springer, Berlin. 221 pp.

Gustafson, F. G. 1936. Inducement of fruit development by growth-promoting chemicals. *Proc. Natl. Acad. Sci.* 22:628–636.

Gustafsson, Ä. 1939. The interrelation of meiosis and mitosis. The mechanism of agamospermy. *Hereditas* 25:289–322.

Guttenberg, H. von. 1947. Studien über die Entwicklung des Wurzelvegetationspunktes bei Dikotyledonen. *Planta* 35:360–396.

de Haan, H. 1927. Length-factors in *Pisum*. *Genetica* 9:481–498.

————. 1930. Contributions to the genetics of *Pisum*. *Genetica* 12:321–440.

de Haan, I. 1936. Polar root formation. *Rec. Trav. Bot. Néerl.* 33:292–309.

Haberlandt, G. 1914. Zur Entwicklungsphysiologie der Rhizoiden. *Sitz. Akad. Wiss., Physik.-Math. Cl.* 1914:384–401.

————. 1921. Wundhormone als Erreger von Zellteilungen. *Beitr. Allg. Bot.* 2:1–54.

————. 1922. Über Zellteilungshormone und ihre Beziehungen zur Wundheilung, Befrüchtung, Parthenogenesis und Adventivembryonie. *Biol. Zentralbl.* 42:145–172.

Hackett, D. P. 1955. Recent studies in plant mitochondria. *Internat. Rev. Cytology* 4:143–196.

Haeckel, E. 1866. *Generelle Morphologie der Organismen*. G. Reimer, Berlin. 2 vols.

Haerdtl, H. 1927. Die Wirkung mechanischer Inanspruchnahme auf Bau und Biegungsfestigkeit der Blattstiele. *Bot. Archiv* 18:61–92.

Hagemann, A. 1931. Untersuchungen an Blattstecklingen. *Gartenbauwiss.* 6:69–195.

Halbsguth, W. 1953. Über die Entwicklung der Dorsiventralität bei *Marchantia polymorpha* L. Ein Wuchsstoffproblem? *Biol. Zentralbl.* 72:52–104.

Hall, W. C. 1949. Effects of photoperiod and nitrogen supply on growth and reproduction in the gherkin. *Plant Physiol.* 24:753–769.

―――. 1950. Growth and development of buckwheat under different temperature gradients. *Bot. Gaz.* 111:331–343.

Haller, M. H., and J. R. Magness. 1925. The relation of leaf area to the growth and composition of apples. *Proc. Amer. Soc. Hort. Sci.* 22:189–196.

Halma, F. F. 1934. Scion influence in *Citrus. Jour. Pomol. and Hort. Sci.* 12:99–104.

Hämmerling, J. 1936. Regenerationsversuche an kernhaltigen und kernlosen Zellteilen von *Acetabularia Wettsteinii. Biol. Zentralbl.* 54:650–665.

―――. 1946. Neue Untersuchungen über die physiologischen und genetischen Grundlagen der Formbildung. *Naturwiss.* 33:337–342; 361–365.

―――. 1955. Neuere Versuche über Polarität und Differenzierung bei *Acetabularia. Biol. Zentralbl.* 74:545–554.

Hammett, F. S. 1936. *The nature of growth: A logistic inquiry.* Science Press Printing Co., Lancaster, Pa. 59 pp.

―――― and L. Walp. 1943. The differentiation-forwarding effect of l-proline on eggs of *Fucus. Growth* 7:199–215.

Hammond, B. L. 1936. Regeneration of *Podostemon ceratophyllum. Bot. Gaz.* 97:834–845.

Hammond, Dorothy. 1941. The expression of genes for leaf shape in *Gossypium hirsutum* L. and *Gossypium arboreum* L. I. *Amer. Jour. Bot.* 28:124–150.

Hamner, K. C., and J. Bonner. 1938. Photoperiodism in relation to hormones as factors in floral initiation and development. *Bot. Gaz.* 100:388–431.

―――. 1944. Photoperiodism in plants. *Ann. Rev. Biochem.* 13:575–590.

Hänsel, H. 1953. Vernalization of winter rye by negative temperatures and the influence of vernalization upon the lamina length of the first and second leaf in winter rye, spring barley, and winter barley. *Ann. Bot.*, n.s. 17:417–432.

Hanson, H. C. 1917. Leaf-structure as related to environment. *Amer. Jour. Bot.* 4:533–560.

Hanstein, J. 1868. Die Scheitelzellgruppe im Vegetationspunkt der Phanerogamen. *Festschr. Niederrhein. Gesell. Natur und Heilkunde, Bonn* 1868:109–143.

Harder, R., and H. von Witsch. 1940*a*. Über die Bedeutung des Alters für die photoperiodische Reaktion von *Kalanchoë Blossfeldiana. Planta* 31:192–208.

―――― and ――――. 1940*b*. Über die Einwirkung von Kurztagsblättern auf im Langtag befindlicher Blätter und Stengelteile der gleichen Pflanze. *Planta* 31:523–558.

―――― and Brigitte Springorum. 1947. Beobachtungen über Metaplasin und Blühhormonwirkungen bei *Rudbeckia. Biol. Zentralbl.* 66:147–165.

―――. 1948. Vegetative and reproductive development of *Kalanchoë Blossfeldiana* as influenced by photoperiodism. *Soc. Exper. Biol. Symposium* II:117–138.

――――, Maria Westphal, and Gertrud Behrens. 1949. Hemmung der Infloreszenzbildung durch Langtag bei der Kurztagspflanze *Kalanchoë Blossfeldiana. Planta* 36:424–438.

Harris, J. A. 1909. The correlation between length of flowering stalk and number of flowers per inflorescence in *Northoscordum* and *Allium. Rept. Missouri Bot. Gard.* 20:105–115.

———. 1918. The interrelationship of the number of stamens and pistils in the flowers of *Ficaria. Biol. Bull.* 34:7–17.

Harrison, G. J. 1931. Metaxenia in cotton. *Jour. Agr. Res.* 42:521–544.

Harrison, R. G. 1945. Relations of symmetry in the developing embryo. *Trans. Connecticut Acad. Arts and Sci.* 36:277–330.

Hartmann, F. 1932. Untersuchungen über Ursachen und Gesetzmässigkeit exzentrischen Dickenwachstums bei Nadel- und Laubbäume. *Forstwiss. Centralbl.* 54:497–517; 547–566; 581–590; 622–634.

———. 1942. *Das statische Wuchsgesetz bei Nadel- und Laubbäume. Neue Erkenntnis über Ursache, Gesetzmässigkeit und Sinn des Reaktionsholzes.* Springer, Vienna. 111 pp.

———. 1943. Die Frage der Gleichgewichtsreaktion von Stamm und Wurzel heimischer Waldbäume. *Biol. Gen.* 17:367–418.

Hartsema, Annie M. 1926. Anatomische und experimentelle Untersuchungen über des auftreten von Neubildungen an Blättern von *Begonia rex. Rec. Trav. Bot. Néerl.* 23:305–361.

Hatcher, E. S. J. 1945. Auxin production during development and ripening of the anther and carpel of spring and winter rye. *Ann. Bot.,* n.s. 9:235–266.

Haupt, W. 1954. Die Übertragung blühfordender Prinzipien bei *Pisum sativum* durch Pfropfung. *Zeitschr. Bot.* 42:125–134.

———. 1956. Gibt es Beziehungen zwischen Polarität und Blütenbildung? *Ber. Deutsch. Bot. Ges.* 69:61–66.

———. 1957. Photoperiodische Reaktion bei einer als tagneutral geltenden Sorte von *Pisum sativum. Ber. Deutsch. Bot. Ges.* 70:191–198.

Hawker, Lilian E. 1957. *The physiology of reproduction in fungi.* Cambridge University Press. 128 pp.

Heald, F. D. 1898. A study of regeneration as exhibited by mosses. *Bot. Gaz.* 26:169–210.

Hegler, R. 1893. Über den Einfluss des mechanischen Zugs auf das Wachstum der Pflanze. *Beitr. Biol. Pflanzen* 6:383–432.

Heimsch, C., G. S. Rabideau, and W. G. Whaley. 1950. Vascular development and differentiation in two maize inbreds and their hybrid. *Amer. Jour. Bot.* 37:84–93.

———. 1951. Development of vascular tissues in barley roots. *Amer. Jour. Bot.* 38:523–537.

——— and Helen J. Stafford. 1952. Developmental relationships of the internodes of maize. *Bull. Torrey Bot. Club* 79:52–58.

Heinicke, A. J. 1935. To what extent is the McIntosh apple influenced by the food materials synthesized by Northern Spy leaves? *Proc. Amer. Soc. Hort. Sci.* 33:336–337.

Heitz, E. 1940. Die Polarität keimender Moossporen. *Verhandl. Schweiz. Naturforsch. Ges.* 120:168–170.

Hering, F. 1896. Über Wachstumskorrelationen in Folge mechanischer Hemmung des Wachsens. *Jahrb. Wiss. Bot.* 29:132–170.

Hertwig, R. 1908. Über neue Probleme der Zellenlehre. *Arch. Zellforsch.* 1:1–32.

Heslop-Harrison, J. 1952. A reconsideration of plant teratology. *Phyton* 4:19–34.

Heslop-Harrison, J. 1956. Auxin and sexuality in *Cannabis sativa*. *Physiol. Plantarum* 9:588–597.

———— and Y. Heslop-Harrison. 1957. The effect of carbon monoxide on sexuality in *Mercurialis ambigua* L. fils. *New Phytol.* 56:352–355.

Heyn, A. N. J. 1931. Der Mechanismus der Zellstreckung. *Rec. Trav. Bot. Néerl.* 28:113–244.

————. 1939. Some remarks on the mechanism of spiral growth of the sporangiophore of *Phycomyces* and a suggestion for its further explanation. *Proc. K. Akad. Wetenschap. Amsterdam, Sect. Sci.*, 42:431–437.

————. 1940. The physiology of cell elongation. *Bot. Rev.* 6:515–574.

Hibbard, R. P. 1907. The influence of tension on the formation of mechanical tissue in plants. *Bot. Gaz.* 43:361–382.

Hicks, Phyllis A. 1928a. Distribution of the carbon-nitrogen ratio in the various organs of the wheat plant at different periods of its life history. *New Phytol.* 27:108–116.

————. 1928b. Chemistry of growth as represented by carbon-nitrogen ratio. Regeneration of willow cuttings. *Bot. Gaz.* 86:193–209.

Hieke, K. 1942. Zur Alkaloidführung der Pfropfpartner bei heteroplastischen Solanaceenpfropfungen. *Planta* 33:185–205.

Himmel, W. J. 1927. A contribution to the biophysics of *Podophyllum* petioles. *Bull. Torrey Bot. Club* 54:419–451.

Hirmer, M. 1922. *Zur Lösung des Problems der Blattstellungen*. G. Fischer, Jena. 109 pp.

————. 1931. Zur Kenntnis der Schraubenstellungen im Pflanzenreich. *Planta* 14:132–206.

Höfler, K. 1934. Regenerationsvorgänge bei *Griffithsia Schousboei*. *Flora* 127:331–344.

Hofmeister, W. 1863. Zusätze und Berichtigungen zu den 1851 veröffentlichen Untersuchungen der Entwicklung höherer Kryptogamen. *Jahrb. Wiss. Bot.* 3:259–293.

————. 1868. Allgemeine Morphologie der Gewächse. In *Handbuch der Physiologischen Botanik* 1:405–664. Engelmann, Leipzig.

Hofmeyr, J. D. 1938. Genetical studies of *Carica Papaya*. I. The inheritance and relation of sex and certain plant characteristics. II. Sex reversal and sex forms. *Dept. Agr. and For. South Africa Sci. Bull.* 187. 64 pp.

Hofsten, Angelica von, and B. von Hofsten. 1958. Factors influencing cell division and vegetative morphogenesis of *Ophiostoma multiannulatum*. *Physiol. Plantarum* 11:106–117.

Holdsworth, H., and P. S. Nutman. 1947. Flowering responses in a strain of *Orobanche minor*. *Nature* 160:223–224.

Holle, H. G. 1876. Über den Vegetationspunkt der Angiospermen-Wurzeln, insbesondere die Haubenbildung. *Bot. Zeit.* 34:241–255.

Holmes, S. J. 1948. *Organic form and related biological problems*. University of California Press, Berkeley. 169 pp.

Holzer, K. 1952. Untersuchungen zur karyologischen Anatomie der Wurzel. *Oesterr. Bot. Zeitschr.* 99:118–155.

Hough, J. S. 1953. Studies on the common spangle gall of oak. *New Phytol.* 52:149–177; 218–228; 229–237.

Houghtaling, Helen B. 1935. A developmental analysis of size and shape in tomato fruits. *Bull. Torrey Bot. Club* 62:243–252.

Howard, H. W. 1949. Potato grafting experiments. I. The effect of grafting scions of Epicure on the short-day species *Solanum demissum. Jour. Genet.* 49:235–241.

Howell, M. J., and S. H. Wittwer. 1955. Further studies on the effects of 2,4-D on flowering in the sweet potato. *Proc. Amer. Soc. Hort. Sci.* 66:279–283.

Hoxmeier, Sister Mary C. 1953. Buffer capacity and pH of press sap in relation to dioecism of phanerogams. *Proc. Iowa Acad. Sci.* 60:167–175.

Huber, B. 1924. Die Beurteilung des Wasserhaushaltes der Pflanze. Ein Beitrag zur vergleichenden Physiologie. *Jahrb. Wiss. Bot.* 64:1–120.

———. 1926. Ökologische Probleme der Baumkrone. *Planta* 2:476–488.

———. 1928. Weitere quantitative Untersuchungen über das Wasserleitungssystem der Pflanzen. *Jahrb. Wiss. Bot.* 67:877–959.

Hurd, Annie M. 1920. Effect of unilateral monochromatic light and group orientation on the polarity of germinating *Fucus* spores. *Bot. Gaz.* 70:25–50.

Hurd-Karrer, Annie M. 1926. A concentration gradient in corn stalks. *Jour. Gen. Physiol.* 9:341–343.

Huskins, C. L. 1948. Segregation and reduction in somatic tissues. I. Initial observations on *Allium cepa. Jour. Hered.* 39:310–325.

——— and K. C. Cheng. 1950. Segregation and reduction in somatic tissues. IV. Reductional groupings induced in *Allium cepa* by low temperature. *Jour. Hered.* 41:13–18.

Hutchinson, J. B. 1934. The genetics of cotton. X. The inheritance of leaf shape in Asiatic *Gossypiums. Jour. Genet.* 28:437–513.

Huxley, J. S. 1932. *Problems of relative growth.* MacVeagh, New York, 276 pp.

———. 1935. Chemical regulation and the hormone concept. *Biol. Rev.* 10:427–441.

Iljin, W. S. 1957. Drought resistance in plants and physiological processes. *Ann. Rev. Plant Physiol.* 8:257–274.

Imai, Y. 1930. A genetic monograph on the leaf form of *Pharbitis nil. Zeitschr. Ind. Abst. Vererb.* 55:1–107.

——— and B. Kanna. 1934. Some remarks on fasciation of *Pharbitis nil. Jour. Coll. Agr. Univ. Tokyo* 12:409–419.

Imamura, S. 1931. Über die Dorsiventralität der unifazialen Blätter von *Iris japonica* Thunb. und ihre Beeinflussbarkeit durch Schwerkraft. *Mem. Coll. Sci. Kyoto Imp. Univ., B,* 6:271–331.

Irmak, L. R. 1956. The size of chloroplasts in young and mature organs. *Rev. Fac. Univ. Istanbul, Ser. B., Sci. Nat.* 21:139–143.

Isbell, C. L. 1931. Regenerative capacities of leaf and leaflet cuttings of tomato and of leaf and shoot cuttings of potato. *Bot. Gaz.* 92:192–201.

Iterson, G. van. 1907. *Mathematische und mikroskopisch-anatomische Studien über Blattstellungen nebst Betrachtungen über den Schalenbau der Miliolinen.* G. Fischer, Jena. 331 pp.

Iterson, G. van, Jr., and A. D. J. Meeuse. 1941. The shape of cells in homogeneous plant tissues. *Proc. K. Ned. Akad. Wetenschap. Amsterdam, Sect. Sci.,* 44:770–778.

Jablonski, J. R., and F. Skoog. 1954. Cell enlargement and cell division in excised tobacco pith tissue. *Physiol. Plantarum* 7:16–24.

Jaccard, P. 1910. Wundholzbildung im Mark von *Picea excelsa. Ber. Deutsch. Bot. Ges.* 28:62–72.

———. 1914. Structure anatomique de racines hypertendues. *Rev. Gén. Bot.* 25(bis):359–372.

Jackson, R. T. 1899. Localized stages in development in plants and animals. *Mem. Boston. Soc. Nat. Hist.* 5:89–153.

Jacobs, M. R. 1939. The vegetative reproduction of forest trees. I. Experiments with cuttings of *Pinus radiata* Don. Commonw. For. Bur. Australia Bull. 25. 28 pp.

———. 1945. The growth stresses of woody stems. Commonw. For. Bur. Australia Bull. 28. 67 pp.

———. 1954. The effect of wind sway on the form and development of *Pinus radiata* Don. *Australian Jour. Bot.* 2:35–51.

Jacobs, W. P. 1947. The development of the gynophore in the peanut plant, *Arachis hypogaea* L. I. The distribution of mitoses, the region of greatest elongation and the maintenance of vascular continuity in the intercalary meristem. *Amer. Jour. Bot.* 34:361–370.

———. 1951. Studies on cell-differentiation: The role of auxin in algae, with particular reference to rhizoid-formation in *Bryopsis*. *Biol. Bull.* 101:300–306.

———. 1952. The role of auxin in differentiation of xylem around a wound. *Amer. Jour. Bot.* 39:301–309.

——— and B. Bullwinkel. 1953. Compensatory growth in *Coleus* shoots. *Amer. Jour. Bot.* 40:385–392.

———. 1954. Acropetal auxin transport and xylem regeneration—a quantitative study. *Amer. Nat.* 88:327–337.

———. 1955. Studies on abscission: The physiological basis of the abscission-speeding effect of intact leaves. *Amer. Jour. Bot.* 42:594–604.

———. 1956. Internal factors controlling cell differentiation in the flowering plants. *Amer. Nat.* 90:163–169.

——— and Ielene B. Morrow. 1957. A quantitative study of xylem development in the vegetative shoot apex of *Coleus*. *Amer. Jour. Bot.* 44:823–842.

Jaffe, L. 1955. Do *Fucus* eggs interact through a CO_2-pH gradient? *Proc. Natl. Acad. Sci.* 41:267–270.

———. 1956. Effect of polarized light on polarity of *Fucus*. *Science* 123:1081–1082.

Jahn, E. 1941. Untersuchungen über die Zellzahl und Zelllänge in der Epidermis der Internodien von *Vicia faba*. *Beih. Bot. Centralbl.* 60, Abt. A:417–482.

Janczewski, E. 1874. Recherches sur l'accroissement terminal des racines dans le Phanérogames. *Ann. Sci. Nat. Bot.* V, 20:162–201.

———. 1885. Organisation dorsiventrale dans les racines des orchidées. *Ann. Sci. Nat. Bot.* VII, 2:55–81.

Janick, J., and E. C. Stevenson. 1955. Genetics of the monoecious character in spinach. *Genetics* 40:429–437.

Janse, J. M. 1906. Polarität und Organbildung bei *Caulerpa prolifera*. *Jahrb. Wiss. Bot.* 42:394–460.

———. 1910. Über Organveränderung bei *Caulerpa prolifera*. *Jahrb. Wiss. Bot.* 48:73–110.

———. 1914. Les sections annulaires de l'écorce et le suc descendant. *Ann. Jard. Bot. Buitenzorg* 28:1–92.

Jenkins, J. M., Jr. 1954. Some effects of different day-lengths and temperatures upon bulb formation in shallots. *Proc. Amer. Soc. Hort. Sci.* 64:311–314.

Jensen, W. A. 1955. A morphological and biochemical analysis of the early phases of cellular growth in the root tip of *Vicia faba*. *Exper. Cell. Res.* 8:506–522.

——— and L. G. Kavaljian. 1958. An analysis of cell morphology and the periodicity of division in the root tip of *Allium cepa*. *Amer. Jour. Bot.* 45:365–372.

Johansen, D. A. 1930. Embryonal manifestations of fasciation in *Clarkia elegans*. *Bot. Gaz.* 90:75–91.

———. 1950. *Plant embryology*. Chronica Botanica, Waltham, Mass. 305 pp.

Johnson, M. A. 1951. The shoot apex in gymnosperms. *Phytomorphology* 1:188–204.

Johnston, E. S. 1937. Growth of *Avena* coleoptile and first internode in different wave-length bands of the visible spectrum. *Smithsonian Misc. Coll.* 96, no. 6, pp. 1–19.

Jones, D. F. 1921. The indeterminate growth factor in tobacco and its effect upon development. *Genetics* 6:433–444.

———. 1934. Unisexual maize plants and their bearing on sex differentiation in other plants and in animals. *Genetics* 19:552–567.

———. 1938. Translocation in relation to mosaic formation in maize. *Proc. Natl. Acad. Sci.* 24:208–211.

———. 1957. Gene action in heterosis. *Genetics* 42:93–103.

Jones, H. 1955. Heterophylly in some species of *Callitriche*, with especial reference to *Callitriche intermedia*. *Ann. Bot.*, n.s. 19:225–245.

Jones, K. L. 1947. Studies on *Ambrosia*. IV. Effects of short photoperiod and temperature on sex expression. *Amer. Jour. Bot.* 34:371–377.

Jørgensen, C. A., and M. B. Crane. 1927. Formation and morphology of *Solanum* chimaeras. *Jour. Genet.* 18:247–273.

———. 1928. The experimental formation of heteroploid plants in the genus *Solanum*. *Jour. Genet.* 19:133–211.

Jost, L. 1935. Wuchsstoff und Zellteilung. *Ber. Deutsch. Bot. Ges.* 53:733–750.

———. 1942. Über Gefässbrücken. *Zeitschr. Bot.* 38:161–215.

Kaan Albest, Anita von. 1934. Anatomische und physiologische Untersuchungen über die Entstehung von Siebrohrenverbindungen. *Zeitschr. Bot.* 27:1–94.

Kaeiser, Margaret, and K. D. Stewart. 1955. Fiber size in *Populus deltoides* Marsh in relation to lean of trunk and position in trunk. *Bull. Torrey Bot. Club* 82:57–61.

Karzel, R. 1924. Untersuchungen über die Regeneration von Sprossspitzen. *Jahrb. Wiss. Bot.* 63:111–141.

Kaufman, P. B. 1955. Histological responses of the rice plant (*Oryza sativa*) to 2,4-D. *Amer. Jour. Bot.* 42:649–659.

Kearney, T. H. 1929. Development of the cotton boll as affected by removal of the involucre. *Jour. Agr. Res.* 38:381–393.

Keeble, F. 1912. Gigantism in *Primula sinensis*. *Jour. Genet.* 2:163–188.

———, M. G. Nelson, and R. Snow. 1930. The integration of plant behaviour. II. The influence of the shoot on the growth of roots in seedlings. *Proc. Roy. Soc. London, B*, 106:182–188.

Kehr, A. E., Y. C. Ting, and J. C. Miller. 1953. Induction of flowering in the Jersey type sweet potato. *Proc. Amer. Soc. Hort. Sci.* 62:437–440.

———, and H. H. Smith. 1954. Genetic tumors in *Nicotiana* hybrids. *Brookhaven Symposia in Biol.* 6:55–76.

Kelly, J. 1927. Fasciation in *Phlox Drummondii*. The origin and nature of fasciation in *Phlox*. *Jour. Hered.* 18:323–327.

Kelvin, Lord. 1887. On the division of space with minimum partition area. *Phil. Mag.* 24:503–514.

———. 1894. On homogeneous division of space. *Proc. Roy. Soc. London* 55:1–16.

Kerl, Irmgard. 1937. Über Regenerationsversüche an Fruchtkörpern und andere Entwicklungsphysiologische Untersuchungen bei *Pyronema confluens*. *Zeitschr. Bot.* 31:129–174.

Kerns, K. R., and J. L. Collins. 1947. Chimeras in pineapple. Colchicine-induced tetraploids and diploid-tetraploids in the Cayenne variety. *Jour. Hered.* 38:323–330.

Kienholz, R. 1932. Fasciation in red pine. *Bot. Gaz.* 94:404–410.

Killian, K. 1911. Beiträge zur Kenntnis der Laminarien. *Zeitschr. Bot.* 3:433–494.

Kisser, J. 1939. Über die Wirkungen carcinogener Substanzen bei Pflanzen. *Ber. Deutsch. Bot. Ges.* 57:506–515.

Klebs, G. 1903. *Willkürliche Entwicklungsänderungen bei Pflanzen. Ein Beitrag zur Physiologie der Entwicklung.* Jena. 166 pp.

———. 1904. Über Probleme der Entwicklung. *Biol. Zentralbl.* 24:257–267; 289–305; 449–465; 481–501; 545–559; 601–614.

———. 1906. Über künstliche Metamorphosen. *Abhandl. Naturforsch. Ges. Halle* 25.

———. 1913. Über das Verhaltnis der Aussenwelt zur Entwicklung der Pflanzen. Eine theoretische Betrachtung. *Sitz. Heidelberg Akad. Wiss., Math.-Nat. Kl.* 47 pp.

Klein, Deana T. 1948. Influence of varying periods of light and dark on asexual reproduction of *Pilobolus kleinii*. *Bot. Gaz.* 110:139–147.

Klein, R. M., and G. K. K. Link. 1955. The etiology of crown-gall. *Quart. Rev. Biol.* 30:207–277.

———. 1958. Activation of metabolic systems during tumor-cell formation. *Proc. Natl. Acad. Sci.* 44:350–354.

Klein, W. H., and A. C. Leopold. 1953. The effects of maleic hydrazide on flower initiation. *Plant Physiol.* 28:293–298.

Kleinmann, A. 1923. Über Kern- und Zellteilung im Cambium. *Bot. Archiv* 4:113–147.

Klieneberger, E. 1918. Über die Grösse und Beschaffenheit der Zellkerne mit besonderer Berücksichtigung der Systematik. *Beih. Bot. Centralbl.* 35:219–278.

Knapp, E. 1930. Ist die Entwicklung des Lebermoosperianths von der Befruchtung abhängig? *Planta* 12:354–361.

———. 1931. Entwicklungsphysiologische Untersuchungen an Fucaceen-Eiern. I. Zur Kenntnis der Polarität der Eier von *Cystosira barbata*. *Planta* 14:731–751.

Knapp, R. 1956. Untersuchungen über die Wirkung täglicher Temperaturschwankungen auf Wachstum, Blütenentwicklung und Fertilität. *Ber. Deutsch. Bot. Ges.* 69:399–412.

Kniep, H. 1907. Beiträge zur Keimungs-Physiologie und -Biologie von *Fucus*. *Jahrb. Wiss. Bot.* 44:635–724.

Knight, T. A. 1811. On the causes which influence the direction of the growth of roots. *Phil. Trans. Roy. Soc. London* 1811:209–219.

Knudson, L. 1913. Observations on the inception, season, and duration of cambium development of the American larch. *Bull. Torrey Bot. Club* 40:271–293.

Kny, L. 1889. Umkehrversuche mit *Ampelopsis quinquefolia* und *Hedera Helix*. *Ber. Deutsch. Bot. Ges.* 7:201–204.

———. 1894. On correlation in the growth of roots and shoots. *Ann. Bot.* 8:265–280.

————. 1902. Über den Einfluss von Zug und Druck auf die Richtung der Scheidewände in sich theilenden Pflanzenzellen. (Zweite Mittheilung.) *Jahrb. Wiss. Bot.* 37:55–98.

Kocher, V. 1941. Untersuchungen über die Blattstickstoffgehalt beider Geschlechter von *Melandrium album* unter besonderer Berücksichtigung des Blattalters. *Mitteil. Naturforsch. Ges. Bern* 1941:111–168.

Koepfli, J. B., K. V. Thimann, and F. W. Went. 1938. Phytohormones: Structure and physiological activities. *Jour. Biol. Chem.* 122:763–780.

Kögl, F., A. J. Haagen-Smit, and H. Erxleben. 1933. Über ein Phytohormon der Zellstreckung. *Zeitschr. Physiol. Chem.* 214:241–261.

Kohlenbach, H. W. 1957. Die Bedeutung des Heteroauxins für die Entwicklung der Dorsiventralität der Brutkörperkeimlinge von *Marchantia polymorpha* L. *Biol. Zentralbl.* 76:70–125.

Köhler, F. 1935. Beitrag zur Kenntnis der Sexualreaktionen bei *Mucor mucedo* (Bref.). *Planta* 23:358–378.

Kondratenko, F. 1940. (Analysis of populations of winter-rye according to length of vernalization stage.) In Russian, with English summary. (*Soviet Plant Industry Record*) 1:27–34.

Konishi, M. 1956. Studies on development of flowering stalks in long-day plants in relation to auxin metabolism. *Mem. Coll. Agr. Kyoto Univ.* 75:1–70.

Korody, Elisabeth. 1938. Studien am Spross-Vegetationspunkt von *Abies concolor, Picea excelsa* und *Pinus montana. Beitr. Biol. Pflanzen* 25:23–59.

Kostoff, D. 1929. Acquired immunity in plants. *Genetics* 14:37–77.

———— and J. Kendall. 1929. Studies on the structure and development of certain cynipid galls. *Biol. Bull.* 56:402–458.

————. 1930*a*. Tumors and other malformations on certain *Nicotiana* hybrids. *Zentralbl. f. Bakteriol.* 81:244–260.

————. 1930*b*. Chromosomal aberrants and gene mutations in *Nicotiana* obtained by grafting. *Jour. Genet.* 22:399–418.

———— and N. S. Arutiunova. 1936. Die Grösse der Zellen in den F_1 Bastarden und deren Eltern in Zusammenhang mit der Grösse der Bastarde. *Zeitschr. Zellforsch. Mikrosk. Anat.* 24:427–438.

Kostrum, Gertrud. 1944. Entwicklung der Keimlinge und Polaritätsverhalten bei Chlorophyceen. *Oesterr. Bot. Zeitschr.* 93:172–221.

Kowalewska, Z. 1927. Über Sprossregenerate an isolierten Keimblättern von Bohnen und Erbsen. *Bull. Internat. Acad. Polonaise Sci. et Lett., Cl. Sci. Math. et Nat., Ser. B.*, 1927:713–718.

Krabbe, G. 1886. *Das gleitende Wachstum bei der Gewebebildung der Gefässpflanzen.* Borntraeger, Berlin. 100 pp.

Krafczyk, H. 1931. Die Zygosporenbildung bei *Pilobolus crystallinus. Ber. Deutsch. Bot. Ges.* 49:141–146.

Kramer, P. J. 1945. Absorption of water by plants. *Bot. Rev.* 11:310–355.

————. 1955. Water relations of plant cells and tissues. *Ann. Rev. Plant. Physiol.* 6:253–272.

Kranz, G. 1931. Zur Kenntnis der wechselnden Blattform des Efeus und ihrer Ursachen. *Flora* 125:289–320.

Kraus, E. J., and H. R. Kraybill. 1918. Vegetation and reproduction with special reference to the tomato. *Oregon Agr. Exp. Sta. Bull. 149.* 90 pp.

Kraus, G. 1867. Die Gewebespannung des Stammes und ihre Folgen. *Bot. Zeit.* 25:105–112; 113–119; 121–126; 129–133; 137–142.

————. 1869. Über die Ursachen der Formänderungen etiolirender Pflanzen. *Jahrb. Wiss. Bot.* 7:209–260.

Kreh, W. 1925. Über den Einfluss der Schwerkraft auf der Entstehung der Dorsiventralität bei den Pilzhüten. *Zeitschr. Pilzkunde* 4:48–50.

Krenke, N. P. 1933. *Wundkompensation, Transplantation und Chimären bei Pflanzen.* Springer, Berlin. 934 pp.

———. 1940. *Theory of cyclic ageing and rejuvenescence of plants.* Moscow. 32 pp. (In Russian. Citation from Ashby.)

Kribs, D. A. 1928. Length of tracheids in jack pine in relation to their position in the vertical and horizontal axes of the tree. *Minnesota Agr. Exp. Sta. Tech. Bull. 54.* 14 pp.

Krieg, A. 1908. *Beiträge zur Kenntnis der Kallus- und Wundholzbildung geringelter Zweige und deren histologischen Veränderungen.* A. Stuber, Würzburg. 68 pp.

Kroll, G. H. 1912. Kritische Studien über die Verwertbarkeit der Wurzelhaubentypen für die Entwicklungsgeschichte. *Beih. Bot. Centralbl.* 28, Abt. 1:134–158.

Kuhn, E. 1941. Untersuchungen zur Frage einer hormonalen oder zellularen Geschlechtsdifferenzierung bei Blütenpflanzen. (Pfropfungen bei zweihäusigen Arten.) *Planta* 32:286–342.

Kuijper, J., and L. K. Wiersum. 1936. Occurrence and transport of a substance causing flowering in the soybean. *Proc. K. Ned. Akad. Wetenschap. Amsterdam* 39:1114–1122.

Künning, H. 1950. Untersuchungen über die Wirkstoffregulation der Kambiumtätigkeit. *Planta* 38:36–64.

Kupfer, Elsie. 1907. Studies in plant regeneration. *Mem. Torrey Bot. Club* 12:195–241.

Kupila, Sirkka. 1958. Anatomical and cytological comparison of the development of crown gall in three host species. *Ann. Bot. Soc. 'Vanamo'* 30:1–89.

Kurosawa, E. 1926. Experimental studies on the secretion of *Fusarium heterospermum. Trans. Nat. Hist. Soc. Formosa* 16:213–227.

Küster, E. 1899. Über Stammverwachsungen. *Jahrb. Wiss. Bot.* 33:487–512.

———. 1903a. Über zwei einheimische Milbengallen: *Eriophyces diversipunctatus und E. fraxinicola. Flora* 92:380–395.

———. 1903b. Beobachtungen über Regenerationserscheinungen an Pflanzen. *Beih. Bot. Centralbl.* 14:316–326; 15:421–426.

———. 1904. Beiträge zur Kenntnis der Wurzel- und Sprossbildung an Stecklingen. *Jahrb. Wiss. Bot.* 40:279–302.

———. 1910. Über organoide Gallen. *Biol. Zentralbl.* 30:116–128.

———. 1911. *Die Gallen der Pflanzen.* Leipzig.

———. 1925. *Pathologische Pflanzenanatomie.* 3d ed. G. Fischer, Jena. 558 pp.

———. 1930. Anatomie der Gallen. In Linsbauer, *Handbuch der Pflanzenanatomie.* Borntraeger, Berlin. 197 pp.

———. 1931. *Über Zonenbildung in kolloidalen Medien. Beiträge Entwicklungsmech. Anat. Pflanzen,* Heft 1, 2d ed. Jena.

———. 1949. *Die Gallenprobleme im Lichte neuer Forschungen. Giessener Naturwiss.* Vortrage 4. W. Schmitz, Giessen. 32 pp.

Labyak, L. F., and F. X. Schumacher. 1954. The contribution of its branches to the main-stem growth of loblolly pine. *Jour. Forestry* 52:333–337.

Ladefoged, K. 1952. The periodicity of wood formation. *K. Danske Videnskab. Selskab. Biol. Skrift* 7:1–98.

Laibach, F., and O. Fischnich. 1935. Künstliche Wurzelneubildung mittels Wuchsstoffpaste. *Ber. Deutsch. Bot. Ges.* 53:528–539.

——— and ———. 1936. Über Blattbewegungen unter dem Einfluss von künstlich zugeführtem Wuchsstoff. *Biol. Zentralbl.* 56:62–68.

——— and F. J. Kribben. 1951. Der Einfluss von Wuchsstoff auf das Geschlecht der Blüten bei einer monözischen Pflanze. *Beih. Biol. Pflanzen* 28:64–67.

———. 1953. Wuchsstoff und Blütenbildung. *Beitr. Biol. Pflanzen* 29:129–141.

Laing, S. 1948. Variation in tracheid length from the pith outwards in the wood of the genus *Larix* with a note on variation in other anatomical features. *Forestry* 22:222–237.

Lal, K. N., and O. N. Mehrotra. 1949. Studies in crop physiology: cell size characteristics of sugar-cane varieties in relation to drought resistance. *Bot. Gaz.* 111:193–210.

La Motte, C. 1937. Morphology and orientation of the embryo of *Isoetes*. *Ann Bot.*, n.s. 1:695–715.

Lamprecht, H. 1949. Die Vererbung verschiedener Infloresenztypen bei *Pisum*. *Agr. Hort. Genet.* 7:112–133.

Lance, A. 1952. Sur la structure et le fonctionnement du point végétatif de *Vicia faba* L. *Ann. Sci. Nat. Bot.* XI, 13:301–339.

Lang, A. 1947. Beiträge zur Genetik des Photoperiodismus. II. Photoperiodismus und Autopolyploidie. *Zeitschr. Naturforsch.* 2*b*:36–44.

——— and G. Melchers. 1947. Vernalisation und Devernalisation bei einer zweijährigen Pflanze. *Zeitschr. Naturforsch.* 2*b*:444–449.

———. 1952. Physiology of flowering. *Ann. Rev. Plant Physiol.* 3:265–306.

———. 1957. The effect of gibberellin upon flower formation. *Proc. Natl. Acad. Sci.* 43:709–717.

Lange, F. 1927. Vergleichende Untersuchungen über die Blattentwicklung einiger *Solanum*-Chimären und ihrer Elterarten. *Planta* 3:181–281.

Larsen, P. 1953. Influence of gravity on rate of elongation and on geotropic and autotropic reactions in roots. *Physiol. Plantarum* 6:735–774.

La Rue, C. D. 1933. Regeneration in mutilated seedlings. *Proc. Natl. Acad. Sci.* 19:53–63.

———. 1935. Vegetative reproduction in *Eleocharis rostellata*. *Papers Michigan Acad. Sci. Arts and Letters* 21:105–117.

———. 1942. The rooting of flowers in sterile culture. *Bull. Torrey Bot. Club* 69:332–341.

———. 1954. Studies on growth and regeneration in gametophytes and sporophytes of gymnosperms. *Brookhaven Symposia in Biol.* 6:187–207.

Lawton, Elva. 1932. Regeneration and induced polyploidy in ferns. *Amer. Jour. Bot.* 19:303–333.

———. 1936. Regeneration and induced polyploidy in *Osmunda regalis* and *Cystopteris fragilis*. *Amer. Jour. Bot.* 23:107–114.

League, Elizabeth A., and V. A. Greulach. 1955. Effects of daylength and temperature on the reproduction of *Vaucheria sessilis*. *Bot. Gaz.* 117:45–51.

Leake, H. M. 1911. Studies in Indian cotton. *Jour. Genet.* 1:204–272.

Lebedincev, Elisabeth. 1927. Physiologische und anatomische Besonderheiten der in trockener und in feuchter Luft gezogenen Pflanzen. *Ber. Deutsch. Bot. Ges.* 45:83–96.

Lebèque, A. 1952. La polyembryonie chez les Angiospermes. *Bull. Soc. Bot. France* 99:329–367.

Lehmann, E. 1936. Versuche zur Klärung der reziproken Verschiedenheiten von *Epilobium*-Bastarden. I. Der Tatbestand und die Möglichkeit seiner

Klärung durch differente Wuchsstoffbildung. *Jahrb. Wiss. Bot.* 82:657–668.

Lehmann, R. 1926. Untersuchungen über die Anatomie der Kartoffelknolle unter besonderer Berücksichtigung des Dickenwachstums und der Zellgrösse. *Planta* 2:87–131.

Lek, H. A. A. van der. 1925. *Over de wortelvorming van houtige stekken.* (Root development in woody cuttings, with English summary.) Veenman and Sons, Wageningen. 230 pp.

Leopold, A. C. 1951. Photoperiodism in plants. *Quart. Rev. Biol.* 26:247–263.

———— and Frances S. Guernsey. 1953*a*. Auxin polarity in the coleus plant. *Bot. Gaz.* 115:147–154.

———— and ————. 1953*b*. Flower initiation in Alaska pea. I. Evidence as to the role of auxin. *Amer. Jour. Bot.* 40:46–50.

———— and ————. 1954. II. Chemical vernalization. *Amer. Jour. Bot.* 41:181–185.

————. 1955. *Auxins and plant growth.* University of California Press, Berkeley. 354 pp.

Levine, M. 1936. Plant tumors and their relation to cancer. *Bot. Rev.* 2:439–455.

————. 1940. Plant responses to carcinogenic agents and growth substances; their relation to crown gall and cancer. *Bull. Torrey Bot. Club* 67:199–226.

Lewcock, H. K. 1937. Acetylene to induce flowering in pineapple. *Queensland Agr. Jour.* 48:532–543.

Lewis, F. T. 1923. The typical shape of polyhedral cells in vegetable parenchyma and the restoration of that shape following cell division. *Proc. Amer. Acad. Arts and Sci.* 58:537–552.

Libbert, E. 1954, 1955. Das Zusammenwirken von Wuchs- und Hemmstoffen bei der korrelativen Knospenhemmung. I and II. *Planta* 44:286–318; 45:68–81.

————. 1956. Untersuchungen über die Physiologie der Adventivwurzelbildung. I. Die Wirkungsweise einiger Komponenten des "Rhizokalinkomplexes." *Flora* 144:121–150.

Liernur, A. G. M. 1927. *Hexenbesen: Ihre Morphologie, Anatomie und Entstehung.* Rotterdam. 57 pp.

Lilleland, O., and J. G. Brown. 1939. The relationship of fruit size in unthinned apricot trees to crop and season. *Proc. Amer. Soc. Hort. Sci.* 37:165–172.

Lillie, R. S. 1945. *General biology and philosophy of organism.* University of Chicago Press. 215 pp.

Lindegren, C. C., and S. A. Haddad. 1954. Growth rates of individual yeast cells. *Genetica* 27:45–53.

Lindemuth, H. 1904. Über Grösserwerden isolierter ausgewachsener Blätter nach ihrer Bewurzelung. *Ber. Deutsch. Bot. Ges.* 22:171–174.

Lindstrom, E. W. 1928. Linkage of size, shape and color genes in *Lycopersicum. Zeitschr. Ind. Abst. Vererb.* Supplementband 2:1031–1057.

Link, G. K. K., and Virginia Eggers. 1946*a*. Mode, site, and time of initiation of hypocotyledonary bud primordia in *Linum usitatissimum* L. *Bot. Gaz.* 107:441–454.

———— and ————. 1946*b*. The effect of indoleacetic acid upon initiation and development of hypocotyledonary bud primordia in flax. *Bot. Gaz.* 108:114–129.

Linnemann, G. 1953. Untersuchungen über den Markstrahlanteil am Holz der Buche. *Ber. Deutsch. Bot. Ges.* 66:37–63.

Linser, H., W. Frohner, and R. Kirschner. 1955. Veränderungen von Blattmorphologie und Blattfolge bei *Erodium cicutarium* unter dem Einfluss von Phenoxyessigsäurederivativen. *Ber. Deutsch. Bot. Ges.* 68:46–51.

Liverman, J. L. 1955. The physiology of flowering. *Ann. Rev. Plant Physiol.* 6:177–210.

Livingston, B. E. 1900. On the nature of the stimulus which causes the change of form in polymorphic green algae. *Bot. Gaz.* 30:289–317.

Loeb, J. 1920. Quantitative laws in regeneration. I. *Jour. Gen. Physiol.* 2:297–307.

———. 1924. *Regeneration from a physicochemical viewpoint.* McGraw-Hill, New York. 143 pp.

Lohwag, K. 1939. Verwachsungsversüche an Fruchtkörpern von Polyporaceen. *Ann. Mycologici* 37:169–180.

Loiseau, J.-E. 1954. Suppression expérimentale d'une hélice foliaire chez *Impatiens Roylei* Walp. *Compt. Rend. Acad. Sci. Paris* 238:149–151.

Loomis, W. E. 1932. Growth-differentiation balance *vs* carbohydrate-nitrogen ratio. *Proc. Amer. Soc. Hort. Sci.* 29:240–245.

——— (ed.). 1953. *Growth and differentiation in plants.* Iowa State College Press, Ames, Iowa. 458 pp.

Lopriore, G. 1892. Über die Regeneration gespaltener Wurzeln. *Ber. Deutsch. Bot. Ges.* 10:76–83.

———. 1895. Vorläufige Mittheilung über die Regeneration gespaltener Stammspitzen. *Ber. Deutsch. Bot. Ges.* 13:410–414.

Lorbeer, G. 1930. Geschlechtsunterschiede im Chromosomensatz und in der Zellgrösse bei *Sphaerocarpos Donnellii* Aust. *Zeitschr. Bot.* 23:932–956.

Löve, A., and Doris Löve. 1946. Experiments on the effects of animal sex hormones on dioecious plants. *Arkiv för Botanik* 32A, 13:1–60.

——— and ———. 1949. The geobotanical significance of polyploidy. I. Polyploidy and latitude. *Portugaliae Acta Biologica, Sér. A, Goldschmidt Vol.,* pp. 273–352.

Love, H. H., and C. E. Leighty. 1914. Variation and correlation of oats. I. Studies showing the effect of seasonal changes on biometrical constants. *Cornell Agr. Exp. Sta. Mem. 3.* 70 pp.

Luckwill, L. C. 1939. On the factors affecting the mean seed weight of tomato fruits. *New Phytol.* 38:181–189.

———. 1957. Hormonal aspects of fruit development in higher plants. *Soc. Exper. Biol. Symposium* XI:63–85.

Lund, E. J. 1923. Electrical control of organic polarity in the egg of *Fucus*. *Bot. Gaz.* 76:288–301.

———. 1931. Electrical correlation between living cells in cortex and wood in the Douglas fir. *Plant Physiol.* 6:631–652.

———, R. I. Mahan, and A. H. Hanszen. 1945. Electric control of polar growth in roots of *Allium cepa*. *Proc. Soc. Exper. Biol. and Med.* 60:326–327. Also pp. 186–197 in Lund's general volume (1947).

——— (and collaborators). 1947. *Bioelectric fields and growth.* University of Texas Press, Austin. 391 pp.

Lund, H. A. 1956. Growth hormones in the styles and ovaries of tobacco responsible for fruit development. *Amer. Jour. Bot.* 43:562–568.

Lundegårdh, H. 1915. Experimentell-morphologische Beobachtungen. *Flora* 107:433–449.

494 Bibliography

Lundegårdh, H., 1931. *Environment and plant development.* (Trans. by E. Ashby.) E. Arnold, London. 330 pp.

Lutman, B. F. 1934. Cell size and structure in plants as affected by various inorganic elements. *Vermont Agr. Exp. Sta. Bull. 383.* 54 pp.

Lyon, C. B., and C. R. Garcia. 1944. Anatomical responses of tomato stems to variations in the macronutrient anion supply. (Also, same title but for cation supply.) *Bot. Gaz.* 105:394–405; 441–456.

MacDaniels, L. H., and O. F. Curtis. 1930. The effect of spiral ringing on solute translocation and on the structure of the regenerated tissues of the apple. *Cornell Univ. Agr. Exp. Sta. Mem. 133.* 31 pp.

MacDougal, D. T. 1903a. The influence of light and darkness upon growth and development. *Mem. New York Bot. Gard.* 2:1–319.

———. 1903b. Some correlations of leaves. *Bull. Torrey Bot. Club* 30:503–512.

Machlis, L. 1958. Evidence for a sexual hormone in *Allomyces. Physiol. Plantarum* 11:181–192.

MacVicar, R., and B. Esther Struckmeyer. 1946. The relation of photoperiod to the boron requirement of plants. *Bot. Gaz.* 107:454–461.

Magnus, W. 1906. Über die Formbildung der Hutpilze. *Arch. Biontol.* 1:85.

———. 1914. *Die Entstehung der Pflanzengallen verursacht durch Hymenopteren.* G. Fischer, Jena. 160 pp.

Maheshwari, Nirmala. 1958. *In vitro* culture of excised ovules of *Papaver somniferum. Science* 127:342.

Maheshwari, P. 1950. *An introduction to the embryology of angiosperms.* McGraw-Hill, New York, 453 pp.

Mahlstede, J. P., and D. P. Watson. 1952. An anatomical study of adventitious root development in stems of *Vaccinium corymbosum. Bot. Gaz.* 113:279–285.

Makarova, N. A. 1943. (Changes in the leaf structure of flax as a result of excluding certain mineral elements from the nutrient solution.) In Russian. *Sovetskaya Botanika* 1943:56–62.

Malinowski, E. 1934. Effect of the relative length of day and night on hybrid vigor in *Phaseolus vulgaris. Polish Agr. and For. Ann.* 33:50–58. (Citation from Burkholder, 1936.)

Maltzahn, K-E. von. 1957. A study of size differences in two strains of *Cucurbita pepo.* I. Gross size differences. II. Histological and cellular size differences. *Canadian Jour. Bot.* 35:809–830; 831–844.

Marchal, Él. and Ém. 1907, 1909, 1911. Aposporie et sexualité chez les mousses. *Bull. Acad. Roy. Belgique Cl. Sci.* 1907:765–789; 1909:1249–1288; 1911:750–778.

Margalef, R. 1953. Estudios experimentales sobre las modificaciones inducidas por diferentes temperaturas en células de cloroficeas. *Publ. Inst. Biol. Aplicada* 12:5–78.

Martin, J. P. 1942. Stem galls of sugarcane induced with insect extracts. *Science* 96:39.

Mason, T. G. 1922. Growth and correlation in sea island cotton. *West Indian Bull.* 19:214–238.

Massart, J. 1917. Sur la polarité des organes végétaux. *Bull. Biol. France et Belgique* 51:475–483.

Masters, M. T. 1869. *Vegetable teratology, an account of the principal deviations from the usual construction of plants.* Hardwicke, London. 534 pp.

Mather, K. 1948. Nucleus and cytoplasm in differentiation. *Soc. Exper. Biol. Symposium* II:196–216.

Matzke, E. B. 1929. A morphologic study of the variations in *Stellaria aquatica* with special reference to symmetry and sterility. *Bull. Torrey Bot. Club* 56:471–534.

———. 1946. The three-dimensional shape of bubbles in foam. An analysis of the role of surface forces in three-dimensional cell shape determination. *Amer. Jour. Bot.* 33:58–80.

———. 1950. In the twinkling of an eye. *Bull. Torrey Bot. Club* 77:222–227.

——— and Regina M. Duffy. 1955. The three-dimensional shape of inter-phase cells within the apical meristem of *Anacharis densa. Amer. Jour. Bot.* 42:937–945.

——— and ———. 1956. Progressive three-dimensional shape changes in dividing cells within the apical meristem of *Anacharis densa. Amer. Jour. Bot.* 43:205–225.

Mäule, D. 1896. Der Faserverlauf in Wundholz. *Bibl. Bot.* 6:1–32.

Maximov, N. A. 1929. *The plant in relation to water.* G. Allen & Unwin, London. 451 pp.

———. 1931. The physiological significance of the xeromorphic structure of plants. *Jour. Ecol.* 19:273–282.

McCallum, W. B. 1902. On the nature of the stimulus causing the change of form and structure in *Proserpinaca palustris. Bot. Gaz.* 34:93–108.

———. 1905. Regeneration in plants. I and II. *Bot. Gaz.* 40:97–120; 241–263.

McClintock, Barbara. 1929. A 2*n*-1 chromosomal chimera in maize. *Jour. Hered.* 20:218.

McClintock, J. A. 1937. The effect of stocks on the yield of Grimes apples. *Proc. Amer. Soc. Hort. Sci.* 35:369–371.

McGahan, M. W. 1955. Vascular differentiation in the vegetative shoot of *Xanthium chinense. Amer. Jour. Bot.* 42:132–140.

McKinney, H. H. 1940. Vernalization and the growth-phase concept. *Bot. Rev.* 6:25–47.

McPhee, H. C. 1924. The influence of environment upon sex in hemp, *Cannabis sativa* L. *Jour. Agr. Res.* 28:1067–1080.

McVeigh, Ilda. 1934. Vegetative reproduction in *Camptosorus rhizophyllus. Bot. Gaz.* 95:503–510.

———. 1937. Vegetative reproduction of the fern sporophyte. *Bot. Rev.* 3:457–497.

———. 1938. Regeneration in *Crassula multicava. Amer. Jour. Bot.* 25:7–11.

Meeuse, A. D. J. 1938. Development and growth of the sclerenchyma fibers and some remarks on the development of the tracheids in some monocotyledons. *Rec. Trav. Bot. Néerl.* 35:288–321.

———. 1942. A study of intercellular relationships among vegetable cells with special reference to "sliding growth" and to cell shape. *Rec. Trav. Bot. Néerl.* 38:18–140.

Mehrlich, F. P. 1931. Factors affecting growth from the foliar meristems of *Bryophyllum calycinum. Bot. Gaz.* 92:113–140.

Meier, Florence E. 1934. Effects of intensities and wave lengths of light on unicellular green algae. *Smithsonian Misc. Coll.* 92(6):1–27.

———. 1936. Growth of a green alga in isolated wave-length regions. *Smithsonian Misc. Coll.* 94(17):1–12.

Meijknecht, J. G. 1955. On the ideal value of varying characters. *Acta Bot. Neerl.* 4:273–320.

Melchers, G. 1937. Die Wirkung von Genen, tiefen Temperaturen und Blühenden Pfropfpartnern auf die Blühreife von *Hyoscyamus niger* L. *Biol. Zentralbl.* 57:568–614.

Melchers, G. 1938. Die Auslösung von Blütenbildung an zweijährigen Pflanzen im ersten Sommer durch implantierte Reiser selbst nicht blüfähiger Kurztagpflanzen in Langtagbedingungen. *Naturwiss.* 26:496.

—— and A. Lang. 1948. Die Physiologie der Blütenbildung. *Biol. Zentralbl.* 67:105–174.

Mer, É. 1886. Des modifications de structure subies par une feuille de Lierre agée de sept ans, détachée du rameau et enracinée. *Bull. Soc. Bot. France* 33:136–141.

Mericle, L. W. 1950. The developmental genetics of the Rg mutant in maize. *Amer. Jour. Bot.* 37:100–116.

Messeri, Albina. 1948. L'evoluzione della cerchia legnosa in *Pinus halepensis* in Bari. *Nuovo Giorn. Bot. Ital.* 55:111–132.

Meves, F. 1917. Historisch-kritische Untersuchungen über die Plastosomen der Pflanzenzellen. *Arch. Mikr. Anat.* 89:249–323.

Meyer, A. 1935. Zwischen Scylla und Charybdis. Holistische Antikritik von Mechanismus und Vitalismus. *Acta Biotheoretica* 1:203–218.

Meyer, B. S. 1938. The water relations of plant cells. *Bot. Rev.* 4:531–547.

Meyer, D. E. 1953. Über das Verhalten einzelner isolierter Prothalliumzellen und dessen Bedeutung für Korrelation und Regeneration. *Planta* 41:642–645.

Michaelis, P. 1938. Über die Konstanz des Plasmons. *Zeitschr. Ind. Abst. Vererb.* 74:435–459.

Michener, H. D. 1938. The action of ethylene on plant growth. *Amer. Jour. Bot.* 25:711–720.

Miehe, H. 1905. Wachstum, Regeneration und Polarität isolierter Zellen. *Ber. Deutsch. Bot. Ges.* 23:257–264.

Miller, C., and F. Skoog. 1953. Chemical control of bud formation in tobacco stem segments. *Amer. Jour. Bot.* 40:768–773.

——. 1954. The influence of cobalt and sugars upon the elongation of etiolated pea stem segments. *Plant Physiol.* 29:79–82.

Miller, Helena A., and R. H. Wetmore. 1946. Studies in the developmental anatomy of *Phlox Drummondii* Hook. I. The embryo. III. The apices of the mature plant. *Amer. Jour. Bot.* 32:588–599; 33:1–10.

Millington, W. F., and Emma L. Fisk. 1956. Shoot development in *Xanthium pennsylvanicum*. I. The vegetative plant. *Amer. Jour. Bot.* 43:655–665.

Mirskaja, Ljuba. 1926. Veränderungen an Pflanzen, hervorgerufen durch Entfernung der Blüten. *Oesterr. Bot. Zeitschr.* 75:85–95.

——. 1929. Über Regenerationsvorgänge an Vegetationspunkten von *Tradescantia guianensis*. *Planta* 8:27–35.

Misra, P. 1939. Observations on spiral grain in the wood of *Pinus longifolia* Roxb. *Forestry* 13:118–133.

——. 1943. Correlation between excentricity and spiral grain in the wood of *Pinus longifolia*. *Forestry* 17:67–80.

Möbius, M. 1920. Über die Grösse der Chloroplasten. *Ber. Deutsch. Bot. Ges.* 38:224–232.

Moewus, F. 1940. Carotinoid-Derivate als geschlechtsbestimmende Stoffe von Algen. *Biol. Zentralbl.* 60:143–166.

——. 1947. Über Morphologische Geschlechtsuntershiede bei *Valeriana dioica*. *Zeitschr. Naturforsch.* 2b:313–316.

——. 1951. Zur Genetik und Physiologie der Kern- und Zellteilung. II. Über den Synchronismus der Kernteilungen bei *Protosiphon botryoides. Beitr. Biol. Pflanzen* 28:36–63.

Mohr, H. 1956. Die Abhängigkeit des Protonemawachstums und der Protonemapolarität bei Farnen von Licht. *Planta* 47:127–158.

Molè-Bajer, Jadwiga. 1951, 1953. Influence of hydration and dehydration on mitosis. I and II. *Acta Soc. Bot. Poloniae* 21:73–94; 22:33–44.

Molisch, H. 1930. *Pflanzenphysiologie als Theorie der Gärtnerei.* 6th ed. G. Fischer, Jena. 367 pp.

Molliard, M. 1895. Recherches sur les Cécidies florales. *Ann. Sci. Nat. Bot.* VIII, 1:67–245.

Moner, J. G. 1954. Evidence for a swarming substance which stimulates colony formation in the development of *Pediastrum duplex* Mayen. *Biol. Bull.* 107:236–246

Monschau, M. 1930. Untersuchungen über das Kernwachstum bei Pflanzen. *Protoplasma* 9:536–575.

Montfort, C., and L. Müller. 1951. Grundsätzliches zur Lebenrhythmik der Mistel (*Viscum album* L.) im jährlichen Längenzuwachs und in der Blattgestaltung. *Ber. Deutsch. Bot. Ges.* 64:297–303.

Moquin-Tandon, A. 1841. *Éléments de tératologie végétale, ou histoire abrégée des anomalies de l'organisation dans les végétaux.* Paris. 403 pp.

Moreland, C. F. 1934. Factors affecting the development of the cotyledonary buds of the common bean, *Phaseolus vulgaris. Cornell Univ. Agr. Exp. Sta. Mem. 167.* 28 pp.

Moskov, B. S. 1939. Transfer of photoperiodic reaction from leaves to growing points. *Compt. Rend. (Doklady) Acad. Sci. USSR.* 24:489–491.

Mothes, K., and A. Romeike. 1955. Nicotin als Ursache der Unverträglichkeit von Pfropfungen. *Flora.* 142:109–131.

Mühldorf, A. 1951. *Die Zellteilung als Plasmateilung.* Springer, Vienna. 194 pp.

Muir, W. H., A. C. Hildebrandt, and A. J. Riker. 1954. Plant tissue cultures produced from single isolated cells. *Science* 119:877–878.

———, ———, and ———. 1958. The preparation, isolation and growth in culture of single cells from higher plants. *Amer. Jour. Bot.* 45:589–597.

Mullenders, W. 1947. L'origine du phloème interxylémien chez *Stylidium* et *Thunbergia.* Étude anatomique. *Cellule* 51:5–48.

Müller-Stoll, W. R. 1947a. Beobachtungen über Wuchsform und Zapfenbildung bei vegetativ vermehrten Fichten. *Züchter* 17/18:422–430.

———. 1947b. Der Einfluss der Ernährung auf die Xeromorphie der Hochmoorpflanzen. *Planta* 35:225–251.

———. 1952. Über Regeneration und Polarität bei *Enteromorpha. Flora* 139:148–180.

Münch, E. 1938. Untersuchungen über die Harmonie der Baumgestalt. *Jahrb. Wiss. Bot.* 86:581–673.

Müntzing, A. 1936. The evolutionary significance of autopolyploidy. *Hereditas* 21:263–378.

——— and S. Akdik. 1948. The effect on cell size of accessory chromosomes in rye. *Hereditas* 34:248–250.

Murneek, A. E. 1926. Effects of correlation between vegetative and reproductive functions in the tomato (*Lycopersicon esculentum* Mill.). *Plant Physiol.* 1:3–56.

———. 1937. Biochemical studies of photoperiodism in plants. *Missouri Agr. Exp. Sta. Res. Bull. 268.* 84 pp.

Murneek, A. E. 1940. Length of day and temperature effects in *Rudbeckia*. *Bot. Gaz.* 102:269–279.

―――― and R. O. Whyte (eds.). 1948. *Vernalization and photoperiodism, a symposium*. Chronica Botanica, Waltham, Mass. 193 pp.

――――. 1948. History of research in photoperiodism. In Murneek and Whyte (eds.), *Vernalization and photoperiodism, a symposium*. Pp. 39–61.

――――. 1954. The embryo and endosperm in relation to fruit development, with special reference to the apple, *Malus sylvestris*. *Proc. Amer. Soc. Hort. Sci.* 64:573–582.

Murray, C. D. 1927. A relationship between circumference and weight in trees and its bearing on branching angles. *Jour. Gen. Physiol.* 10:725–729.

Muzik, T. J., and C. D. La Rue. 1954. Further studies on the grafting of monocotyledonous plants. *Amer. Jour. Bot.* 41:448–455.

Näf, U. 1953. Some contributions to the development of the gametophytic phase of the fern *Onoclea sensibilis* L. (Section D. The relation of environmental gradients to the induction of form and polarity in the gametophyte.) Thesis, Yale University. 189 pp.

――――. 1956. The demonstration of a factor concerned with the initiation of antheridia in polypodiaceous ferns. *Growth* 20:91–105.

Navashin, M. 1931. Chromatin mass and cell volume in related species. *Univ. California Publ. Agr. Sci.* 6:207–230.

Naylor, A. W., and E. A. Davis. 1950. Maleic hydrazide as a plant growth inhibitor. *Bot. Gaz.* 112:112–126.

――――. 1953. Reactions of plants to photoperiod. In W. E. Loomis (ed.), *Growth and differentiation in plants*. Pp. 149–178.

Naylor, E. E. 1932. The morphology of regeneration in *Bryophyllum calycinum*. *Amer. Jour. Bot.* 19:32–40.

―――― and Betty Johnson. 1937. A histological study of vegetative reproduction in *Saintpaulia ionantha*. *Amer. Jour. Bot.* 24:673–678.

――――. 1940. Propagation of *Hyacinthus* by leaf cuttings. *Bull. Torrey Bot. Club* 67:602–606.

――――. 1941. The proliferation of dandelions from roots. *Bull. Torrey Bot. Club* 68:351–358.

Needham, J. 1936. *Order and life*. Yale University Press, New Haven, Conn. 175 pp.

Neeff, F. 1914. Über Zellumlagerung. Ein Beitrag zur experimentellen Anatomie. *Zeitschr. Bot.* 6:465–547.

――――. 1922. Über polares Wachstum von Pflanzenzellen. *Jahrb. Wiss. Bot.* 61:205–283.

Neel, J. 1940. Correlated growth in the leaf of *Begonia argenteo-guttata*. *Growth* 4:237–240.

Neilson-Jones, W. 1925. Polarity phenomena in seakale roots. *Ann. Bot.* 39:359–372.

――――. 1934. *Plant chimaeras and graft hybrids*. Methuen, London. 136 pp.

――――. 1937. Chimaeras: A summary and some special aspects. *Bot. Rev.* 3:545–562.

Nemec, B. 1905. *Studien über Regeneration*. Borntraeger, Berlin. 387 pp.

Newcombe, F. C. 1895. The regulatory formation of mechanical tissue. *Bot. Gaz.* 20:441–448.

Newman, I. V. 1956. Pattern in meristems of vascular plants. I. Cell partition in living apices and in the cambial zone in relation to the concepts of initial cells and apical cells. *Phytomorphology* 6:1–19.

Nickell, L. G. 1948. Heteroplastic grafts. *Science* 108:389.

――――. 1956. The continuous submerged cultivation of plant tissue as single cells. *Proc. Natl. Acad. Sci.* 42:848–850.

Nickerson, W. J., and Z. Mankowski. 1953. Role of nutrition in the maintenance of yeast-shape in *Candida. Amer. Jour. Bot.* 40:584–592.

―――― and C. W. Chung. 1954. Genetic block in the cellular division mechanism of a morphological mutant of a yeast. *Amer. Jour. Bot.* 41:114–120.

Niedergang-Kamien, Ethel, and F. Skoog. 1956. Studies on polarity and auxin transport in plants. I. Modification of polarity and auxin transport by triiodobenzoic acid. *Physiol. Plantarum* 9:60–73.

Nienburg, W. 1922a. Die Keimungsrichtung von Fucuseiern und die Theorie der Lichtperzeption. (Vorläufige Mitteilung.) *Ber. Deutsch. Bot. Ges.* 40:38–40.

――――. 1922b. Die Polarisation der Fucus-Eier durch das Licht. *Wiss. Meeresunters., Abt. Helgoland* 15, *N.F.,* Abhandl. 7.

――――. 1924. Die Wirkung des Lichtes auf die Keimung der Equisetumspore. *Ber. Deutsch. Bot. Ges.* 42:95–99.

Nilson, E. B., V. A. Johnson, and C. O. Gardner. 1957. Parenchyma and epidermal cell length in relation to plant height and culm internode length in winter wheat. *Bot. Gaz.* 119:38–43.

Nitsch, J. P. 1950. Growth and morphogenesis of the strawberry as related to auxin. *Amer. Jour. Bot.* 37:211–215.

――――. 1951. Growth and development *in vitro* of excised ovaries. *Amer. Jour. Bot.* 38:566–577.

――――. 1952. Plant hormones in the development of fruits. *Quart. Rev. Biol.* 27:33–57.

――――, E. B. Kurtz, Jr., J. L. Liverman, and F. W. Went. 1952. The development of sex expression in cucurbit flowers. *Amer. Jour. Bot.* 39:32–43.

Njoku, E. 1956a. The effect of light intensity on leaf shape in *Ipomoea caerulea. New Phytol.* 55:91–110.

――――. 1956b. The effect of defoliation on leaf shape in *Ipomoea caerulea. New Phytol.* 55:213–228.

――――. 1957. The effect of mineral nutrition and temperature on leaf shape in *Ipomoea caerulea. New Phytol.* 56:154–171.

Nobécourt, P. 1939. Sur la pérennité et l'augmentation de volume des cultures des tissus végétaux. *Compt. Rend. Soc. Biol.* 130:1270–1271.

Noll, F. 1888. Über den Einfluss der Lage auf die morphologische Ausbildung einiger Siphoneen. *Arb. Bot. Inst. Würzburg* 3:466–476.

Nordhausen, M. 1903. Über Sonnen- und Schattenblätter. *Ber. Deutsch. Bot. Ges.* 21:30–45.

Northcott, P. L. 1957. Is spiral grain the normal growth pattern? *For. Chron.* 33:335–352.

Northen, H. T. 1942. Relationship of dissociation of cellular proteins by auxin to growth. *Bot. Gaz.* 103:668–683.

Nutman, P. S. 1952. Studies on the physiology of nodule formation. III. Experiments on the excision of root-tips and nodules. *Ann. Bot.,* n.s. 16:79–101.

Nysterakis, F., and Simonne Quintin. 1955. Quelques considérations évolutives à la suite des modifications par l'auxine des trachéides d'*Araucaria excelsa. Compt. Rend. Acad. Sci. Paris* 240:658–661.

Oehlkers, F. 1955. Blattstecklinge als Indikatoren für blütenbildende Substanzen. *Zeitschr. Naturforsch.* 10b:158–160.

Oehm, G. 1924. Studien über Riesen- und Zwergformen einheimischer Pflanzen. *Beih. Bot. Centralbl.* 40, *Abt.* 1:237–292.

Oexemann, S. W. 1942. Relation of seed weight to vegetative growth, differentiation, and yield in plants. *Amer. Jour. Bot.* 29:72–81.

Opatowski, I. 1946. On oblique growth of trees under the action of winds. *Bull. Math. Biophys.* 8:41–49.

O'Rourke, F. L. 1942. The influence of blossom buds on rooting of hardwood cuttings of blueberry. *Proc. Amer. Soc. Hort. Sci.* 40:332–334.

Oserkowsky, J. 1942. Polar and apolar transport of auxin in woody stems. *Amer. Jour. Bot.* 29:858–866.

Ossenbeck, C. 1927. Kritische und experimentelle Untersuchungen an *Bryophyllum. Flora* 122:342–387.

Owen, F. V., E. Carsner, and M. Stout. 1940. Photothermal induction of flowering in sugar beets. *Jour. Agr. Res.* 61:101–124.

Palser, Barbara F., and W. J. McIlrath. 1956. Responses of tomato, turnip and cotton to variations in boron nutrition. II. Anatomical responses. *Bot. Gaz.* 118:53–71.

Pandey, K. K. 1956. Studies in autotetraploids of linseed (*Linum usitatissimum*). I. Growth rate. *Lloydia* 19:120–128.

Parke, R. V. 1959. Growth periodicity and the shoot tip of *Abies concolor. Amer. Jour. Bot.* 46:110–118.

Parker, M. W., and H. A. Borthwick. 1950. Influence of light on plant growth. *Ann. Rev. Plant Physiol.* 1:43–58.

Parr, T. J. 1940. *Asterocelanium variolosum* Ratzeburg, a gall-forming coccid, and its effect upon the host trees. *Yale School Forestry Bull.* 46. 49 pp.

Partanen, C. R., I. M. Sussex, and T. A. Steeves. 1955. Nuclear behavior in relation to abnormal growth in fern prothalli. *Amer. Jour. Bot.* 42:245–256.

Passmore, Sara G. 1934. Hybrid vigour in reciprocal crosses in *Cucurbita Pepo. Ann. Bot.* 48:1029–1030.

Pearl, R., and F. M. Surface. 1915. Growth and variation in maize. *Zeitschr. Ind. Abst. Vererb.* 14:97–203.

———. 1939. *The natural history of population.* Oxford University Press, New York. 416 pp.

Pearsall, W. H. 1923. Correlations in development. *Ann. Bot.* 37:261–275.

——— and Alice M. Hanby. 1925. The variation of leaf form in *Potamogeton perfoliatus. New Phytol.* 24:112–120.

——— and ———. 1926. Factors affecting the development and form of leaves. *Ann. Bot.* 40:85–103.

———. 1927. On the relative sizes of growing plant organs. *Ann. Bot.* 41:549–556.

Pearse, H. L. 1939. Plant hormones and their practical importance in horticulture. *Imper. Bur. Hort. Plantation Crops Tech. Commun.* 12:1–88.

Peebles, R. H., and T. H. Kearney. 1928. Mendelian inheritance of leaf shape in cotton. *Jour. Hered.* 19:235–238.

Penfound, W. T. 1931. Plant anatomy as conditioned by light intensity and soil moisture. *Amer. Jour. Bot.* 18:558–572.

Pennington, L. H. 1910. The effect of longitudinal compression upon the production of mechanical tissue in stems. *Bot. Gaz.* 50:257–284.

Penzig, O. 1921. *Pflanzen-Teratologie.* 2d ed. Jena.

Petit, J. 1952. Sur la détermination du sexe chez *Cannabis sativa* dans les conditions expérimentales du phytotron de Liége. *Bull. Soc. Roy. Sci. Liége* 11:464–476.

Pfeffer, W. 1871. Studien über Symmetrie und specifische Wachsthumsursachen. *Arb. Bot. Inst. Würzburg* 1:77–98.

———. 1900–1906. *The physiology of plants.* 2d ed. Clarendon Press, Oxford. 3 vols.

Pfeiffer, Norma E. 1926. Microchemical and morphological studies of effect of light on plants. *Bot. Gaz.* 81:173–195.

Philipson, W. R. 1948. Studies in the development of the inflorescence. IV. The capitula of *Hieracium boreale* Fries and *Dahlia gracilis* Ortg. V. The raceme of *Lobelia Dortmanna* L., and other campanulaceous inflorescences. *Ann. Bot.,* n.s. 12:65–75; 147–156.

———. 1949. The ontogeny of the shoot apex in dicotyledons. *Biol. Rev.* 24:21–50.

———. 1954. Organization of the shoot apex in dicotyledons. *Phytomorphology* 4:70–75.

Phinney, B. O. 1956. Growth response of single-gene dwarf mutants in maize to gibberellic acid. *Proc. Natl. Acad. Sci.* 42:185–189.

Pierce, W. P. 1937. The effect of phosphorus on chromosome and nuclear volume in a violet species. *Bull. Torrey Bot. Club* 64:345–354.

Pilet, P-E. 1952. Problème hormonal concernant l'*Endophyllum Sempervivi* Lév. parasite du *Sempervivum tectorum* L. *Ber. Schweiz. Bot. Ges.* 62:269–274.

Pilkington, Mary. 1929. The regeneration of the stem apex. *New Phytol.* 28:37–53.

Pirschle, K. 1939. Weitere Untersuchungen über die Auswirkung eines Genabhängigen Wirkstoffs bei *Petunia* in einem Pfropfversuch auf alteren Unterlagen. *Zeitschr. Ind. Abst. Vererb.* 76:512–534.

———. 1940. Ist der *d*-Stoff von *Petunia* artspezifisch? *Biol. Zentralbl.* 60:318–326.

Plantefol, L. 1948. *La théorie des hélices foliaires multiples. Fondements d'une théorie phyllotaxique nouvelle.* Masson, Paris. 154 pp.

Plateau, J. A. F. 1873. *Statique expérimentale et théorique des liquides soumis aux seules forces moléculaires.* Paris. 2 vols.

Platt, A. W., J. G. Darroch, and H. J. Kemp. 1941. The inheritance of solid stem and certain other characters in crosses between varieties of *Triticum vulgare. Sci. Agr.* 22:216–224.

Plempel, M. 1957. Der Sexualstoffe der Mucoraceae. Ihre Abtrennung und die Erklärung ihrer Funktion. *Arch. Mikrobiol.* 26:151–174.

Plett, W. 1921. Untersuchungen über die Regenerationserscheinungen an Internodien. Dissertation, Hamburg.

Plumb, G. H. 1953. The formation and development of the Norway spruce gall caused by *Adelges abietis. Connecticut Agr. Exp. Sta. Bull.* 566. 77 pp.

Pohjakallio, O. 1953. On the effect of day-length on the yield of potato. *Physiol. Plantarum* 6:140–149.

Polster, H. 1938. Kohlhydrat/Stickstoff-Verhältnis und Blütenbildung. *Beitr. Biol. Pflanzen* 25:228–260.

Pomplitz, R. 1956. Die Heteromorphie der Früchte von *Calendula arvensis* unter besonderer Berücksichtigung der Stellungs- und Zahlenverhältnisse. *Beitr. Biol. Pflanzen* 32:331–369.

Pont, J. W. 1934. Inverted polarity in *Salix babylonica. Rec. Trav. Bot. Néerl.* 31:210–222.

Poole, C. F., and P. C. Grimball. 1939. Inheritance of new sex forms in

Cucumis melo L. *Jour. Hered.* 30:21–25.

Popesco, C. T. 1949. Le changement des caractères biologiques gegnes sous l'influence du greffage entre *Phaseolus vulgaris* et *Sophora japonica*. *Botaniste* 34:329–335.

Popham, R. A., and A. P. Chan. 1950. Zonation in the vegetative stem tip of *Chrysanthemum morifolium* Bailey. *Amer. Jour. Bot.* 37:476–484.

———. 1951. Principal types of vegetative shoot apex organization in vascular plants. *Ohio Jour. Sci.* 51:249–270.

———. 1955a. Zonation of primary and lateral root apices of *Pisum sativum*. *Amer. Jour. Bot.* 32:267–273.

———. 1955b. Levels of tissue differentiation in primary roots of *Pisum sativum*. *Amer. Jour. Bot.* 42:529–540.

———. 1958. Cytogenesis and zonation in the shoot apex of *Chrysanthemum morifolium*. *Amer. Jour. Bot.* 45:198–206.

Popoff, M. 1908. Experimentelle Zellstudien. *Arch. Zellforsch.* 1:244–379.

Popp, H. W. 1926. Effect of light intensity on growth of soy beans and its relation to the auto-catalyst theory of growth. *Bot. Gaz.* 82:306–319.

Potter, G. F., and T. G. Phillips. 1927. Statistical analysis of data on fruit spur composition. *Proc. Amer. Soc. Hort. Sci.* 24:197–201.

Powers, L. 1939. Studies on the nature of the interactions of the genes differentiating quantitative characters in a cross between *Lycopersicon esculentum* and *L. pimpinellifolium*. *Jour. Genet.* 39:139–170.

Prakken, R. 1938. Zwei verschiedene Fälle somatischer Spaltung in der Blütenepidermis heterozygoter Pflanzen. *Genetica* 20:453–457.

Prantl, K. 1874. Untersuchungen über die Regeneration des Vegetationspunktes an Angiospermenwurzeln. *Arb. Bot. Inst. Würzburg* 1(4):546–562.

Prat, H. 1935. Recherches sur la structure et le mode de croissance des chaumes. *Ann. Sci. Nat. Bot.* X, 17:81–145.

———. 1948, 1951. Histo-physiological gradients and plant organogenesis. *Bot. Rev.* 14:603–643; 17:693–746.

Preston, R. D. 1948. Spiral growth in sporangiophores of *Phycomyces*. *Biochim. et Biophys. Acta* 2:155–166.

———. 1949. The development of spiral grain in conifers. *Forestry* 23:48–55.

———. 1952. *The molecular architecture of plant cell walls*. Wiley, New York. 211 pp.

Prévot, P. C. 1938. Relation entre l'épiderme et les autres tissus de la feuille dans la néoformation des bourgeons chez *Begonia rex* Putz. *Bull. Soc. Roy. Sci. Liége* 7:288–294.

———. 1939. La néoformation des bourgeons chez les végétaux. *Mem. Soc. Roy. Sci. Liége*, 4 série 3:175–342.

———. 1940. Recherches sur le métabolisme de diverses régions de la racine. *Lejeunia* 4:37–43.

Pridham, A. M. S. 1942. Factors in the rooting of cuttings and the growth of young plants. *Proc. Amer. Soc. Hort. Sci.* 40:579–582.

Priestley, J. H. 1926a. Problems of vegetative propagation. *Jour. Roy. Hort. Soc.* 51:1–16.

———. 1926b. Light and growth. II. On the anatomy of etiolated plants. *New Phytol.* 25:145–170.

——— and C. F. Swingle. 1929. Vegetative propagation from the standpoint of plant anatomy. *U.S. Dept. Agr. Tech. Bull. 151.* 98 pp.

———. 1930. Studies in the physiology of cambial activity. II. The concept of sliding growth. III. The seasonal activity of the cambium. *New Phytol.* 29:96–140; 316–354.

———, Lorna I. Scott, and Marjorie E. Malins. 1933. A new method of studying cambial activity. *Proc. Leeds Phil. Soc., Sci. Sect.* 2:365–374.

———, ———, and ———. 1935. Vessel development in the angiosperm. *Proc. Leeds Phil. Soc., Sci. Sect.* 3:42–54.

———. 1945. Observations on spiral grain in timber. *Amer. Jour. Bot.* 32:277–284.

Purvis, O. N. 1953. Photoperiodism and vernalization in cereal plants. *Proc. Linnean Soc. London* 164:136.

Quinby, J. R., and R. E. Karper. 1954. Inheritance of height in *Sorghum*. *Agronomy Jour.* 46:211–216.

Quinlan, Mildred S., and K. B. Raper. 1959. Myxobacteria. Chapter in Vol. XV of the *Encyclopedia of Plant Physiology*. Springer, Heidelberg.

Radley, Margaret. 1958. The detection of substances similar to gibberellic acid in higher plants. *Ann. Bot.*, n.s. 22:297–307.

Randolph, L. F. 1941. Genetic characteristics of the B chromosomes in maize. *Genetics* 26:608–631.

———, E. C. Abbe, and J. Einset. 1944. Comparison of shoot apex and leaf development and structure in diploid and tetraploid maize. *Jour. Agr. Res.* 69:47–76.

Raper, J. R. 1939. Sexual hormones in *Achlya*. I. Indicative evidence for a hormonal coordinating mechanism. *Amer. Jour. Bot.* 26:639–650.

———. 1950. Sexual hormones in *Achlya*. VII. The hormonal mechanism in homothallic species. *Bot. Gaz.* 112:1–24.

———. 1952. Chemical regulation of sexual processes in the thallophytes. *Bot. Rev.* 18:447–545.

———. 1957. Hormones and sexuality in lower plants. *Soc. Exper. Biol. Symposium* XI:143–165.

Raper, K. B. 1940a. The communal nature of the fruiting process in the Acrasieae. *Amer. Jour. Bot.* 27:436–448.

———. 1940b. Pseudoplasmodium formation and organization in *Dictyostelium discoideum*. *Jour. Elisha Mitchell Sci. Soc.* 56:241–282.

———. 1941. Developmental patterns in simple slime molds. *Third Growth symposium. Growth* 5(Suppl.):41–76.

———. 1956. Factors affecting growth and differentiation in simple slime molds. *Mycologia* 48:169–205.

Rasdorsky, W. 1925. Über die Reaktion der Pflanzen auf die mechanische Inanspruchnahme. *Ber. Deutsch. Bot. Ges.* 43:332–352.

———. 1931. Zur Frage über die baumechanischen Autoregulationen bei den Pflanzen. (Erwiderung und Betrachtungen anlässlich eines Sammelreferats.) *Beih. Bot. Centralbl.* 47, Abt. 1:192–254.

Rashevsky, N. 1944. Studies in the physicomathematical theory of organic form. *Bull. Math. Biophys.* 6:1–59.

———. 1955. Life, information theory and topology. *Bull. Math. Biophys.* 17:229–235.

———. 1958. A contribution to the search of general mathematical principles in biology. *Bull. Math. Biophys.* 20:71–93.

Rathfelder, O. 1954. Anatomische Untersuchungen an *Pulsatilla*. II. Protoxylementwicklung. *Flora* 141:379–388.

———. 1955. Anatomische Untersuchungen zu Castan's "Polarisationsumkehr" bei *Pisum sativum*. *Ber. Deutsch. Bot. Ges.* 68:227–232.

Rauh, W. 1937. Die Bildung von Hypocotyl und Wurzelsprossen und ihre Bedeutung für die Wuchsformen der Pflanzen. *Nova Acta Leop.* 4:395–553.

Raven, C. P. 1943. Sur les notions de "gradient" et "champ" dans l'embryologie causale. *Acta Biotheoretica* 7:135–146.

Reed, E. 1923. Hypothesis of formative stuffs as applied to *Bryophyllum calycinum. Bot. Gaz.* 75:113–142.

Reed, H. S. 1921. Correlations and growth in the branches of young pear trees. *Jour. Agr. Res.* 21:849–876.

———. 1927. Growth and differentiation in plants. *Quart. Rev. Biol.* 2:79–101.

Reeve, R. M. 1948. The "tunica-corpus" concept and development of shoot apices in certain dicotyledons. *Amer. Jour. Bot.* 35:65–75.

Reiche, Hildegard. 1924. Über Auslösung von Zellteilungen durch Injektion von Gewebesäften und Zelltrümmern. *Zeitschr. Bot.* 16:241–278.

Reid, Mary E. 1924. Relation of kind of food reserves to regeneration in tomato plants. *Bot. Gaz.* 77:103–110.

———. 1929. Growth of seedlings in light and in darkness in relation to available nitrogen and carbon. *Bot. Gaz.* 87:81–118.

———. 1941. Relation of vitamin C to cell size in the growing region of the primary root of cowpea seedlings. *Amer. Jour. Bot.* 28:410–415.

Reinders-Gouwentak, Cornelia A., and J. H. van der Veen. 1953. Cambial activity in *Populus* in connection with flowering and growth hormone. *Proc. K. Akad. Wetenschap. Amsterdam, Sect. Sci.,* 56:194–201.

Reinert, J. 1956. Dissociation of cultures from *Picea glauca* into small tissue fragments and single cells. *Science* 123:457–458.

Reinke, J. 1880. *Lehrbuch der allgemeinen Botanik mit Einschluss der Pflanzenphysiologie.* Berlin.

———. 1922. Grundlagen einer Biodynamik. *Abhandl. Theoret. Biol.* 16:1–160.

Rettig, H. 1929. Über den Einfluss der Luftfeuchtigkeit auf die Entwicklung und die Gewebedifferenzierung der Pflanzen. *Bot. Archiv* 25:128–172.

Reuter, Lotte. 1955. Protoplasmatische Pflanzenanatomie. *Protoplasmatologia* 11(2):1–131.

Richards, F. J. 1948. The geometry of phyllotaxis and its origin. *Soc. Exper. Biol. Symposium* II: 217–245.

———. 1950. Phyllotaxis: its quantitative expression and relation to growth in the apex. *Phil. Trans. Roy. Soc. London, B,* 235:509–564.

Richards, O. W., and A. J. Kavanagh. 1943. The analysis of the relative growth gradients and changing form of growing organisms, illustrated by the tobacco leaf. *Amer. Nat.* 77:385–399.

——— and ———. 1945. The analysis of growing form. In Clark and Medawar (eds.), *Essays on growth and form.* Clarendon Press, Oxford. Pp. 227–229.

Richardson, S. D. 1953. Studies of root growth in *Acer saccharinum.* I. The relation between root growth and photosynthesis. *Proc. K. Akad. Wetenschap. Amsterdam, Sect. Sci.,* 56:185–193.

Rick, C. M. 1952. The grafting relations of wilty dwarf, a new tomato mutant. *Amer. Nat.* 86:173–184.

Rickett, H. W. 1920. Regeneration in *Sphaerocarpos Donnellii. Bull. Torrey Bot. Club* 47:347–357.

Riehm, E. 1904. Beobachtungen an isolierten Blättern. *Zeit. Naturwissenschaften* 77:281–314.

Rietsema, J., Sophie Satina, and A. F. Blakeslee. 1953a. The effect of sucrose on the growth of *Datura stramonium* embryos *in vitro*. *Amer. Jour. Bot.* 40:538–545.

——, ——, and ——. 1953*b*. The effect of indole-3-acetic acid on *Datura* embryos. *Proc. Natl. Acad. Sci.* 39:924–933.

——, Benigna Blondel, Sophie Satina, and A. F. Blakeslee. 1955. Studies on ovule and embryo growth in *Datura*. I. A growth analysis. *Amer. Jour. Bot.* 42:449–455.

Riker, A. J., E. Spoerl, and Alice E. Gutsche. 1946. Some comparisons of bacterial plant galls and of their causal agents. *Bot. Rev.* 12:57–82.

—— and others. 1958. Symposium on plant tumors. *Proc. Natl. Acad. Sci.* 44:338–368.

Riley, H. P., and Dorothy Morrow. 1942. Cell size in developing ovaries of *Iris fulva*. *Bot. Gaz.* 104:90–98.

Rink, W. 1935. Zur Entwicklungsgeschichte, Physiologie und Genetik der Lebermoosgattungen *Anthoceros* und *Aspiromitus*. *Flora* 130:87–130.

Rippel, A. 1919. Der Einfluss der Bodentrockenheit auf den anatomischen Bau der Pflanzen, insbesondere von *Sinapis alba*. *Beih. Bot. Centralbl.* 36, *Abt.* 1:187–260.

Röbbelen, G. 1957. Über Heterophyllie bei *Arabidopsis thaliana* (L.) Heynh. *Ber. Deutsch. Bot. Ges.* 70:39–44.

Robbins, W. J. 1957. Gibberellic acid and the reversal of adult *Hedera* to a juvenile state. *Amer. Jour. Bot.* 44:743–746.

Robbins, W. R., G. T. Nightingale, L. G. Schermerhorn, and M. A. Blake. 1929. Potassium in relation to the shape of the sweet potato. *Science* 70:558.

Roberts, R. H., and B. Esther Struckmeyer. 1946. The effect of top environment and flowering upon top-root ratios. *Plant Physiol.* 21:332–344.

—— and ——. 1948. Anatomical and histological changes in relation to vernalization and photoperiodism. In Murneek and Whyte (eds.), *Vernalization and photoperiodism, a symposium.* Pp. 91–100.

——. 1949. Theoretical aspects of graftage. *Bot. Rev.* 15:423–463.

——. 1954. The role of photoperiod in flowering. VIIIe *Congr. Internat. Bot., Rapp. et Comm. Sect.,* 11:349–350.

Robertson, T. B. 1923. *The chemical basis of growth and senescence.* Lippincott, Philadelphia. 389 pp.

Rodríguez, A. G. 1932. Influence of smoke and ethylene on the fruiting of the pineapple (*Ananas sativus*). *Jour. Dept. Agr. Porto Rico* 16:5–18.

Rogers, W. S., A. Beryl Beakbane, and Carol P. Field. 1939. The influence of "stem builder" intermediates on apple root systems. *Jour. Pomol. and Hort. Sci.* 17:20–26.

—— and ——. 1957. Stock and scion relations. *Ann. Rev. Plant Physiol.* 8:217–236.

de Ropp, R. S. 1951*a*. The crown-gall problem. *Bot. Rev.* 17:629–670.

——. 1951*b*. Experimental induction and inhibition of overgrowths in plants. In F. Skoog (ed.), *Plant growth substances.* Pp. 381–390.

——. 1955. The growth and behaviour *in vitro* of isolated plant cells. *Proc. Roy. Soc. London, B,* 144:86–93.

Rosa, J. T. 1928. The inheritance of flower types in *Cucumis* and *Citrullus*. *Hilgardia* 3:233–250.

Rosenwinge, L. K. 1889. Influence des agents extérieurs sur l'organisation polaire et dorsiventrale des plantes. *Rev. Gén. Bot.* I:53, 123, 170, 244, 304.

Rösler, P. 1928. Histologische Studien an Vegetationspunkt von *Triticum vulgare*. *Planta* 5:28–69.

Ross, H. 1932. *Praktikum der Gallenkunde: Enstehung, Entwicklung, Bau der durch Tiere und Pflanzen hervorgerufenen Gallbildungen sowie Ökologie der Gallenerreger*. Springer, Berlin. 304 pp.

Roth, Ingrid. 1957. Relation between the histogenesis of the leaf and its external shape. *Bot. Gaz.* 118:237–245.

Rouffa, A. S., and J. E. Gunckel. 1951. A comparative study of vegetative shoot apices in the Rosaceae. *Amer. Jour. Bot.* 38:290–300.

Rübel, E. 1920. Experimentelle Untersuchungen über die Beziehungen zwischen Wasserleitungsbahn und Transpirationsverhältnissen bei *Helianthus annuus* L. *Beih. Bot. Centralbl.* 37, *Abt.* 1:1–62.

Rüdiger, W. 1952. Über die Beziehungen des Langen-Breiten-Index der Zellen und Organe bei Gigaspflanzen und ihren kleinzelligen Ausgangsformen. *Ber. Deutsch. Bot. Ges.* 65:239–245.

Ruge, U. 1952. Über die Bedeutung des Chlorophylls für die Entwicklung der Adventivwurzeln. *Ber. Deutsch. Bot. Ges.* 65:338–340.

Russell, E. S. 1933. The limitations of analysis in biology. *Proc. Aristotelian Soc.* 33:147–158.

Sacher, J. A. 1955. Cataphyll ontogeny in *Pinus lambertiana*. *Amer. Jour. Bot.* 42:82–91.

Sachs, J. 1859. Physiologische Untersuchungen über die Keimung der Schminkbohne (*Phaseolus multiflorus*). *Sitz. Akad. Wiss. Wien, Math.-Nat.* 37:57–119.

———. 1878. Über die Anordnung der Zellen in jüngsten Pflanzentheilen. *Arb. Bot. Inst. Würzburg* 2:46–104.

———. 1880–1882. Stoff und Form der Pflanzenorgane. *Arb. Bot. Inst. Würzburg* 2:452–488; 689–719.

———. 1893. Über einige Beziehungen der specifischen Grösse der Pflanzen zu ihrer Organisation. *Flora* 77:49–81.

Sagromsky, Herta. 1949. Weitere Beobachtungen zur Bildung des Spaltöffnungsmusters in der Blattepidermis. *Zeitschr. Naturforsch.* 4b:360–367.

Sahni, B. 1925. The ontogeny of vascular plants and the theory of recapitulation. *Jour. Indian Bot. Soc.* 4:202–216.

Salisbury, E. J. 1927. On the causes and ecological significance of stomatal frequency, with special reference to the woodland flora. *Phil. Trans. Roy. Soc. London, B*, 215:1–65.

Salisbury, F. B. 1955. The dual role of auxin in flowering. *Plant Physiol.* 30:327–334.

Sanio, K. 1872. Über die Grösse der Holzzellen bei der gemeinen Kiefer (*Pinus silvestris*). *Jahrb. Wiss. Bot.* 8:401–420.

———. 1873. Anatomie der gemeinen Kiefer (*Pinus silvestris* L.). *Jahrb. Wiss. Bot.* 9:50–126.

Sankewitsch, E. 1953. Untersuchungen von Röntgenmorphosen bei *Nicotiana rustica* L. *Beitr. Biol. Pflanzen* 29:1–74.

Satina, Sophie, and A. F. Blakeslee. 1926. Studies on biochemical differences between (+) and (−) sexes in *Mucors*. 2. A preliminary report on the Manoilov reaction and other tests. *Proc. Natl. Acad. Sci.* 12:191–196.

———, ———, and A. G. Avery. 1940. Demonstration of the three germ layers in the shoot apex of *Datura* by means of induced polyploidy in periclinal chimeras. *Amer. Jour. Bot.* 27:895–905.

—— and ——. 1941. Periclinal chimeras in *Datura stramonium* in relation to development of leaf and flower. *Amer. Jour. Bot.* 28:862–871.

—— and ——. 1943. Periclinal chimeras in *Datura* in relation to the development of the carpel. *Amer. Jour. Bot.* 30:453–462.

——. 1944. Periclinal chimeras in *Datura* in relation to development and structure (A) of the style and stigma, (B) of calyx and corolla. *Amer. Jour. Bot.* 31:493–502.

——. 1945. Periclinal chimeras in *Datura* in relation to the development and structure of the ovule. *Amer. Jour. Bot.* 32:72–81.

——, J. Rappaport, and A. F. Blakeslee. 1950. Ovular tumors connected with incompatible crosses in *Datura*. *Amer. Jour. Bot.* 37:576–586.

Sax, Hally J. 1938. The relation between stomata counts and chromosome numbers. *Jour. Arnold Arboretum* 19:437–441.

Sax, K. 1953. Interstock effects in dwarfing fruit trees. *Proc. Amer. Soc. Hort. Sci.* 62:201–204.

——. 1954. Stock and scion relationship in graft incompatibility. *Proc. Amer. Soc. Hort. Sci.* 64:156–158.

—— and A. Q. Dickson. 1956. Phloem polarity in bark regeneration. *Jour. Arnold Arboretum* 37:173–179.

Schaffalitzky de Muckadell, M. 1954. Juvenile stages in woody plants. *Physiol. Plantarum* 7:782–796.

Schaffner, J. H. 1931. The fluctuation curve of sex reversal in staminate hemp plants induced by photoperiodicity. *Amer. Jour. Bot.* 18:424–430.

Schander, H. 1952. Untersuchungen über umweltbedingte Eigenschaften des Samens und Keimlings von Apfel und Birne. *Angew. Bot.* 26:165–180.

Schechter, V. 1935. The effect of centrifuging on the polarity of an alga, *Griffithsia bornetiana*. *Biol. Bull.* 68:172–179.

Scheibe, A. 1956. Über gengesteuerte Formbildungsprozesse beim Sprossaufbau der Erbse. *Angew. Bot.* 30:129–134.

Schenck, H. 1916. Über Verbänderungen an Nadelhölzern. *Mitt. Deutsch. Dendrol. Ges.* 25:37–52.

Schilling, E. 1915. Über hypertrophische und hyperplastische Gewebeswucherungen an Sprossachsen, verursacht durch Paraffine. *Jahrb. Wiss. Bot.* 55:177–258.

Schimper, C. F. 1836. Geometrische Anordung der um eine Achse peripherische Blattgebilde. *Verhandl. Schweiz. Ges.* 1836:113–117.

Schkwarnikow, P. K. 1934. Über die Grösse der meristematischen Zellen von trisomen Pflanzen von *Crepis tectorum*. *Planta* 22:375–392.

Schlenker, G., and G. Mittmann. 1936. Versüche zur Klärung der reziproken Verschiedenheiten von *Epilobium*-Bastarden. IV. Internodienwachstum und Zellstreckung bei *Epilobium hirsutum* unter dem Einfluss synthetischer beta-indolylessigsäure. *Jahrb. Wiss. Bot.* 83:315–323.

Schlösser, L-A. 1935. Beitrag zu einer physiologischen Theorie der plasmatischen Vererbung. *Zeitschr. Ind. Abst. Vererb.* 69:159–192.

Schmidt, A. 1924. Histologische Studien an phanerogamen Vegetationspunkten. *Bot. Archiv.* 8:345–404.

Schmitt, F. O. 1956. Macromolecular interaction patterns in biological systems. *Proc. Amer. Phil. Soc.* 100:476–486.

Schneider, E. 1926. Über die Gewebespannung der Vegetationspunkte. *Ber. Deutsch. Bot. Ges.* 44:326–328.

Schoch-Bodmer, Helen, and P. Huber. 1951. Das Spitzenwachstum der Bastfasern bei *Linum usitatissimum* und *Linum perenne*. *Ber. Schweiz. Bot. Ges.* 61:377–404.

Schopfer, W. H. 1950. Morphogénèse et vitamines. *L'Année Biol.* 26:583–595.

Schoser, G. 1956. Über die Regeneration bei den Cladophoraceen. *Protoplasma* 47:103–134.

Schoute, J. C. 1902. *Die Stelär-Theorie.* P. Noordhoff, Groningen. 182 pp.

———. 1913, 1914. Beiträge zur Blattstellungslehre. I. Die Theorie. II. Über verästelte Baumfarne und die Verästelung der Pteropsida im allgemeinen. *Rec. Trav. Bot. Néerl.* 10:153–325; 11:95–193.

———. 1936. Fasciation and dichotomy. *Rec. Trav. Bot. Néerl.* 33:649–669.

Schramm, R. 1912. Über die anatomischen Jugendformen der Blätter einheimischer Holzpflanzen. *Flora* 104:225–295.

Schrank, A. R. 1957. Bioelectrical implications in plant tropisms. *Soc. Exper. Biol. Symposium* XI:95–117.

Schratz, E. 1927. Über Korrelationen zwischen Zellgrösse und Chloroplastenmasse bei Moosen. *Jahrb. Wiss. Bot.* 66:748–772.

Schrödinger, E. 1944. *What is life?* Cambridge University Press. 91 pp.

Schroeder, C. A. 1953a. Spirality in *Citrus. Bot. Gaz.* 114:350–352.

———. 1953b. Growth and development of the Fuerte avocado fruit. *Proc. Amer. Soc. Hort. Sci.* 61:103–109.

Schröter, H-B. 1955. Über das Vorkommen von Nikotin in *Zinnia elegans* und über die Bedeutung dieses Alkaloids für die interfamiliäre Pfropfung *Zinnia* auf *Nicotiana. Arch. Pharmaz. und Ber. Deutsch. Pharm. Ges.* 288:141–145.

Schüepp, O. 1917. Über den Nachweis von Gewebespannung in der Sprossspitze. *Ber. Deutsch. Bot. Ges.* 35:703–706.

———. 1926. Meristeme. In Linsbauer, *Handbuch der Pflanzenanatomie.* Bd. 4. Borntraeger, Berlin. 115 pp.

———. 1945. Allometrie und Metamorphose. Konstruktion eines Schemas eines einfachen Fiederblattes. *Verhandl. Naturforsch. Ges. Basel* 56:261–271.

———. 1946. Geometrische Betrachtungen über Wachstum und Formwechsel. *Ber. Schweiz. Bot. Ges.* 56:629–655.

———. 1952. Wachstum und Zellanordnung im Sprossgipfel erläutert am Beispiel des Springbrunnentypus von *Microcycas. Ber. Schweiz. Bot. Ges.* 62:592–627.

Schulman, E. 1956. *Dendroclimatic changes in semiarid America.* University of Arizona Press. 142 pp.

Schumacher, W. 1933. Untersuchungen über die Wanderung des Fluoreszeïns in der Siebröhren. *Jahrb. Wiss. Bot.* 77:685–732.

———. 1936. Untersuchungen über die Wanderung des Fluoreszeïns in der Haaren von *Cucurbita pepo. Jahrb. Wiss. Bot.* 82:507–533.

Schwabe, W. W. 1951, 1954. Factors controlling flowering in the chrysanthemum. II. Day-length effects on the further development of inflorescence buds and their experimental reversal and modification. IV. The site of vernalization and translocation of the stimulus. *Jour. Exper. Bot.* 2:223–237; 5:389–400.

———. 1958. Effects of photoperiod and hormone treatment on isolated rooted leaves of *Kalanchoë Blossfeldiana. Physiol. Plantarum* 11:225–239.

Schwanitz, F., and H. Pirson. 1955. Chromosomengrösse, Zellgrösse und Zellenzahl bei einigen diploiden Gigaspflanzen. *Züchter* 25:221–229.

Schwarz, W. 1927. Die Entwicklung des Blattes bei *Plectranthus fruticosus* und *Ligustrum vulgare* und die Theorie der Periklinalchimären. *Planta* 3:499–526.

———. 1930. Der Einfluss der Zug-, Knick- und Bewegungsbeanspruchung auf das mechanische Gewebesystem der Pflanzen. *Beih. Bot. Centralbl.* 46, *Abt.* 1:306–338.

———. 1933. Die Strukturänderungen sprossloser Blattstecklinge und ihre Ursachen. Ein Beitrag zur Kausalanalyse der Gewebebildung. *Jahrb. Wiss. Bot.* 78:92–155.

Schwarzenbach, F. H. 1956. Die Beeinflussing der Viviparie bei einer Grönlandische Rasse von *Poa alpina* L. durch den jahreszeitlichen Licht- und Temperaturwechsel. *Ber. Schweiz. Bot. Ges.* 66:204–223.

Schwendener, S. 1878. *Mechanische Theorie der Blattstellung.* Engelmann, Leipzig. 107 pp.

———. 1898. *Gesammelte botanische Mittheilungen.* Borntraeger, Berlin, 2 vols. 872 pp.

Scott, D. R. M., and S. B. Preston. 1955. Development of compression wood in eastern white pine through the use of centrifugal force. *For. Sci.* 1:178–182.

Scully, N. J., M. W. Parker, and H. A. Borthwick. 1945. Interaction of nitrogen nutrition and photoperiod as expressed in bulbing and flower-stalk development of onion. *Bot. Gaz.* 107:52–61.

Seeliger, R. 1924. Topophysis und Zyklophysis pflanzlicher Organe und ihre Bedeutung für die Pflanzenkultur. *Angew. Bot.* 6:191–200.

Sensarma, P. 1957. On the vascularization of the leaf and its associated structures in *Muntingia calabura. Bot. Gaz.* 119:116–119.

Setchell, W. A. 1905. Regeneration among kelps. *Univ. California Publ. Bot.* 2:139–168.

Shaffer, B. M. 1957. Aspects of aggregation in cellular slime molds. I. Orientation and chemotaxis. *Amer. Nat.* 91:19–35.

Shank, D. B. 1945. Effects of phosphorus, nitrogen and soil moisture on top-root ratios of inbred and hybrid maize. *Jour. Agr. Res.* 70:365–377.

Sharman, B. C. 1945. Leaf and bud initiation in the Gramineae. *Bot. Gaz.* 106:269–289.

Shields, Lora M. 1950. Leaf xeromorphy as related to physiological and structural influences. *Bot Rev.* 16:399–447.

——— and W. K. Mangum. 1954. Leaf nitrogen in relation to structure of leaves of plants growing in gypsum sand. *Phytomorphology* 4:27–38.

Shirley, H. L. 1929. The influence of light intensity and light quality upon the growth of plants. *Amer. Jour. Bot.* 16:354–390.

Shull, G. H. 1910. Inheritance of sex in *Lychnis. Bot. Gaz.* 49:110–125.

———. 1914. Duplicate genes for capsule form in *Bursa bursa-pastoris. Zeitschr. Ind. Abst. Vererb.* 12:97–149.

Sierp, H. 1913. Über die Beziehungen zwischen Individuengrösse, Organgrösse und Zellengrösse, mit besonderer Berücksichtigung des erblichen Zwergwuchses. *Jahrb. Wiss. Bot.* 53:55–124.

Sifton, H. B. 1944. Developmental morphology of vascular plants. *New Phytol.* 43:87–129.

Silberschmidt, K. 1935. Die Abhängigkeit des Pfropferfolges von der systematischen Verwandschaft der Pärtner. *Zeitschr. Bot.* 29:65–137.

Silow, R. A. 1939. The genetics of leaf shape in diploid cottons and the theory of gene interaction. *Jour. Genet.* 38:229–276.

Simak, M. 1953. Beziehungen zwischen Samengrösse und Samenzahl in verschieden grösse Zapfen eines Baumes (*Pinus silvestris*). *Meddeland. Statens Skogsforskn. Inst.* 43:1–15.

Simon, S. 1904. Untersuchungen über die Regeneration der Wurzelspitze. *Jahrb. Wiss. Bot.* 40:103–143.

———. 1908. Experimentelle Untersuchungen über die Entstehung von Gefässverbindungen. *Ber. Deutsch. Bot. Ges.* 26(Festschrift):364–396.

Simon, S. V. 1920. Über die Beziehungen zwischen Stoffstauung und Neubildungsvorgängen in isolierten Blättern. *Zeitschr. Bot.* 12:593–634.

———. 1929. Über Gewebeveränderungen in den Stielen abgetrennter bewurzelter Blätter von *Begonia Rex*. *Jahrb. Wiss. Bot.* 70:368–388.

———. 1930. Transplantationsversüche zwischen *Solanum melongena* und *Iresine Lindeni*. *Jahrb. Wiss. Bot.* 72:137–160.

Simonis, W. 1952. Untersuchungen zum Dürreeffekt. I. Morphologische Struktur, Wasserhaushalt, Atmung und Photosynthese feucht und trocken gezogener Pflanzen. *Planta* 40:313–332.

Simons, R. K. 1956. Comparative anatomy of leaves and shoots of Golden Delicious and Jonared apple trees grown with high and low moisture supply. *Proc. Amer. Soc. Hort. Sci.* 68:20–26.

Singleton, W. R. 1946. Inheritance of indeterminate growth in maize. *Jour. Hered.* 37:61–64.

———. 1951. Inheritance of "corn grass," a macromutation in maize, and its possible significance as an ancestral type. *Amer. Nat.* 85:81–96.

Sinnott, E. W., and I. W. Bailey. 1914. Nodal anatomy and the morphology of stipules. *Amer. Jour. Bot.* 1:441–453.

———. 1921. The relation between body size and organ size in plants. *Amer. Nat.* 55:385–403.

———. 1930. The morphogenetic relationships between cell and organ in the petiole of *Acer*. *Bull. Torrey Bot. Club* 57:1–20.

———, Helen Houghtaling, and A. F. Blakeslee. 1934. The comparative anatomy of extra-chromosomal types in *Datura stramonium*. *Carnegie Inst. Washington Publ. 451*. 50 pp.

———. 1935. Evidence for the existence of genes controlling shape. *Genetics* 20:12–21.

———. 1936a. The relation of organ size to tissue development in the stem. *Amer. Jour. Bot.* 23:418–421.

———. 1936b. A developmental analysis of inherited shape differences in cucurbit fruits. *Amer. Nat.* 70:245–254.

———. 1937. The relation of gene to character in quantitative inheritance. *Proc. Natl. Acad. Sci.* 23:224–227.

———. 1939. A developmental analysis of the relation between cell size and fruit size in cucurbits. *Amer. Jour. Bot.* 26:179–189.

——— and R. Bloch. 1939. Changes in intercellular relationships during the growth and differentiation of living plant tissues. *Amer. Jour. Bot.* 26:625–634.

——— and ———. 1941. Division of vacuolate plant cells. *Amer. Jour. Bot.* 28:225–232.

———. 1942. An analysis of the comparative rates of cell division in various parts of the developing cucurbit ovary. *Amer. Jour. Bot.* 29:317–323.

——— and R. Bloch. 1943. Development of the fibrous net in the fruit of various races of *Luffa cylindrica*. *Bot. Gaz.* 105:90–99.

———— and Alicelia H. Franklin. 1943. A developmental analysis of the fruit in tetraploid as compared with diploid races of cucurbits. *Amer. Jour. Bot.* 30:87–94.

————. 1944. Cell polarity and the development of form in cucurbit fruits. *Amer. Jour. Bot.* 31:388–391.

————. 1945a. The relation of cell division to growth rate in cucurbit fruits. *Growth* 9:189–194.

————. 1945b. The relation of growth to size in cucurbit fruits. *Amer. Jour. Bot.* 32:439–446.

———— and R. Bloch. 1945. The cytoplasmic basis of intercellular patterns in vascular differentiation. *Amer. Jour. Bot.* 32:151–156.

————. 1952. Reaction wood and the regulation of tree form. *Amer. Jour. Bot.* 39:69–78.

————. 1955. Stalk diameter as a factor in fruit size. *Jour. Arnold Arboretum* 36:267–272.

————. 1958. The genetic basis of organic form. *Ann. New York Acad. Sci.* 71:1223–1233.

Sinoto, Y. 1925. Notes on the histology of a giant and an ordinary form of *Plantago. Bot. Mag. Tokyo* 39:159–166.

Sirks, M. J. 1915. Die Natur der pelorischen Blüte. *Zeitschr. Ind. Abst. Vererb.* 14:71–79.

Skok, J., and N. J. Scully. 1955. Nature of the photoperiodic responses of buckwheat. *Bot. Gaz.* 117:134–141.

Skoog, F. 1940. Relationships between zinc and auxin in the growth of higher plants. *Amer. Jour. Bot.* 27:939–951.

———— (ed.). 1951. *Plant growth substances.* University of Wisconsin Press, Madison, 476 pp.

———— and C. Tsui. 1951. Growth substances and the formation of buds in plant tissues. In F. Skoog (ed.), *Plant growth substances.* Pp. 263–285.

———— and C. O. Miller. 1957. Chemical regulation of growth and organ formation in plant tissues cultured *in vitro.* In *Soc. Exper. Biol. Symposium* XI:118–131.

Smirnov, E., and A. N. Zhelochovtsev. 1931. Das Gesetz der Altersveränderungen der Blattform bei *Tropaeolum majus* L. unter verschiedenen Beleuchtungsbedingungen. *Planta* 15:299–354.

Smith, E. F., Nellie A. Brown, and C. O. Townsend. 1911. Crown-gall of plants: its cause and remedy. *U.S. Dept. Agr. Bur. Plant Ind. Bull.* 213. 215 pp.

————. 1917. Mechanism of tumor growth in crown gall. *Jour. Agr. Res.* 8:165–186.

Smith, Harriet E. 1946. *Sedum pulchellum:* a physiological and morphological comparison of diploid, tetraploid and hexaploid races. *Bull. Torrey Bot. Club* 73:495–541.

Smith, H. B. 1927. Annual versus biennial growth habit and its inheritance in *Melilotus alba. Amer. Jour. Bot.* 14:129–146.

Smith, H. H. 1943. Studies on induced heteroploids of *Nicotiana. Amer. Jour. Bot.* 30:121–130.

————. 1950. Developmental restrictions on recombination in *Nicotiana. Evolution* 4:202–211.

Smith, K. M. 1920. Investigation on the nature and cause of the damage to plant tissue resulting from the feeding of capsid bugs. *Ann. Appl. Biol.* 7:40–55.

512 *Bibliography*

Smith, W. H. 1950. Cell-multiplication and cell-enlargement in the development of the flesh of the apple-fruit. *Ann. Bot.*, n.s. 14:23–38.

Smith, W. K. 1943. Propagation of chlorophyll-deficient sweet clover hybrids as grafts. *Jour. Hered.* 34:135–140.

Smuts, J. C. 1926. *Holism and evolution.* Macmillan, New York. 362 pp.

Snow, Mary, and R. Snow. 1934. The interpretation of phyllotaxis. *Biol. Rev.* 9:132–137.

—— and ——. 1935. Experiments on phyllotaxis. Part III. Diagonal splits through decussate apices. *Phil. Trans. Roy. Soc. London, B*, 225:63–94.

—— and ——. 1937. Auxin and leaf formation. *New Phytol.* 36:1–18.

—— and ——. 1942. The determination of axillary buds. *New Phytol.* 41:13–22.

—— and ——. 1947. On the determination of leaves. *New Phytol.* 46:5–19.

—— and ——. 1952. Minimum areas and leaf determination. *Proc. Roy. Soc. London, B*, 139:545–566.

Snow, R. 1935. Activation of cambial growth by pure hormones. *New Phytol.* 34:347–360.

——. 1937. On the nature of correlative inhibition. *New Phytol.* 36:283–300.

——. 1940. A hormone for correlative inhibition. *New Phytol.* 39:177–184.

——. 1945. Plagiotropism and correlative inhibition. *New Phytol.* 44:110–117.

——. 1950. Experiments on bijugate apices. *Phil. Trans. Roy. Soc. London, B*, 235:291–310.

——. 1955. Problems of phyllotaxis and leaf determination. *Endeavour* 14:190–199.

Söding, H. 1934. Über die Bedingungen fur die Entstehung der Sonnenblätter. *Ber. Deutsch. Bot. Ges.* 52:110–120.

——. 1936. Über den Einfluss von Wuchsstoff auf das Dickenwachstum der Bäume. *Ber. Deutsch. Bot. Ges.* 54:291–304.

——. 1940. Weitere Untersuchungen über die Wuchsstoffregulation der Kambiumtätigkeit. *Zeitschr. Bot.* 36:113–141.

——. 1952. *Die Wuchsstofflehre. Ergebnisse und Probleme der Wuchsstoffforschung.* Thieme, Stuttgart. 304 pp.

Solereder, H. 1905. Über Hexenbesen auf *Quercus rubra*, nebst einer Zusammenstellung der auf Holzpflanzen beobachteten Hexenbesen. *Naturwiss. Zeitschr. Forst- und Landwirtschaft* 2:17–24.

Sorauer, P. 1899. Über Intumescenzen. *Ber. Deutsch. Bot. Ges.* 17:456–460.

Sorokin, Helen, and Anna L. Sommer. 1929. Changes in the cells and tissues of root tips induced by the absence of calcium. *Amer. Jour. Bot.* 16:23–39.

——. 1955. Mitochondria and spherosomes in the living epidermal cell. *Amer. Jour. Bot.* 42:225–231.

Sossountzov, I. 1953, 1954. Action du glycocolle sur le développement in vitro des colonies prothalliennes de *Gymnogramme calomelanos*, Filicinée Polypodiacée. I. Morphologie générale des colonies. II. Morphologie générale, sexualité et dimensions des prothalles constitutifs des colonies prothalliennes. *Physiol. Plantarum* 6:723–734; 7:1–15. (Reports continued in 7:383–396 and 726–742.)

Souèges, R. 1934–1939. *Exposés d'embryologie et de morphologie végétales.* Vols. I–X. Hermann, Paris. (Many other papers, chiefly in *Bull. Soc. Bot. France* and *Compt. Rend. Acad. Sci. Paris.* See Maheshwari, 1950, for references.)

Southwick, L. 1937. Malling stock influence on fruit size and shape. *Proc. Amer. Soc. Hort. Sci.* 35:359–361.

Sprague, G. F. 1953. Heterosis. In W. E. Loomis (ed.), *Growth and differentiation in plants*. Pp. 113–136.

Springer, Eva. 1935. Über Apogame (vegetative entstandene) Sporogone an der bivalenten Rasse des Laubmooses *Phascum cuspidatum. Zeitschr. Ind. Abst. Vererb.* 69:249–262.

Sproston, T., and D. C. Pease. 1957. Influence of thermoperiods on production of the sexual stage of the fungus *Sclerotinia trifoliorum. Trans. New York Acad. Sci.* 20:199–204.

Spurr, A. R. 1949. Histogenesis and organization of the embryo in *Pinus strobus. Amer. Jour. Bot.* 36:629–641.

――――. 1957. The effect of boron on cell-wall structure in celery. *Amer. Jour. Bot.* 44:637–650.

Spurr, S. H., and M. J. Hyvärinen. 1954*a*. Compression wood in conifers as a morphogenetic phenomenon. *Bot. Rev.* 20:551–560.

―――― and ――――. 1954*b*. Wood fiber length as related to position in tree and growth. *Bot. Rev.* 20:561–575.

Stahl, E. 1885. Einfluss der Beleuchtungsrichtung auf die Theilung der Equisetumsporen. *Ber. Deutsch. Bot. Ges.* 3:334–340.

Stanfield, J. F. 1944. Chemical composition of roots and tops of dioecious *Lychnis* in vegetative and flowering phases of growth. *Plant Physiol.* 19:377–383.

Stant, Margaret Y. 1954. The shoot apex of some monocotyledons. II. Growth organization. *Ann. Bot.,* n.s. 18:441–447.

Stebbins, G. L., Jr. 1938. Cytological characteristics associated with the different growth habits in the dicotyledons. *Amer. Jour. Bot.* 25:189–198.

Steeves, T. A., and I. M. Sussex. 1957. Studies on the development of excised leaves in sterile culture. *Amer. Jour. Bot.* 44:665–673.

―――― and W. R. Briggs. 1958. Morphogenetic studies on *Osmunda cinnamonea* L. The origin and early development of vegetative fronds. *Phytomorphology* 8:60–72.

Steffen, K. 1956. Endomitosen im Endosperm von *Pedicularis palustris* L. *Planta* 47:625–652.

Steil, W. N. 1939, 1951. Apogamy, apospory and parthenogenesis in the pteridophytes. *Bot. Rev.* 5:433–453; 17:90–104.

Stein, Emmy. 1939. Über einige Pfropfversüche mit erblichen, durch Radium-Bestrahlung erzeugten Varianten von *Antirrhinum majus, Antirrhinum siculum* und *Solanum lycopersicum. Biol. Zentralbl.* 59:59–78.

Stein, O. L. 1956. A comparison of embryonic growth rates in two inbreds of *Zea mays* L. and their reciprocal hybrids. *Growth* 20:37–50.

Steinberg, R. A. 1953. Low temperature induction of flowering in a *Nicotiana rustica* × *N. Tabacum* hybrid. *Plant Physiol.* 28:131–134.

Steinecke, F. 1925. Zur Polarität von *Bryopsis. Bot. Archiv* 12:97–118.

Stephens, S. G. 1944. The genetic organization of leaf-shape development in the genus *Gossypium. Jour. Genet.* 46:28–51.

――――. 1948. A comparative developmental study of a dwarf mutant in maize, and its bearing on the interpretation of tassel and ear structure. *Ann. Missouri Bot. Gard.* 35:289–299.

Sterling, C. 1945. Growth and vascular development in the shoot apex of *Sequoia sempervirens* (Lamb.) Endl. I. Structure and growth of the shoot apex. *Amer. Jour. Bot.* 32:118–126.

Steward, F. C., R. H. Wetmore, J. F. Thompson, and J. P. Nitsch. 1954. A quantitative chromatographic study of nitrogenous components of shoot apices. *Amer. Jour. Bot.* 41:123–134.

———, ———, and J. K. Pollard. 1955. The nitrogenous components of the shoot apex of *Adiantum pedatum. Amer. Jour. Bot.* 42:946–948.

———, Marion O. Mapes, and Joan Smith. 1958. Growth and organized development of cultured cells. I. Growth and division of freely suspended cells. *Amer. Jour. Bot.* 45:693–703.

———, ———, and Kathryn Mears. 1958. II. Organization in cultures grown from freely suspended cells. *Amer. Jour. Bot.* 45:705–708.

Stewart, W. N. 1948. A study of the plastids in the cells of the mature sporophyte of *Isoetes. Bot. Gaz.* 110:281–300.

Stiefel, S. 1952. Über Erregungsvorgänge bei der Einwirkung von photischen und mechanischen Reizen auf *Coprinus*-Fruchtkörper. *Planta* 40:301–312.

Stingl, G. 1905. Untersuchungen über Doppelbildung und Regeneration bei Wurzeln. *Oesterr. Bot. Zeitschr.* 55:219–225; 260–263.

———. 1908. Uber regenerative Neubildungen an isolierten Blättern phanerogamer Pflanzen. *Flora* 99:178–192.

Stolwijk, J. A. J. 1954. Wave length dependence of photomorphogenesis in plants. *Mededeel. Landbouwhoogesch. Wageningen* 54:181–244.

Stoudt, H. N. 1934. Gemmipary in *Byrnesia weinbergii. Amer. Jour. Bot.* 21:562–572.

———. 1938. Gemmipary in *Kalanchoë rotundifolia* and other Crassulaceae. *Amer. Jour. Bot.* 25:106–110.

Stoutemyer, V. T., and A. W. Close. 1946. Rooting cuttings and germinating seeds under fluorescent and cold cathode lighting. *Proc. Amer. Soc. Hort. Sci.* 48:309–325.

Stowe, B. B., and T. Yamaki. 1957. The history and physiological action of the gibberellins. *Ann. Rev. Plant Physiol.* 8:181–216.

Strasburger, E. 1877. *Über Befruchtung und Zelltheilung.* Dufft, Jena. 108 pp.

———. 1882. *Über den Bau und das Wachstum der Zellhäute.* Fischer, Jena. 264 pp.

———. 1893. Über die Wirkungssphäre der Kerne und die Zellgrösse. *Histologische Beit.* 5:97–124.

———. 1900. Versüche mit diöcischen Pflanzen in Rücksicht auf Geschlechtsverteilung. *Biol. Zentralbl.* 20:657–665; 689–698; 721–731; 753–785.

Straub, J. 1940. Quantitative und qualitative Verschiedenheiten innerhalb von polyploiden Pflanzenreihen. *Biol. Zentralbl.* 60:659–669.

———. 1948. Zur Organisation der Zelle. Die Abhängigkeit der Zellgrösse von der Beleuchtungsstärke und der Konzentration der Kulturlösung. *Biol. Zentralbl.* 67:479–489.

———. 1954. Das Licht bei der Auslösung der Fruchtkörperbildung von *Didymium eunigripes* und die Übertragung der Lichtwirkung durch das tote Plasma. *Naturwiss.* 41:219–220.

Street, H. E., and E. H. Roberts. 1952. Factors controlling meristematic activity in excised roots. I. Experiments showing the operation of internal factors. *Physiol. Plantarum* 5:498–509.

Strugger, S. 1957. Schraubig gewundene Fäden als sublichtmikroskopische Strukturelemente des Cytoplasmas. *Ber. Deutsch. Bot. Ges.* 70:91–108.

Sunderland, N., and R. Brown. 1956. Distribution of growth in the apical region of the shoot of *Lupinus albus. Jour. Exper. Bot.* 7:127–145.

Sussex, I. M. 1955. Experimental investigation of leaf dorsiventrality and orientation in the juvenile shoot. *Phytomorphology* 5:286–300.

Sussman, M. 1952. An analysis of the aggregation stage in the development of the slime molds, Dictyosteliaceae. II. Aggregative center formation by mixtures of *Dictyostelium discoideum* wild type and aggregateless variants. *Biol. Bull.* 103:446–457.

———. 1955. "Fruity" and other mutants of the cellular slime mold, *Dictyostelium discoideum:* a study of developmental aberrations. *Jour. Gen. Microbiol.* 13:295–309.

Swamy, B. G. L. 1946. Inverted polarity of the embryo sac of angiosperms and its relation to the archegonium theory. *Ann. Bot.,* n.s. 10:171–183.

Swarbrick, T., and R. H. Roberts. 1927. The relation of scion variety to character of root growth in apple trees. *Wisconsin Agr. Exp. Sta. Res. Bull.* 78. 23 pp.

———. 1928. Factors governing fruit bud formation. VIII. The seasonal elongation growth of apple varieties on some vegetative rootstocks, and its possible relation to fruit bud formation. *Jour Pomol. and Hort. Sci.* 7:100–129.

———. 1930. Rootstock and scion relationship. Some effects of scion variety upon the rootstock. *Jour. Pomol. and Hort. Sci.* 8:210–228.

Swingle, C. F. 1927. Graft hybrids in plants. *Jour. Hered.* 18:73–94.

———. 1940, 1952. Regeneration and vegetative propagation. *Bot. Rev.* 6:301–355; 18:1–13.

Swingle, W. T. 1928. Metaxenia in the date palm. Possibly a hormone action by the embryo or endosperm. *Jour. Hered.* 19:257–268.

Takashima, R., H. Kawahara, and H. Hara. 1951. On the morphoregulative effects of supersonics on germination and growth of seeds and growth of sprouts. *Bull. Exper. Biol.* 1:1–6.

Talbert, Charlotte M., and A. E. Holch. 1957. A study of the lobing of sun and shade leaves. *Ecology* 38:655–658.

Tammes, Tine. 1903. Die Periodicität morphologischer Erscheinungen bei den Pflanzen. *Verhandl. K. Akad. Wetenschap. Amsterdam* 9:1–148.

Tartar, V. 1956. Pattern and substance in *Stentor. Soc. Devel. and Growth, Symposium* 14:73–100.

Tatum, E. L., R. W. Barratt, and V. M. Cutter, Jr. 1949. Chemical induction of colonial paramorphs in *Neurospora* and *Syncephalastrum. Science* 109:509–511.

Tellefsen, Marjorie A. 1922. The relation of age to size in certain root cells and in vein-islets of the leaves of *Salix nigra. Amer. Jour. Bot.* 9:121–139.

Tenopyr, Lillian A. 1918. On the constancy of cell shape in leaves of varying shape. *Bull. Torrey Bot. Club* 45:51–76.

Teodoresco, E. C. 1929. Observations sur la croissance des plantes aux lumières de diverse longueurs d'onde. *Ann. Sci. Nat. Bot.* X, 11:201–336.

Terby, Jeanne. 1933. Cas d'orientation des figures de division les unes par rapport aux autres au sein d'un plasmodium. *Bull. Acad. Roy. Belgique, Cl. Sci.,* 19:1198–1206.

Therman, Eeva. 1956. Dedifferentiation and differentiation of cells in crown gall of *Vicia faba. Caryologia* 8:325–348.

Thimann, K. V., and F. Skoog. 1934. On the inhibition of bud development and other functions of growth substance in *Vicia Faba. Proc. Roy. Soc. London, B,* 114:317–339.

——— and Jane Behnke. 1947. The use of auxins in the rooting of woody cuttings. *Cabot Foundation Publ.* (Harvard) 1:1–272.

Thimann, K. V. 1948. Plant growth hormones. In Pincus and Thimann (eds.), *The hormones: physiology, chemistry, and applications.* Academic Press, New York. Pp. 5–74.

———. 1951. Studies on the physiology of cell enlargement. *Tenth Growth Symposium. Growth* 15 (*Suppl.*):5–22.

———. 1954a. The physiology of growth in plant tissues. *Amer. Scientist* 42:589–606.

———. 1954b. Correlations of growth by humoral influences. VIIIe Congr. *Internat. Bot., Rapp. et Comm. Sect.,* 11:114–128.

———. 1956. Promotion and inhibition: twin themes of physiology. *Amer. Nat.* 90:145–162.

———. 1957. Growth and growth hormones in plants. *Amer. Jour. Bot.* 44:49–55.

Thomas, J. B. 1939. Electrical control of polarity in plants. *Rec. Trav. Bot. Néerl.* 36:373–437.

Thompson, D'Arcy W. 1942. *On growth and form.* 2d ed. Cambridge Univ. Press. 1116 pp.

Thompson, H. C. 1953. Vernalization of growing plants. In W. E. Loomis (ed.), *Growth and differentiation in plants.* Pp. 179–196.

Thompson, M. T. 1915. In E. P. Felt (ed.), *An illustrated catalog of American insect galls.* Nassau, N.Y. 116 pp.

Thomson, Betty F. 1954. The effect of light on cell division and cell elongation in seedlings of oats and peas. *Amer. Jour. Bot.* 41:326–332.

Tieghem, P. van. 1887. Recherches sur la disposition des radicelles et des bourgeons dans les racines des Phanérogames. *Ann. Sci. Nat. Bot.* VII, 5:130–151.

———. 1888. Sur le réseau de soutien de l'écorce de la racine. *Ann. Sci. Nat. Bot.* VII, 7:375–378.

——— and H. Douliot. 1888. Recherches comparatives sur l'origine des membres endogènes dans les plantes vasculaires. *Ann. Sci. Nat. Bot.* VII, 8:1–660.

Tingley, Mary A. 1944. Concentration gradients in plant exudates with reference to the mechanism of translocation. *Amer. Jour. Bot.* 31:30–38.

Tischler, G. 1918. Untersuchungen über die Riesenwuchs von *Phragmites communis* var. *Pseudodonax.* *Ber. Deutsch. Bot. Ges.* 36:549–558.

———. 1951. *Allgemeine Pflanzenkaryologie.* Pt. 2. *Kernteilung und Verschmelzung.* Borntraeger, Berlin. 1040 pp.

Titman, P. W., and R. H. Wetmore. 1955. The growth of long and short shoots in *Cercidiphyllum. Amer. Jour. Bot.* 42:364–372.

Tobler, F. 1904. Über Eigenwachstum der Zelle und Pflanzenform. Versüche und Studien an Meeresalgen. *Jahrb. Wiss. Bot.* 39:527–580.

———. 1929. Zur Kenntnis der Wirkung des Kaliums auf den Bau der Bastfaser. *Jahrb. Wiss. Bot.* 71:26–51.

Tobler, Margarete. 1931. Zur Variabilität des Zellvolumens einer Sippenkreuzung von *Funaria hygrometrica* und deren bivalenten Rassen. *Zeitschr. Ind. Abst. Vererb.* 60:39–62.

Torrey, J. G. 1950. The induction of lateral roots by indoleacetic acid and root decapitation. *Amer. Jour. Bot.* 37:257–264.

———. 1952. Effects of light on elongation and branching in pea roots. *Plant Physiol.* 27:591–602.

———. 1953. The effect of certain metabolic inhibitors on vascular tissue differentiation in isolated pea roots. *Amer. Jour. Bot.* 40:525–533.

————. 1955. On the determination of vascular patterns during tissue differentiation in excised pea roots. *Amer. Jour. Bot.* 42:183–198.

————. 1957a. Cell division in isolated single plant cells *in vitro*. *Proc. Natl. Acad. Sci.* 43:887–891.

————. 1957b. Auxin control of vascular pattern in regenerating pea root meristems grown *in vitro*. *Amer. Jour. Bot.* 44:859–870.

Townsend, G. F., and C. C. Lindegren. 1954. Characteristic growth patterns of the different members of a polyploid series of *Saccharomyces*. *Jour. Bacteriol.* 67:480–483.

Transeau, E. N. 1916. The periodicity of freshwater algae. *Amer. Jour. Bot.* 3:121–133.

Trécul, A. 1853. Accroissement des végétaux dicotylédonées ligneux, reproduction du bois et de l'écorce par le bois decortiqué. *Ann. Sci. Nat. Bot.* III, 19:157–192.

Troll, W. 1928. *Organisation und Gestalt im Bereich der Blüte*. Springer, Berlin. 413 pp.

Trombetta, Vivian V. 1939. The cytonuclear ratio in developing plant cells. *Amer. Jour. Bot.* 26:519–529.

————. 1942. The cytonuclear ratio. *Bot. Rev.* 8:317–336.

Truscott, F. H. 1958. On the regeneration of new shoots from isolated dodder haustoria. *Amer. Jour. Bot.* 45:169–177.

Tschermak-Woess, Elisabeth, and Gertrude Hasitschka. 1953a. Veränderungen der Kernstrucktur während der Endomitose, rhythmisches Kernwachstum und verschiedenes Heterochromatin bei Angiospermen. *Chromosoma* 5:574–614.

———— and ————. 1953b. Über Musterbildung in der Rhizodermis und Exodermis bei einigen Angiospermen und einer Polypodiacee. *Oesterr. Bot. Zeitschr.* 100:646–651.

———— and Ruth Doležal. 1953. Durch Seitenwurzelbildung induzierte und spontane Mitosen in der Dauergeweben der Wurzel. *Oesterr. Bot. Zeitschr.* 100:358–402.

———— and Gertrude Hasitschka. 1954. Über die endomitotische Polyploidisierung im Zuge der Differenzierung von Trichomen und Trichozyten bei Angiospermen. *Oesterr. Bot. Zeitschr.* 101:79–117.

————. 1956. Karyologische Pflanzenanatomie. *Protoplasma* 46:798–834.

Tukey, H. B. 1933. Embryo abortion in early-ripening varieties of *Prunus avium*. *Bot. Gaz.* 94:433–468.

———— and K. D. Brase. 1933. Influence of the scion and of an intermediate stem-piece upon the character and development of roots of young apple trees. *New York (Geneva) Agr. Exp. Sta. Tech. Bull. 218.* 50 pp.

———— and J. O. Young. 1939. Histological study of the developing fruit of the sour cherry. *Bot. Gaz.* 100:723–749.

Tukey, L. D. 1952. Effect of night temperature on growth of the fruit of the sour cherry. *Bot. Gaz.* 114:155–165.

Tulecke, W. 1957. The pollen of *Ginkgo biloba: In vitro* culture and tissue formation. *Amer. Jour. Bot.* 44:602–608.

Tupper-Carey, Rose M. 1930. Observations on the anatomical changes in tissue bridges across rings through the phloem of trees. *Proc. Leeds Phil. Soc., Sci. Sect.,* 2:86–94.

Turing, A. M. 1952. The chemical basis of morphogenesis. *Phil. Trans. Roy. Soc. London, B,* 237:37–72.

Ullrich, J. 1953. Variationsstatistische Untersuchungen an Blättern. *Ber. Deutsch. Bot. Ges.* 66:322–332.

Umrath, K., and A. Soltys. 1936. Über die Erregungssubstanz der Papilionaceen und ihre zellteilungsauslösende Wirkung. *Jahrb. Wiss. Bot.* 84:276–289.

———. 1953. Geschlechtsbedingte Unterschiede in der Blattform. *Phyton* 4:290–299.

Ungerer, E. 1926. *Die Regulationen der Pflanzen.* 2d ed. Springer, Berlin. 363 pp.

Uphof, J. C. T. 1924. On mendelian factors in radishes. *Genetics* 9:292–304.

Ursprung, A. 1912. Über die Polarität bei *Impatiens Sultani. Beih. Bot. Centralbl.* 28, Abt.1:307–310.

Van Fleet, D. S. 1952. The histochemical localization of enzymes in vascular plants. *Bot. Rev.* 18:354–398.

———. 1954a. The significance of the histochemical localization of quinones in the differentiation of plant tissues. *Phytomorphology* 4:300–310.

———. 1954b. Cell and tissue differentiation in relation to growth (plants). *Soc. Devel. and Growth, Symposium* 11:111–129.

Van Overbeek, J. 1935. The growth hormone and the dwarf type of growth in corn. *Proc. Natl. Acad. Sci.* 21:292–299.

———. 1936. "Lazy," an a-geotropic form of maize. *Jour. Hered.* 27:93–96.

———. 1938. Auxin distribution in seedlings and its bearing on the problem of bud inhibition. *Bot. Gaz.* 100:133–166.

——— and L. E. Gregory. 1945. A physiological separation of two factors necessary for the formation of roots on cuttings. *Amer. Jour. Bot.* 32:336–341.

———. 1946. Control of flower formation and fruit size in the pineapple. *Bot. Gaz.* 108:64–73.

———, S. A. Gordon, and L. E. Gregory. 1946. An analysis of the functions of the leaf in the process of root formation in cuttings. *Amer. Jour. Bot.* 33:100–107.

——— and H. J. Cruzado. 1948. Flower formation in the pineapple plant by geotropic stimulation. *Amer. Jour. Bot.* 35:410–412.

Vardar, Y., and P. Acarer. 1957. Auxin in relation to the development of epiphyllous buds in *Bryophyllum. Phyton* 8:109–118.

Vazart, B. 1955. La parthénocarpie. *Bull. Soc. Bot. France* 102:406–443.

Venning, F. D. 1949. Stimulation by wind motion of collenchyma formation in celery petioles. *Bot. Gaz.* 110:511–514.

———. 1953. The influence of major mineral nutrient deficiencies on growth and tissue differentiation in the hypocotyl of Marglobe tomato, *Lycopersicon esculentum* Mill. *Phytomorphology* 3:315–326.

Vince, Daphne. 1956. Studies of the effects of light quality on the growth and development of plants. II. Formative effects in *Lycopersicon esculentum* and *Pisum sativum. Jour. Hort. Sci.* 31:16–24.

Vischer, W. 1915. Experimentelle Beiträge zur Kenntnis der Jugend- und Folgeformen xerophiler Pflanzen. *Flora* 108:1–72.

Vlitos, A. J., and W. Meudt. 1955. Interactions between vernalization and photoperiod in spinach. *Contrib. Boyce Thompson Inst.* 18:159–166.

Vöchting, H. 1878. *Über Organbildung im Pflanzenreich.* Max Cohen, Bonn. 258 pp.

———. 1906. Über Regeneration und Polarität bei höhern Pflanzen. *Bot. Zeit.* 64:101–148.

———. 1908. *Untersuchungen zur experimentellen Anatomie und Pathologie des Pflanzenkörpers.* H. Laupp, Tubingen. 318 pp.

———. 1918. *Untersuchungen zur experimentellen Anatomie und Pathologie des Pflanzenkörpers.* II. *Die Polarität der Gewächse.* Tubingen. 333 pp.

Von Schrenk, H. 1905. Intumescences formed as a result of chemical stimulation. *Ann. Rept. Missouri Bot. Gard.* 16:125–148.

Wagenbreth, D. 1956. Leguminoseenpfropfungen und Wirtsspezifität der Knollchenbakterien. *Flora* 144:84–97.

Wagner, N. 1936. Über die Mitosenverteilung in Wurzelspitzen bei geotropschen Krümmungen. *Planta* 25:751–773.

———. 1937. Wachstum und Teilung der Meristemzellen in Wurzelspitzen. *Planta* 27:550–582.

Wain, R. L., and F. Wightman (eds.). 1956. *The chemistry and mode of action of plant growth substances.* Academic Press, New York. 312 pp.

Wakanker, S. M. 1944. Influence of size of seed piece upon the yield of potatoes. *Jour. Amer. Soc. Agron.* 36:32–36.

Wakker, J. H. 1886. Die Neubildungen an abgeschnittenen Blättern von *Caulerpa prolifera. Versl. Meded. K. Akad. Wetenschap. Amsterdam* 3:251–264.

Wald, G. 1958. Innovation in biology. *Sci. American* 199:100–113.

Wallace, R. H. 1928. Histogenesis of intumescences in the apple induced by ethylene gas. *Amer. Jour. Bot.* 15:509–524.

Wallace, T. 1950. *Trace elements in plant physiology.* Chronica Botanica, Waltham, Mass. 144 pp.

Walter, H. 1955. The water economy and the hydrature of plants. *Ann. Rev. Plant Physiol.* 6:239–252.

Wanner, H. 1944. The zonal gradation of respiratory intensity in the root. *Arkiv Bot.* 31A, 9:1–9.

Ward, M., and R. H. Wetmore. 1954. Experimental control of development in the embryo of the fern *Phlebodium aureum. Amer. Jour. Bot.* 41:428–434.

Wardlaw, C. W. 1945. The shoot apex in pteridophytes. *Biol. Rev.* 20:100–114.

———. 1947. Experimental investigations of the shoot apex of *Dryopteris aristata. Phil. Trans. Roy. Soc. London, B,* 232:343–384.

———. 1948. Preliminary observations on tensile stress as a factor in fern phyllotaxis. *Ann. Bot.,* n.s. 12:97–109.

———. 1949a. Leaf formation and phyllotaxis in *Dryopteris aristata* Druce. *Ann. Bot.,* n.s. 13:163–198.

———. 1949b. Experiments on organogenesis in ferns. *Ninth Growth Symposium. Growth* 13 (*Suppl.*):93–131.

———. 1950. The comparative investigation of apices of vascular plants by experimental methods. *Phil. Trans. Roy. Soc. London, B,* 234:583–602.

———. 1952a. *Phylogeny and morphogenesis.* Macmillan, London. 536 pp.

———. 1952b. *Morphogenesis in plants.* Methuen, London. 176 pp.

———. 1952c. The nutritional status of the apex and morphogenesis. *Ann. Bot.,* n.s. 16:207–218.

———. 1953a. A commentary on Turing's diffusion-reaction theory of morphogenesis. *New Phytol.* 52:40–47.

———. 1953b. Comparative observations on the shoot apices of vascular plants. *New Phytol.* 52:195–209.

———. 1955a. *Embryogenesis in plants.* Methuen, London. 381 pp.

Wardlaw, C. W. 1955*b*. Leaf symmetry and orientation in ferns. *Ann. Bot.,* n.s. 19:389–399.

———. 1955*c*. The chemical concept of organization in plants. *New Phytol.* 54:302–310.

——— and Elizabeth G. Cutter. 1956*a*. The effect of shallow incisions on organogenesis in *Dryopteris aristata* Druce. *Ann. Bot.,* n.s. 20:39–56.

———. 1956*b*. Further investigations on the effect of undercutting fern leaf primordia. *Ann. Bot.,* n.s. 20:121–132.

———. 1957*a*. On the organization and reactivity of the shoot apex in vascular plants. *Amer. Jour. Bot.* 44:176–185.

———. 1957*b*. The reactivity of the apical meristem as ascertained by cytological and other techniques. *New Phytol.* 56:221–229.

Wardrop, A. B. 1956. The distribution and formation of tension wood in some species of *Eucalyptus. Australian Jour. Bot.* 4:152–166.

Wareing, P. F. 1951. Growth studies in woody species. IV. The initiation of cambial activity in ring-porous species. *Physiol. Plantarum* 4:546–562.

———. 1956. Photoperiodism in woody plants. *Ann. Rev. Plant Physiol.* 7:191–214.

Warmke, H. E., and A. F. Blakeslee. 1940. The establishment of a 4*n* dioecious race in *Melandrium. Amer. Jour. Bot.* 27:751–762.

———. 1946. Sex determination and sex balance in *Melandrium. Amer. Jour. Bot.* 33:648–660.

——— and Germaine L. Warmke. 1950. The role of auxin in the differentiation of root and shoot primordia from root cuttings of *Taraxacum* and *Cichorium. Amer. Jour. Bot.* 37:272–280.

Wassink, E. C., and J. A. J. Stolwijk. 1952. Effects of light of narrow spectral regions on growth and development of plants. *Proc. K. Ned. Akad. Wetenschap., Ser. C,* 55:471–488.

——— and ———. 1956. Effects of light quality on plant growth. *Ann. Rev. Plant Physiol.* 7:373–400.

Way, D. W. 1954. The relationship of diameter to regenerative organ differentiation in apple roots. *Proc. K. Ned. Akad. Wetenschap., Ser. C,* 57:601–605.

Weaver, H. L. 1946. A developmental study of maize with particular reference to hybrid vigor. *Amer. Jour. Bot.* 33:615–624.

Webber, J. M. 1940. Polyembryony. *Bot. Rev.* 6:575–598.

Weber, Friedl. 1941. Kurzzellen-Schliesszellen von *Iris japonica. Protoplasma* 35:140–142.

Wehnelt, B. 1927. Untersuchungen über das Wundhormon der Pflanzen. *Jahrb. Wiss. Bot.* 66:773–813.

Weide, A. Über die Regenerationsleistungen der Callithamnien. *Arch. Protistenk.* 91:209–221.

Weier, T. E. 1932. The structure of the bryophyte plastid with reference to the Golgi apparatus. *Amer. Jour. Bot.* 19:659–672.

Weiss, F. E. 1930. The problem of graft hybrids and chimeras. *Biol. Rev.* 5:231–271.

Weiss, P. 1950. Perspectives in the field of morphogenesis. *Quart. Rev. Biol.* 25:177–198.

———. 1956. The compounding of complex macromolecular and cellular units into tissue fabrics. *Proc. Natl. Acad. Sci.* 42:819–830.

Weissenböck, K. 1939. Membranregeneration plasmolysierter *Vaucheria*-Protoplasten. *Protoplasma* 32:44–91.

Wellensiek, S. J. 1949. (The prevention of graft-incompatibilty by own foliage on the stock.) *Mededeel. Landbouwhoogesch. Wageningen* 49:257–272.

Wenck, Ursula. 1952. Die Wirkung von Wuchs- und Hemmstoffen auf die Blattform. *Zeitschr. Bot.* 40:33–51.

Went, F. W. 1928. Wuchsstoff und Wachstum. *Rec. Trav. Bot. Néerl.* 25:1–116.

———. 1929. On a substance, causing root formation. *Proc. K. Akad. Wetenschap. Amsterdam* 32:35–39.

———. 1932. Eine botanische Polaritätstheorie. *Jahrb. Wiss. Bot.* 76:528–557.

——— and K. V. Thimann. 1937. *Phytohormones.* Macmillan, New York. 294 pp.

———. 1938. Specific factors other than auxin affecting growth and root formation. *Plant Physiol.* 13:55–80.

———. 1939. The dual effect of auxin on root formation. *Amer. Jour. Bot.* 26:24–29.

———. 1941. Polarity of auxin transport in inverted *Tagetes* cuttings. *Bot. Gaz.* 103:386–390.

———. 1944. Thermoperiodicity in growth and fruiting of the tomato. *Amer. Jour. Bot.* 31:135–150.

———. 1945. The relation between age, light, variety and thermoperiodicity of tomatoes. *Amer. Jour. Bot.* 32:469–479.

———. 1948. Thermoperiodicity. In Murneek and Whyte (eds.), *Vernalization and photoperiodism, a symposium.* Pp. 145–157.

———. 1951a. Twenty years of plant hormone research. In F. Skoog (ed.), *Plant growth substances.* Pp. 67–79.

———. 1951b. The development of stems and leaves. In F. Skoog (ed.), *Plant growth substances.* Pp. 287–298.

———. 1953. The effect of temperature on plant growth. *Ann. Rev. Plant Physiol.* 4:347–362.

———. 1954. Thermoperiodicity and photoperiodism. VIIIe *Congr. Internat. Bot., Rapp. et Comm. Sect.,* 11:335–340.

Werner, O. 1931. Die Maispflanze auf einem trockenharten Wurzelfaden voll wachsend. *Biol. Gen.* 7:689–710.

Wershing, H. F., and I. W. Bailey. 1942. Seedlings as experimental material in the study of "redwood" in conifers. *Jour. Forestry* 40:411–414.

Westerdijk, Johanna. 1906. Zur Regeneration der Laubmoose. *Rec. Trav. Bot. Néerl.* 3:1–66.

Westergaard, M. 1940. Studies on cytology and sex determination in polyploid forms of *Melandrium album. Dansk. Bot. Arkiv* 10:1–131.

Wetmore, R. H. 1943. Leaf-stem relationships in the vascular plants. *Torreya* 43:16–28.

——— and C. W. Wardlaw. 1951. Experimental morphogenesis in vascular plants. *Ann. Rev. Plant Physiol.* 2:269–292.

———. 1954. The use of "in vitro" cultures in the investigation of growth and differentiation in vascular plants. *Brookhaven Symposia in Biol.* 6:22–38.

——— and S. Sorokin. 1955. On the differentiation of xylem. *Jour. Arnold Arboretum* 36:305–317.

———. 1956. Growth and development in the shoot system of plants. *Soc. Devel. and Growth, Symposium* 14:173–190.

Wetter, C. 1952. Beitrag zur Polaritätsproblem leptosporangiater Farne. *Biol. Zentralbl.* 71:109–113.

Wettstein, D. von. 1953. Beeinflussung der Polarität und undifferenzierte Gewebebildung aus Moossporen. *Zeitschr. Bot.* 41:199–226.

Wettstein, F. von. 1924. Morphologie und Physiologie des Formwechsels der Moose auf genetischer Grundlage. I. *Zeitschr. Ind. Abst. Vererb.* 31:1–236.

———. 1938. Zellgrössenregulation und Fertilwerden einer polyploiden *Bryum*-Sippe. *Zeitschr. Ind. Abst. Vererb.* 74:34–53.

——— and K. Pirschle. 1938. Über die Wirklung heteroplastischer Pfropfungen und die Übertragung eines Gen-bedingten Stoffes durch Pfropfung ben *Petunia. Biol. Zentralbl.* 58:123–142.

Whaley, W. G. 1939. Inheritance of leaf and flower characters in the nasturtium. *Jour. Hered.* 30:335–341.

——— and C. Y. Whaley. 1942. A developmental analysis of inherited leaf patterns in *Tropaeolum. Amer. Jour. Bot.* 29:195–200.

———. 1950. The growth of inbred and hybrid maize. *Growth* 14:123–154.

——— and J. H. Leech. 1950. The developmental morphology of the mutant "corn grass." *Bull. Torrey Bot. Club* 77:274–286.

Whitaker, D. M. 1937. Determination of polarity by centrifuging eggs of *Fucus furcatus. Biol. Bull.* 73:249–260.

———. 1940. Physical factors of growth. *Growth* 4 (*Suppl.*):75–90.

White, D. J. B. 1954. The development of the runner-bean leaf with special reference to the relation between the sizes of the lamina and of the petiolar xylem. *Ann. Bot.,* n.s. 18:327–335.

White, O. E. 1916. The nature, causes, distribution and inheritance of fasciation with special reference to its occurrence in *Nicotiana. Zeitschr. Ind. Abst. Vererb.* 16:49–185.

———. 1948. Fasciation. *Bot. Rev.* 14:319–358.

White, P. R. 1939. Potentially unlimited growth of excised plant callus in an artificial nutrient. *Amer. Jour. Bot.* 26:59–64.

——— and A. C. Braun. 1942. A cancerous neoplasm of plants. Autonomous bacteria-free crown-gall tissue. *Cancer Research* 2:597–617.

———. 1944. Transplantation of plant tumors of genetic origin. *Cancer Research* 4:791–794.

———. 1945. Metastatic (graft) tumors of bacteria-free crown galls on *Vinca rosea. Amer. Jour. Bot.* 32:237–241.

———. 1951. Neoplastic growth in plants. *Quart. Rev. Biol.* 26:1–16.

——— and W. F. Millington. 1954. The structure and development of a woody tumor affecting *Picea glauca. Amer. Jour. Bot.* 41:353–361.

Whyte, L. L. 1954. *Accent on form.* Harpers, New York. 198 pp.

Whyte, R. O. 1939. Phasic development of plants. *Biol. Rev.* 14:51–87.

———. 1948. History of research in vernalization. In Murneek and Whyte (eds.), *Vernalization and photoperiodism.* Pp. 1–38.

Wiedersheim, W. 1903. Über den Einfluss der Belastung auf die Ausbildung von Holz- und Bastkörper bei Trauerbäumen. *Jahrb. Wiss. Bot.* 38:41–69.

Wiesner, J. 1868. Beobachtungen über den Einfluss der Erdschwere auf Grössen- und Formverhältnisse der Blätter. *Sitz. Kais. Akad. Wiss., Mat.-Nat. Cl., Wien* 58:369–389.

———. 1892*a.* Vorläufige Mittheilungen über die Erscheinung der Exotrophie. *Ber. Deutsch. Bot. Ges.* 10:552–561.

———. 1892*b. Die Elementarstruktur und das Wachstum der lebenden Substanz.* Wien.

———. 1892*c.* Untersuchungen über den Einfluss der Lage auf die Gestalt der

Pflanzenorgane. 1. Die Anisomorphie der Pflanze. *Sitz. Kais. Akad. Wiss., Mat.-Nat. Cl., Wien* 101:657–705.

———. 1895. Über Trophieen nebst Bemerkungen über Anisophyllie. *Ber. Deutsch. Bot. Ges.* 13:481–495.

Wildt, W. 1906. Über die experimentelle Erzeugung von Festigkeitselementen in Wurzeln und deren Ausbildung in verschiedenen Nährboden. Dissertation, Bonn. 34 pp.

Williams, B. C. 1947. The structure of the meristematic root tip and origin of the primary tissues in the roots of vascular plants. *Amer. Jour. Bot.* 34:455–462.

Williams, S. 1937. Correlation phenomena and hormones in *Selaginella*. *Nature* 139:966.

Wilson, C. M. 1952. Sexuality in the Acrasiales. *Proc. Natl. Acad. Sci.* 38:659–662.

———. 1953. Cytological study of the life cycle of *Dictyostelium*. *Amer. Jour. Bot.* 40:714–718.

——— and I. K. Ross. 1957. Further cytological studies in the Acrasiales. *Amer. Jour. Bot.* 44:345–350.

Wilson, G. E., and K. C. Cheng. 1949. Segregation and reduction in somatic tissues. II. The separation of homologous chromosomes in *Trillium* species. *Jour. Hered.* 40:2–6.

Wilson, Katherine S., and C. L. Withner, Jr. 1946. Stock-scion relationships in tomatoes. *Amer. Jour. Bot.* 33:796–801.

Wilson, K. 1955. The polarity of the cell wall of *Valonia*. *Ann. Bot.*, n.s. 19:289–292.

Wilton, Ocra C., and R. H. Roberts. 1936. Anatomical structure of stems in relation to the production of flowers. *Bot. Gaz.* 98:45–64.

Winkler, H. 1900. Über Polarität, Regeneration und Heteromorphose bei *Bryopsis*. *Jahrb. Wiss. Bot.* 35:449–469.

———. 1902. Über die Regeneration der Blattspreite bei einigen *Cyclamen*-Arten. *Ber. Deutsch. Bot. Ges.* 20:81–87.

———. 1903. Über regenerative Sprossbildung auf den Blättern von *Torenia asiatica*. *Ber. Deutsch. Bot. Ges.* 21:96–107.

———. 1907a. Über die Umwandlung des Blattstieles zum Stengel. *Jahrb. Wiss. Bot.* 45:1–82.

———. 1907b. Über Pfropfbastarde und pflanzliche Chimären. *Ber. Deutsch. Bot. Ges.* 25:568–576.

———. 1909. Weitere Mitteilungen über Pfropfbastarde. *Zeitschr. Bot.* 1:315–345.

———. 1933. Entwicklungsmechanik oder Entwicklungsphysiologie der Pflanzen. *Handw. Nat. Wiss.* 3:620–649.

Wipf, Louise, and D. C. Cooper. 1940. Somatic doubling of chromosomes and nodular infection in certain Leguminosae. *Amer. Jour Bot.* 27:821–824.

Withrow, Alice P., and R. B. Withrow. 1943. Translocation of the floral stimulus in *Xanthium*. *Bot. Gaz.* 104:409–416.

Witsch, H. von, and Anna Flügel. 1952. Über Polyploidieerhöhung im Kurztag bei *Kalanchoë Blossfeldiana*. *Zeitschr. Bot.* 40:281–291.

Wittwer, S. H., and F. G. Teubner. 1957. The effects of temperature and nitrogen nutrition on flower formation in the tomato. *Amer. Jour. Bot.* 44:125–129.

Wolf, F. A. 1947. Growth curves of oriental tobacco and their significance. *Bull. Torrey Bot. Club* 74:199–214.

Woltereck, Ilse. 1928. Experimentelle Untersuchungen über die Blattbildung amphibischer Pflanzen. *Flora* 123:30–61.

Woodford, E. K., K. Holly, and C. C. McCready. 1958. Herbicides. *Ann. Rev. Plant Physiol.* 9:311–358.

Woodger, J. H. 1929. *Biological principles.* Harcourt, Brace, London, 498 pp.

———. 1930, 1931. The "concept of organism" and the relation between embryology and genetics. *Quart. Rev. Biol.* 5:1–22 and 438–463; 6:178–207.

Worsdell, W. C. 1915. *The principles of plant teratology.* Robert Hardwicke, London.

Woyciki, S. 1954. On the origin of the *Retinospora* forms of *Thuja, Biota* and *Chamaecyparis. Acta Soc. Bot. Poloniae* 23:443–458.

Wright, C. 1873. On the uses and origin of arrangements of leaves in plants. *Mem. Amer. Acad. Arts and Sci.* 9:379–415.

Wulff, E. 1910. Über Heteromorphose bei *Dasycladus clavaeformis. Ber. Deutsch. Bot. Ges.* 28:264–268.

Yampolsky, C. 1957. Further experiments with male and female grafts of *Mercurialis annua. Bull. Torrey Bot. Club* 84:1–8.

Yapp, R. H. 1912. *Spiraea Ulmaria* and its bearing on the problem of xeromorphy in marsh plants. *Ann. Bot.* 26:815–870.

Yarbrough, J. A. 1932. Anatomical and developmental studies of the foliar embryos of *Bryophyllum calycinum. Amer. Jour. Bot.* 19:443–453.

———. 1936a. The foliar embryos of *Tolmiea Menziesii. Amer. Jour. Bot.* 23:16–20.

———. 1936b. The foliar embryos of *Camptosorus rhizophyllus. Amer. Jour. Bot.* 23:176–181.

———. 1936c. Regeneration in the foliage leaf of *Sedum. Amer. Jour. Bot.* 23:303–307.

Yarwood, C. E. 1946. Detached leaf culture. *Bot. Rev.* 12:1–56.

Yates, Ruth C., and J. T. Curtis. 1949. The effect of sucrose and other factors on the shoot-root ratio of orchid seedlings. *Amer. Jour. Bot.* 36:390–396.

Young, B. S. 1954. The effects of leaf primordia on differentiation in the stem. *New Phytol.* 53:445–460.

Young, H. E., and P. J. Kramer. 1952. The effect of pruning on the height and diameter growth of loblolly pine. *Jour. Forestry* 50:474–479.

Zalenski, V. 1904. Materials for the study of the quantitative anatomy of different leaves on the same plant. *Mem. Polytech. Inst. Kiev* 4:1–203. (In Russian. Citation from Maximov.)

Zeeuw, D. de, and A. C. Leopold. 1956. The promotion of floral initiation by auxin. *Amer. Jour. Bot.* 43:47–50.

Zeller, O. 1954. Beginn der Blütenphase bei den Infloreszenzknospen einiger Kern- und Steinobstsorten. *Angew. Bot.* 28:178–191.

Zepf, E. 1952. Über die Differenzierung des Sphagnumblattes. *Zeitschr. Bot.* 40:87–118.

Zimmerman, P. W., and A. E. Hitchcock. 1929. Root formation and flowering of dahlia cuttings when subjected to different day lengths. *Bot. Gaz.* 87:1–13.

———, W. Crocker, and A. E. Hitchcock. 1933a. Initiation and stimulation of roots from exposure of plants to carbon monoxide gas. *Contrib. Boyce Thompson Inst.* 5:1–17.

——— and A. E. Hitchcock. 1933b. Initiation and stimulation of adventitious roots caused by unsaturated hydrocarbon gases. *Contrib. Boyce Thompson Inst.* 5:351–369.

—— and W. F. Wilcoxon. 1935. Several chemical growth substances which cause initiation of roots and other responses in plants. *Contrib. Boyce Thompson Inst.* 7:209–229.

—— and A. E. Hitchcock. 1936. Tuberization of artichokes regulated by capping stem tips with black cloth. *Contrib. Boyce Thompson Inst.* 8:311–315.

—— and ——. 1942. Substituted phenoxy and benzoic acid growth substances and the relation of structure to physiological activity. *Contrib. Boyce Thompson Inst.* 12:321–343.

—— and ——. 1951a. Rose "sports" from adventitious buds. *Contrib. Boyce Thompson Inst.* 16:221–224.

——. 1951b. Formative effects of hormone-like growth regulators. In F. Skoog (ed.), *Plant growth substances.* Pp. 175–183.

Zimmermann, W. 1923. Zytologische Untersuchungen an *Sphacelaria fusca.* Ag. Ein Beitrag zur Entwicklungsphysiologie der Zelle. *Zeitschr. Bot.* 15:113–175.

——. 1929. Experimente zur Polaritätsproblem. *Arch. Entwicklungsmech. Organ.* 116:669–688.

Name Index

Black, L. M., 290
Blackburn, Kathleen B., 429
Blackman, V. H., 16
Blair, D. S., 260
Blake, M. A., 505
Blakeslee, A. F., 59, 89, 185, 221, 222, 270, 272, 273, 296, 430, 437, 440, 446, 447
Blaringhem, L., 279, 282
Blaser, H. W., 91, 271
Bloch, R., 25, 77, 82, 118, 130, 131, 135, 171, 190–193, 197, 218, 219, 240–242, 277, 282, 403, 404
Blondel, Benigna, 19
Boell, E. J., 73, 74, 140
Böhme, H., 262
Boke, N. H., 65
Bond, G., 197, 311
Bond, T. E. T., 278, 280
Bonner, D. M., 395
Bonner, James, 397, 398, 403, 408, 409, 412
Bonner, John T., 20–22, 224–226, 228, 229, 406
Bonnet, C., 151
Boodle, L. A., 245
Bopp, M., 195
Bordner, J. S., 347
Borgström, G., 123, 311, 385
Bormann, J., 250
Borowikow, G. A., 134
Borriss, H., 18, 21, 309, 346
Borthwick, H. A., 282, 308, 314, 322, 366, 397
Bosshatd, H. H., 80
Bouillenne, R., 394
Bouygues, H., 50
Bower, F. O., 360
Boysen-Jensen, P., 190, 223, 375
Brabec, F., 270
Bradford, F. C., 259
Bradley, Muriel V., 442
Brain, E. D., 40
Brase, K. D., 259, 260
Braun, A., 151, 153
Braun, Armin C., 291–294, 407
Brauner, L., 355
Bravais, A., 151
Bravais, L., 151
Brenchley, Winifred E., 368
Brian, P. W., 410
Briggs, W. R., 187
Brink, R. A., 273
Broadbent, D., 42
Brotherton, W., Jr., 310
Brown, A. B., 404
Brown, J. G., 98
Brown, Nellie A., 290
Brown, R., 21, 29, 41, 42, 68, 78

Brown, W. V., 336
Bruhn, W., 214
Brumfield, R. T., 28, 76, 77, 268
Brush, W. D., 349
Bücher, H., 351, 352
Buchholz, J. T., 110, 206, 235, 236
Budde, H., 33, 111
Bullwinkel, B., 99, 100
Bünning, E., 118, 131, 133, 160, 192, 199, 200, 230, 322, 337, 343, 346, 347, 435
Burgeff, H., 400
Burkholder, P. R., 30, 31, 308, 309, 315, 364, 365, 380, 381, 383
Burns, G. P., 216, 353
Burpee, D., 425
Burr, H. S., 361, 455
Burström, H., 40, 41, 341, 412
Bussmann, K., 170, 355
Butler, L., 422
Buvat, R., 68, 232

Cain, S. A., 329
Cajlachjan, M. C., 397
Camefort, H., 68, 159
Camus, G., 72, 219, 405
Carlson, Margery C., 245, 247, 250
Carrière, E. A., 250
Carsner, E., 339
Carter, W., 284, 285
Carvalho, A., 189
Castan, R., 126
Castle, E. S., 21, 149, 165, 166, 310
Chalk, L., 37
Champagnat, P., 101, 387
Champion, H. G., 166
Chan, A. P., 64
Chandler, W. H., 339
Chandraratna, M. F., 432
Chao, Marian D., 18
Chapman, H. W., 320
Charles, D. R., 417
Chattaway, M. Margaret, 37
Chaudri, J. J., 343
Cheng, K. C., 274
Chester, K. S., 261
Cheuvart, C., 221
Child, C. M., 101, 140, 145, 231, 453, 454
Chowdhury, K. A., 86, 201
Christensen, Hilde M., 437
Chrysler, M. A., 237
Chung, C. W., 43
Church, A. H., 151, 153, 159, 163
Clark, H. E., 398
Clark, W. G., 361, 385
Cleland, R., 412
Close, A. W., 321
Clowes, F. A. L., 76–79

Subject Index